LIVING AND WORKING

IN

SPAIN

A SURVIVAL HANDBOOK

by

David Hampshire

First Published 1995
Second Edition 1998
Reprinted 1998

Survival Books Limited, Suite C, Third Floor
Standbrook House, 2-5 Old Bond Street
London W1X 3TB, United Kingdom
Tel. (44) 171-493 4244, Fax (44) 171-491 0605
E-mail: survivalbooks@computronx.com
Internet: computronx.com/survivalbooks

British Library Cataloguing in Publication Data
A CIP record for this book is available from the British Library
ISBN 0 9519804 2 4

Printed and bound in Great Britain by Page Bros (Norwich) Ltd., Mile Cross Lane, Norwich, Norfolk NR6 6SA, UK.

ACKNOWLEDGEMENTS

My sincere thanks to all those who contributed to the successful publication of this book, in particular the many people who provided information and took the time and trouble to read and comment on the many draft versions. I would especially like to thank my chief researcher Susan Mitchell for her invaluable help. I would also like to thank Charles Peard Clarke, Ron and Pat Scarborough, Louise Stapleton, Pam Miller, Charles King, Sarah Sherman, John Knight, Veronica Orchard, Adèle Kelham and everyone else who contributed in any way and whom I have omitted to mention. Also a special thank you to Jim Watson (tel. UK 01788-813609) for the superb cartoons, fine illustrations and the beautiful cover.

By the same publisher:

Buying a Home Abroad
Buying a Home in Florida
Buying a Home in France
Buying a Home in Portugal
Buying a Home in Spain
Living and Working in America
Living and Working in Australia
Living and Working in Britain
Living and Working in France
Living and Working in New Zealand
Living and Working in Switzerland

What Readers and Reviewers Have Said About Survival Books

When you buy a model plane for your child, a video recorder, or some new computer gizmo, you get with it a leaflet or booklet pleading 'Read Me First', or bearing large friendly letters or bold type saying 'IMPORTANT - follow the instructions carefully'. This book should be similarly supplied to all those entering France with anything more durable than a 5-day return ticket. — It is worth reading even if you are just visiting briefly, or if you have lived here for years and feel totally knowledgeable and secure. But if you need to find out how France works then it is indispensable. Native French people probably have a less thorough understanding of how their country functions. — Where it is most essential, the book is most up to the minute.

Living France

We would like to congratulate you on this work: it is really super! We hand it out to our expatriates and they read it with great interest and pleasure.

ICI (Switzerland) AG

Rarely has a 'survival guide' contained such useful advice — This book dispels doubts for first-time travellers, yet is also useful for seasoned globetrotters — In a word, if you're planning to move to the US or go there for a long-term stay, then buy this book both for general reading and as a ready-reference.

American Citizens Abroad

It's everything you always wanted to ask but didn't for fear of the contemptuous put down — The best English-language guide — Its pages are stuffed with practical information on everyday subjects and are designed to complement the traditional guidebook.

Swiss News

A complete revelation to me — I found it both enlightening and interesting, not to mention amusing.

Carole Clark

Let's say it at once. David Hampshire's *Living and Working in France* is the best handbook ever produced for visitors and foreign residents in this country; indeed, my discussion with locals showed that it has much to teach even those born and bred in *l'Hexagone*. — It is Hampshire's meticulous detail which lifts his work way beyond the range of other books with similar titles. Often you think of a supplementary question and search for the answer in vain. With Hampshire this is rarely the case. — He writes with great clarity (and gives French equivalents of all key terms), a touch of humor and a ready eye for the odd (and often illuminating) fact. — This book is absolutely indispensable.

The Riviera Reporter

The ultimate reference book — Every conceivable subject imaginable is exhaustively explained in simple terms — An excellent introduction to fully enjoy all that this fine country has to offer and save time and money in the process.

American Club of Zurich

What Readers and Reviewers Have Said About Survival Books

What a great work, wealth of useful information, well-balanced wording and accuracy in details. My compliments!

Thomas Müller

This handbook has all the practical information one needs to set up home in the UK — The sheer volume of information is almost daunting — Highly recommended for anyone moving to the UK.

American Citizens Abroad

A very good book which has answered so many questions and even some I hadn't thought of — I would certainly recommend it.

Brian Fairman

A mine of information — I might have avoided some embarrassments and frights if I had read it prior to my first Swiss encounters — Deserves an honoured place on any newcomer's bookshelf.

English Teachers Association, Switzerland

Covers just about all the things you want to know on the subject — In answer to the desert island question about *the one* how-to book on France, this book would be it — Almost 500 pages of solid accurate reading — This book is about enjoyment as much as survival.

The Recorder

It's so funny — I love it and definitely need a copy of my own — Thanks very much for having written such a humourous and helpful book.

Heidi Guiliani

A must for all foreigners coming to Switzerland.

Antoinette O'Donoghue

A comprehensive guide to all things French, written in a highly readable and amusing style, for anyone planning to live, work or retire in France.

The Times

A concise, thorough account of the DO's and DON'Ts for a foreigner in Switzerland — Crammed with useful information and lightened with humourous quips which make the facts more readable.

American Citizens Abroad

Covers every conceivable question that might be asked concerning everyday life — I know of no other book that could take the place of this one.

France in Print

Hats off to Living and Working in Switzerland!

Ronnie Almeida

CONTENTS

14. FINANCE 271

15. LEISURE 319

IMPORTANT NOTE

Spain is a large country with myriad faces and many ethnic groups, religions and customs. Although ostensibly the same throughout the country, many rules and regulations are open to local interpretation, and are occasionally even formulated on the spot. Laws and regulations have also been changing at a considerable rate in recent years following Spain's change of government in 1996.

I cannot recommend too strongly that you always check with an official and reliable source (not always the same) before making any major decisions or undertaking an irreversible course of action. However, don't believe everything you're told or read, even, dare I say it, herein!

To help you obtain further information and verify data with official sources, useful addresses and references to other sources of information have been included in all chapters and in appendices A and B. Important points have been emphasised throughout the book **in bold print**, some of which it would be expensive or even dangerous to disregard. **Ignore them at your peril or cost!** Unless specifically stated, the reference to any company, organisation, product or publication in this book *doesn't* constitute an endorsement or recommendation. Any reference to any place or person (living or dead) is purely coincidental. There's no Spanish city named Seville.

AUTHOR'S NOTES

- Whenever references are made to the Spanish language, this means Castilian, spoken as a first or second language throughout Spain. Other official languages in Spain include Basque, Catalan and Galician (see **Language** on page 44).

- Spanish place names (shown in brackets below) are often changed when written in English. In many cases this means just dropping an accent, e.g. Cadiz (Cádiz), Cordoba (Córdoba), Malaga (Málaga), San Sebastian (San Sebastián) and Valencia (València), while other changes are more pronounced, e.g. Andalusia (Andalucía), Alicante (Alacant), Majorca (Mallorca), Seville (Sevilla) and Zaragossa (Zaragoza).

- Times in timetables are shown using the 24-hour clock, e.g. 10am is shown as 1000 and 10pm as 2200 (see page 422).

- **Prices quoted should be taken as estimates only**, although they were mostly correct when going to print and fortunately don't usually change overnight. Most prices are quoted inclusive of value added tax (*IVA incluido*), which is the method used when quoting prices in this book (unless indicated), although prices are sometimes quoted exclusive of tax (*más IVA*).

- His/he/him/man/men, etc. also mean her/she/her/woman/women, etc. (no offence ladies). This is done simply to make life easier for both the reader and (in particular) the author, and **isn't** intended to be sexist.

- The Spanish translation of many key words and phrases is shown in brackets in *italics*.

- Warnings and important points are shown in **bold** type.

- Frequent references are made in this book to the European Union (EU) which comprises Austria, Belgium, Denmark, Finland, France, Germany, Greece, Ireland, Italy, Luxembourg, the Netherlands, Portugal, Spain, Sweden and the United Kingdom. The EU countries plus Iceland, Liechtenstein and Norway comprise the European Economic Area (EEA).

- Lists of Useful Addresses and Further Reading are contained in **Appendices A** and **B** respectively.

- For those unfamiliar with the metric system of weights and measures, conversion tables are included in **Appendix C**.

- A map of Spain showing the regions and provinces is contained in **Appendix D**.

- A **Service Directory** containing the names, addresses, telephone and fax numbers of companies and organisations doing business in Spain is contained in **Appendix E**.

INTRODUCTION

Whether you're already living or working in Spain or only thinking about it — this is **THE BOOK** you've been looking for. Forget about all those glossy guide books, excellent though they are for tourists; this amazing book was written especially with you in mind and is worth its weight in saffron! *Living and Working in Spain* is designed to meet the needs of anyone wishing to know the essentials of Spanish life including immigrants, temporary foreign workers, businessmen, students, retirees, long-stay tourists, holiday home owners and even extra terrestrials. However long your intended stay in Spain, you'll find the information contained in this book invaluable.

As anyone who has lived in Spain knows only too well, accurate, up-to-date information for foreigners *Living and Working in Spain* is difficult to find, particularly in the English language. My aim in writing this book was to help fill this void and provide the comprehensive *practical* information necessary for a relatively trouble-free life. You may have visited Spain as a tourist, but living and working there is a another matter altogether. Adjusting to a different environment and culture and making a home in any foreign country can be a traumatic and stressful experience, and Spain is no exception.

You need to adapt to new customs and traditions and discover the Spanish way of doing things, for example finding a home, paying bills and obtaining insurance. For foreigners in Spain, finding out how to overcome the everyday obstacles of life has previously been a case of pot luck. **But no more!** With a copy of *Living and Working in Spain* to hand you'll have a wealth of information at your fingertips. Information is derived from a variety of sources, both official and unofficial, not least the hard won personal experiences of the author, his friends, colleagues and acquaintances. *Living and Working in Spain* is a comprehensive handbook on a wide range of everyday subjects and represents the most up-to-date source of general information available to foreigners in Spain. It isn't, however, simply a monologue of dry facts and figures, but a practical and entertaining look at life in Spain.

Adapting to life in a new country is a continuous process and although this book will help reduce your beginner's phase and minimise the frustrations, it doesn't contain all the answers (most of us don't even know the right questions). What it *will* do is help you make informed decisions and calculated judgments, instead of uneducated guesses and costly mistakes. **Most important of all it will help you save time, trouble and money and repay your investment many times over.**

Although you may find some of the information a bit daunting, don't be discouraged. Most problems occur once only and fade into insignificance after a short time (as you face the next half a dozen!). The majority of foreigners in Spain would agree that, all things considered, they relish living there. A period spent in Spain is a wonderful way to enrich your life, broaden your horizons and hopefully please your bank manager. I trust this book will help you avoid the pitfalls of life in Spain and smooth your way to a happy and rewarding future in your new home.

¡Mucha suerte!

David Hampshire
October 1997

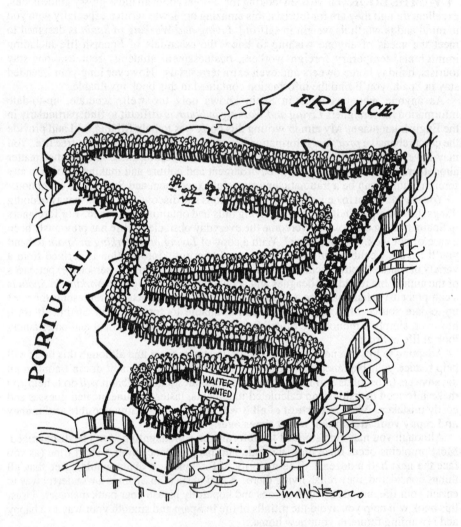

1.

FINDING A JOB

Finding a job in Spain isn't easy, particularly outside the major cities where unemployment is very high in most regions. Furthermore, if you don't qualify to live and work in Spain by birthright or as a national of a European Union (EU) country (see page 22), obtaining a residence card can be even more difficult than finding work. Americans and other foreigners without the automatic right to work in Spain must have their employment approved by the Spanish Ministry of Labour (*Ministerio de Trabajo*) and obtain a visa before entering Spain. EU nationals have the same employment rights as Spanish citizens, as do Spanish nationals in other EU countries.

Spain attracts a relatively low number of migrants who total around 500,000, compared with some 2.5m in Britain, 3.5m in France and 5.5m in Germany. In fact, Spain has fewer foreign residents (less than 1 per cent) in relation to the total population than any other EU country, although there's a large floating population of unregistered foreign 'residents'. Over two-thirds of foreign residents in Spain come from Europe, 95 per cent from EU countries. Many Spaniards also work abroad, notably in France, Germany and Switzerland, and Spain imports (low-paid) workers from Morocco, Poland and Portugal. Spain is a key entry point for North African immigrants into Europe which causes considerable problems with illegal immigrants.

Employment Prospects: You shouldn't plan on obtaining employment in Spain unless you have a firm job offer, special qualifications or experience for which there's a strong demand. If you want a good job, you must usually be well qualified and speak fluent Spanish. If you plan to arrive in Spain without a job, you should have a detailed plan for finding employment and try to make some contacts before you arrive. Being attracted to Spain by its weather and lifestyle is understandable, but doesn't rate highly as an employment qualification. It's almost impossible to find work in rural areas (apart from low paid farm work) and it isn't easy in cities and large towns, particularly if your Spanish isn't fluent.

Many people turn to self-employment or starting a business to make a living, although this path is strewn with pitfalls for the unwary. **Many foreigners don't do sufficient homework before moving to Spain.** While hoping for the best, you should prepare for the worst case scenario and ensure that you have a contingency plan and sufficient funds to last until you're established. Before arriving in Spain you should dispassionately examine your motives and credentials. What kind of work can you realistically expect to do in Spain? What are your qualifications and experience? Are they recognised in Spain? How good is your Spanish (or other languages)? Unless your Spanish is fluent, you won't be competing on equal terms with the Spanish (you won't anyway, but that's a different matter!). Spanish employers aren't usually interested in employing anyone without, at the very least, an adequate working knowledge of Spanish. Are there any jobs in your profession or trade in the area where you wish to live? Could you be self-employed or start your own business? The answers to these and many other questions can be quite disheartening, but it's better to ask them *before* moving to Spain, rather than afterwards.

Unemployment: Spain's strong economic recovery in the last few years has had little effect on its unemployment rate, which stubbornly remains the highest in western Europe at over 20 per cent (around double the EU average, three times that of the US and some 10 times that of the Pacific rim). However, Spain's unemployment figures have fallen in recent years and are distorted by the large number of people working illegally in the 'black' (cash) economy, although 'real' unemployment in some areas is much higher than the national average (as high as 40 per cent). Unemployment is particularly high among the young and is the highest in the EU. Over 50 per cent of the 16 to 19 age group are unemployed and some 40 per cent of the 20 to 24 age group (more women are unemployed than men). The unemployed are often unskilled or even illiterate, although some 30 per cent of university graduates are also unemployed. Some 60 per cent of the total have been unemployed for more than a year. Only some 40 per cent of the population is employed in Spain, compared with, for example, over 60 per cent in Denmark.

The biggest increase in unemployment in recent years has been in the service and construction industries, the 'engines' of growth in Spain in recent years. Spain has traditionally exported workers (Spain's most successful export) to other European countries, although even this lifeline has dried up in the last few years as companies have slashed their workforces and unemployment has risen. In fact, unemployment in Spain has been exacerbated by returning emigrants, particularly in regions such as Andalusia. Apart from the debilitating effects on the Spanish economy, unemployment is extremely expensive due to Spain's relatively high social security benefits. Reducing unemployment is the most urgent task facing Spain and the one issue on which all politicians agree.

Economy: Spain has experienced an economic 'miracle' in the last few decades, during which it has been transformed from a basically agricultural country into a modern industrial nation. However, the booming 1980s have been followed by a slump (the severity of which shocked Spain's business and political leaders to the core), although there has been a recovery in the last few years. The recession coincided with Spain becoming a full member of the EU and highlighted the country's lack of competitiveness, low productivity and high production costs. Over-manning is common in Spain, particularly in the civil service and state-owned industries, which are renowned for their inefficiency. The spiralling increase in business costs, particularly labour costs, eroded Spain's competitiveness and led to a loss of confidence among national and international investors.

Industrial Relations: Spain has had more strikes (*huelgas*) and lost more production days due to strikes in the last 10 years than any country in the EU (which highlights the lack of communication between workers and management in Spain). However, industrial relations have improved dramatically in recent years (the number of working hours lost to strikes in 1996 dropped by around 20 per cent compared with 1995 and was the lowest number of strikes since 1990) as high unemployment has sapped the unions' bargaining power. Despite the squeeze on pay rises to meet the ERM criteria and qualify for the single currency, there has been little industrial unrest in the last few years, and in 1997 the unions and employers signed an historic agreement to exchange high redundancy payments for more permanent jobs.

Workforce: Spanish workers have an affluent lifestyle compared with just a decade ago and employees enjoy high salaries (particularly executives and senior managers) and good working conditions. Spain has a reasonably self-sufficient labour market and doesn't require a large number of skilled or unskilled foreign workers. Women have professional and salary equality with men, although they still fill most low-paid jobs. However, workers' security has been seriously eroded in recent years with an increasing number of workers employed on short-term, rather than indefinite employment contracts. Many Spaniards (particularly low-paid civil servants) now hold down two jobs and work overtime and extra shifts in order to pay their bills. The recession has also reversed the long-established trend of workers leaving the countryside for the cities and factories, and in recent years unemployed workers have returned to their rural roots to scratch a 'living' from the soil.

Spain and the EU

Spain became a full member of the European Union (EU) on 1st January 1986, joining Belgium, Denmark, France, Germany, Greece, Ireland, Italy, Luxembourg, the Netherlands, Portugal (who joined at the same time as Spain) and the United Kingdom. The bulk of the union's legislation was immediately applicable to Spain, although it was granted certain transition periods which expired at the end of 1992. The EU was enlarged to 15 members in 1995 with the entry of Austria, Finland and Sweden. The European Economic Area (EEA) was formed on the 1st January 1994 and comprises the EU member countries plus Iceland, Liechtenstein and Norway.

Nationals of all EU states have the right to work in Spain or any other member state without a work permit, providing they have a valid passport or national identity card and comply with the member state's laws and regulations on employment. EU nationals are entitled to the same treatment as Spanish citizens in matters of pay, working conditions, access to housing, vocational training, social security and trade union rights, and families and immediate dependants are entitled to join them and enjoy the same rights. The Single European Act, which came into effect on 1st January 1993, created a single market with a more favourable environment for stimulating enterprise, competition and trade, and made it easier for EU nationals to work in other EU countries.

There are still some barriers to full freedom of movement of workers and the right to work within the EU. For example some jobs require applicants to have specific skills or vocational qualifications, and qualifications obtained in some member states aren't recognised in others. Mutual acceptance of all EU educational and professional qualifications by all member states will make it easier to study, train and work abroad, and eventually all equivalent professional qualifications will be recognised throughout the union. In a number of trades and professions, member states are already required to recognise qualifications and experience obtained elsewhere in the EU (see below). There are, however, restrictions on employment in the civil service, when the right to work may be limited in certain cases on the grounds of public policy, health or security.

QUALIFICATIONS

The most important qualification for working in Spain is the ability to speak Spanish fluently (see page 44). Once you have overcome this hurdle you should establish whether your trade or professional qualifications and experience are recognised in Spain. Theoretically, all qualifications recognised by professional and trade bodies in any EU country should be recognised in Spain. However, recognition varies from country to country and in certain cases foreign qualifications aren't recognised by Spanish employers, professional or trade associations. All academic qualifications should also be recognised, although they may be given less prominence than equivalent Spanish qualifications, depending on the country and the educational establishment that awarded them. A ruling by the European Court in 1992 declared that where EU examinations are of a similar standard, with just certain areas of difference, then individuals should only be required to take exams in those particular areas. EU citizens may become public employees, for example teachers and postal workers, and fill other civil service positions in Spain, with the exception of the military and police.

Professionals whose training was compulsory (regulated by statute, statutory instrument or a professional college) and consisted of at least three years degree level training plus job-based training, can have their qualifications recognised automatically in member states. They are, however, subject to any professional codes and limitations in force, e.g. in Spain a medical practitioner must have his qualifications accepted by the medical college of the province where he intends to practise and by any controlling specialist bodies. He must also show that he is in good standing with the professional authorities in his country of origin. However, professional colleges (*colegios*) in Spain can no longer act as either open or covert obstacles to the practise of professions by EU citizens holding recognised qualifications issued in another EU country.

All EU member states issue occupation information sheets containing a common job description with a table of qualifications. These cover a large number of trades and are intended to help someone with the relevant qualifications look for employment in another EU country. Occupations in many industries are officially recognised including those in hotel and catering; motor vehicle repair and maintenance; construction; electrical/electronics; agriculture; metalworking; the textile industry; commerce; clerical and administration; chemicals; the food industry; tourism; transportation; and public works.

Information regarding the official validation of qualifications and the addresses of Spanish professional bodies is obtainable from the education department of Spanish embassies. A direct comparison between foreign qualifications and those recognised in Spain can be obtained from any Spanish employment office (*oficina de empleo*) where there's a representative of the National Academic Recognition Information Centre (NARIC). In Britain, information can be obtained from the Comparability Co-Ordinator, Occupational Standards Branch - OS5, Room E454, The Training Agency, Moorfoot, Sheffield S1 4PQ, UK (tel. 01742-704144).

GOVERNMENT EMPLOYMENT SERVICE

The state-run National Employment Institute (*Instituto Nacional de Empleo/INEM*) is the only employment and recruitment agency permitted to operate in Spain for permanent work. INEM operates some 700 offices (*oficinas de empleo*) throughout Spain, providing both local and national job listings. Jobs in the local province are advertised on a bulletin board, with perhaps a few national positions requiring specialised experience, training or qualifications. INEM offices also provide a comprehensive career resource library including Spanish company listings, trade publications and a wide range of reference books. If you have a residence card (*residencia*), without which you may receive no help, a personal counsellor is assigned to your case. In addition to offering a job placement service, INEM also provides assistance to those wishing to start a business or be self-employed.

INEM services are available to all EU nationals and foreign residents in Spain. Unemployed foreigners must register as job seekers (*demandantes de empleo*) after which they receive a document permitting them to legally remain in Spain for six months while seeking employment. Note, however, that INEM offices are usually unhelpful to foreign job seekers unless you speak fluent Spanish, have already been employed in Spain, or are unemployed and receiving unemployment benefit. Being a government department, INEM isn't service-oriented and the quality of service and co-operation varies depending on the region, office and the person handling your case. Most Spanish employers advertise in daily newspapers for personnel. The *Servicio de Empleo y Acción Formativa/Promoción Profesional Obrera (SEAF/PPO)* of the Ministry of Labour reviews such advertising and sends qualified applicants to apply for the positions described.

There's also a European Employment Service (EURES) network, the members of which include all EU countries. Member states exchange information on job vacancies on a regular basis and you can also have your personal details circulated to the employment service in selected countries, e.g. to the INEM in Spain. Details are available in local employment service offices in each member country, where advice on how to apply for jobs is provided. Note, however, that it isn't a reliable or quick way to find a job in Spain, and with high Spanish unemployment, an application through EURES is protracted and seldom successful.

RECRUITMENT AGENCIES

Private employment agencies in Spain may operate only as temporary employment bureaux (*empresas de trabajo temporal*) and there aren't yet any fully operational private employment agencies. Most agencies are based in the major cities and deal only with enquiries from within Spain. In addition to general temporary agencies handling a range of industries and professions, there are also agencies specialising in particular fields such as accounting, banking, computer personnel, construction, engineering and technical staff, hotel and catering staff, industrial recruitment, insurance, nannies and nursing, sales, and secretarial and office staff. Temporary recruitment agencies such as Manpower are common in cities and large towns, and generally hire office staff and unskilled and semi-skilled labour. Many secretarial jobs are for bi-lingual or tri-lingual secretaries with word processing experience (an agency will usually test your written language and typing or word processing skills).

To be employed by a temporary agency, you must be legally eligible to work in Spain and have a social security card (see page 256). You need to register with most agencies, which entails completing a registration form and providing a curriculum vitae and references (you can register with any number of agencies). Always ensure you know exactly how much, when and how you will be paid. Your salary should include a payment in lieu of holidays and a deduction for unemployment insurance. Because of the long annual holidays in Spain and generous maternity leave, companies often require temporary staff and a temporary job can frequently be used as a stepping stone to a permanent position. Note that private recruitment agencies in Spain are prohibited from offering anything other than temporary work. Agencies are listed in the Yellow Pages under *Oficinas de Empleo*.

Executive recruitment and search companies (head-hunters) are also common in cities and large towns, and have traditionally been used by large Spanish companies to help recruit staff, particularly executives, managers and professionals. Agents place advertisements in daily and weekly newspapers and trade magazines but don't usually mention the client's name, not least to prevent applicants from approaching the company directly, thus depriving the agency of its fat fee. Unless you're a particularly outstanding candidate (Superman/Superwoman) with half a dozen degrees, six languages and valuable experience, sending an unsolicited CV to a head-hunter is usually a waste of time. There are also recruitment agencies in other European countries that recruit executives, managers and professionals for employers in Spain.

SEASONAL JOBS

Most seasonal jobs last for the duration of the summer tourist season (May to September), although a few are available in the small Spanish winter sports' industry (December to April) and some are simply casual or temporary jobs for a few weeks only. Spanish fluency is required for all but the most menial and worst paid jobs, and is equally or more important than experience and qualifications (although fluent Spanish alone won't guarantee you a well paid job). Seasonal jobs include most trades in hotels and restaurants; couriers and representatives; various jobs in holiday camps and campsites; work in ski resorts; sports instructors (e.g. tennis, golf and assorted water sports); jobs in bars, clubs and discos (particularly on the *costas* and in the Balearic and Canary Islands); fruit and grape picking and other agricultural jobs; and diverse jobs in the construction industry. If you aren't an EU national, it's essential to check whether you're eligible to work in Spain before your arrival and whether you need a visa (see page 65). Check with a Spanish embassy or consulate in your home country well in advance of your visit. Foreign students in Spain can obtain a temporary work permit for part-time work during the summer holiday period and school terms.

Hotels & Restaurants: Hotels and restaurants are by far the largest employers of seasonal workers and jobs are available year round, from hotel managers to kitchen hands. Experience, qualifications and fluent Spanish are required for all the better and higher paid positions, although a variety of jobs are available for the untrained and inexperienced. Note that if accommodation with cooking facilities or full board isn't provided with a job, it can be expensive and difficult to find. Ensure that your salary is sufficient to pay for accommodation, food and other living expenses, and hopefully save some money (see **Cost of Living** on page 315).

Couriers and Representatives: One of the best sources of seasonal work for foreigners is as a courier or representative for a foreign package holiday company and various jobs at holiday camps and campsites. Competition for jobs is fierce and Spanish fluency is usually necessary, even for employment with foreign tour operators. Most companies have age requirements, the minimum usually being 21, although many companies prefer employees to be older. To find out which companies operate in Spain, check the brochures in your local travel agents or consult a trade travel directory in your local library. Make applications well before the season starts, e.g. for summer work you should apply in November or December as many positions are filled by January or February. Major British companies operating in Spain include Eurocamp (Canute Court, Toft Road, Knutsford, Cheshire WA16 0NL, UK), Canvas Holidays Ltd. (12 Abbey Park Place, Dunfermline, Fife KY12 7PD, UK), Club Cantabrica Holidays (146-148 London Road, St. Albans, Herts. AL1 1PQ, UK), Keycamp Holidays (92-96 Lind Road, Sutton, Surrey SM1 4PL, UK) and Seasun/Tentrek Holidays (71/71 East Hill, Colchester, Essex CO1 2QW, UK).

Further Reading: There are many books for those seeking seasonal jobs abroad including *Summer Jobs Abroad* by David Woodworth and *Work Your Way Around the World* by Susan Griffith (both published by Vacation Work). The Central Bureau for Educational Visits & Exchanges (Seymour Mews House, Seymour Mews, London W1H 9PE, UK, tel. 0171-486 5101) publish various books for young job seekers including *Home From Home*, *A Year Between*, *Teach Abroad* and *Working Holidays*, an annual guide to job opportunities in over 100 countries, including Spain. *A Year Off, A Year On* is published by CRAC Learning Materials, Hobsons Publishing plc, Bateman Street,

Cambridge CB2 1LZ, UK. An invaluable book for anyone looking for a job in a ski resort is *Working in Ski Resorts - Europe*, by Victoria Pybus & Charles James (Vacation Work). Note that although a summer job in Spain might be a working holiday to you with lots of sunbathing and little work, to your employer it means exactly the opposite. Long hours and low pay are par for the course and you're often required to work 10 hours a day with only one day a week free. Due to the large number of unemployed, unskilled workers in Spain, it's difficult to find work in the construction and farming (e.g. fruit or grape picking) industries and when found, work is hard and low paid. Unemployment is high in resort areas, although foreigners can often find work in bars, clubs and other tourist-oriented businesses where fluent English (or other foreign language fluency) is an advantage. Bear in mind that seasonal workers have few rights and little legal job protection in Spain, and can generally be fired without compensation at any time. See also **Recruitment Agencies** on page 24 and **Temporary & Casual Work** on page 28.

TEACHING ENGLISH

English teachers are in huge demand in Spain, where learning English (and other foreign languages) has become *de rigueur* in the last decade. There are over 20,000 English-language teachers in Spain and due to the constant demand and high turnover, those with a TEFL (Teaching English as a Foreign Language) or ESL (English as a Second Language) certificate can sometimes find a job on the spot, although you shouldn't rely on it. In fact, due to the high demand for teachers in some cities, some schools don't insist on formal teaching qualifications and a graduate native English speaker can get a job without other qualifications (although Americans aren't as popular as Britons).

Private Language Schools: There are numerous private language schools in Spain (which has the largest number of language schools of any country in Europe) offering English classes for both adults and children. The quality of schools and rates of pay vary considerably, and contracts should be carefully examined before committing yourself. Salaries are low and are usually between 90,000 to 120,000 ptas a month or around 1,000 ptas an hour, although board and lodging may be subsidised by the school (and salaries can be supplemented by giving private lessons). Hours are long and anti-social (depending on whether you're a night owl) and schools often exploit teachers, many of whom work illegally without work permits. Teachers are usually employed on short-term contracts, which may run parallel with school terms (September to June).

Many foreign international language schools have branches in Spain, including Berlitz, International House and Linguarama, and often require applicants to attend their own teacher-training courses. Many teaching jobs, particularly those in smaller schools, are advertised locally in Spain only and those advertised abroad tend to be for the larger schools, international agencies and government institutions. Information about language schools in Spain is provided by Spanish consulates or you can write to the Association of Language Teaching Institutions (*Asociación de Centros de Enseñanza de Idiomas*), C/Sagasta, 27, 28004 Madrid. Language schools are listed in Yellow Pages under *Idiomas* or *Escuelas de Idiomas*.

Private Tuition: There's a high demand for private English teachers in Spain and many teachers employed in language schools supplement their income by giving private lessons. You can advertise in local schools, universities and retail outlets, and once you're established, additional students can usually be found through word of mouth. The demand for private lessons is particularly strong during the summer months (e.g. for children who failed their end of term English examination). The rate for private lessons varies considerably depending on the city or area and the competition, and is usually around 1,500 ptas an hour. You could also try placing an advertisement in a Spanish newspaper or magazine offering private lessons.

The British Council: The British Council recruits English language teachers and supervisory staff for two-year placements in its language centres in Barcelona, Bilbao, Granada, Las Palmas, Madrid, Oviedo, Palma de Mallorca, Segovia, Seville and Valencia. It's necessary to have an RSA diploma or PGCE in TEFL and two years' experience for most positions. For managerial posts, postgraduate qualifications and a minimum of five years' experience are required. For information contact the British Council, Recruitment Section, Central Management of Direct Teaching, 10 Spring Gardens, London SW1A 2BN, UK (tel. 0171-389 4931). The British Council also recruits English teachers and teachers of other subjects on behalf of British and international schools in Spain. Applicants must be trained teachers with at least two years' experience. For information contact the Overseas Educational Appointments Department, British Council, 65 Davies Street, London W1Y 2AA, UK (tel. 0171-389 7660). The British Council publishes *Teaching Overseas*, a free publication explaining how it recruits its teachers abroad. The British Council ETRC, Santa Barbara 10, 28004 Madrid, can provide a list of major English-language schools in Spain.

Language Assistants: The language assistants scheme enables students from Britain and more than 30 other countries to spend a year working in a school or college in Spain assisting language teachers. Assistants spend 12 to 15 hours a week in the classroom under the supervision of the English (or other language) teacher, helping students improve their command of English and gain an insight into the English way of life. Graduates and undergraduates aged 20 to 30 of any discipline with the relevant foreign language qualification, e.g. at least A-level standard in the UK, are eligible to apply. Students aged 18 to 20 with an A-level or equivalent qualification in Spanish can apply for a position as a junior language assistant at secondary schools in Spain from January to June. Information and applications must be made to the Assistants Department, Central Bureau for Educational Visits & Exchanges, Seymour Mews House, Seymour Mews, London W1H 9PE, UK (tel. 0171-486 5101).

Publications: For more information obtain a copy of *Teaching English Abroad* by Susan Griffith (Vacation Work) or *Teaching English as a Foreign Language and Teaching Abroad* published by AGCAS, Central Services Unit, Armstrong House, Oxford Road, Manchester M1 7ED, UK (tel. 0161-236 8677). One of the best resources for English teachers is the monthly *EFL Gazette* (10 Wrights Lane, London W8 6TA, UK), who also publish the *EFL Guide*.

Teaching Other Subjects: Other teaching jobs are few and far between in Spain and Spanish qualifications are often required to teach in state schools, even though schools can no longer insist on Spanish teaching qualifications under EU regulations. Jobs are also available in international and foreign schools teaching American, British and other foreign children. Jobs in Spain are advertised in the *Times Educational Supplement* (Fridays) and through the European Council of International Schools, 21B Lavant Street, Petersfield, Hampshire GU32 3EW, UK (tel. 01730-268244). Jobs for teachers are also listed in *Working Holidays* (see page 25).

Translators & Interpreters: Those who are fluent in Spanish and English (and other languages) can also find work as translators and interpreters. The best job prospects for translators are in the major cities, where most translation work involves business correspondence (although it can be low paid and you need a computer). It's also worthwhile contacting major exporters who need to translate their technical and other documentation into English and other languages. Translation agencies are listed in Yellow Pages under *Traductores*.

TEMPORARY & CASUAL WORK

Temporary and casual work in Spain is usually for a fixed period, ranging from a few hours to a few months, or it may be intermittent. Casual workers may be employed on a daily, first-come, first-served basis. Work often entails heavy labouring and is therefore intended mostly for males, although if you're a female Schwarzenegger there's usually no discrimination against the 'fairer' sex. Anyone looking for casual unskilled work in Spain must usually compete with unskilled Spaniards and North Africans, who are usually prepared to work for less money than anyone else, although nobody *should* be paid less than the minimum salary (see page 32). Many employers illegally pay temporary staff cash-in-hand without making deductions for social security (see **Illegal Working** on page 43). Temporary and casual work includes the following:

• Office work, which is well paid if you're qualified and the easiest work to find in major cities due to the large number of temporary secretarial and office staff agencies (see page 24). You must be fluent in Spanish.

• Work in the construction industry can be found by applying at building sites and through industrial recruitment agencies (such as Manpower). Note, however, that the building industry has been in a slump for the last few years and jobs are difficult to find and poorly paid.

• Jobs in shops during the height of the tourist season and during Christmas and annual sales in major cities.

• Doing promotion work for bars, restaurants and other businesses in the summer season, which usually consists of handing out leaflets to tourists.

• Gardening jobs in private gardens, public parks, and for landscape gardeners and garden centres, particularly in spring and summer.

• Peddling ice cream, cold drinks, food or suntan lotion in summer, e.g. on beaches.

• Work touting for timeshare property companies can be found in many resorts during the summer season (and throughout the year in some areas), although it usually involves dubious practices and high-pressure sales methods (and is usually on a commission basis only). Note, however, that touting for timeshare customers in public has been banned in some resorts, although it's often carried out under another guise, e.g. market research or free prize draws.

• Various jobs are available in ports including yacht-minding, crewing, servicing, cleaning and boat delivery. Work as a deck-hand on a yacht pays well and usually also includes tips. You should have private medical insurance.

• Market research which entails asking people personal questions either in the street or house to house (an ideal job for nosy parkers with fluent Spanish).

• House sitting which involves caring for a house and garden (possibly including a pet) while the owners are away. Not usually paid, but provides free accommodation.

- Modelling at art colleges; both sexes are usually required and not just the body beautiful.

- Nursing and auxiliary nursing in hospitals, clinics and nursing homes (temporary staff are often employed through nursing agencies to replace permanent staff at short notice). The best-paid nursing jobs are in private clinics and hospitals, or working directly for private patients in their own homes.

- Newspaper, magazine and leaflet distribution.

- Courier work (own transport required — motorcycle, car or van).

- Driving jobs, including coach and truck drivers, and ferrying cars for manufacturers and car rental companies.

- Miscellaneous jobs such as office cleaners, baby-sitters and labourers are available from a number of agencies specialising in temporary work.

Temporary jobs are advertised on notice boards in supermarkets, expatriate clubs, churches and organisations, and in expatriate newsletters and newspapers. See also **Recruitment Consultants** on page 24 and **Seasonal Jobs** on page 25.

VOLUNTARY WORK

Voluntary work (as described here) is primarily to enable students and young people to visit Spain for a few weeks or months to learn about the country and its people at first hand. The minimum age requirement for volunteers is 16 to 18 and you must usually be under 30, although some organisations have no upper age limit. No special qualifications are required and the minimum length of service is usually a few weeks. Handicapped volunteers are welcomed by many organisations. Voluntary work is (naturally) unpaid and you must usually pay a registration fee, which includes personal liability and health insurance, and your own travel costs to and from Spain and to the workcamp. Although meals and accommodation are normally provided, you may be expected to contribute towards the cost of board and lodging. The usual visa regulations apply to voluntary workers (you will be informed when applying whether you need a visa), although work or residence permits aren't necessary.

Much voluntary work in Spain takes place in international workcamps which provide the opportunity for young people to live and work together on a range of projects including agriculture, archeology, building, conservation, environmental, gardening, handicrafts, restoration of buildings and monuments, social welfare and community projects. Camps are usually run for two to four weeks between April and October, although some operate all year round. Work is unskilled or semi-skilled and is for around five to eight hours a day, five or six days a week. The work is usually physically quite demanding and accommodation, which is shared with your fellow slaves, is fairly basic. Most workcamps consist of volunteers from several countries and English is often the common language.

Archaeological and conservation projects are coordinated in Spain by the *Instituto de la Juventud, Servicio Voluntario Internacional (SVI) de España*, C/José Ortega y Gasset, 71, 28006 Madrid (tel. (91) 401 6652). The SVI publish a handbook entitled *Campos de Trabajo* (work camps) containing details in English and Spanish of over 100 two-week projects throughout Spain. Many Spanish voluntary organisations are listed in *Working Holidays* published by the Central Bureau (see page 25). The Central Bureau also publishes *Volunteer Work*, containing information on over 100 organisations recruiting volunteers for projects in over 150 countries worldwide (including Spain). Another useful guide is the *International Directory of Voluntary Work* (Vacation Work), a guide to residential and non-residential voluntary work throughout the world.

JOB HUNTING

When looking for a job (or a new job) in Spain, it's best not to put all your eggs in one basket, as the more job applications you make the better your chances of finding the right job. Contact as many prospective employers as possible, either by writing, telephoning or calling on them in person. Whatever job you're looking for, it's important to market yourself appropriately, which will depend on the type of job or position you're seeking. For example, the recruitment of executives and senior managers is often handled by recruitment consultants who advertise in the Spanish national press and trade magazines. At the other end of the scale, unskilled manual jobs requiring no previous experience may be advertised at INEM employment offices, in local newspapers and on notice boards, and the first suitable applicant may be offered the job on the spot. Job hunting includes the following resources:

Newspapers: Obtain copies of Spanish national and regional newspapers, all of which contain 'situations vacant' (*trabajo vacante* or *ofertas de empleo*) sections on certain days, e.g. Sundays. Most professions and trade associations publish journals containing job offers (see *Benn's Media Directory Europe*). Jobs are also advertised in various English-language publications including the *International Herald Tribune*, *Wall Street Journal Europe*, *The European* (weekly) and *Overseas Jobs Express*. The expatriate Spanish press (see page 389) also contains 'Situations Vacant' and 'Situations Wanted' small ads. You can place an advertisement in 'Situations Wanted' (*demanda*) columns in most publications. Publicitas Limited can help you place an advertisement in Spanish publications and has offices in many countries, e.g. Publicitas Ltd., 517-523 Fulham Road, London SW6 1HD, UK (tel. 171-385 7723). It's best to place an advert in the middle of the week and to avoid the summer and other holiday periods.

When writing for jobs, address your letter to the personnel director or manager and include your curriculum vitae (in Spanish), and copies of all references and qualifications. If possible, offer to attend an interview and state when you will be available. Letters should be tailored to individual employers and be professionally translated if your Spanish isn't perfect. Note, however, that Spanish companies are notoriously bad at answering letters and you should follow up letters with a telephone call.

Employment Offices: Visit local INEM offices in Spain (see page 23). Jobs on offer are mainly non-professional skilled, semi-skilled and unskilled jobs, particularly in industry, retailing and catering.

Recruitment Agencies: Apply to international recruitment agencies acting for Spanish companies. These companies mainly recruit executives and key personnel, and many have offices worldwide including major Spanish cities. Contact recruitment agencies in Spain (see page 24) for temporary positions. Note that many Spanish agencies find positions for Spanish and EU nationals only or non-EU foreigners with a residence card (*residencia*).

Unsolicited Job Applications: Apply to American, British and other multi-national companies with offices or subsidiaries in Spain, and make written applications direct to Spanish companies. Useful addresses can usually be obtained from regional and local chambers of commerce (*Cámara Oficial de Comercio e Industria*) and other organisations in Spain. Spanish companies are listed by products, services and provinces in *Kompass Spain*, available at libraries in Spain and main libraries and Spanish Chambers of Commerce abroad. Making unsolicited job applications to targeted companies is naturally a hit and miss affair. It can, however, be more successful than responding to advertisements as you aren't usually competing with other applicants. Some companies recruit a large percentage of employees through unsolicited résumés. When writing from abroad, enclosing an international reply coupon may help elicit a reply.

Networking: Networking (which originated in the USA) consists of making business and professional contacts. It's particularly useful in Spain, where it's common to use personal contacts for everything from looking for a job to finding accommodation. It's difficult for most foreigners to make contacts among the Spanish and therefore many turn to the expatriate community. If you're already in Spain, contact or join expatriate social clubs, churches, societies and professional organisations. Finally, don't forget to ask friends and acquaintances working in Spain if they know of an employer looking for someone with your experience and qualifications.

WORKING WOMEN

The number of working women in Spain has increased considerably in the last 20 years and some 40 per cent of Spanish women under 40 now work full or part-time. The number of women in the professions has steadily increased over the years in line with the increase in the number of women graduates (which now exceeds those of men). Women represent around 40 per cent of the working population and two thirds of Spain's unemployed.

Nowadays professional women are quite common in Spain, particularly doctors and lawyers, and there's less sexism in the professions than in other Latin countries. Career women are commonplace and accepted in many fields which were previously closed to them, although they still have difficulty reaching senior management positions. However, the 'glass ceiling' for professional women in Spain is no worse than in most other western countries (although macho Spanish men often feel threatened by female bosses). Spanish employers are often reluctant to hire women in responsible positions, particularly if they think they're planning a family, not least because they must provide generous, paid maternity leave. Women are protected by law against discrimination on the grounds of their sex.

A woman doing the same or broadly similar work to a man and employed by the same employer, is legally entitled to the same salary and other terms of employment. However, women in Spain occupy most poorly paid jobs and their salaries are generally around 20 per cent lower than men's. This largely reflects the fact that most women work in lower paid industries and hold lower paid positions than men, rather than discrimination. Most women are employed in distribution and transport, nursing and health care, education, secretarial professions, and service industries such as retailing. However, although there's no official discrimination, in practice it's often not the case. The fact that 'the best man for the job may be a woman' isn't often acknowledged by Spanish employers (or employers anywhere) and women must generally be twice as qualified as men to compete on equal terms. However, the situation has improved considerably in recent years and women are exploited less in Spain than in some other western European countries. Spain celebrates a 'day of the working woman' (March 8th) and there are associations of business women (AMECO) in many provinces.

Sexual harassment isn't widespread in Spain, although women must usually tolerate a certain amount of (usually innocent) flirting, which is an accepted part of Spanish life and isn't taken too seriously. Most remarks are intended as a compliment and are acknowledged by Spanish women in a perfunctory manner. If, however, you do receive and refuse a sexual advance from your boss, it will rarely result in the loss of your job as it's difficult to fire employees in Spain.

SALARY

It's often difficult to determine the salary (*sueldo*) you should command in Spain as salaries aren't often quoted in job advertisements, except in the public sector, where employees are paid according to fixed grades and salaries are public knowledge. Salaries vary considerably for the same job in different parts of Spain. Those working in major cities such as Madrid and Barcelona are generally the highest paid, primarily due to the high cost of living, particularly accommodation. If you're able to negotiate your own salary, then you should ensure that you receive the salary and benefits commensurate with your qualifications and experience (or as much as you can get!). If you have friends or acquaintances working in Spain or who have worked there, ask them what an average or good salary is for your particular trade or profession. When comparing salaries you must take into account compulsory deductions such as tax and social security, and also consider the cost of living (see page 315).

Salaries for managers and professionals compare favourably with other western countries and are among the highest in Europe. Directors usually earn between 10 and 25m ptas a year depending on the size of the company and middle managers between 6m and 10m ptas. Salaried professionals earn around 6m ptas. Spanish blue-collar workers earn less than their counterparts in most other western European countries (only Greek and Portuguese workers earn less), e.g. some 55 per cent less than German workers, 30 per cent less than the French and around 10 per cent less than British workers. However, their productivity is usually much lower than in most EU countries.

For many employees, particularly executives and senior managers, their remuneration is much more than what they receive in their monthly pay packets. Many companies offer a number of benefits for executives and managers including a company car (rarer in Spain than in some other European countries); private health insurance and health screening; paid holidays; private school fees; inexpensive or interest-free home and other loans; rent-free accommodation; free public transport tickets; free or subsidised company restaurant; sports or country club membership; non-contributory company pension; stock options; bonuses and profit-sharing schemes; complementary tickets for sports events and shows; and 'business' conferences in exotic places (see also **Executive Positions** on page 51).

Spain has a statutory minimum wage (*salario mínimo interprofesional*), which was 66,630 ptas a month (2,221 ptas a day) in 1997 for an unskilled worker aged over 18 and 59,130 ptas a month (1,971 ptas a day) for someone aged under 18. Minimum salaries are set for all workers under collective labour agreements. Most workers receive more than the minimum salary and less than 500,000 employees are directly affected by minimum wage rates. However, an increase in the minimum wage usually serves as a benchmark for wage demands. Unskilled workers (particularly women) are usually employed at or near the minimum wage, while semi-skilled and skilled workers receive a premium of up to 100 per cent. Note, however, that minimum salaries don't mean much in Spain, particularly in the expatriate community where many people work illegally and get paid cash in hand. Most employees in Spain receive a month's extra salary (*pagas extraordinarias*) twice a year, at Christmas and before the August summer holiday. Salaries in most industries in Spain are decided by collective bargaining between employers and unions.

Throughout the 1980s Spanish employees enjoyed huge wage increases far in excess of inflation, and the average salary doubled. However, salaries remained largely static during the recession and pay increases are now often linked to increased productivity. In recent years the government has frozen civil service pay and reduced government spending, which, along with the booming economy, has lead to increased prosperity and a more positive outlook than anyone would have dared dream possible a few years ago.

SELF-EMPLOYMENT

If you're an EU-national or a permanent resident with a *residencia* (see page 67), you can be self-employed (*trabajador autónomo*) or work as a sole trader (*empresa individual*) in Spain. If you want to work as self-employed in a profession or trade in Spain, you must meet certain legal requirements and register with the appropriate organisation, e.g. a professional must become a member of the relevant professional college (*colegio*). However, these colleges serve no real purpose today and the Spanish consumer organisation (OCU) has suggested that they be abolished. Under Spanish law every self-employed person must have an official status and it's illegal simply to hang out a sign and start business.

Members of some professions and trades must possess professional qualifications (see page 22) and certificates recognised in Spain, and are usually required to sit a written examination in Spanish. You're subject to any professional codes and limitations in force, e.g. a medical practitioner must have his qualifications accepted by the medical college of the province where he intends to practise and any controlling specialist bodies before he can practise in Spain. You must also show that you're in good standing with the professional authorities in your own country. In certain professions, such as lawyers, it's unusual to be permitted to practise in Spain without Spanish qualifications.

As a self-employed person you don't have the protection of a limited company should your business fail, although there are certain tax advantages. It may be advantageous to operate as a limited company, for example an SL (see page 38). Always obtain professional advice before deciding whether to operate as a sole trader or form a company in Spain, as it has far-reaching social security, tax and other consequences. All self-employed persons must register for income tax, social security and VAT (IVA), and anyone with an income in Spain requires a fiscal identification number (*Número de Identificación Fiscal/NIF*), obtainable from your local national police station (*comisaría de policía nacional*).

Social Security: There's a special social security scheme (*régimen especial de autónomos*) for self-employed workers. If you're self-employed and employ others, you must register your business in the general social security scheme and must affiliate all your employees and comply with the requirements of the *Inspección Provincial de Trabajo*. Social security contributions for the self-employed are higher than for salaried employees and you receive less benefits (which encourages illegal working). In 1997 they were a minimum of around 30,000 ptas a month irrespective of income. You receive a book of payment slips from your social security office and payments can be made directly by your bank. Note that as a self-employed person in Spain, you aren't entitled to unemployment benefit should your business fail. Furthermore, if you have two unconnected part-time jobs, you officially require two sets of papers and must pay social security twice!

Registration Tax: You must register as a self-employed worker or professional at your local town hall (*ayuntamiento*) for the *Impuesto sobre Actividades Económicas (IAE)*, which is a 'tax on economic activities' that replaced the fiscal licence (*licencia fiscal*). The costs of IAE, which roughly equates to a business licence, varies considerably and can be from 10,000 to over 50,000 ptas a year, depending on your profession or business (there are around 1,000 categories) and where it's located. It also depends on other factors, such as whether you work alone or employ staff and the size and location of your business premises. Registration must be made at least 10 days prior to starting business. A fee is payable for the licence (*abono de la declaración-liquidación de alta*), which is issued for six months or one year. Once you have registered for IAE you must apply for a residence card (*residencia*) at the nearest national police station with a foreigner's department.

Value Added Tax: All self-employed persons must register for valued added tax (*Impuesto sobre el Valor Añadido/IVA*), irrespective of income, and levy VAT at 16 per cent on all services or goods. VAT must be declared and paid quarterly.

STARTING A BUSINESS

Most foreigners find Spain a frustrating country in which to do business. The bureaucracy associated with starting a business there is staggering and ranks among the most pernicious in the western world. For foreigners the red tape is almost impenetrable, especially if you don't speak Spanish, as you will be inundated with official documents and must be able to understand them. It's only when you come up against the full force of Spanish bureaucracy that you understand what it *really* means to be a foreigner in Spain! It's difficult not to believe that the authorities' sole purpose in life is to obstruct business (in fact it's to protect their own jobs). Patience and tolerance are the watchwords when dealing with Spanish bureaucrats (and will also do wonders for your blood pressure). Although many foreigners find it hard to believe, things have improved considerably in recent years and the regulations and procedures have become less onerous (it's true!) since Spain joined the EU. Despite the red tape, Spain is traditionally a country of small companies and sole traders, and there are some 1.5m family-run businesses (of all sizes) employing over 80 per cent of the working population. Among the best sources of help and information are your local chamber of commerce (*Cámara de Comercio*) and town hall (*ayuntamiento*).

Work Permits: An EU national doesn't require a work permit to start a business in Spain. However, a non-EU citizen wishing to start a business in Spain must make an investment of the equivalent of around US$100,000 in order to be granted a work permit. A licence issued for a business owned by a non-EU national may be conditional on the employment of a minimum number of EU citizens (the authorities can no longer insist that you employ Spanish nationals). Businesses that create jobs are welcomed with open arms, particularly in areas with high unemployment.

Avoiding the Crooks: In addition to problems with the Spanish authorities, assorted crooks and swindlers are unfortunately fairly common in Spain, particularly in resort areas. You should always have a healthy suspicion regarding the motives of anyone you do business with in Spain (unless it's your mum or spouse), particularly your fellow countrymen. It's generally best to avoid partnerships as they rarely work and can be a disaster. In general, you should trust nobody and shouldn't sign anything or pay any money before having a contract checked by a lawyer. It's a sad fact of life that foreigners who prey on their fellow countrymen are common in Spain. In most cases you're better off dealing with a long-established Spanish company with roots in the local community (and therefore a good reputation to protect), rather than your compatriots. Note that if things go wrong you may be unprotected by Spanish law, the wheels of which grind extremely slowly (when they haven't fallen off completely!).

Research: BEWARE! For many foreigners, starting a business in Spain is one of the quickest routes to bankruptcy known to mankind. In fact, the majority of foreigners who open businesses in Spain would be better off investing in lottery tickets, when they would at least have a chance of receiving a return on their investment! Many would-be foreign entrepreneurs leave Spain with literally only their shirts on their backs, having learnt the facts of Spanish business life the hard way. **If you aren't prepared to thoroughly research the market and obtain expert business and legal advice, then you shouldn't even think about starting a business in Spain (or anywhere else for that matter).**

The key to starting or buying a successful business in Spain is exhaustive research, research and yet more research (plus innovation, value for money and service). It's an absolute must to check out the level of competition in a given area. Note that even when competition is light, there may be insufficient custom to sustain another business. A saturation of trades and services is common in Spain, particularly in resort areas where there's a glut of bars, cafés, restaurants and retail outlets catering to tourists. **Your chances of making a living from a bar, restaurant or retail outlet in a resort area are practically zero, as there's simply too much competition and too few customers to go around.**

In resort areas, some foreigners (e.g. bar and restaurant owners) will do almost anything to lure their competitors' customers, even reducing prices to below cost. In winter you may be lucky to take a few thousand pesetas a day in a bar and it often isn't worthwhile even opening your doors. In some areas you may have to put up with petty laws, which are often selectively enforced on foreign businesses by local police and officials (particularly in resort areas). The Spanish survive only because they invariably own their business premises, have low overheads and live inexpensively. If you're convinced that you have what it takes, don't burn your bridges and sell up abroad, but rent a home in Spain and spend some time doing research before taking the plunge. You should also lease your business premises (at least initially), rather than buying them outright. However, before doing so it's imperative to ensure that you fully understand your rights regarding possible future rent increases and the renewal and termination of a lease.

Generally speaking you shouldn't consider running a business in Spain in a field in which you don't have previous experience. It's often advisable to work for someone else in the same line of business (even without pay) to gain experience, rather than jump in at the deep end. Always thoroughly investigate an existing or proposed business before investing any money. **As any expert (and many failed entrepreneurs) will tell you, Spain isn't a country for amateurs, particularly amateurs who don't speak fluent Spanish.** It isn't always necessary to speak English if your customers are exclusively expatriates, although it's important that at least one partner or employee speaks fluent

Spanish. Otherwise you will need to pay a secretary or business agent to do simple tasks that you could easily do yourself.

Many small businesses in Spain exist on a shoe string, with owners living from hand to mouth, and certainly aren't what could be considered thriving enterprises. Self-employed businessmen usually work extremely long hours, particularly those running bars or restaurants (days off are almost impossible in the high season), often for little financial reward. As in most countries, many people choose to be self-employed for the lifestyle and freedom it affords (no clocks or bosses), rather than the money. It's important to keep your plans small and manageable and work well within your budget, rather than undertake a grandiose scheme.

Many foreigners start businesses in Spain on a whim and a prayer with little business acumen or money and no Spanish. They're simply asking for trouble! **It's pitiful (but all too common) to see newcomers working all the hours under the sun struggling to make a living from a business that's doomed to failure.** Bear in mind that when a couple operate a business together it can put an intolerable strain on their relationship and many marriages fail under the pressures. Many people come to Spain with a grand design without doing their homework (research, marketing, etc.), lose all their money, hang on desperately for a few months or years trying to scrape a living in the expatriate community and are eventually forced to return home much wiser and poorer, having learnt the facts of Spanish business life the hard way. **It pays to be brutally honest with yourself before making the decision to run a business in Spain, where the unpalatable truth is that there's a foreign sucker born every minute!**

Legal Advice: Before establishing a business or undertaking any business transactions in Spain, it's important to obtain legal advice to ensure that you're operating within the law. There are severe penalties for anyone who ignores the regulations and legal requirements. Expert legal advice is also necessary to make the most of any favourable tax and business breaks, and make sense of the myriad rules and regulations. It's imperative to ensure that contracts are clearly defined and water-tight before making an investment, as if you become involved in a legal dispute it's likely to take years to resolve. Before starting a business in Spain you should obtain advice from a lawyer (*abogado*) and an accountant (*asesor fiscal*), and engage an official agent (*gestor*) to shepherd you through the minefield of red tape (see page 410). Many Spanish lawyers, accountants and agents speak English and other languages (lists can be obtained from embassies and consulates in Spain).

Opening Licence & Other Permits: If your business requires premises such as a shop, workshop or offices, you require a business 'opening' licence (*licencia de apertura*) from the local municipal council before starting business. The cost of an opening licence varies considerably depending on the type of business, for example from 10,000 ptas for a small shop, 100,000 ptas for a bar or restaurant and up to 650,000 ptas for a bank branch (although it's unlikely you will be opening a bank). To obtain an opening licence you require a lease or title deed for the premises and a receipt for registration tax or IAE (see page 34).

If a business may create a risk or inconvenience to the local community, e.g. a bar or discotheque, the council will insist that you fulfill certain requirements before it grants an opening licence. Note that you won't be granted a licence if the business is likely to cause a nuisance or if there are already deemed to be sufficient businesses of that kind in the area. A licence application isn't necessary if the business premises are to be used for the same purpose as previously, e.g. a bar or restaurant, although you will need to register the ownership of the business in your name. Note that you may have to wait up to six months for your opening licence to be issued. Many businesses operate without a licence and some continue to operate without one for years, although they are increasingly being closed by the local authorities. To sell or serve alcohol and food you require a health licence, and establishments that serve food need to also undergo sanitary and technical inspections, and employees must obtain a food handler's medical certificate (possibly even when no food is served!).

Tax: Spanish companies are assigned a fiscal identity number which is used for all tax purposes. Small businesses (such as a shop or restaurant) are initially taxed on a modular system (*modulos*) where tax is estimated based on the size of premises, number of tables in a restaurant, number of employees and other factors. You pay business tax on the estimated amount each quarter and receive a refund or pay the amount outstanding at the end of the tax year. After the first year you can choose whether to continue with the modular system or pay tax on your actual earnings by the direct estimation (*estimación directa*) method, which requires maintaining detailed records.

All Spanish limited companies must file corporate tax returns which are submitted to the provincial tax headquarters (*Delegación de Hacienda*) in the area where the business is registered (*domicilio fiscal*). Various returns must be made including corporation tax, personal income tax, income tax of sole proprietors and value added tax. Corporation tax at 35 per cent is levied on profits. Surcharges and interest are levied for late payment of tax and huge fines are imposed for tax infringements. On the other hand, if you overpay your tax you can claim a refund when you make your annual tax declaration.

Grants: There are a wide range of investment incentives available to anyone planning to establish a business in Spain, both from the Spanish government and the European Union. Incentives include investment subsidies, tax relief, low-interest or interest-free loans, social security rebates and reduced registration tax during the start-up period. No special incentives are offered to foreign investors. However, the Spanish government provides seminars for prospective foreign investors including advice from banks, and lectures from established business people and representatives of companies with subsidiaries in Spain. There are government incentives for investment in 'economic promotion zones' (*zonas de promoción económica*), which include all autonomous regions except for Madrid, Rioja, Catalonia and Valencia; 'declining industrial zones' (*zonas industrializadas en declive (ZID)*) which include certain areas of Asturias, the Basque country, Cantabria and Galicia; and 'urgent re-industrialisation zones' (*zonas de urgente reindustrialización*), including Aragón, Asturias, the Canary Islands, Cantabria, Castilla-La Mancha, Castilla-León, Galicia and Murcia.

Further Information: Most international accountants have offices throughout Spain and are an invaluable source of information (in English and other languages) on subjects such as forming a company, company law, taxation and social security. Many publish free booklets concerning doing business in Spain including *A Guide to Business in Spain* available from Arthur Anderson 1 Surrey Street, London WC2R 2PS, UK (tel. 0171-438 3000), *Doing Business in Spain*, published by Ernst & Young, Beckett House, 1 Lambeth Palace Road, London SE1 7EU, UK (tel. 0171-928 2000) and *Doing Business in Spain* (again) from Price Waterhouse, Southwark Towers, 32 London Bridge Street, London SE1 9SY, UK (tel. 0171-939 3000).

The Spanish Ministry of Economy and Commerce publishes a series of booklets in English entitled *A Guide to Business in Spain*. Booklets in the series include *Foreign Investment*, *Forms of Business Organisations* and *Labour Legislation*. They are obtainable from Spanish embassies and also direct from the *Ministerio de Economía y Comercio*, Dirección General de Transacciones Exteriores, C/Almagro, 34, 28010

Madrid. Many countries maintain chambers of commerce in Spain, which are an invaluable source of information and assistance. Each province also has its own chamber of commerce, each with an international department. For information contact the Association of Spanish Chambers of Commerce, *Consejo Superior de Cámaras de Comercio, Industria y Navegación de España*, C/Claudio Coello, 19, 28001 Madrid (tel. (91) 575 3400).

Limited Companies: Companies cannot be purchased 'off the shelf' in Spain and it usually takes a number of months to set up a company. Incorporating a company in Spain takes longer and is more expensive and complicated than in most other European countries (those bureaucrats again!). There are a number of different types of 'limited companies' or business entities in Spain and choosing the right one can be difficult. **Always obtain professional legal advice regarding the advantages and disadvantages of different limited companies.**

A Spanish business may assume various legal entities. Most small businessmen operate as sole traders (*empresas individuales*), and must register with the appropriate trade association, pay a small entrance fee and a monthly subscription. A small company is usually a 'private limited company' (*Sociedad Limitada/SL*) and a larger limited company is usually a 'public company' (*Sociedad Anónima/SA*). Other business entities include a general partnership (*Sociedad Regular Colectiva/SRC*), a limited partnership (*Sociedad Comanditaria*), and a joint venture between a Spanish and foreign company (*Asociación de Empresas en Participación*).

Sociedad de responsabilidad Limitada (SL): An SL is the simplest and most common form of limited company in Spain. It doesn't have any public shares and the capital is divided among the shareholders, of whom there can be a maximum of 50. The minimum capital required is 500,000 ptas. Its constitution process is simpler than an SA (see below) and only two founders are required, although its statutes are more restrictive.

Sociedad Anónima (SA): An SA is similar to a British limited company (plc) or an American corporation (Inc.). To form an SA requires a minimum share capital of 10m ptas and at least three shareholders, who can be companies or individuals of any nationality. An SA must have at least 50 employees and a committee on which workers are represented (*comité de empresa*). Only one director is necessary, who may be a foreigner *and* a non-resident.

Wealth Warning: Whatever people may tell you, working for yourself isn't easy and it requires a lot of hard work (self-employed people generally work much longer hours than employees); a sizeable investment and sufficient operating funds (under-funding is the major cause of business failures); good organisation (e.g. bookkeeping and planning); excellent customer relations; and a measure of luck (although generally the harder you work, the more 'luck' you will have). Don't be seduced by the apparent relaxed way of life in Spain — if you want to be a success in business you cannot play at it.

However, although there are numerous failures for every success story, many foreigners *do* run successful businesses in Spain. Those who make a go of it do so as a result of extensive market research, wise investments, excellent customer relations and most important of all, a lot of hard work. One way *not* to make money is to answer one of the tempting advertisements that occasionally appear in English-language publications in Spain, e.g. "50,000 ptas daily. Interested? Then let me show you how. For full details send 1,000 pesetas to . . ." On the other hand, placing an advertisement in a newspaper and getting 50 suckers a day to send you 1,000 ptas may well be a quick way to get rich!

Buying an Existing Business

It's much easier to buy an existing business in Spain (or anywhere else) than it is to start a new one. The paperwork for taking over an existing business is complicated enough, without doing it from scratch. Taking over an established business is also less of a risk than starting something new. Note, however, that buying an existing business that's a going concern isn't easy. Most people in Spain simply don't sell thriving businesses without a good reason, at least not at a cost-effective price. The Spanish aren't in a habit of buying and selling businesses, which are usually passed from generation to generation. If you plan to buy a business, always obtain an independent valuation (or two). Try to find out why the previous owner is selling as there may be a hidden motive, for example a thriving small grocery shop will probably become worthless if a supermarket opens around the corner. It's essential to check local planning permission for rival businesses, roads, factories, public works, housing developments and anything else that may affect your business.

Never sign anything you don't understand 100 per cent and without obtaining independent professional advice from local business experts such as accountants and banks. However, don't expect their advice to be totally unbiased or totally accurate. Always ensure that turnover claims can be substantiated and aren't inflated (a common practice). It goes without saying that you should never take actual or projected turnover or profit figures at face value, particularly when they are provided by someone with an interest in selling a business, e.g. an agent or the owner. However, it's true that the declared turnover for tax purposes is usually lower than actual turnover. The only way to verify the turnover is to spend some time working with the owner or tenant assessing the income at first hand.

It's important to note when buying a business property in Spain, that all debts against the property are automatically transferred to the property's new owners (as with domestic property). **Beware!** Get your lawyer to check whether there are any charges against a business. Many bars and restaurants are sold leasehold and often leases are too expensive to allow the leaseholder to make a profit. Note that there's no statutory security of tenure under the law of industrial leases and if you rent business premises, it's essential to take legal advice regarding the lease. When buying a business in Spain, two prices are usually quoted; one for the lease/business and a monthly rental. The lease is usually a life lease (*traspaso*), although leases can also be from two to 20 years. The lease should limit future rent increases to the rate of inflation, otherwise if your business is a huge success your landlord can hold you to ransom by demanding an extortionate rent. Business leases must be paid in cash and loans aren't usually available. It's important to obtain *all* necessary licences before signing a lease or purchase contract, or the contract should be conditional on licences being issued.

There are specialist business agents throughout Spain and many real estate agents also sell businesses. Businesses are also advertised for sale through the Spanish and English-language press in Spain (see page 389), and local chambers of commerce can also offer advice and provide contacts.

Starting a New Business

Most people are far too optimistic about the prospects of a new business in Spain and over-estimate income levels (it sometimes takes years to make a profit). Be realistic or even pessimistic when estimating your income, and overestimate the costs and underestimate the revenue (then reduce it by another 50 per cent!). While hoping for the best, you should plan for the worst and have sufficient funds to last until you're established. New projects are rarely (if ever) completed within budget.

Capital: Make sure you have sufficient working capital and that you can survive until a business takes off. If possible you should have enough capital to last a year without taking any money out of a business. Spanish banks are usually wary of lending to new businesses, especially businesses run by foreigners (would you trust a foreigner?). Lenders usually require a detailed business plan plus security, and a loan may be restricted to the amount of capital you put into a business. If you wish to borrow money to buy property or for a business venture in Spain, you should carefully consider where and in what currency to raise finance.

Location: Choosing the location for a business is usually more important than the location for a home. As is often said, the three most important points when starting a retail business are location, location and location, e.g. you're asking to fail if you open a bar or restaurant targeted at foreigners or tourists in an area where there are neither. Depending on the type of business, you may need access to motorways and rail links or to be located in a popular tourist area or near local attractions. Local plans regarding communications, industry and major building developments, e.g. housing complexes and new shopping centres, may also be important. Plans regarding new motorways and rail links are usually available from the local town hall.

Employees: Hiring employees is a big step in Spain and should be taken into account *before* starting a business. You must enter into a contract under Spanish labour law and employees enjoy extensive rights. If you're planning to hire staff, you should use the services of a 'labour lawyer' (*asesor laboral*), who's a specialist in employment and self-employment law. Note that it's expensive to hire full-time employees in Spain. In addition to their salary you must pay an additional around 30 per cent in social security payments, pay two extra months' salaries (see page 53), and give employees 30 days paid holiday and 14 paid public holidays each year. Each employee will cost you at least 120,000 ptas a month, based on a low salary of 75,000 ptas a month plus the additional 30 per cent for social security. **You should also take care when employing someone part-time, such as a gardener or maid.** See also **Social Security** on page 254 and **Chapter 2.**

Type of Business: The most common businesses operated by foreigners in Spain include hotels and other accommodation (particularly in rural areas, where grants are available to encourage 'rural tourism'); caravan and camping sites; farming; catering (e.g. bars, cafés and restaurants); shops and franchises; hairdressers; property development, sales and letting; garden centres; sports centres and tuition (e.g. tennis, golf, squash, bowling, snooker or pool hall, gymnasiums, water and aerial sports, and horse riding); social clubs; business and secretarial services; English-language schools; translations and interpreting; car, motorcycle and bicycle sale and rentals; boat sales and rentals; nursing homes; secondhand furniture stores; new and secondhand book shops and lending libraries; kennels and catteries; discotheques and night clubs; and satellite television, to name but a few examples. The majority of businesses established by foreigners in Spain are linked to the leisure and catering industries, followed by property investment and development, and providing for the miscellaneous needs of foreign residents.

TRAINEES & WORK EXPERIENCE

Spain is a participant in an international trainee (*aprendiz*) programme designed to give young people the opportunity for further education and occupational training, and to enlarge their professional experience and knowledge of languages. The programme has exchange agreements with Austria, Belgium, Canada, Denmark, Finland, Germany, Ireland, Luxembourg, the Netherlands, New Zealand, Norway, Sweden, Switzerland, the United Kingdom and the USA. If you're aged between 18 and 30 (USA 21 to 30) and have completed your vocational training (minimum of two years), you may be eligible for a position as a trainee in Spain. The trainee agreement covers most occupations and employment must be in the occupation in which you were trained. Positions are usually granted for one year and in exceptional circumstances can be extended for a further six months. Information about the trainee programme can be obtained from INEM offices (see page 23) in Spain and government employment offices abroad.

Technical and commercial students, who wish to gain experience by working in industry and commerce in Spain during their holidays, can apply to the International Association for the Exchange of Students for Technical Experience (IAESTE) in over 60 countries. Applicants must possess a working knowledge of Spanish and be currently enrolled at an educational institution as a full-time student of engineering, science, agriculture, architecture or applied arts, *or* be undergraduates in their penultimate year of study and aged between 19 and 30. In Britain, applicants should apply to IAESTE, Imperial College, South Kensington, Prince Consort Road, London SW7 2NA, UK (tel. 0171-589 5111). Most foreign trainees in Spain are sponsored by employers or colleges under exchange arrangements. For information about trainee and work experience schemes in Spain, contact your country's national employment services agency or the national trade association for the industry in which you wish to train, who may be able to put you in contact with a suitable Spanish employer.

PETRA: PETRA is an EU-sponsored programme providing support for 16-27 year-olds to benefit from vocational training and work experience in another EU country. Placements are for from three weeks to 12 months and are targeted at young people in vocational training, young workers, young jobseekers, and those taking part in an advanced training programme after starting work. Applications must be submitted through relevant training organisations or colleges.

AU PAIRS

Single males and females aged between 18 and 30 (ages may vary depending on the agency or employer) are eligible for a job as an au pair. The au pair system provides young people with an excellent opportunity to travel, improve their Spanish, and generally broaden their education by living and working in Spain. However, the main aim of the au pair system is to give young people the opportunity to learn a foreign language in a typical family environment.

Au pairs in Spain are accepted from most countries. If you're an EU national you need a valid passport only and it's unnecessary to arrange an au pair position before arriving in Spain. In fact it's often better *not* to do so. Some agents allow you to meet families in Spain, before making a decision. This is advisable as you can interrogate the family, inspect their home and your accommodation, and meet the children who will make your life heaven or hell! If you arrive in Spain without a position you can usually find one within a few weeks. Applicants from non-EU countries *must* obtain a visa (see page 65) before arriving in Spain and require an offer of a position from a Spanish family. This must be presented to your local Spanish embassy or consulate (with your passport) in order to obtain a visa.

Au pairs are usually contracted to work for a minimum of six months and a maximum of one year. Most families require an au pair for at least the whole school year, from September to June. The best time to look for an au pair position is therefore before the beginning of the school year in September. You should apply as early as possible and not later than one month prior to your preferred start date or at least two months if you need a visa. There are also summer au pair programmes of two to three months, for which enrolment must usually be made before 31st March. Au pairs employed for the summer only aren't required to attend Spanish lessons.

Au pairs are only placed with Spanish-speaking families with children in Spain. Duties consist of *light* housework including simple cooking for children; clothes washing (with a machine) and ironing (for children only); washing up and drying dishes (if the family doesn't have a dishwasher); making beds; dusting; vacuum cleaning; and other light jobs around the home. To enjoy life as an au pair you should be used to helping around the house and enjoy working with children. An au pair isn't a general servant or cook (although you may be treated as one) and you aren't expected to look after physically or mentally handicapped children.

As an au pair you receive free meals and accommodation and have your own room. Usually you're housed with the family, although this may not always be possible. Working hours are officially limited to 30 a week, five hours a day (morning or afternoon), six days a week, plus a maximum of three evenings' baby-sitting. You should have at least one full day (usually Sunday) and three evenings free each week, and should be free to attend religious services. In some families, au pairs are expected to holiday with the family, though you may be free to take Christmas or Easter holidays at home. Choose a wealthy family and you may be taken on exotic foreign holidays. For your labours you're paid the princely (princessly?) sum of between 6,000 and 7,000 ptas (in cities) per week 'pocket money'. You're required to pay your own fare to Spain (and back). A family employing an au pair must make a declaration to the Spanish social security administration and make monthly contributions. If you're ill or have an accident during your stay in Spain, you can obtain treatment under the Spanish social security health system (see page 237). If you aren't covered by Spanish social security, your family must take out private health insurance and pay at least half the premium.

An au pair position can be arranged privately with a family or through an agency, either in Spain or abroad. Au pair positions can also be found through magazines (such as the British *Lady* magazine) and newspapers, but you're usually better off using an agency. The best agencies vet families, make periodic checks on your welfare, help you overcome problems (either personal or with your family), and may organise cultural activities (particularly in major cities). Agencies will send you an application form (questionnaire) and usually ask you to provide character (moral) references, a medical certificate, school references and a number of passport-size photographs. Au pairs must usually have had a high school education (or equivalent) and have a good basic knowledge of Spanish. Au pairs *must* attend Spanish language classes (see page 166) organised for foreign students. An application form can sometimes be completed in your own language, although it's better to complete it in Spanish, even if it means obtaining help (forms are often printed only in Spanish). In addition to regular au pair positions, some agencies offer positions where a room is provided in exchange for around 10 hours work a week (e.g. for full-time students). Agencies charge a registration fee of around 10,000 ptas.

The au pair system has been referred to uncharitably (or aptly?) as a minefield of guilt-ridden mothers, lecherous fathers and spoilt brats (probably by an ex-au pair who was badly bitten by a child!). Your experience as an au pair will depend entirely on your family. If you're fortunate enough to work for a warm and friendly host family, you will have a wonderful experience, lots of free time, and may even enjoy wonderful holidays in Spain or abroad. Many au pairs grow to love their children and families and form lifelong friendships. On the other hand, abuses of the au pair system are common in all countries and you may be treated as a servant or slave rather than a member of the family, and be expected to work long hours and spend most evenings baby-sitting. Many families employ an au pair simply because it costs much less than the salary of the lowest-paid nanny. If you have any questions or complaints about your duties, you should refer them to the agency that found you your position (if applicable). **There are many families to choose from and you should never remain with a family if you're unhappy at the way you're treated.** You're usually required to give notice if you wish to go home before the end of your agreement, although this won't apply if the family has abused the contract.

Au pair agencies in Britain are listed in the *Au Pair and Nanny's Guide to Working Abroad*, by Susan Griffith (Vacation Work). You should contact a number of agencies and compare registration fees and pocket money, both of which may vary considerably (although the terms of employment should always be the same). Note that it's possible for responsible Spanish-speaking young women, even without experience or training, to obtain employment as a nanny in Spain (and many other countries). Duties are basically the same as an au pair, except that a position as a nanny is a real job with a real salary.

ILLEGAL WORKING

Illegal working (*trabajo ilegal*) thrives in Spain, where it has been estimated that the turnover of the 'black economy' (*economía sumergida*) equals between 20 and 25 per cent of the official GNP, and that real unemployment is much less than the official figure. After Italy, Spain has the largest black (cash) economy in the developed world (it's reckoned to be most widespread in Andalusia, Galicia and Valencia). Official estimates put the numbers of illegal workers at around 500,000, although the real figure could be double this amount (it's estimated that some 300,000 Portuguese alone could be working illegally in Galicia). In recent years there has been an increasing number of illegal immigrants from Asian countries, who pay up to 1.5m ptas to be smuggled into Spain where they are employed in sweatshops.

Many unscrupulous employers use illegal labour in order to pay low wages (below the minimum wage) for long hours and poor working conditions (e.g. in greenhouses employing dangerous pesticides). Abuse is most widespread in industries that traditionally employ casual labour including the building, farming and service industries. Another aspect of illegal working is avoiding payment of 16 per cent value added tax (IVA), which for many makes the difference between a fair price and much too expensive.

In recent years there has been a clamp down on illegal labour and there are large fines (up to 15m ptas) for both employers and workers, and even imprisonment for the most serious offenders. Companies employing illegal foreign labour can be fined for each illegal employee and illegal workers can be deported and barred from entering Spain for up to three years. A foreigner has the right to a hearing before a court when a expulsion order is made. Occasionally amnesties are declared, during which illegal immigrants are given the opportunity to become legal without reprisals or penalties.

It's strictly illegal for non-EU nationals to work in Spain without a work permit. Note that if you use illegal labour or avoid paying IVA, you will have no official redress if goods or services are substandard. If you work illegally and don't pay tax or social security contributions, you will have no entitlement to state insurance against work injuries, health care, unemployment benefits or a state pension.

LANGUAGE

Although English is the *lingua franca* of international commerce and may help you to secure a job in Spain, the most important qualification for anyone seeking employment is the ability to speak good Spanish (or the local regional language). Spanish is the official language of 19 countries and is spoken worldwide by some 285m people. It's the world's second most important commercial language after English and the third most widely spoken after Chinese and English. What most foreigners refer to as Spanish is actually Castilian (*castellano*), which developed into classical Spanish. Castilian is *the* Spanish language, particularly among the educated classes, and is understand by most Spaniards. All references to Spanish in this section (and elsewhere in this book) mean Castilian, spoken by 65 per cent of Spaniards as their first or only language. The main exceptions are the autonomous regions of the Basque country, Catalonia and Galicia, where Basque, Catalan and Galician (respectively) are also official languages (see below). However, most people you meet in Spain are likely to speak or understand Castilian (although they may be unwilling to).

Regional Languages: Regional languages were banned under Franco, schools were forbidden to teach them and books weren't allowed to be published (many existing books were destroyed). Since the death of Franco in 1975 and the large degree of autonomy subsequently ceded to the regions, regional languages have made a strong comeback and are now taught in schools alongside Castilian. Basque, Catalan and Galician all have long-established standardised grammars and Catalan and Galician also have ancient literary traditions. You should *never* make the mistake of calling regional languages dialects. In the Basque country, Catalonia and Galicia, many street and buildings names, road signs, notices, and official documents are posted or printed in Spanish and the regional language. This practice is widespread in Catalonia (particularly Barcelona), where many people are obsessive about speaking Catalan and unnecessary nationalism results in public notices and even restaurant menus being printed only in Catalan. Basque, Catalan and Galician have also been revived by regional television and radio broadcasts, native film industries and extensive schooling.

The dominance of regional languages in autominous regions is causing increasing problems for foreigners and Spaniards from other regions of Spain. It's an important consideration if you're planning to live in Catalonia, Galicia or the Basque lands (particularly if you have school age children), where Spanish is a 'minor' language. In these regions, all communications from the authorities may be in the local language only and officials may refuse to speak any other language. Do you wish to learn Catalan or Basque, particularly if you already speak Spánish? After years of repression, there's a draconian linguistic policy in Catalonia (which is being followed by other regions), which forces Spanish-speaking residents to speak and write Catalan for all official business.

Catalan (*Catalán*) is spoken by some 6.5m people in Catalonia, the Balearics, the principality of Andorra and parts of the French Pyrenees. It's also spoken in Valencia, although less extensively, where there's some doubt over whether a dialect of Catalan or a separate *Valenciana* language is spoken. Catalan is by far the predominant language in Catalonia, where Spanish speakers feel linguistically oppressed in much the same way that Catalan speakers were under Franco. This is particularly noticeable in schools, where all lessons apart from Castilian are conducted in Catalan. However, in Barcelona almost everyone speaks Castilian, while less than half are fluent in Catalan. Most Catalans will readily speak Spanish, particularly to non-Catalans, although some refuse or pretend not to understand Spanish.

Galician (*gallego*) is the language of the northwest province of Galicia. Around 80 per cent of Galicians, some 2.5m people, speak Galician (40 per cent exclusively), which is more prevalent in the countryside than the cities. Like Catalan, Galician is a language and not a dialect, although three dialects of Galician are spoken.

Basque (*euskera* or *vascuence* in Spanish) is spoken by around 500,000 inhabitants of the Basque lands, mostly in rural areas. Although some words are borrowed from Spanish and French, the basic vocabulary and structure of Basque is unique. It's an ancient tongue of unknown origin and first appeared in Latin texts in the 9th century. Basque bears no relation to any other European language and is thought to be the only remaining representative of a pre Indo-European language (a possible link has recently been found between Basque and the ancient Etruscan tongues). To foreigners and anyone but a native speaker it's unfathomable, full of Ks, Xs and Zs and cluttered with consonants.

Other Dialects: In addition to the above official languages, there are also a number of dialects. For example in the Balearics there are *Mallorquín* (Majorca), *Menorquín* (Menorca) and *Ibiçenco* (Ibiza). All three are similar in vocabulary with many words having their origin in Arabic, French, Italian and Portuguese. Many Spanish gypsies, who arrived with the Moors from North Africa, speak *caló*, a language that includes Spanish and elements borrowed from Sanskrit and other European languages.

English: Unlike many other European countries, the majority of Spanish businesses don't use English as a working language, and the vast majority of Spaniards don't speak any foreign languages, particularly older Spaniards and people in rural areas. The amount of English spoken varies hugely depending on the area or city and who you speak to (professionals are more likely to speak English than shop assistants). In resort areas such as the *costas*, Balearic and Canary Islands, English is widely spoken and understood, as is German. It's also understood by many people in Barcelona, though it's spoken little in Madrid and hardly at all in Bilbao.

See also **Language** on page 155 and **Language Schools** on page 166.

2.

WORKING CONDITIONS

W orking conditions in Spain are largely dependent on the 1980 Workers' Statute
(*Estatuto de los Trabajadores*). Other factors include collective agreements
(*convenios colectivos*), an employee's individual employment contract (*contrato de
trabajo*) and an employer's in-house regulations. Salaried foreigners are employed under
the same working conditions as Spanish citizens, although there are different rules for
different categories of employees, e.g. directors, managers and factory workers. As in
many countries, part-time, seasonal and temporary workers aren't protected by
employment laws and have few legal rights. Consequently temporary employment has
increased considerably in recent years as a percentage of total jobs and is around 35 per
cent.

Permanent employees in Spain enjoy excellent employment conditions and social
security benefits, and extensive rights under Spanish law. The Workers' Statute details
the minimum conditions of employment including labour contracts, terms of hiring and
dismissal, working conditions, employee representation and trade union rights. Spain
has a statutory minimum wage (see page 52) and pay and working conditions in many
industries are governed by collective agreements (*convenios colectivos*), negotiated
nationally or regionally for each industry, which stipulate the rights and obligations of
both employees and employers in a particular industry or occupation.

Employees are protected by the workers' statute prohibiting discrimination on the
grounds of sex, marital status, age, race, official languages, social status, religious belief,
political opinion and trade union membership. Discrimination is also illegal with respect
to mental or physical disability, providing a disabled person is able to perform the work
required. Youths aged under 16 cannot be employed and measures must be taken to
protect those aged under 18 including a prohibition on working overtime, night-work,
and doing certain dangerous and unhealthy jobs.

There has traditionally been a link between a labour contract and a job for life in Spain.
However, the situation has changed and Spain's economic problems have been
exacerbated by the unions' uncompromising defence of high wages and rigid employment
terms, which has become outdated in the ever-increasingly competitive world of the
1990s. Spain has the most rigid and costly labour market in Europe and critics claim that
the requirements of the Workers' Statute are a major disincentive to investors and
employers, and restrict employment due to the high cost of hiring and firing employees.
During the recession in the early 1990s and its aftermath, this led many employers to hire
most new employees on short term temporary contracts, rather than permanent ones.
However, an historic agreement was reached between the employers and unions in 1997
whereby unions reduced their entitlement to redundancy payments in return for
permanent jobs.

TERMS OF EMPLOYMENT

Negotiating an appropriate salary is just one aspect of your working conditions. When
negotiating your terms of employment for a job in Spain, the checklists on the following
pages will prove invaluable. The points listed under **General Positions** (below) apply
to most jobs, while those listed under **Executive Positions** (on page 51) usually apply to
executive and senior managerial appointments only.

General Positions

- Salary:
  - Is the salary adequate, bearing in mind the cost of living in Spain (see page 315)? Is it index-linked?
  - Is the total salary (including expenses) paid in pesetas, or will the salary be paid in another country in a different currency, with expenses for living in Spain?
  - When and how often is the salary reviewed?
  - Is the annual salary paid in 14 installments and are annual or end-of-contract bonuses paid (see page 53)?
  - Is overtime paid or time off given in lieu of extra hours worked?
- Relocation expenses:
  - Are removal expenses or a relocation allowance paid?
  - Does the allowance include travelling expenses for all family members?
  - Is there a limit and is it adequate?
  - Are you required to repay your relocation expenses (or a percentage) if you resign before a certain period has elapsed?
  - Are you required to pay for your relocation in advance? This can run into hundreds of thousands of pesetas for normal house contents.
  - If employment is for a limited period only, will your relocation costs be paid when you leave Spain?
  - If you aren't shipping household goods and furniture to Spain, is there an allowance for buying furnishings locally?
  - Do relocation expenses include the legal and agent's fees incurred when moving home?
  - Are the services of a relocation consultant (see page 85) provided?
- Accommodation:
  - Will an hotel or lodging allowance be paid until you find permanent accommodation?
  - Is subsidised or free, temporary or permanent accommodation provided? If so, is it furnished or unfurnished? Some Spanish companies provide subsidised housing.
  - Must you pay for utilities such as electricity, gas and water?
  - If accommodation isn't provided, is assistance given to find suitable accommodation? If so, what sort of assistance?
  - What will accommodation cost?
  - Are your expenses paid while looking for accommodation?
- Working Hours:
  - What are your weekly working hours?
  - Are you required to clock in and out of work?
  - Can you choose to take time off in lieu of overtime or be paid for it?

- Leave entitlement:
  - What is the annual leave entitlement? Does it increase with length of service?
  - What are the paid public holidays? Is Monday or Friday a free day when a public holiday falls on a Tuesday or Thursday respectively? This is usually the case in Spain.
  - Is free air travel to your home country or elsewhere provided for you and your family, and if so, how often?
- Insurance:
  - Is extra insurance cover provided besides obligatory insurance (see **Chapter 13**)?
  - Is free life insurance provided?
  - Is free health insurance provided for you *and* your family (see page 55)?
  - For how long will your salary be paid if you're sick or have an accident?
- Company or supplementary pension:
  - Is a company pension scheme provided? If so, is it contributory or non-contributory? If it's contributory, what percentage of your salary must you pay (see page 260)?
  - Are you required or able to pay a lump sum into your pension fund in order to receive a full or higher pension?
  - Is the pension transportable to another employer?
- Employer:
  - What are his future prospects?
  - Does he have a good reputation?
  - Does he have a high staff turnover?
- Are free or subsidised Spanish lessons provided for you and your spouse?
- Is free transportation or a travel allowance paid from your home to your place of work?
- Is free or subsidised parking provided at your place of work?
- Is a free or subsidised company restaurant provided? If not, is an allowance paid or luncheon vouchers provided? Many companies provide staff restaurants which not only saves you money, but also time.
- Is a company nursery provided or an allowance paid for nursery care?
- Is professional training or education provided or paid for, if necessary abroad?
- Are free work clothes or overalls provided? Is the cleaning or laundering of work clothes paid for?
- Are fringe benefits provided such as subsidised banking services, low interest loans, inexpensive petrol, employees' shop or product discounts, sports and social facilities, and subsidised tickets for social/sports events?
- Do you have a written list of your job responsibilities?
- Have your employment conditions been confirmed in writing?
- If a dispute arises over your salary or working conditions, under the law of which country will your employment contract be interpreted?

Executive Positions

- Is private schooling for your children financed or subsidised? Does it include the cost of a boarding school in Spain or abroad?

- Is your salary index-linked and protected against devaluation? This is particularly important if you're paid in a foreign currency that fluctuates wildly or could be devalued (like the peseta). Are you paid an overseas allowance for working in Spain?

- Are the costs incurred by a move to Spain reimbursed? For example the cost of selling your home, employing an agent to let it for you, or storing household effects.

- Is domestic help provided or a contribution made towards the cost of hiring a servant or cook?

- Is a car provided? With a chauffeur?

- Are you entitled to any miscellaneous benefits, such as membership of a social or sports club or free credit cards?

- Is there a business entertainment allowance?

- Is there a clothing allowance? For example if you arrive in Madrid from the tropics during the winter, you will probably need to buy new winter clothes.

- Is extra compensation paid if you're made redundant or fired? Redundancy or severance payments (see page 59) are compulsory for all employees in Spain (subject to length of service), but executives often receive a generous 'golden handshake' if they're made redundant, e.g. after a takeover. Even bosses who fail miserably and leave by mutual consent (i.e. are sacked) leave with multi-million dollar severance packages (nice work if you can get it!).

EMPLOYMENT CONTRACT

Employees in Spain almost always have an employment contract (*contrato de trabajo*), stating such particulars as job title, position, salary, working hours, benefits, duties and responsibilities, and the duration of employment. Note that the legally binding minimum terms of employment and minimum wages are usually decided by agreement between employers and trade unions, and also apply to employees with individual contracts. There are two main types of employment contract in Spain, an indefinite term contract and a short-term contract, usually for a minimum of one year. All contracts must be written in Spanish. Note that the relationship between employer and employee is legally binding, even if there's no written contract.

To circumvent the difficulties and high costs of dismissing employees in Spain, many employers have relied heavily on temporary contracts (particularly when hiring young workers — over 75 per cent of those aged under 25 have temporary contracts) of from one to three years. An employee can be hired on a succession of one-year contracts for a total of up to three years, after which an employer must either let someone go or hire him permanently. At the end of the three-year period an employer can fire an employee and it costs him nothing, however, if he does it one day later it could cost him millions of pesetas! The system is obviously open to abuse by employers and in the last few years many employers chose to sack employees on short-term contracts rather than give them permanent contracts. However, this has changed under a new agreement between employers and unions signed in 1997, whereby permanent contracts will be provided in exchange for lower redundancy payments.

The salary of an employee hired on a short-term contract mustn't be less than that paid to a similarly qualified person employed in a permanent job. A short-term contract can be terminated before the end of its period in specific circumstances only. For example, when either the employer or employee has committed a serious offence, in the case of an event beyond the control of both parties, or with the agreement of both parties. There are special contracts for seasonal and temporary workers, who have few legal rights. Contracts for seasonal and temporary workers can be issued when a permanent employee is on leave of absence (including maternity or sick leave) or when there's a temporary increase in business. If you're thinking of employing a part-time or temporary employee, e.g. domestic help in your home, take care that you don't get embroiled in Spanish employee legislation, particularly when terminating employment (see **Dismissal & Redundancy** on page 59).

All employment contracts are subject to Spanish labour law and references may also be made to other regulations such as collective agreements. Anything in contracts contrary to statutory provisions and unfavourable to an employee may be deemed null and void. There are usually no hidden surprises or traps for the unwary in a Spanish employment contract. Nevertheless, as with any contract, you should know exactly what it contains before signing it. If your Spanish isn't fluent, you should try to obtain an English translation (your Spanish must be excellent to understand the legal jargon in some contracts) or at least have it translated verbally so that you don't get any nasty surprises later.

EMPLOYMENT CONDITIONS

Employment conditions contain an employer's general rules and regulations regarding working conditions and benefits that are applicable to all employees (unless stated otherwise in your employment contract). Employment conditions are explained in this chapter or a reference is made to the chapter where the subject is covered in more detail.

Validity & Applicability

Employment conditions usually contain a paragraph stating the date from which they take effect and to whom they apply.

Salary & Benefits

Your salary (*sueldo*) is stated in your employment contract and salary reviews, planned increases and cost of living rises may also be included. In job contracts, salaries may be stated in gross or net terms. Salaries are paid weekly, fortnightly or monthly, depending on the employer. If a bonus is paid, such as 13th and 14th month salaries (see below), this is stated in your employment contract. General points, such as the payment of your salary into a bank account and the date of salary payments, may also be included in employment conditions. You receive a pay slip (*nómina de sueldo*) itemising your salary and deductions.

There's a statutory minimum wage (*salario mínimo interprofesional*) in Spain which in 1997 was 66,630 ptas a month (2,221 ptas a day) for an unskilled worker aged over 18 and 59,130 ptas a month (1,971 ptas a day) for someone aged under 18. Most workers receive more than the minimum salary and less than 500,000 employees are actually affected by minimum wage rates. However, an increase in the minimum wage usually serves as a benchmark for wage demands. Salaries in most industries in Spain are decided by collective bargaining between employers and unions. Salary increases are usually in line with the inflation rate, although the government imposed a complete wage freeze for public employees in recent years. Salary increases usually take effect from 1st January. See also **Salary** on page 32.

Extra Months' Salary & Bonuses

Most employers in Spain pay their employees a number of extra months' salaries (*pagas extraordinarias*), usually two — one paid in July before the annual summer holiday and the other in December — which were originally intended to ensure that employees had extra money for their summer and Christmas holidays. Some companies pay as many as 15 or 16 months' salary, although this is exceptional. Extra months' salary aren't mandatory unless part of a collective agreement, when they should be stated in your employment contract. In practice their payment is universal and taken for granted by most employees. In your first and last years of employment, your extra months' salary and other bonuses should be paid pro rata if you don't work a full calendar year. Where applicable, extra months' salary are guaranteed bonuses and aren't pegged to a company's performance (such as with profit-sharing). Senior and middle managers may receive extra bonuses, perhaps linked to profits, equal to around 10 to 20 per cent of their annual salary.

Working Hours & Overtime

The standard working week in Spain is 40 hours and the average with overtime around 43. The normal working day is from 0930 to 1330 and from 1730 until 1930 or 2030, although from June and September the working day may be continuous from 0700 to 1500 (called *horario intensivo*). Sometimes working hours are reduced in summer, e.g. from eight to seven hours a day. Foreign companies (and an increasing number of Spanish companies) often operate from 0830 or 0900 to 1730 or 1800, with a one hour break for lunch. There are usually no scheduled coffee or tea breaks in Spain, although drinks can usually be taken at any time and it's common for workers to pop out for breakfast or a cup of coffee two or three times a day during business hours.

The long afternoon siesta isn't as common as it used to be and many hard-pressed workers and mothers no longer have time for an afternoon nap. In winter, banks and many businesses work on Saturday mornings (they are closed in summer). An attempt has been made to reduce working hours in recent years, in an effort to create more jobs, although this has usually foundered on the employees' refusal to accept any reduction in their wages. When public and annual holidays are taken into account, Spanish workers work less hours a year than those in other EU countries.

Overtime is never compulsory in Spain and cannot exceed 80 hours a year. It must be paid at a premium of not less than 75 per cent of the normal hourly rate, i.e. normal rate plus 75 per cent. Employees cannot be obliged to work on Sundays unless collective agreements state otherwise, although when an employee agrees to work on a Sunday, normal overtime rates are applicable. Overtime may be compensated for by time off rather than extra pay, providing there's a written agreement to that effect. Employees are entitled to a minimum of one and a half days (including Sundays) free each week plus public holidays (see page 56). Twelve hours must elapse between the end of one working day or shift and the start of the next. Salaried employees, particularly executives and managers, aren't generally paid overtime, although this depends on their employment contracts. Managers and executives generally work long hours, even allowing for their often long lunch breaks. Weekends are sacrosanct and few people in Spain work on Saturdays and Sundays unless it's mandatory.

It may come as a nasty surprise to some foreigners to discover that many Spanish employers (including most large companies) require all employees to clock in and out of work. Employees caught cheating the clock are liable to instant dismissal.

Travel & Relocation Expenses

Travel and relocation expenses to Spain depend on your agreement with your employer and are usually included in your employment contract or conditions. If you're hired from outside Spain, your air ticket and other travel costs to Spain are usually paid for by your employer or his representative. In addition you can usually claim any extra travel costs, for example the cost of transport to and from airports. If you travel by car to Spain, you can usually claim a mileage rate or the equivalent air fare cost.

An employer may pay a fixed relocation allowance based on your salary, position and size of family, or he may pay the total cost of removal. The allowance should be sufficient to move the contents of an average house (*castillos* aren't usually catered for) and you must normally pay any excess costs yourself. If you don't want to bring your furniture to Spain or have only a few belongings to ship, it may be possible to purchase furniture locally up to the limit of your allowance (check with your employer). When they're liable for the total cost, a company may ask you to obtain two or three removal estimates.

Generally you're required to organise and pay for the removal in advance. Your employer usually reimburses the equivalent amount in pesetas *after* you have paid the bill, although it may be possible to get him to pay the bill directly or give you a cash advance. If you change jobs within Spain, your new employer may pay your relocation expenses when it's necessary for you to move house. Don't forget to ask, as he may not offer to pay (it may depend on how desperate he is to employ you).

Social Security

All Spanish employees, foreign employees working for Spanish companies and the self-employed must contribute to the Spanish social security (*seguridad social*) system. Social security for employees covers health care (plus sickness and maternity); injuries at work; unemployment insurance; retirement benefits; and invalidity and death benefits. Contributions are calculated as a percentage of your gross income and are deducted at source by your employer. Social security contributions are high and total an average of 30 per cent of gross pay, 75 per cent of which is paid by employers. For full details see **Social Security** on page 254.

Medical Examination

Apart from the employees of a few large Spanish employers, prospective employees in Spain aren't usually required to undergo a pre-employment medical examination, although some employers must pass a psychological examination. A medical examination may be required only for employees in specific occupations, e.g. where good health is of paramount importance for safety reasons, when an examination may be necessary periodically (e.g. every one or two years) or when requested by the employer. Where applicable, an offer of employment is subject to a prospective employee being given a clean bill of health. Medical examinations may also be required as a condition of membership of a company health, pension or life insurance scheme. Some companies insist that key employees have regular health screening, particularly executives and senior managers.

Health Insurance

Most Spanish employers don't provide private health insurance for employees, although they may belong to a group policy offering employees large savings over individual policies. However, some employers, particularly foreign companies, provide free comprehensive private health insurance for executives, senior managers and their families. For further information about health insurance see page 260.

Company Pension Fund

In addition to contributing to social security (which provides a state pension), some employers have a company pension scheme (*plan de pensiones*), although they aren't common in Spain. Where applicable, the maximum tax-deductible annual contribution to a company pension plan is 15 per cent of earnings or a maximum of 750,000 ptas. Most retirement schemes are designed to induce employees to retire at a certain age (e.g. between 60 and 65), although there's no legal requirement for an employee to retire at a particular age. For further information see **Supplementary Pensions** on page 260.

Unemployment Insurance

Unemployment insurance (*pago de desempleo*) is compulsory for all employees of Spanish companies and is covered by social security contributions. For details see page 257.

Salary Insurance

Salary insurance (*pago de seguro*) pays employees' salaries during periods of sickness or after accidents and is provided by social security. After a certain number of consecutive sick days (the number varies depending on your employer), your salary is no longer paid by your employer but by social security, which is one reason why employers pay those astronomical contributions. Employees in Spain don't receive a quota of sick days as in some countries (e.g. the USA) and there's no limit to the amount of time you may take off work due to sickness or accidents. Some employers operate their own unemployment insurance schemes and pay their employees' full salaries for a limited period, usually depending on their length of service.

You're normally required to notify your employer immediately of sickness or an accident that prevents you from working. If you're away from work for longer than two days, you're usually required to produce a doctor's certificate (*certificado de médico*). The actual period is stated in your employment conditions. For information see **Benefits** on page 257.

Annual Holidays

Under Spanish labour law a full-time employee is entitled to one month's (20 working days) paid annual holiday (*vacaciones*). Employers cannot count official Spanish public holidays (see below) as annual holidays. Some collective agreements grant extra holiday for long service. When both annual and public holidays (see below) are taken into account, Spain has the most holidays of any country in the EU.

Most employees take three or four weeks summer holiday between July and August and perhaps a week in winter (often around the Christmas and New Year holiday period) and at Easter. August is traditionally the month for summer holidays, with many businesses closing down entirely for the whole month. When a company closes down during the summer, all employees are obliged to take their holiday at the same time. An office or company that doesn't close in August will usually operate on a skeleton staff. Some businesses close for two to three weeks over Christmas and the New Year, although this is rare nowadays. Before starting a new job, check that any planned holidays will be honoured by your new employer. This is particularly important if they fall within your trial period (usually the first three months), when holidays may not be permitted.

Public Holidays

The central government allows for 14 national and local paid public holidays (*días de fiestas*) a year, more than any other country in Europe. Of the 14, seven are celebrated nationally and five are widely celebrated, although regional authorities can substitute regional or local holidays for any three of these five. The remaining two holidays are regional or municipal holidays to celebrate dates of local importance. The seven national holidays and five most widely celebrated other holidays are listed below:

Date	Holiday
* 1 January	New Year's Day (*Día del Año Nuevo*)
6 January	Epiphany or Holy Kings' Day (*Día de los Reyes Magos*)
19 March	St. Joseph's Day (*Día de San José*)
* March or April	Good Friday (*Viernes Santo*)
*1 May	Labour Day (*Día del Trabajador*)
May/June	Corpus Christi (*Corpus Christi*) - 2nd Thursday after Whitsun
May/June	Ascension Day (*Ascensión*) - Thursday 40 days (6th Thursday) after Easter
25 July	St. James' Day (*Día de Santiago*)
*15 August	Assumption of the Virgin (*Asunción*)
*12 October	Virgin of Pilar or National Day (*Día de Virgen del Pilar*)
* 8 December	Immaculate Conception (*Inmaculada Concepción*)
*25 December	Christmas Day (*Día de Navidad*)

* National Holidays

When a holiday falls on a Saturday or Sunday, another day isn't usually granted as a holiday unless the number of public holidays in a particular year falls below a minimum number. However, when a public holiday falls on a Tuesday or Thursday, the day before or the day after (i.e. Monday or Friday respectively) is usually declared a holiday, although this depends on the employer. This practice is called making a bridge (*hacer un puente*). If a holiday falls on a Wednesday it's common for employees to take the two preceding or succeeding days off, a practice known as making a viaduct (*viaductos*). When two public holidays fall midweek, many people take the whole week off, known as a *superpuente*.

All public offices, banks and post offices are closed on public holidays and only essential work is performed. Note that foreign embassies and consulates in Spain usually observe all Spanish public holidays *plus* their own country's national holidays. Most regions, towns and even neighbourhoods (*barrios*) have their own carnival and feast days (*ferias*). Although these aren't always official public holidays, most local businesses are closed, sometimes for a whole week. Due to the 'floating' nature of some holidays, such as Easter, an official annual public holiday calendar (*calendario laboral*) is published. Public holidays are marked on most calendars, many of which also show saints' days (calendars are distributed free by local businesses such as banks in December/January).

Compassionate & Special Leave of Absence

All Spanish companies must by law provide additional days off for moving house (one day); your own or a family marriage (one day); birth of a child (two days for the father); death of a family member or close relative (two days); and other compassionate reasons. Grounds for compassionate leave are usually defined in collective agreements. Employees who have worked for a company for a number of years may be entitled to take a sabbatical, e.g. for one year (naturally *without* pay!).

Paid Expenses

Expenses (*gastos*) paid by your employer are usually listed in your employment conditions. These may include travel costs from your home to your place of work, which may consist of a second class rail season ticket or the equivalent amount in cash (paid monthly with your salary). Travelling expenses to and from your place of work are tax deductible. Companies without an employee restaurant or canteen may pay a lunch allowance or provide luncheon vouchers. Expenses paid for travel on company business or for training or education may be detailed in your employment conditions or be listed in a separate document.

Trial & Notice Periods

For most jobs in Spain there's a trial period (*período de prueba*) of from 15 days to six months, depending on the type of work and the employer. It's usually 15 working days for unqualified workers, six months for university graduates and three months for other employees. The length of a trial period is usually stated in collective agreements, which impose restrictions on the maximum period. During the trial period, either party may terminate the employment contract without notice or any financial penalty, unless otherwise stated in a collective agreement. Notice periods usually vary with your position and length of service. Generally the higher the position, the longer the notice period. Although many employees prefer to leave immediately after giving notice, they have the right to work their notice period. However, both parties can agree that an employee receives payment in lieu of notice. Compensation must also be made for any outstanding paid annual holidays up to the end of the notice period. See also **Dismissal & Redundancy** on page 59.

Education & Training

Most employers provide education and training schemes for their employees, many of which are subsidised by central government through a reduction in employer social security contributions. The government promotes industrial training through technical colleges and arrangements with various business enterprises. Training may include management seminars, special technical courses, language lessons or any other form of continuing education. However, the vast majority of the average company's training budget is spent on managers and executives rather than the workers.

If you need to learn or improve your language proficiency to perform your job, the cost of language study may be paid or subsidised by your employer. It's in your own interest to investigate courses of study, seminars and lectures, that you believe are of direct benefit to you and your employer. Most employers give reasonable consideration to a request to attend a course during working hours, providing you don't make it a full-time occupation.

Pregnancy & Confinement

Female employees are entitled to excellent employment benefits under Spanish labour law with regard to pregnancy (*embarazo*) and confinement. The family is of fundamental importance in Spain and employers are flexible regarding time off work necessitated by pregnancy. Social security benefits are generous and are designed to encourage large families. Maternity leave is guaranteed for all women irrespective of their length of employment. The permitted leave period is 16 weeks; six weeks prior to birth and 10 weeks following birth. A doctor may authorise additional time off, either before or after the birth, in which case a company must continue to pay your salary. Maternity benefits depend on your length of employment. A husband is allowed two days compassionate leave on the birth of his child and a wife can transfer two weeks of her maternity leave to her husband.

Part-Time Job Restrictions

Restrictions on part-time employment (*media jornada*) may be detailed in your employment conditions. Most Spanish companies don't allow full-time employees to work part-time (i.e. moonlight) for another employer, particularly one in the same line of business. You may, however, be permitted to take a part-time teaching job or similar part-time employment (or you could write a book!).

Changing Jobs & Confidentiality

Companies in a high-tech or highly confidential business may have restrictions on employees moving to a competitor in Spain or within Europe. You should be aware of these restrictions as they are enforceable under Spanish law, although it's a complicated subject and disputes may need to be resolved by a court of law. Spanish law regarding industrial secrets and general employer confidentiality are strict. If you breach this confidentiality you will be dismissed and may be unable to find further employment in Spain.

Retirement

There's no compulsory retirement age in Spain, although the traditional retirement age is 65 for both men and women. This is gradually being lowered to 60 and some companies have pensioned off workers in recent years between the ages of 50 and 55 to reduce costs. Company pension schemes are often designed to induce employees to retire at a specific age, although an employee can be dismissed only if his age restricts his ability to perform his job. If you wish to continue working after you have reached 65, you may be required to negotiate a new employment contract (you should also seek psychiatric help!).

Dismissal & Redundancy

It has traditionally been very difficult to legally dismiss workers in Spain without paying a large redundancy sum (except on specific grounds), although the law has now changed. In addition to obvious reasons such as mutual agreement, death, expiration of contract term and retirement, an employment contract can be terminated for **technological and economic causes**, and for **objective or disciplinary reasons** involving individual employees.

Technological and Economic Grounds: An employee can be made redundant (*despedido*) on technological and economic grounds and *force majeure* only in relation to the collective restructuring of a company's workforce. Technological and economic causes are legally defined terms, when dismissal may be decided unilaterally by the employer, but requires intervention by the labour authorities. A formal procedure must be followed, allowing employees an opportunity to be heard and a restructuring plan to be presented to the labour authorities. Employees can then be dismissed only if the plan is approved. The plan must include an indemnity for each employee, equivalent to 20 days' salary for each year of service up to a maximum of 12 months' salary. In exceptional circumstances this may be paid by the government from a 'salary guarantee fund' (*fondo de garantía salarial*).

Objective Reasons: Objective causes for dismissal include employee ineptitude disclosed after a trial period; the inability to adapt to technological changes after a reasonable period (minimum two months) and retraining; when there's an objectively determined need to eliminate a redundant job position (in companies with less than 50 employees); and justified absences which constitute over 20 per cent of working days in two consecutive months within a 12-month period, provided the total absenteeism in the workplace is over 5 per cent. To dismiss an employee for an objective cause an employer must give the employee an indemnity (immediately on notice of dismissal) of 20 days' salary for each year of service up to a maximum of 12 months' salary.

Disciplinary Reasons: Legal grounds for dismissal for disciplinary reasons include insubordination or disobedience; repeated absenteeism or lateness; physical or verbal abuse of the employer, fellow employees or family members; fraud, disloyalty or abuse of confidence; voluntary and continuous reduction of job productivity; carrying on business on his own account for a third party without the consent of the employer; and habitual drug or alcohol abuse which negatively affects job performance. An employee must be given written notice of dismissal for these causes, stating the effective date of dismissal, without which the dismissal is null and void.

An employee dismissed for objective or disciplinary reasons may challenge the decision in the labour courts (*magistratura de trabajo*). However, it's obligatory to first resort to conciliation between the employee and the employer, during which an agreement can be sought. If an employee was deemed to have been dismissed improperly, then the employer may elect to re-engage the employee or pay compensation. If the employee is re-engaged he's entitled to back pay from the date of dismissal to the date of judgement. If he isn't re-engaged, the compensation previously consisted of back pay plus 45 days' salary for each year of service, up to a maximum of 42 months' salary. This has now been reduced to 33 days' salary a year under a new agreement reached between employers and unions in 1997.

Executives: Top executives can be dismissed without cause, in which case they are entitled to compensation of seven days' salary for each year of service, with a maximum of six months' salary (unless other terms are agreed in their contract). If the dismissal of an executive is successfully challenged in the court and judged to be unjustified, the executive is entitled to compensation of 20 days' salary for each year of service (up to a maximum of 12 months' salary), unless otherwise agreed by contract. Although the minimum compensation for executives is less than that for 'ordinary' employees, it's common practice for contracts to allow for higher compensation than the legal minimum.

If you run a small business and are planning to employ a part-time or temporary employee, take care not to become embroiled in Spanish employee legislation, particularly if you may wish to terminate the employment at short notice. You should get an employee to sign a written statement agreeing to the terms of the termination of employment, otherwise you could be sued for unfair dismissal.

Union Membership

There's not a strong trade union (*sindicato*) movement in Spain and only some 2m of Spain's 15m workers belong to a trade union. However, despite the low union membership, the two main union confederations, the socialist *Unión General de Trabajadores (UGT)* and the Communist *Comisiones Obreras*, play a major role in industrial negotiations. Spanish unions are mainly concerned with negotiations regarding wages, social aspects of work, technical training, and fringe and retirement benefits. Collective labour agreements negotiated between companies, employers' associations and worker representatives are legally binding on all parties. Unions have the right to elect employee delegates to company committees in companies employing between six and 10 people, and are automatic for companies with 10 or more employees. Company committees receive quarterly and annual information on the company's performance, monitor employment affairs and can express opinions on company strategy. Employees aren't obliged to join unions, but all businesses with 50 or more employees are required to have some sort of employee representation. Workers' councils in Spain aren't a joint management-employee structure as they are in some other European countries (e.g. Germany) and neither unions or employees have a say in management decisions.

Spain has had more strikes (*huelgas*) and lost more production days due to strikes in the last 10 years than any country in the EU, although industrial relations have improved considerably in recent years. The government can enforce an imposed settlement (*laudo*) if a strike impairs public services or disrupts important sectors of the economy and industry. With the exception of certain public sector employees, e.g. the police, employees are guaranteed the right to strike under Spanish law and cannot be dismissed for striking.

Sanity Clause

Does the employment contract include a sanity clause? This is particularly important if you have young children. Some people, however, don't believe in sanity clause (particularly scrooges).

3.

PERMITS & VISAS

Before making any plans to live or work in Spain, you must ensure that you have a valid passport (with a visa if necessary) and the appropriate documentation to obtain a residence card or work permit. The free movement of workers between EU countries and Spain became effective on 1st January 1992, after a six-year transition period. Spain can no longer refuse a residence card to any EU citizen, or his family members and dependants, even when they aren't EU citizens. The EU allows the free movement of goods, services, capital and people between member states and any EU citizen has the right to live, study, work or start a business in Spain. Citizens of non-EU countries must obtain a visa from a Spanish consulate in their home country before coming to Spain to work, study or live. All foreigners need a residence card to live in Spain, including EU nationals.

When in Spain you should always carry your foreign identity card, passport or Spanish residence card (or a copy certified by a national police station) and produce it on demand to the authorities (if you don't have it you can be fined). A residence card constitutes an identity card for foreigners, which all Spaniards must carry by law. Permit infringements are taken seriously by the Spanish authorities and there are penalties for breaches of regulations, including large fines, deportation and even imprisonment for flagrant abuses. Spain has been criticised in recent years for its strongarm and repressive tactics with regard to the deportation of illegal African immigrants, who are a huge problem. On the other hand, illegal immigrants are also given residence papers under periodic amnesties.

Immigration is a complex subject and the information in this chapter is intended as a general guide only. You shouldn't base any decisions or actions on the information contained herein without confirming it with an official and (hopefully) reliable source, such as a Spanish consulate.

Spanish Bureaucracy

Spain is infamous for its stifling bureaucracy and it's sometimes difficult to say with any certainty exactly what the correct procedure is for anything. Spanish bureaucrats have a millions ways to make even the most simple procedure complicated beyond imagination and are world class at unhelpfulness and obstruction (they make the French look like amateurs and would even give India a run for its money). However, things have improved since Spain joined the EU and officials aren't always deliberately obstructive, but often make genuine mistakes due to ignorance of the latest rules or regulations (which have been changing at a bewildering pace in the last decade). As a result it's possible for an application to be refused by one person in the morning and approved by another (or even the same) person in the afternoon without any changes.

In many cases it simply takes too long or is impossible to get anything done through 'official' channels and many people give up or turn to unofficial channels, e.g. if you have a friend who knows someone in the administration or can afford to pay someone to 'speed things up a bit' something may happen. Some town halls have backlogs of literally thousands of applications for residence permits, where the stock reply is 'come back next month'. If you're refused a permit you shouldn't accept it as the end of the matter, but should obtain legal advice.

Many people employ a lawyer or *gestor* (see page 410) to act on their behalf. A *gestor* is a professional person who's trained to deal with the reams of paperwork, red tape and petty bureaucracy involved in dealing with government officials. Although it isn't always necessary to employ a lawyer or *gestor* and may result in unnecessary expense, they can usually save you much time and trouble. Some town halls, particularly in municipalities with a lot of foreign residents, have established a special foreigners' department (*departamento de extranjeros*) with staff who speak English and other foreign languages. If such a department exists in your municipality, it's worthwhile obtaining free counsel before going to the expense of employing a *gestor*.

A *gestor's* fees are usually reasonable and lower than a lawyer's, and depend on the complexity of your case. However, the total sum required to make an application, for example for a work permit for a non-EU citizen, can amount to 200,000 ptas when all the costs are taken into account. Before employing a *gestor* to make an application for a permit on your behalf, obtain quotations from a number of *gestors'* offices (*gestorías*) and ensure that all expenses, translations, registrations and certificates are included. For anything other than a straightforward case, it's always advisable to obtain professional help, particularly if you're starting a business, purchasing or renting property for commercial use, or employing staff.

VISAS

All citizens of non-EU countries, including non-EU spouses and other non-EU dependants of EU nationals, must obtain a visa (*visado*) from a Spanish consulate in their home country before coming to Spain to work, study or live. There are various categories of visas including employees, retired pensioners, investors, business people, employees of multinational companies (transferees), teachers, students, extended holidays over 90 days, and those performing cultural or sporting activities. Non-EU nationals planning to take up residence in Spain must obtain a residence visa (*visado de residencia*) before entering the country. The visa is stamped in your passport, which must be valid for a minimum of six months, and is valid for entry into Spain within 60 days of the date of issue. Some nationalities require an in-transit visa when passing through Spanish airports or ports for in-transit stays of less than five days.

Applications for visas must be made to your local Spanish consulate abroad with jurisdiction over your place of residence and must be made in person by you or your authorised representative. Applicants living in a country other than their country of nationality must have been resident there for at least one year. The documentation required for a visa application depends on your reason for coming to Spain and may include:

- * a full passport with a minimum validity period of six months plus a copy of the pages showing your particulars;

- * a number of completed application forms, e.g. four (the number varies);

- * a number of passport-size photographs, e.g. three or four (one of which must be firmly fixed to each application form);

- proof of **private health insurance** if you aren't eligible for health treatment under Spanish social security (see page 254).

- proof of **financial resources** for those planning to retire or start a business in Spain. There's no fixed income required to obtain a visa to retire to Spain, but a minimum income of around 100,000 ptas a month (plus owning a home in Spain) for a retired couple or 1.2m ptas a year is usually required (although the recipient of an EU state pension will qualify even when it's less than this). A minimum investment of 15m ptas (around US$100,000) is usually necessary for a non-EU national wishing to start a business in Spain.

- a certificate of criminal record (*certificado de antecedentes penales*) issued by the police or another official authority from the country or countries where you have lived during the five years prior to the application. This doesn't exist in some countries, although a statement from your local police that you have no criminal record is usually sufficient to meet the requirements.

- **employees** require a pre-contract, stamped and signed by both parties, or a letter on headed notepaper of the prospective employer in Spain;

- **employees** also require a health certificate (*certificado médico*), sold in a tobacconist's (*estanco*) and issued by a doctor, stating that they don't suffer from any contagious or infectious diseases or mental disorders and that they are fit to work;

- **students** require proof of admission from an approved Spanish educational establishment;

- **au pairs** require an agreement with a family in Spain (see page 41).

- a non-EU national married to a Spanish citizen or a foreigner resident in Spain needs a marriage certificate;

- *a small stamped addressed envelope.

* Required by all applicants.

Note that a copy (or copies) are also required of most documents, some of which may require an official stamp (*apostille*) on the back. The certificate of criminal record and the medical certificate are valid for a limited period only, e.g. three months, so don't apply for them too far in advance (if they expire you must obtain new documents). Visas are valid for 60 days from the date of issue. Successful applicants for residence in Spain must apply for a residence card (see page 67) within 15 days of their arrival. Various other documents may be required, depending on the purpose of the visa, many of which must be translated into Spanish. All translations must be made by an official translator approved by your local Spanish consulate, a list of whom will be supplied on request.

Applications usually take six to eight weeks to be approved, although they can take much longer. Successful applicants must collect their visas in person when advised by the consulate that they are ready. You require your passport and the fee of around 8,000 ptas in local currency.

If you require a visa to enter Spain and attempt to enter without one, you will be refused entry. If you're in any doubt as to whether you require a visa to enter Spain, enquire at a Spanish consulate abroad before making plans to travel.

Visitors

Visitors from EU countries, North and South America, Andorra, Costa Rica, Cyprus, the Czech Republic, Gibraltar, Grenada, Hungary, Japan, South Korea, Malta, Monaco, New Zealand, San Marino, the Seychelles, Singapore, Slovakia, Switzerland and some African countries *don't* need a visa for stays in Spain of up to 90 days. Nationals of certain countries including Australia, Bahrain, Kuwait, Malaysia, Oman, Qatar, Saudi Arabia, the United Arab Emirates and Yemen can visit Spain for up to 30 days without a visa. All other nationalities require a visa to visit Spain.

Most visitors require a full passport to visit Spain, although EU nationals and nationals of Andorra, Monaco and Switzerland can enter Spain with a national identity card. The period a visitor can remain in Spain depends on his nationality and is 182 days for EU citizens. A non-EU visitor wishing to remain in Spain for longer than 90 days must obtain a special entry visa (*visado especial de entrada*) at a Spanish consulate before arrival in Spain. Spanish immigration officials may require visitors to produce a return or onward ticket and proof of accommodation, health insurance and financial resources (e.g. 5,000 ptas a day for each day they plan to stay in Spain), although this is unlikely. If you're a non-EU national, it isn't possible to enter Spain as a visitor and change your status to that of an employee, student or resident. You must normally return to your country of residence and apply for a visa, although it's possible to obtain an exemption.

After 90 days, anyone permitted to remain in Spain as a visitor for 90 days must either apply for a 90-day extension (*prórroga de estancia*) or cross the border to a neighbouring country, which permits them to return to Spain for another 90-days. An extension should be applied for at a national police station (*Comisaría de Policía Nacional*) with a foreigners' department (*departamento/oficina de extranjeros*) at least two weeks before the 90-day period has expired. Leaving Spain and re-entering after a brief period is easier than obtaining an extension and is quite legal, although your total stay in Spain mustn't exceed a total of six months (182 days) in a calendar year. However, if you wish to prove you have left, you must have your passport stamped. After 182 days you *must* either leave Spain or apply for a residence card (see below), although if you're unemployed or have insufficient financial means, your application will be refused.

RESIDENCE CARD

A residence card (*tarjeta de residencia*) is required by anyone wishing to work or start a business in Spain or planning to live there for longer than 182 days in a calendar year. Holders of a residence visa (*visado de residencia*) or EU nationals planning to stay longer than 90 days must apply for a residence card (*residencia*) within 15 days of their arrival in Spain. Visitors can apply for a 90-day extension (*permanencia*) and remain in Spain for a maximum of 182 days in a calendar year (only one is granted per calendar year). A person travelling around Spain and staying in different places doesn't need to leave the country or obtain a *permanencia* after three months. However, after staying three months in Spain, a person with a permanent address must either obtain a *permanencia*, leave the country or apply to become a resident.

Where applicable, a residence card holder's dependants are also granted a residence card. Dependants require proof of relationship, e.g. a marriage or birth certificate. Note that under Spanish law, if a husband or wife has a residence card their partner is also considered to be a resident of Spain, i.e. the non-resident spouse of a resident isn't entitled to be treated as a non-resident (unless they are legally separated). A resident of Spain isn't required to remain in Spain for any period of time and can spend as much time out of Spain as he wishes.

Note that, irrespective of whether you have a residence card, if you remain in Spain for more than 182 days in a calendar year you will be regarded as a resident for tax purposes and will be liable to pay income tax on your total worldwide income. However, there are estimated to be tens of thousands of 'eternal tourists' in Spain who live their more or less permanently and never register, some even paying Spanish income tax *without* having a residence card. In recent years local authorities have tried to encourage foreigners spending over 182 days a year in Spain to register as residents, The central and regional governments allocate funds for public services in each municipality according to the number of residents, therefore it isn't surprising that they are anxious that all bona fide residents register. Note that if you remain in Spain for longer than six months a year without becoming a resident, you're can be fined up to 50,000 ptas and be excluded from Spain for three years, although the law isn't strictly enforced, particularly for EU nationals.

Applications

Anyone arriving in Spain and planning to live indefinitely, study, work or start a business, must apply for a residence card within 15 days of arriving in Spain. EU nationals planning to stay for a limited period (e.g. a short-term contract) are issued with a temporary residence card for the period requested. If the period is indefinite a five-year residence card (*tarjeta comunitaria europea* or *tarjeta de residente comunitario*) is issued. Cards for dependants are issued for the same period as the principal applicant (children under 18 may be included on a parent's *residencia*). A non-EU residence card is initially valid for two years or the length of a contract and on renewal is valid for five years. A permanent residence card is available to all foreigners who have held a normal residence permit for a period of six years.

Residence cards for foreigners (*tarjeta de extranjero*) are plastic and colour-coded as follows:

- red: residence permit (*permiso de residencia*) for a non-EU national;
- green: residence and work permit (*tarjeta de residencia y trabajo*) for a non-EU national;
- orange: residence permit for a student (*tarjeta de estudiante*);
- blue: residence permit for an EU national (*regimen comunitario*)
- dark purple: residence permit for a refugee (*tarjeta de refugiado*);
- black: permit for someone who crosses the frontier to work in Spain (*trabajadores fronterizos*).

Residence cards are issued by the foreign nationals office (*Oficina Gubernativa de Extranjeros*) or the provincial central police station (*Comisaría de Policía Provincial*) in the province where the applicant is resident, and applications must be made in person to the nearest national police station (*Comisaría de Policía Nacional*) with a foreigners' department (*departamento/oficina de extranjeros*).

Try to obtain a list of the documents required (and the fee payable) in advance, otherwise you will need to return if you don't have the correct paperwork. Usually the original documents must be accompanied by one or two copies. The documentation required depends on your personal situation and usually includes the following:

- *a passport valid for at least six months and a photocopy of the pages showing your particulars;
- *a marriage or divorce certificate or other papers relating to your marital status plus a Spanish translation;

- *a number (usually three or four) of completed application forms (e.g. form 037 for EU citizens, form 120 for non-EU employed persons and form 140 for non-EU, non-employed persons);
- *a number of passport-size photographs (one for each application form);
- *proof of residence, e.g. your property purchase contract (*escritura*), a long-term rental contract or receipts for rent;
- *the fee, which must be paid via a bank (you will be given a paying-in slip). It depends on your nationality and whether your country has a bilateral agreement with Spain (it's around 1,000 ptas for EU citizens).
- *a medical certificate (*certificado médico*), obtainable from any Spanish doctor;
- a certificate of criminal record (*certificado de antecedentes penales*) declaring that you don't have a criminal record in your home country (you can request a statement from your local police authorities);
- *a certificate of registration (consular inscription) confirming that you're a resident in Spain, available from your country's local consulate in Spain;
- **Retired persons** require proof that they belong to a private health insurance scheme that's valid in Spain (the company must have an office in Spain) or that they have the right to medical treatment under the Spanish public health scheme (see page 237);
- **Employees** require a job contract or an offer of employment in the form of a pre-contract stamped and signed by both parties (or a letter written on the headed paper of the Spanish employer);
- **Self-employed persons** require evidence that they meet the requirements to operate a business or perform a particular profession in Spain (see page 33). A written presentation of a business proposal including estimated investment required, details regarding business premises, number of jobs to be created, estimated income and your salary. Non-EU citizens require proof of their investment in order to be self-employed in Spain.
- **Pensioners and persons of independent means** require evidence of sufficient funds or the receipt of regular monthly pension or other income. The minimum monthly income required is usually considered to be equal to the Spanish minimum monthly wage (66,630 ptas a month in 1997), although the recipient of an EU state pension will qualify. Non-EU nationals must not have a criminal record and need sufficient funds or income for accommodation, living expenses and health care for the family. Non-EU pensioners must have an annual income of US$10,000 plus US$1,700 for each family member, in addition to owning a home in Spain. Working non-EU nationals must show an annual income of US$75,000 plus US$10,000 for each dependent family member (and own a home). They are issued with a *visado de residencia sin finalidad lucrativa*.
- **Dependants** require evidence of their relationship and proof that they will be wholly maintained by the applicant if they are over 21 years of age.
- **Students** require proof of enrolment with a recognised educational establishment, proof of sufficient funds to meet the cost of their studies and living expenses, and proof of health insurance.

- **Au Pairs** require an au pair contract and a certificate of registration for Spanish-language classes (see page 41);

* Required by most applicants. If you're accompanied by any dependants, they also require a passport and photographs.

If you don't have the required documents, you will be sent away to obtain them. Some documents must be translated into Spanish by a notarised translator or notarised by a public notary (*notario*). It isn't advisable to get documents translated or notarised in advance as it's expensive and the requirements may vary depending on the area or office and your nationality. Always check in advance.

When your application for a residence card is approved, you're issued with a receipt (*resguardo*) as proof of your application. It's valid for two months and renewable until your *residencia* is ready for collection. The *resguardo* also permits you to travel abroad and return to Spain without a visa, if applicable. When your *residencia* is ready for collection, you're summoned to the local police station, where a finger-print of your right index finger is taken. You should carry your residence card with you at all times as it constitutes a mandatory identity card for foreign residents in Spain.

Your residence card bears a fiscal number (*número de identificación de extranjero/NIE*), which must be quoted when opening a Spanish bank account or paying Spanish taxes (see page 273). All residents (and non-resident home-owners) must have an NIE, including Spaniards, when it's called the *número de identificación fiscal (NIF)*. Note that a resident in Spain must pay Spanish taxes on his worldwide income, may not own a car on foreign registration plates and must apply for a Spanish driving licence (unless he holds a valid EU driving licence).

The application for the renewal of a *residencia* must be made at least one month before its expiry date. The procedure is the same as for the initial application, although the documents required include (in addition to those listed above) proof of having paid your Spanish income tax, IVA and social security (as applicable). Non-EU citizens also require a certificate of good conduct from the Spanish Ministry of Justice. If you lose your card or the details (such as your address) change, you must report it within one month to a police station or foreigner's office. When you leave Spain for good or cease to be a resident, you can have your residence status cancelled by simply handing your residence card into a police station with a foreigners' department (*departamento de extranjeros*).

WORK PERMITS

Technically an EU resident doesn't require a work permit to work in Spain, but he does require a residence card which is usually issued for five years. A non-EU foreigner who carries out an activity for monetary gain (*fines lucrativos*) in Spain requires a work permit and a residence card (issued simultaneously for the same duration). A work permit (*permiso de trabajo*) for a non-EU national is initially valid for one year, after which a five-year permit may be issued no longer restricting the holder by area, activity, employer or industry. The spouse and children under 21 years of age of a non-EU work permit holder are also granted certain rights to work in Spain. A work permit isn't required to buy a property, make an investment, start a Spanish company or to register a foreign company in Spain, although the person in Spain (who's responsible for a company's activities) must have a work permit. Note that fees for work permits were raised sharply in 1997 and are now between 25,000 and 50,000 ptas (which is mostly paid by employers).

EU Nationals: If you're an EU national you can enter Spain as a tourist and register with the Spanish national employment office *Instituto Nacional de Empleo/INEM* (see page 23) as a job-seeker (*demandante de empleo*). If you visit Spain to look for a job you have 90 days in which to find employment, although if you enter as a visitor you can obtain an extension after 90 days or leave Spain and re-enter for a further 90 days (see page 66). EU nationals receiving unemployment benefit can be paid their benefit in Spain for 90 days, however, if they wish to continue to receive unemployment benefit after this period they must return to their home country. When you're offered a job, you should obtain an employment contract (*contrato de trabajo*), which is necessary when applying for your residence card (see page 51).

Non-EU Nationals: Non-EU nationals must obtain a visa (see page 65) for the purpose of employment before arriving in Spain, the granting of which is subject to the approval of the work permit. When applying for a visa, a copy of the application form, passport and medical certificate certified by the consulate are returned to the applicant as proof of his application. These must be sent by the applicant to the prospective employer in Spain with other relevant documentation, who then applies for a work permit to the provincial office of the Ministry of Labour (*Delagación Provincial del Ministerio de Trabajo*).

A position must have been advertised to EU citizens through the INEM before it can be given to a non-EU citizen and a work permit will be issued only when it's demonstrated that there isn't an unemployed EU citizen available to do the job. The employment of non-EU nationals must be approved by the Ministry of Labour and Social Security (*Ministerio de Trabajo y Seguridad Social*), who can propose the employment of a EU national in place of a non-EU national. Applications must also be approved by the provincial office of the Ministry of Labour, where the prospective employer is registered.

Spain has had a virtual freeze on the employment of non-EU nationals for some years, which has been strengthened in recent years by the high unemployment rate. Before granting or renewing work permits certain factors are taken into account, including the level of unemployment in the relevant profession or activity, the number of vacancies in the profession or trade, and whether a reciprocal agreement exists between Spain and the applicant's country of origin. Certain non-EU nationals are given preference, including those married to Spaniards; persons closely related to a Spaniard or to someone who previously held Spanish nationality; nationals of Latin American countries, Andorra, the Philippines, Equatorial Guinea, Portugal and Jews of Spanish origin; the family of a work permit holder; and those born and living legally in Spain or who have been resident there for the past five years.

Certain categories of employees don't require work permits, including technical personnel invited by the state; foreign teachers invited by Spanish universities; the management of cultural teaching centres of another state or private centres recognised in Spain; civil and military personnel working with the Spanish government; accredited foreign press staff; and members of international scientific missions carrying out investigations in Spain. Temporary and restricted work permits valid for six months (and not renewable) are issued to artists, journalists, performers, professors or other 'skilled' people performing temporary jobs in Spain. A temporary work permit is also required by non-EU students studying in Spain and is available from INEM offices (see page 23). Note, however, that although temporary employment may be permitted for students, it's usually extremely difficult to find work due to Spain's high unemployment.

The type and duration of work permits vary depending on a number of factors including the particular job to be performed, the region and whether the job is permanent or temporary. The following classes of work permits are issued to non-EU nationals:

- **Permit A:** For seasonal or temporary work in a particular area. Valid for a maximum of nine months and not renewable.

- **Permit B:** For employees (*cuenta ajena*) working in a particular profession or trade, for a specified employer in a particular location. Valid for one year and renewable.

- **Permit C:** Unrestricted permit allowing an employee to work anywhere in Spain in any occupation, but not as a self-employed person. Valid for a maximum of three years and renewable.

- **Permit D:** For self-employed persons (*autónomos*) working in a particular activity and location. Valid for one year and renewable.

- **Permit E:** Permits any type of activity, including self-employment, anywhere in Spain. Valid for three years and renewable.

- **Permit F:** Issued to frontier workers who cross the frontier each day to work in Spain. Valid for three years and renewable.

Self-Employed: Prior to 1st January 1993, many EU citizens spent years trying to obtain a self-employed (*cuenta propia* or *autónomo*) work permit, particularly professionals whose qualifications weren't recognised in Spain. Although it's now much easier, applicants may still suffer obstruction and delays from local bureaucrats. Anyone planning to work in a profession such as medicine or law must apply for membership to the relevant professional association in Spain.

A non-EU citizen wishing to be self-employed in Spain must obtain a visa before arriving in Spain. You must show that you're investing around 15m ptas (US$100,000) in foreign currency to start a business or that your professional activities will produce a profit and benefit to Spain. If you can show that you will provide employment for several Spanish (or EU) workers, your chances of obtaining a permit are greatly enhanced. A Spanish consulate may insist that the investment is made, employees are hired and the business ready to operate *before* they grant a visa. For further information see **Self-Employment** on page 33 and **Starting a Business** on page 34.

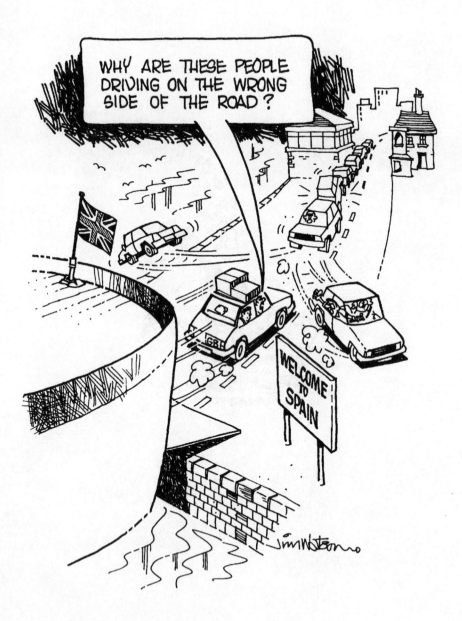

4.

ARRIVAL

On arrival in Spain, your first task will be to negotiate immigration and customs. Fortunately this presents few problems for most people, particularly citizens of a country that's a member of the European Union or the EEA (see page 22). However, non-EU nationals coming to Spain for any purpose other than as visitors usually require a visa (see page 65). Spain is a signatory to the Schengen agreement (named after a Luxembourg village on the Moselle River) which came into effect in 1994 and was intended to introduce an open-border policy between member countries. Other Schengen members are Belgium, France, Germany, Luxembourg, the Netherlands and Portugal, who are expected to be joined by Austria, Greece and Italy. Under the agreement, immigration checks and passport controls take place when you first arrive in a member country, after which you can travel freely between member countries.

If you're travelling to Spain by road, you should bear in mind that not all border posts are open 24-hours a day. Some of the smaller posts open only from early morning until some time in the evening and times may vary depending on the season. If you plan to enter Spain via a minor border post, check the opening times in advance. In addition to information regarding immigration and customs, this chapter also contains a list of tasks that must be completed before (or soon after) arrival in Spain, and includes suggestions for finding local help and information. Note that in Spain you should always carry your foreign identity card, passport or Spanish residence card (or a copy certified by a Spanish police station).

IMMIGRATION

Under the Schengen agreement which came into effect in 1994, Spain operates an open-border policy with most of its European Union (EU) partners. When you arrive in Spain from another EU country, there are usually no immigration checks or passport controls, which take place when you arrive in an EU country from outside the EU. If you're a non-EU national and arrive in Spain by air or sea from outside the EU, you must go through immigration (*imigración*) for non-EU citizens.

Non-EU citizens are required to complete an immigration registration card, which are provided on aircraft, ships, trains and at land border crossings. If you have a single-entry visa (see page 65) it will be cancelled by the immigration official. **If you require a visa to enter Spain and attempt to enter without one, you will be refused entry.** Some people may wish to get a stamp in their passport as confirmation of their date of entry into Spain. If you're a non-EU national coming to Spain to work, study or live, you may be asked to show documentary evidence.

Immigration officials may ask non-EU visitors to produce a return ticket, proof of accommodation, health insurance and financial resources, e.g. cash, travellers cheques and credit cards. Spanish regulations require visitors to have a minimum of 5,000 ptas per day on entry to Spain or a total of 50,000 ptas, although this doesn't apply to visitors on pre-paid package holidays (this rule was brought in mainly to deter illegal immigrants from Morocco). The onus is on visitors to show that they are genuine and that they don't intend to breach Spanish immigration laws. Immigration officials aren't required to prove that you will breach the immigration laws and can refuse you entry on the grounds of suspicion only. Young people may be liable to interrogation, particularly 'strange looking' youths or coloureds, and will find it advantageous to carry international credit and charge cards, a return or onward travel ticket, a student identity card, and a letter from an employer or educational establishment stating that they are on holiday.

CUSTOMS

The Single European Act, which came into effect on 1st January 1993, created a single trading market and changed the rules regarding customs (*aduanas*) for EU nationals. The shipment of personal (household) effects to Spain from another EU country isn't subject to customs formalities, although an inventory must be provided. Note, however, that all persons arriving in Spain from outside the EU (including EU citizens) are still subject to customs checks and limitations on what may be imported duty-free. There are no restrictions on the import or export of Spanish or foreign banknotes or securities, although if you enter or leave Spain with 1m ptas or more in cash or negotiable instruments (see page 274), you must make a declaration to Spanish customs.

Information about the following can be found on the page indicated: duty-free allowances (see page 393), pets (see page 415) and vehicles (see page 193). Further information can be obtained from the Dirección General de Aduanas, Ministerio de Economía y Hacienda, Guzman el Bueno, 137, 28071 Madrid (tel. (91) 554 3200).

Visitors

Visitors' belongings aren't subject to duty or VAT when they are visiting Spain for up to six months (182 days). This applies to the import of private cars, camping vehicles (including trailers or caravans), motorcycles, aircraft, boats and personal effects. Goods may be imported without formality, providing their nature and quantity doesn't imply any commercial aim. All means of transport and personal effects imported duty-free mustn't be sold or given away in Spain, and must be exported before the expiration of the visitor's stay in Spain. If you cross into Spain by road you may drive slowly through the border post without stopping unless asked to do so. However, any goods and pets that you're carrying mustn't be subject to any prohibitions or restrictions (see page 78). Customs officials can still stop anyone for a spot check, e.g. to check for drugs or illegal immigrants.

If you arrive at a seaport by private boat there are no particular customs formalities, although you must produce the boat's registration papers on request. A vessel registered outside the EU may remain in Spain for a maximum of six months in any calendar year, after which it must be exported or imported (when duty and tax must be paid). However, you can get the local customs authorities to seal (*precintar*) your foreign-registered boat while you're absent from Spain and unseal it when you wish to use it, thus allowing you to keep it in Spain all year round (although you can use it for six months of the year only). Foreign-registered vehicles and boats mustn't be lent or rented to anyone else while in Spain.

Primary or Secondary Residence

EU nationals planning to take up permanent or temporary residence in Spain are permitted to import their furniture and personal effects free of duty or taxes, providing they were purchased tax-paid within the EU or have been owned for at least six-months. Non-EU nationals must have owned and used all goods for at least six months to qualify for duty-free import. You require an application form for a primary (*cambio de residencia*) or secondary (*vivienda secundaria*) residence (as applicable), available from Spanish consulates, plus a detailed inventory (in Spanish) of the items to be imported, showing their estimated value in pesetas. All items to be imported should be included on the list, even if some are to be imported at a later date. These documents must be signed and presented to a Spanish consulate with the owner's passport. If the owner isn't present when the effects are cleared by customs in Spain, a photocopy of the principal pages of his passport are necessary, which must be legalised by the local Spanish embassy.

Permanent Residence: Applicants importing personal effects for a permanent home must present their residence card (*residencia*) to the consulate, or if the permit hasn't yet been granted, evidence that an application has been made. **Non-EU citizens** must provide Spanish customs with a bank guarantee (of up to 60 per cent of the value of their belongings) until the residence card is granted in the following 12 months. The deposit 'exempts' the holder from customs duties and is returned when a residence card has been obtained (see below). **Note that you have one year in which to obtain a residence card and request the return of your deposit. If you take longer than one year without obtaining an extension, you may lose your deposit!**

Secondary Residence: Applicants importing personal effects for a secondary residence must present the title deed (*escritura*) of a property that they own in Spain or a rental contract (lease) for a minimum period of two years.

Non-EU citizens must provide a bank guarantee (see above) issued by a bank in Spain to ensure that the goods will remain in the same dwelling, that the property won't be sub-let by the foreign owner or lessee, and that it will be reserved for his (or his family's) exclusive use. The deposit must be paid into a Spanish bank, which issues a certificate for the customs office stating the funds have been received. The deposit is returned after two years. When the two-year period has expired, you must obtain a certificate from your local town hall verifying that the goods are still in your possession. When customs receive the certificate they will issue you with a document authorising the bank to release your funds. Note that it can take some time to get your deposit returned.

Your goods must be imported within three months of your entry into Spain and may be imported in one or a number of consignments, although it's best to have one only. If there's more than one consignment, subsequent consignments should be cleared through the same customs office. Goods imported duty-free mustn't be sold in Spain within two years of their importation and if you leave Spain within two years, everything imported duty-free must be exported or the duty paid.

If you use a shipping company to transport your belongings to Spain, they will usually provide all the necessary forms and take care of the paperwork. Always keep a copy of all forms and communications with customs officials, both with Spanish customs officials and officials in the country from where you're shipping your belongings. Note that if the paperwork isn't in order, your belongings may end up incarcerated in a Spanish customs storage depot for a number of months. If you personally import your belongings, you may need to employ a customs agent (*agente de aduanas*) at the point of entry to clear them. You should have an official record of the export of valuables from any country, in case you wish to re-import them later.

Prohibited & Restricted Goods

Certain items are subject to special regulations in Spain and in some cases their import and export is prohibited or restricted. This applies in particular to animal products; plants (see below); wild fauna and flora and products derived from them; live animals; medicines and medical products (except for prescribed drugs and medicines); firearms and ammunition; certain goods and technologies with a dual civil/military purpose; works of art and collectors' items.

If you're unsure whether any goods you're importing fall into the above categories, you should check with Spanish customs. If you're planning to import sports guns into Spain you must obtain a certificate from a Spanish consulate abroad, which is issued on production of a valid firearms' licence. The consular certificate must be presented to the customs authorities on entry into Spain and can be used to exchange a foreign firearms' licence for a Spanish licence when taking up residence.

To import certain types of plants into Spain, you must obtain a health certificate. There's usually a limit on the number of plants that can be imported, although when they are included in your personal effects they aren't usually subject to any special controls. Visitors arriving in Spain from 'exotic' regions, e.g. Africa, South America, and the Middle and Far East, may find themselves under close scrutiny from customs officials seeking illegal drugs.

RESIDENCE CARD

A foreigner (legally) residing in Spain for longer than 182 days must apply for a residence card (see page 67). If you come to Spain with the intention of remaining longer than 182 days (e.g. as an employee, student or a non-employed resident), you must apply for a residence card within 15 days of your arrival. EU nationals who visit Spain with the intention of finding employment or starting a business normally have up to 182 days to find a job and apply for a residence card. Once employment has been found, an application must be made for a residence card. Note that if you don't have a regular income or adequate financial resources, your application will be refused. Failure to apply for a residence card within the specified time is a serious offence and can result in a heavy fine and deportation.

EMBASSY REGISTRATION

Nationals of some countries are required to register with their local embassy or consulate after taking up residence in Spain. Registration isn't usually mandatory, although most embassies like to keep a record of their country's citizens who are resident in Spain. However, non-EU residents may require a certificate (consular inscription) from their country's consulate in Spain declaring that they are registered with them as residing in Spain, in order to obtain a residence card. Many countries, particularly European countries with a lot of residents in Spain, maintain consulates throughout Spain which are an important source of local information for residents and can often provide valuable contacts. See **Appendix A** for addresses.

FINDING HELP

One of the major problems facing new arrivals in Spain is how and where to get help with day to day problems, for example, finding accommodation, schooling, insurance and so on. **This book was written in response to this need.** However, in addition to the comprehensive information provided herein, you will also need detailed *local* information. How successful you are at finding local help depends on your employer, the town or area where you live (e.g. residents of resort areas are far better served than those living in rural areas), your nationality, Spanish language proficiency and your sex (women are usually better provided for than men).

There's an abundance of information available in Spanish, but little in English and other foreign languages. An additional problem is that much of the available information isn't intended for foreigners and their particular needs. You may find that your friends and colleagues can help, as they can often offer advice based on their own experiences and mistakes. **But take care!** Although they mean well, you're likely to receive as much false and conflicting information as accurate (it may not necessarily be wrong, but may not apply to your particular situation).

Your local town hall (*ayuntamiento*) may be a good source of information, but you usually need to speak Spanish to benefit and may be sent on a wild goose chase from department to department. However, town halls in areas where there are many foreign residents often have a foreigners' department (*departamento de extranjeros*) where staff speak Spanish and English, and possibly other languages such as Danish, French, German, Norwegian and Swedish (an advantage of living somewhere where there are many other foreigners). Some foreigners' departments also publish useful booklets in English and other languages. Note that a foreigner's department can help you save on fees that you would otherwise have to pay to a legal professional such as a *gestor* or a lawyer. Some companies employ staff to help new arrivals or contract this job out to a relocation consultant (see page 85): however, most Spanish employers are totally unaware of (or not interested in) the problems and difficulties faced by foreign employees and their families.

A wealth of valuable information is available in major cities and resort towns, where foreigners are well-served by English-speaking clubs and expatriate organisations. Contacts can also be found through many expatriate magazines and newspapers (see page 389). Most consulates provide their nationals with local information including details of lawyers, translators, doctors, dentists, schools, and social and expatriate organisations.

CHECKLISTS

Before Arrival

The following checklist contains a summary of the tasks that should (if possible) be completed before your arrival in Spain:

- Obtain a visa, if necessary, for you and all your family members (see **Chapter 3**). Obviously this *must* be done before arrival in Spain.

- If possible, visit Spain prior to your move to compare communities and schools, and organise schooling for your children (see **Chapter 9**).

- Find temporary or permanent accommodation and buy a car. If you purchase a car in Spain, register it and arrange insurance (see page 195 and 203).

- Arrange for shipment of your personal effects to Spain (see page 96).

- Arrange health insurance for yourself and your family (see page 260). This is essential if you won't be covered by Spanish social security.

- Open a bank account in Spain and transfer funds (you can open an account with many Spanish banks abroad). It's best to obtain some pesetas before your arrival in Spain, as this will save you having to change money on arrival.

- Compile and update your personal records, including those relating to your family's medical, dental, educational (schools), insurance (e.g. car insurance), professional and employment history.
- Obtain an international driver's licence, if necessary.
- Obtain an international credit or charge card, which will be invaluable during your first few months in Spain.

Don't forget to bring all your family's official documents with you including birth certificates; driver's licences; marriage certificate, divorce papers or death certificate (if a widow or widower); educational diplomas, professional certificates and job references; school records and student ID cards; employment references; medical and dental records; bank account and credit card details; insurance policies; and receipts for any valuables. You also need the documents necessary to obtain a residence card (see page 67) plus certified copies, official translations and numerous passport-size photographs (students should take at least a dozen).

After Arrival

The following checklist contains a summary of tasks to be completed after arrival in Spain (if not done before arrival):

- On arrival at a Spanish airport or port, have your visa cancelled and your passport stamped, as applicable.
- If you don't own a car, you may wish to rent one for a week or two until you buy one locally (see page 224). Note that it's practically impossible to get around in rural areas without a car.
- Apply for a residence card at your local town hall within 15 days of your arrival (see page 67).
- Register with your local consulate (see page 79).
- Do the following within the next few weeks:
  - register with your local social security office (see page 256);
  - open a bank account at a local bank and give the details to your employer (see page 279);
  - arrange schooling for your children (see **Chapter 9**);
  - find a local doctor and dentist (see **Chapter 12**);
  - arrange whatever insurance is necessary (see **Chapter 13**) including:
    * health insurance (see page 260);
    * car insurance (see page 203);
    * household insurance (see page 264);
    * third-party liability insurance (see page 267).

5.

ACCOMMODATION

In most areas of Spain, finding accommodation to rent or buy isn't difficult, providing that your requirements aren't too unusual. There are, however, a few exceptions. For example in major cities such as Madrid and Barcelona rented accommodation is in high demand and short supply, and rents can be astronomical. Accommodation accounts for around 25 per cent of the average Spanish family's budget, but can be up to 50 per cent in the major cities. Property prices and rents in Spain vary considerably depending on the region and city. For example, an apartment renting for 40,000 ptas a month in Seville will cost 100,000 ptas a month in Madrid and Barcelona, and at least 60,000 ptas a month in most other northern cities. In cities and large towns, apartments are much more common than detached houses, which are rare and prohibitively expensive.

The average Spaniard lives with his parents until the age of around 30, including some 50 per cent of those aged between 25 and 30. However, around 80 per cent of Spaniards own their own homes, compared with some 70 per cent in Britain and Italy, 55 per cent in France, 45 per cent in Germany and just 40 per cent in Switzerland. Around one in every 12 Spanish families also owns a second home in Spain and the number is increasing annually. There are some 1.2m foreign property owners in Spain, which is Europe's favourite country for second homes, particularly among buyers from the Benelux countries, Britain, Germany and Scandinavia. Most foreigners are concentrated on the Mediterranean coast (the *costas*) and in the Balearic and Canary Islands. Officially some 20 per cent of foreign property owners in Spain are residents, the majority of whom are retired, although the real figure is much higher as many foreigners fail to register as residents.

Property prices soared throughout Spain in the 1980s, when rising prices in the north and northeast created problems for many aspiring homeowners, particularly in the major cities where property prices rose by up to 40 per cent a year. In resort areas, rising prices were fuelled by the high demand for holiday homes, particularly from foreigners. However, as the world recession deepened in the early 1990s, prices in most resort areas plummeted as the stream of buyers dried up, leaving developers and agents with a glut of unsold properties, many of which remained unsold years after being built. Prices in the major cities have remained fairly stable, being less dependent on foreign buyers and the vagaries of the world economic climate.

The cost of many properties in resort areas (both new and re-sale) were reduced by some 50 per cent during the recession compared with the heyday of the 1980s, driven down by repossessions, distress sales and bankruptcies. However, by 1997 the property market had made a robust recovery, particularly the medium and top price brackets, although the bottom end of the market remained fairly flat. Property remains excellent value in most areas, particularly for foreigners paying in currencies which have made large gains against the peseta in recent years. The stockpile of new properties in resort areas had mostly been sold by 1997 and the increasing number of new foreign buyers (e.g. from eastern Europe, particularly Russia, Hong Kong and South Africa) gave rise to hopes that a new property 'boom' was imminent.

You have probably heard a number of horror stories concerning property transactions in Spain, most of which are unfortunately true. Nevertheless, buying property in Spain isn't the lottery it once was and most problems in recent years have been due to bankruptcies rather than outright fraud. **However, it's vital to obtain expert, independent legal advice and beware of fraudsters when buying and selling property in Spain.**

TEMPORARY ACCOMMODATION

On arrival in Spain, you may find it necessary to stay in temporary accommodation for a few weeks or months, e.g. before moving into permanent accommodation or while waiting for your furniture to arrive. Some employers provide rooms or self-contained apartments for employees and their families, although this is rare and is for a limited period only. Many hotels and hostels cater for long-term guests and offer reduced weekly and monthly rates. In most areas, particularly in Madrid and other large cities, self-contained, service apartments are widely available with private bathrooms and kitchens. These are cheaper and more convenient than hotels, particularly for families, and are usually let on a weekly basis. In cities and resorts, self-catering holiday accommodation (see page 327) is widely available, though it's prohibitively expensive during the main holiday season (June-August).

For information about hotels, bed and breakfast, self-catering and budget accommodation, see **Chapter 15**.

RELOCATION CONSULTANTS

If you're fortunate enough to have your move to Spain paid for by your employer, it's likely that he will engage a relocation consultant to handle the details. There are fewer relocation consultants in Spain than in most other western European countries and those that exist usually deal exclusively with corporate clients rather than individuals. Fees are usually around 40,000 ptas per day or you can choose a package of services for a set fee, e.g. 400,000 ptas. The main service provided by relocation consultants is finding accommodation to rent or buy and arranging viewing. Other housing services include conducting negotiations, drawing up contracts, arranging mortgages, organising surveys and insurance, and handling the house move. Relocation consultants also provide reports on local schools, health services, public transport, sports and social facilities, and other amenities and services. Some companies provide daily advice and assistance, e.g. helping clients in their dealings with local officials and businesses.

Finding rental accommodation for single people or couples without children can usually be accomplished in a few weeks, while housing families may take up to four weeks, depending on the location and requirements. You should usually allow at least two months between your initial visit and moving into a purchased property in Spain.

BUYING PROPERTY

Buying property in Spain is usually a good long-term investment and is preferable to renting. However, if you're staying for a short term only, say less than three years, then you may be better off renting. For those staying longer than this, buying is usually the better option, particularly as buying a house or apartment is generally no more expensive than renting in the long term and could yield a handsome profit (or a loss!). Property in Spain is relatively inexpensive compared with many other European countries, although the fees associated with a purchase add around 10 per cent to the cost.

One of the things which attracts many buyers to Spain is the relatively low cost of property compared with many other European countries, which generally offers excellent value for money. However, although more Spaniards own their own homes than the inhabitants of many other EU countries, the Spanish don't generally buy property as an

investment and you shouldn't expect to make a quick profit when buying property in Spain. Property values generally increase at an average of around 3 or 4 per cent (if you're lucky) a year or in line with inflation, meaning that you must own a house for around three years simply to recover the fees associated with buying. Property prices rise faster than average in some fashionable areas, although this is generally reflected in higher purchase prices. The stable property market in Spain acts as a discouragement to speculators wishing to make a quick profit and capital gains tax (see page 308) can also take a large chunk out of any profit made on the sale of a second home.

As when buying property anywhere, it's never advisable to be in too much of a hurry. Have a good look around in your preferred area(s) and make sure you have a clear picture of the relative prices and the types of properties available. There's a huge variety of properties in Spain ranging from derelict farmhouses requiring complete restoration to new luxury apartments and villas with all modern conveniences. If after discussing it at length with your partner one of you insists on a new luxury apartment in Marbella and the other a 17th century *castillo* in Galicia, the easiest solution may be to get a divorce! Some people set themselves impossible deadlines in which to buy a property or business (e.g. a few days or a week) and often end up bitterly regretting their impulsive decision. Although it's common practice, mixing a holiday with a property purchase isn't advisable, as most people are inclined to make poor business decisions when their mind is on play rather than work.

It's a wise or lucky person who gets his choice absolutely right first time, which is why most experts recommend that you rent before buying unless you're absolutely sure of what you want, how much you wish to pay and where you want to live. To reduce the chances of making an expensive error when buying in an unfamiliar region, it's often prudent to rent for 6 to 12 months, taking in the worst part of the year (weather-wise). This allows you to become familiar with the region and the weather, and gives you plenty of time to look around for a permanent home at your leisure. There's no shortage of properties for sale in Spain (indeed, in many resort areas there's a glut) and whatever kind of property you're looking for, you will have an abundance from which to choose. Wait until you find your 'dream' home and then think about it for another week or two before signing a contract.

Publications & Exhibitions: Invaluable reading for anyone planning to buy a home in Spain is our sister publication *Buying a Home in France* (Survival Books) written by yours truly, David Hampshire (see page 463). A comprehensive list of other reference books is contained in **Appendix B**. Overseas Property Match (532 Kingston Road, Raynes Park, London SW20 8DT, UK, tel. 0181-542 9088) publish *World of Property* a quarterly publication containing many properties for sale in Spain (and other countries) and organise property exhibitions in the south and north of England. Other international property exhibitions that include Spain are organised by Homebuyer Events Ltd., Mantle House, Broomhill Road, London SW18 4JQ, UK (tel. 0181-877 3636). Property is also advertised for sale in many newspapers and magazines in Spain and abroad (see page 389 and **Appendix A**).

Independent Advice and Information: A useful source of information for foreign property buyers in Spain is the Institute of Foreign Property Owners (*Instituto de Propietarios Extranjeros SL*), Apartado de Correos 418, Avda. Fermín Sanz Orrio, 15, 2ª Pta. 9, 03590 Altea (Alicante), tel. (96) 584 2312. The *Instituto* publishes an English-language magazine (*Boletín informativo*) for members containing valuable information including an early warning system for owners who are the subject of official municipal notices concerning tax and other debts. The *Instituto* styles itself as the 'the voice of foreign home owners in Spain' and provides free advice to members about buying and renting property, a free document check and legal scrutiny of contracts (for a small fee).

RENTED ACCOMMODATION

If you're planning to stay in Spain for a few years only (say less than three), then renting is usually the best solution. It's also the answer for those who don't want the trouble, expense and restrictions associated with buying a property. **In fact, it's prudent for anyone looking for a permanent home in Spain to rent for a period until you know exactly what you want, how much you wish to pay and where you want to live.** This is particularly important for retirees who don't know Spain well, when renting allows you to become familiar with an area, its weather, amenities and the local people; to meet other foreigners who have made their homes in Spain and share their experiences; and not least, to discover the cost of living at first hand. Note that this section is concerned with long-term rentals of six months or longer and *not* short-term holidays rentals (for information about holiday rentals see **Self-Catering** on page 327).

If you're looking for a property in a resort area, long-term rentals are good value, particularly during the winter months. Some people even rent long term (or even 'permanently') as an alternative to buying, as it saves them tying up their capital and can be surprisingly inexpensive in many regions (some people let out their family homes abroad and rent one in Spain, when it's even possible to make a profit). Renting also affords you maximum flexibility should you wish to move to another region in Spain, return home or even move to another country. In today's uncertain financial climate, there can be considerable risks associated with buying, particularly if you're unsure of your future plans.

Renting isn't as common in Spain as it is in many other European countries with the exception of the major cities, where the majority of people live in rented accommodation. In cities, most rental properties are small one or two-roomed apartments, and large apartments and houses are difficult to find and prohibitively expensive. Most rental properties in Spain are let unfurnished, particularly for lets longer than one year. Furnished (*amueblado*) properties are difficult to find in cities, although they are common in resort areas, particularly for lets of less than one year. If you're looking for a home for less than a year, then you're better off renting a furnished apartment or house. Note that 'unfurnished' doesn't simply mean 'without furniture' in Spain. An unfurnished property, particularly in major cities, is usually an 'empty shell' with no light fixtures, curtain rods or even a television aerial. There's also no cooker, refrigerator or dishwasher and there may even be no kitchen units, carpets or kitchen sink! Always ask before viewing as you may save yourself a wasted trip. If the previous tenant has fitted items such as carpets and kitchen cupboards, he may ask you to reimburse him for the cost. You should be prepared to negotiate the price and make sure that you receive value for money.

See also **Temporary Accommodation** on page 85 and **Self-Catering** on page 327.

Finding a Rental Property

Your success or failure in finding a suitable rental property depends on many factors, not least the type of rental you're looking for (a one-bedroom apartment is easier to find than a four-bedroom detached house), how much you want to pay and the area where you wish to live. Finding a property to rent in Madrid or Barcelona is similar to the situation in London or Paris, where the most desirable properties are often found through personal contacts. There are a number of ways of finding a property to rent, including the following:

- Ask your friends, relatives and acquaintances to help spread the word, particularly if you're looking in the area where you already live. A lot of rental properties, particularly in major cities, are found by word of mouth. You can also look out for 'to rent' (*se alquila*) signs in windows in your local neighbourhood. If you're looking for an apartment in a block in Madrid or Barcelona, it's prudent to ask the porter (*portero*) if there are any vacancies in a building or if anything is coming vacant soon.

- Check the advertisements in local Spanish newspapers and magazines under *alquiler*. If you cannot speak Spanish, you may prefer to respond to advertisements in expatriate newspapers and magazines (see page 389), where advertisers are likely to speak English or other foreign languages. In major cities there are property newspapers and magazines. There's little jargon or abbreviations in Spanish rental ads and most can be deciphered without too much trouble.

- Visit accommodation and letting agents. Most cities and large towns have estate agents (*Agentes Propiedad Inmobiliaria*) who also act as letting agents for owners. It's often better to deal with an agent than directly with owners, particularly concerning contracts and legal matters. Some agents advertise abroad in property publications and many companies handling holiday rentals also offer longer term rentals, particularly during the winter. Note that agents usually charge commission equal to a half or one month's rent for long-term rentals. If you wish to avoid agency fees ask before viewing, as advertisers who appear to be private individuals are often agencies.

- Check the advertisements in shop windows and on notice boards in shopping centres, supermarkets, universities and colleges, and company offices.

* Obtain copies of newsletters published by churches, clubs and expatriate organisations, and also check their notice boards.

To find accommodation through advertisements in local newspapers you must usually be quick off the mark. Buy the newspaper as soon as it's published and start phoning straight away. You must be available to inspect properties immediately or at any time. Even if you start phoning at the crack of dawn, you're still likely to find a queue when you arrive to view a choice property in Madrid or Barcelona. The best days for advertisements are usually Fridays and Saturdays. Advertisers may be private owners, real-estate managers or letting agencies (particularly in major cities). You can insert a 'rental wanted' advertisement in many newspapers and on notice boards, but don't count on success using this method.

Rental Costs

Rental costs in Spain vary considerably depending on the size (number of bedrooms), quality and age of a property, and the facilities provided. However, the most significant factor affecting rents is the region of Spain, the city and the particular neighbourhood. In major cities, particularly Madrid and Barcelona, rental accommodation is in high demand and short supply, and rents are high. A two bedroom, unfurnished apartment (e.g. 75 square metres) which rents for around 100,000 ptas a month in Madrid or Barcelona, costs around 50 per cent less in most smaller cities, and rural and resort areas. Rents are lowest in small towns and rural areas, although good rented accommodation is often difficult to find. As a general rule, the further a property is from a large city or town (or town centre), public transport or other facilities, the cheaper it is. Many Spanish families live in communal high-rise property developments called *urbanizaciones* (which surround Spanish cities), where rents are much lower than in city centres. Rents are also dictated by supply and demand and are naturally higher in cities than in rural and resort areas (except for short lets during the high season).

Rents are calculated according to the number of bedrooms (*dormitorios*) and the floor area (in square metres). In cities, an apartment with a terrace or balcony is usually more expensive. Generally the higher an apartment is in a block, the more expensive it is (you pay for the view, the extra light, the absence of street noise, increased security and the rarified air). However, if a block doesn't have a lift, apartments on lower floors may be the most expensive. A *rough* guide to rents is show below:

Property	Monthly Rent (Ptas)	
	Resort Area	Major City
studio	from 30,000	50,000
2-bedroom apartment	from 40,000	75-100,000
3-bedroom apartment	from 50,000	100-150,000 +
2/3 bedroom townhouse	from 50,000	100-200,000 +
3+ bedroom villa with pool	from 90,000	200,000 ++

The rents listed above are for good quality new or recently renovated properties and with the exception of villas, usually don't include a garage. **They don't include apartments located in the central area of cities or properties in exclusive residential areas, where the sky's the limit.** It's possible in some areas to find cheaper, older apartments, but they are rarer, generally smaller and don't usually contain the standard 'fixtures and fittings' of a modern apartment. Rents in resorts are similar for both furnished and unfurnished properties, although some owners and agents charge 10 to 20 per cent more for a furnished property. In cities, most properties are let unfurnished. Expect to pay up to 50 per cent more (than the rents indicated above) for a furnished property in a city. Note that if the rent of your principal residence is over 10 per cent of your total income and your income is less than 3.5m ptas a year for a single person and 5m ptas for a couple, you can deduct 15 per cent of your rental payments (maximum 100,000 ptas) from your Spanish income tax.

Extra Costs: Long-term contracts usually require tenants to pay gas, electricity and telephone bills, and may also include community (*comunidad*) fees, property taxes (IBI) and water rates, although these are usually paid by the owner. However, if these charges aren't specifically mentioned in your contract, they are the landlord's responsibility. If a property has a telephone installed you must usually pay a deposit, e.g. 100,000 ptas. Always have a contract checked by a lawyer if you don't understand it. Long-term tenants must take out third party insurance (see page 264) for a property they are renting.

Seasonal Letting: Rents for short-term lets, e.g. less than one year, are usually higher than for longer lets, particularly in popular resort areas where most properties are let furnished as self-catering holiday accommodation. However, many agents let furnished holiday homes in resort areas (except for the Canaries) at a considerable reduction during the 'low season', which may extend from October to May. Some holiday letting agents divide the rental year into three seasons, e.g. low (October to March), medium (April to June) and high (July to September). The rent for a one or two-bedroom furnished apartment or townhouse during the low season ranges from between 40,000 and 60,000 ptas a month for a minimum one or two-month let. Rent is usually paid one month in advance with one month's rent as a deposit (which is forfeited if you leave before the end of the contract). Lets of less than one month are more expensive, e.g. 20,000 ptas per week for a two-bedroom apartment in the low season, which is some 25 to 50 per cent of the rent in the high season. Note that many hotels and hostels also offer special low rates for long stays during the low season (see **Chapter 15**).

Rental Contracts

A rental contract (*contrato de arrendamiento*) is necessary when renting any property in Spain, whether long or short term. A short-term or temporary (*arriendo de temporada* or *contrato de arrendamiento de finca urbana amueblada, por temporada*) contract is usually for holiday letting (although it also applies to lets of up to a year) and provides tenants with less rights than a long-term (*arriendo de viviendas*) contract. You can rent a property without a contract, although it's always advisable to have a written contract. Rental contracts are usually standard state-sponsored tenant/landlord agreements available from tobacconists (*estancos*). If you don't understand a contract you should have it checked by a lawyer before signing it. When a landlord accepts a rent payment there's an implicit contract, although this is only for the period for which you have paid. You should receive a written receipt for all rental payments.

Pre-1985: Until 9th May 1985, a tenant was 'protected' and could extend his rental contract indefinitely and his rent could be increased only by the rate of inflation each year, irrespective of market rents. Rented properties could even be handed down to children, with the result that there are today over 750,000 Spanish families paying ridiculously low rents (e.g. just a few thousand pesetas a month) with little prospect of the landlord recovering his property. Some owners have been trying to reclaim their property for over 20 years, which led to a new law in 1995 (see below) which will eventually end 'protected tenants' rights under the old law.

From 1985: The law concerning rental contracts was changed in 1985 and ended previous extremely rigid tenant protection. From 9th May 1985, rental contracts were for fixed periods and at the end of the contract the tenant can be offered a new contract at the same or a higher rent. As is often the case, the new law went too far in the opposite direction and offered tenants too little security, while landlords were free to increase rents at will. Contracts signed before 9th May 1985 were unaffected.

From 1995: A new law of urban lettings (*Ley de Arrendamientos Urbanos*) came into effect on 1st January 1995 and has breathed some life into the long term rental market by balancing the rights of both landlords and tenants. This law will eventually eradicate the draconian law which made it all but impossible for landlords to get rid of tenants and allowed them to remain in a property in perpetuity for a derisory rent, but will also give new tenants adequate security. Pre-1995 contracts held by protected tenants will be gradually increased to market levels over 5 or 10 years depending on the tenant's income. If the tenant earns less than 4.6m ptas a year his rent can be gradually increased to market levels over 10 years; if he earns more than this sum, his rent can be increased to the market level over five years. The right to pass on the tenancy remains, but is limited to a spouse or child and is more restrictive, and a landlord will eventually be able to take possession of his property.

Under the new law a rental contract for a principal home has a minimum duration of five years and is renewable annually by mutual consent. A contract is tacitly increased for one year if the tenant doesn't give the landlord 30 days' notice before the end of a year and rent increases are limited to the rise in the consumer price (inflation) index (*Indice de Precios al Consumo/IPC*). If a landlord wishes to recover a property for his own use he can refuse to extend the contract beyond five years. A tenant must pay a deposit of one month's rent against damages, which is held by an independent agency. Tenants may be required to pay property tax (IBI) and community fees if it's specified in the contract. **Note that if you're a landlord you must be careful not to fall into the trap whereby you sign a temporary contract, say for one year, which is later interpreted by a court as a long-term contract valid for five years. This is common practice when the tenant is a resident of Spain and is the reason why many foreigners refuse to rent to Spaniards.**

A tenant can be evicted under certain circumstances, although the owner may require a court order (*demanda de desahucio*) to force him to leave the property. Reasons for eviction include failure to pay the rent, damage to property, use of property for immoral purposes, subletting a property without permission from the owner, and causing a serious nuisance to neighbours. A tenant can terminate the contract (and is entitled to compensation) if the landlord has caused changes or disturbances in the property, doesn't carry out the repairs necessary to keep the property in adequate condition, or doesn't offer the services stated in the contract.

If you have a complaint regarding a long-term rental, you should report it to the local municipal consumers' information office (*Oficina Municipal de Información al Consumidor/*OMIC). If they're unable to help you, they will direct you to the office where you can make a formal complaint.

INVENTORY

When renting a property you may be required to complete and sign an inventory (*inventario*) of the fixtures, fittings and furnishings and make a report of its general condition. This usually includes the condition of fixtures and fittings, the state of furniture and carpets, etc. (if furnished), the cleanliness and state of the decoration, and anything missing or in need of repair. Don't sign the inventory until after you've moved in. If you find a serious fault after signing the inventory, send a registered letter to your landlord asking for it to be attached to the inventory.

An inventory document should be provided by your landlord or letting agent and normally includes every single item in a furnished property. Note, however, that many rental companies in resort areas in Spain are negligent when it comes to providing an inventory. This it to your advantage, as the landlord or agent can hardly charge you for breakages or missing items when no inventory was provided. If an inventory isn't provided, you can ask for one to be prepared and annexed to the lease. Where applicable, an inventory should be drawn up both when moving in and when vacating rented accommodation. If the two inventories don't correspond, the tenant must make good any damages or deficiencies or the landlord can do so and deduct the cost from the tenant's deposit. Note that although Spanish landlords are no worse than landlords in most other countries, some will use any excuse to prevent repaying a deposit. When leaving rented accommodation you may be required to pay for cleaning, unless you leave it in a spotless condition. Check that you aren't overcharged; the going rate is usually less than 1,000 ptas an hour, although some landlords may try to charge you 2,000 ptas or more an hour.

When moving into a property that you have purchased, you should also make an inventory of the fixtures and fittings, and check that the previous owner hasn't absconded with anything which was included in the contract or paid for separately, e.g. carpets, light fittings, curtains, fitted cupboards, kitchen appliances, doors or walls.

HOME SECURITY

When moving into a new home (rented or purchased) it's usually wise to replace the locks (or lock barrels) as soon as possible, as you have no idea how many keys are in circulation for the existing locks. This is true even for new homes, as builders often give keys to sub-contractors. If you let a home it's advisable to change the external lock barrels regularly, e.g. annually. If they aren't already fitted, it's wise to fit high security (double cylinder or dead bolt) locks. Most modern apartments in Spain are fitted with an armoured door (*puerta blindada*) with individually numbered, high security locks with three sets of levers. Extra keys for these locks cannot always be cut at a local hardware store and you may need to obtain details from the previous owner or your landlord.

In areas with a high risk of theft (e.g. most resort areas and major cities), your insurance company may insist on extra security measures such as two locks on all external doors, internal locking shutters, and security bars or metal grilles (*rejillas*) on windows and patio doors on ground and lower floors, e.g. the first and second floors of high and low-rise buildings. A policy may specify that all forms of protection on doors must be employed when a property is unoccupied and that all other forms (e.g. shutters) must also be used after 2200 hours and when a property is left empty for two or more days.

You may wish to have a security alarm fitted, which is usually the best way to deter thieves and may also reduce your household insurance (see page 264). It should include all external doors and windows, internal infra-red security beams, and may also include a coded entry keypad (which can be frequently changed and is useful for clients if you let) and 24-hour monitoring (with some systems it's even possible to monitor properties remotely from another country). With a monitored system, when a sensor (e.g. smoke or forced entry) detects an emergency or a panic button is pushed, a signal is sent automatically to a 24-hour monitoring station. The person on duty will telephone to check whether it's a genuine alarm and if he cannot contact you someone will be sent to investigate. Some developments and urbanisations have security gates and are patrolled 24-hours a day by security guards, although they often have little influence on crime rates and may instill a false sense of security.

You can deter thieves by ensuring that your house is well lit at night and not conspicuously unoccupied. External security 'motion detector' lights (that switch on automatically when someone approaches); random timed switches for internal lights, radios and televisions (although these aren't much use in an area which suffers frequent power cuts); dummy security cameras; and tapes that play barking dogs triggered by a light or heat detector, may all help deter burglars. In rural areas it's common for owners to fit two or three locks on external doors, alarm systems, grilles on doors and windows, window locks, security shutters and a safe for valuables. The advantage of grilles is that they allow you to leave windows open without inviting criminals in (unless they are *very* slim). Note, however, that security grilles must be heavy duty, as the bars on cheap grilles can be prised apart with a car jack. Many people also wrap a chain around security grilles and secure them with a padlock when a property is unoccupied, although a better solution is to fit a metal security bracket which cannot be cut with boltcutters. You can fit UPVC (toughened clear plastic) security windows and doors, which can survive an attack with a sledge-hammer without damage, and external steel security blinds (which can be electrically operated), although both of these are expensive. A dog can be useful to deter intruders, although it should be kept inside where it cannot be given poisoned food. Irrespective of whether you actually have a dog, a warning sign showing an image of a fierce dog may act as a deterrent. You should have the front door of an apartment fitted with a spy-hole and chain so that you can check the identity of visitors before opening the door. **Remember, prevention is better than cure as stolen property is rarely recovered.**

Holiday homes are particularly vulnerable to thieves, especially in rural areas, and are often ransacked. No matter how secure your door and window locks, a thief can usually gain entry if he's sufficiently determined, often by simply smashing a window or even breaking in through the roof or by knocking a hole in a wall in a rural area! In isolated areas thieves can strip a house bare at their leisure and an un-monitored alarm won't be a deterrent if there's no-one around to hear it. If you have a holiday home in Spain, it inadvisable to leave anything of real value (monetary or sentimental) there and to have comprehensive insurance for your belongings (see page 264). One 'foolproof' way to protect a home when you're away is to employ a house-sitter to look after it. This can be done for short periods or for six months (e.g. during the winter) or longer if you have a holiday home in Spain. It isn't usually necessary to pay someone to house-sit for a period of six months or more, when you can usually find someone to do it in return for free accommodation. However, you must take care whom you engage and obtain references.

An important aspect of home security is ensuring you have early warning of a fire, which is easily accomplished by installing smoke detectors. Battery-operated smoke detectors can be purchased for around 1,000 ptas and should be tested periodically to ensure that the batteries aren't exhausted. You can also fit an electric-powered gas detector that activates an alarm when a gas leak is detected. When closing up a property for an extended period, e.g. over the winter, you should ensure that everything is switched off and that it's secure. If you vacate your home for a long period, you may also be obliged to notify a caretaker, landlord or insurance company, and to leave a key with a caretaker or landlord in case of emergencies. If you have a robbery, you should report it immediately to your local police station where you must make a statement (*denuncia*). You will receive a copy, which is required by your insurance company if you make a claim.

MOVING HOUSE

After finding a home in Spain it usually takes only a few weeks to have your belongings shipped from within continental Europe. From anywhere else it varies considerably, e.g. around four weeks from the east coast of America, six weeks from the US west coast and the Far East, and around eight weeks from Australasia. Customs clearance is no longer necessary when shipping your household effects between European Union (EU) countries. However, when shipping your effects from a non-EU country to Spain, you should enquire about customs formalities in advance. If you fail to follow the correct procedure you can encounter problems and delays, and may even be wrongly charged duty or even fined. The relevant forms to be completed by non-EU citizens depend on whether your Spanish home will be your main residence or a second home. Removal companies usually take care of the paperwork and ensure that the correct documents are provided and properly completed (see **Customs** on page 77).

It's advisable to use a major shipping company with a good reputation. For international moves it's best to use a company that's a member of an international organisation such as the International Federation of Furniture Removers (FIDI) or the Overseas Moving Network International (OMNI), with experience in Spain. Members of FIDI and OMNI usually subscribe to an advance payment scheme providing a guarantee, whereby if a member company fails to fulfill its commitments to a client the removal is completed at the agreed cost by another company or your money is refunded. Some removal companies have subsidiaries or affiliates in Spain, which may be more convenient if you encounter problems or need to make an insurance claim. If you engage a shipping company in Spain, it's wise to avoid small unregistered companies ('man and van'), as some have been known to disappear with their clients' worldly possessions (on the other hand, some are very reliable). A Spanish shipping company should have a Spanish business address, a registered licence number, a VAT (IVA) number and must be licensed to do removals in Spain. For information about Spanish removal companies contact the Asociación de Empresarios de Guardamuebles y Mundanzas, Apartado de Correos 5154, 29080 Malaga.

You should obtain at least three written quotations before choosing a company, as rates vary considerably. Moving companies should send a representative to provide a detailed quotation. Most companies will pack your belongings and provide packing cases and special containers, although this is naturally more expensive than packing them yourself. Ask a company how they pack fragile and valuable items, and whether the cost of packing cases, materials and insurance (see below) are included in a quotation. If you're doing your own packing, most shipping companies will provide packing crates and boxes. Shipments are charged by volume, e.g. the square metre in Europe and the square foot in the USA. You should expect to pay from 1m to 1.5m ptas to move the contents (say 40m3) of a three to four bedroom house within western Europe, e.g. from the UK to the south of Spain. If you're flexible about the delivery date, shipping companies will usually quote a lower fee based on a 'part load', where the cost is shared with other deliveries. This can result in savings of 50 per cent or more compared with a 'special' delivery. Whether you have an individual or shared delivery, always obtain the maximum transit period in writing, otherwise you may have to wait months for delivery!

Make sure that you fully insure your belongings during shipment with a well established insurance company. Don't insure with a shipping company that carries its own insurance as they will usually fight every peseta of a claim. Insurance premiums are usually 1 to 2 per cent of the declared value of your goods, depending on the type of cover chosen. It's prudent to make a photographic or video record of valuables for insurance purposes. Most insurance policies cover for 'all-risks' on a replacement value basis. Note, however, that china, glass and other breakables can usually be included in an 'all-risks' policy only when they're packed by the removal company. Insurance usually covers total loss or loss of a particular crate only, rather than individual items (unless they were packed by the shipping company). If there are any breakages or damaged items, they must be noted and listed before you sign the delivery bill (although it's obviously impractical to check everything on delivery). If you need to make a claim be sure to read the small print, as some companies require clients to make a claim within a few days, although seven is usual. Send a claim by registered mail. Some insurance companies apply an 'excess' of around 1 per cent of the total shipment value when assessing claims. This means that if your shipment is valued at 4m ptas and you make a claim for less than 40,000 ptas, you won't receive anything.

If you're unable to ship your belongings directly to Spain, most shipping companies will put them into storage and some offer a limited free storage period prior to shipment, e.g. 14 days. **If you need to put your household effects into storage, it's imperative to have them fully insured as warehouses have been known to burn down!** Make a complete list of everything to be moved and give a copy to the removal company. Don't include anything illegal (e.g. guns, bombs, drugs or pornography) with your belongings as customs checks can be rigorous and penalties severe. Provide the shipping company with *detailed* instructions on how to find your Spanish address from the nearest motorway or main road and a telephone number where you can be contacted.

After considering the shipping costs, you may decide to ship only selected items of furniture and personal effects, and buy new furniture in Spain. If you're importing household goods from another European country, it's possible to rent a self-drive van or truck, but bear in mind that if you rent a vehicle outside Spain you will need to return it to the country where it was hired. If you plan to transport your belongings to Spain personally, check the customs requirements in the countries you must pass through. Most people find it isn't advisable to do their own move unless it's a simple job, e.g. a few items of furniture and personal effects only. It's no fun heaving beds and wardrobes up stairs and squeezing them into impossible spaces! If you're taking pets with you, you may need to get your vet to tranquilise them, as many pets are frightened (even more than people) by the chaos and stress of moving house.

Bear in mind when moving home that everything that can go wrong often does, so allow plenty of time and try not to arrange your move to your new home on the same day as the previous owner is moving out. That's just asking for fate to intervene! **Last but not least, if your Spanish home has poor or impossible access for a large truck you must inform the shipping company (the ground must also be firm enough to support**

a heavy vehicle). Note that if large items of furniture need to be taken in through an upstairs window or balcony, you may need to pay extra. See also **Customs** on page 77 and the **Checklists** on page 80.

GARBAGE DISPOSAL

There's little recycling (*reciclaje*) in Spain, where most garbage (*basura*) goes into landfill sites, although more municipalities are now incinerating it. The problem of landfill sites (some of which pollute ground water used for household consumption) is a serious and growing problem and many municipalities have a shortage of available sites. When buying a property in Spain, make sure that you aren't within 'smelling' distance of the local rubbish dump (or that one isn't planned a block away), as they are sometimes located close to residential areas.

Some municipalities recycle glass, paper, cardboard, aluminium, cans, batteries and other materials, although there are usually too few collection points (widespread recycling would not only pay for itself, but would help reduce the chronic unemployment). Some municipalities publish leaflets detailing where and when to dump your household garbage. The amount of waste produced per head in Spain is fortunately one of the lowest in the EU, although little effort is made to educate citizens regarding recycling and waste reduction. Although the dumping of garbage is strictly forbidden, many people dump their rubbish in the countryside (particularly large items such as refrigerators and stoves) and the Spanish seem to have little respect for their environment.

Garbage collection is efficient in most towns and cities, although in some rural areas residents are required to take their garbage to a collection point, which may be located some kilometres away from an urbanisation. However, most community properties (urbanisations) have communal skips or garbage bins where residents are required to deposit their rubbish in sealed plastic bags. Bins are usually emptied daily (at night) except on Sundays. In some areas, residents have personal bins which they put out at night and take in the morning. If this is the case ask your neighbours when you should put out your rubbish for collection, as some municipalities levy fines if rubbish is put out for collection too early, e.g. before 2100. By the year 2002 residents in municipalities with over 5,000 inhabitants will have to deposit different types of rubbish in separate containers.

Most municipalities charge an annual fee for garbage collection, which varies depending on whether you live in a town or a rural area, e.g. from 5,000 to 20,000 ptas a year. Costs are usually reduced for the elderly on low incomes. Check with your town hall and have the bill sent to your bank and paid directly by them, as (like all municipal bills) if you don't pay it on time it's increased by 20 per cent.

ELECTRICITY

Spain's main electricity companies (which include Endesa, Iberdrola, Union-Fenosa, Sevillana, Fecsa and Hydrocantábrico) are monopolies and make huge profits, although plans are afoot to introduce some much needed competition. Endesa is Spain's largest producer (and Europe's third largest), producing half of Spain's electricity.

Registration: Immediately after buying or renting a property (unless utilities are included in the rent), you must sign a contract with the local electricity company. This usually entails a visit to the company's local office to register. You need to take with you some identification (passport or residence card) and the contract and bills paid by the previous owner (and a good book, as queues can be long). If you have purchased a home in Spain, the real estate agent may arrange for the utilities to be transferred to your name or go with you to the offices (no charge should be made for this service). Make sure all previous bills have been paid and that the contract is put into your name from the day you take over, otherwise you will be liable for debts left by the previous owner. If you're a non-resident owner, you should also give your foreign address in case there are any problems requiring your attention, such as your bank refusing to pay the bills. You may need to pay a deposit. Some electricity companies have service lines where foreign customers can obtain information in English and German in addition to Spanish.

Wiring Standards: Most modern properties (e.g. less than 20 years old) in Spain have good electrical installations. However, if you buy an old home you may be required to obtain a certificate (*boletín*) from a qualified electrician stating that your electricity installation meets the required safety standards, even when the previous owner already had an electricity contract. You should ensure that the electricity installations are in good condition well in advance of moving house, as it can take some time to get a new meter installed or be reconnected. If you buy a rural property (*finca rústica*), there are usually public guarantees of services such as electricity (plus water, sewage, roads, telephone, etc.) and you aren't obliged to pay for the installation of electricity lines or transformers, only the connection to your property.

Connection Costs: The cost of electricity connection (*acometida*) and the installation of a meter is usually between 15,000 and 30,000 ptas, although it varies considerably depending on the region, power supply and the type of meter installed. When you buy a community property, the cost of connection to utility services is included in the price of the property and it's illegal for developers to charge buyers extra for this.

Meters: In an old apartment block there may be a common meter, with the bill being shared among the apartment owners according to the size of their apartments. It's obviously advisable to have your own meter, particularly if you own a holiday home that's occupied for a few months of the year only. Meters for an apartment block or community properties may be installed in the basement of an apartment block in a special room or may be housed in a meter 'cupboard' in a stair well or outside a group of properties, e.g. in an apartment or townhouse development. You should have free access to your meter and should be able read it (some meters don't have a window to allow you to read the consumption).

Plugs, Fuses & Bulbs

Depending on the country you have come from, you will need new plugs (*enchufes*) or a lot of adaptors. Plug adaptors for most foreign electrical apparatus can be purchased in Spain, although it's wise to bring some adaptors with you, plus extension cords and multi-plug extensions that can be fitted with Spanish plugs. There's often a shortage of electric points in Spanish homes, with perhaps just one per room (including the kitchen), so multi-plug adaptors may be essential. Most Spanish plugs have two round pins, possibly with an earth built into the plug, although most sockets aren't fitted with earth contacts. Sockets in modern properties may also accept three-pin plugs (with a third earth pin), although few appliances are fitted with three-pin plugs.

Small, low-wattage electrical appliances such as table lamps, small TVs and computers, don't require an earth. However, plugs with an earth must always be used for high-wattage appliances such as electric fires, kettles, washing machines and refrigerators. These plugs must always be used with earthed sockets, although they also fit non-earthed, two-pin sockets. Electrical appliances that are earthed have a three-core wire and must never be used with a two-pin plug without an earth socket. **Always make sure that a plug is correctly and securely wired, as bad wiring can be fatal.**

In modern properties, fuses (*fusibles*) are of the earth trip type. When there's a short circuit or the system has been overloaded, a circuit breaker is tripped and the power supply is cut. If your electricity fails, you should suspect a fuse has tripped off, particularly if you have just switched on an electrical appliance (usually you will hear the power switch off). Before reconnecting the power, switch off any high-power appliances such as a stove, washing machine or dishwasher. Make sure you know where the trip switches are located and keep a torch handy so you can find them in the dark (see **Power Supply** below).

Electric light bulbs in Spain are of the Edison type with a screw fitting (of which there are two sizes). If you have lamps requiring bayonet bulbs you should bring some with you, as they cannot be readily purchased in Spain. You can, however, buy adaptors to convert from bayonet to screw fitting (or vice versa). Bulbs for non-standard electrical appliances (i.e. appliances that aren't made for the Spanish market) such as refrigerators and sewing machines may not be available in Spain, so bring some spares with you.

Power Supply

The electricity supply in most of Spain is 220 volts AC with a frequency of 50 hertz (cycles). However, some areas still have a 110 volt supply and it's even possible to find dual voltage 110 and 220 volt systems in the same house or the same room! All new buildings have a 220 volt supply and the authorities have mounted a campaign to encourage home owners with 110 volt systems to switch to 220 volts. Note that not all appliances, e.g. televisions made for 240 volts, will function with a power supply of 220 volts. Spain is committed to introducing the international standard (adopted in 1983) of 230 volts AC by the year 2003.

Power cuts are frequent in many areas of Spain. When it rains heavily the electricity supply often becomes *very* unstable, with frequent power cuts lasting from a few micro seconds (just long enough to crash a computer) to a few hours or even a number of days. If you use a computer it's advisable to fit an uninterrupted power supply (UPS) with a battery backup (costing around 20,000 ptas), which allows you time to shut down your computer and save your work after a power failure. If you live in an area where cuts are frequent and rely on electricity for your livelihood, e.g. for operating a computer, fax machine and other equipment, you may need to install a back up generator. **Even more important than a battery backup is a power surge protector for appliances such as TVs, computers and fax machines, without which you risk having equipment damaged or destroyed.** In remote areas you *must* install a generator if you want electricity as there's no mains electricity, although some people make do with gas and oil lamps (and without television and other modern conveniences). Note that in many urbanisations, water is provided by an electric pump and therefore if your electricity supply is cut off, so is your water supply.

If the power keeps tripping off when you attempt to use a number of high-power appliances simultaneously, e.g. an electric kettle and a heater, it means that the power rating (*potencia*) of your property is too low. This is a common problem in Spain. If this is the case, you may need to contact your electricity company and ask them to uprate the power supply in your property (it can also be downgraded if the power supply is more than you require). The power supply increases by increments of 1.1kW, e.g. 2.2kW, 3.3kW, 4.4kW, 5.5kW, etc. Note, however, that it can take some time to get your power supply changed. The power supply rating is usually shown on your meter (and on bills). Your standing charge (see **Tariffs** below) depends on the power rating of your supply, which is why owners tend to keep it as low as possible, e.g. many holiday homes have a power rating of just 3.3kW.

Converters & Transformers

Assuming that you have a 220 volt power supply, if you have electrical equipment rated at 110 volts AC (for example, from the USA) you will require a converter or a step-down transformer to convert it to 220 volts. If you have a 110 volt supply, you can buy converters or step-up transformers to convert appliances rated at 220 volts to 110 volts. However, some electrical appliances are fitted with a 110/220 volt switch. Check for the switch, which may be inside the casing, and make sure it's switched to 220 volts *before* connecting it to the power supply. Converters can be used for heating appliances, but transformers are required for motorised appliances. Total the wattage of the devices you intend to connect to a transformer and make sure that its power rating *exceeds* this sum.

Generally all small, high-wattage, electrical appliances, such as kettles, toasters, heaters, and irons need large transformers. Motors in large appliances such as cookers, refrigerators, washing machines, driers and dishwashers, will need replacing or fitting with a large transformer. In most cases it's simpler to buy new appliances in Spain, which are of good quality and reasonably priced, and sell them when you leave if you cannot take them with you. Note also that the dimensions of cookers, microwave ovens, refrigerators, washing machines, driers and dishwashers purchased abroad, may differ from those in Spain, and therefore may not fit into a Spanish kitchen.

An additional problem with some electrical equipment is the frequency rating, which in some countries, e.g. the USA, is designed to run at 60Hz (Hertz) and not Europe's 50Hz. Electrical equipment *without* a motor is generally unaffected by the drop in frequency to 50Hz (except televisions). Equipment with a motor may run okay with a 20 per cent drop in speed; however, automatic washing machines, cookers, electric clocks, record players and tape recorders must be converted from the US 60Hz cycle to Spain's 50Hz cycle. To find out, look at the label on the back of the equipment. If it says 50/60Hz it should be okay; if it says 60Hz you can try it, but **first ensure that the voltage is correct as outlined above.** Bear in mind that the transformers and motors of electrical devices designed to run at 60Hz will run hotter at 50Hz, so make sure that apparatus has sufficient space around it to allow for cooling.

Tariffs

Electricity used to be inexpensive in Spain, although the cost has increased considerably in recent years and is now similar to most other EU countries. The actual charges will depend on your local electricity company (the rates shown in the example below are those charged by Sevillana de Electricidad in Andalusia). The tariff depends on your power rating (*potencia*), which for domestic users with a power rating of up to 15kW is 2.0 (above 15kW it's 3.0). This tariff is used to calculate your bi-monthly standing charge. For example, if your power rating is 4.4kW this is multiplied by the tariff of 2.0 and then multiplied by the standing charge rate per kW (e.g. 279 ptas), i.e. 4.4 x 2.0 x 279, making a standing charge of 2,455 ptas. The standing charge is payable irrespective of whether you use any electricity during the billing period.

The actual consumption is charged per kW, e.g. 15.84 ptas in Andalusia (Sevillana de Electricidad). To save on electricity costs, you can switch to night tariff (*tarifa nocturna*) and run high-consumption appliances overnight, e.g. storage heaters, water heater, dishwasher and washing machine (which can be operated by a timer). If you use a lot of water, it's better to have a large water heater (e.g. 150 litres) and heat water overnight on a timer system. If you use electricity for heating, you can install night storage heaters which run on the cheaper night tariff. The night tariff rate consists of paying 3 per cent more than the normal tariff during the day and evening (from 0700 to 2300), but provides a reduction of 55 per cent for electricity used overnight (between 2300 and 0700). Value added tax at 16 per cent must be added to all charges.

Electricity Bills

Electricity bills are sent out every two months, usually after meters have been read. However, electricity companies are permitted to make an estimate of your consumption every second period without reading the meter. You should learn to read your electricity bill and check your consumption, to ensure that your electricity company isn't overcharging you. The most important figures on bills (which have recently been made more consumer friendly) are:

Item	Description
POTEN	standing charge (*potencia*, see above)
L. ANT./LEC. ANT.	previous meter reading (*lectura anterior*)
L. ACT./LEC. ACT.	actual meter reading (*lectura actual*)
ESTIMADA	estimated reading (this will replace *L. ACT./LEC. ACT.* when your meter hasn't been read)
CONSUMO	number of kW consumed during the period
ENERG	energy (*energía*) consumption (kW) multiplied by the charge per kW and the total
ALQUILER/ EQUIPOS MEDIDA	meter rental charge
PER	the period of the bill
IVA	VAT at 16 per cent
FECHA DE FACTURA	date of bill
TOTAL (A PAGAR)	the total to pay

It's advisable to pay all your utility bills by direct debit (*transferencia*) from a Spanish bank account. If you own a holiday home in Spain, you can have your bills sent to an address abroad. Bills should then be paid automatically on presentation to your bank, although some banks cannot be relied on 100 per cent. Both the electricity company and your bank should notify you when they have sent or paid a bill. Alternatively you can pay bills at a post office, local banks (listed on the bill) or at the electricity company's office (in cash).

Electricity companies aren't permitted to cut your electricity supply without authorisation from the proper authorities, e.g. the Ministry of Industry and Energy, and without notifying the owner of a property. If you're late paying a bill, you should be sent a registered letter requesting payment and stating that the power will be cut on a certain date if you don't pay. If you disagree with a bill, you should notify the *Servicio Territorial, Ministerio de Industria y Energía* in writing, who will refuse your electricity company permission to cut your supply if your complaint is founded. If your supply is cut off, you must usually pay to have it reconnected (*enganche*).

GAS

Mains gas is available in major cities only in Spain, although with the recent piping of gas from North Africa (Algeria and Libya) it may soon be more widely available. When moving into a property with mains gas, you must contact the local gas company to have the gas switched on, the meter read and to sign a supply contract. As with electricity, you're billed every two months and bills include VAT (IVA) at 16 per cent. Like all utility bills, gas bills can be paid by direct debit (*transferencia*) from a Spanish bank account. In rural areas, bottled gas is used and costs less than half that of mains gas in most northern European countries. Many people use as many gas appliances as possible including cooking, hot-water and heating. You can have a combined gas hot-water and heating system (providing background heat) installed, which is relatively inexpensive to install and run.

In most areas of Spain, gas bottles (*bombonas*) are delivered to homes by Repsol Butano (the company responsible for distributing gas bottles), for which a contract is required. You must pay a deposit of around 4,000 ptas and an exchange bottle costs around 1,000 ptas (prices fluctuate frequently). A contract is drawn up only after a safety inspection has been made of the property where the gas appliance is to be used. In some areas you must exchange your bottles at a local supplier. Keep a spare bottle handy and make sure you know how to change them (get the previous owner or a neighbour to show you). A bottle used for cooking only, will last an average family around six to eight weeks.

You must have your gas appliances serviced and inspected at least every five years. If you have a contract with Repsol Butano, they will do this for you or it will be done by your local authorised distributor. Some distributors will try to sell you a package which includes third party insurance and free parts should they be required, although it isn't necessary to have this insurance and is a waste of money. Beware of 'bogus' gas company representatives calling unannounced to inspect gas appliances. Most are usually legitimate companies, but their charges are extortionate and they will give you a large bill for changing tubing and regulators (which usually don't need changing at all), and demand payment in cash on the spot. If you wish you can let them make an inspection and give you an estimate (*presupesto*) for any work that needs doing, but don't let them do any work done or pay them any money before checking with your local Repsol Butano distributor. Incidentally, plastic tubes have an expiry date printed on them and you can buy them cheaply at a hardware store (*ferretería*) and change them yourself.

WATER

Water, or rather the lack of it, is a major concern in Spain and the price paid for all those sunny days. Like some other countries that experience regional water shortages, Spain as a whole has sufficient water, but it isn't distributed evenly. There's (usually) surplus rainfall in the northwest and centre and a deficiency along most of the Mediterranean coast and in the Balearic and Canary islands. In the Canaries there's a permanent water shortage and most drinking water is provided by desalination plants, while in the Balearics 20,000 wells are employed to pump water to the surface (there are also desalination plants in Majorca and Ibiza). In 1995, there were plans to build a desalination plant on the Costa del Sol (85 per cent of the cost was to be paid by the EU), although this was shelved when the drought was broken in the winter of 1995/96.

On the Costa del Sol, purification plants recycle waste water from urban areas for crop irrigation and watering golf courses. The shortages are exacerbated in resort areas, where the local population swells five to tenfold during the summer tourist season, the hottest and driest period of the year. The government has drawn up a national hydrological plan (*plan hidrológico nacional*) to solve water shortages and pipe water from northern Spain to eastern and southern coastal areas, although it's still on the drawing board. Meanwhile Spain's regions openly fight over the allocation of water, particularly for crop irrigation (intensive and often wasteful agricultural irrigation accounts for around 80 per cent of all water used in some areas).

In summer 1995 the reservoirs in southern and eastern Spain were almost empty after four years of severe drought (the worst this century), during which millions of people had to endure water rationing. In some areas the water table had dropped so low that sea-water has penetrated the underground wells. The drought was broken in the winter of 1995/96 followed by even heavier rainfall in 1996/97, when months of torrential rain (the heaviest on record) caused widespread flooding throughout Spain. Water shortages are exacerbated by poor infrastructure (some 40 per cent is lost due to leaking pipes) and wastage due to poor irrigation methods. There's also surprisingly little emphasis on water conservation in Spain, particularly considering the frequent droughts. For example, the Costa del Sol uses double the national average per person (500 litres a day) for its numerous swimming pools, lawns, gardens and golf courses, and people in towns and cities consume some 300 litres of water per person, per day (one of the highest figures in Europe). At the same time, hundreds of rural towns and villages have water on tap for just a few hours a day during the summer months and farmers regularly face ruin due to the lack of water for irrigation. However, domestic consumption has reduced in many regions as a result of the sharp increase in water costs in recent years, and people have learnt to use less water during the prolonged drought. **In Spain, water is a precious resource and not something simply to pour down the drain!**

Restrictions: During water shortages, local municipalities may restrict the water consumption or cut off supplies altogether for days at a time. Restrictions can be severe and householders may be limited to as little as three cubic metres a month, which is sufficient for around 10 baths or 20 showers. You can forget about watering the garden or washing your car unless you have a private water supply. If a water company needs to cut your supply, e.g. to carry out maintenance work on pipes and other installations, they will usually notify you (or your urbanisation) in advance so that you can store water for cooking. In some areas, water shortages can create low water pressure, resulting in insufficient water to take a bath or shower. Note that in many developments, water is provided by electric pump and therefore if your electricity is cut off, so is your water supply. In urbanisations the tap to turn water on or off is usually located outside properties and therefore if your water goes off suddenly you should check that someone hasn't switched it off by mistake. In the hotter parts of Spain, where water shortages are common, water tankers, with the words 'drinking water' (*agua potable*) on the side, deliver water to homes. Some properties don't have a mains supply at all, but a storage tank (*depósito*) that's filled from a tanker. If you have a storage tank, water will be pumped into it and you will be charged by the litre, plus a delivery charge.

Check the Supply: One of the most important tasks before renting or buying a home in Spain is to investigate the reliability of the local water supply (over a number of years) and the cost. Ask your prospective neighbours and other local residents for information. In most towns and cities, supplies are adequate, although there may be cuts in summer. It's inadvisable to buy a property where the water supply is controlled by the developer (e.g. he owns the private water company), some of whom charge extortionate rates or charge owners for a minimum quantity, even when they're non-residents. A developer may also cut off your water illegally if you refuse to pay the bill and you may receive little or no satisfaction from the courts.

In rural areas there are often severe shortages in summer unless you have your own well. Note, however, that a well containing water in winter may be bone dry in summer and you may have no rights to extract water from a water channel (*acequia*) running alongside your land. Dowsing (finding water by holding a piece of forked wood) is as accurate as anything devised by modern science (it has an 80 per cent success rate) and a good dowser can also estimate the water's yield and purity to within 10 or 20 per cent accuracy. Before buying land without a water supply, engage an experienced douser with a successful track record to check it. Although rare, some people in remote areas have spent a fortune (e.g. 10m ptas or more) ensuring a reliable, year-round, water supply, which may need to be piped from many kilometres away.

Storage Tanks: If you have a detached house or villa, you can reduce your water costs by collecting and storing rain water and having a storage tank (*depósito*) installed. Tanks can be both roof-mounted or installed underground, which are cheaper and can be any size, but require an electric pump. Check whether a property has a water storage tank or whether you can install one. Most modern properties have storage tanks which are usually large enough to last a family of four for around a week or even longer with careful use. It's also possible to use recycled water from baths, showers, kitchen and apparatus such as washing machines and dish washers, to flush toilets or water a garden. Note that in recent years it has become common to have a storage tank installed that refills itself automatically when the water supply is restored after having been cut off.

Contracts: After buying or renting a property (unless utilities are included in the rent), you should arrange for the water contract to be registered in your name. Always check in advance that all water bills have been paid by the previous owner, otherwise you will be liable for any debts. You must usually visit the local town hall to register your ownership and have the water contract transferred to your name. Take along some identification (passport or residence card) and the previous contract and bills paid by the former owner. When registering, non-resident owners should also give their foreign address in case there are any problems requiring the owners attention, such as your bank refusing to pay water bills.

Hot Water: Water heating in apartments may be provided by a central heating source for the whole building or apartments may have their own water heaters. If you install your own water heater, it should have a capacity of at least 75 litres. Many holiday homes have quite small water boilers, which are often inadequate for more than two people. If you need to install a water heater or change to a larger water heater, you should consider the merits of both electric and bottled gas heaters. An electric water boiler with a capacity of 75 litres (sufficient for two people) costs from 20,000 to 40,000 ptas and usually takes between 60 and 90 minutes to heat water to 40 degrees in winter.

A gas flow-through water heater is more expensive to purchase and install than an electric water boiler, but you get unlimited hot water immediately whenever you want it and there are no standing charges. Ensure that a gas heater has a capacity of 10 to 16 litres per minute if you want it for a shower. A gas heater costs from 15,000 to 40,000 ptas (although there's little difference in quality between the cheaper and more expensive heaters), plus installation costs. Note that a gas water heater with a permanent flame may use up to 50 per cent more gas than one without one. A resident family with a constant consumption is better off with an electric heater operating on the night-tariff (see page 101), while non-residents using a property for short periods will find a self-igniting gas heater more economical. Solar energy can also be used to provide hot water (see page 108).

Connection Costs & Standing Charges: Water is a local matter in Spain and is usually controlled by local municipalities, many of which have their own wells. In some municipalities, water distribution is the responsibility of a private company. The cost of connection to the local water supply for a new home varies considerably from around 10,000 ptas up to 75,000 ptas (when a private company controls the distribution) or even 250,000 pesetas in an isolated area. In most municipalities there's a standing quarterly charge or a monthly charge for a minimum consumption (*canón de consumo*), e.g. 14 cubic metres a month or 1,000 ptas a month plus IVA at 7 per cent, even if you don't use any water during the billing period. Water shortages don't stop municipalities from levying high standing charges for water consumption that's sometimes non-existent.

Water Rates: The cost of water in Spain has risen dramatically in recent years (as a result of drought) and in some towns, water bills have increased by over 300 per cent or more. The cost of water varies considerably from municipality to municipality and from region to region, and is an average of around 120 ptas per m3 on the mainland to between 300 and 500 ptas per m3 in the Canaries and some parts of the Balearics (where drinking water is often provided by desalination plants and is expensive). In most areas tariffs start with a low basic charge of below 50 ptas per cubic metre (e.g. for the first 15 to 50m3 a month), but can become prohibitively expensive above this consumption. In some municipalities the top rate applies only above a fairly large consumption figure, e.g. 150m3. Some municipalities levy a standing charge, which is usually for a minimum amount of water per quarter or month, e.g. 45m3 a quarter or 15m3 a month), whether any water is used or not (which hits non-residents hardest).

Some municipalities levy a quarterly surcharge (*canón de servicio*) and regional governments may also levy a charge for water purification. Sometimes a higher water rate is charged for holiday home owners or owners in community developments, where the water supply isn't controlled by the local municipality, while in others the cost of water is included in community fees. Water bills usually include sewerage and may also include rubbish collection (e.g. when a city provides all services), in which case the cost of rubbish collection may be calculated on how much water you use (a large family will usually use more water and also create more rubbish). There's also a rental charge for the water meter, e.g. around 300 ptas per quarter plus VAT (IVA). Always check your water bill carefully as overcharging on bills is widespread (people have been know to have been charged for air when the water was switched off!). Sometimes water company meters show a huge disparity (increase!) in consumption compared with a privately installed meter (when confronted with the evidence water companies may simply refuse to answer). Some municipalities arbitrarily levy higher tariffs on certain urbanisations, although this is illegal. Pensioners receive discounts of from 50 to 75 per cent on their water and sewage bills in some municipalities.

To reduce your water costs, you can buy a 'water saver' which mixes air with water, thus reducing the amount of water used. The cost of fitting an apartment with water savers is around 6,000 ptas only, which can be recouped in six months through lower water bills. For information contact RST Water Savers, Aquarium Park, Local 22, Playa Levante, Calpe, Alicante (tel. (96) 583 6222). RST water savers can also be purchased from stores such as El Corte Inglés and Hipercor.

Water Bills: Bills are generally sent out quarterly. If you don't pay your water bill on time you should receive an 'enforced collection' (*recaudación ejecutiva*) letter requesting payment of your bill (plus a surcharge) within a number of days. If you don't pay your bill your water supply can be cut off, although this doesn't usually happen until customers are around a year in arrears. However, many thousands of people have their water supply cut off each year for non-payment. If your supply is cut you must pay a reconnection fee, e.g. 5,000 ptas, plus any outstanding bills.

Water Quality: Water is supposedly safe to drink in all urban areas, although it can be of poor quality (possibly brown or rust coloured), full of chemicals and taste awful. Many residents prefer to drink bottled water, of which over 3,000 million litres are consumed each year in Spain. In rural areas, water may be extracted from mountain springs and taste excellent, although the quality standards applied in cities are usually absent and it may be of poor quality. Water in rural areas may also be contaminated by the fertilisers and nitrates used in farming, and by salt water in some coastal areas. If you're in any doubt about the quality of your water you should have it analysed. **Note that although boiling water will kill any bacteria, it won't remove any toxic substances contained in it.** You can install filtering, cleansing and softening equipment to improve its quality. You can also install a water purification unit costing around 200,000 ptas to provide drinking water. Note, however, that purification systems operating on the reverse osmosis system waste three times as much water as they produce. Obtain expert advice before installing a system as not all equipment is effective.

Many areas of Spain have hard water containing high concentrations of calcium and magnesium. Water is very hard (*muy dura*) in the east, hard (*dura*) in the north and most of the south, and soft in the northwest (e.g. Galicia), and central and western regions. You can install a water softener which will prevent the build-up of scale in water heaters (which increases heating costs) and water pipes, and damages electric heaters and other appliances. Costs vary considerably and can be hundreds of thousands of pesetas for a sophisticated system, which also consumes large quantities of water for regeneration. Note that it's necessary to have a separate drinking water supply if you have a water softener installed in your home.

Sewage: Surprisingly for a western industrialised country, some 60 per cent of the population isn't connected to a sewage treatment system, with untreated waste water going straight into the ground, rivers or the sea. In some areas there are no sewage plants and sewage is drained into cesspools (*pozos negros*) or septic tanks (*fosas sépticas*) which are emptied by tankers. Septic tanks can cause problems in summer is some buildings, for example when holiday homes are fully occupied and the septic tank isn't emptied frequently. Note that cesspools are illegal in many areas and properties must be connected to mains drainage. Most sewage treatment deficiencies are found in central Spain and along the northern Atlantic coast, although raw sewage is dumped into the sea throughout the country. A special tax (*canón*) is levied in many areas to pay for the installation of sewage treatment plants, and towns with 15,000 inhabitants or more are expected to have a sewage treatment system by the year 2001 and municipalities of between 2,000 and 15,000 people by the year 2006.

HEATING & AIR-CONDITIONING

Central heating (*calefacción*) is essential in winter in northern and central Spain and isn't a luxury in most other areas. If you're used to central heating and like a warm house in winter, you will almost certainly miss central heating, even on the Costa del Sol (especially if there are more winters like 1995/96 and 1996/97). Central heating systems in Spain may be powered by oil, gas (mains or bottled), electricity, solid fuel (usually wood) or even solar power. Oil-fired central heating isn't common in Spain due to the high cost of heating oil and the problems associated with storage and deliveries. In rural areas, many houses have open wood-burning fireplaces and stoves, which may be combined with a central heating system. Whatever form of heating you use, it's important to have good insulation, without which up to 60 per cent of the heat generated is lost through the walls and roof. Note that many properties in Spain don't have good insulation and builders don't always adhere to current regulations. In cities, apartment blocks may have a central heating system providing heating for all apartments, the cost of which is divided among the tenants. If you're a non-resident or absent from Spain for long periods, you should choose an apartment with a separate heating system, otherwise you will be contributing towards your neighbours' heating bills.

Electric Heating: Electric heating isn't particularly common in Spain as it's too expensive and requires good insulation and a permanent system of ventilation. It's advisable to avoid totally electric apartments in regions with a cold winter, such as Madrid, as the bills can be astronomical. However, a system of night-storage heaters operating on night tariff can be economical. Some stand-alone electric heaters are also expensive to run and are best suited to holiday homes. If you rely on electricity for your heating, you should expect to pay between 10,000 and 20,000 ptas a month during the coldest months, i.e. November to February. An air-conditioning system (see below) with a heat pump (which can be electrically or gas operated) provides cooling in summer and economical heating in winter. Note that if you have electric central heating or air-conditioning, you may need to uprate your power supply (see page 100).

Gas Heating: Stand-alone gas heaters using standard gas bottles cost from 10,000 to 20,000 ptas and are an economical way of providing heating in areas that experience mild winters (such as the Costa del Sol). Note that gas heaters must be used only in rooms with adequate ventilation (inspected and approved by Repsol Butano) and it can be dangerous to have too large a difference between indoor and outdoor temperatures. Gas poisoning due to faulty ventilation ducts for gas heaters (e.g. in bathrooms) isn't uncommon in Spain. It's possible to install a central heating system operating from standard gas bottles, which costs around 300,000 ptas for a small home (Primus of Sweden is one of the leading manufacturers). Mains gas central heating is popular in cities and is the cheapest to run.

Solar Energy: The use of solar energy to provide hot water and heating (with a hot-air solar radiator) is surprisingly rare in Spain, where the amount of energy provided by the sun each year per square metre is equivalent to eleven gas bottles (the sun provides around 8,000 times the world's present energy requirements annually!). A solar power system can be used to supply all your energy needs, although it's usually combined with an electric or gas heating system, as it cannot usually be relied upon year-round for heating and hot water. If you own a home on Spain's Mediterranean coast (or on the islands), solar energy is a viable option and the authorities (both regional and national governments) offer grants and interest-free finance to encourage home owners to install solar energy systems.

The main drawback is the high cost of installation, which varies depending on the region and how much energy you require. A 400 litre hot-water system costs around 300,000 to 400,000 ptas and must be installed by an expert. The advantages are no running costs, silent operation, maintenance-free and no (or very small) electricity bills. A system should last 30 years (it's usually guaranteed for 10 years) and can be uprated to provide additional power in the future. Solar power can also be used to heat a swimming pool. Continuous advances in solar cell and battery technology are expected to dramatically increase the efficiency and reduce the cost of solar power, which is forecast to become the main source of energy worldwide in the next century. A solar power system can also be used to provide electricity in a remote rural home, where the cost of extending mains electricity is prohibitive.

Air-Conditioning: In some regions of Spain, summer temperatures can reach over 40C (104F) and although properties are built to withstand the heat, you may wish to install air-conditioning (*aire acondicionado*). Note, however, that there can be negative effects if you suffer from asthma or respiratory problems. You can choose between a huge variety of air-conditioners, fixed or moveable, indoor or outdoor installation, and high or low power. Air-conditioning units cost from around 100,000 ptas (plus installation) for a unit (2,000 frigorías) sufficient to cool an average sized room. When comparing prices, don't forget to include the cost of installation. An air-conditioning system with a heat pump provides cooling in summer and economical heating in winter. Some air-conditioners are noisy, so check the noise level before buying one. Many people fit ceiling fans for extra cooling in the summer (costing from around 10,000 ptas), which are standard fixtures in some new homes (as is air-conditioning in luxury homes),

Humidifiers: Note that central heating dries the air and may cause your family to develop coughs and other ailments. Those who find the dry air unpleasant can purchase a humidifier to add moisture to the air. These range from simple water containers hung from radiators to expensive electric or battery-operated devices. Humidifiers that don't generate steam should be disinfected occasionally with a special liquid available from chemists (to prevent nasty diseases).

6.

POST OFFICE SERVICES

There's a post office (*oficina de correos*) in most towns and at major railway stations, airports and ports in Spain, a total of over 6,000 (a list is provided). In addition to the usual post office services, a limited range of other services are provided including telegrams, fax and telex transmissions, and domestic and international giro money orders. The post office also operates a savings bank (*Caja Postal*) which may be located in a separate building to a post office. Telephones aren't available in most Spanish post offices. Unlike almost all other European post offices, the Spanish post office produces few leaflets and brochures and you may even have difficulty obtaining a tariff. You shouldn't expect post office staff to speak English or other foreign languages, although main post offices may have an information desk with multilingual staff. The identifying colour used by the Spanish post office (and most European countries) is yellow, which is the colour of Spanish post boxes (*buzones*), post office signs and mail vans. Postpersons (*carteros*) don't usually wear uniforms in Spain.

The Spanish mail (*correo*) delivery service has a reputation for being one of the slowest and most unreliable in Europe, with deliveries taking anything from a few days to a few weeks or months (or mail disappearing altogether). Delivery times are well below the EU average and while deliveries within and between major cities are adequate, deliveries to (and between) small towns and rural areas in different provinces can be very slow. In some areas deliveries are delayed or stop altogether when the local post person goes on holiday! It's advisable to send all international mail by air mail (*por correo aéreo*). There's a cheaper surface mail (*por barco* or *correo ordinario*) service outside Europe but it takes eons, e.g. six weeks or more to North America. Delivery times in Europe vary considerably depending on the countries concerned and where letters are posted in Spain (possibly even the post box used). Letters may arrive quicker when posted at a main post office (but don't count on it).

Although letters posted in Spain often arrive at European destinations in two to four days, it's advisable to allow around seven days. Air mail letters between Spain and North America usually take five to 10 days, although you should allow up to two weeks. Sending letters by express (*exprés/urgente*) post isn't the answer as there's no guarantee they will arrive earlier than ordinary post. **Note that although international mail delivery can be fast, delivery times can never be relied upon.** The only guaranteed way to send something urgently, within Spain or internationally, is by courier (*mensajería* or *transportes*), e.g. the post office's EMS *postal exprés* service or by private couriers (or to send letters by fax). Most European post offices are models of efficiency compared with the Spanish post office, which loses over 100,000 items of mail each year, and Spanish business is badly affected by the failings of the country's postal system (many businesses routinely send important mail by courier).

There are usually long, slow-moving, queues at post offices, most of which have a number of windows, each handling a different service and possibly with different business hours. In main post offices there may be one window for stamps (*venta de sellos*), another to register a letter or send an express letter (*Certificados - Postal Exprés*) and yet another to prepare and mail a parcel (*Prep. Paquete*). There are also various windows (in main post offices) for Giro current accounts (e.g. *Cuentas Corrientes, Cuentas de Ahorro*), telegraphs (*Incendias Telégrafos*), and telegrams and telex (*Telegram y Telex Burofax*). In smaller post offices there may be a few windows only, for example one dealing with stamps, small parcels and registered and express letters (*Venta de sellos, paquetes, certificados, urgentes*), another for giros and telegraphs (*Giro nacional y internacional, telégrafos*) and a third for wrapping and mailing large parcels (*Entrega de paquetes*). If you want to buy stamps only, it's quicker to buy them from a tobacconist's (*estanco*), although they don't always have postal scales (or may not be able to tell you the postage cost).

Complaints (*quejas*) about the mail service can be made at any post office and don't need to be made at the post office where the problem occurred or originated (if applicable). In the case of loss of mail, the person sending the mail must make the complaint. If you don't receive satisfaction you can take a complaint to the *Jefatura Provincial de Correos* or even the *Inspección General de Correos*, Plaza de la Cibeles s/n, 28014 Madrid. Two different types of complaints forms (*hojas de reclamaciones*) are available in post offices, depending on the nature of the complaint. If you have a complaint about bad service, the service *may* be improved but no compensation will be paid.

Postal and telegraphic tariffs and are listed in a free booklet entitled *Tarifas Postales y Telegráficas* obtainable from post offices and a more comprehensive guide is available for 300 ptas. Note, however, that compared with most other countries the system of postage rates is inordinately complicated (it could only have been conceived by a civil servant with too much time on his hands).

BUSINESS HOURS

Business hours (*horas de oficina*) at main post offices in major cities are usually from between 0800 and 0900 until 2100 or 2200, Monday to Friday and from 0900 to 1400 (or later) on Saturdays. Main post offices in major towns don't close for lunch and may also provide limited services outside normal business hours. Some post offices in major cities also open for a period on Sundays, although the range of services may be limited. There are also post offices at international airports, which are generally open during the mornings only. There are mobile post offices in some areas which usually operate from around 1000 to 1300. In small towns and villages, post offices usually open from 0830 or 0900 until between 1200 and 1430, Monday to Friday, and from 0930 to 1300 on Saturdays. Note also that some services may be available at post offices for a limited number of hours each day only, including sending telegrams and faxes; the preparation, mailing and collection of parcels; and poste restante (*lista de correos*).

LETTER POST

There are two domestic mail rates in Spain, one for local mail in the same town or city (*urbana*) and another for mail to other destinations (*interurbana*). There's a special low (and very slow) rate for domestic publicity mail (*publicorreo*) starting at 16 ptas for 20g to all destinations. International letter rates depend on the destination as shown in the table below. Rates for letters (*cartas*) and postcards (*tarjetas postales* or *postales*) are the same to all destinations. The maximum weight for domestic and international letters is 2kg.

The cost of posting a letter in Spain is as follows:

Weight	Spain*	Europe	Surface Mail	Rest of the World Airmail (see notes below)			
				America	Asia	Africa	Oceania
up to 20g	21/32	65	65	123	169	65	169
up to 50g#	32/45	151	151	267	359	223	359
up to 100g	38/70	184	184	387	548	310	548

* The first rate shown for letters within Spain is local mail (*urbana*), the second for 'national' mail (*interurbana*).

Airmail

America   North and South America.

Asia   Letters to Bangladesh, China, Japan, Kampuchea, Korea, Laos, Malaysia, Mongolia, Myanmar, Singapore, Taiwan, Thailand and Vietnam. Rates for all other Asian countries are the same as for America. There's a special low rate for mail to the Philippines.

Africa   Rate shown apply to Algeria, Morocco and Tunisia only. Rates for all other African countries are the same as for America.

Oceania   Rates are the same as the countries listed under **Asia**.

General Information

- When sending letters or parcels to or from Spain, *always* ensure that they are securely sealed or wrapped, otherwise they may arrive in tatters. When sending anything heavy, always use strong cloth envelopes (e.g. Tyvek), which even the Spanish post office has a problem tearing to shreds (also ask your correspondents to use them when sending mail to you). Note that you aren't supposed to use coloured envelopes (although they are sold in Spain!), e.g. to send birthday cards, and a post office may refuse to sell you a stamp (although you can buy a stamp from a tobacconist's and drop the letter in a post box and it should be delivered). Spanish envelopes often have perforated flaps for easy opening.

- If you live in an apartment block in a town or city your mail will be placed in your mail box (make sure that it has a lock) located in a central area such as the foyer. Often mailboxes aren't big enough for magazines and large packets, which are left in a common storage space. If you prefer, you can arrange to have a post office box (see page 119) and collect your mail from the post office. Postpersons aren't required to deliver parcels weighing over 500g, which must usually be collected from a post office (parcels up to 10kg will be delivered on payment of a surcharge).

- Letters are delivered once a day to your door if your letter box is placed on a public road, although in rural areas you may receive a delivery around three times a week only. If you have no letter box outside your house, you will need to install one at the boundary of your property on the street (often a number of boxes are grouped together at the end of a road). In rural areas there isn't a home postal delivery (*reparto*) service and mail must be collected from a local post office, a postal 'depot' or even a store, which functions as a mail drop off and collection point. Post for rural urbanisations is usually deposited in numbered mail boxes, which may be located many kilometres away (this may be something you wish to take into account before buying or renting a home in Spain).

- In addition to post offices, stamps are also sold by tobacconist's (*tabacos* or *estancos*), shown by a sign of a letter 'T' on a stylised tobacco leaf, hotels and some shops. Shops selling postcards don't usually sell stamps. Stamps are always sold at face value and no surcharge is added. Main post offices also have vending machines that print postage labels (*Estampillas*) for the amount required. Stamps purchased at main post offices are usually printed postage labels of the 'peel-off' type, i.e. they don't need to be moistened. Official fiscal stamps (*papeles del estado*), used to legalise documents, pay government taxes and motoring fines are sold exclusively by tobacconist's.

- A domestic and international express service (*urgente*) is available for urgent mail, which can be deposited in special red mailboxes at main post offices in major cities. Express mail guarantees 48-hour delivery within Spain, although there's no such guarantee for international mail, which can take up to 10 days to European destinations (or the same as ordinary mail). The express mail surcharge (payable in addition to ordinary postage) for a letter weighing up to 20 grammes is 173 ptas for local mail (same town), 194 ptas for other Spanish destinations and 216 ptas for international mail.

- You should affix an airmail (*por avión*) label or use airmail envelopes for international air mail, although this isn't necessary for mail between European countries, as most mail is automatically sent by air. Aerogrammes (*aerogramas*) are available from post offices and cost 76 ptas to anywhere in the world.

- Post boxes (*buzones*) in Spain are bright yellow with red stripes circling the base and are usually free standing. In cities, post boxes may have two slots, one for local mail (*ciudad* or *localidad*) and the other for other provinces and international mail (*provincias y extranjero*). There may also be separate boxes for Madrid (*Madrid Capital*), local province or provinces (*provincias*), the rest of Spain (*resto España*) and international (*extranjero*) mail (however, rumour has it that they all end up in the same receptacle!). There are also red mail boxes at main post offices in cities for express (*urgente*) mail. You may also see green post boxes which are reserved for the use of postal staff.

Post boxes can sometimes be scarce and difficult to locate, although there's always one outside a post office or railway station. It's best to post letters at main post offices or railway stations as collections are more frequent and delivery may be expedited. Note that during the winter in resort areas some post boxes may be emptied infrequently, irrespective of the collection times (*horas de recogida*) posted on them, which may be hand written and illegible (some post boxes look abandoned and any mail deposited in them may still be there in a year's time!). Some urbanisations have a box (which may be marked *Sólo Para Recogida de Correo para su Despacho*) where you can deposit letters for collection by the postperson.

- The international postal identification for Spanish postal or zip codes (*el distrito postal*) is 'E', which is placed before the post code (as shown below), although its use isn't mandatory or widespread. Spain uses a five-digit post code, where the first two digits indicate the postal route and the last three the town. Small villages often use the post code of a nearby town, when the village name should be included in the address before the post code. Freepost (*franqueo en destino*), where the addressee pays the cost of postage, is available to large companies only in Spain and isn't as widely used as in many other countries.

Spanish addresses (*dirección*) often include a number of abbreviations, for example 'C/España, 33, 3° dcha'. This means España street (C/ is short for *calle* meaning street) number 33, third floor (3°) on the right (*derecha* or *dcha*). An apartment on the left (when facing the front of an apartment block) is indicated as *izda* (*izquierda*) and one in the centre is *cto* (*centro*). Often a house will have no street number, indicated by s/n (*sin número*). On many roads (*carretera* or *ctra*) the address includes a kilometre marker, e.g. N-340, km 148 or N-V, km 64. Others may include '*ctra* town 1-town 2, km 25', meaning 25km along the road between town 1 and town 2 or 'ctra de town, km 7' means 7km along the road from town (name). Confusion may arise over the use of regional languages (Basque, Catalan or Gallego) in street and town names, which replace or are written alongside their Castilian (Spanish) counterparts. A typical Spanish address is shown below:

> Sr. Don Pulpo
> C/Pescado, 16
> E-12345 Fruta del Mar
> Spain/España

The Spanish post office publishes a guide to postal codes (*guía código postal*) costing 225 ptas, listing each street in cities and individual houses in small villages.

- If a letter is unable to be delivered due to being wrongly addressed or the addressee having moved, it will be stamped 'return' (*devuelto*) or 'return to sender' (*a su procendencia*). A box headed *devuelto* may be stamped on the reverse of a letter stating the reason for non-delivery. You should write your name and address on the back of all letters and parcels marked 'sender' (*remitente/rte*), as the Spanish post office won't usually open mail to obtain a return address. If you send mail with insufficient postage (*insuficiencia de franqueo*), the addressee must pay double the amount that's under paid for national mail and the underpaid amount plus 76 ptas for international mail.

- If you want your mail to be redirected (*reexpedir*) by the post office, you must present your local post office with your name and your old and new addresses. There's no official form and you shouldn't rely on any mail being redirected, but should give all your correspondents your new address and make private arrangements for mail sent to your old address to be redirected.

- The Spanish post office provides a service for stamp collectors and publishes leaflets for new editions (in English, French, German and Spanish). For information contact Correos y Telégrafos, Servicio Filatélico, Palacio de Communicaciones, 28070 Madrid (tel. (91) 396-2552/396-2170).

Finally, carefully check all your mail and don't throw anything away unless you're certain it's junk mail (unsolicited mail, circulars, newspapers, etc.). It isn't unknown for foreigners to throw away important bills and correspondence during their first few weeks in Spain. Look between the pages of junk mail for 'real' mail.

REGISTERED & RECORDED MAIL

You can send important letters and parcels by registered mail (*certificado*), obtain proof of delivery (*aviso recibo*) and send items by cash on delivery (*reembolso*) both in Spain and abroad. You're required to complete a form on which you insert your name and address (*remitente*) and the name and address of the destination (*destinario*). The sender's address must be written on the back of registered mail, for which you will receive a receipt. Note that in main post offices you must usually buy stamps at one window and complete the registration at another. The registration fee (plus postage) for national letters and parcels is 140 ptas and for international mail 162 ptas. Proof of delivery (*aviso recibo*) costs 54 ptas for domestic mail (also for Gibraltar and the Philippines) and 108 ptas for international mail. Cash on delivery (*reembolso*) costs 119 ptas for national mail and 162 ptas for international mail, which must also be registered.

Registered letters require a signature and proof of identity on delivery, normally from the addressee. If the addressee is absent when delivery is made, a notice is left and the letter must be collected from the local post office (see **Mail Collection** on page 118). Registration is common in Spain when sending official documents and important communications. You can insure (*seguro*) registered domestic and international mail. The cost for domestic mail is 1 per cent of the declared value up to a maximum of 500,000 ptas. If you have a complaint about registered mail (plus giros or postage to be paid by the receiver) you can make a claim (*reclamaciones reglamentarias*) and obtain compensation. Compensation (*indemnizaciones*) is paid for the loss or damage of registered mail (*pérdida o sustracción de certificado*), e.g. 3,672 ptas for domestic mail. Compensation for a package sent *postal exprés* is 8,316 ptas (plus postage costs) and for an item with a declared value is up to 50,000 ptas.

Spanish courier services offer similar services at competitive prices for letters and parcels, and some companies (such as Seur) have branches in most cities and large towns.

PARCEL POST

Parcels (*paquetes*) are usually dealt with at a separate window in main post offices. The post office offers a range of parcel services, both domestic and international. Parcel services are also provided by Spanish railways and airlines, and by international courier companies such as DHL and UPS. International letters and small packets (*pequeños paquetes*) are limited to a maximum weight of 2kg, as are periodicals (*periódicos*). There's also a national small packet rate for parcels weighing up to 500g. Domestic and international parcels containing printed matter (*impresos*), e.g. books and magazines, are limited to 5kg (and take 'for ever' to be delivered). Domestic and international parcels are limited to a maximum of 20kg. Parcels to non-EU addresses abroad must have an international customs label (*impreso para la aduana*) affixed to them (these are no longer required for parcels sent within the EU).

The standard surface domestic parcel service (*paquete postal*) costs 173 ptas up to 1kg, 270 ptas between 1 and 2kg, 324 ptas between 2 and 3kg, 621 ptas for 10kg and 1,431 ptas for 20kg. There's also a fast domestic airmail parcel service (*paquete azul*) costing 459 ptas up to 1kg, 486 ptas from 1 to 2kg, 513 ptas for 2 to 3kg, 810 ptas for 10kg and 1,620 ptas for 20kg. An international small packet (*pequeño paquete*) service is available costing 110 ptas up to 100 grammes, 220 ptas (100 to 250gr), 421 ptas (250 to 500g), 703 ptas (500 to 1,000g) and 1,231 ptas for 1,000 to 2,000g (the maximum permitted weight) for surface (*superficie*) mail. **If required, the cost of airmail must be added to the surface rates listed above.** When mailing small parcels; newspapers and magazines; books and brochures; or other printed matter, use a post office window marked *entrega paquetes, reembolso.*

Parcels posted in Spain must be securely packaged. A post office will make up your parcel and seal it at a special window in main post offices (*Prep. Paquete*). This is an inexpensive service costing 100 to 200 ptas (depending on size) and ensures that parcels comply with regulations.   Boxes, padded bags, large envelopes and other packing materials aren't generally sold at post offices in Spain, but are available from stationery stores.

The fastest and most convenient way to send domestic or international letters or parcels is via the post office's *postal exprés/EMS* service (serving around 160 countries). Within Spain EMS packages up to 20kg are guaranteed to arrive at their destination within 24 hours and mail sent to EU countries is usually guaranteed delivery within 48 hours, depending on the country. The maximum time for delivery to any country is three or four days. Although it's expensive, it's up to 50 per cent cheaper than private courier services, e.g. an item weighing up to 1kg costs 3,564 ptas to EU and other western European countries (zone 1); 4,860 to eastern Europe, the Mediterranean and North Africa (zone 2); 5,940 ptas to North America (zone 3); and 7,560 ptas to the rest of the world (zone 4). Items can be insured for up to 500,000 ptas.

Spanish railways also operate an express package and parcel service within Spain (24-hour) and to most European countries. Charges vary depending on the speed of delivery, the distance, and whether the package is to be collected or delivered. The Spanish state-owned airline, Iberia, provides domestic standard and express (guaranteeing airport-to-airport delivery within four hours) freight services between airports, plus optional delivery at the receiving end. Packages should be delivered a minimum of three hours prior to an aircraft's departure time. Many private courier and transport companies also provide an express parcel delivery service, both nationally and internationally.

MAIL COLLECTION

If the postperson calls with mail requiring a signature or payment when nobody is at home, he will leave a collection form (*aviso*). This also applies to mail weighing over 500g, which must usually be collected from a post office (although parcels up to 10kg will be delivered on payment of a surcharge). Mail is kept at the post office for one month, after which it's returned to the sender, therefore if you're going to be away from home for longer than this you should ask the post office to hold your mail. There's no charge for this service.

To collect mail, you must present the collection form at your local post office or postal 'depot', the address of which is written on the form. In large post offices there may be a special window (*Lista, Poste Restante*). You need some form of identification, for example, your passport, residence card (*residencia*) or Spanish driving licence. A post office may refuse to give letters to a spouse addressed to his or her partner, or to give letters to a house owner addressed to his tenants or guests.   You can give someone authorisation to collect a letter or parcel on your behalf by entering the details on the back of the collection form in the box marked *autorización*, for which both the addressee's and collector's identification is required.

You can receive mail at any post office in Spain via the international *poste restante* (general delivery) service, called *lista de correos* in Spain. If you choose a large town or city, always address mail to the main post office (*Correo Central*) to avoid confusion. Sometimes a post office will display a list of people for whom they have poste restante mail. Letters should be addressed as follows:

> Blenkinsop-Smith, Marmaduke Cecil
>
> Lista de Correos
>
> Correo Central
>
> Post Code, City Name (Province)
>
> Spain/España

Mail sent to a poste restante address is returned to the sender if it's unclaimed after 30 days. Identification (e.g. a passport) is necessary for collection and there's no fee. Mail can be forwarded from one main post office to another.

If you have an American Express card or use American Express traveller's cheques, you can have mail sent to an American Express office in Spain. Standard letters are held free of charge (registered letters and packages aren't accepted). Mail, which should be marked 'client mail service', is kept for 30 to 90 days before being returned to the sender. Mail can be forwarded to another office or address, for which there's a charge. Other companies also provide mail holding services for customers, e.g. Thomas Cook and Western Union.

You can obtain a post office box (*apartado particular*) at most post offices for an annual fee of 2,430 ptas. If you have a post box, all your mail will be stored there and the postperson will no longer deliver to your home. Post boxes are allocated on a first come, first served basis and may be unavailable. You can arrange to be informed when registered or express mail arrives. There's a window in a post office where you can register to receive all types of correspondence, packages and money orders (*giro postal*), which can also be forwarded to another post office in the same city for no charge. Proof of identity must be provided to collect mail.

POSTCHEQUE ACCOUNTS

The Spanish post office provides a range of cheque and savings accounts through the national savings bank (*Caja Postal Argentaria*) including tax-free savings accounts, house purchase, savings and retirement plans. In rural areas where the nearest bank may be many kilometres away, many people use the post office as their local bank. Post office accounts provide the same services as bank accounts including international money transfers (by mail and telegraph to many countries), payment of bills, and cheque, cash and debit cards. Post office account holders are issued with a (free) cash card for withdrawals from automated teller machines (ATMs) located outside main post offices and most banks. Withdrawals made at an ATM displaying the *Servired* sign are free of charge; however, if you use an ATM at a bank not belonging to the *Servired* network you will be charged 400 ptas for the transaction.

Cash transfers can be made both within Spain and internationally, with a postal giro (*giro postal*), by completing a form at any post office. You can choose between an ordinary giro (*giro ordinario*) taking around two to three days within Spain (five to seven days international) and an urgent giro (*giro urgente*) which takes around two hours within

Spain (four hours international). You're required to complete a form and pay the amount to be transferred plus the fee in cash. Fees for national giro payments depend on whether the recipient has a post office giro account and whether the payment is sent by mail or made by telephone. There are set fees plus a percentage of the amount being transferred. The fee for international giros depends on the destination and is calculated as a percentage of the amount sent, e.g. 2 per cent (the highest fee charged is to Britain, which is 3 per cent).

There are usually various giro windows in main post offices including sending ordinary giros (*giro ordinario admisión*), sending urgent and international giros (*giro urgente y internacional admisión*), paying for ordinary giros (*giro ordinario pago*) and paying for urgent and international giros (*giro urgente y internacional pago*). Note that it isn't possible to make giro transfers to some countries and some countries accept ordinary giro payments only. Domestic postal giros are useful for sending money to someone in Spain when you don't have a Spanish bank account or when sending money to someone else without a Spanish bank account. Some companies insist on payment by postal giro, as the cost of processing bank cheques is prohibitive.

If you have a post office account in another European country and a postcheque guarantee card, you can cash postcheques at main post offices at a special counter marked *caja postal de ahorros* or *reintegros* (hours of service may be restricted). The maximum value per cheque is 25,000 ptas. There's a standard charge for each cheque and you aren't charged a commission. Note that postcheques *cannot* be used to pay for goods or services in Spain, e.g. in hotels, shops or restaurants.

7.

TELEPHONE

The Spanish telephone service is operated by the *Compañia Telefónica Nacional de España (CNTE)*, better known simply as *Telefónica*, which has recently been privatised (the remaining government stake was sold in 1997). Spain has one of the lowest numbers of telephones per head of population (around 400 telephones per 1,000 people) in the EU, with a total of around 15m lines in service. The Spanish aren't habitual telephone users (it's too expensive) and don't usually spend hours on the telephone (many businessmen prefer to meet in person or exchange letters, rather than conduct business over the telephone). However, the last few years has seen the cost of mobile phones fall considerably and Spain is now one of the fastest-expanding countries in the EU for mobile phones.

Telefónica's monopoly is due to end on 1st January 1998 when the European Union's liberalisation of the telecommunications industry comes into force and new companies such as Retevision enter the market. Because of its market dominance, Spain has traditionally had some of the highest call rates in the EU, particularly for domestic calls. However, with the opening of the market to competitors, telephone bills are expected to halve in Spain (and across Europe) in the next few years. International call charges have already been reduced in recent years in order to compete with callback companies, which proliferate in Spain (see page 132).

Although Telefónica lags behind the best telephone companies in Europe in terms of quality of service and value for money, there has been a significant improvement in recent years, with less than 1 per cent of calls having problems and most faults being fixed within 24 hours. The waiting time for new telephone installations has also fallen dramatically and is now similar to other EU countries. Telefónica has made a huge investment in advanced technology (such as fibre-optics) in the last decade or so in order to bring its service up to the best European and North American standards (it has also linked up with British Telecom and American telecommunications company MCI to expand into new markets).

Where applicable, all costs listed in this chapter are exclusive of value added tax (*IVA*), unless otherwise stated. **Information regarding EMERGENCY NUMBERS is provided on page 137 and local emergency number are listed at the front of telephone directories (White and Yellow Pages).**

INSTALLATION & REGISTRATION

When moving into a new home in Spain which has a telephone line, you must have the account transferred to your name. If you're planning to move into a property without an existing telephone line, you will need to have one installed (although it isn't compulsory!). To have a telephone installed or reconnected, you must usually visit the local Telefónica office. Take along your passport or residence card (*residencia*), proof of your address such as a recent electricity bill, and a copy of your property deed (*escritura*) or rental contract. If you're renting and don't have a residence permit (*residencia*) you must pay a deposit of around 32,400 ptas. Note that staff don't usually speak English. If you're taking over a property from the previous occupants, you should arrange for the telephone account to be transferred to your name from the day you take possession. Before buying or renting a property, check that all the previous bills have been paid, otherwise you may find yourself liable for them.

Telephone installation used to be a lengthy affair with waiting lists from a few months to several years. Not surprisingly, homes with a telephone were in high demand and those who couldn't do without a telephone (e.g. businesses) were often forced to purchase a mobile telephone (see page 136). However, the situation has improved dramatically in recent years and the waiting list is now down to an average of around seven days and Telefónica will even give you a free telephone if you have to wait longer than 15 days for your installation. Note that if you're renting a property, getting a telephone installed can be a problem and you may have to ask your landlord to arrange it for you and pay a deposit. The cost of a having a private telephone line installed was among the most expensive in Europe, although it has now been reduced to 24,250 ptas. If you buy or rent a property a long distance away from existing installations, you may be charged for the cost of erecting posts and lines to your property. There are various types of lines but unless you have special requirements you should request a private line (*línea individual*).

You aren't required to rent a telephone from Telefónica and it doesn't pay to rent a telephone long term (it's usually worthwhile only if you wish to test a telephone or change it frequently). The cost of the cheapest model (*Arquero*) from Telefónica is 5,900 ptas, although you can buy telephones from phone shops for less. You can choose from a wide range of all-singing, all-dancing models, which can be rented or purchased from Telefónica or purchased from retailers. Note that if you're using a callback service (see page 132) you should buy a phone with a memory (unless you like dialling around 20 numbers every time you make a call). Cordless phones (from around 10,000 ptas) are useful as they can be used throughout the house or garden (e.g. when you're lying in the sun). All telephones must be approved (*aprobado*) by Telefónica, which means that you cannot officially buy a telephone abroad and use it in Spain.

Temporary Disconnection: If you're leaving your Spanish home for an extended period, you can have Telefónica disconnect your line temporarily. Note, however, that this can be done for up to three months a year only and you need to provide the exact dates for disconnection and reconnection in writing. You must continue to pay the standing charge plus 500 ptas for the disconnection and 500 ptas for the reconnection.

Telefónica has an *Oficina Comercial* in each province or an *Oficina de Atención al Usuario* where you can make a complaint. If you don't receive a reply within one month you can take your complaint to the *Delegación del Gobierno en Telefónica*, Javier Nadal Ariño, Valverde, 2, 28004 Madrid (tel. (91) 531 5349).

USING THE TELEPHONE

There are no town codes as such in Spain but each province has its own area code number (*prefijo* or *códigos territoriales*), listed below. Major cities (and provinces) have a two-digit provincial code e,g, Madrid (91), Barcelona (93), Bilbao (94), Seville (95) and Valencia (96), followed by a seven-digit number. There are plans to extend this system throughout Spain, although at present most provinces have a three-digit area code followed by a six-digit number. The provincial code is usually shown in brackets before a subscriber's number, unless it's obviously a local number. The codes listed below are shown on a map in telephone directories (the provinces are also shown on the map in **Appendix D**):

Alava	945	La Coruña	981	Navarra	948
Albacete	967	Cuenca	969	Orense	988
Alicante	96	Giupúzcoa	943	Palencia	979
Almería	950	Gerona (Guarana)	972	Pontevedra	986
Asturias	98	Granada	958	La Rioja	941
Avila	920	Guadalajara	949	Salamanca	923
Badajoz	924	Huelva	959	Sta. Cruz Tenerife	922
Baleares	971	Huesca	974	Segovia	921
Barcelona	93	Jaén	953	Seville	95
Bizkaia (Vizcaya)	94	Las Palmas	928	Soria	975
Burgos	947	León	987	Tarragona	977
Cáceres	927	Lleida (Lérida)	973	Teruel	978
Cadiz	956	Lugo	982	Toledo	925
Cantabria	942	Madrid	91	Valencia	96
Castellón	964	Malaga	95	Valladolid	983
Ceuta	956	Melilla	95	Zamora	980
Ciudad Real	926	Murcia	968	Zaragossa	976
Córdoba	957				

The code for Andorra is 9738 and the code for Gibraltar 9567. When making a domestic call in the same province, i.e. to a number with the same provincial code, don't dial the code number. However, to make a call to another province, the provincial code must be dialled. When making an international call to Spain, the first digit, i.e. the 9, is dropped, e.g. the code for Madrid from abroad is 1 and the code for Barcelona is 3. To make an international call from Spain, first dial 07 to obtain an international line. When you hear the international tone, dial the country code, e.g. 44 for Britain, the area code *without* the first zero and the subscriber's number. To make a call to a country where there isn't international direct dialling (IDD) you must dial 9198 for European countries, Algeria, Lebanon, Syria or Tunisia and 9191 for all other countries.

Numbers beginning with 900 are free, although they aren't widely used in Spain and aren't nearly as common as in Britain or (particularly) the USA. Don't confuse 900 numbers with other numbers beginning with 9 (e.g. 903 and 906 information numbers) which are expensive and used by companies providing services such as weather forecasts, and financial and health information. The most expensive 903/906 numbers cost 137 ptas for three minutes (reduced rate), 171 ptas (normal rate) and 194 ptas (peak rate), plus IVA. Pornographic 'sex' chat lines were banned in 1993 after a scandal over selling prostitution by telephone, but not until many consumers (including many children) had ran up bills of hundreds of thousands of pesetas. However, 903/906 sex lines have been replaced by the proliferation of even more expensive international (07) sex lines advertised in national newspapers (one boy ran up a bill for 4m ptas!).

The tones used in Spain are similar to other European countries, e.g. the dialling tone (*señal para marcar*) is a low continuous tone (similar to Britain and the USA), a ringing tone is a repeated long tone and the engaged (busy) signal is a series of rapid pips. If you get a recorded message (which is often incomprehensible) after dialling, it may be telling you that all lines are engaged and to try again later. It's best to try again immediately and if you cannot get through, try again in five or 10 minutes. The message may also be telling you that the number you've dialled doesn't exist (e.g. *el número marcado no existe*). If this happens, check that the number is correct and re-dial; if you're dialling an international number, make sure you haven't dialled the first zero of the area code. To make a reverse charge (collect) call (*cobro revertido*) within Spain dial 009, or 008 for another EU country. Person-to-person (*persona a persona*) calls can also be made via the operator. A surcharge is made for both reverse charge and person-to-person calls. These calls can also be made to certain countries via the Home Direct service (see page 132). As with anything requiring interaction with the operator, this can be a slow process and it may be easier to make a short direct call and ask the party to call you back.

The usual Spanish response when answering the telephone is *¡diga!* or *¡dígame!* (hello or literally 'speak to me'). The caller will usually preface what he has to say with *¡oiga!* (listen). 'I'm trying to connect you' is *le pongo/paso con* and 'go ahead' may be simply *adelante*. A call is *una llamada* and to call is *llamar*. Other useful words include 'to answer the telephone' (*coger*), hang up (*colgar*), dial (*marcar*), connect me (*me pone con*) and wrong number (*número equivocado*).

In Spain, telephone numbers are usually dictated on the telephone two digits at a time. If someone asks you to spell (*deletrear*) something on the telephone, such as your name, you should use the telephone alphabet. Obviously to use it you need to be able to pronounce the alphabet in Spanish and the names listed below. For example if your name's Smith you say, S (essay) para Sábado, M (emay) para Madrid, I (ee) para Inés, T (tay) para Tarragona y H (achay) para Historia.

A (ah)	Antonio	N (enay)	Navarra
B (bay)	Barcelona	Ñ (enyay)	Ñoño
C (thay)	Carmen	O (oh)	Oviedo
CH (chay)	Chocolate	P (pay)	Paris
D (day)	Dolores	Q (ku)	Querido
E (ay)	Enrique	R (eray)	Ramón
F (efay)	Francia	S (essay)	Sábado
G (zhay)	Gerona	T (tay)	Tarragona
H (achay)	Historia	U (oo)	Ulises
I (ee)	Inés	V (oo-bay)	Valencia
J (hota)	José	W (oo-bay-doblay)	Washington
K (kah)	Kilo	X (ekiss)	Xiquina
L (elay)	Lorenzo	Y (ee greeyayga)	Yegua
LL (elyay)	Llobregat	Z (thayta)	Zaragossa
M (emay)	Madrid		

CUSTOM & OPTIONAL SERVICES

Telefónica provides a range of custom and optional services (*líneas multíservicios*), although to take advantage of them your telephone must be connected to a digital exchange and you must have a touch-tone telephone. Most custom or optional services have a 1,000 ptas initial fee (*alta inicial*), which is sometimes waived, plus a 50 to 150 ptas monthly charge (*abono mensual*). They include the following:

Multi-Frequency dialling tone (*marcación multifrecuencia*) consists of several superimposed audiotones for better quality internet connections. An initial fee of 1,000 ptas plus 50 ptas a month.

Make a call without dialling (*llamada sin marcar*). Initial fee of 1,000 ptas plus 150 ptas a month.

Divert calls when engaged (*desvío si comunica*) by informing the exchange to divert calls to another number when your number is engaged. An initial fee of 1,000 ptas plus 100 ptas a month.

Divert calls when your away (*desvío por ausencia*) allows you to divert calls to another number when your telephone isn't answered within 15 seconds. An initial fee of 1,000 ptas plus 100 ptas a month.

Divert calls when you change address (*desvío en bajas y cambio de domicilio*) can be done for two months (1,200 ptas fee), six months (7,500 ptas fee) or indefinitely (7,000 ptas fee plus a monthly charge of 3,500 ptas).

Information about a change of number (*información de cambio de número*). An initial fee of 1,000 ptas plus 100 ptas a month.

Call transfer (*desvío inmediatio*) allows you to divert calls to another telephone number automatically, e.g. from home to office (or vice versa) or to a mobile telephone. Telefónica will also arrange to have calls automatically transferred to another number in the event that you move house or office and change your telephone number. An initial fee of 1,000 ptas plus 100 ptas a month.

Call waiting (*llamada en espera*) lets you know when another caller is trying to contact you (you will hear two short pips on the line) when you're already making a call and allows you to speak to him without terminating your current call. An initial fee of 1,000 ptas plus 100 ptas a month.

Three-way conversation (*llamada a tres*) allows you to hold a three-way conversation, either in Spain or abroad. An initial fee of 1,000 ptas plus 100 ptas a month.

CHARGES

Line rental and call charges in Spain are among the highest in Europe, although they have been reduced in recent years. Telephone charges in Spain include line rental; telephone and other equipment rentals; credit card calls; and general call charges. If you have a private line (*línea individual*), the monthly line rental or service charge (*cuota de abono*) is 1,242 ptas (levied bi-monthly). Handicapped persons and those aged 65 or over with an income below the Spanish minimum pension pay a reduced tariff and receive a number of free calls. A reduction is also granted on the monthly standing charge and on the installation charge.

There are two primary tariffs in Spain: national and international. National (i.e. domestic) tariffs are divided into local/metropolitan calls (*metropolitana*), calls within your province (*provincial*) and calls outside your province (*nacional/interprovincial*). The initial connection fee is 5.70 ptas for local calls, 11.40 ptas for provincial calls and 17.10 ptas for national/interprovincial calls. The length of calls are billed by the 'tariff unit' (*pasos*), at a cost of 5.70 ptas per unit. There are three tariff (*tarifa*) periods for domestic calls:

Peak (*horas punta*) hours are from 0800 to 1700 hours from Monday to Friday and 0800 to 1400 on Saturdays (only Spain within the EU sets the 'peak' period all day, i.e. from 0800 to 1700 Monday to Friday *and* on Saturdays).

Normal (*normal*) hours are from 1700 to 2200, Monday to Friday.
Reduced (*reducida*) hours are from 2200 to 0800 Monday to Friday, 1400 to 2400 on Saturdays and all day on Sundays and national public holidays (calls are charged at around 30 per cent less than 'peak' calls). Note that Spain has the shortest periods for reduced rates for international calls of any country in Europe.

The amount of time allocated per unit for automatic (self-dialled) calls depends on the distance and time of the call (tariff), as shown in the table below:

Call Type	Tariff/Duration (in seconds)		
	Peak	Normal	Reduced
metropolitan	180.0	180.0	240.0
provincial	20.0	22.9	46.0
national	7.2	10.7	20.6

Note that there's a surcharge for operator connected calls, the tariffs for which are shown in telephone directories. You can buy or rent a telephone with a built-in meter (*contador*), which records the units used, or have a separate counter installed to monitor the cost of calls or to check unauthorised use, e.g. by baby-sitters, guests, burglars and children (alternatively you can buy a telephone with a lock). A counter is also useful if you suspect Telefónica of overcharging (i.e. even more than they do usually).

BILLS

Telefónica bills you every two months and allows you 20 days to pay your bill (*factura*). Bills include value added tax (IVA) at 16 per cent. Itemised bills (*factura detallada*) are provided listing all numbers called (except for metropolitan calls) with the date and time, duration, number of units and the charge. Bills can be paid in cash at certain banks, via a bank account or in cash at a Telefónica office. Simply present the bill with your payment (you will receive a receipt). You can also have your telephone bill paid by direct debit (*transferencia*) from a bank account, which is advisable for holiday-home owners as it ensures that you aren't disconnected for non-payment. If your bill isn't paid within 20 days, your line may be cut without further warning, although a new system has been introduced whereby lines with unpaid bills are reduced to incoming calls only for 10 days, prior to cutting the service completely. When a debtor tries to dial a number (during the 10-day period) he hears a recorded message warning him of the impending cut. If your line is cut, there's a reconnection fee which depends on the amount owing and the elapsed period, after which it should be reconnected within two working days.

If you complain about your bill being too high, Telefónica will install a counter on your telephone for a number of days to check for a malfunction. If the test fails to discover any line problems, Telefónica won't reduce your bill. Note that you must pay your telephone bill, even if the amount is contested, otherwise Telefónica may cut your line. If you're unable to pay the whole amount of a contested bill, you should pay your usual amount and contest the rest. Non-payment of telephone bills is a huge problem in Spain, particularly by government departments, and Telefónica is getting tough and increasingly cutting lines.

Telephone bills includes the following details (reading from top to bottom, left to right):

Item	Description
Núm. abono	your telephone number
Hoja	page number
Factura n°.	bill number
Fecha emisión	date of billing
Titual/Domicilio/Población	name/address/town (of subscriber)
D.N.I.-C.I.F.	number of your identity card (*Documento Nacional de Identidad*) or fiscal number (*Código de Indentificación Fiscal*)
Domicilio de Pago	bank account from where bill is paid
Detalle de conceptos	details of bill
Importe (Ptas.)	amount (pesetas)
1. Cuotas de Abono.	standing charges (including those below)
- Línea Individual	private line
- Equipo Principal Teide	telephone rental
2. Cuotas de Publicidad Guías	charge for publicity in the phone book
3. Varios	other services
4. Conferencias a Través de Operadora	operator assisted calls
5. Servicio Automático de DD-MM-YY a DD-MM-YY (NUM/PASOS)	automatic services from 'date' to 'date' (number of calls/units)
- Llamadas Metropolitanas	local calls
- Llamadas Provinciales (P)	provincial calls
- Llamadas Interprovinciales (N)	inter-provincial calls
- Llamadas Internacionales (I)	international calls
- Llamadas a Moviline* (L)	calls to mobile phones (* or Movistar)
- Resto Llamadas (R)	other calls (such as directory enquiries)
Precio del Paso	unit cost
Total Importes	total amount
I.V.A. Aplicable (16%)	VAT at 16 per cent
Total a Pagar	total payable
Lamadas Recogidas en Servicio Automático (Excepto Metropolitanas)	- itemised calls (except local calls)
- Abonado/Llamado	number called
- Fecha	date
- Hora Inicio	time (start)
- Duración (mmmm:ss)	duration (minutes and seconds)
- Pasos	units

- Importe (Ptas.)   total cost

INTERNATIONAL CALLS

It's possible to make direct IDD (International Direct Dialling) calls from Spain to most countries, from both private and public telephones. A full list of IDD country codes is shown in the information pages (*páginas informativas*) of your local White Pages, plus area codes for main cities and tariffs. To make an international call you must first dial 07 to obtain an international line. When you hear the (high-pitched) international dialing tone dial the country code (e.g. 44 for Britain), the area code *without* the first zero (e.g. 71 for central London) and the subscriber's number. For example to call the central London number 123-4567 from Spain you would dial 07-44-71-123-4567. To make a call to a country where there isn't international direct dialling (IDD) you must dial 9198 for European countries, Algeria, Lebanon, Syria or Tunisia, and 9191 for all other countries.

The initial connection fee for all international calls is 28.50 ptas and the cost of each 'tariff unit' (*paso*) is 5.70 ptas. There are just two tariff periods for international calls to most countries; normal from 0800 to 2200 daily and reduced (30 per cent reduction) from 2200 to 0800 daily (even Saturdays and Sundays are charged at normal rates by Telefónica!). There's also a **super reduced** (*super reducida*) tariff to the USA (including Alaska and Hawaii), Canada and parts of the Caribbean from 0300 to 0800, costing 65 ptas a minute to the US and 80 ptas to Canada. There are a range of tariffs for international calls, depending on the country called, as shown below:

Tariff	Cost Per Minute (Ptas)	
	Normal	Reduced
1 Andorra	54	45
2. EU, Switzerland	65	58
3. Iceland, Norway	71	61
4. Czech Republic, Faroe Islands, Hungary, Malta, Poland & Slovakia	65	58
5. Rest of Europe & North Africa	99	80
6. USA (except Alaska)	85	75
7. Alaska, Canada, Hawaii, Part of the Caribbean	99	85
8. Argentina, Chile, Mexico Nicaragua, Peru, Venezuela	175	125
9. Rest of the Americas	180	125
10 Australia, India, Japan, etc.	185	170
11 Saudi Arabia, China Pakistan & Senegal	199	179
12 Rest of the World	230	179

Calls to Gibraltar are charged at the domestic rate for interprovincial calls. Note that there's a high surcharge for operator connected international calls, the tariffs for which are shown in telephone directories.

Spain subscribes to a Home Direct (*Servicio Directo País*) service that enables you to call a number giving you direct and free access to an operator in the country you're calling, e.g. for Britain dial 900-990044 (BT) or 900-990944 (Mercury). The operator will connect you to the number required and will also accept credit card calls. Countries with the home direct service include Australia, Belgium, Brazil, Canada, Chile, Denmark, Finland, France, Germany, Guatemala, Hong Kong, Indonesia, Ireland, Japan, South Korea, Norway, the Netherlands, Portugal, Sweden, the United Kingdom, Uruguay and the USA. Note, however, that this can be expensive, particularly when making reverse charge calls.

To obtain an operator from one of the three major US telephone companies call 900-990011 (AT&T), 900-990014 (MCI) or 900-990013 (Sprint). You're connected directly with a US operator and you can place calls with a domestic USA telephone card or ask for a collect (reverse charge) call. Information about the Home Direct service is provided in the 'international communications' (*Comunicaciones Internacionales*) section of telephone directories. International calls can be made from Telefónica telephone offices (*locutorios públicos*) in major towns and cities (see **Public Telephones** on page 133), where you can pay for calls costing over 500 ptas with a credit card.

Callback Companies: An increasing number of expatriates (and Spaniards) make use of a callback service such as those provided by I.T.S. Europe (tel. (95) 277-2057), Euronet International (tel. (95) 258-6256) and Telegroup Global Access (tel. (971) 676293) in Spain. Subscribers 'call' a number (e.g. in Britain or the USA) and can make international calls over leased UK or USA lines at up to 75 per cent less than Telefónica's rates.

Internet 'Telephone' Services: The success of the Internet is built on the ability to gather information from computers around the world by connecting to a nearby service for the cost of a local telephone call. If you have correspondents or friends who are connected to the Internet, you can make international 'calls' for the price of a local telephone call to an Internet provider. Once on the Internet there are no other charges, no matter how much distance is covered or time is spent on-line. Internet users can buy software from companies such as Quarterdeck and Vodaltec (costing around 10,000 ptas) that effectively turns their personal computer into a voice-based telephone (both parties must have compatible computer software). You also need a sound card, speakers, a microphone and a modem, and access to a local Internet provider (costing from around 1,000 ptas a month plus connection costs). While the quality of communication isn't as good as using a telephone (it's similar to using a CB radio) and you need to arrange call times in advance, making international 'calls' costs virtually nothing. The Internet can also be used to send electronic mail (e-mail) messages.

DIRECTORIES

Telephone directories (*Guías Telefónicas*) in Spain are published by province, with each province having its own telephone book and code number (see page 126). Some provinces have more than one volume, e.g. the Madrid 'white' (*Sección Alfabética*) and Yellow Pages (*Páginas Amarillas*) both consist of two volumes. The directories for the province where you reside or have your business are provided free of charge. If you want other directories they are available from provincial Telefónica offices at around 500 ptas each.

Directory White Pages contain a number of information pages (*páginas informativas*), including **emergency** and useful local numbers; Telefónica service numbers; telephones for sale and rent; tariffs; national and international codes and costs; instructions on how to use the telephone (in English, French, German and Italian); bills; directories; mobile telephones; and tourist information. The second section in the White Pages is the alphabetical list of subscribers. Yellow Pages contain useful local numbers at the front, a list of towns covered by the directory and local information. Blue pages (*Páginas azules*) are also published in Spain and contain an alphabetical index of streets and subscribers by street number. New directories are published every few years (although not all at the same time) and information contained in them is often out of date. *Euro Pages* is a European business directory containing some 150,000 suppliers (tel. 900-131131 for information). In some areas, there are English-language directories (e.g. the English Speaker's Telephone Directory or ESTD for the Costa del Sol and Gibraltar - tel. (956) 776958). Other free local telephone directories are also published in some areas. *Hola* English Yellow Pages are available in Madrid (tel. (91) 345 4972).

When you have a telephone installed, your name and number is automatically included in the next edition of your local telephone directory. You can choose to have an unlisted number (*no registrado*), for which there's no charge. Subscribers are listed in the White Pages under their town or village (*ciudad*) and not alphabetically for the whole of a province. When looking for a subscriber's number, you must know the town, not just the province where they live. You will receive little or no help from directory enquiries unless you know the town where the subscriber is located.

Dial 003 for provincial and national directory enquiries and 025 for international enquiries. International operators may speak English or other foreign languages, but don't expect national operators to speak anything but Spanish. There's a charge of 45.6 ptas domestic directory enquiries and 171 ptas for international enquiries. Trying to obtain international numbers from directory enquiries is time-consuming and costly, and it may be easier to call someone abroad and ask them to find the number for you. Telefónica telephone offices (see below) contain a full set of Spanish telephone directories.

PUBLIC TELEPHONES

Public telephones (*cabinas Telefónicas* or *teléfonos públicos*) are located in bus depots, railway stations and airports; bars, cafés and restaurants; motorway rest areas; various business premises; and in streets in towns and villages. Public telephones aren't found in post offices with the exception of a few main post offices in major cities. All payphones allow International Direct Dialling (IDD) and international calls can also be made via the operator. Most old-style call boxes have been replaced by new 'vandal-proof' telephones. All public telephones accept coins and many also except telephone and credit cards such as Visa, Amex, Diners Club and 4B (there are no public telephone boxes in Spain accepting telephone cards only).

Telephone cards (*Tarjetas Telefónicas*) costing 1,000 or 2,000 ptas (including an extra 100 ptas free) are available from post offices, newsagents, tobacconists and some retailers, and save you having to find change or carry around piles of coins. The procedure for using public telephones depends on whether you're using an old style telephone or a new one. The instructions for using modern public telephones are as follows:

1. Lift the receiver and check that there's a dialling tone, as some public telephones don't work. Insert coins or a telephone card (*inserte moneda o tarjeta*) will be displayed on the LCD display. If you wish to see instructions in English, French or German, press the top 'select language' (*selección de idioma*) button below the display (depicting a flag marked with an 'L') until the language you require is displayed. Thereafter follow the instructions on the display. You can increase or lower the volume by pressing the 'volume' (*volumen*) button, which is the third button down below the display. Instructions on how to use the telephone are also posted in telephone boxes in English, French, German and Spanish. A selection of national and international code numbers are also posted in some public telephones.

2. Insert coins, a telephone card or a credit card (minimum charge 200 ptas). Telephones accept 500, 200, 100, 50, 25, 10 and 5 peseta coins. You must insert at least 20 ptas for a local call, 50 ptas for a national call (to another province) and 100 ptas or more for a long-distance or international call. If you insert too little you will be unable to make your call. If you dial the wrong number or don't insert coins fast enough, you must start again and the message 'please wait' (*por favor, espere*) may be displayed. Make sure you have plenty of 100 peseta coins for international calls. Don't insert large denomination coins for short local calls as they will be lost unless you have a number of calls to make (see below). If you have a problem inserting coins or coins don't register on the LCD display, press the coin return button next to the coin slot.

   If you're using a telephone card (*tarjeta Telefónica*), simply insert it in the card slot and dial. The message 'Dial Number Credit XXXX' will be displayed. As your call continues the remaining credit on your card is displayed. When you have finished your call, hang up the receiver and remove your card when 'Remove Card Credit XXXX' is displayed. When using an American Express or Diners Club card, insert your card, remove it when instructed, listen for the dial tone and dial.

3. After you have inserted your money or card the instruction 'Dial number - credit XXXX' (*marque número - crédito XXXX*) will be displayed (where 'XXXX' is the amount inserted in coins). The credit amount is permanently displayed as you insert more coins or coins are used. If you're making an international call, dial 07 and wait for the second dial tone before dialling the country code and number.

4. Insert new coins as necessary (a high pitched tone indicates when more money is needed). If you're using a telephone card and your credit expires, press the 'card change' (*cambio de tarjeta*) button and insert a new card. If you don't have a new card, you can continue your call by pressing the manual payment button (*bóton cobro manual*) and inserting coins.

5. If you wish to make another call, don't hang up the receiver but press the button marked 'R' located beneath the handset rest. This ensures that any partly used coins aren't lost.

6. When you have finished your call(s) hang up the receiver. Any completely unused coins will be returned in the coin box (partly used coins are lost). Don't forget to retrieve your telephone card or credit card.

In old-style public telephones you place coins in the sloping groove at the top of the payphone. Coins drop into the box one by one (or are supposed to - they don't always drop automatically) and you must add more coins as they are used. You can receive calls and make reverse charge (collect) calls from modern public call boxes only. When making an emergency call from a public telephone, you must insert at least 20 ptas or a telephone card.

Telefónica Booths: The least expensive place to make telephone calls (apart from private telephones) is from Telefónica offices in major towns. These may be open from 0800 or 0900 until 2400 on working days (*laborables*) and on Sundays and public holidays (*domingos y festivos*) from 0800 until 2200 (however Sunday hours vary considerably and cabins are often open for a few hours only). In small towns, Telefónica cabins (*locutorios públicos*) are franchised businesses, where you pay a 35 per cent surcharge on all calls. These blue cabins have shorter business hours than Telefónica offices, e.g. 1000 to 1400 and 1700 to 2200 daily. Most credit cards are accepted in payment for calls costing over 500 ptas including Visa, Eurocard, Mastercard, Access, Electron and telephone cards. Reverse charge calls can be made. You can make a number of calls in succession and receive an itemised receipt which includes the surcharge and IVA. Offices keep a full set of telephone directories.

Private Booths: In cities and resort towns there are private telephone kiosks (*centros Telefónicas* or *cabinas*) which are leased from Telefónica by private companies. They charge a high commission on calls and don't handle reverse charge (collect) calls, as they don't make any money on them. Many businesses in resort areas (such as restaurants) also have telephone booths and may also offer a fax service. **Note, however, that (according to the Spanish Consumers Union, UCE) some operators charge extortionate rates that can be over 1,000 per cent higher than Telefónica rates.** El Corte Inglés department stores provide communications centres where calls can be made in sound-proof cabins.

Private Telephones: Bars, cafés and restaurants also set their own charges, although they are usually reasonable and only slightly more expensive than public telephones. Many bars and restaurants have green or red payphones with an LCD credit display which reduces as coins are used. Some bars and restaurants still have telephones where you buy tokens (*fichas*) instead of using coins. Many businesses also allow customers to make calls on metered telephones and make a surcharge on calls. To make a call from an hotel room, you may be able to dial direct or you may need to make a call via the hotel receptionist. However, making calls from hotels is best avoided as they levy a high surcharge in addition to the cost of calls. There are free SOS telephones on motorways and main highways in Spain for use in the event of accidents, breakdowns and other emergencies.

You can obtain a telephone calling card (*Tarjeta Personal*) from Telefónica costing 100 ptas a month. Cards can be used from any public or private telephone, with calls being charged to your Spanish telephone account. To use a Telefónica card you dial 083 and give your card number and personal identity number (PIN). **Take care when using telephone calling cards and make sure that nobody discovers your PIN, as card fraud is rife.** For more information dial 900-667788 (free).

MOBILE TELEPHONES

Mobile telephones (*telefonía móvil*) were relatively slow to take off in Spain, although in the last few years prices have fallen dramatically and sales have rocketed, making Spain one of the fastest-expanding countries in the EU for mobile phones. In 1997, there were over 3m users and this is expected to exceed 5m by the year 2000. All the major population centres (some 90 per cent of the population) are covered by both analogue and digital networks, although sparsely populated areas aren't served. Spain has both analogue (Moviline) and digital (Airtel and Movistar) networks, although the analogue Moviline network will close down in 2007. Moviline covers 90 per cent of the country and 98 per cent of the population, while both Airtel and Movistar cover around 75 per cent of the country.

One of the reasons for the initial lack of interest was the high cost of phones and calls and poor service (lines were hopelessly overloaded at certain times), although the service has improved considerably and is now on a par with that of other countries. It's hard to imagine now, but mobile phones cost as much as 500,000 ptas when they were first introduced and only a few years ago they were still selling for between 50,000 and 100,000 ptas. The latest phones are much lighter and smaller (they can easily be popped in a pocket or bag or attached to a belt) and cost as little as 10,000 ptas or are even given away free or for a few thousand pesetas with special promotions. Many people choose a mobile phone because the cost of connection is less than a standard 'cable' phone and is instantaneous, you can move house and retain the same number, and you can use the phone almost anywhere, both in Spain and internationally.

Tariffs have fallen dramatically due to the price war that has been raging between the two service providers in the last few years. Before buying a phone or signing up for a service, compare the prices of the various services offered by all providers. In 1997, connection to GSM Airtel cost around 3,500 ptas and the typical monthly service charge some 4,000 ptas a month, depending on the particular tariff chosen. If you plan to use the phone a lot you should choose a tariff with a low call cost, which will have a higher monthly service charge. On the other hand, if you place to use the phone infrequently or mainly for incoming calls, you should choose a tariff with a low monthly service charge and higher call rates.

A typical tariff is Airtel's *plan profesional* which has a 4,000 ptas monthly service charge. There's a 20 ptas connection fee (*establecimiento de la llamada*) for each call, with domestic calls costing 40 ptas a minute during normal hours (from 0700 to 2100 Monday to Friday) and 17 ptas a minute during reduced hours (from 2100 to 0700 Monday to Friday and from 2100 Friday to 0700 Monday, weekends and public holidays). Calls to other Airtel users are cheaper (30 ptas a minute normal rate, 10 ptas reduced rate) and there are further reductions for high usage. For international calls within Europe there's a 50 ptas connection fee and calls cost 80 ptas a minute during normal hours (from 0800 to 2200) and 70 ptas during reduced hours (from 2200 to 0800). Note that calls to a mobile phone (e.g. numbers prefixed with 907, 908, 909, 929, 939, 970 and 989) from a 'fixed' phone cost more than when calling another 'fixed' phone.

With international roaming, GSM digital phones can be used in over 40 countries including all EU countries plus Andorra, Australia, Bahrain, Cyprus, Estonia, Hong Kong, Hungary, Iceland, Indonesia, Latvia, Liechtenstein, Morocco, Norway, Qatar, Russia, Singapore, South Africa, Switzerland and Turkey.

NUISANCE CALLS

If you receive nuisance (or obscene) calls, you should do the following:

* hang up as soon as you realise it's a nuisance call;
* don't provide any information to an unknown caller;
* tell your children not to give any information to strangers;
* tell your children that if anyone asks for their mother or father when you aren't at home, they should say that you're unable to come to the telephone at the moment (e.g. you're in the bath/shower) and they **mustn't** tell callers that you aren't at home.
* if you need assistance in dealing with nuisance calls or if you're receiving persistent nuisance calls, you should report it to your local police who will contact Telefónica (if necessary Telefónica will arrange for the operator to intercept your calls).

Note that it's an offence to make nuisance calls in Spain (telephone salespersons please note!).

EMERGENCY NUMBERS

Emergency numbers (*Servicios de Urgencia*) are listed at the front of all telephone directories (White and Yellow Pages). They include civil protection (*Protección Civil*), fire (*Bomberos*), red cross (*Cruz Roja*), ambulance (*Ambulancias*), police (*Policía*), civil guard (*Guardia Civil*), local/municipal police (*Policía Local/Municipal*), urgent health services (*Servicio de Salud - Urgencias*), social security (*Seguridad Social*), first aid posts (*Casas de Socorro*), maritime rescue and security (*Salvamento y Seguridad Marítima*), drug addiction (*Fundación de Ayuda contra la Drogadicción*), poison information (*Información Toxicológica*) and SOS or the Samaritans (*Teléfono de la Esperanza*). Note that there are few national emergency numbers in Spain, although 062 for the *guardia civil*, 091 for national police and 092 for local municipal police are valid throughout Spain.

You should make a note of your local emergency numbers such as your doctor, hospital, ambulance, fire and police and keep them by your telephone(s). When reporting a medical emergency, you should state the type of emergency, e.g. accident (*accidente*), serious illness (*enfermedad grave*), heart attack (*ataque cardiaco*) and whether an ambulance (*ambulancia*) or doctor (*médico*) is required. Calls to emergency numbers cost one unit or *paso* (5.7 ptas) from private telephones. You need to insert at least 20 ptas or a telephone card when using a public telephone, although your money is returned when the emergency service answers. There are free SOS telephones on motorways and main highways in Spain. For gas, electricity and water emergency numbers, look in your local directory under *Otros Servicios de Interés*. Dial 002 to report telephone breakdowns or line problems. See also **Emergencies** on page 235.

SERVICE NUMBERS

Useful service numbers are listed at the front of all telephone directories (White and Yellow Pages) after the emergency numbers in the information pages (*Páginas Informativas*) under the heading 'other services of interest' (*Otros Servicios de Interés*). They include regional government information (*información ciudadano*), water (*agua*), electricity (*electricidad*), gas, airports (*aeropuerto*), post offices (*correos*), rail (*RENFE*), bus (*estación de autobuses*), telegrams (*telegramas por teléfono*) and road information (*ayuda en carretera*). Local useful telephone numbers (*teléfonos útiles*) are listed in English-language and other expatriate newspapers and magazines, generally by town, and usually include local emergency and hospital numbers.

The following Telefónica and general information numbers can be dialled throughout Spain:

Number	Service
002	telephone technical assistance
003*	directory enquiries - provincial and national
004	Telefónica commercial enquiries
005	Operator assisted calls - rest of the world
008	Operator assisted calls - Europe, Algeria, Libya, Morocco, Tunisia and Turkey
009	Operator assisted calls - domestic (Spain)
025*	directory enquiries - international
091	**Police (national)**
092	**Police (local)**
093*	time
094	local weather (general weather for Spain can be obtained by dialling 91-532 69 40)
095*	news (RNE)
096*	automatic alarm call (*aviso y despertador*)
097*	sports information (*información deportiva*)
098*	miscellaneous information (*información diversas*)
099*	manual alarm call (*servicio despertador a través de operadora*)

*   Calls to these numbers cost from 8 to 30 units (one unit or *paso* costs 5.7 ptas).

TELEGRAMS, TELEX & FACSIMILE

Telegrams (*telegramas*), telexes and faxes can be sent from any post office in Spain. Main post offices have a separate 'telegram and telex' desk or window (*Telegram y Telex Burofax*) often with a telex and fax cabin (*Cabina Telex/Burofax*). Note that business hours for these services may be restricted. Telegrams can also be sent from a private telephone (the number is listed under *telegramas por teléfono* in your local telephone directory), but don't expect the telephone operator to speak English or other foreign languages. To avoid mistakes when sending telegrams or spelling words on the telephone, use the phonetic table of code names for individual letters (shown on page 127).

Telegrams: The cost of sending a domestic telegram is 9 ptas per word with a minimum charge (*percep. fija*) of 313 ptas for home delivery (*domicilio*) or 157 ptas for collection from a post office (*no domicilio*). Telegrams to European addresses (*continental*) cost 49 ptas for ordinary (*ordinario*) telegrams and 98 ptas per word for urgent (*urgente*) telegrams with a minimum charge of 1,512 or 3,024 ptas respectively. European telegrams include all European countries plus Algeria, Egypt, Israel, Jordan, Lebanon, Libya, Morocco, Syria, Tunisia and Turkey. There's no minimum charge for telegrams to intercontinental destinations, but they must contain a minimum of seven words at 162 ptas per word for ordinary telegrams and 324 ptas per word for urgent telegrams. You can also send radio telegrams from Spain.

Fax: There has been a huge increase in the use of fax (facsimile) machines in Spain during the last five years, helped by lower prices, the proliferation of international callback companies (see page 132), and the unreliability of the Spanish post office (a fax machine is handy for sending and receiving letters, etc.). They can be purchased from Telefónica and purchased or rented from telephone and business equipment retailers (shop around and compare prices). If you're planning to take a fax machine with you to Spain, check that it will work there or that it can be modified. Most fax machines made for other European countries will operate in Spain, although getting them repaired locally may be impossible unless the same machine is sold in Spain. A TeleAdapt fax connector is available that remedies the incompatibility problem of foreign (e.g. British) fax machines when they are connected to the telephone system in Spain. For information contact TeleAdapt Ltd., The Technology Park, Colindeep Lane, London NW9 6TA, UK (tel. 0181-233 3000).

Public fax services (*Burofax*) are provided by main post offices in most towns, from where you can send and receive faxes (you can also have them delivered to your home). Telexes and faxes can also be sent from major hotels, business offices (providing 'business services') and newsagents (*papelerías*), which may be cheaper than using a post office and is certainly simpler (note, however, that some levy high charges). The cost of receiving faxes at private offices is usually around 100 ptas a page. The telex number of any Spanish company can be obtained via a directory (*Lista Oficial de Abonados al Servicio Telex*) available at main post offices. **Beware of bogus fax bills purporting to be from Telefónica. This is a Europe-wide scam and often includes 'the right to inclusion in an annual directory of fax owners'. The giveaway is the address, which is usually abroad!**

Telex: A dedicated telex line costs 22,680 ptas for the connection and a 7.020 ptas monthly line rental fee. Telexes cost 38 ptas per minute within Spain and 65 ptas per minute within Europe. Telexes can be sent via post offices and from major hotels and business offices (providing 'business services').

8.

TELEVISION & RADIO

Spanish television isn't renowned for its quality, although it has improved in recent years and is probably not much worse than the rubbish dished up in most other European countries. In addition to terrestrial TV, satellite TV reception is excellent in most areas of Spain and is particularly popular among the expatriate community (not that much of it's output is any better than Spanish TV). Cable TV isn't common in Spain compared with northern European countries, although it's expected to have between 2.5m and 5m subscribers by the year 2001. However, digital TV will soon be available in Spain which will allow hundreds of channels to be transmitted by satellite and cable. Spanish radio (including many expatriate stations) is generally excellent and the equal of most other European countries. The government still has a major stake in public TV and its policy towards independent broadcasters is far from neutral, which was highlighted by a dispute over TV soccer rights and digital TV.

The Spanish are avid TV viewers (over 90 per cent of Spanish homes have a colour TV) and according to surveys rate around fourth in Europe (after Portugal, the UK and Italy) in average viewing time per day, per head (around 3.5 hours). Some 90 per cent of Spaniards over the age of 14 watch TV every day and most get their news from the TV (only some 10 per cent of Spaniards buy a newspaper). Spain produces some of the worst TV in Europe, much of which is termed 'junk TV' (*telebasura*) by its critics, with sex and violence prominent even during children's viewing times. Like people in most countries, the Spanish complain endlessly about their TV. The most common complaints concern the endless diet of imbecile game shows; dreary talk shows; poorly-dubbed foreign programmes and films (the Spanish dub everything, even including foreign names, and show the words of songs sung in foreign languages, e.g. English, with subtitles); too much violence; amateur presentation; and a surfeit of advertising. The consolation is that there's no TV or radio licence in Spain (so at least the rubbish is 'free')!

TELEVISION

The standards for television reception in Spain **aren't the same as in some other countries**. Due to the differences in transmission standards, television sets and video recorders operating on the British (PAL-I), French (SECAM) or North American (NTSC) systems won't function in Spain. Spain (along with most other continental European countries) uses the PAL-BG standard. It's possible to buy a multi-standard European TV (and VCR) containing automatic circuitry that switches between different systems. Some multi-standard TVs also handle the North American NTSC standard and have an NTSC-in jack plug connection allowing you to play back American videos. A standard British, French or US TV won't work in Spain, although British TVs can be modified. The same goes for a 'foreign' video recorder, which won't operate with a Spanish TV unless the VCR is dual-standard. Some people opt for two TVs, one to receive Spanish TV programmes and another (i.e. SECAM or NTSC) to playback their favourite videos.

If you decide to buy a TV in Spain, you will find it advantageous to buy one with teletext, which apart from allowing you to display programme schedules, also provides a wealth of useful and interesting information. A portable colour TV can be purchased in Spain from around 20,000 ptas for a 36cm (14 inch) with remote control. A 55cm (21 inch) TV costs between 35,000 and 80,000 ptas depending on the make and features, and a 63cm (25 inch) model between 80,000 and 140,000 ptas. Nicam, a high quality, digital TV stereo sound system, is available in most areas of Spain.

It's possible to rent a TV, video recorder (VCR) or video camera in Spain, particularly in resort areas, although most rentals are intended for long-term visitors and holidaymakers rather than for residents. The fee for TV or VCR rental is around 3,500 ptas for the first week and 1,500 ptas for subsequent weeks, or 5,000 ptas for the first week and 2,500 ptas for subsequent weeks for both a TV and a VCR. Video cameras can be rented for around 4,500 ptas per day. There are usually special rates for long-term rentals, e.g. 4,000 ptas a month for a TV or VCR for a minimum rental period of four months. Note, however, that it's cheaper to buy a TV in the long term, as you can buy a small portable TV for around 20,000 ptas and could easily sell it for at least half this amount if it's no longer required. There's a deposit of from 10,000 to 15,000 ptas on all rentals. VAT (IVA) at 16 per cent must be added to all rates.

TV Stations

There has been a revolution in Spanish television (and radio) since the death of Franco in 1975 and the lifting of censorship in the 1980s, since when a number of new TV stations have been established. The introduction of commercial TV provided much needed competition for the state-run channels and has helped improve the choice, if not always the quality. Most areas of Spain receive five channels with a standard external aerial, although those with an in-house 'cable' system may receive 10 or more. Spanish TV consists of a surfeit of moronic game shows (the staple diet of popular TV, although it isn't obligatory to watch them), chat shows, football, basketball and bullfighting, although there are also excellent news programmes, documentaries, and wildlife and history programmes. Football reigns supreme in Spain, where TV companies pay a staggering sum to televise live football matches, which has had a significant effect on the restaurant trade (live matches are screened six nights a week). One thing you can be sure of, whatever is showing on one of the three main channels, a similar programme will be showing on the others (called counter-programming).

Soap operas (*culebrones*) such as *Hosta Royal Manzanares*, *La Casa de Los Líos*, *La Parodia Nacional* and *Médico de Familia* are hugely popular and regularly attract audiences of up to 20m. Other popular programmes include *Espejo Secreto* (candid camera), *Hoy es Posible* (magazine) and *Corazón, Corazón* (gossip). Popular current affairs programmes include *Informe Semanal* (TVE-1) and *Los Reporteros* (Canal Sur), and chat shows such as *¿Quién Sabe Donde?* (who knows where?) and *Lo Que Nesesitas Es Amor* (what you need is love) are also popular. Television news (Newscasters and presenters are well-known personalities), both domestic and international, is comprehensive and upbeat and contains regular items about the arts (e.g. ballet or opera). There's generally no censorship on normal television and 'sexy' and risqué programmes are commonplace, particularly on Tele 5. Risqué programmes include *Discoteca de Verano* and *Su Media Naranja*, where couples are asked intimate questions (often leading to heated arguments). However, sometimes the programmers go too far and a new TV programme in 1997, *Esta Noche Sexo* (Sex Tonight), created a furore (Spain is still a staunchly Catholic country). The main Spanish TV stations are:

TVE: TVE (*Televisión Española*) was established as a state monopoly in 1956 and heavily censored under Franco. Despite the increased competition, TVE remains Spain's largest and most popular TV network (although the opposition is gaining ground), with its two channels TVE-1 and TVE-2 claiming around 30 per cent of viewers. TVE-1 places the emphasis on light entertainment such as game and chat shows, music shows, comedy, soap operas, children's shows, news and films. TVE-2 puts more emphasis on sports, live cultural broadcasts, regional shows, serials, documentaries and films. Not surprisingly, TVE-1 attracts around double the audience of TVE-2. Both TVE channels broadcast from 0800 until 0100 from Monday to Thursday and round the clock from Friday until Monday morning.

Antena 3 went on the air in January 1990. Its output consists of fairly conservative programming aimed at a family audience. Antena 3 shows better quality programmes than most stations and has around 25 per cent of the TV audience (not far behind TVE).

Telecinco (tele-5) claims to be Spain's entertainment channel and broadcasts popular children's programmes and American soaps. It specialises in soft porn, terrible game shows, and films saturated with ads (making watching them almost impossible).

Canal Plus is modeled on the French station of the same name (although they have no connection) and much of its output (particularly evening films) is scrambled. Many films are fairly recent and are often screened with the original soundtrack and Spanish subtitles. It also shows live sports events including a Spanish first division soccer match every Sunday evening (two hours after the kick-off of other matches being played) and an English Premiership soccer match on Saturday afternoons. It offers decoders to subscribers (over 600,000) for a refundable deposit of 9,000 ptas, a connection fee of 6,000 ptas plus a monthly subscription of 3,660 ptas (includes a monthly programme schedule). More expensive digital TV services are also provided.

Regional Stations: There are regional channels broadcasting in the local language in the Basque country, Catalonia, Galicia, and others in Andalusia, Madrid and Valencia. Most are controlled and sponsored by regional governments and serve as supplements to the national network (and most are deeply in debt). Some municipalities also have their own local stations.

Expatriate TV: Spain has a number of television stations for foreigners, for example Mediterranean International Television (MITV) and the Entertainment Channel on the Costa del Sol. MITV broadcasts on UHF band channel 51 (between Canal+ and TVE2) and can be received from Gibraltar to Fuengirola and further eastwards. On the Costa Blanca there's Mediterrania This Week. All these stations have limited viewing hours and programmes can be extremely amateurish. The Gibraltar television channel GBC (showing BBC programmes) can also be received in southern Spain, for which a decoder is necessary. However, there have been numerous complaints about poor reception and you're better off with satellite TV.

Scheduling of programmes in Spain can be extremely 'flexible', with programmes often being shown half an hour earlier or later than scheduled and sometimes not at all. Programme times published in the daily press vary from newspaper to newspaper and often don't agree with the actual broadcast times. Even news programmes don't start on time and some programmes are delayed by as much as an hour or cancelled with no apology or reason given. All Spanish TV channels carry advertising and there's a continuous battle for advertising revenue. Although advertising time has increased considerably in recent years, advertising revenue has decreased. Advertising is pervasive and there's even advertising during live sports events such as soccer matches (at the bottom of the screen) whenever the ball goes out of play (TV soccer is also obsessed with replays, which are often shown while play is continuing).

TV programmes are listed in all Spanish newspapers and in special TV guides such as *Tele-Indiscreta* (the best-selling publication in Spain). Some Spanish TV programmes are also listed in English-language newspapers and magazines, along with satellite TV programmes.

Satellite Television

Some 15 geostationary satellites are positioned over Europe, carrying hundreds of TV stations, broadcasting in a variety of languages. Although there are millions of homes with satellite dishes in Europe, Spain has a few hundred thousand only, mostly owned by expatriates. Although it wasn't the first in Europe (which was Eutelsat), the European satellite revolution took off with the launch of the Astra 1A satellite in 1988 (operated by the Luxembourg-based Sociéte Européenne des Satellites or SES), positioned 36,000km (22,300 miles) above the earth. TV addicts (easily recognised by their antennae and square eyes) are offered a huge choice of English and foreign-language stations which can be received throughout most of Spain with an 80cm (or smaller) dish and receiver (costing from around 50,000 ptas). Since 1988 three more Astra satellites have been launched, increasing the number of available channels to 64. An added bonus is the availability of foreign radio stations via satellite, including all the popular British Broadcasting Corporation (BBC) stations (see **Satellite Radio** on page 148).

The next revolution will be digital TV, which will dramatically increase the number of available channels, as 10 digital channels can be broadcast on the same satellite transponder which currently carries just one. Sky will eventually change over to digital and viewers will require a digital decoder, although there's likely to be a transition period of a few years during which programmes will be transmitted in analog for existing viewers. In the future it's expected that viewers will be able to receive TV stations from around the world via the Internet for the cost of a local phone call.

Astra Satellites: Among the many English-language stations available on Astra are Sky One and Two, Sky Movies Plus, Sky Movies Gold, Sky News, Sky Sports, UK Gold, the Movie Channel, Eurosport, CNN, NBC Superchannel, the Adult Channel, Lifestyle, The Children's Channel, The Disney Channel, Filmnet and Discovery. Other stations broadcast in Dutch, German, Japanese, Swedish and various Indian languages. There are a number of pan-European TV channels including European Business News, BBC World, CNN (Euronews), Eurosport, NBC Superchannel and MTV. Of these only Eurosport has a significant audience (around 13m a week). A few stations such as Eurosport are multi-language and viewers can select the soundtrack language, e.g. English, Dutch, German or Spanish. The signal from many stations is scrambled (the decoder may be built into the receiver) and viewers must pay a monthly subscription fee to receive programmes. You can buy pirate decoders for some channels. The best served by clear (unscrambled) stations are German-speakers (most German stations on Astra are clear).

Sky Television: Astra receivers contain a Videocrypt decoder and must pay a monthly subscription to receive any Sky stations except Sky News (which isn't scrambled). Various subscription packages are available costing from around 2,000 ptas to over 5,000 ptas a month for the premium package offering all movie channels plus Sky Sports. To receive scrambled channels such as Sky Movies Plus, Sky Movies Gold, the Movie Channel, the Adult Channel and Sky Sports, you need an address in Britain. Subscribers are sent a coded 'smart' card (similar to a credit card), which must be inserted in the decoder to switch it on (cards are periodically updated to thwart counterfeiters).

Sky won't send smart cards to overseas viewers as they have the copyright for a British-based audience only (overseas home owners need to obtain a card through a friend or relative in Britain or from a local satellite installation company). When you load your card into your decoder it may display a message asking you to phone Sky before they will activate your card. If this happens you should get a friend in the UK to call Sky after you have inserted your card in the decoder and tuned to Sky One. Give your friend in the UK your Sky card and contract numbers and if they are asked to do anything to the decoder they should simply say they are calling from the office. **There used to be a constant battle between TV companies such as Sky and the pirates, although in November 1995 Sky introduced new high-tech cards which immediately invalidated all pirate cards.** Since this time the market for pirate cards has died and it's now virtually impossible to obtain pirate Sky cards, which cost as much as genuine Sky cards. Sky produce new cards around every 12 to 18 months which invalidates all existing cards.

Eutelsat: Eutelsat (owned by a consortium of national telephone operators) was the first company to introduce satellite TV to Europe (in 1983) and it now runs a fleet of seven communications satellites carrying TV stations to over 50m homes. Until 1995 they broadcast primarily advertising-based, clear-access cable channels. However, following the launch in March 1995 of their Hot Bird 1 satellite (to be followed by two more over the next few years), Eutelsat is set to become a major competitor to Astra. The English-language stations on Eutelsat include Eurosport, Euronews, MTV, BBC World, European Business News, NBC Superchannel, Sci-Fi Channel and Worldnet. Other stations broadcast in Arabic, French, German, Italian, Polish, Spanish and Turkish.

BBC Worldwide Television: If you wish to receive the BBC satellite TV stations, BBC Prime (general entertainment) and BBC World (24-hour news and information) you need access to the Intelsat VI and Eutelsat II F1 satellites respectively. BBC Prime is encrypted and requires a D2-MAC decoder and a smartcard costing around 5,000 ptas and an annual 15,000 ptas subscription fee plus VAT (total around 20,000 ptas). Smartcards are available from TV Extra, PO Box 304, 59124 Motala, Sweden (tel. 46-141-56060). BBC World is clear (un-encrypted) and is financed by advertising revenue. For more information and a programming guide contact BBC Worldwide Television, Woodlands, 80 Wood Lane, London W12 0TT, UK (tel. 0181-576 2555). The BBC publish a monthly magazine, *BBC On Air*, containing comprehensive information about BBC Worldwide Television programmes (see page 148)

Equipment: A satellite receiver should have a built-in Videocrypt decoder (and others such as Eurocrypt, if required) and be capable of receiving satellite stereo radio. With a 1.2 or 1.5 metre motorised dish, you can receive hundreds of stations in a multitude of languages from around the world. If you wish to receive satellite TV on two or more TVs, you can buy a satellite system with two or more receptors. To receive stations from two or more satellites simultaneously, you need a motorised dish or a dish with a double feed antenna (dual LNBs). There are numerous satellite sales and installation companies in Spain, many of which advertise in the expatriate press. Shop around and compare prices. Alternatively you can import your own satellite dish and receiver and install it yourself. **Before buying a system, ensure that it can receive programmes from all existing and planned satellites.**

Location: To receive programmes from any satellite, there must be no obstacles between the satellite and your dish, i.e. no trees, buildings or mountains must obstruct the signal, so check before renting or buying a home. Before buying or erecting a satellite dish, check whether you need permission from your landlord or the local authorities. Some towns and buildings (such as apartment blocks) have strict laws concerning the positioning of antennae, although generally owners can mount a dish almost anywhere without receiving any complaints. Dishes can usually be mounted in a variety of unobtrusive positions and can be painted or patterned to blend in with the background.

Communities: Note that when an apartment or townhouse is advertised as having satellite television, it often means that it has a communal system and not its own satellite dish. Satellite stations are received via a communal satellite dish (or a number) and transmitted via cable to all properties in an urbanisation. Only a limited number of programmes are usually available and no scrambled programmes may be included. Only two English-language stations are currently unscrambled on Astra: Sky News and Eurosport, although some urbanisations pay to receive more.

Programme Guides: Many satellite stations provide teletext information and most broadcast in stereo. Sky satellite programme listings are provided in a number of British publications such as *What Satellite, Satellite Times* and *satellite TV* (the best), which are available on subscription. Satellite TV programmes are also listed in expatriate newspapers and magazines in Spain. The annual *World Radio and TV Handbook* (Billboard) contains over 600 pages of information and the frequencies of all radio and TV stations worldwide.

Videos

Video films are popular in Spain (some 4m homes have VCRs) and there are video rental shops in all towns, many of which also rent VCRs and TVs. Video films are expensive to buy in Spain and there's little available in English (Spanish video rental shops may have a few English-language titles only). However, there are English-language rental shops in main cities and resort areas, where English-language films can be rented from around 300 ptas a day. If you aren't a permanent resident with proof of your address, you usually need to pay a deposit, e.g. 5,000 ptas and show your passport. Rental costs can sometimes be reduced by paying a monthly membership fee or a lump sum in advance. If you have a large collection of SECAM or NTSC video tapes, you can buy a multi-standard TV and VCR, or have a separate TV and video to play back your favourite videos.

BBC Television has leapt on the profitable video bandwagon and produces three-hour videos of its best programmes (including entertainment, humour, sport, natural history, news and current affairs), available on subscription. For information write to Video World, Subscription Dept., 3-4 Hardwick Street, London EC1R 4RY, UK.

RADIO

Spanish radio was strictly controlled in the Franco era and censorship wasn't ended until 1978, since when there has been a huge growth in the number of stations. The Spanish are a nation of radio listeners and spend more time listening to the radio than they do watching TV (which is saying something). Spain has an estimated 35m radios (for 40m people) and radio has a regular average daily audience of 16m people (much higher than in most other European countries).

There are numerous high-quality, public and private, local, regional, national and foreign radio stations in Spain. Among the most popular national radio stations are SER, RNE (*Radio Nacional de España*, created under Franco in 1937), Antena 3 (the largest national network), COPE (*Cadena de Ondas Populares Españolas*, owned by the church and the second largest network of private stations) and Onda Cero. In the autonomous regions many stations broadcast in the local regional language. Most stations and networks broadcast on FM, rather than medium wave (there are no long-wave stations in Spain).

There's a wealth of excellent FM stations in the major cities and resort areas, although in remote rural areas you may be lucky to receive one or two FM stations clearly. Spain has many excellent music stations playing mainly American and British pop songs, although relaxing classical or 'easy listening' music is rare on Spanish radio. RNE 2 is one of the few stations to play classical music around the clock. As in all countries, Spanish radio stations plumb the depths to unearth their banal DJs, who babble on (and on) at a zillion words a minute in a secret language intelligible only to other DJs and teenagers (when you can understand Spanish DJs, you're ready to go native).

English & Other Expatriate Radio: There are English and other foreign-language commercial radio stations in major cities and resort areas (e.g. Radio Coastline and Onda Cero International on the Costa del Sol) where the emphasis is on music and chat with some news. Some expatriate stations broadcast in a variety of languages (not simultaneously) including English, Dutch, German and various Scandinavian languages at different times of the day. Unfortunately (or inevitably), expat radio tries to be all things to all men (and women) and not surprisingly falls short, particularly with regard to music, where it tries to cater for all tastes. However, it generally does a good job and is popular with senior citizens. The main drawback of expatriate radio (and all commercial radio) is its agonising, amateurish ads, which are obtrusive and repetitive, and make listening a chore. English-language radio programmes are published in the expatriate press in Spain (see page 389).

BBC: The BBC World Service is broadcast on short wave on several frequencies (e.g. short wave 12095, 9760, 9410, 7325, 6195, 5975 and 3955 Khz) simultaneously and you can usually receive a good signal on one of them. The signal strength varies depending on where you live in Spain, the time of day and year, the power and positioning of your receiver, and atmospheric conditions. The BBC World Service plus BBC Radio 1, 2, 3, 4 and 5 are also available on the Astra (Sky) satellite. For a free BBC World Service programme guide and frequency information write to BBC World Service, BBC Worldwide, PO Box 76, Bush House, Strand, London WC2B 4PH, UK (tel. 0181-752 5040). The BBC publish a monthly magazine, *BBC Worldwide*, containing comprehensive information about BBC world service radio and television programmes. It's available on subscription (from the above address) and from some newsagents in Spain.

Satellite Radio: If you have satellite TV, you will also be able to receive a wide range of satellite stereo radio stations if you have a stereo tuner or receiver. You can also receive digital radio via the Astra satellite with a DMX satellite receiver in conjunction with a Sky decoder connected to your hi-fi system. Ask a satellite expert for advice regarding equipment and installation. Satellite radio stations are listed in British magazines such as the *Satellite Times*. If you're interested in receiving radio stations from further afield, obtain a copy of the *World Radio TV Handbook* (Billboard).

9.

EDUCATION

Although Spain's state schools lag behind the best in Europe, the Spanish educational system has improved dramatically in the last few decades. Prior to the 1980s, there were insufficient places in state schools in many areas and parents who could afford it were forced to pay for private education (many children just didn't attend school). However, since those dark days the education budget has increased considerably (although still one of the lowest in the EU as a percentage of total public spending) and education is compulsory for all children aged between 6 and 16. The Spanish take education very seriously and have a deep respect and thirst for learning that isn't found in many other countries. In the highly competitive labour market of the 1990s, both parents and students are acutely aware that academic qualifications and training are of vital importance to obtain a good job.

Spain's state-funded school system (*escuela pública*) is supported by a comprehensive network of private schools (*escuelas privadas*), including many foreign and international schools. Around one third of Spain's schoolchildren attend private schools, most of which are co-educational day schools. Education in Spain is almost exclusively co-educational and is entirely free, from nursery school through to university (and includes the children of foreign residents). Over 90 per cent of children aged four or five attend nursery school and over 55 per cent of students remain in full-time education until they are 18, with around 25 per cent going on to vocational training and 30 per cent to university. Education standards at Spain's finest universities are comparable with the best in Europe, although they are generally extremely overcrowded. Families who can afford it often send their children to foreign universities, particularly American universities, where courses are shorter and more flexible than in Spain.

Critics of the Spanish education system complain that its teaching methods are too traditional and unimaginative, with the emphasis on learning by rote. It has also been plagued by poor teacher training, badly motivated and poorly paid teachers, and a high student failure rate, although all have improved in the last decade. One of the main criticisms voiced is that children and parents must make an irrevocable choice between an academic or vocational career at age 14, which many consider is too young. This will be changed to 16 under the *Ley Orgánica de Ordenación General del Sistema Educativo (LOGSE)* reforms currently being introduced. At present the average number of years schooling is lower in Spain than in many other European countries.

Generally the younger a child is when he enters the Spanish system, the easier he will cope. Conversely the older he is, the more problems he will have adjusting, particularly as the school curriculum is more demanding. Teenagers in particular often have considerable problems learning Spanish and adjusting to Spanish school life. Many foreign parents prefer to educate younger children in Spanish nursery and primary schools, where they quickly learn Spanish, and to send children of secondary school age to a private school. For many children the experience of schooling and living in a foreign land is a stimulating change and a challenge they relish, and it offers invaluable cultural and educational experiences. Children become 'world' citizens and are less likely to be prejudiced against foreigners and foreign ideas. This is particularly true when they attend an international school with pupils from different countries, although many state schools also have pupils from a number of countries and backgrounds, particularly in some resort towns on the *costas*. Before making major decisions about your children's future education, it's important to consider their ability, character and individual requirements.

Spain's educational system underwent profound (and long overdue) reforms in the 1980s and early 1990s, during which period it was in a constant state of development. Most changes were necessary, although some have been controversial and haven't met with universal support from parents and teaching staff. The most contentious reforms were those instituted under the *Ley Orgánica del Derecho a la Educación (LODE)*), which prompted fierce opposition from the church and demonstrations by middle class parents, whose privileged position was threatened. LODE has made education in Spain more egalitarian and accessible and was one of the most important laws introduced by the Socialists during their first term in office. Other important reforms include the 'Fundamental Law for the General Organisation of the Education System' (*Ley Organica de Ordención del Sistema Educativo/LOGSE*) passed on 3rd October 1990, which won't be fully implemented until the year 2000. LOGSE contains a complete reorganisation of state education, introduces a new compulsory secondary education (CSE), modifies the school curriculum and makes important changes in vocational education.

Information about Spanish schools, both state and private, can be obtained from Spanish embassies and consulates abroad, and from foreign embassies, educational organisations and government departments in Spain. Information about local schools can be obtained from town halls (*ayuntamientos*). The Ministry of Education and Science (*Ministerio de Educación y Ciencia*) provides a general information service at their central office: *Servicio de Información*, Iniciativas y Reclamaciones, C/Alcalá, 34, 28014 Madrid (tel. (91) 532 1300). The autonomous regions also have their own education offices in regional capitals.

In addition to a detailed look at the Spanish state school system and private schools, this chapter also contains information about higher education and language schools.

STATE OR PRIVATE SCHOOL ?

If you're able to choose between state and private education, the following checklist will help you decide:

- How long are you planning to stay in Spain? If you're uncertain, then it's best to assume a long stay. Due to language and other integration problems, enrolling children in Spanish state schools is advisable for a minimum of one or two years only, particularly for teenage children who aren't fluent in Spanish.

- Bear in mind that the area where you choose to live will affect your choice of school(s). For example it's usually necessary to send your child to a state school near your home and if you choose a private day school, you must take into account the distance and travelling time from your home to the school.

- Do you know where you're going when you leave Spain? This may be an important consideration with regard to your child's language of tuition and system of education in Spain. How old is your child and what age will he be when you plan to leave Spain? What future plans do you have for his education and in which country?

- What educational level is your child at now and how will he fit into a private school or the Spanish state school system? The younger he is, the easier it will be to place him in a suitable school.

- How does your child view the thought of studying in Spanish? What language is best from a long-term point of view? Is schooling available in Spain in his mother tongue?

- Will your child require your help with his studies, and more importantly, will you be able to help him, particularly with his Spanish?

- Is special or extra tutoring available in Spanish or other subjects, if necessary?

- What are the school hours? What are the school holiday periods? How will the school holidays and hours affect your and your family's work and leisure activities?
- Is religion an important aspect in your choice of school? Religion is no longer a mandatory subject in Spanish schools.
- Do you want your child to go to a co-educational or a single-sex school? Spanish state schools are usually co-educational.
- Should you send your child to a boarding school? If so, in which country?
- What are the secondary and further education prospects in Spain or another country? Are Spanish examinations or the examinations set by prospective schools in Spain recognised in your home country or the country where you plan to live after leaving Spain? If applicable, check whether the Spanish *bachillerato* examination (see page 160) is recognised as a university entrance qualification in your home country.
- Does a prospective school have a good academic record? Most schools provide exam pass rate statistics.
- How large are the classes? What is the pupil-teacher ratio? The legal maximum size of classes in state schools is 40 pupils, which is much larger than in private schools.

Obtain the opinions and advice of others who have been faced with the same decisions and problems as yourself, and collect as much information from as many different sources as possible before making a decision. Speak to students, teachers and the parents of children attending the schools on your short list. Finally, you should discuss all the alternatives with your child before making a decision. See also **Choosing a Private School** on page 162.

STATE SCHOOLS

Although state-funded schools are termed public schools (*escuelas públicas*) in Spain, the term 'state' has been used in preference to public in this book. This is to prevent confusion with the term 'public school', used in the USA to refer to a state school, but which in Britain refers to a private fee-paying school. The state school system in Spain differs considerably from the school systems in, for example, Britain and the USA, particularly regarding secondary education.

Spain's state schools have undergone profound changes in the last decade and standards, which were low, are now the equal of those in most of the rest of Europe. State education is the responsibility of the Ministry of Education and Science (*Ministerio de Educación y Ciencia*), although authority can be delegated to regional governments. Of the 17 autonomous regions, seven (Andalusia, the Basque Lands, the Canary Islands, Catalonia, Galicia, Navarre and Valencia) have responsibility for their own education system (including higher education). State education is free but parents must usually pay for school books (which are expensive, although they are provided free in certain cases), school supplies, and extra-curricular activities such as sports and arts and crafts. Pupils usually go to local village (*pueblo*) nursery and primary schools, although attending secondary school may entail travelling long distances (buses are provided).

For most Spanish children, school starts with nursery or pre-school (*preescolar*) at the age of 4 or 5. Compulsory education (*escolaridad obligatoria*), termed the basic general education (*Educación General Básica/EGB*), begins at six years of age in a primary school (*escuela primaria*) and lasts for eight years. At the age of 14 (equivalent to eighth grade) pupils receive a school-leaving certificate, which determines the course of their future education. Those with high marks are awarded a *título de graduado escolar* certificate and attend a higher secondary school to study for their baccalaureate (*bachillerato*). Less academically-gifted pupils are awarded a school certificate (*certificado de escolaridad*) and attend a vocational school (*formación profesional*) providing specialised training for a specific career (see page 159).

A general criticism of Spanish state schools made by many foreigners is the lack of extracurricular activities such as sport, music, drama, and arts and crafts. State schools don't have school clubs or sports teams and if children want to do team sports they must usually join a local club. However, although not part of the curriculum, sports and other activities are generally organised through parents' and sports associations. Fees are low and activities usually take place directly after school.

Attending a state school helps children integrate into the local community and learn the local language, and is highly recommended if you plan to remain in Spain indefinitely. Although it may not appeal initially, given the choice many foreign children prefer to attend Spanish school and become part of the local community. Note that while it's fairly easy to switch from a state school to a private school, the reverse isn't true. If you need to move a child from a private school to a state school (e.g. due to financial reasons), it can be difficult for a child to adjust, particularly a teenager. Having made the decision to send a child to a state school, you should stick to it for at least a year to give it a fair trial. It may take your child this long to fully adapt to a new language, the change of environment and the different curriculum.

There are also special state schools in Spain for pupils with special education needs, e.g. learning difficulties due to psychological, emotional or behavioural problems and slow learners. However, pupils are taught in special education units or schools only when their needs cannot be catered for in a mainstream school.

Language

There are many considerations to take into account when choosing an appropriate school in Spain, not least the language of study. The only schools in Spain using English as the teaching language are foreign and international private schools. A number of multilingual international schools also teach pupils in both English and Spanish. If your children attend any other school, they must study all subjects in Spanish. For most children, studying in Spanish isn't such a handicap as it may appear at first, particularly for those aged below ten. The majority of children adapt quickly to a new language and most become reasonably fluent within three to six months (if only it was so easy for adults!). However, all children don't adapt equally well to a change of language and culture, particularly children aged over 10 (at around 10 years of age children begin to learn languages more slowly), many of whom have great difficulties during their first year. Children who are already bilingual, such as Dutch and Scandinavian children, usually have little problem learning Spanish, while American and British children tend to find it more difficult. Spanish children are generally friendly towards foreign children, who often acquire a 'celebrity status' (particularly in rural schools) which helps their integration.

Some state schools provide intensive Spanish lessons ('bridging classes') for foreign children, although this depends on the school and the province or region. It may be worthwhile inquiring about the availability of extra Spanish classes before choosing where to live. Foreign children are tested and put into a class suited to their level of Spanish, even if this means being taught with younger children. Children who don't read and write Spanish are often set back a year to compensate for their lack of Spanish and different academic background. Once a child has acquired a sufficient knowledge of spoken and written Spanish he's assigned to a class appropriate to his age.

If your local school doesn't provide extra Spanish classes, your only choice will be to pay for private lessons or send your children to another (possibly private) school, where extra Spanish tuition is provided. Some parents send children to an English-speaking school for a year, followed by a move to a bilingual or Spanish school, while other parents believe it's better to throw their children in at the deep end, rather than introduce them gradually. It all depends on the character, ability and wishes of each child. Whatever you decide, it will help your children enormously if they have intensive Spanish lessons before arriving in Spain.

An added problem in some regions is that state schools teach most lessons in a regional language such as Basque, Catalan and Galician, although parents may be offered a choice of teaching language. Learning a regional language can be a huge problem, not only for foreign children but also for Spanish-speaking children. However, immersion courses in the local language are usually offered to Spanish-speaking children. If you live in an area where education is dominated by a regional language, you may need to consider educating your child in a private school. For example in Catalonia children aged between three and eight are taught in Catalan only. After the age of nine they are taught Spanish for an average of three hours a week only, which is the same amount of time allocated to foreign languages. As a consequence, Spanish speakers in Catalonia (totalling around one third of residents) now feel 'culturally persecuted' in the same way that Catalans were under Franco when the Catalan language was banned. This discrimination is contrary to EU law and many believe it doesn't represent the bilingual and tolerant character of the Catalonian people, and may actually be contrary to the best interests of its children.

See also **Language** on page 44 and **Language Schools** on page 166.

Enrolment

Enrolment in a Spanish school requires an interview and in rare cases an examination. New arrivals in Spain must have their children's education record officially verified through a process known as homologation (*homologación*) or convalidation. This is an expensive and lengthy process involving the confirmation of credits and marks for each year of schooling. It can be *very* expensive, e.g. 50,000 to 200,000 ptas, depending on the number of years to be convalidated. In some countries there may be only one 'public notary' (*notario público*) authorised to carry out the necessary work and consequently he usually charges the earth. Without the necessary paperwork a child won't be accepted at a state school, irrespective of his qualifications (foreign qualifications such as the British GCSE aren't recognised in Spain). If possible, this process should be completed before arriving in Spain, as a child may not be accepted at a school until the official papers (confirming convalidation) have been received and stamped by the Spanish Department of Education.

In Spain, children must attend a state school within a certain distance of their home, so if you have a preference for a particular school, it's important to buy or rent a home within that school's catchment area. Town halls and provincial Ministry of Education offices can provide a list of local schools at all levels. To enrol a child in a Spanish school you must provide your town hall with the following documents:

- your child's birth certificate or passport, with an official Spanish translation (if necessary);
- proof of immunisation;
- proof of residence in the form of an electricity or telephone bill in your name. If you don't have any bills (lucky you!) a rent receipt, lease or proof of ownership (*escritura*) is acceptable.
- proof of convalidation (see above);
- a passport-size photograph (for a student ID card) for a child entering secondary school.

School Hours & Holidays

The academic year in Spain runs from the first week in September to the end of June, with the main holidays at Christmas, Easter and the long summer break. School hours vary depending on the particular school and are usually from 0900 until 1600 with a one hour break for lunch, although an increasing number of schools don't have a lunch break and finish classes for the day at 1400. Lessons are usually divided into teaching periods of 45 minutes. Some schools offer school lunches, although many children bring a packed lunch or go home for lunch if they live nearby. Most schools provide a subsidised bus service to take children to and from their homes in outlying regions. State schools and communities usually provide an after school nursery (*guardería*) for working mothers.

Spanish school children have long school holidays (*vacaciones escolares*) compared with many other countries. School terms are fixed and are generally the same throughout the country, although they may be modified in autonomous regions to take account of local circumstances and special events (such as local fiestas). The school year is made up of three terms, each averaging around 11 weeks. The following table shows the main school holidays for the 1997 school year (all dates inclusive):

Holiday	Dates
Christmas and New Year (*Navidad y Año Nuevo*)	23rd December to 8th January
Spring (*primavera*)	3rd to 13th April
Summer (*verano*)	20th June to 5th September

Schools are also closed on public holidays when they fall within term time. Pupils transferring from primary to secondary school are given an additional two weeks summer holiday, which usually includes an 'end of school' trip (*viaje de estudios*) with their fellow pupils. School holiday dates are published by schools and local communities well in advance, thus allowing parents plenty of time to schedule family holidays during the school holidays. Normally you aren't permitted to withdraw a child from classes during the school term except for visits to a doctor or dentist, when the teacher should be informed in advance.

Pre-School

Spain has a long tradition of state-funded pre-school (*preescuelar*), with over 90 per cent of children aged four or five attending for at least one year before starting compulsory schooling. The term pre-school embraces play school, nursery school (*guardería*), kindergarten (*jardín de la infancia*) and infant school (*escuela infantil*). Under the LOGSE reforms, pre-school education is divided into two cycles; cycle one (*ciclo 1º*) for ages one to three and cycle two (*ciclo 2º*) for ages four to six. Attendance is voluntary and free in public centres in many areas. Note, however, that the provision of public and private pre-school facilities varies considerably depending on the town and the region, particularly regarding state schools. In addition to state-funded schools, there are also many private fee-paying nursery schools, usually taking children aged from two to six, some of which are an integral part of a larger primary school. Arrangements are generally flexible and parents can choose attendance during mornings or afternoons, all day, or on selected days only. Many schools provide transport to and from homes. Fees are generally low and schools are popular, well organised and good value for money.

Note that some nursery schools are more nurseries than schools and are simply an inexpensive way for parents to obtain supervised childcare. The best pre-schools are designed to introduce children to the social environment of school and concentrate on the basic skills of coordination, encouraging the development of self-awareness and providing an introduction to group activities. Exercises include arts and crafts (e.g. drawing, painting and pottery), music, dancing, educational games, perceptual motor activities and listening skills. Children are also taken on outings and it's common to see groups of small children 'roped' together for their own protection being shepherded by a teacher. During the final years of nursery school, the rudiments of reading, writing and arithmetic are taught in preparation for primary school. Note that by the year 2000 there are plans to teach English from the age of three or four in state schools in the regions where Madrid still controls education.

Nursery school is highly recommended, particularly if your children are going to continue with a state education. After one or two years of nursery school they will be integrated into the local community and will have learnt Spanish in preparation for primary school. Research (in many countries) has shown that children who don't attend pre-school are at a distinct disadvantage when they start primary school.

Primary School

Compulsory education (*escolaridad obligatoria*), termed the basic general education (*Educacion General Básica/EGB*), begins at age six in a primary school (*escuela primaria*) and lasts for eight years. Primary school is split into three cycles: *ciclo inicial/1º* (years 1-2), *ciclo medio/2º* (years 3-5) and *ciclo superior/3er* (years 6-8). Under the new LOGSE reforms (see page 152), primary education will end at age 12. There will still be three cycles, although the second and third cycles will each consist of two instead of three years (3-4 and 5-6 respectively).

The primary curriculum includes natural and social sciences; Spanish and an autonomous language (if applicable); literature; mathematics; religion; arts; physical education; and a foreign language (usually English or French), which is compulsory from the second cycle. In most schools pupils have five evaluations (*evaluaciones*) each year and exams at the end of each cycle. If a child fails to achieve the required standard set for a particular cycle, he may be required to repeat the previous year unless he can pass a further exam in the autumn (many private and state schools offer 'recovery' classes during the summer holidays to help pupils catch up). The opinion of the teachers, tutors, inspectors and the sector's psychological and pedagogical team are taken into account when deciding whether a pupil must repeat a year. Pupils aren't required to repeat more than one year during their primary education.

On completion of their last year of primary school before the age of 14, pupils undergo a selection process that determines the course of their future schooling and career possibilities (one of the most criticised features of the Spanish educational system). Pupils with high marks receive a *título de graduado escolar*, which is a prerequisite to attending a higher secondary school to study for the baccalaureate (*bachillerato*) examination. Pupils who don't earn the *título* are awarded a *certificado de escolaridad* which qualifies them to undergo a two-year vocational training course at a vocational training establishment (*Centro de Formación Profesional*).

Secondary School

Under the LOGSE educational reforms (see page 152), a new educational stage called Compulsory Secondary Education (*Enseñanza Secundaria Obligatoria/ESO*) has been created for pupils aged from 12 to 16, which completes their compulsory education. It provides pupils with more specialised training than previously and prepares them for the baccalaureate (*bachillerato*) or vocational training. The four years of compulsory secondary school are divided into two two-year cycles, with the curriculum containing both compulsory and optional subjects. Compulsory subjects during the first cycle (*ciclo 1er*) include natural and social sciences; history and geography; physical education; plastic and visual arts; Spanish and an autonomous community language (if applicable); literature; mathematics; Catholic religion (or study periods for non-Catholics); music; technology; and foreign languages. During the last year of the first cycle, pupils must choose two optional subjects from natural sciences; plastic and visual arts; music; and technology. A second foreign language, classical culture and other optional subjects can be studied for at least one year during the second cycle (*ciclo 2°*).

As with primary education, a pupil can be required to repeat a year. Upon completion of CSE, pupils who have achieved the set standards are awarded a 'graduate of secondary education' (*graduado en educación secundaria*) certificate enabling them to study for the baccalaureate or undergo specialised intermediate-grade vocational training. All pupils, whether or not they have achieved the course objectives, receive a document stating the school years completed, the marks obtained in each subject, and recommendations regarding their academic and vocational future.

As with a primary school, the secondary school that a child may attend is largely determined by where he lives. In some rural areas there's little or no choice of schools, while in Madrid and other cities there are usually a number of possibilities. Naturally the schools with the best reputations and exam results are the most popular, and are therefore the most difficult to which to gain acceptance. Parents should plan well ahead, particularly if they wish their child to be accepted at a superior school.

Vocational Training

Vocational training (*formación profesional/FP*) has traditionally been reserved for less academically-gifted pupils who failed to achieve the standards required to study for the baccalaureate (*Bachillerato Unificado y Polivalente/BUP*). Vocational training consists of two two-year phases, the first of which is compulsory for pupils who don't study for the BUP. The first phase of FP (*primero grado* or FP1) provides a general introduction to a career such as clerical work, electronics or hairdressing, while the second FP2 phase (*segundo grado*) provides specialised vocational training. FP2 pupils divide their time between school studies and practical on-the-job training in commerce or industry. Vocational training is free for most pupils, whether training takes place in a public centre or a private institution financed by the state. Vocational training courses have a strong practical emphasis and accept pupils from the age of 14 (16 under LOGSE).

Upon completion of the new CSE programme (see above), pupils who have been awarded a *graduado en educación secundaria* certificate can choose specialised intermediate-grade vocational training rather than study for the baccalaureate. In the past, around two thirds of pupils took the BUP and one third the FP course, although as vocational training has become more important in Spain's fiercely competitive job market, the number taking the FP course has increased.

One of the main problems with the FP1 course has been the high ratio of dropouts and the low value placed on the FP1 certificate by employers. Pupils who complete the FP2 course receive a 'technical specialist' (*técnico especialista*) certificate, which has more value in the job market. One of the most important LOGSE reforms concerns vocational training, which is of vital importance to Spain's economic future. At present there's little interaction between educational establishments and the labour market, and vocational training has long been discredited as only for those who aren't bright enough to pursue an academic career. Under LOGSE, new higher-grade vocational training courses will be introduced, enabling successful pupils to take specialist baccalaureate courses and proceed to higher education.

The Baccalaureate

The Spanish baccalaureate (*Bachillerato Unificado y Polivalente/BUP*) provides pupils with three years academic training to prepare them for higher education, specialised higher-grade vocational training or to start a career. The first and second years are divided equally between the natural sciences, mathematics, languages and the humanities; in the third year pupils take optional specialist subjects. Under LOGSE reforms the compulsory core subjects are Spanish; an autonomous regional language (if applicable); literature; a foreign language; history; philosophy; and physical education. Four broad specialities are established in the arts, natural sciences, technology, and the humanities and social sciences. Some subjects are obligatory in order to follow certain higher-grade vocational training and university courses.

Successful pupils who fail no more than two subjects in their final examinations are awarded the *título de bachiller* (called simply *bachiller*). The *bachiller* permits entrance to a one-year pre-university course (*Curso de Orientacíon Universitaria/COU*) or the second stage of vocational training (see above). Pupils must pass an entrance examination in all subjects to undertake a COU course or vocational training at the second level. Pupils who fail the *bachillerato* are awarded a certificate of attendance and can proceed to vocational training. The *bachillerato* is recognised as an entrance qualification by universities throughout the world, providing the student's language proficiency in the language of study is up to the required standard.

PRIVATE SCHOOLS

There's a wide range of private schools (*escuelas privadas*) in Spain including parochial (mostly Catholic) schools, bilingual schools, international schools and a variety of foreign schools, including American and British schools. Together they educate around a third of all children. Most private schools in Spain are co-educational, Catholic day schools, although a number of schools (including some American and British schools) take weekly or term boarders. Like state schools, most private schools operate a five-day Monday to Friday timetable, with no Saturday morning classes. Private schools in Spain teach a variety of syllabi, including the British GCSE and A level examinations, the American High School Diploma and college entrance examinations (e.g. ACT, SAT, achievement tests and AP exams), the International Baccalaureate (IB) and the Spanish *bachillerato*.

Most Spanish private schools, i.e. schools teaching wholly in Spanish, are state-subsidised and follow the Spanish state-school curriculum. Some international schools are also subsidised and follow a totally bi-lingual (English/Spanish) curriculum and are authorised to accept Spanish pupils. They must teach the Spanish curriculum including the *Educación General Basica (EGB), Bachillerato Unificado y Polivalente (BUP), Curso de Orientacíon Universitaria (COU)* and the *selectividad* (university entrance examination). They provide the opportunity for children to become completely bilingual and to choose between a Spanish and English-language university or career. To receive state subsidies and accept Spanish pupils, 25 per cent of a school's total number of pupils must be Spanish and at least 20 per cent in each class. As a condition of receiving government funding, schools with Spanish pupils are subject to inspection by the Spanish school authorities. Many international private schools have mixed Spanish and foreign student bodies, e.g. one third American or British students, one third Spanish and one third other nationalities, although the they may be called American or British.

Private school fees in Spain vary considerably depending on, among other things, the quality, reputation and location of a school, and are low compared to the cost of private education in northern Europe and North America. Not surprisingly, schools located in Madrid and Barcelona are among the most expensive. Fees at subsidised Spanish schools are around 75,000 ptas a year, whereas fees at independent foreign schools range from around 250,000 ptas a year to well over 1m ptas a year at senior schools (particularly for boarders). Fees don't usually include registration, books, materials, laundry, insurance, extra-curricular activities, excursions, meals and transport (most private schools provide school buses). You should allow around 100,000 a term for meals and other extras. Most private schools subscribe to insurance schemes covering accidents both in school and during school-sponsored activities. Some schools award scholarships and offer grants to help parents pay fees, depending on their financial circumstances.

Your choice of foreign schools will depend on where you live in Spain. There's a good choice of English-speaking schools (accepting children aged from 3 to 18) in Madrid, Barcelona, Palma de Mallorca, Tenerife and on the *costas*. For example there are British schools in Alicante, Barcelona, Cadiz, Fuengirola, Lanzarote, Las Palmas, Madrid, Palma de Mallorca, Marbella, Tenerife, Torremolinos and Valencia. In other cities and areas there may be one English-speaking school only or none at all. In addition to American and British schools there are also French, German, Swedish and other foreign-language schools in Spain. Under Spanish law, all foreign schools must be approved by their country's embassy in Spain.

Private foreign and international schools have smaller classes and a more relaxed, less rigid regime and curriculum than Spanish state schools. They provide a more varied and international approach to sport, culture and art, and a wider choice of academic subjects. Many also provide English-language summer school programmes combining academic lessons with sports, arts and crafts, and other extra-curricular activities. Their aim is the development of a child as an individual and the encouragement of his unique talents, rather than teaching on a production-line system. This is made possible by small classes allowing teachers to provide pupils with individually tailored lessons and tuition. The results are self-evident and many private secondary schools have a near 100 per cent university placement rate. On the other hand, one of the major problems of private foreign-language education in Spain is that children can grow up in cultural 'ghettos' and be illiterate as far as the Spanish language and culture are concerned. Although attending a private school may be advantageous from an academic viewpoint, integration into Spanish society can be severely restricted.

You should make applications to private schools as far in advance as possible, as some international schools have waiting lists for places. You're usually requested to send school reports, exam results and other records. Before enrolling your child in a private school, make sure that you understand the withdrawal conditions in the school contract. It's advisable to check whether a school is recognised by the Spanish education authorities and whether it belongs to an accredited organisation. Most British schools in Spain belong to the National Association of British Schools in Spain (NABS), whose members are visited and approved by British school inspectors. Advice about British English-language schools in Spain can be obtained from the British Council, C/Almagro, 5, 28010 Madrid (tel. (91) 337 3500). For information about American schools in Spain, write to the *Instituto de Cooperación Ibero-americana*, Avenida de los Reyes Católicos 4, 28003 Madrid. Information is also obtainable from embassies in Spain.

Choosing a Private School

The following checklist is designed to help you choose an appropriate private school in Spain:

* Does the school have a good reputation? How long has it been established?

* Does the school have a good academic record? For example, what percentage of pupils obtain good examination passes and go on to good universities? All the best schools provide exam pass-rate statistics.

* What does the curriculum include? What examinations are set? Are examinations recognised both in Spain and internationally? Do they fit in with your future education plans? Ask to see a typical pupil's timetable to check the ratio of academic to non-academic subjects. Check the number of free study periods and whether they are supervised.

* How large are the classes and what is the pupil/teacher ratio? Does the stated class size tally with the number of desks in the classrooms?

* What are the classrooms like? For example their size, space, cleanliness, lighting, furniture and furnishings. Are there signs of creative teaching, e.g. wall charts, maps, posters and pupils' work on display.

* What are the qualification requirements for teachers? What nationalities are the majority of teachers? Ask for a list of the teaching staff and their qualifications.

- What is the teacher turnover? A high teacher turnover is a particularly bad sign and usually suggests poorly paid teachers or poor working conditions.

- What extras must you pay? For example, lunches, art supplies, sports equipment, excursions, clothing, health and accident insurance, text books and stationery. Some schools charge extra for every little thing.

- Which countries do most pupils come from?

- Is religion an important consideration in your choice of school?

- Are intensive English or Spanish lessons provided for children who don't meet the required standard?

- What standard and type of accommodation is provided? What is the quality and variety of food provided? What is the dining room like? Does the school have a dietician?

- What languages does the school teach as obligatory or optional subjects? Does the school have a language laboratory?

- What is the pupil turnover?

- What are the school terms and holiday periods? Private school holidays are usually longer than state schools (e.g. four weeks at Easter and Christmas and 10 weeks in the Summer) and they often don't coincide with state school holiday periods.

- If you're considering a day school, what are the school hours? Is transportation provided?

- What are the withdrawal conditions, should you need or wish to remove your child? A term's notice is usual.

- What sports instruction and facilities are provided? Where are the sports facilities located?

- What are the facilities for art and science subjects, for example arts and crafts, music, computer studies, biology, science, hobbies, drama, cookery and photography? Ask to see the classrooms, facilities, equipment and pupils' projects.

- What sort of excursions and supervised school holidays are organised?

- What medical facilities does the school provide, e.g. infirmary, resident doctor or nurse? Is medical and accident insurance included in the fees?

- What kinds of punishments are applied and for what offences?

- What reports are provided for parents and how often?

- **Last but not least (unless someone else is paying), what are the fees?**

Before making a final choice, it's important to visit the schools on your short list during term time and talk to teachers and pupils (if possible, also speak to former pupils and their parents). Where possible, check out the answers to the above questions in person and don't rely on a school's prospectus or director to provide the information. If you're unhappy with the answers, look elsewhere.

Finally, having made your choice, keep track of your child's progress and listen to his complaints. Compare notes with other parents. If something doesn't seem right, try to establish whether the complaint is founded or not, and if it is, take action to have the problem resolved. Never forget that you or your employer is paying a lot of money for your child's education and you should ensure that you receive good value. See also **State or Private School?** on page 153.

HIGHER EDUCATION

Spain has 36 universities (*universidades*), 32 state-run and 4 private universities run by the Catholic church. Spain also has a number of non-university higher education institutes for physical education, civil marine, tourism, dramatic art and dance, and song and music, plus a number of highly rated business schools (usually American). Although few Spanish universities are world-renowned, Spain has a long history of university education, with the university system dating back to the middle ages and the oldest university (Salamanca) founded in 1218 (prior to which, the Moors had 'universities' in Spain long before anyone else had even thought of them). The largest and most highly regarded Spanish universities are Complutense in Madrid and Central in Barcelona, with student bodies of around 90,000 and 70,000 respectively.

The number of university students in Spain exploded in the 1960s and 1970s and today numbers over a million, a figure generally considered to be too high for a country with a population of 40m. Overcrowding is a huge problem, particularly in first year classes (you usually need to arrive early just to get a seat at a lecture). However, many students drop out after the tough exams set at the end of the first year. The number of female students has increased by around 40 per cent in the last decade and they now outnumber male students (more women also complete their courses and obtain degrees than men). Foreign students comprise only some 3 per cent of students at Spanish universities, with a third coming from EU countries. In general, the academic year runs from October to June.

There are four different types of university establishments in Spain: **university schools** (*escuelas universitarias*) where 'short-term' three-year courses are offered; **university colleges** (*colegios universitarios*) where the first three years of study leading to a *licenciado* is completed; **faculties** (*facultades*) where long-term courses are offered in all academic disciplines (except technical courses); and **higher technical schools of engineering and architecture** (*escuela superior de ingeniería y arquitectura*) where long-term technical courses are completed. The Spanish university system is rigidly structured and students must choose a fixed curriculum and aren't permitted to change universities during their studies (except for family or health reasons).

Studies at Spanish universities are divided into three cycles. The first cycle or three-year diploma is termed a *diplomado* or *licenciado*, depending on the type of college and the course. Students who complete a three-year vocational course (e.g. for teachers and nurses) at an *escuela universitaria* are awarded a *diploma*, which is much less highly regarded than a purely academic course (although this is changing as more students choose vocational courses). Twice as many students take academic as vocational courses. A second cycle diploma is called a *licenciatura* or *tesina*, awarded after five or six years study at a *facultad*, and is equivalent to an American or British MA or MSc. An *ingeniero superior y arquitecto* degree is awarded after a five or six-year course of study at a higher technical school, the first three years of which may be completed at a *colegio universitario* (a university college affiliated to a university). The third cycle of studies is a PhD (doctorate) programme, which results in the academic title of *doctor* or *Doctor en Filosofía y Letras*.

Competition for places at Spanish universities is high as there are too few places for all the students wishing to attend. Spanish students must pass the Spanish *bachillerato* examination, successfully complete a one-year introductory course (*Curso de Orientación Universitaria/COU*) and pass an entrance examination (*selectividad* or *prueba de acceso a la Universidad*) before being accepted. Entrance examinations are usually set in July by individual universities, with results being announced in August.

EU nationals are entitled to compete for places at Spanish universities on equal terms with Spanish nationals, as are Spanish nationals in other EU countries. In addition, a percentage of places at most universities, e.g. 5 per cent, are allocated to foreign non-EU students. Applications must be submitted to universities and addressed to the student secretariat (*vice-rectorado de alumnos*). In general qualifications that are accepted as entry requirements in a student's home country are accepted in Spain. Spanish universities accept British A-levels as an entrance qualification, but an American high school diploma isn't usually accepted. American students must usually have spent two years at college or hold a BA, BBA or BSc degree. For information about the recognition of EU diplomas in Spain, contact the *Ministerio de Educación y Ciencia*, Subdirección General de Cooperación Internacional, Centro de Información sobre Reconocimiento de Títulos y Movilidad de Estudiantes, Paseo de Prado, 28, 4ª Planta, 28014 Madrid (tel. (91) 230 2000).

Students with foreign qualifications must have them approved by a process known as convalidation or homologation (*homologación*) by the Spanish Department of Education and Science in Spain or a Spanish embassy abroad. After this has been done they must usually take the university entrance examination for foreigners (*selectividad para extranjeros*). The National Open University holds this examination in Spanish embassies in some countries, particularly when a large number of applicants are involved. All foreign students require a thorough knowledge of Spanish, although preparatory courses are provided. **Note that in autonomous regions where there's a second official language (e.g. the Basque Country, Catalonia and Galicia), courses may be conducted in the local language.**

In most regions, university fees (*tasas*) are set by the Spanish Ministry of Education and Science. In autonomous regions with responsibility for their own education, fees are set annually by the university council and the local regional government. Private universities under the auspices of the Catholic church set their own fees. Grants and scholarships are available to Spanish and foreign students (around one in seven students receives a grant). Spanish university fees are low for residents and EU nationals, e.g. from 40,000 to 75,000 ptas a year, depending on the faculty and location. This may be an important consideration if you don't qualify for a grant and must pay for your own university education abroad. Note that a disadvantage of moving to Spain is that foreign children resident in Spain may be classified as overseas students by their home countries, making them no longer eligible for grants and possibly liable to pay fees (or higher fees). If you live permanently in Spain and plan to study in another EU country such as Britain, you aren't required to pay tuition fees, but won't be eligible for a living expenses grant.

Students should expect to pay 50,000 to 75,000 ptas a month for meals and accommodation. There's a huge difference in the cost of living between cities and regions, with Madrid and Barcelona the most expensive. Finding a part-time job to help pay your living expenses is extremely difficult in Spain and shouldn't be relied upon. Some universities have their own student halls of residence (*colegios mayores*), although places are in high demand and short supply. The availability and cost of private rented accommodation (see page 89) depends on the particular university and where it's located.

Spanish students under the age of 28 and registered at a Spanish institute of higher education are covered for health insurance by a students' insurance fund. This fund also covers many foreign students under reciprocal agreements, including those from EU countries. Students over the age of 28 and others who aren't covered must have private health insurance.

Many Spanish students attend the nearest university to their home and treat university as an extension of school, particularly in Madrid and other large cities where accommodation is expensive. Most students face the choice of either living with their parents or subsisting in a depressing university residence or cheap room (most choose to live at home). Spanish students don't usually work during their studies or during holidays and most go home at weekends. Few university facilities are open at weekends, when foreign students must amuse themselves. Note that like Spanish state schools, universities offer few extra-curricular, sports and social activities.

In addition to Spanish higher education establishments, there are also a number of US universities with faculties in Spain including the Schiller International University, the St. Louis University, the University of Southern Mississippi (all in Madrid) and the Boston University (Zaragossa). All classes at American universities are taught in English. The European university has branches in Barcelona and Madrid. Many foreign university students (and Spanish students abroad) can study in Spain under European Union exchange programmes for periods ranging from a few weeks to several months. If you're heading for Barcelona (or anywhere in Catalonia), ensure that a course is conducted in Spanish (Castilian) and not Catalan.

Information about higher education in Spain can be obtained from the cultural sections of Spanish embassies abroad and from the University Council (*Consejo de Universidades*), Secretaría General, Ciudad Universitaria s/n, 28040 Madrid (tel. (91) 449 6665). A useful book entitled *Higher Education in the European Community* (Kogan Page) is published by the Commission of the European Communities and describes the Spanish system of higher education and lists all universities and the courses offered. It's available from Official Publications, European Community, 5, rue du Commerce, BP 1003, 2985 Luxembourg and from EU government publishing offices (e.g. HMSO in Britain).

LANGUAGE SCHOOLS

If you don't speak Spanish, it's advisable to enrol in a course at a local language school, preferably before arriving in Spain. If you're working in Spain you will usually have little choice about learning Spanish; in fact you're unlikely to obtain a job interacting with Spaniards if you don't speak good Spanish. If you're planning to work in Spain you may wish to obtain a formal qualification in Spanish for non-native speakers of Spanish (*Diplomas de Español Como Lengua Extranjera*), administered by the Spanish Ministry of Education, the Instituto Cervantes and the University of Salamanca. Information is available from the above institutions or Spanish embassies, and examinations are held worldwide at three levels (beginner, intermediate and advanced). Diplomas are particularly useful when formal evidence of Spanish proficiency is required, e.g. for employment or study in Spain.

Although it isn't always *essential* for retirees and residents who live and work among the expatriate community to learn Spanish, it certainly makes life easier and less frustrating. Unfortunately many residents (particularly British retirees) make little effort to learn Spanish beyond the few words necessary to buy the weekly groceries and order a cup of coffee, and live as if they were on a brief holiday. **However, for anyone living in Spain permanently, learning Spanish should be seen as a necessity, not an option.** It's vital to get stuck into learning Spanish **as soon as possible after you arrive** and to avoid foreign 'ghettos' and live among the Spanish if you want to learn the language.

If you're a retiree, you ought to make an effort to learn at least the rudiments of Spanish so that you can understand your bills, use the phone, deal with servicemen, and communicate with your local town hall (plus performing myriad other 'daily' chores). If you don't learn Spanish, you will be continually frustrated in your communications and will be constantly calling on friends and acquaintances to assist you, or even paying people (such as *gestores*, see page 410) to do jobs you could quite easily do yourself. **However, the most important and serious purpose of learning Spanish is that in an emergency it could save your life or that of a loved one!** Learning Spanish also helps you to appreciate the Spanish way of life and make the most of your time in Spain, and opens many doors that remain firmly closed to resident 'tourists'. One of the bonuses of learning Spanish in Spain is that you will also discover the secrets of how to enjoy Spanish life and all it has to offer.

Although it isn't easy, even the most non-linguistic (and oldest) person can acquire a working knowledge of Spanish. All that's required is a little hard work and some help and perseverance (particularly if you have only English-speaking colleagues and friends). You won't just 'pick it up' (apart from a few words), but must make a real effort to learn. Although learning any language isn't easy, learning Spanish is simpler than learning many other languages because it's written phonetically with all letters pronounced. If you have difficulty learning Spanish, you could try the 'suggestological method' where the structure is assimilated while you're under deep relaxation — apparently it really works!

Methods: Most people can teach themselves a great deal through the use of books, tapes, videos and even CD-ROM computer-based Spanish courses. However, even the best students require some help. Teaching Spanish is a big business in Spain, with classes offered by language schools (Spain has the highest number in Europe); Spanish and foreign colleges and universities; private and international schools; foreign and international organizations; local associations and clubs; chambers of commerce and town halls; and private teachers. Classes range from language courses for complete beginners, through specialised business or cultural courses, to university-level seminars leading to recognised diplomas. Most Spanish universities offer language courses all year round, including special summer courses. These are generally cheaper than language schools, although classes may be much larger. If you already speak some Spanish but need conversational practice, you may wish to enrol in an art or craft course at a local institute or club.

Language Schools: There are language schools (*escuelas de idiomas*) in all Spanish cities and large towns. Most offer a range of classes depending on your current language ability, how many hours you wish to study a week, how much money you want to spend and how quickly you wish to learn. Courses are usually open to anyone over the age of 18 and some also accept students aged from 14. Courses are graded according to ability, e.g. beginner, intermediate or advanced, and usually last from 2 to 16 weeks. All schools offer free tests to help you find your correct level and a free introductory lesson.

Don't expect to become fluent in a short time unless you have a particular flair for learning languages or already have a good command of Spanish. Unless you desperately need to learn quickly, it's usually better to arrange your lessons over a long period.

However, don't commit yourself to a long course of study, particularly an expensive one, before ensuring that it's the right course for you. Courses generally fall into the following categories:

extensive	4-15	hours per week
intensive	15-30	"
total immersion	30-40	"

Some schools offer combined courses where language study is linked with optional subjects including business Spanish; Spanish art and culture; reading and commentary of a daily newspaper; conversation; Spanish history; and traditions and folklore. Many schools combine language courses with a range of social and sports activities such as horse riding, tennis, windsurfing, golf, skiing, hang-gliding and scuba-diving.

The most common language courses in Spain are intensive courses providing four hours tuition a day from Monday to Friday (20 hours a week). The cost of an intensive course is usually quite reasonable, e.g. 30,000 to 45,000 ptas for a two week course, 35,000 to 50,000 ptas (three weeks) and 40,000 to 65,000 ptas (four weeks). The highest fees are charged in the summer months, particularly during July and August. Commercial courses are generally more intensive and expensive, e.g. 80,000 ptas for two weeks and a total of 60 hours tuition. Courses that include accommodation are often excellent value and many schools arrange home stays with a Spanish family (full or half board), or provide apartment or hotel accommodation. Accommodation with a host family typically costs 10,000 to 15,000 ptas a week for half board.

For those for whom money is no object (hopefully your employer!), there are total immersion courses where study is for eight hours a day, five days a week. Whichever course you choose, you should shop around as tuition fees vary considerably. You may wish to check that a school is a member of a professional association such as the *Asociación para la Enseñanza del Español como Lengua Extranjera (ASELE)*. Free courses are organised for resident foreigners in some provinces, e.g. Alicante and Malaga, by the Spanish department of the *Escuela Oficial de Idiomas*.

Private Lessons: You may prefer to have private lessons, which are a quicker although more expensive way of learning Spanish. The main advantage of private lessons is that you learn at your own speed and aren't held back by slow learners or dragged along by the class genius. One way to get to know the Spanish and improve your Spanish is to find a Spanish partner wishing to learn English (or your mother tongue), called a 'language exchange' *(intercambio)*. Partners get together on a regular basis during which half the time is spent speaking English (or another foreign language) and half speaking Spanish. You can advertise for a private teacher or partner in local newspapers, on bulletin and notice boards (in shopping centres, supermarkets, universities, clubs, etc.), and through your and your spouse's employers. Don't forget to ask your friends, neighbours and colleagues if they can recommend a private teacher. Private Spanish teachers often advertise in English-language publications in Spain. Private lessons cost from around 2,000 ptas an hour at a school and between 1,000 and 2,000 ptas an hour from an experienced private tutor (1,000 ptas is the going rate in many resort areas).

Further Information: Information about Spanish language schools can be obtained from the *Departamento de Español para Extranjeros*, Escuela Oficial de Idiomas, Jesús Maestro s/n, 28003 Madrid (tel. (91) 254 4492). A list of Spanish language schools in Spain can be obtained from the Instituto Cervantes which has offices in many countries including Britain (102 Eaton Square, London SW3 2RP, UK, tel. 0171-235 1485). The

Instituto also runs Spanish language classes in some 30 countries. The list may also contain organisations arranging courses, exchange visits and home stays in Spain for both children and adults. A guide entitled 'Spanish Courses for Foreigners in Spain' (*Cursos de Español para Extranjeros en España*) is available from the Servicio de Publicaciones, Ministerio de Educación y Ciencia, Ciudad Universitaria s/n, 28040 Madrid.

A useful book for anyone wishing to visit Spain to study the Spanish language and culture is *Study Holidays*, containing practical information on accommodation, travel, and sources of bursaries, grants and scholarships. It's published by the Central Bureau, Seymour Mews House, Seymour Mews, London W1H 9PE, UK (tel. 0171-486 5101). One of the best sources for Spanish language-learning books and materials in Britain is European Schoolbooks Ltd., The Runnings, Cheltenham, Glos. GL51 9PQ, UK (tel. 01242-245252). For further information about the Spanish language, see **Language** on page 44 and page 155.

10.

PUBLIC TRANSPORT

Public transport (*transporte público*) is generally excellent in Spanish cities, most of which have efficient urban bus and rail services, some supplemented by underground railways (*metros*) and trams. Spanish railways (RENFE) provide an efficient and reasonably fast rail service, particularly between cities served by AVE high-speed trains. Spain has comprehensive intercity bus and domestic airline services and is also served by frequent international coaches, trains and airline services. On the debit side, rail services are non-existent in many areas and buses are sometimes infrequent in coastal resorts and rural areas, where it's often essential to have your own transport.

Urban transport in major cities such as Madrid and Barcelona is inexpensive and efficient, and rates among the best in the world. Services include comprehensive bus routes, *metros* and extensive suburban rail networks. Systems are totally integrated and the same ticket (sold at tobacconists) can be used for all services. A range of commuter and visitor tickets are also available. There are travel agencies (such as *Viajes Ecuador*, *Viajes Halcón* and *Viajes Melia*) in all major cities and large towns, and specialist agencies for young travellers such as *Viajes TIVE*. Students with an International Student Identity Card (ISIC) card receive a 30 per cent discount on selected Iberia flights and a 15 per cent discount on buses. Pensioners aged 65 or over also receive discounts on most forms of public transport (if you aren't offered a discount, don't forget to ask). A free travel map (*mapa de comunicaciones*) is available from the SNTO.

TRAINS

The Spanish rail network is operated by the state-owned company *Red Nacional de los Ferrocarriles Españoles (RENFE)* which operates 14,738km (9,158miles) of track and 2,500 stations. The RENFE network takes in all major cities, although it doesn't run to many small towns, and is supplemented by a few suburban networks such as the FFCC city lines in Barcelona and private narrow-gauge railways. Little freight is transported by train both within Spain or to other EU countries, compared with the tens of thousands of tonnes shipped by road. Like most state-owned businesses in Spain, the railways were grossly under-funded under Franco and RENFE remains western Europe's most idiosyncratic railway (many lines are still single track), despite huge investments in new rolling stock. The safety of Spain's rail network was questioned when in 1997 two major accidents within the space of 12 hours left 20 dead and over 100 seriously injured.

Spain's railway network is well below average by European standards, particularly regarding punctuality, although they are also one of the continent's cheapest. However, RENFE has undergone a comprehensive modernisation programme in the last decade during which journey times have been reduced by up to 50 per cent. In 1992, a high speed *Tren de Alta Velocidad Española (AVE)* service was introduced between Madrid and Seville (2 hours 25 minutes) for the World Fair. The AVE (which also means big bird in Spanish) employs 'disguised' French TGV trains running on special lines and travelling at speeds of up to 300kph (185mph). Full refunds are offered if an AVE train is more than five minutes late arriving at its destination!

The AVE service is to be extended between Madrid and Barcelona and will eventually comprise part of a Europe-wide, high-speed rail network due for completion around the year 2005 (unlike other Spanish trains, AVE trains run on European standard-gauge track). It may also be extended south to Malaga and possibly as far as Marbella. There are three classes of AVE trains: first (*club*), 'business' (*preferente*) and tourist (*turista*), plus sleeping accommodation for international travel. AVE trains are air-conditioned and equipped with reclining seats, TVs (films are screened), a restaurant and cafeteria, a drinks/refreshment trolley service and, in first class, free newspapers and the AVE magazine (*revista de paisajes*). Other first-class, long-distance (*largo recorrido*) trains include the *Talgo 200* which has first and tourist class seats and is similarly equipped to AVE trains (although slower).

RENFE operate a mind-boggling variety of trains, most with different services and fare structures. Spanish trains vary greatly in speed, with the fastest comparable to Europe's best and the slowest travelling at about the same speed as a city bus. In general, fast trains stop at main stations only, while slow local train stops at all stations. One of the fastest trains is the *talgo* (*tren articulado ligero goicoechea oriol*) which also includes *talgo* sleepers (*coches-cama*). A *talgo* TEE (trans-europa express) is a fast train operating on international routes. IC (intercity) are air-conditioned fast trains and the ELT (*electrotren*) and TER are both comfortable and fast, but are slower (and make more stops) than a *talgo*. A TAF is a diesel express used on secondary routes and slower than a *talgo* or TER.

There are also a huge variety of slow, local, short-distance trains classified variously as *tranvía* (also a tram), *semi-directo*, *correo* (mail train), *automotor*, *omnibús* and *ferrobús*. Suburban commuter trains (*cercanías*) are second class only and stop at all stations. A regional express (*reg. exp.*) or *interurbano* is a second class air-conditioned diesel train and an *exprés* is a slow night train, usually with sleeping cars. A *rápido* is a daytime version of the *exprés*. Despite the names, the *exprés* and *rápido* aren't particularly fast. Night trains (*estrellas*) are slow trains with various types of couchettes (*literas*) and beds (many long-distance trains run overnight). Car trains run to all parts of Spain (e.g. you can transport your car by train from Barcelona, Bilbao or Madrid to Malaga) and include an *autoexpreso*, which carries cars, motorcycles, light boats and canoes, and (on some routes) there's a *motoexpreso* carrying motorcycles only. If you aren't in a hurry, it's advisable to compare the cost of slow trains with fast trains, as the savings are considerable. Slow trains are excellent for tourists as they allow plenty of time to enjoy the sights.

Trains usually have first and second class carriages, although there's a bewildering variety of fares within each class and for different train types. Spanish fares are low by European standards, with the base fare around 45 ptas per 10km for second class and 65 ptas per 10km for first class. However, supplements can increase fares by up to 80 per cent. Fares are graded according to a train's speed and comfort and there are surcharges (*suplementos*) on fast trains including TER, *talgo*, Inter-City and ELT trains. A smaller supplement is payable on *rápido* class trains. A first class ticket costs around 50 per cent more than second class.

International Trains: Spain also has many international services, although they are slow and expensive compared with air travel. There are direct trains to many western European cities (e.g. Geneva, Milan, Montpellier, Paris and Zurich) and there's even a train from Madrid to Moscow taking around three days. International trains usually have two classes, first (*gran clase*) and tourist (*turista*), plus sleeping cars (*coches camas*) with a choice of individual compartments or couchettes. At border stops it may be necessary to change trains due to Spain's wider gauge (1,676mm) than the rest of Europe (1,435mm), except for *Talgo* and TEE trains which have adjustable axles. Beware of thieves on overnight international trains as there have been robberies on overnight trains in recent years, particularly those travelling between France and Spain.

Spanish Network & Main Stations: The Spanish railway system is centred on Madrid, from where three main lines radiate out to other parts of the country (two extend to the French border and the other to Andalusia and the Levante). Consequently there are good links between Madrid and other cities, although to get to a destination without going via Madrid often requires a circuitous journey. Madrid has three main stations (*estaciones*). **Chamartín** (the largest) serves Albacete, Alicante, Barcelona, Bilbao, Cadiz, Cartagena, Cordoba, Irún, Malaga, Santander, Seville, Soria, Zaragossa, Portugal and France. **Atocha** station (south of the Prado museum) serves Castilla-La Mancha, Andalusia and Extremadura, including Almeria, Badajoz, Cadiz, Ciudad Real, Cordoba, Cuenca, Granada, Mérida, Salamanca, Toledo, Valencia, plus Portugal. **Príncipe Pío** (or **Norte**) serves Coruña, León, Lugo, Ovense, Oviedo, Salamanca, Vallodolid and Zamora. The main stations in Barcelona are **França** and **Sants** (the most important), which has a link to Barcelona airport. Trains to all major Spanish cities and to France (via Gerona) leave from Sants, while França has daily international trains to Geneva, Milan, Paris and Zurich. Note that in smaller towns, stations are often located a few kilometres from the centre and there may be no bus service.

Tourist Trains: Spain has a number of 'tourist' trains, many of which run on narrow-gauge lines. The *Al-Andalus Express* is a unique travel experience on a luxurious converted 1920s train and a wonderful introduction to Spain, with the round trip commencing in Seville and taking in Cordoba, Granada, Malaga, Ronda and Jerez. However, with the six day journey costing up to 300,000 ptas (including food and excursions), it isn't for those on a tight budget. *El Transcantábrico* is another 1920s train operating between León and Ferrol in the north of Spain along the longest stretch of narrow-gauge railway in Europe (1,000km/625miles). It takes in stunning mountain scenery and offers excursions to a number of enchanting villages and towns during its week-long journey. Although not a tourist train, one of the most spectacular train journeys in southern Spain is on the RENFE line from Ronda to Jimena de la Frontera (British built in the 1890s).

Other trains include the independent FGV narrow-gauge line (1915) operating the *Costa Blanca Exprés* running along the Costa Blanca from Denia to Alicante (93km) and the *Limón Exprés* operating between Benidorm and Gata de Gorgos. A coal-burning steam train (*Tren de la Fresa*) with wooden seats runs from Madrid to Aranjuez on Saturdays, Sundays and public holidays from May to October. In Majorca, railway enthusiasts can enjoy a trip on the vintage (circa 1900) train running from Palma to Sóller (the only other train in the Balearics runs from Palma to Inca). It travels through tunnels and mountains and provides some of the best views on the island. From Sóller an equally ancient tramcar runs through orange and lemon groves to Puerto de Sóller. RENFE organise many day and weekend excursion trains including 'ski trains' such as the *Sierra Nevada* from Madrid to Granada and the *Tren Blanco Estrella Pirineo* from Madrid to Jaca or Canfranca in the Pyrenees. An interesting book for train buffs is *Spain and Portugal by Train* by Norman Renouf (Bradt Publications).

General Information

- All AVE and long-distance trains have a bar-buffet and/or a restaurant car (*coche restaurante*) with waiter service. Medium distance trains have a refreshment trolley (*carrito de restauración*) offering drinks and snacks at your seat. Note that rail catering is expensive and isn't of good quality by Spanish standards (many passengers prefer to provide their own picnic).

- Main railway stations provide a variety of services including an information booth; tourist office; post office; accommodation service; luggage lockers and storage; wash, shower and brush-up facilities; car rental; telephones; cafeterias and restaurants; bank with ATMs; currency exchange; photocopiers; instant passport photograph machines; and assorted shops and kiosks.

- All trains have smoking (*fumadores*) and non-smoking (*no fumadores*) carriages. Smoking is forbidden in sleeping cars and couchettes and in all local trains, except in the corridors (if there is one). Smoking is permitted on platforms and most stations have smoking and non-smoking waiting rooms (*salas de espera*). When booking a ticket, you should specify whether you want a seat in a non-smoking or a smoking carriage.

- Public telephones are available on AVE and other fast trains and permit both domestic and international calls. They must be used with a Telefónica phone card available from train cafeterias.

- Platforms (*andénes*) aren't always clearly numbered, so always make sure you're waiting at the correct one. Lines often have different numbers from platforms, which can be confusing. The destination of trains is usually written or displayed on the outside of carriages.

- Car parks are often provided close to railway stations, where long-term parking costs around 1,500 per day for a car (monthly season tickets are available to commuters).

- You can rent a car from many main railway stations in Spain (see page 224) and leave it at another major city station. Cars can be reserved at travel agencies at the same time as your rail journey.

- Beware of baggage thieves when travelling on trains and always try to store your bags in an overhead rack where you can keep an eye on them.

- Self-service luggage lockers (*consignas*) and left-luggage offices have returned at major railway stations after being closed during ETA's bombing campaign of the 1970s and 1980s. Lockers large enough for large suitcases or backpacks cost around 200 to 400 ptas per day. Main stations also have left luggage offices open from around 0800 until 2200. Luggage forwarding up to 20 kg is free for long-distance rail passengers.

Buying Tickets

Buying train tickets (*billetes*) in Spain can be extremely confusing as there's a baffling range of fares (*precios, importes*) and trains to choose from. Confusion is widespread and ticket office clerks aren't always familiar with the variety of special tickets and reductions available. **You should always double check to ensure that you pay the lowest possible fare for a journey.** Fares for long-distance and high-speed trains such as AVE are published in leaflets available from stations and RENFE offices. Children under four years of age travel free (including sleeping accommodation) and those aged between 4 and 12 travel for half fare.

Tickets can be purchased at station ticket windows (*taquillas de billetes*); from ticket machines (*máquinas de billetes*) accepting cash and credit cards; at RENFE offices; and from RENFE appointed travel agents. A single ticket is *un billete de ida* and a return (round trip) *ida y vuelta*. There may be an information (*información*) or international information window at major stations, where staff may speak English and other foreign languages. A ticket must always be purchased and validated *before* boarding a train, unless there's no ticket office (or it's closed) at the station where you're boarding. It's possible to buy a ticket on a train from the ticket collector/conductor (*revisor*), although you may need to pay a surcharge, depending on the type of train and the length of your journey.

Ticket Offices: It usually pays to avoid station ticket windows, where there are usually long queues, and buy your ticket at a RENFE office or a travel agent. Ticket windows at stations usually open around an hour before train departures (or in some cases, a few minutes before a train is due to arrive) and usually close around 10 minutes before the departure time. To purchase a ticket at some stations you must take a number from a machine and wait for it to be called (so you must understand Spanish numbers). At main stations, there are a number of ticket windows which may include *regionales y cercanías* (local trains) and *largos recorridos* (long-distance trains), each with *venta anticipada* (advance tickets) or *venta inmediata* (imminent departure — for tickets purchased from two hours before departure) windows. There's also a window for international tickets (*billetes internacionales*) at some stations in Madrid and Barcelona. A computerised RENFE ticket shows the train number (*N° Tren*), carriage (*coche*), seat number (*N° Plaza*) and whether it's a smoking or non-smoking (*fuma/no fuma*) seat.

Ticket Classes: There are two classes on most long-distance trains, first class (*primera clase* shown as *1ª*) and second class (*segunda clase* shown as *2ª*). On some services, such as fast AVE trains, there are three fare classes: *turista* (tourist), *preferente* (business) and *club* (first). Some trains such as IC and TEE international trains are first class only. A supplement (*suplemento*) is payable on InterCity (IC), *talgo* and TER trains (shown by an 'S' in timetables).

Fare Calendar: One of the major factors influencing the cost of a long-distance rail ticket is the day on which you travel. In 1994, RENFE replaced their old calendar of 'blue days' (*días azules*) with a new calendar. This divides the year into three seasons: low (*bajo*) season (green), mid (*medio*) season (yellow) and high (*alto*) season (red), with 205, 142 and 18 days respectively. Green days are the cheapest days on which to travel and red days, which mainly occur just before or after public holidays or long weekends, the most expensive. Saturdays are the cheapest day to travel (particularly if they fall on a green or yellow day), Mondays to Thursdays are slightly more expensive, and Fridays and Sundays are the most expensive. The two most expensive months in which to travel are July and August, when all days are designated as yellow or red.

There are also different fares for each 'type of train' (*tipo de tren*) on a particular day, classified as 'valley' (*valle*), 'plain' (*llano*) and 'peak' (*punta*) according to demand. The difference between the cheapest and most expensive fare can be as much as 150 per cent. Apart for the extra cost, it's best to avoid travelling on public holidays or over long weekends (*puentes*), when the whole nation takes to the rails (those that aren't on the roads).

Reservations: Reservations can be made on routes over 200km between two months and one hour before departure and cost 200 ptas. On AVE trains, open tickets (*billetes abiertos*) are valid for six months; bookings can be made 10 minutes before train departures. Many stations have advance booking offices, although it's usually better to book at a RENFE office or a RENFE-appointed travel agent (*agencias de viajes*), displaying the blue and yellow RENFE logo. Seats should be reserved as far in advance as possible (at least 24 hours), particularly during the main tourist season and before public holidays.

RENFE's central reservation service in Madrid is open from 0900 to 2100 each day (tel. (91) 429 8228). When a reservation is made by telephone you're given a code number. You must then go to any station or RENFE travel agent within two days of making the reservation, quote this number and pay for your ticket. Tickets can be paid for with cash, eurocheques and various credit and charge cards including Access, Visa, Mastercard, Eurocard and *tarjeta 4B*. Note that seat and (in particular) sleeper reservations are compulsory on many long-distance trains. Rail tickets purchased abroad must be stamped before each journey, either at a RENFE office or at a station before departure.

Ticket Change & Cancellation: It's possible to change the date and time of travel on pre-booked tickets. There's a surcharge of 10 per cent of the cost of a ticket to change it and a 15 per cent surcharge to cancel a ticket and receive a refund (25 per cent if the train is classified as a *llano* or *punta* and the cancellation is made less than 24 hours before departure). **Note that refunds are made only on tickets purchased with credit cards.** You can change the departure date of a ticket with a reserved seat without penalty up to a few hours before the scheduled departure. Cancellation and refund of a ticket incurs a penalty of 10 per cent of the fare for AVE and Talgo trains, and 200 ptas for *largo recorrido* trains, and can be done up to 15 minutes before departure.

Season & Special Tickets

Many season tickets (*abonos*) and special discount (*descuento*) tickets are available in Spain. These include discounts for students and youths (16 to 25); senior citizens; handicapped passengers; commuters; groups; and holiday and excursion tickets. Most special tickets can be changed or cancelled. Information is obtainable from information and ticket offices at any railway station.

Senior Citizens & Handicapped Passengers: Senior citizens aged over 60 and handicapped passengers can obtain a gold pass (*tarjeta dorada*) for 500 ptas a year offering discounts of 45 per cent on suburban trains (*cercanías*), 40 per cent on regional trains, 35 per cent on long distance (*valle*) trains, and 25 per cent on AVE and Talgo 200 *llano* and *punta* long-distance trains. A 'rail europ senior card' (*Tarjeta Rail Europ Senior*) is also available for 3,000 ptas a year and provides reductions of 30 to 50 per cent on international fares.

Commuters: There are various commuter tickets in Spain including monthly season tickets (*abonos mensuales*) offering discounts of up to 40 per cent. For further information enquire at any RENFE ticket office.

Youths: A *carnet joven* (national student card) is available from local municipal youth departments for 500 ptas for students aged between 12 and 26 and provides a 20 per cent discount on RENFE regional trains, but no discount on AVE or Talgo trains. A passport or residence card (*residencia*) and a passport-size photograph are required.

Families: A family card (*tarjeta de familia*) is available for families and provides special discounts on green days (see **Fare Calendar** on page 176). Discounts depend on the number of children in a family, e.g. 20 per cent for four children, 40 per cent for seven children and 50 per cent for the *categoría de honor* of 10 children. The family group must include a minimum of three people, two of whom must be adults, and can be used only for journeys over 100km. The first adult pays full price, the second adult travels at a 50 per cent discount and children (aged 4 to 12) travel at a 75 per cent discount.

Children: On AVE trains there's a 40 per cent discount for children aged from 4 to 11. Children under four travel free on all trains.

Groups: Groups of 10 to 25 people receive a 15 per cent discount on AVE trains (for groups above 25, contact RENFE).

International Tickets: Holders of a Eurailpass, Eurodomino or tourist card (*tarjeta turística*) receive reductions of 60 per cent (*club*), 65 per cent (*preferente*) and 85 per cent (*turista*) on AVE trains. *Club* and *preferente* discounts are applicable only to holders of first class tickets. Student discounts of up to 40 per cent are available from offices of Wasteels.

Timetables

If you're a regular rail user, you should obtain route maps (*mapas de carreteras*) and timetables (*horarios*) on arrival in Spain. However, bear in mind that most times are *approximate* only, and with the exception of timetables for fast (e.g. AVE) and international trains, they shouldn't be relied upon. At major stations, arrivals (*llegadas*) and departures (*salidas*) are shown on large electronic boards. It's always wise to double-check departure times and not rely on announcements (that's if you can understand the often garbled messages). You also shouldn't trust the list of trains posted at a station, but confirm trains and times at the ticket or information office. When you buy a rail ticket with a reserved seat, the train number and departure time are printed on it.

Rail timetables are published in national, regional and local versions, and also for individual routes and train types (e.g. long-distance). RENFE publish a variety of special guides and information, plus an 'Atlas of Spanish Railways' (*Atlas de Ferrocarriles Españoles*) containing a selection of maps of Spain. Train timetables (*horarios de trenes*) are printed for most major domestic and international rail routes, often in the form of a handy pocket card. A commuter train schedule for Madrid costs around 150 ptas at station news kiosks. RENFE also publish a 200-page rail guide, *Guía RENFE*, costing 200 ptas and containing a schedule of major national and international rail routes (*grandes relaciones*). It's published twice annually at the end of May and at the end of September and is available from main stations or from RENFE, *Dirección de Información*, Madrid-Chamartín, 28036 Madrid (tel. (91) 323 2121).

Before planning a trip, it's advisable to check the fare calendar (see page 176) and, if possible, avoid travelling on red days. Note that many services operate daily (*diario*) or on working days (*laborables*) only, which may include Saturdays, and a limited service is operated on Sundays and holidays (*domingos y festivos*).

METROS

There are underground railway systems (*metros*) in Madrid, Barcelona and Valencia, where public transport tickets and passes permit travel on all modes of public transport including *metro*, bus and suburban rail services. *Metros* offer the quickest way to get around these cities, although they are crowded during rush hours, and trains that aren't air-conditioned can become very hot and uncomfortable. No smoking is permitted on *metro* trains or in stations, which are clean and safe (crime is rare on Spanish *metros*).

Madrid has the largest and oldest *metro* system in Spain with 10 lines and 126 stations covering most of the city, operating from 0600 until 0130. The fare is 130 ptas per journey and 645 ptas for a 10-journey ticket (*bonometro*). Special tickets are available including a cheap day return, a *metrocard* allowing three or five days unlimited use, and weekly and monthly passes for commuters. A free map (*plano del metro*) showing the lines in different colours is available from ticket offices. Tickets are sold at station ticket booths and from machines. The *metro* is easy to use; simply note the end station of the line you want and follow the signs. When entering or leaving a train, car doors must be opened manually by pressing a button. Apart from Sundays and late at night, trains run around every five minutes. However, no timetable is published and the only clue to the arrival of the next train is a green timer indicating the departure time of the *last* train.

Barcelona's *metro* is one of the world's most modern and best designed systems, although it has just four lines: L1 (red), L3 (green), L4 (yellow) and L5 (blue), with a fifth line planned. Large areas of the city aren't covered by the *metro* (particularly within the Eixample area) and despite having a few lines only, most connections require long walks between platforms (not recommended if you're carrying heavy baggage). Stations are indicated at street level by a large 'M' within a diamond. Trains are frequent and run every three or four minutes at peak times. There's piped music on platforms to keep you entertained while waiting for trains, most of which are air-conditioned.

A map (*xarxa de metro* in Catalan) is available from tourist offices and at ticket windows in stations (there's also a *metro* map on the back of the free tourist office city map). Lines are marked in colours, and connections between lines (*correspondencia*) and between metro and rail systems (*enlace*) are clearly indicated. Stops are announced over an intercom and illuminated panels show where the train has come from, the station you're approaching, and as the train departs after stopping, the next station (an excellent idea which should be adopted in all metro trains). Flashing red chevrons at the end of each carriage indicate which side of the train to exit from. Announcements on trains (and in stations) are made in Spanish (Castilian) and not in Catalan.

A single journey costs 130 ptas and a T-1 (*tarjeta multiviaje*) pass costs 700 ptas and is valid for 10 journeys on the *metro* and city buses, and can also be used on the blue tramway (*Tibidabo*), the Montjuïc funicular railway and Catalan railways Generalitat (FFCC) city lines (although the latter three modes of transport require a further cancellation of the pass, i.e. each trip costs the equivalent of two bus or *metro* journeys). A T-2 pass is also available for 680 ptas and allows 10 journeys on the *metro*, but cannot be used on buses. One, three and five-day passes are also available.

Tickets and passes can be purchased from automatic ticket machines at most stations, ticket windows, and from savings banks and special sales' outlets. If you purchase a multi-trip ticket, it must be inserted in the slot of an automatic gate, which clips off a segment of the ticket, illuminates a flashing yellow light and releases the gate. Always keep your pass or ticket until you leave the metro, as riding without a ticket incurs a 5,000 ptas fine, payable on the spot. The *metro* is open from 0500 (0600 on Sundays) and closes at 2300 (surprisingly early) from Monday to Thursday, 2400 on Sundays, and 0100 on Fridays, Saturdays and the day before public holidays.

Barcelona also has the *Ferrocarrils de la Generalitat de Catalunya*, commonly referred to as the Generalitat or FFCC, a small underground train service within the city operated by the provincial government of Catalonia. You can use the T-1 and T-2 passes on the FFCC or buy tickets from machines in stations.

Valencia: has a new *metro* system (opened in 1988) consisting of just eight stations in the city centre, although there are plans to extend it to the suburbs. Tickets cost from around 100 to 350 ptas.

BUSES & TRAMS

There are excellent bus (*autobús*) services in all major cities and towns in Spain and comprehensive long-distance 'coach' (*autocar*) services between major cities. Buses are the cheapest and most common form of public transport in Spain and most coastal towns and rural villages are accessible by bus only. The quality and age of buses vary considerable from luxurious modern buses in most cities to old ramshackle relics in some rural areas. Private bus services are often confusing and uncoordinated and buses usually leave from different locations rather than a central bus station (*estación de autobuses*), e.g. Madrid has eight bus stations and most cities have two or more (possibly located on the outskirts of town). There are left luggage offices (*consignas*) at central bus stations. Note that smoking isn't permitted on most buses.

Before boarding a bus at a bus terminal you must usually buy a ticket from the ticket office or a machine. Otherwise you buy a single ticket from the driver or conductor as you enter the bus (they usually give change for small banknotes). Passengers usually enter a bus from a front door (marked *entrada*) and dismount from a centre or side exit (*salida*). Most buses are driver-only operated, although some city buses (e.g. blue buses in Madrid) have the entrance at the rear where you pay a conductor who sits by the door. You must usually signal before the stop (*parada*) where you wish to get off by pressing a button (which activates a bell in the driver's cab).

City Buses: Most bus services in cities run from around 0600 until between 2200 and midnight, when a night service normally comes into operation (which is usually more expensive than day buses). There's usually a 10-minute service on the most popular routes during peak hours and an hourly night service, although services are considerably reduced on Sundays and public holidays. City buses are often very crowded and buses that aren't air-conditioned can be uncomfortable in the summer (some urban buses are air-conditioned). Most city buses don't have a lot of seats, so as to provide maximum standing room. There are numerous bus routes in major cities and it can be difficult to find your way around by bus. Urban buses are generally very slow and although there are special bus and taxi lanes in some cities (e.g. Madrid), there are still frequent traffic jams. Consequently many people prefer to use the *metro* (e.g. in Barcelona or Madrid) or taxis (which are inexpensive). In Madrid, a single bus trip costs 130 ptas and a 10-trip ticket (*bonobús*) is available for 645 ptas. Fares are similar in other cities and there are reductions for pensioners and students. Tickets are available from bus offices and tobacconists.

Bus and *metro* fares are the same in Madrid and tickets can be used on both systems. In Barcelona, a 10-ride T-1 pass can be used on all urban public transport including the *metro* (see page 178). In Madrid and Barcelona (and some other cities) tickets are valid for an entire bus route, but not for transfers to other buses. Day and multi-day passes allowing unlimited travel are also available, plus a range of season tickets (*abono*), e.g. for a week, month or a year. In some cities (such as Madrid) those aged between 15 and 25 can buy a youth card (*carnet joven*) providing discounts on public transport and other discounts (e.g. entrance fees to museums). Multi-ride tickets and passes must be stamped in a special machine on boarding a bus and there are on-the-spot fines for anyone found riding without a valid ticket. Routes are numbered and terminal points are shown on buses and displayed on signs at stops in most cities. Bus timetables and route maps are available from bus company offices, bus stations and tourist offices. Tourist buses are provided in major cities, most of which follow a circular route, and bus companies offer excursions throughout Spain (packages often include meals, sightseeing and ferry travel).

Rural Buses: In rural and resort areas, bus services are often operated by the local municipality and services are usually irregular, e.g. four to six buses a day on most routes, although some have an hourly service (there may be no service during the lunch break, e.g. 1330 and 1500). The first bus departs at anytime between 0630 and 0900 and the last bus may depart as early as 1600 or 1700 on some routes (most last buses depart before 2100). However, bus services are usually reliable and run on time. Small towns can often be reached only via their provincial capital and in the centre of Spain it's almost impossible to get from one city to another without going via Madrid. Local bus timetables may be published in free newspapers and magazines.

Long-Distance Buses: In addition to local city and rural bus companies, there are also many long-distance bus companies in Spain including Auto Res, Continental and Enatcar (the largest). Inter-city buses are usually faster than trains and cost a little less. Fares on long-distance routes are around 750 ptas per 100km. Long-distance bus companies are usually privately owned and fares are quite competitive. The most luxurious buses are comfortable and offer air-conditioning, films and possibly free soft drinks.

International Buses: There are regular international bus services between Spain's major cities and many European cities. For example Eurolines runs coach services from Britain to some 45 destinations in Spain. Journeys are very long, e.g. from London it's 26 hours to Barcelona and 32 hours to Madrid, and fares are often little cheaper than flying (it's worth comparing bus fares with the cheapest charter flights). Unless you have a fear of flying or a love of coach travel, you may find one or two days spent on a bus a nightmare. Buses are, however, comfortable and air-conditioned, and are equipped with toilets and video entertainment. Most services operate daily during the summer holiday season and three or four times a week out of season. Discounts are provided for students and youths on some routes. Bookings can be made at travel agents in Spain and abroad. Typical return fares with Eurolines are Barcelona-London around 25,000 ptas and Alicante-London around 30,000 ptas.

Trams: Few Spanish cities have retained their trams, although air-conditioned trams were reintroduced in Valencia in 1994 after an absence of 20 years and Barcelona, Malaga and Zaragossa are also thinking of reintroducing them.

FERRIES & SHIPS

Regular car and international ferry services operate all year round between Spain and Britain and Morocco, and domestic ferries run between the mainland and the Balearics, the Canaries, and Spain's North African enclaves of Ceuta and Melilla. Spain's most important ports include Algeciras, Almeria, Barcelona, Bilbao, Cadiz, Las Palmas (Gran Canaria), Palma de Mallorca, Santander, Santa Cruz (Tenerife) and Valencia.

Two companies, Brittany Ferries and P&O, operate ferry services between Britain and Spain. Ships provide a variety of facilities and services including a choice of bars and restaurants (book early for a table during peak hours); swimming pool; jacuzzi; sauna; cinemas; shops; hairdressing salon; photographic studio; medical service; children's playroom; and evening entertainment including a nightclub, casino, discotheque and musical entertainment. There are more shops and diversions on P&O, which also tends to have the best service and entertainment.

Both Brittany Ferries and P&O have three fare tariffs (depending on the time of the year) and offer a choice of single fares, minicruises (spending around five hours in Spain or Britain), minibreaks (five days abroad), 8-day returns (up to eight days abroad) and standard return fares. Children aged under four travel free and those aged from four to 14 travel for half fare. It's advisable to book well ahead when travelling during peak periods and at any time when you require a luxury cabin. If possible, it's best to avoid travelling during peak times, when ships can be uncomfortably crowded.

Travelling between Britain and Spain by ferry will save you around 1,200km (750miles) of driving compared with travelling via France. Ferries can also be a cheaper way to travel, particularly with children and a car, as you don't pay expensive air fares for children or (if you bring your car with you) for car rental at your destination. Travelling from Britain to southern Spain by road (via France) entails spending three full days driving and making two overnight stops, plus meals and petrol costs, although it usually works out cheaper than the ferry.

Note that the seas are often rough between Spain and Britain (the Bay of Biscay is famous for its storms) and travel isn't advisable during bad weather if you're a bad sailor (sailings may be delayed due to bad weather in the Bay of Biscay). When seas are rough, there's absolutely no respite from sea sickness and the journey will be a nightmare (if you take a minicruise during BAD weather you will have just a few hours respite from the rolling seas before having to endure the return journey!). Check the weather report and be prepared to travel via France or fly. If you do travel by ferry, always keep a good supply of seasickness pills handy!

Brittany Ferries operate a year-round, twice-weekly service between Plymouth or Portsmouth in Britain to the Spanish port of Santander. The British port of departure, and days and times of sailings vary depending on the time of year. In December 1996 and January 1997 the service operated between Portmouth and Santander. There was no service in February 1997. From March until November the service operated between Plymouth and Santander. Always check the British port of departure and times carefully. The journey time is 24 hours between Plymouth and Santander, when one night is spent on board ship, and 30 to 31.5 hours between Portsmouth and Santander (two nights on board). The ferry serving the route is the 32,000 tonne *Val de Loire*, with a capacity of 2,140 passengers and 570 cars.

The cost (1997) for a car, motorhome, minibus or van (up to 6.5m in length) including driver is from £276 to £484 (depending on the season) for a standard return. The cost of a cabin isn't included in the fare and is from £18 to £23 sharing a four-berth cabin, and from £52 to £120 for a two to four-berth private cabin, which are well worth the extra cost. The best cabins are in the Salon Commodore (Commodore Class) which has 14 luxurious wood-panelled suites (£94 to £120) and an exclusive lounge bar overlooking the bow. Reclining seats are also available at a cost of £4 to £6. Foot passengers pay from £87 to £145 for a standard return. Food and drinks are quite expensive, particularly bar drinks and snacks, although Britanny ferries have better food and restaurants than P&O. For reservations telephone UK 0990-360260. Brittany Ferries run a Spanish Property Owners Club for frequent travellers, offering savings of up to one-third off single and standard return fares.

P&O Ferries operate a year-round, twice-weekly service between Portsmouth in Britain to the Spanish port of Bilbao (the ferry port is actually at Santutzi, around 13km/8miles to the northwest of the city centre). The route is served by the P&O ferry *Pride of Bilbao*, the largest cruise ferry operating out of Britain (capacity 2,500 passengers, 600 cars). Departures from Portsmouth are at 2000 on Tuesdays and Saturdays, arriving in Bilbao at 0800 on Thursdays and Mondays respectively. Departures from Bilbao are 1230 on Mondays and 1230 and 1800 on Thursdays. The

1230 departures arrive in Portsmouth at 1630 on Tuesdays and Fridays respectively and the 1800 Thursday departure at 0830 on Saturdays. The journey time is 36 hours from Portsmouth and 28 hours from Bilbao (38.5 hours for the 1800 departure). Ferries operate throughout the year.

The cost (1997) for the smallest vehicle (up to 6.5m in length) is £275 to £485 including the driver. The cost of a cabin isn't included in the fare and is from £30 sharing a four-berth cabin, and from £60 to £175 for a two to four-berth private cabin, which are well worth the extra cost. A luxury cabin offers a double bed, two easy chairs, writing desk, TV, shower, toilet, washbasin, two large windows and room service. Foot passengers pay from £85 to £145 for a standard return. For reservations telephone UK 0990-980555. One of the best travel deals around is offered by P&O, whose preference shareholders owning at least 600 £1 shares receive discounts of up to 50 per cent on all P&O sailings.

Other International Ferry Services: There are frequent car ferry services from Algeciras to Tangier and Ceuta (hourly, one and a half hours). There's also an hourly service from Algeciras to Tangier in summer taking two and a half hours (note, however, there are long delays in summer when thousands of Moroccan migrant labourers return home). There's also a ferry service from Gibraltar to Tangier, a summer hydrofoil service from Tarifa to Tangier, and ferry services to Melilla (North Africa) from Almeria and Malaga. Ferry services also operate from Barcelona to Livorno and Sicily (Italy) and from Palma de Mallorca and Ibiza to Sète in France (June to September only).

Domestic Ferries: Domestic ferry services operate from mainland ports to the main Balearic and Canary islands and are supplemented by inter-island services. Services include Barcelona to Palma, Ibiza and Mahón; Gandía to Ibiza and Formentera; and Valencia to Palma, Ibiza and Mahón. Services operate from Cadiz on the mainland to Tenerife, Las Palmas, Lanzarote and Fuerteventura in the Canaries. Tickets should be purchased in advance, particularly in summer, but can also be bought on board, when a surcharge is payable. There are various tariffs depending on the type of seat required (*couchettes* are available on night trips). The fare from the mainland to the Balearics (8 to 10 hours from Barcelona) is from around 5,500 ptas single (reclining seat), some 15,000 ptas for a cabin and around 12,500 ptas for a car. Ferries carry cars, boat-trailers, buses and trucks, and are equipped with restaurants and coffee shops, large bar-lounges, televisions, discotheques and shops. Note that ferries are very crowded in summer, with erratic schedules and a range of fares (shop around for the best deal).

There are regular inter-island ferries in the Balearics and Canaries including a fast (two hours) hydrojet service between Palma de Mallorca and Ibiza, and a regular ferry service from Ibiza to Formentera. Frequent inter-island ferry services also operate in the Canaries, including a hydrofoil service between all the islands. Most domestic routes to and from the mainland and the Balearic and Canary islands are operated by Compañía Transmediterránea (C/Pedro Muñoz Seca, 2, 28001 Madrid, tel. (91) 431 0700), known simply as *la Tras*. Transmediterránea offers retirees aged 65 or over a 25 per cent discount on fares outside the high season to the Balearics, the Canaries and Africa, and a 40 per cent discount to those living in the Balearics and the Canaries.

Cruises: A number of companies operate cruise ships calling at Spanish ports. In winter, many ships operate out of Malaga, Spain's main cruise port, and ships also call at Las Palmas and Lanzarote in the Canaries and at Gibraltar (which is also a major cruise port). The Cunard Princess offers winter cruises of 10 to 14 days from November to March out of Malaga calling at Madeira, Las Palmas, Lanzarote, Tenerife, Casablanca and Tangier. The cost starts at around 100,000 ptas for 10 days and groups of 10 or more receive a 20 per cent discount. At the other end of the cruise range, those with *very* deep pockets may wish to take a trip on the *Crystal Harmony*, promoted as the world's most luxurious cruise ship, calling at Malaga a few times a year. Most cruise lines offer large discounts for early bookings on winter cruises, e.g. a general 40 per cent reduction or a 50 per cent reduction for the second person. For information contact H.M. Bland, The Cruise Club, 1st Floor, Cloister Building, PO Box 554, Gibraltar (tel. 956-777221), Trident Cruises, PO Box 544, Gibraltar (tel. 956-742895) or your travel agent.

TAXIS

Taxi ranks (*paradas de taxi*) are located outside railway stations, at airports, and at main intersections in towns and cities. In major cities you can hail a taxi in the street, but in small towns they are available only at taxi ranks. You can also call a radio-taxi in most towns and cities, but you must pay for the taxi's journey to the pick-up point (taxi ranks also have phones). It's advisable to book on the day you want a taxi, preferably close to the time required (if you book too far in advance a taxi may not appear at the desired time). In cities and many towns you can rent luxury chauffeur-driven cars (*grandes turismos*), either by the hour or for a fixed fee for a particular journey.

Spanish taxi drivers are a pleasant surprise to many foreigners, particularly if you come from a country where taxi drivers are surly, rude and dishonest, as they generally take passengers by the most direct route and don't usually over-charge. What's more Spanish taxis are relatively inexpensive and many people routinely use them when shopping. Even more astounding is that contrary to the practice in most other countries, it isn't usual to tip taxi drivers in Spain.

Madrid has around 15,000 licensed taxis (one of the highest densities in the world) which are black or white with a horizontal red stripe on the side and have the city's coat of arms on their doors. Taxis usually have a maximum capacity of four passengers. Tariffs are controlled and the fares for the most popular destinations are often displayed on a board at taxi ranks (particularly when taxis have no meters). All taxis levy a standing charge, a charge per kilometre, a surcharge and/or higher kilometre rates at night and on Sundays, and various surcharges, e.g. for baggage, pets, etc. Note that many taxis won't carry dogs. There are special taxis for handicapped passengers which can carry wheelchairs in many towns (ask when booking).

In Madrid there's a 170 ptas standing charge plus 50 to 75 ptas per kilometre. Supplementary charges include an airport pick-up fee of 350 ptas, a 150 ptas fee for journeys terminating at bus and main railway stations, and 50 ptas per item of baggage. There's a supplement of 150 ptas on Sundays and public holidays and between the hours of 2300 and 0600. In Barcelona the first six minutes or 1.9km cost 235 ptas, after which the tariff (*tarifa*) depends on the zone, the time, and the day of the week, and is between around 90 and 110 ptas per km.

You should only hail a taxi that's travelling in the direction you wish to go, as they won't usually do U-turns. A *libre* (free) sign or a green light at night indicates that a taxi is for hire. If a taxi is displaying a red sign with the name of a local neighbourhood, it means the taxi driver is on his way home and isn't obliged to pick up passengers unless their destination is on his route. If you go outside a city's limits (shown by a *limite taxi* sign), you may be required to pay double the fare shown on the meter (e.g. in Madrid).

In all cities and major urban areas, taxis are fitted with meters (but make sure that the driver switches it on). If a taxi has no meter, you should always agree the fare before starting a journey. If you aren't fluent in Spanish, it's advisable to write down your destination, so that there's no misunderstanding. Taxis without meters have fixed rates for popular destinations and various distances (which may be posted). **Beware of illegal unlicensed and unmetered taxis operating in main cities and preying on foreign visitors.** If you think you have been cheated ask for an official receipt (*recibo oficial*) showing the taxi licence number, start and finish points of the journey, the date and time, and the driver's signature. Send it to the local licensing authority with your complaint.

AIRLINE SERVICES

Most major international airlines provide scheduled services to Madrid and many also fly to Barcelona and other Spanish cities. The Spanish state-owned (but soon to be privatised) national airline, Iberia, is Spain's major international carrier. Although not rated as one of the world's best airlines, it has an excellent safety record and its standard of service has improved considerably in recent years. Iberia's fares have also become more competitive, although like most European carriers it still makes huge losses. Like many other nationalised airlines, Iberia is kept aloft by public subsidies, and employees constantly use the threat of strikes to obstruct urgently required cost-cutting measures (salaries, perks and other benefits can boost top pilots' salaries to some 70m ptas a year!). However, co-operation agreements with British Airways and American Airlines should help drag Iberia into the 21st century.

The remaining restrictions on air travel within the European Union (EU) were lifted in 1997 and EU airlines can now fly where and when they want (providing they can get landing and take off slots). Increased competition from airlines such as Air Europa (Spanish-owned) has forced Iberia to reduce its fares and it now provides competitive fares to over 25 major European cities. A price war between Iberia and independent airlines such as Air Europa and Spanair on domestic routes has also hit Iberia hard, particularly on the Madrid-Barcelona route. To add to Iberia's woes, the British airline Virgin plans to enter the Spanish market with their Virgin Express European service. Ticketless reservations (you just receive a confirmation number) will be possible by phone with a credit card or via travel agents.

Scheduled Flights: Iberia has good connections to North, Central and South America and throughout Europe, but doesn't offer many flights to the rest of the world apart from a few cities such as Cairo, Tel Aviv, Tokyo and a number of countries in North and West Africa. All transatlantic flights from North America travel via Madrid. If you're unable to get a direct intercontinental flight to Spain, it's usually advisable to fly via London, from where there are daily flights to airports throughout Spain. Fares on scheduled flights to and from Spain have fallen in recent years due to increased competition, although they are still high compared with charter fares. However, if you're unable to obtain a cheap charter flight, Iberia's scheduled apex flights are good value for money and will allow you to fly more or less when you want. Iberia have low (*baja*) and high (*alta*) season fares on most routes.

Charter Flights: Cheap charter flights to Spain are common from many European countries, particularly Britain, Germany and the USA. Around 70 per cent of people visiting Spain from Britain do so on charter aircraft (Britain and Spain are the only countries in the world with such a high percentage of charter flights). The cheapest Spanish destinations from Britain are Malaga, Alicante and Palma de Mallorca, with return fares from as little as £70 in low season rising to £100 to 150 in the peak season (mid-June to mid-September). If you're travelling from Britain to the western Costa del Sol or the Costa de la Luz, you can also fly via Gibraltar (fares are similar to flights to Malaga). Charter flights from New York to Madrid cost around $800. It's often cheaper for North Americans and others travelling on intercontinental flights to fly to London and get a charter flight from there, particularly outside the summer high season. Return fares from Spain are usually more expensive than from Britain, with typical return fares around 25,000 ptas to London and 35,000 ptas to Amsterdam, Frankfurt and Paris.

It's worth shopping around for the best price. In Britain, check the advertisements in the London *Time Out* entertainment magazine and British Sunday newspapers such as the *Sunday Times* and the *Observer*. In the USA, the best place to look for advertisements for inexpensive flights is the *New York Times*. In Britain, those aged under 26 qualify for discount charter flights offered by student travel agents such as Academic Travel, Campus Travel, STA Travel and USIT. It's also advisable to shop around local travel agents.

The negative aspect of charter flights is that charter agents and companies can be unreliable. Some agents seem to advertise low fares as bait (they are always 'sold out') and then try to sell you a more expensive flight. You should always reconfirm a flight and the departure time in advance, as it isn't unusual to arrive at an airport to find that the flight time has been changed (e.g. the flight has already departed) or that you aren't on the passenger list. If you're asked to pay an extra fee to be 'added to the passenger list', you should protest vociferously and if forced to pay, should demand a refund later. Charter flights are largely unregulated in Britain and over-booked flights are common due to the number of people involved in the chain (naturally charter companies deny any responsibility).

As a general rule, the further in advance you buy your ticket, the cheaper it will be (and the greater the penalty for cancelling), although late bookings can also be good value. The main disadvantage of charter flights is that they usually have fixed return dates and a maximum of four weeks between the outward and return flights. Most charter flights restrict stays to 7, 14, 21 or 28 days, although you can always throw away the return ticket (it may still be cheaper than a single fare on a scheduled flight). It's advisable to take out insurance against missing your flight as there are no refunds for charter flights. Note that charter tickets are non-transferable and it's illegal to use a ticket issued in someone else's name. A common 'dodge' used to be to buy a cheap return to Spain and sell the return flight to someone else. This is now more difficult (or impossible) as tickets are checked against passports when boarding and if the ticket and passenger's name don't match, the flight will be refused (and you can be prosecuted).

Domestic Flights: There are a number of airlines offering domestic services in Spain including Iberia, Aviaco (*Aviación y Comercio*), Air Europa and various small airlines such as Binter Canarias and Binter Mediterránea (subsidiaries of Iberia). Aviaco covers most of the same routes as Iberia and along with charter companies such as Air España (Palma), Aviación y Comercio (Madrid) and Euskal Air (Vitoria) are cheaper than Iberia. Air Europa's domestic fares are also lower than Iberia's. Single flights are available to most domestic destinations from 8,000 to 12,000 ptas and cheaper night (*nocturno*) flights are available to some cities. Youth fares are also available at large discounts. Flights to the Balearics from the mainland are only slightly more expensive than ferries, although you usually need to reserve well in advance during the peak summer season.

Most domestic flights are routed via Madrid or Barcelona, so it can be difficult to get a direct flight between regional cities. There are frequent flights between Spain's international airports and regional airports, with Iberia operating flights from Barcelona and Madrid to around 20 domestic airports. There's a half-hourly or hourly 'air bridge' (*puente aéreo*) shuttle service between Barcelona and Madrid, carrying over 2m passengers a year. Tickets for Iberia domestic flights can be purchased from machines at airports (using a credit card). Private aircraft and helicopters can be rented from most Spanish airports to almost anywhere in Spain.

Fares: When buying a ticket in Spain for an international or domestic flight, it pays to shop around for the best deal. Whatever your destination, it's advisable to consult a travel agent, who can explain the various options available and may be able to offer a range of inexpensive flights. In addition to first, business and tourist class tickets, airlines offer a variety of discount fares including superpex, apex, superapex, weekend returns, youth and senior citizens (Iberia and Aviaco tourist class tickets are available at a 25 per cent discount for those over 65), students, families, children and groups. Scheduled airlines often offer bigger child discounts than charter airlines. Note that scheduled flights booked at short notice can considerably increase the fare, regardless of the availability of seats. Special offers for frequent fliers are provided by Iberia ('Iberia Plus') and most international airlines. Note that although cheap fares are widely advertised in Spain, they are often unavailable on the dates when you want to fly (that's if they ever existed!) and you may be offered much more expensive flights.

Iberia are rarely the cheapest but offer competitive special offers and promotional flights. These include 'open-jaw' flights that allow you to fly into one airport and out of another; a *Bravo* ticket allowing two people to fly for the price of one; and minifares (*tarifas-minis*) offering savings of up to 60 per cent on certain domestic flights. If you buy a return transatlantic ticket with Iberia, you're entitled to purchase a *Visit Spain* pass providing unlimited domestic air travel during your stay in Spain. It must be purchased before arrival in Spain and costs around $250. These offers may also be matched by other airlines. Some flights have restrictions, e.g. they must be booked in advance, are available only on certain days of the week, and the period in between flights must include a Saturday night. Iberia offers special promotional fares (e.g. 'citysavers') which may undercut charter fares, particularly to Barcelona and Madrid.

If you're planning a trip abroad during school holidays, book well in advance, particularly if you're heading for a popular destination such as London, Paris or New York.

Airports

The main Spanish airport for intercontinental flights is Madrid's Barajas airport, served by direct flights from most European and North and South American cities. Barcelona is also a major international airport, although Palma de Mallorca airport is the second busiest airport in Spain after Madrid, handling over 7m passengers a year (mainly summer charter flights). Madrid is the hub of Spanish domestic flights and typical flight times are: Barcelona (55 minutes), Bilbao (50 minutes), Seville (50 minutes), Valencia (30 minutes), Palma de Mallorca (one hour) and the Canary Islands (2 hours 30 minutes).

International flights are available from many of Spain's 'regional' airports including Alicante, Almeria, Avilés, Bilbao, Fuenteventura, Gerona, Granada, Gran Canaria, Ibiza, Jerez de la Frontera, La Coruña, Lanzarote, Las Palmas, Malaga, Melilla, Menorca, Murcia, Palma de Mallorca, Rues (Tarragona), San Sebastían, Santander, Santiago de Compostela, Seville, Tenerife, Valencia, Vigo, Vitoria and Zaragossa. Other domestic airports include Ampurias (Gerona), Badajoz, Burgos, Cáceres, Cordoba, Logroño, Mahón (Menorca), Oviedo (Asturias), Puigcerdà, Pamplona, Salamanca, Seu d'Urgell and Valladolid.

Madrid's *Aeropuerto de Barajas* is located 15km outside the city on the N-11 and is one of Europe's six major airports, although it's a little dated compared with Barcelona's modernised airport. It has separate international and domestic terminals. Madrid has difficulty handling the increasing number of flights and there are often delays, with incoming flights sometimes diverted to the Torrejón military air base 12km away. There are regular bus and train services to Madrid city centre and a taxi to the city costs around 2,000 ptas. For information telephone (91) 408 5200/408 5457.

Barcelona's *El Prat de Llobregat*, located 14km (9 miles) from the city centre, was virtually rebuilt from 1989 to 1991 (for the 1992 Olympics) and is now one of the finest airports in the world. The fastest way to the city is by RENFE train, costing around 200 ptas (around twice as much as the bus). A taxi to the city centre costs around 2,500 ptas. For information telephone (93) 379 2454.

Many Spanish airports have been expanded and modernised in recent years including Barcelona, Malaga and Seville, although you should expect delays at major airports during the summer high season (the worst airports for delays in summer include Alicante, Malaga, Palma, Ibiza and Mahon, particularly at weekends). Always carefully check your baggage on collection and report any damage immediately. Most airports have sufficient baggage trolleys, although you usually need a 100 pta coin to use one, and porters (who charge an official rate per piece of baggage) are also usually available to carry bags. All major Spanish airports have duty-free shops, although some are open only during the main tourist season. Note that it's usually cheaper to buy alcohol in a local liquor store or supermarket. There's no airport departure tax in Spain. Secure 24-hour parking is provided at or near most Spanish airports, where parking fees are usually reasonable, e.g. 300 to 600 ptas a day, with discounts for two weeks or longer.

HOLIDAY & VISITOR'S PASSES

There are a variety of rail tickets for visitors to Spain and Spanish residents travelling by train in Europe. A wide range of rail passes are also available, some of which are sold only in certain countries, e.g. Canada and the USA, or to non-residents of Spain. Passes include a tourist card (*tarjeta turista*), *Eurodomino*, *Spain Rail 'n Drive Pass* and Route 26 passes (under 26 year-olds). A range of Eurail passes, allowing travel in 17 countries and valid for 15, 25, 30, 60 or 90 days, are available for those with their permanent residence outside Europe, including the Eurailpass, the Eurail Flexipass, Eurail Youthpass (under 26), the Eurail Saverpass and the Eurail Flexi Saverpass. The Inter-Rail Pass is valid for one month for those under 26, and 15 days or one month for those aged over 26. It allows unrestricted, second-class rail travel in 27 European countries including Britain, Ireland and Morocco, and discounts of up to 50 per cent in the country where it's purchased. The Inter-Rail pass is better value than Eurail passes and is available to those with their permanent residence in Europe (but must be purchased in your country of permanent residence).

Both Inter-Rail and Eurail passes are valid on all RENFE trains, although supplements are payable. For example you must pay extra to travel on an express train such as a *talgo* and sometimes on *expreso* and *rápido* trains or on rail bus services. Surcharges seem to be random and may depend on individual conductors. It's advisable to reserve a ticket in advance, in return for which you will receive a computer-printed ticket that usually satisfies conductors. Note that international railpasses aren't valid on Spain's private railway lines such as those operated by FEVE. Free Eurail/Inter Rail timetables and a wide range of brochures and maps are available from offices selling passes.

A tourist card (*tarjeta turística*) is available to non-residents and allows unlimited first or second class travel for 8, 15 or 22 consecutive days' travel on scheduled RENFE trains and on international trains with the exception of the Paris-Madrid *talgo* service. There are also flexi-tickets allowing four days travel in any 15-day period or nine days travel in any 30-day period. North Americans can buy a *Spain Rail 'n Drive Pass*. Reservation fees and supplements for fast trains and sleepers are payable, although holders of 1st class tourist cards are exempt from paying 2nd class couchette supplements on domestic RENFE trains. There's a 50 per cent reduction for children aged 4 to 11. Cards are valid for one year, although you must state the day on which you wish the card to commence, either at the time of purchase or within six months of purchase. Validation can be carried out at main railway stations, RENFE offices or RENFE appointed travel agents. BIGE tickets are available to those aged under 26 and offer savings of up to 50 per cent off normal fares. Tickets are available at student centres such as *Viajes de Jóvenes y Estudiantes*, Fernando el Católico, 88, 28015 Madrid, which also has offices in other Spanish cities.

An excellent book for European rail travellers is *Europe by Train* by Katie Woods and George McDonald (Fontana). It covers accommodation, visas, food, sights, customs and even the idiosyncracies of local transport. *Europe by Eurail* by George and Laverne Ferguson provides tips on planning a European tour using a Railpass and other passes, making day trips from selected base cities. Thomas Cook publish a wide range of books, guides and maps for train travellers. These include a *European Timetable*, which is much more than a collection of train times and contains information on shipping services, customs regulations, visa requirements and town plans. Thomas Cook Publications publish a number of other useful maps and timetables for European and world travellers including a *Rail Map of Europe*, the *Railpass Guide* and the *Overseas Timetable* (rail, bus and shipping services outside Europe). All publications are available direct from Thomas Cook Publishing, PO Box 227, Peterborough PE3 6SB, UK (tel. 01733-505821).

11.

MOTORING

Motoring in Spain has altered dramatically in the last few decades, during which period the number of cars has vastly increased and roads have been improved beyond recognition. The traffic on Spanish roads doubled between 1980 and 1990 and today is 30 times what it was in 1960, although only some 65 per cent of Spanish households own a car, which is less than in northern European countries. In addition to building new roads and by-passes to avoid town centres, existing roads have been widened, lanes added for heavy traffic, and signs and road markings improved. The road network covers over 300,000km (around 200,000miles), of which around 6,000km (3,728miles) are motorways (*autopistas*). Although still covering a smaller proportion of the country than motorways in most northern European countries, there are plans to extend the motorway network to some 10,000km (6,214miles) by the year 2000.

Spanish motorways are mostly toll roads built by private companies and are among Europe's finest. Unfortunately, they are also among the world's most expensive roads and consequently main trunk roads (*carreteras*) are jammed by drivers who are reluctant (or cannot afford) to pay the high motorway tolls. The road-building programme (and provision of parking spaces) has, however, failed to keep pace with the increasing number of cars on Spanish roads (it's hard to believe that Spain has a lower density of vehicles than most other European countries). In contrast to the generally excellent motorways and trunk roads, roads in rural areas and small towns are often dreadful (or even dangerous) and full of potholes.

Driving long distances is usually cheaper than using public transport in Spain, particularly when your car runs on diesel fuel, the costs are shared between a number of people and you avoid motorways. In any case, unless you're travelling between major cities you will have little choice but to drive yourself, as public transport is generally poor in rural areas. However, if you're travelling long distances, you'll find it quicker and certainly less stressful to take the train or fly. Those travelling to Spain from Britain may prefer to take the ferry (see page 181) to northern Spain rather than drive through France. If you live in a city, particularly Madrid or Barcelona (where public transport services are excellent), a car is a liability, while in rural areas it's a necessity.

Driving can be enjoyable in rural areas, particularly outside the tourist season, when it's possible to drive for miles without seeing another motorist (or a caravan). However, driving in Spain's major cities is a nightmare and to be avoided if at all possible. As a result of the *siesta*, Spain has four rush hours (*horas puntas*): 0800-0930, 1230-1430, 1530-1600 and 1830-2000; the quietest period is usually between 1500 and 1700 when most people are having their *siesta*. Traffic jams (*atascos*) are particularly bad in cities such as Madrid and Barcelona, where the rush 'hour' lasts all day. Madrid, where the average traffic speed fell from over 50 kph (31 mph) in 1980 to below 20 kph (11 mph) in 1994, is to be avoided at any time. Jams are common on coastal roads and in resort towns during summer. There is, however, a positive side to traffic jams, which reduce traffic speeds and accidents, thus contributing to the Spaniards' longevity.

Bottlenecks and traffic jams are horrendous at the start and end of holiday periods, particularly in summer on roads heading south out of Madrid and Barcelona, when some 12m Spaniards and foreigners take to the roads on their annual holidays. Anyone who has driven in Spain won't be surprised to learn that it has one of the worst accident records in the EU (only Portugal has a worst per capita record in western Europe), with over 4,000 deaths a year, although it has fallen in recent years (due to increased vigilance by the Guardia Civil and a national advertising campaign). Traffic accidents are the single biggest cause of death among young Spaniards. Eccentric and impatient drivers, *machismo*, drunken (around a third of drivers in fatal accidents are over the alcohol limit) and drugged motorists and pedestrians, blazing hot weather, stray animals, vehicles without lights, badly marked roads and sharp bends without crash barriers, all contribute to the hazards of driving in Spain. **The most important point to bear in mind when driving in Spain is to drive defensively and always expect the unexpected from other road users.** For information about car ferries see page 181.

CAR IMPORTATION

Car importation is a topical subject among expatriates (and the expatriate press) in Spain, particularly as the rules and regulations have been changing at a bewildering pace in the last decade. Importing a car into Spain involves the usual battle with Spanish bureaucracy, although the paperwork has been reduced considerably in recent years. However, many people still find the red tape forbidding and employ a *gestor* (see page 410) to do it for them. In the past the Spanish authorities have tried to discourage the personal import of vehicles by erecting an almost impenetrable barrier of paperwork and taxes. However, under threats from the EU, the process has been simplified, although it still involves mountains of forms and can take a number of months (and can cost up to around 125,000 ptas plus any taxes due!). The regulations vary depending on whether you're an EU resident or not. The procedure for the importation of a caravan or motorcycle with an engine capacity over 49cc is the same as for a car, although mopeds with engines below 49cc can be freely imported as part of your personal possessions and require no special paperwork.

Residents: A permanent resident of Spain isn't permitted to operate a car on foreign registration plates and must import it and operate it on Spanish plates. Vehicles registered outside the EU cannot generally be operated in Spain or any other EU country by EU residents (although there are a few exceptions). A vehicle imported tax and duty free into Spain mustn't be sold, rented or transferred within one year of its registration. The importation of right-hand drive (RHD) cars was prohibited in 1991, but this was subsequently reversed after protests from British residents to the European Commission. However, registration of a RHD vehicle in Spain applies only to new residents already owning a RHD vehicle, and doesn't apply to residents of Spain who aren't permitted to purchase a RHD vehicle abroad and register it in Spain. However, many resident foreigners continue to illegally drive foreign-registered cars long after they have become residents without any apparent problems.

Homologation: Homologation (*homologación*) is the name given to the procedure whereby vehicles must comply with certain safety and other requirements before they can be registered. Homologation is no longer necessary for vehicles previously registered in an EU country, although a standardisation certificate (*ficha reducida*) is required, which can be issued by any licensed Spanish engineer. However, a vehicle imported from a country outside the EU must still undergo homologation. It must be certified by the manufacturer or an officially recognised laboratory and undergo a test before it can be registered in Spain. This costs between 20,000 and 60,000 ptas, depending on the make of car. It's a long and annoying process and the information demanded by the local authorities often varies depending on the province or region of Spain.

Taxes: The following taxes and duty must be paid when importing a vehicle into Spain:

- Value added tax (IVA) at 16 per cent is payable on cars imported from outside the EU or on a tax-free car (on which VAT hasn't previously been paid) imported from an EU country.

- A special registration tax (*impuesto municipal sobre circulación de vehículos*) of 12 per cent (11 per cent in the Canaries) is payable on vehicles imported into Spain, and is calculated on the vehicle's current value (based on the original market price in Spain). The exception is petrol-engined vehicles with a capacity of less than 1,600cc and diesel-engined vehicles under 2,000cc, on which the tax is 7 per cent. The tax also includes four-wheel drive vehicles which were previously taxed at a lower rate. **However, from 1st January 1997 EU residents coming to live in Spain and importing a car they have owned for at least six months are no longer required to pay this tax.**

- Import duty of 10 per cent is payable on vehicles imported from outside the EU.

The amount payable for each of the above taxes is based on the original price of the vehicle with a reduction for each year of its age up to 10 years, e.g. 80 per cent after the first year, 70 per cent after two years, 50 per cent after five years, reducing to 20 per cent after 10 years. Anyone wishing to import a vehicle into Spain must be a permanent resident or must own property in Spain. For residents, the application must be accompanied by a certificate from the *Dirección de la Seguridad del Estado* showing the date of issue of the applicant's first residence card and stating that he has continuously lived in Spain from the date of issue. An application to import a car should be made as soon as possible after receipt of the residence card (*residencia*). During this period you must apply for an import licence to the Ministry of Economy and Finance (*Ministerio de Economía y Hacienda*), Castellana, 162, Madrid.

After you have completed the importation procedure you mustn't drive your car until the Ministry of Transport has issued temporary (green) registration plates (see page 195). These are valid for a limited period and allow you to drive to the nearest testing station for an ITV test (see page 197), which must be passed before you receive a standard registration number.

EU Non-Residents: Non-residents of Spain resident in another EU country can bring a vehicle registered in another EU country to Spain and can use it without any time limits and without paying Spanish taxes. However, the period of use is determined by the length of time that a non-resident is permitted to remain in Spain, which is six months (182 days) in a calendar year. This means that it's possible to use a vehicle in Spain for up to one year continuously when the period includes the last six months of one year and the first six months of the following year. The vehicle must be road-legal in its home country, meaning that it must be inspected (for roadworthiness) and taxed each year in its country of registration.

Persons Resident Outside the EU: A person resident outside the EU may temporarily import a vehicle registered outside the EU for a total period of six months (which needn't be continuous) within a calendar year. Under certain strict conditions and for certain persons only, the six-month period can be extended, e.g. for those regularly crossing into EU territory to work, full-time students from outside the EU, and persons from outside the EU on a special mission for a specified period in an EU country. This exemption is applicable only to persons resident outside the EU and the vehicle can be used only by the owner, his spouse, parents and children (who must also be non-residents). Note, however, that it's necessary for non-EU citizens to have a foreign-registered vehicle 'sealed' (*precintado*) by customs during periods of absence from Spain.

Tourist Plates: It's possible for non-residents to purchase a vehicle on tourist plates under Spain's special tourist scheme (*regimen especial*) and renew them indefinitely. However, since 1st January 1993 it's no longer possible for EU residents to buy a vehicle on tourist plates without paying VAT and renew the plates *after* they have become Spanish residents. Spanish road tax must be paid on all cars kept in Spain on tourist plates. Most car dealers will handle the registration and renewal of tourist plates, as will a *gestor*. There's an annual fee for the renewal and extensions of tourist plates plus the *gestor's* fees (if a *gestor* is employed to do the paperwork).

EU Citizens: EU citizens who aren't residents of Spain can, however, still buy cars on tourist plates, but must pay Spain's 16 per cent IVA. They are exempt from paying Spain's special registration tax unless they become residents (when the registration tax becomes payable, less a reduction for each year of the vehicle's age). There's no limit on the period a car purchased free of registration tax can be kept in Spain. The owner of a vehicle on tourist plates must be a non-resident without any Spanish income and must pay for the vehicle in foreign currency (it also cannot be purchased on credit terms). Under the new regulations, tourist plates are only of real benefit to EU residents when they buy an expensive car and keep it for a number of years (due to the cost of renewing the registration and *gestor's* fees).

Non-EU Citizens: Non-EU citizens can continue to purchase tax-free vehicles on Spanish tourist plates and operate them for six months each year (the maximum stay permitted for non-residents). The six months needn't be continuous and can be divided into any number of visits. Providing that you don't work in Spain, you can apply to renew your tourist plates indefinitely. A non-EU national must, however, make a sworn statement (*declaración jurada*) that he doesn't reside in Spain for more than six months a year. A non-EU resident pays around 25,000 a year for tourist plates for a car manufactured in Spain and around 35,000 ptas for a foreign-manufactured car, but doesn't pay VAT, registration tax or import duty. Non-EU citizens cannot renew their tourist plates if they become residents of Spain. Note that a vehicle on tourist plates owned by a non-EU citizen can be used only by the registered owner or his immediate family members and must be 'sealed' (*precintado*) by customs during periods of absence from Spain. **Anyone who illegally drives a vehicle on foreign or tourist plates can be fined up to 150,000 ptas and the vehicle can be confiscated.**

CAR REGISTRATION

When you import a car into Spain or buy a new or secondhand car, it must be registered (*matriculación*) at the local provincial traffic department (*jefatura provincial de tráfico*) in the province where you're resident. If you import a car, you must obtain customs clearance and, if it's imported from a country outside the EU, it must undergo a homologation inspection before it can be registered (see page 193). When you buy a car from a dealer in Spain he will usually arrange for the issue of the registration certificate (*permiso de circulación*) or the transfer of ownership. If you buy a car privately you can do the registration yourself or you can employ a *gestor* to do it for you.

When you buy a secondhand car you must apply for a new registration certificate within 10 days of purchase at the *vehículos* counter of the local traffic department. The following documents are required:

- a completed application form (*notificación de transferencia de vehículos*), obtainable from the local provincial traffic department;

- the current registration document (*permiso de circulación*) with the transfer of ownership listed on the reverse, including the seller's signature;

- the road tax receipt for the current year and a photocopy;

- the current ITV test certificate (see page 197) with the technical sheet and a photocopy;

- a receipt for the payment of transfer tax (see page 200);

- your resident card (*residencia*) or a photocopy or the title deeds (*escritura*) of your Spanish home if you aren't a Spanish resident;

- the receipt for the registration fee of 9,650 ptas (payable at a *Caja Postal* and not at the traffic department);

- a stamped self-addressed envelope (for the return of the new registration document).

If a person other than the new owner makes the application, he must provide written authorisation from the owner and supply his own resident card and a copy.

Change of Address or Loss of Document: If you change your address, you must apply to have the address on your registration document changed (there's no fee). If you lose or damage your registration document, you must apply for a new one and pay a fee of 1,000 ptas. Always make a copy of your registration document and keep it in a safe place.

Licence & Residence: EU nationals aren't required to have a Spanish driving licence (see page 201) to buy or operate a Spanish-registered car, although non-EU residents must have a Spanish driving licence. It's usually necessary to be either a Spanish resident or own a home in Spain in order to operate a car on Spanish plates, although you can also obtain a certificate (*certificado de empadronamiento*) stating that you're a registered inhabitant of a municipality. This isn't a residence permit but a registration certificate stating that you live in a particular municipality. Note that an EU resident is prohibited from driving a vehicle registered in a country outside the EU and that Spanish residents aren't permitted to operate a vehicle on foreign registration plates.

De-Registration: When a vehicle is stolen or scrapped you should complete a *baja* form available from your local provincial traffic department. You require the same documents as for registration (listed above), with the exception of the receipt for payment of transfer tax, or a sworn statement that you no longer have them, and the fee of 925 ptas. If a vehicle has been stolen, a copy of the police report (*denuncia*) is required. The *baja* ensures that you no longer receive road tax bills or traffic fines, even if someone else puts the vehicle back on the road.

Spanish Registration Plates: The first one or two letters of a Spanish registration plate denote the province where the vehicle is registered (see table below), followed by four numerals and one or two more letters, indicating the age of the car. Since 1st July 1995, Spanish registration plates have incorporated the EU flag and a 'E' for España. Tourist plates have an M plus numerals and a number and date of expiry in red. Green plates signify an imported vehicle or one previously on tourist plates awaiting standard plates. When a non-resident with a vehicle on tourist plates becomes a resident, he has three months from the date of receipt of his residence card to change to standard plates.

In Spain, the original registration remains permanently with a car. If you buy a secondhand car in Spain, it's best to buy one that's registered in the province where you live, otherwise you will be stuck with the registration that comes with the car, which may 'identify' you as a person from a 'strange' province (which could be a problem in some areas). For example because of traditional rivalry, cars with Madrid number plates are difficult to sell in Catalonia and vice versa (most people prefer to drive a car bearing the prefix of their home province). In future plates will bear just three letters and four numbers and won't show the province of registration.

There are 58 registration letters: 50 for the mainland and island provinces plus the North African protectorates of Ceuta (CE) and Melilla (ML); the army (*Ejército de Tierra/ET*), air force (*Fuerzas Aéreas/EA*), and navy (*Fuerzas Navales/FN*); civil guard (*Parque Guardia Civil/PGC*), ministry of public works (*Ministerio de Obras Públicas/MOP*) and general civil service vehicles (*Parque Móvil Ministerios/PMM*); as shown below:

A	Alicante	GE	Gerona (Girona)	PGC	Parque Guardia Civil
AB	Albacete	GR	Granada	PM	Baleares
AL	Almeria	GU	Guadalajara	PMM	Parque Móv. Min.
AV	Avila	H	Huelva	PO	Pontevedra
B	Barcelona	HU	Huesca	S	Santander
BA	Badajoz	J	Jaén	SA	Salamanca
BI	Vizcaya	L	Lérida (Lleida)	SE	Seville
BU	Burgos	LE	León	SG	Segovia
C	Coruña	LO	Logroño	SO	Soria
CA	Cadiz	LU	Lugo	SS	Guipózcoa
CC	Cáceres	M	Madrid	T	Tarragona
CE	Ceuta	MA	Malaga	TE	Teruel
CO	Córdoba	ML	Melilla	TF	Tenerife
CR	Ciudad Real	MOP	Minis. Obras. Púb.	TO	Toledo
CS	Castellón	MU	Murcia	V	Valencia
CU	Cuenca	NA	Navarra	VA	Vallodolid
EA	Fuerzas Aéreas	O	Oviedo	VI	Alava
ET	Ejército de Tierra	OR	Orense	ZA	Zamora
FN	Fuerzas Navales	P	Palencia	Z	Zaragossa
GC	Gran Canaria				

TECHNICAL INSPECTION (ITV)

All cars over four years old must have an annual control test (*Inspección Técnica de Vehículos/ITV*), carried out at an authorised test station. Motorcycles are first tested after five years, after which it's due annually. There are ITV test stations in all major towns (listed in Yellow Pages under *Automóviles Inspección Técnica de Vehículos*). Make an appointment to avoid a long wait or a wasted journey. The test fee is 4,790 ptas. Most garages will get your car tested for you, although if you ask a garage to take your car in for a test, make sure that you don't pay for unnecessary repairs, either before or after the test.

If a vehicle fails the test you receive a blue form listing the faults and you're given 15 days to have it repaired and re-tested. If possible get the ITV examiner to write down the repairs necessary to pass the test, otherwise you could receive a large bill for unnecessary repairs. Tests aren't exhaustive or rigorous and consequently old wrecks that should have been consigned to the scrap heap decades ago flourish in Spain, particularly in rural areas. If a vehicle is involved in a serious accident, it must usually undergo an ITV test after repair to establish whether the repairs have been carried out correctly. When your car has passed the test you're given a certificate showing the month and year when the test is next due, which must be displayed in the top right-hand corner of your windscreen. Certificates are a different colour for each year. You can be fined up to 250,000 ptas for failing to display a valid ITV certificate. You also receive an ITV card (*tarjeta de inspección técnica de vehículos*).

Note that the Spanish ITV test has no value in other EU countries. If you operate a car in Spain that's registered in another EU country, it must be tested in accordance with the law of the country where it's registered in order to be legal in Spain. If you import a car into Spain, it must pass the ITV test before it can be registered on Spanish plates.

BUYING A CAR

Cars are more expensive in Spain than in most other EU countries and up to double the cost in the USA. However, although cars are more expensive to buy, they depreciate slower than in most other European countries, so the extra you pay when buying a car is usually gained when you sell it. Spanish-made cars are generally cheaper than imported cars, due to import taxes and duty. If you do high mileage, it's worth considering buying a diesel car, as diesel fuel costs around 20 per cent less than petrol in Spain (it's also cheaper in most other EU countries). In order to buy a Spanish-registered car you need a residence card (*residencia*), a deed (*escritura*) or rental contract for a Spanish property, or a certificate of residence (*certificado de empadronamiento*) in a Spanish community. Note, however, that the regulations may be interpreted differently by the authorities depending on the province. It's also possible for non-residents to buy a tax-free car on Spanish plates and operate it for up to six months of the year in Spain (see page 193).

New Cars

Although sales have increased slightly in the last few years, Spain generally remains a buyers' market for new cars and you may be able to drive a hard bargain. The prices of most new cars are around 10 to 20 per cent higher in Spain than in many other EU countries and the choice is more restricted, although some models are cheaper. The taxes on new cars are higher in Spain than in any other EU country due to the registration tax of 12 per cent, which is charged in addition to VAT (IVA) at 16 per cent. Most new cars are sold at list price, although you should still shop around for the best deal as dealers compete in offering discounts, guarantees, financing terms and special sales. To boost new car sales and reduce the number of old cars on Spanish roads (over 35 per cent are over 10 years old), anyone who has owned a car which is over 10 years old for more than one year is given a discount of 80,000 ptas (against the registration tax) when buying a new car. The new vehicle must be purchased within six months of scrapping the old vehicle.

Residents can buy cars on hire purchase (instalment plan), although those who aren't property owners usually need to provide a financial guarantee or obtain a guarantor. You will also need a certificate from your Spanish bank stating that you pay your bills regularly, a copy of your employment contract and a copy of your previous year's tax return. The down payment varies depending on the dealer and payments can be spread over one to four years. After making the down payment, you'll be asked to sign a number of 'bills of exchange' (*letras de cambio*), usually one for each monthly instalment due. These are like cheques or individual direct debit advices and are addressed directly to your bank for payment. Most car dealers also sell car insurance, although you should shop around as you will probably get a better deal elsewhere.

It's possible to buy a new tax-free car in another EU country, e.g. from the factory of a European manufacturer or from an exporter in countries such as Belgium, Denmark (usually the cheapest due to high local taxes), Greece and the Netherlands, and personally import it into Spain. In some countries (e.g. Britain) you can buy a tax-free car up to six months before exporting it. Personally importing any car from the USA is usually much cheaper than buying the same car in Spain or elsewhere in Europe. However, before importing a car from outside the EU, you should ensure that it's manufactured to Spanish specifications, or you will encounter problems getting it through the homologation (*homologación*) inspection (see page 193). There's no longer any import duty on cars imported from other EU countries, although you must pay Spain's special registration tax (*impuesto municipal sobre circulación de vehículos*) and 16 per cent VAT (if VAT hasn't already been paid in another EU country).

Used Cars

Used or secondhand (*de segundo mano*) cars in Spain are more expensive than in many other EU countries, as new cars are more expensive and cars hold their value better. It often pays to buy a used car that's around two years old, as depreciation in the first one or two years is considerable (high mileage cars, particularly rental cars, are good value). Note, however, that older cars in Spain (outside of their warranty period) aren't always well maintained. You must take extra care when buying a used car on foreign plates as many are 'clocked' (the odometer is turned back so that it appears to have done less kilometres/miles that it has); make sure that a car has a genuine service history that confirms the kilometres or miles shown on the clock. You must pay registration tax to transfer a foreign registered car to Spanish plates. There are many cowboys in Spain (often foreigners) selling old cosmetically improved lemons (the small ads in the expatriate press are full of them) and it's generally better to buy from a reputable dealer, even if you pay a bit more, and obtain a warranty. If you intend to buy a used car in Spain, whether privately or from a garage, check the following:

- that it has a current ITV test certificate (see page 197), if applicable;
- that it hasn't been involved in a major accident and suffered structural damage;
- that the chassis number tallies with the registration document (*permiso de circulación*), which should be in the name of the seller when a car is purchased privately (check his identity card or passport);

- that the service coupons have been completed and stamped, and that servicing has been carried out by an authorised dealer;

- that you receive a 'transfer of ownership' (*transferencia*) form from the seller. The form is available from the provincial traffic department (*jefatura provincial de tráfico*).

- whether a written guarantee is provided.

Car dealers usually give warranties on used cars of from three to 12 months, depending on the age of the car and the particular model. Used car dealers, rather than franchised dealers, have the same dreadful (and usually well-deserved) reputation in Spain as in other countries, and caution must be taken when buying from them. When you're buying a used car from a garage, always try to negotiate a reduction, particularly when you're paying cash and aren't trading in another vehicle. When you buy a car from a dealer, he will arrange the transfer of ownership, usually for a small fee. Alternatively you can employ a *gestor* to handle the transfer or do it yourself at the local provincial traffic department.

It may pay you to personally import a used car from another EU country or even from North America. The procedure for importing cars from EU countries has been eased in recent years and it's no longer necessary for a car to undergo a homologation inspection. A saving of 20 to 25 per cent can be made on used cars purchased in some countries, e.g. Belgium or Germany, and savings of up to 50 per cent on imports from the USA (although the paperwork involved in US imports is a nightmare).

When you buy a secondhand car in Spain you must obtain the registration document (*permiso de circulación*); the ITV test certificate (see page 197) plus the technical sheet and a photocopy; the road tax receipt and a photocopy; and a receipt for the payment of transfer tax (see page 200). You have 15 days to register the vehicle in your name.

There are various motoring journals advertising used cars including *Solo Auto* (monthly) and *Coche Actual* (bi-monthly) in addition to most daily newspapers. There are also free magazines in some areas, such as *Motor en Mano* on the Costa del Sol. All national and local (including free) newspapers carry advertisements for used cars, as do expatriate newspapers, which include foreign-registered cars. Secondhand car prices vary depending on the region of Spain and are generally higher in remote areas and the islands than they are in Madrid and other major cities.

SELLING A CAR

When selling a car in Spain, you must obtain and complete a 'transfer of ownership' (*notificación de transferencia de vehículos*, usually simply called a *transferencia*) form, available from the provincial traffic department (*jefatura provincial de tráfico*). The form must be completed in duplicate, one copy of which is given to the buyer and the other sent to the traffic department. When you sell a secondhand car in Spain, a 'transfer tax' is levied called ITP (*impuesto sobre transmisiones patrimoniales y actos jurídicos documentados*), which is 4 per cent of the fiscal value. The fiscal value of a car when new is decided by the tax office, which publishes a list of values for all new cars sold in Spain. The fiscal value is reduced each year (e.g. to 88 per cent when a vehicle is between one and two years old) until it's 10 or more years old, when the fiscal value is reduced to 10 per cent of the new value. The tax should be paid by the buyer, although it's the responsibility of the seller to pay the tax. Most sellers include the tax in the sales price (so check in advance what it will be).

The tax must be declared on form 620 (*compra-venta de vehículos usados entre particulares*), obtainable from a tobacconist's (*estanco*) or tax office (*hacienda*), and paid within 30 days of selling your car. Payment is made at the provincial tax office (*Consejería de Hacienda*) of the regional government, e.g. the *Junta de Andalucía*. The tax declaration can also be made by a *gestor*. Other points to note when selling a car are:

- Complete, sign and date the reverse of the registration document (*permiso de circulación*) under the section *transferido*. For additional protection you could register the sale with your local *jefatura provincial de tráfico*. Some people recommend that you don't leave the transfer of a vehicle to the buyer, but go with him to the *jefatura provincial de tráfico* and register the vehicle in his name before you give him the documents or keys. Failing this you can de-register the car yourself (see page 196). This will ensure that from the date of the sale you will no longer be liable for road tax and won't be responsible for parking fines and motoring offences committed by the new owner.

- You must give the buyer the registration document (*permiso de circulación*); the ITV test certificate (see page 197) plus the technical sheet and a photocopy; the road tax receipt for the current year and a photocopy; and a receipt for the payment of transfer tax (see page 200).

- Inform your insurance company.

- If selling your car privately, insist on payment in cash or with a banker's draft (*letra de cambio*), which is standard practice in Spain. If you cannot tell a banker's draft from a personal cheque, insist on cash. **Never accept a personal cheque.**

- Include in the receipt that you're selling the car in its present condition (as seen) without a guarantee (*sin garantía*), the price paid and the car's kilometre reading.

The best place to advertise a car for sale is in local newspapers, expatriate newspapers, on free local notice boards, and in the Friday and Saturday editions of major newspapers. Many people also put a for sale (*se vende*) notice on their car with a telephone number and park it in a prominent place.

Finally, you should be wary of thieves posing as buyers, who, given half a chance will steal your car. Never allow a prospective buyer to drive your car alone or even to sit in the driving seat when you aren't in the car (unless you retain the ignition keys). There have been a number of cases of crooks driving off with cars after duping the owner into getting out of the car. Usually it's the last that's seen of the 'buyer' or your car.

DRIVING LICENCE

The minimum age for driving in Spain is 18 for a car or a motorcycle with an engine capacity over 125cc and 14 for a motorcycle (moped) up to 50cc (16 for a motorcycle up to 125cc). There's also a maximum age of 65 for obtaining your first licence. This applies to first-timers only and doesn't apply to foreigners aged over 65, e.g. retired residents, who can exchange their foreign licence for a Spanish licence (*permiso de conducción*). Non-residents can drive in Spain on a foreign or international driving licence for a maximum of six months in a calendar year. EU residents can drive on their existing EU licence until it expires, but non-EU residents must obtain a Spanish driving licence after one year.

Most foreign driving licences are recognised in Spain, although some foreign licence holders, e.g. licences printed in Arabic or Chinese, require a Spanish translation (available from Spanish consulates) or an international licence. Americans also need a Spanish translation (notarised by the American consulate or any American consulate in Spain) of their American licence or an international driving licence. An international driving licence is obtainable in Spain from the Royal Automobile Club of Spain (*Real Automóvil Club de España*) on presentation of a valid foreign driving licence, passport and two photographs. Note, however, that if a non-resident obtains an international driving licence in Spain, it will be valid only for driving *outside* Spain. Holders of licences issued by countries without a reciprocal agreement with Spain must take a Spanish written and/or practical driving test. The written test can be taken in English and other foreign languages. If in doubt, consult a Spanish consulate abroad or your country's embassy or consulate in Spain.

Non-EU Residents can drive in Spain with a foreign or international licence for up to one year, after which they must obtain a Spanish driving licence, even when they don't currently drive in Spain. It's no longer necessary for EU citizens to obtain a Spanish driving licence and they can continue driving in Spain with their foreign EU licence until it expires, when they must apply for a Spanish driving licence.

To apply for a Spanish driving licence (or a renewal) you require the following:

- a completed application form TASA 2.3 (*Solicitud de Carnet del Permiso de Conducir*), available from the *información-impresos* counter at the local provincial traffic department (*Jefatura Provincial de Tráfico*);

- your Spanish residence card (*residencia*) and a photocopy;

- your current foreign driving licence and a photocopy. Non-EU citizens require an official translation and a certificate of equivalence (*certificado de equivalencia*) available from the Royal Automobile Club of Spain (see page 226). Your current Spanish licence is required for a renewal.

- the registration number of a Spanish registered vehicle or a sworn statement that you don't own a vehicle with Spanish registration (not required for renewals);

- one passport-size photograph. Non-EU citizens require three passport-size photographs, one of which must be signed on the back by the doctor performing the medical examination (see below).

- the fee of 2,450 ptas (there's no fee for drivers over 70), payable at a Caja Postal, which also applies to renewals and the replacement of a lost or damaged licence. If a Spanish licence is being renewed and is over 30 days out of date, an additional fee of around 1,000 ptas is payable.

- Holders of non-EU driving licences require a medical certificate of fitness to drive (see below) and a stamped self-addressed envelope.

If a person other than the new owner makes the application, he must provide written authorisation from the owner and supply his own resident card and copy.

Medical Certificate: Holders of non-EU driving licences require a medical certificate to obtain a Spanish driving licence. The medical examination is carried out in special clinics (*Centros de Reconocimento Médico para Conductores*) open from 1000 to 1400 and from 1600 to 2000, Monday to Friday. The examination consists of eyesight, hearing, pulse and blood pressure tests, plus tests for speed of reaction, judgement of the speed of other vehicles and acuteness of visual identification. If you wear glasses or contact lenses you will be tested with them and your licence with be annotated to indicate this (note also that you must carry a spare pair when driving). The examination takes around half an hour and costs 3,400 ptas for those aged under 70 and 800 ptas for those aged 70 or over. The medical certificate is valid for 90 days and the examination should be performed around one month before you make your application for a licence (or a renewal). **A passport-size photograph is required.**

It usually takes two to three months to obtain a Spanish licence. You're given an official receipt for your application and a copy of your foreign licence, which is valid until you receive your Spanish licence. When you receive your Spanish licence, your foreign licence is returned to the issuing authority abroad. If you change your address, you must apply to have the address on your licence changed (there's no fee). A Spanish driving licence is a standard (pink) EU licence and contains a photograph. Note, however, that although it has the EU logo on it, it isn't an EU licence and must be replaced by a national licence after it expires if you move permanently to another EU country.

Licence Validity: The validity period of a Spanish licence depends on your age and the type of licence held, e.g. a motorcycle (A-1/A-2) or car (B-1) licence is valid for 10 years if you're aged under 45 and for five years if you're aged between 45 and 70. A driver aged over 70 must renew his licence annually and have an annual medical examination. A commercial, passenger vehicle or heavy goods licence must be renewed every five years up to the age of 45, every three years from age 46 to 60, and every two years from age 61 to 70. A motorist aged over 70 must renew his licence annually. There's no licence point system in Spain for traffic offences, although one may be introduced.

You can use a *gestor* (see page 410) to obtain a Spanish driving licence or the services of a Spanish motoring organisation such as the Royal Automobile Club of Spain (see page 226). A *gestor* will charge you 5,000 to 10,000 ptas for the work involved. You must carry your foreign or Spanish driving licence at all times when driving in Spain (see **Traffic Police** on page 211). Note that many Spaniards drive without a valid licence or when their licence is suspended, although they are liable for a fine of up to 250,000 ptas.

CAR INSURANCE

Under Spanish law, all motor vehicles plus trailers and semi-trailers must be insured when entering Spain. However, it isn't mandatory for cars insured in most European countries to have an international insurance 'green' card (see below) in Spain. Motorists insured in an EU country, the Czech Republic, Hungary, Liechtenstein, Norway, Slovakia and Switzerland are automatically covered for third-party liability in Spain. The following categories of car insurance are available in Spain:

Third-Party (*responsabilidad civil obligatoria* or *seguro obligatorio*): Third-party insurance is compulsory and is the minimum insurance required by law. It costs from around 25,000 ptas a year to insure against the minimum third party claims of up to 56m ptas for personal injury and 16m ptas for damage to third-party property. Extra cover can be purchased (see **Third-Party Personal/Property Limits** below). Roadside assistance (*asistencia en viajes*), glass cover (*rotura de lunas*) and legal expenses (*defensa penal*) in the event of a court case may be included in basic third-party cover or can be included for an additional premium.

Third-Party, Fire & Theft (*responsabilidad civil obligatoria, incendio y robo*): Third-Party, fire and theft insurance, known in some countries as part comprehensive, includes cover against fire (*incendio*), natural hazards (e.g. rocks falling on your car), theft (*robo*), broken glass (e.g. windscreen), legal expenses (*defensa penal*), and possibly damage or theft of contents (although this is rare). Insurance against the theft of a radio or stereo system is usually available from the manufacturer only, e.g. for one year after purchase (it may be included in the purchase price) or under a separate (very expensive) insurance policy. Fire cover may be able to be taken out independently, although theft cover may be available with fire cover only.

Full Comprehensive (*todo riesgo*): Full comprehensive insurance covers all the risks listed under third-party, fire and theft (above), and includes damage to your own vehicle irrespective of how it's caused. **Note that some insurance companies don't provide full comprehensive cover for vehicles older than two or three years (although you can get comprehensive cover on vehicles up to 10 years of age).** Full comprehensive insurance may be compulsory for lease and credit purchase contracts. Spanish insurance doesn't usually pay for a replacement car when your car is being repaired after an accident.

Third-Party Personal/Property Limits: The minimum third-party cover required by Spanish law is 56m ptas for bodily injury and 16m ptas for third-party property damage. You should always make sure that you fully understand the cover provided for the driver and passengers and that it meets your needs. You can choose to pay an extra premium for additional cover up to a specified or unlimited amount (*ilimitada*), which is highly recommended. Unlimited third-party cover usually costs around 5,000 ptas extra a year. Note that a driver and his family don't count as third parties and must be insured separately.

Driver & Passenger Insurance: Driver and passenger insurance (*seguro de ocupantes*) is usually optional in Spain and can be added to insurance policies. Driver protection allows the driver of a vehicle involved in an accident to claim for bodily injury to himself, including compensation for his incapacity to work or for his beneficiaries should he be killed. There are usually various levels of driver and passenger accident insurance, e.g. from 1 to 4m ptas for a driver for death and permanent disability and unlimited medical assistance.

Premiums: Insurance premiums in Spain are among the lowest in the EU, although they vary considerably depending on numerous factors including the type of insurance; your car, age and accident record; and the area where you live. Cars are divided into eight categories in Spain, based on their performance (power), the cost of repairs, where they are used, whether they are garaged and what they are used for, e.g. business or pleasure. Premiums are highest in Madrid and other major cities and lowest in rural areas. Some premiums are based on the number of kilometres driven each year. Full comprehensive insurance is generally available on cars under three years old only, although some companies offer full comprehensive insurance on vehicles up to 10 years of age. Insurance companies must give two month's notice of an increases in premiums, otherwise you can pay the same premium for another year.

In addition to the many Spanish insurance companies, car insurance is available from a number of foreign insurance companies in Spain, including direct insurance companies who don't use agents, such as the British Direct Line insurance company. Among the cheapest insurers for residents in Spain are the Expat Club and ExtranDirect, both of which are underwritten by Royal Insurance. Always shop around and obtain a number of quotations. **When choosing a company, bear in mind that a number of Spanish**

car insurance companies have gone bust in recent years, leaving tens of thousands of motorists blissfully unaware that they no longer had any insurance!

Some companies don't insure high performance vehicles, while others offer special low-cost policies for experienced older drivers, e.g. those over 50 or 55, with a good safety record. Premiums vary from around 25,000 ptas a year for third-party insurance for a small family saloon, to 150,000 ptas or more a year for full comprehensive insurance for a high-performance sports saloon (such as a BMW). Short term policies for periods of less than one year are available from some companies, although premiums are high, e.g. 50 per cent of the annual rate for three months and 70 per cent of the annual rate for six months. Value added tax (IVA) at 16 per cent is payable on insurance premiums.

Excess Premiums: You can reduce your premium by choosing to pay a voluntary excess (*franquicia*), e.g. the first 10,000, 15,000, 30,000 or 50,000 ptas of a claim. Special insurance can be purchased for contents and accessories such as an expensive car stereo system. Drivers with less than two or three years experience usually pay a penalty (*multa*) and drivers under a certain age, e.g. 25, also pay higher premiums. Drivers aged over 70 may also pay a penalty. Some insurance companies refuse to insure young drivers aged under 23 because their accident rate is so high. If you're convicted of drunken or dangerous driving, your premium will be increased considerably.

No-Claims: A foreign no-claims bonus (*bonificación/sistema bonus-malus*) is usually valid in Spain, but you must provide written evidence from your present or previous insurance company, not just an insurance renewal notice. You may need an official Spanish translation. Always insist on having your no-claims bonus recognised, even if you don't receive the same percentage reduction as you received abroad (shop around). If you haven't had car insurance for the previous two years, you aren't usually entitled to a no-claims bonus in Spain. The no-claims bonus in Spain isn't always as generous as in some other countries, although some companies offer 10 per cent a year up to five years and 5 per cent for the next two years, making a total discount of 60 per cent after seven years. Foreign insurance companies may offer a more generous no-claims bonus than Spanish companies, some of which offer a maximum of 50 per cent only (or less). If you have an accident, you're usually required to pay a penalty (*multa*) or your bonus is reduced, e.g. one accident may lose you two years' no-claims bonus. You can usually pay an extra premium to protect your no-claims bonus. No-claims bonuses usually also apply to a second family car. Some insurance companies give additional discounts of from 10 to 20 per cent for experienced drivers and you may also receive a discount (e,g, 5 per cent) if a vehicle is garaged overnight.

Claims: In the event of an accident, claims are decided on the information provided in accident report forms (*declaración de siniestro de automóvil*) completed by drivers, reports by insurance company experts and police reports (see also **Accidents** on page 218). You must notify your insurance company of a claim within a limited period, e.g. two to five days. If you have an accident, the damage must usually be inspected and the repair authorised by your insurance company's expert, although sometimes an independent expert's report may be permitted. An inspection may be unnecessary for minor repairs. Note that when a vehicle is a total loss, a Spanish insurance company may pay only a percentage of its 'book' value, which is less than its actual value.

If your car is stolen you must report it to the local police immediately and submit a copy of the police report with your claim. After reporting your car stolen, 30 days must elapse before an insurance company will consider a claim. Note that some Spanish insurance companies are very slow to pay claims (delays can run into years) and you may be better off insuring with a foreign company. There's little communication or co-operation between insurance companies in Spain and trying to recover uninsured losses is a nightmare. Some insurance companies have 24-hour helplines for claims, both in Spain and abroad.

Cancellation: Spanish insurance companies are forbidden by law to cancel third-party cover after a claim, except in the case of drunken driving or when a driver is subsequently disqualified from driving. A company can, however, refuse to renew your policy at the end of the current period, although they must give you 15 days notice. Note that if you have an accident while breaking the law, e.g. drunken driving or illegal parking, your comprehensive insurance may be automatically downgraded to third party only. This means that you must pay for your own repairs and medical expenses. If you wish to cancel your car insurance at the end of the current term, you must notify your insurance company in writing by registered letter and usually give two month's notice. You may cancel your insurance before the term has expired if the premium is increased, the terms are altered, or your car has been declared a total loss or stolen. If you cancel your policy during the term of the insurance, e.g. you sell your car, and don't take out another policy, your insurance company isn't required to give you a refund.

Green Cards: All Spanish and most insurance companies in western Europe provide an automatic 'green' card (*certificado internacional de seguro de autómovil*), which extends your normal insurance cover (e.g. full comprehensive) to other European countries. This doesn't include cars insured in Britain, where insurance companies usually provide a green card for limited periods only (e.g. 30 or 45 days) and for a maximum number of days a year, e.g. 90. However, you should shop around, as some companies allow drivers a green card for up to six months a year. Green cards are also expensive. This is to discourage the British from driving on the continent, where they are a menace and a danger to all road users (most of them don't know their left from their right, particularly the politicians!). If you're British and have full comprehensive insurance, it's wise to have a green card when visiting Spain.

If you drive a British-registered car and spend over six months a year on the continent, you may need to take out a special (i.e. expensive) European insurance policy or obtain insurance with a European company. Another alternative is to insure with a British insurance company in Spain. Note that from 1995, EU rules require all vehicles be insured in their country of registration. For example, if you keep a British-registered car in Spain, you can insure it through an insurance agent in Spain, but it must be with a UK-based insurance company. Similarly, if you have a Spanish-registered car, it must be insured with a Spanish insurance company (or a foreign insurance company with an office in Spain).

Breakdown Insurance: Spanish insurance companies provide an optional accident and breakdown service (*asistencia en viaje*), adopted by some 75 per cent of Spanish motorists. The breakdown service usually covers the policy-holder, his spouse, single dependent children, and parents and grand-parents living under the same roof. The 24-hour telephone number of the breakdown service's head office is shown on a card, which should be kept in your vehicle. If you break down anywhere in Spain, you simply call the emergency number, give your location and a recovery vehicle will be sent to your aid. Although accidents are covered anywhere in Spain, in the event of a breakdown you need to be a certain distance from your home, e.g. 15 or 25km. The insurance provides for transportation in the event of a breakdown or illness, in which case transportation to hospital (if necessary) plus medical treatment is recompensed up to a limited amount, e.g. 60,000 ptas. An interest free loan is provided in the case of a robbery and an emergency message service. The retrieval of your vehicle is also guaranteed from within Spain or abroad. If you're unable to find spare parts locally, your insurance company will arrange to have them shipped to you (at your expense).

Motorists driving without insurance is a huge problem in Spain where an (astonishing) estimated 1.5 to 2 million drivers are without insurance (Spain has more insurance fraud than any other EU country). However, driving without obligatory insurance (*seguro obligatorio*) is a serious offence in Spain, for which you can be fined up to 500,000 ptas or even imprisoned. You must carry your insurance documents when driving and can be fined 10,000 ptas for not having them if you're stopped by the police. See also **Insurance Contracts** on page 253.

ROAD TAX

All Spanish registered vehicles must pay road tax (*impuesto municipal sobre vehículos de tracción mecánica*). Like all Spanish taxes, road tax has increased in the last decade, although it's still lower than in other EU countries. Tax levels are set by individual municipalities and vary from town to town depending on their size; rates are higher in municipalities with over 100,000 inhabitants, which may double the minimum tax rate. Minimum and maximum limits are established by law, between which municipalities set their own rates. The tax is based on the fiscal horsepower (*potencia fiscal*) of your car, as calculated for tax purposes. For a vehicle of less than 8 fiscal horsepower/HP (*caballos fiscales*) the tax is usually between 2,000 and 4,000 ptas, 8 to 12 HP between 5,000 and 10,000 ptas, 12 to 16 HP between 12,000 and 20,000 ptas and above 16 HP between 15,000 and 23,000 ptas. Among the cheapest provinces are Tarragona, Ibiza and Castellon, and among the most expensive are Las Palmas and Majorca. Note that it's advisable to check your bill as some town halls overcharge by up to 100 per cent by using the wrong formula to calculation the horsepower. Motorcyclists also pay road tax.

Payment: Road tax must be paid to your local authority, usually sometime between March and May. Contact your local town hall to find out when and how it must be paid and to obtain a payment form. Announcements are made on municipal notice boards and in local newspapers and banks, and the town hall may send you a reminder (but don't count on it). It can be paid in person at the town hall collection or tax office (*recaudación* or *oficina municipal de impuestos*), in certain local banks and by mail. You can also pay via your bank by direct debit. It's best to pay at a local bank or by mail as there are usually long queues at the town hall. There's a late payment surcharge (*recargo*) of 5 per cent in the first month and 20 per cent thereafter, and the unpaid sum will also be liable to interest. When a vehicle is purchased, the tax payable is calculated pro rata for the current tax year. If a car is unused for a whole calendar year then you can have it's registration temporarily suspended (*baja temporal*) at your provincial traffic department. However, if a vehicle is used for just one month in a year, then tax must be paid for the whole year.

Non-Payment: Some people have been able to avoid paying road tax for many years, although municipalities are now clamping down on non-payers. The cars of non-payers can be impounded by local police on authority from town halls. Unlike many other countries, a road tax certificate isn't displayed inside your car's windscreen or on your registration plates. However, you should keep the receipt for your road tax in your car with your other car documents as the local police may ask to see it. Note that a Spanish-registered car is automatically recorded by your local municipality when you register your ownership with the provincial traffic department (*Jefatura Provincial de*

Tráfico), so local municipalities have a record of all Spanish-registered cars located in their area.

GENERAL ROAD RULES

The following general road rules may help you adjust to driving in Spain. Don't, however, expect other motorists to adhere to them (many Spanish drivers make up their own 'rules', which are infinitely variable).

- You may have already noticed that the Spanish drive on the right-hand side of the road (when not driving in the middle). It saves confusion if you do likewise! If you aren't used to driving on the right, take it easy until you're accustomed to it. Be particularly alert when leaving lay-bys, T-junctions, one-way streets and petrol stations, as it's easy to lapse into driving on the left. It's helpful to have a reminder (e.g. 'keep right!') on your car's dashboard.

- All motorists must carry a red warning triangle (two if the vehicle has nine or more seats and weighs over 3,500kg) and a full set of spare bulbs and fuses. You must have a spare wheel and the tools for changing a wheel. It's advisable (but not mandatory) to carry a fire extinguisher and a first-aid kit.

- In towns you may be faced with a bewildering array of signs, traffic lights, road markings, etc. If you're ever in doubt about who has priority, always give way to trams, buses and all traffic coming from your RIGHT. Emergency (ambulance, fire, police) and public utility (electricity, gas, telephone, water) vehicles attending an emergency have priority on all roads.

- Most main roads are designated priority roads (*prioridad de paso*), indicated by one of two signs. The most common priority sign is a yellow diamond on a white background, in use throughout most of Europe. The end of priority (*fin de prioridad*) is shown by the same sign with a black diagonal line through it. The other sign is triangular and displays a broad vertical arrow with a thinner horizontal line through it or a road entering the main road from the left or right. On secondary roads *without* priority signs and in built-up areas, you must give way to vehicles coming from your RIGHT. **Failure to observe the priority rule is the cause of many accidents.**

  Priority is indicated at most road junctions by a sign, e.g. all secondary roads have either a stop sign or a give way sign, often with the words *ceda el paso* (give way) beneath it. Give way may also be indicated not by a sign, but by a triangle painted on the road. When roads have equal status and no priority is indicated, traffic coming from the right has priority. The priority to the right rule usually also applies in car parks, but never when exiting *from* car parks or dirt tracks. If you're ever in doubt about who has the right of way, it's wise to give way (particularly to large trucks!).

- On roundabouts (traffic circles), you must give way to traffic approaching from your right unless there's a give way sign (which may be painted on the road). Traffic flows anti-clockwise round roundabouts and not clockwise as in Britain and other countries that drive on the left. Although the British think roundabouts are marvellous (we spend most of our time going round in circles), they aren't so popular on the continent of Europe, although they have become more common in recent years.

- The wearing of seat belts in Spain is *compulsory* on all roads at all times (not only outside of towns as was previously the law) and includes passengers in rear seats when seat belts are fitted (rear seat belts have been compulsory in new vehicles in Spain since 1st July 1994). Children aged under 12 must travel in the back seats of cars unless the front seat is fitted with an approved child seat. Failure to wear a seat belt can result in an on-the-spot fine of 15,000 ptas and subsequent offences may mean increased fines or even the loss of your licence. If you're wise you will not only use your seat belt at all times, but will also buy a car fitted with an air bag. If you have an accident and aren't wearing your seat belt, your insurance company can refuse to pay a claim for personal injury. **Note, however, that rear seat lap belts without a shoulder strap (such as fitted in the rear seats of many cars) can cause serious internal and back injuries, and should be avoided if at all possible (by children as well as adults).**

- Don't drive in bus, taxi or cycle lanes unless necessary to avoid a stationary vehicle or an obstruction. Bus drivers get irate if you drive in their lanes, identified by a continuous yellow line parallel to the kerb (you can be fined for doing so). Be sure to keep clear of tram lines and outside the restricted area, marked by a line.

- For left-hand turns off a main road with traffic lights, there's often a specially marked filter lane to the *right*, where you wait to cross the main road at right angles.

- The use of horns are forbidden at night in towns, when lights should be flashed to warn other motorists or pedestrians. In towns, horns should be used only in emergencies, day or night. If you use a horn 'unnecessarily', e.g. to wake the driver in front when the traffic lights change to green, you can be fined up to 10,000 ptas (although this is rare).

- Headlamps must be used when driving at night, in poor visibility during daylight and in tunnels at any time (you're reminded by a sign). Your main beam must be dipped (*luces de cruce*) at night when following a vehicle or when a vehicle is approaching from the opposite direction. Failure to dip your lights can result in a fine. Note that headlight flashing has a different meaning in different countries. In some countries it means 'after you' and in others 'get out of my way' (almost always the case in Spain). It may also mean 'I am driving a new car and haven't yet worked out what all the switches are for'! Spanish drivers sometimes warn motorists of police radar traps and road blocks (although this is illegal) and accidents by flashing their headlights. A vehicle's hazard warning lights may be used to warn other drivers of an obstruction, e.g. an accident or a traffic jam.

- Most traffic lights are situated on posts at the side of the road, although they may also be suspended above the road. The sequence of Spanish traffic lights (*semáforos*) is usually red, green, amber (yellow) and back to red. Amber means stop at the stop line; you may proceed only if the amber light appears after you have crossed the stop line or when stopping may cause an accident. However, take care before stopping at an amber light when a vehicle is close behind you, as Spanish drivers routinely drive through amber lights and may be taken by surprise if you stop (and ram you).

  Flashing amber lights at the side of the road usually indicate that you're approaching traffic lights or a built-up area with a restricted speed limit (e.g. 50 kph). When entering many towns there are flashing amber traffic lights designed to slow traffic. Double flashing amber lights mounted vertically are simply a warning to slow down, although some have a red light mounted above them that changes to red if you approach them too fast, e.g. more than 50 kph. This is an excellent if irritating way of slowing down traffic, except for the fact that many Spanish drivers are impervious to red lights and simply ignore them. You shouldn't follow their example as if you're observed by the police you will be heavily fined (e.g. from 15,000 to 100,000 ptas). If you approach an amber light at over 50 kph it will change to red and will revert to amber when you slow your speed. You can usually anticipate it and there's no need to stop or slow below 50 kph.

An amber or green filter light, usually flashing and with a direction arrow, may be shown in addition to the main signal. This means that you may drive in the direction shown by the arrow, but must give priority to pedestrians or other traffic. In towns, individual lanes sometimes have their own traffic lights showing either a green arrow or a red cross indicating 'no entry' (for traffic travelling in the opposite direction). Flashing amber lights are a warning to proceed with caution and may indicate you must give way to pedestrians. Occasionally you will see a flashing red light, meaning stop or no entry, e.g. at a railway level crossing. Two red lights mounted vertically one above the other indicate 'no entry'.

• White lines mark the delineation of traffic lanes (not that these mean anything to some Spanish drivers). A solid single line or two solid lines means no overtaking (*adelantar*) in either direction. A solid line to the right of the centre line, i.e. on your side of the road, means that overtaking is prohibited in your direction. You may overtake only when there's a single broken line in the middle of the road or double lines with a broken line on your side of the road. No overtaking is also shown by the international sign of two cars side by side (one red and one black). Overtaking is prohibited within 100m of a blind hill and on roads where visibility is less than 200m. It's illegal to overtake on an inside lane on a multi-lane road unless traffic is being channeled in a different direction.

Note that when overtaking in Spain you must always indicate before you pull out and again when returning to your lane. Drivers of trucks, buses and other commercial vehicles in Spain will often indicate with their right-hand indicator when it's safe to overtake. However, always take a good look in case they are making a right-hand turn! The left-hand indicator means 'do not overtake'. Always check your rear view and wing mirrors carefully before overtaking, particularly as Spanish motorists seem to appear from nowhere and zoom past at a 'zillion' miles an hour, especially on country roads. If you drive a right-hand drive car, take extra care when overtaking — the most dangerous manoeuvre in motoring (it's advisable to have a special overtaking mirror fitted to your car). Note that you're forbidden to overtake a stationary tram when passengers are boarding or alighting. Illegal overtaking can result in a fine of 35,000 ptas or more and a suspended licence.

• Take care when approaching a railway crossing, indicated by a sign with a large 'X' or an engine in a triangle. You must take particular care at crossings without barriers, which can be *very* dangerous. Approach a railway level crossing slowly and **STOP**:

   – as soon as the barrier or half-barrier starts to fall;

   – as soon as the red warning lights are illuminated or flashing or a warning bell rings;

   – when a train approaches!

Your new car may be built like a tank, but it won't look so smart after a scrap with a locomotive.

• Be particularly wary of moped (*ciclomotor*) riders and cyclists. It isn't always easy to see them, particularly when they are hidden by the blind spots of a car or are riding at night without lights. Many young moped riders seem to have a death wish and tragically many lose their lives each year in Spain. They are constantly pulling out into traffic or turning without looking or signalling. **Follow the example set by Spanish motorists, who, when overtaking mopeds and cyclists, ALWAYS give them a wide . . . . WIDE berth.** If you knock them off their bikes you may have a difficult time convincing the police that it wasn't your fault; far better to avoid them (and the police). It's also common to encounter tractors, horses, donkeys and sheep in rural areas. Keep an eye out for them and give them a wide berth.

- An 'E' (España) nationality plate (*nacionalidad*) must be affixed to the rear of a Spanish-registered car when motoring abroad and drivers of foreign registered cars in Spain must have the appropriate nationality plate affixed to the rear of their cars. You can be fined on the spot for not displaying it, although it isn't often enforced judging by the number of cars without them.

- Miscellaneous rules:
  - Three-point turns and reversing into side streets is forbidden in towns. U-turns can be made on main roads where signposted.
  - Studded tyres and snow chains may be used in winter in mountainous areas. Snow chains are compulsory on some roads in winter, indicated by a sign.
  - Cars must not be overloaded, particularly roofracks, and the luggage weight shouldn't exceed that recommended in manufacturers' handbooks (except for North Africans!).
  - Drivers towing (*con remolque*) a caravan or trailer must display a sign of a yellow triangle on a blue background on the front of their vehicle. Note that towing a broken down vehicle is permitted only by a tow truck.
  - Anti-glare blinds and stickers aren't permitted on the rear window unless mirrors are fitted on both sides of the car.
  - A dog must be restrained in a car and not running free.
  - The use of hand-held telephones and the wearing of audio headphones is illegal when driving, for which you can be fined up to 50,000 ptas (although it's more likely to be 5,000 ptas).

- All motorists in Spain must be familiar with the Spanish highway code (*Código de la Circulación*), available from bookshops throughout Spain.

TRAFFIC POLICE

In towns, the local municipal police (*policía municipal*) are responsible for traffic control, while on Spain's highways the guardia civil (*guardia civil de tráfico*) undertake the task, patrolling in cars, motorcycles and helicopters. Motorcycle police always patrol in pairs (*parejas*), at least one of whom is usually a trained mechanic and the other trained in first-aid. They will stop and help anyone in trouble. Always follow the instructions of traffic police and be prepared to stop. Police in towns blow whistles and wave their arms about a lot — if you don't know what's going on, follow the example of other motorists and hope that they know what they are doing!

On-the-spot fines (*multas*) of up to 50,000 ptas can be imposed for a range of traffic offences including speeding, overtaking without indicating, travelling too close to the car in front, not being in possession of your car papers and not wearing a seat belt. However, a Spaniard or Spanish resident driving a Spanish-registered vehicle with a Spanish driving licence isn't required to pay on-the-spot fines. On the spot fines are common practice when dealing with non-resident foreigners, whose vehicles can be impounded or immobilised if they're unable to pay a fine. The police may escort you to a bank or hotel where you can obtain money or change foreign currency to pesetas. **Note that the police can also impound a foreign-registered cars if they believe that it's used permanently in Spain (you will need to prove that you live abroad, which may be difficult).**

Motoring offences are classified as minor (*leve*), serious (*grave*) and very serious (*muy grave*). Minor offences carry fines of up to 15,000 ptas, serious offences fines of from 15,000 to 50,000 ptas, and very serious offences fines of up to 100,000 ptas and an automatic licence suspension. For minor offences, residents (and foreigners who pay on-the-spot) receive a 20 per cent discount if they pay the fine within 10 days, after which fines must be paid within 30 days. The 20 per cent discount doesn't apply to serious offences. A *boletín de denuncia* is issued specifying the offence and the fine (check that it's the same as the amount demanded). Fines can be paid at any post office via a post office money order (*giro postal*) or at the local traffic department. **Always ensure that you receive a receipt for all payments.** Some communities offer young traffic offenders (e.g. moped riders) the option of doing community service rather than paying traffic fines, which means that parents no longer have the obligation to pay their children's traffic fines.

Note that if notification of a fine is sent to your holiday home in Spain while you're abroad, you property in Spain can eventually be embargoed for non-payment. Your driving licence may also be suspended without your knowledge and your name listed in the provincial official bulletin (*Boletín Oficial*), although this form of notification has been deemed insufficient by courts (but it's still in wide use). If over 60 working days elapse between an offence and you receiving official notification of it, the fine is invalid and you shouldn't be required to pay it.

The police often set up check points and stop motorists at random to check their identification and car papers (and also to look for drugs or terrorists). Vehicles coming towards you may warn you of a police radar trap or road block by flashing their headlights, although this is illegal. You should always carry your passport or residence card (*residencia*), driving licence (Spanish if held), vehicle registration papers (*permiso de circulación*) and insurance certificate. If a vehicle isn't registered in your name, you also need a letter of authorisation from the owner. It's advisable to make a copy of your car papers and keep the *originals* with you (at all times) or lock them in the glove box of your car.

Police have stepped up their patrols in many areas and may impose fines for the slightest and most obscure infringements. Fines can be astronomical even for the most trifling of offences, such as not carrying your original driving licence, which can carry a 40,000 ptas fine. New laws in recent years have increased maximum fines to 250,000 ptas for serious offences. In certain cases, such as not having the original of your driving licence with you, the fine can be recovered from your local provincial traffic department (*jefatura provincial de tráfico*) on production of your original driving licence. Note, however, that even when you're fined illegally (a fairly common practice), it can take eons to get your money back.

You can appeal against a fine and there are instructions in English on the back of the *boletín de denuncia* explaining how to do this. A written appeal (in any language) must be made within 10 days of an (alleged) offence to the provincial traffic department in the province where the offence took place. The police will decide whether to uphold your appeal and there's no appeal against their decision, so unless you have a foolproof case it's a waste of time and money. You need the assistance of a notary, lawyer or barrister, which can incur costs of 100,000 ptas or more (to avoid a fine of say 20,000 ptas).

Note that in some provinces the authorities embargo and seize cars when road taxes and traffic fines are unpaid. This seizure can be expensive for non-residents, who can have their vehicles towed away and stored (at their owner's expense) for a number of months while they are abroad. The names of those embargoed are listed in official bulletins (*boletines oficiales*) displayed at town halls.

SPANISH ROADS

Spanish roads have improved considerably in recent years and Spain's best roads are now among the finest in Europe. However, in contrast to the excellent new motorways (*autopistas*) and trunk roads, many secondary roads in rural areas and small towns are full of potholes and in dreadful or even dangerous condition. Some main highways are also in poor condition with surprising undulations and dips, and they aren't always up to the standards of roads in northern Europe. Heavy rains in the winters of 1995/96 and 1996/97 exposed defects in many roads in southern Spain, including some relatively new roads, some of which were built with inferior materials (due to corruption) or badly engineered. When it rains heavily the roads in many towns, even main roads, can be treacherous due to inadequate drainage, and heavy rainfall also causes widespread floods, rock falls, landslides and subsidence.

In recent years there has been a huge road-building scheme in Spain, particularly of motorways, which now cover some 6,000km (3,728miles). Spanish motorways are indicated by blue or green signs and often have a motorway symbol on them. Most are toll roads (*autopistas de peajes*) and are the most expensive in Europe (Spain has the third largest network of toll motorways in Europe after France and Italy). Tolls vary as each motorway has its own fee structure and usually average around 15 ptas per kilometre (the European average is around 11 ptas per km) for a family car, or double the cost of petrol to travel the same distance! The toll from La Jonquera on the French border to Alicante on the A7/E15 motorway is around 8,000 ptas and consequently is avoided by most motorists. However, although you may need to take out a second mortgage to drive on them, motorways are Spain's safest roads (you cannot get hit by a Spaniard overtaking on a blind bend).

A ticket is issued automatically at the motorway entrance (or shortly afterwards) and when you reach another toll-booth or exit from the motorway you hand your ticket to the attendant (the toll due is usually shown on a display). Tolls may also be levied at intermediate points. On some stretches, e.g. around cities, tickets aren't issued and a fixed toll is charged. On these roads there may be unmanned toll-booths for those with the correct change, shown by the sign *Automático - importe exacto*. Throw the correct amount into the 'basket' and wait for the red light to change to green and the barrier to rise. Regular commuters can buy a season pass (*tarjeta de la autopista*) offering savings of 10 to 25 per cent. Passes allow you to go through an automatic gate where you insert your pass in a machine.

All motorways have service areas with a petrol station, cafeteria or coffee shop, toilets, telephones, and possibly a restaurant and shops. Some have repair workshops, exchange facilities, information offices and motels. As always in Spain, be careful not to leave anything of value visible inside your car when you park. Most motorway operators provide free maps. Motorway exits (*salidas* or *sortidas* in Catalan) are marked on maps, as are service and rest stops (*apartaderos*). Motorway maps and toll information is available from ASETA, C/Estébanez Calderón, 3, 28020 Madrid (tel. (91) 571 6258).

For many Spaniards, driving on motorways is too expensive and the traffic density is usually low. However, the same cannot be said of main trunk roads (*carreteras*) running parallel to the motorways, which are jammed by drivers who are reluctant or cannot afford to pay the high motorway tolls. Toll motorways in Spain (and other countries) are a luxury for the wealthy few and the high tolls simply discourage most motorists (particularly truckers) from using them and add to the congestion on other roads. Even an offer of half price for trucks attracts few takers. If you need to get from A to B in the shortest possible time, then there's no alternative to the motorway, apart from taking a plane or train. However, if you aren't in too much of a hurry, want to save money *and* wish to see something of Spain, you should avoid motorways. The money saved on tolls can pay for a good meal or an (inexpensive) hotel room.

Many dual carriageways (*autovías*), such as the E5/N-IV south of Madrid, have the appearance of motorways and the same maximum speed limit (120 kph). However they also have left and right turns and crossing roads in some places, so take care. The sign *cambio de sentido* (change direction) on a dual carriageway is an opportunity to reverse your direction by way of an under or over-pass, e.g. when you have missed your turn off. On national highways there are special 'crawler' lanes on gradients for heavy goods vehicles and other slow-moving vehicles. On single lane highways you shouldn't expect to cover more than around 70-80 kph. Bear in mind that travelling on secondary roads (particularly mountain roads) invariably takes a lot longer than travelling on national routes and usually takes twice or three times as long to reach your destination (even if the distance is less than half). Mountain passes in Spain are usually open all year, although some are closed intermittently. Most are narrow with hairpin bends, no road markings and unprotected roadsides with sheer drops, and aren't recommended for timid or nervous drivers, particularly in winter.

Emergency SOS telephones, mounted on orange posts, are sited approximately every 5km on motorways and other main roads. Each telephone is individually numbered and directly connected to the local police station, which will send out a breakdown van or tow truck (*grúa*) with first-aid equipment. There are fixed (reasonable) charges for emergency repairs and towing. If you have broken down and call from an ordinary telephone, you should ask the operator for the 'rescue service' (*auxilio en carretera*). The *Guardia Civil* also provide roadside assistance on main roads throughout Spain, as do motoring organisations (see page 226). If you break down on a motorway, you must park your car on the hard shoulder and place an emergency triangle 30 metres behind your vehicle, visible at a distance of 100 metres. Two triangles (one in front and one behind) are required for vehicles with nine or more seats or weighing over 3,500kg. Never remain in your car when it's parked on the hard shoulder as it's extremely dangerous. Note that you're only permitted to stop on the hard shoulder in an emergency (e.g. not for a 'call of nature').

The main national (*nacional*) highways, with the prefix 'N' and the number in white lettering on a red background, radiate out from Madrid to the coast or the Spanish border. The principal roads are indicated by Roman numerals, i.e. the N-I to San Sebastian, the N-II to Barcelona, the N-III to Valencia, the N-IV to Cadiz, the N-V to Badajoz and the N-VI to La Coruña. Other major roads are identified by Arabic numbers, e.g. N-401. All main roads have kilometre stones located on the right hand side. Distances on the national roads listed above are calculated from the Puerta del Sol in Madrid and shown on red and white kilometre stones at the side of the road. The starting point of national roads without Roman numerals isn't so easy to determine, but is indicated on kilometre stones at the edge of the road. Some national highways are also designated as European highways and have the prefix 'E', e.g. the E5 running from the French border at Hendaye to Algeciras. Local main roads have the prefix 'C' (*comarcales*) and other minor roads are unnumbered or prefixed with the first two letters of the province, followed by a number.

In general, signposting in Spain is reasonable, even in most rural areas, thanks largely to the vast numbers of tourists who invade Spain each summer. Most road signs are international, although Spain still has many Spanish and local idiosyncracies. In some areas you will find that direction signs disappear, or everywhere is signposted except where you want to go. Signs out of towns are often non-existent. It's always advisable to have a good map, particularly when you aren't travelling on main roads. In major cities it's advisable to park your car (if you can find a parking space) and use public transport. You should be wary of entering small towns and villages, where streets are narrow and often come to a dead end (when you will need to reverse out). It's better to park on the edge of town.

Driving in Madrid is the motoring equivalent of hell and should be avoided at all costs. In and around Madrid and other main cities signs can be extremely confusing, due to the sheer number of roads and destinations signposted. Look out for the road number as well as the name of your destination. Often only road numbers *or* towns are listed, and not both. When travelling north to south on the E5/N-IV you should follow the signs for Algeciras and Ocaña. Travelling south to north on the same road follow the signs for the E5 and the N-I to Burgos.

Spanish roads are classified as follows and are identified by their prefix:

Prefix	Classification
A (*autopista*)	toll motorways — usually marked blue or red/yellow on maps;
E (*carretera europea*)	European 'motorway' standard highways traversing a number of countries, e.g. the E5 running from the French-Spanish border to Algeciras;
N (*carretera nacional*)	national trunk roads (*carreteras de gran circulación*) usually marked in red or yellow on maps;
C (*carretera comarcal*)	main secondary roads (*carreteras de segundas*), usually marked in green or yellow on maps;
MA (*carretera autonómica*)	minor roads (*carreteras de terceras*) with two letters indicating the province, e.g. MA = Malaga, followed by a number. Usually marked in yellow or white on maps.

General road information can be obtained by telephoning (91) 742 1213 or (91) 535 2222 for information about specific routes. See also **Road Maps** on page 224.

SPANISH DRIVERS

Like all Latins, a Spaniard's personality often changes the moment he gets behind the wheel of a car, when even many tolerant and patient people become motoring anarchists. Many Spaniards are frustrated racing drivers and they rush around at breakneck speed (totally out of character with their celebrated *mañana* attitude) in their haste to reach their destination (or the next life). To many Spaniards, driving is like a bullfight and an opportunity to demonstrate their machismo to their wives and girfriends. Foreign-registered cars (observing speed limits) are like red rags to a bull to some Spaniards who *must* overtake them immediately, irrespective of their speed, the prevailing speed limit, solid white lines or traffic coming from the opposite direction.

When driving in Spain you should regard all drivers as totally unpredictable and always drive defensively (**although it should be noted, that not all Spanish drivers are bad or incompetent**). Among the most eccentric drivers' various idiosyncracies are a total lack of lane discipline (lane markings are treated as optional), overtaking with reckless abandon on blind bends, failure to use mirrors or indicators (very common when exiting from a motorway or dual carriageway), driving through red lights and the wrong way up one way streets, and parking anywhere it's illegal. Many drivers routinely park too close to other cars and bang their doors up against them, damaging the paintwork.

The Spanish drive on both the right <u>and</u> on the left side of the road — that's when they aren't driving in the middle. When driving on narrow country roads, always stay on your own side of the road at all times unless you can see a long distance ahead (if you don't, you can bet your life that around the next blind corner will be a large truck with poor brakes). Some Spanish drivers are confused by roundabouts (as are many other Europeans) and they don't always give way to traffic already on roundabouts when entering them (previously traffic on a roundabout had to give way to traffic entering it). When driving at night, watch out for bicycles, motorcycles, donkeys, and horse and carts without lights. Maniacs on ear-splitting motorcycles and mopeds are a menace to everyone in towns. Motorists should also keep a wary eye out for pedestrians, particularly older people, who often walk across the road without looking.

Although they aren't among Europe's worst tail-gaters, some Spanish drivers will sit a few metres (centimetres) from your bumper trying to push you along irrespective of traffic density, road and weather conditions, or the speed limit. Always try to leave a large gap between your vehicle and the one in front. This isn't just to give you more time to stop should the vehicles in front decide to come together, but also to give the inevitable tail-gater behind you more time to stop. **The closer the car is behind you, the further you should be from the vehicle in front.** Failure to maintain a safe distance from the vehicle in front can result in a fine of between 15,000 and 100,000 ptas.

Many Spanish motorists have little respect for traffic rules (any semblance of road discipline is purely coincidental), particularly anything to do with parking (in towns a car is a device used to create parking spaces). A good sign of a nation's motoring competence is the number of cars with dents or accident damage. In Spain nearly every car has a dent in it ('fender benders' are a way of life in Spanish cities). The most civilised 'Spanish' drivers are to be found in the north of Spain (e.g. Catalonia), where most drivers follow the rules and even stop at red lights. In contrast to most car drivers, Spanish truck drivers are competent and courteous, and most use their right-hand indicators to signal when it's safe to overtake and warn you when there's an oncoming vehicle by using their left-hand indicator. Motorists also use their hazard warning lights when forced to slow rapidly, e.g. for an accident or road works.

Adding to the general confusion and hazards on Spanish roads are thousands of tourists and retirees, whose driving habits vary from exemplary to suicidal and include many (such as the British) who don't even know which side of the road to drive on! Driving in cities can be absolutely chaotic and is to be avoided if at all possible. Inexperienced drivers should take extra care in Spain as the accident rate for foreigners is quite high, particularly in Spanish cities. The Germans and the French have the most accidents, being speed-crazy like the Spanish (the sensible British drive more defensively).

Don't be too discouraged by the road hogs and tail-gaters on Spanish roads. Driving in Spain can be a pleasant experience, particularly when you're using rural roads, which are relatively traffic-free most of the time. If you come from a country where traffic drives on the left, you will quickly get used to driving on the 'wrong' side of the road. Just take it easy at first and bear in mind that there are other motorists around just as confused as you are!

MOTORCYCLES

Somewhat surprisingly, given Spain's excellent weather, large touring motorcycles (*motos* or *motocicletas*) aren't particularly common on Spain's roads. However, mopeds (*ciclomotores*), scooters and small motorcycles are a scourge in towns and cities, where their noise may drive you crazy (noise levels are restricted but not enforced). Approved crash helmets (*casco*) must be worn at all times by all moped and motorcycle riders and passengers (previously helmets weren't necessary in urban areas), although you will see many riders not wearing them. Failure to wear a helmet can result in a fine of 15,000 ptas, although judging by the number of offenders this law isn't enforced by the police (it isn't unusual to see a whole family on a motorcycle, including children and babies, without a helmet between them!).

Dipped headlamps must be used at all times by all motorcyclists except moped riders. When parking a motorcycle in a city, always lock it securely (if possible, chain it to an immovable object). Take extra care when parking in a public place overnight, particularly in major cities, where bike theft is rife. Mopeds and motorcycles of all sizes can be rented throughout Spain. Note that rental insurance doesn't always include theft. You must usually leave your driving licence as security (it isn't advisable to leave your passport as if the bike breaks down or is stolen, you may have trouble getting it back).

Mopeds: A teenager can ride a moped at the age of 14 with an engine capacity of up to 50cc capable of a maximum speed of 60 kph. However, he must be a Spanish resident, otherwise the age limit is 16. Riders aged under 16 must pass a simple examination on the rules of the road and obtain written parental consent. Mopeds require a permit and plates issued by your local town hall (*ayuntamiento*) after passing the test (if applicable) and presentation of your residence card and moped documents. The (LCC) permit costs around 600 ptas and the plates around 1,000 ptas. Third party insurance isn't obligatory but accident insurance can be obtained from various insurance companies. No licence, registration or road tax is required for a moped with an engine capacity below 50 cc. Mopeds aren't permitted on motorways and riders must use cycle paths where provided. Two-stroke petrol (*mezcla*) is available at most petrol stations.

Note that mopeds and motorbikes can be lethal in the wrong hands (many teenagers have little more road sense than hedgehogs and rabbits) and many riders are killed each year in Spain. If you have a child with a moped or motorcycle, it's important to impress upon him the need to take care and not take unnecessary risks, e.g. always observe traffic signs, and signal before making manoeuvres. Car drivers often cannot see or avoid moped riders, particularly when they speed out of side streets without looking or ride at night without lights.

Motorcycles: At 16, youths can ride a light motorcycle (*moto* or *motocicleta*) with an engine capacity of up to 125cc, requiring an A1 licence. At age 18 a motorcycle (with an engine capacity) over 125cc may be ridden, for which an A motorcycle licence (*licencia de conducción de ciclomotores*) is required. A motorcycle licence (A1/A) is valid for 10 years if you're aged under 45 and for five years if you're aged between 45 and 70. A rider aged over 70 must renew his licence annually. Speed limits are the same for motorcycles above 75cc as for cars and they are also permitted to use motorways (tolls are lower than for cars). All motorcycles must be registered with the *Jefatura Provincial de Tráfico*. A motorcycle over 500cc must have a manufacturer's certificate, industry certificate, appraiser's certificate and town hall registration. Third party insurance is necessary for bikes over 75cc, costing around 30,000 ptas a year. Motorcycles must have their first technical inspection (*Inspección Técnica de Vehículos/ITV*) after five years and thereafter it's required annually (see page 197).

ACCIDENTS

If you're unfortunate enough to be involved in a car accident (*accidente de tráfico*) in Spain, the procedure is as follows:

1. Stop immediately. If a vehicle is blocking the road, switch on your hazard warning lights or place a warning triangle at the edge of the road 30 metres behind your car, with a visibility of 100 metres. If necessary, for example, when the road is partly or totally blocked, turn on your car's headlights and direct traffic around the hazard. In bad visibility, at night, or in a blind spot, try to warn oncoming traffic of the danger, e.g. with a torch or by waving a warning triangle up and down.

2. If anyone is injured, immediately call for an ambulance. If someone has been injured more than superficially or extensive damage has been caused, the police (*guardia civil*) must be called to the scene. Don't move an injured person unless it's absolutely necessary to save him from further injury and don't leave him alone except to call an ambulance. Cover him with a blanket or coat to keep him warm. **Note that, where necessary, all motorists are required to stop and help at the scene of a serious accident.**

3. If there are no injuries and damage to vehicles or property isn't serious, it's unnecessary to call the police to the accident scene. Note that contacting the police may result in someone being fined for a driving offence. If another driver has obviously been drinking or appears incapable of driving, call the police. Note that you must never leave the scene of a serious accident as it's a serious offence in Spain.

4. If either you or the other driver(s) involved decides to call the police, don't move your vehicle or allow other vehicles to be moved. In an accident where someone has been injured or killed, any vehicles involved mustn't be moved until the police have been informed. If it's necessary to move vehicles to unblock the road, mark their positions with chalk. Alternatively take photographs of the accident scene or make a drawing showing the position of all vehicles involved before moving them. There's a space for this on the Spanish insurance accident report form (see below).

5. Check whether there are any witnesses to the accident and take their names and addresses, particularly noting those who support *your* version of what happened. Write down the registration numbers of all vehicles involved and their drivers' names, addresses and insurance details. Give any other drivers involved your name, address and insurance details, if requested.

6. If you have caused material damage, you must inform the owner of the damaged property as soon as possible. If you cannot reach him, contact the nearest police station (this also applies to damage caused to stationary vehicles when parking or manoeuvering).

7. If you're detained by the police ask someone you're travelling with to contact anyone necessary as soon as you realise you're going to be detained. **Don't sign a statement, particularly one written in Spanish, unless you're <u>certain</u> you understand and agree with every word.**

8. In the case of an accident involving two or more vehicles, it's standard practice for drivers to complete an accident report form (*declaración de siniestro de automóvil*) provided by Spanish insurance companies (always keep one in your car). This form is an 'amicable statement', where drivers agree (more or less) on what happened and who was at fault. It isn't obligatory to complete an accident report form and if your Spanish isn't up to it you should refuse. You may, however, complete it in English or another language if you wish. It's important to check the details included on forms completed by other drivers against official documents, particularly those relating to a driver's identity, driving licence, car registration and insurance details. If the police attend the scene of an accident, they will make their own report.

9. Your insurance company must be notified of an accident within 24 to 48 hours and a delay may affect a claim. If you're involved in an accident, you have two months to bring a charge against other parties involved. This involves going to a local police station and making a statement (*atestado*), after which the insurance companies will determine the outcome. Bear in mind that if a court case is required to decide the outcome, it can take years before the case is heard. Note that, in the absence of evidence to the contrary, a foreigner may be 'automatically' blamed for an accident involving a Spanish driver.

DRIVING & DRINKING

As you're no doubt well aware, driving and drinking don't mix. Alcohol is a major factor in a high percentage of Spain's road accidents (around a third of drivers in fatal accidents are over the alcohol limit), particularly those that occur late at night. The amount you can drink and remain below the limit depends on whether you regularly imbibe and your sex and weight. A man weighing around 75kg can usually drink around half a bottle of wine with a meal and remain below the limit. Your alcohol level rises considerably if you drink on an empty stomach, which is why the Spanish eat lots of bread!

Random breath tests (*alcohol-tests*) can be carried out by the police at any time (they are more widespread during the Christmas and New Year holiday period) and motorists who are involved in accidents or who infringe motoring regulations are routinely given alcohol and drug tests. In Spain, you're no longer considered fit to drive when your blood alcohol concentration exceeds 80mg of alcohol per 100ml of blood, the same as in most other European countries (there are lower levels for drivers of goods vehicles and public passenger vehicles). Drunken driving can result in a fine of up to 100,000 ptas, suspension of your licence and even imprisonment. Drivers who refuse to take a breath test are liable to a prison sentence of six months to one year.

Despite the high number of accidents involving drunken drivers in Spain, drunken driving doesn't carry the same stigma as it does in many other European countries and drunken drivers are treated leniently (in comparison). Penalties usually depend on the level of alcohol in your blood and whether you're involved in an accident. **If you have an accident while under the influence of alcohol, your car and health insurance could be nullified. This means you must pay your own and any third party's car repairs, medical expenses and other damages.** Your car insurance will also be increased dramatically.

CAR THEFT

All European countries have a problem with car theft and thefts from cars, and Spain's is among the worst (particularly thefts from cars). **Foreign-registered vehicles, especially camper vans and mobile homes are popular targets.** If you drive anything other than a worthless heap you should have theft insurance, which includes your car stereo and personal belongings. If you drive a new or valuable car it's wise to have it fitted with an alarm, an engine immobiliser (preferably of the rolling code variety with a transponder arming key) or other anti-theft device, and to also use a visible deterrent such as a steering or gear change lock. It's particularly important to protect your car if you own a model that's desirable to professional car thieves, e.g. most new sports and executive models (BMW and Mercedes are favourites), which are often stolen by crooks to order. In the south of Spain, stolen cars often find their way to Africa and may already be on a ferry by the time their owners report them stolen.

Few cars are fitted with deadlocks (Fords are one notable exception) and most can be broken into in seconds by a competent thief. However, a good security system won't usually prevent someone from breaking into your car or even stop it being stolen, but it *will* make it more difficult and may persuade a thief to look for an easier target. Radios, cassette and CD players attract thieves like bees to a honey jar in Spanish cities and coastal resorts. If you buy an expensive stereo system, always buy one with a removable unit or with a removable control panel that you can pop in a pocket. However, never forget to remove it (and your mobile telephone), even when parking for a few minutes. You will notice that Spanish cars parked in cities rarely have stereos in them.

Thieves often smash windows (in Spain, BMW is short for 'break my window') to steal stereo systems and other articles from cars, even articles of little worth such as sunglasses or cigarettes. When leaving your car unattended, store any valuables (including clothes) in the boot (trunk). Note, however, that storing valuables in the boot isn't foolproof. If a car is empty a thief may be tempted to force open the boot with a crowbar. Many people leave the boot of their car open (and empty) to avoid having it broken open, as it can be expensive to repair. Some people also leave their cars unlocked and use a steering lock or an engine immobiliser to discourage car thieves. It's never advisable to leave your original car papers in your car (which will help a thief dispose of it). When parking overnight or when it's dark, it's advisable to park in a secure overnight car park or garage, or at least in a well-lit area.

Other Scams: Note that thieves in Spain operate various scams which include pretending that you have a flat tyre (they may even puncture your tyre in slow moving or stopped traffic) or that fuel is leaking from beneath your car. While they are pretending to help fix your car they steal your belongings (women are popular targets). View any strangers offering to help you with suspicion. Some criminals specialise in robbing motorists at motorway toll booths and there are also incidences of highway piracy where gangs deliberately bump or ram cars to force drivers to stop (usually late at night when there's little traffic about). **Be on your guard!**

If your car is stolen or anything is stolen from it, report it to the police in the area where it was stolen. You can report it by telephone but must go to the station to complete a report (*denuncia*). Don't, however, expect the police to find it or even take any interest in your loss. Report a theft to your insurance company as soon as possible.

PETROL

Leaded petrol is usually sold in two grades, normal (92 octane), which isn't always available, and super or premium grade (98 octane). Unleaded petrol (*sin plomo*) is widely available in Spain, often in both normal (95 octane) and super (98 octane) grades. Diesel fuel (*gasóleo*) is available at all petrol stations (*gasolineras*) and many also sell a mixture (*mezcla*) for two-stroke engines. Note that there aren't many petrol stations in rural areas off the main highways, so it's advisable to keep your tank topped up when touring. You're permitted to carry a can containing 10 litres of petrol.

There are three main petrol companies in Spain: Campsa, Repsol and Cepsa and petrol prices were previously fixed by the government. However, this is no longer the case (it was against EU policy) and where there are a number of petrol stations in a town it's worth shopping around for the lowest price. Prices per litre are around 95 ptas for diesel, 115 ptas for unleaded and 120 ptas for super leaded. Most petrol stations are open continuously (they don't close for a *siesta*) from around 0700 to 2200 or 2300, except on fiesta days, when opening hours are severely curtailed. In large towns, local petrol stations operate a rota to ensure that at least one station is open 24-hours a day. Many service stations are open 24 hours on motorways and other main highways (although some close over night).

Self-service (*autoservicio*) stations are the exception rather than the rule in Spain, although they are common on motorways and other main highways and are becoming commonplace in towns. When paying at self-service petrol stations, simply tell the cashier your pump number. Most petrol stations don't provide any services and it's unnecessary to tip unless an extra service is performed such as checking your oil or tyre pressures, when a tip of around 50 ptas is sufficient. If you need oil (*aceite*) or water (*agua*) ask the attendant. When not filling your tank (*lleno por favor*), petrol is usually purchased in multiples of 1,000 ptas; to ask for '1,000 (2,000, 3,000) pesetas worth' simply say *'dame mil (dos mil, tres mil) pesetas por favor'*. To prevent robberies some stations don't give change at night and you must fill up to exact cash amounts. However, most (but not all) stations accept credit cards such as Mastercard or Visa, and most major chains also provide their own credit cards.

Many cars that aren't fitted with a catalyser can run quite safely on unleaded petrol, possibly indicated by a label inside your petrol filler flap or stated in your car's handbook. If you're in doubt ask the Spanish importer or a dealer for your make of car. A car fitted with a catalyser must never be filled with leaded petrol. To do so will damage the catalyser, which is expensive to repair or replace. Filling some cars (particularly high-performance cars) with unleaded petrol can damage the engine. If you accidentally fill a car fitted with a catalyser with leaded fuel, it's possible to have the tank and fuel system drained without it causing any damage, providing that you don't drive it. To prevent errors, petrol pumps and pipes are colour coded, green for unleaded and red for leaded. The nozzles of leaded (super) petrol pumps in Spain are also usually larger than those of unleaded pumps and won't fit the petrol filler hole of a car fitted with a catalyser. Nevertheless, pay attention, particularly when a garage attendant is filling your car. You should also take care not to fill a petrol-engined car with diesel, a common error among foreigners in Spain.

Many petrol stations provide services such as car washes, vacuum cleaners and air (although machines are often out of order), and routine servicing and repairs are also carried out at some stations. Petrol stations usually have toilets or there's a bar/café or restaurant nearby, and many have a shop or vending machines for soft drinks, beer, confectionery, snacks and cigarettes.

SPEED LIMITS

The following speed limits (*límites de velocidades*) apply to cars and motorcycles in Spain:

Road	Speed Limit
Motorways (*autopistas*)	120 kph (75 mph)
Dual Carriageways (*autovías*)	100 kph (62 mph)
Other Main Roads (*carreteras*)	90 kph (56 mph)
Built-Up Areas/Towns	50 kph (31 mph) or as signposted, e.g. 20 kph in
(*vías urbanas*)	some residential areas.

Cars towing caravans and trailers are restricted to a maximum of 80 kph (50 mph) on motorways and dual carriageways, and 70 kph (43 mph) on all other roads (unless a lower speed limit is in force). Note that mandatory speed restrictions are shown on signs with black figures on a white background and a red rim. Recommended speed limits, e.g. at sharp bends on main highways, are shown on square signs with white figures on a blue background. The RACE motoring organisation has proposed raising the speed limit on dual carriageway roads to 130kph and to 140kph on motorways.

Most Spanish drivers routinely speed everywhere, particularly on rural roads, and it has been estimated that only some 15 per cent of Spanish drivers observe speed limits. Many drivers are reluctant to slow for 50 kph limits in towns, particularly on national highways running through towns, and are often irritated by motorists who do so. However, speed limits are more rigidly enforced in towns, particularly in resort areas, where tourists are among the main contributors to the town halls' coffers. Radar controls are in use throughout Spain and Spanish drivers often flash their headlights to warn other motorists of speed traps, although it's illegal. Speed limits are also enforced by motorcycle traffic police operating in pairs.

Speeding fines (*multas*) depend on an offender's speed above the speed limit and usually range from 15,000 to 50,000 ptas, although if speeding is considered to be dangerous the fine can be up to 100,000 ptas. If you're caught speeding on a motorway below 196kmh you will automatically lose your licence for a month; between 196kph and 235kph and you lose your licence for two months and over 235kph it's three months. If a driver has a 'bad' driving record (e.g. six or more offences in a 12-month period) or a speeding offence is particularly dangerous, he's likely to lose his licence for a period of up to three months. If you're a non-resident the police will insist on a fine being paid on the spot and if you're unable to pay your car will be impounded (see **Traffic Police** on page 211).

You can contest a conviction, but unless you have a foolproof case you would be wise to simply pay the fine. However, if the fine seems unusually high without good reason, you should question it or take legal advice. If you're caught in an unmanned radar trap you will be sent a photograph of your number plate, which is deemed to be irrefutable proof of speeding.

GARAGES & REPAIRS

When buying (or importing) a car in Spain, you should take into account the local service facilities, as not all cars can be easily serviced. All the main European manufacturers are well represented in Spain, but garages (*garajes* or *talleres de reparaciones*) servicing North American and some Japanese cars are few and far between. If you drive a 'rare' car, it's advisable to carry a basic selection of spare parts, as service stations in Spain may not stock them and you may have to wait several weeks for them to be sent from abroad.

The quality of repair work is usually of a high standard and prices are very competitive (many garages offer fixed prices for routine servicing). However, you shouldn't rely on a Spanish garage to repair a car when they say they will as it's common for repairs to take days (or even weeks) longer than scheduled due to the Spanish *mañana* attitude (although it may also be due to a lack of spare parts). You should receive a three month or 2,000km guarantee for any major work done and should get back any parts that have been changed. Always ask for a written estimate (*presupuesto*) before getting a car repaired after an accident (you can be billed for this, although it isn't usual).

Unlike garages in most other western European countries, Spanish mechanics may try to repair parts rather than simply replacing them. This is because labour has traditionally been cheaper than spare parts, although this is changing fast, particularly in the cities. Mechanics can often come up with creative solutions to problems if parts are unavailable. It's generally cheaper to have your car serviced at a local village garage rather than at a main dealer, although the quality of work may vary considerably from garage to garage. Note that when a car is under warranty it must usually be regularly serviced by an approved dealer in order not to invalidate the warranty. However, if you need urgent assistance, particularly with an exotic foreign car, you're more likely to receive sympathetic help from a small local garage than a large dealer. Garages in Spain are 'generally' open from 0800 or 0900 until 1900 or 2000 and close for *siesta* from 1300 or 1400 until 1500 or 1600. In major cities there are garages providing 24-hour breakdown assistance (at a price).

Service stations in Spain rarely provide a free 'loan car' (*coche prestado*) while yours is being serviced or repaired, although you can usually rent a car from a large garage for a reasonable fee. Some garages will collect your car from your home or office and deliver it after a service, or alternatively will drop you off at a rail or bus station or in a local town and pick you up when your car is ready for collection.

ROAD MAPS

A huge variety of road maps (*mapas de carreteras*) are available in Spain, including the following:

- Michelin map (990) covers Spain and Portugal (1cm to 10km) and a set of six maps (440 to 446) covering the mainland in more detail (1cm to 4km). The Canary Islands are shown on a separate map.

- An excellent official map of Spanish roads (*España Mapa Oficial de Carreteras*) is published by the Ministry of Public Works (*Ministerio de Obras Públicas de Carreteras/MOPU*) and available from most bookshops. It includes street plans, an alphabetic list of towns and villages, emergency telephone numbers and petrol stations.

- The *Motoring Atlas of Spain* (Michelin) and the *Road Atlas of Spain* (Hamlyn) are priceless.

- The Campsa petrol company produces a book of maps (*Guía Campsa*) which contains detailed road maps and a guide to hotels and restaurants in major cities.

- Motorway maps are distributed free by the operators and a general map (*Autopistas de España*) can be obtained by post from ASETA, C/Estébanez Calderón, 3, 28020 Madrid (tel. (91) 571 6258).

- A free map of Spain (*Mapa de Comunicaciones*) is obtainable from Spanish National Tourist Offices abroad and free town and city maps are available from local tourist offices in Spain. Town maps are also available from bookshops, news agencies and kiosks.

Unfortunately Spain has no large-scale maps for rural areas with comprehensive street indexes. You must put your trust in 'St.' Christopher the patron saint of travellers, although he may not be able to help much, since he's had his sainthood revoked by the Pope (if he fails you, try St. Jude, the patron saint of lost causes). A map showing the regions and provinces of Spain is included in **Appendix D**.

CAR RENTAL

Car rental (*alquiler de coches*) companies such as ATESA, Avis, Budget, Europcar, Hertz and Thrifty have offices in most cities and at major airports. ATESA are generally cheaper than the major international companies, although the cheapest of all are small local rental companies. Car rental companies are listed in Yellow Pages under *Automóviles Alquiler* and local companies are listed by town. You may be approached at airports by representatives of local companies, most of whom are reputable (but check their credentials). If you're a visitor, it's advisable to reserve a rental car before arriving in Spain, particularly during peak periods (more visitors rent cars in Spain than any other European country). When booking in advance, remember to specify an automatic model if you're unused to a manual (stick-shift) gearbox, as most rental cars in Spain are manual. Fly-drive deals are available through most airlines and travel agents.

Car rental in Spain is the cheapest in Europe, due mainly to the cut-throat competition, particularly during off-peak periods. The rates of major international companies vary little, although you may get a better deal by booking in advance. One of the advantages of hiring with a national company is that you can rent a car in one town and drop it off in another, although you should check the cost of this service. Although cheaper, small local companies require you to return the car to the office you got it from or to the local airport. When comparing rates, check that prices are fully inclusive of insurance and taxes (IVA at 16 per cent), that insurance cover (including personal accident) is adequate and that there are no hidden costs. Some companies don't offer unlimited kilometres (*kilometraje ilimitado*), which usually works out more expensive unless you plan to drive relatively few kilometres. If required, check in advance that you're permitted to take a car out of Spain, e.g. to France or Portugal, as you may need extra insurance.

At the top end of the market, Hertz charge around 30,000 ptas for their cheapest group A cars, such as an Opel Corsa (without air-conditioning), for seven days rental including unlimited mileage, collision damage waiver (CDW) and value added tax. Business tariffs are even higher. At the other extreme, small local companies in resort areas charge as little as 12,000 ptas a week (around 2,000 ptas a day) in winter, e.g. from 15th November to 30th April, for a small Seat or Opel, rising to around 20,000 ptas a week in summer. **Note, however, that some inexpensive rental companies cut corners on maintenance and repairs, and cars can sometimes be unsafe to drive.**

It's also possible to find inexpensive rental cars in winter from major companies such as Hertz, as they must often reduce prices to compete. Shop around for the best deal. Most companies have special low rates for weekend rentals, e.g. from 1600 on Friday to 1200 on Monday, and for rentals of 14 days or longer. When comparing prices always check any extras that aren't included in the basic price such as collision damage waiver/CDW (*cobertura de daños por colisión*), theft cover (*cobertura contra robo*), personal accident insurance/PAI (*asistencia por lesiones personales*), airport tax (*cargo de aeropuerto*), roof rack, baby seat, air-conditioning, additional drivers and value added tax (IVA).

When choosing a rental car, bear in mind that if you're touring you should ensure that you have sufficient power for mountain driving, e.g. at least a 1.6 litre engine for two people and their luggage. If you're going to be doing a lot of driving in summer, air-conditioning is a must. When parking overnight or at any time in cities, don't leave any valuables in your car (see page 220). Always carefully check a car (e.g. for body damage and to ensure that everything works) and the contract before setting out.

To rent a car in Spain you must usually be at least 21 years old, which is increased to 25 for certain cars. Note that most companies have an upper age limit, e.g. 65. Drivers must produce a valid licence (a copy isn't acceptable) and some drivers require an international driving licence. If more than one person will be driving, all the drivers' names must be entered on the rental agreement. If a credit card isn't used, there's usually a high cash deposit and possibly the whole rental period must be paid in advance. **When paying by credit card carefully check your bill and your statement, as extra unauthorised charges aren't unknown.** It may be possible to sign a credit card authorisation slip and then pay by cash when you return the car. However, if you do this, you must make sure that you obtain (and destroy) the credit card payment slip.

MOTORING ORGANISATIONS

There are a number of motoring organisations in Spain, although membership isn't as large as in many other European countries. Breakdown insurance is also provided by insurance companies in Spain and most motorists take advantage of the low rates offered. Spain has two national motoring organisations: *Real Automóvil Club de España (RACE)*, C/José Abascal, 10, 28003 Madrid (tel. (91) 447 3200), the largest and most famous, and *Real Automobil Club de Catalunya (RACC)*, C/Santaló, 8, 08021 Barcelona (tel. (93) 200 3311). Services and fees are similar and both have agreements with foreign organisations such as the AA, AAA, ACI, ADAC, AvD, DTC, RAC and the TCI.

Membership of the RACE costs around 5,000 ptas for initial registration plus an annual fee of some 12,000 ptas. A breakdown must happen at least 25km (15km in the Balearics and Canaries) from your home and there's a limit of three 'free' breakdowns each year, after which a fee is charged. RACE will transport your vehicle to a garage and will make alternative travel arrangements if you break down while on holiday. Assistance outside Spain is provided within 60 days of leaving Spain only. Other services include assistance in obtaining a driving licence, licence plates and vehicle importation; insurance and financial services; comparative running costs and reliability information for popular cars; tourism (hotel discounts), leisure and sports services; an information service; and legal advice.

PARKING

Parking (*estacionamiento/aparcamiento*) in most Spanish towns and cities is a nightmare, although it isn't usually as expensive as in many other European countries. However, there's restricted parking in all cities and towns and parking is prohibited altogether in certain areas. Note that in many small towns and villages it's advisable to park on the edge of town and walk to the centre, as many towns are difficult to navigate with narrow and dead-end streets commonplace. When buying a property in Spain, it's important to investigate the parking facilities; few Spanish apartments and townhouse developments have underground or lock-up garages or even adequate off-road parking facilities, particularly in towns.

Parking regulations vary depending on the area of a city, the time of day, the day of the week, and whether the date is odd or even. In many towns, parking is permitted on one side of the street for the first half of the month (blue and red parking restriction sign marked '1-15') and on the other side for the second half of the month (sign marked '16-31'). In one-way streets parking may be permitted on the side with even numbers on even-numbered days and on the side with odd numbers on odd-numbered days. Parking should always be in the same direction as the traffic flow in one-way streets or on the right-hand side of roads with two-way traffic (parking must also be diagonal in some streets). Some cities have on-street resident parking areas, marked with black bands on telephone and street lighting posts. Residents must buy a parking card from the town hall (proof of residence is required) and display it in their windscreen. Some towns have zones where parking is regulated during working hours (*horas laborables*), when you need a permit covering the period you intend to stay.

Meters and Ticket Machines: In most Spanish cities, individual parking meters (*parquímetros*) have been replaced by ticket machines (*expendedor de tickets de estacionamiento*). These are often located in areas designated as blue zones (*zonas* *azules*), indicated by blue street markings with blue ticket machines. Parking must usually be paid for from 0900 until 1400 and from 1600 or 1630 until 2000, Monday to Friday, and from 0900 until 1400 on Saturdays. Parking is free on Sundays and public holidays. Parking costs from around 50 to 125 ptas per hour, depending on the town. You can usually park from 30 minutes up to a maximum period of two hours. Buy a ticket for the period required and place it behind your windscreen where it can be seen by the parking attendant.

If you exceed your time, you can often cancel it by paying a penalty (*anulación aviso de sanción*) of around 500 ptas (purchased in ticket form from a ticket machine) and either 'posting' it in a special slot in the ticket machine, displaying it in your car window or giving it to the parking attendant (if you can find him). This must, however, be done within a limited period, otherwise you must pay a fine of up to 5,000 ptas.

In some towns an *ORA ZONA* system is operated, whereby parking tickets for 30, 60 and 90 minutes, costing 25, 50 and 75 ptas respectively, are sold by tobacconists (*estancos*) and other retail outlets. Look out for the *ORA ZONA* signs. You punch holes in the ticket indicating the date and time you parked and display it in your car window. Some towns operate a monthly card system costing around 2,000 ptas a month.

Car Parks: Apart from on-street parking, there are off-road car parks in cities and towns, although these are rarely adequate. Parking rates vary considerably and are usually from around 100 ptas an hour or 1,200 ptas for 24 hours. However, in resort areas there are often public car parks where you pay as little as 100 ptas for all day parking. Spaces available in a multi-storey or underground car park (*aparcamiento subterráneo*) are indicated by a 'free' (*libre*) sign at the entrance, while *completo* indicates that it's full. Many multi-storey car parks have video security. If you park in a multi-storey car park, make a note of the level and space number where you park your car (it can take a long time to find your car if you have no idea where to start looking!). On entering most car parks you take a ticket from an automatic dispenser, usually by pressing a button. You must usually pay *before* collecting your car, either at a cash desk (*cajero*) or in a machine. You cannot usually pay at the exit. After paying you usually have around 15 minutes to find the exit, where you insert your ticket in the slot of the exit machine in the direction shown by the arrow on the ticket.

Fines: Parking fines (*multas*) have skyrocketed in recent years and there have been many reports of bogus fines where previous free parking zones are changed almost overnight without warning (or streets become temporary 'no-parking' zones *after* you have parked). Many town halls have allegedly targeted the motorist as a way of buying their way out of bankruptcy, particularly through extortionate parking fines. In Malaga alone, around 1m ptas a day (300m ptas a year) is collected in parking fines, with unsuspecting tourists often the victims. A fine of 15,000 ptas (less 20 per cent for prompt payment) is common for a minor parking infringement, which is astronomical considering the relatively low cost of living in Spain.

Residents are allowed 15 days to pay or formally protest a fine. A fine may be drastically increased if you don't pay within the prescribed period. If your car is towed away, you must pay a towing fee of between 5,000 and 7,500 ptas in addition to the parking fine. Non-residents must first pay the fine (in cash) before paying the towing (*grúa*) charge, usually at two different places. A large number of cars are towed away in Spain, particularly as most Spaniards don't pay parking fines (in Madrid, only a fraction of parking fines are paid). If your car is towed away there may be an adhesive sticker by the side of the road indicating this. You will need to ask a policeman or parking warden the location of the car pound. Wheel clamps (*cepos*) have been introduced in recent years in some cities. When they were first used in Madrid they almost caused a riot and many motorists attacked them with sledgehammers! They aren't, however, used to prevent illegal parking in private parking areas or on private land, as in some other countries.

Parking Signs: On-street parking is forbidden in many streets in the centre of main cities. *Estacionamiento Prohibido* means parking is forbidden or restricted and may be accompanied by the sign of a red circle with a blue background and a red line through it. No parking may also be indicated by yellow, red or white kerb or road markings. A blue and white curbstone indicates that you can stop briefly but cannot park. No parking signs also indicate the direction (shown by an arrow), i.e. left or right of the sign, where it's illegal to park. If parking is illegal in both directions, a sign will have two arrows. A tow-away zone is usually shown by a sign of a hoist on the back of a truck and the words *retirada grúa*.

Some no parking signs have a large 'E' (for *Estacionamiento*) with a diagonal line through it (any sign with a diagonal line means something is prohibited). In many towns, private entrances and garage doors usually have a 'no parking' (*prohibido estacionar* or *vado permanente*) sign accompanied by a police permit number enforcing the parking restriction. Parking in front of this sign may mean a fine or that your car is towed away or clamped. Many streets in Spanish villages and towns are very narrow and cars are invariably parked opposite garages making access even tighter. If someone blocks your car in a town, they will usually be shopping or working locally. You should ask around the local shops and businesses or ask a parking attendant for help before calling the police. Failing that, leaning on your horn (although illegal) may help. Some people leave their cars in neutral and the handbrake off when they double park, so that drivers of other parked cars can move it if necessary (however, don't do this on a hill!).

Like all Latins, Spaniards are parking anarchists and are world champions at the art of 'creative' parking. They will park on footpaths, pedestrian crossings, corners, in front of entrances and exits, in fact, almost anywhere it's illegal. Double parking is commonplace, although triple parking or completely blocking the road is frowned upon and not recommended.

In some cities you may encounter unofficial parking 'attendants' who will demand a fee to 'look after' your car. This may be simply a protection racket as if you refuse to pay they may damage your car. However, they usually want around 50 ptas only and although there's no guarantee that your car will be safe, it may reduce the risk of having it broken into. In some areas (e.g. outside Gibraltar) there are parking touts, who will demand a parking fee (e.g. 2,000 ptas) and take your money and run. Note that official parking attendants (*guardacoches*) are usually uniformed.

PEDESTRIAN ROAD RULES

Pedestrian crossings (*pasos para peatones*) in Spain are distinguished by black and white stripes on the road but aren't usually illuminated, e.g. by flashing or static lights. In towns, pedestrian crossings are usually combined with traffic lights. Motorists are required by law to stop for a pedestrian waiting at a pedestrian crossing *only* if he signals his intention to cross by giving a clear hand-signal or placing one foot on the crossing. **However, it's never safe to assume that you have the right of way at a pedestrian crossing in Spain, particularly in cities.** Only cross when the road is clear in both directions or a driver stops.

At a pedestrian crossing with pedestrian lights, pedestrians are supposed to wait for a green light (or green man) before crossing the road (sometimes you must press a button), regardless of whether there's any traffic. The green light may be accompanied by an intermittent audible signal which may give a few short bleeps just before the light changes to red. A blinking green light means don't cross, otherwise you may get caught in no man's land in the middle of the road when the traffic lights turn green. You can be fined for crossing the road at the wrong place or ignoring pedestrian lights and crossings, although most people cross when the road is clear even if the pedestrian light is red.

Usually pedestrians must share footpaths with bikes, skate boards, rollerskates, assorted animals and the occasional moped, at the same time as keeping an eye out for broken paving stones and open manholes and drains. Note that paving stones and tiles can be slippery and dangerous when wet, and in country areas many roads have loose gravel and stones on which it's easy to loose your footing. Many towns and cities have pedestrian streets (*zona peatonal*) barred to traffic and occasional roads barred to pedestrians (shown by a sign). Footpaths are rare outside towns, although there may be a narrow 'hard shoulder'. Pedestrians must use footpaths where provided or may use a bicycle path when there's no footpath. Where there's no footpath or bicycle path, you should usually walk on the left side of the road facing the oncoming traffic. However, on narrow country roads it's advisable to walk on the side of the road which affords the best view of oncoming traffic, as many roads have blind corners and drivers often drive close to the edge of the road.

MOTOR BREAKDOWN INSURANCE

Motor breakdown insurance (*seguro de asistencia en carretera*) in Spain and other European countries is provided by Spanish car insurance companies (see page 203) and Spanish motoring organisations (see page 226). If you're motoring abroad or you live abroad and are motoring in Spain, it's important to have motor breakdown insurance (which may include holiday and travel insurance), including repatriation for your family and your car in the event of an accident or breakdown. In Britain, National Breakdown provides *free* continental breakdown cover for members taking out their top two levels of British cover, otherwise it costs around £50 for two weeks.

Most foreign breakdown companies provide multi-lingual 24-hour centres where assistance is available for motoring, medical, legal and travel problems. Some organisations also provide economical annual motoring policies for those who frequently travel abroad, e.g. owners of holiday homes in Spain. When motoring in Europe, don't assume that your valuables are safe in the boot of your car, particularly if the boot can be opened from inside the car. Check that your insurance policy covers you for items stolen from your car.

SPANISH ROAD SIGNS

Although Spain generally adheres to international standard road signs, there are also many unique signs with instructions or information in Spanish. Some of the most common are listed below:

Spanish	English
¡Alto!	stop!
Apagar Luces	switch off lights
Aparcamiento	parking
Autopista (de peaje)	motorway (toll)
Bandas Sonoras	sleeping policeman
Calzada Deteriorada	bad road
Calzada Estrecha	narrow road
Cambio de Sentido	change direction
Ceda el Paso	give way/yield
Centro Ciudad	city centre
Cruce Peligroso	dangerous crossroads
Cuidado	caution
Curva Peligrosa	dangerous bend
Desprendimientos	landslides
Despacio	slow
Desvío/Desviación	diversion/detour
Dirección única	one way
Escalón Lateral	drop at edge of road
Encender Luces	switch on lights
Escuela	school
Estacionamiento Prohibido	parking prohibited
Gasolinera	petrol station
Grúa	tow-away area
Obras	roadworks
Paso Prohibido	no entry
Peligro	danger
Prohibido Adelantar	no overtaking/no passing
Prohibido Aparcar	no parking
Puesto de Socorro	first-aid post
Ronda	ringroad
Salida (de camiones)	exit (for trucks)

12.

HEALTH

The quality of health care and health care facilities in Spain is generally good and at their best are the equal of any country in Europe. Spanish medical staff are highly trained (Spain actually has a surfeit of doctors, many of whom are unemployed) and major hospitals are equipped with the latest high-tech equipment. Health care costs per head in Spain are among the lowest in the European Union (only Portugal and Greece are lower) and Spain spends a relatively small percentage of its GDP on health (around 7 per cent). However, hospital nursing care and post-hospital assistance are below what northern Europeans and North Americans take for granted, and spending on preventive medicine is low. Public and private medicine operate alongside each other in Spain and complement each other, although public health facilities are limited in some areas. An important contribution is also made by voluntary organisations such as the Red Cross which provides an important service and is funded totally by voluntary contributions and membership subscriptions.

Spain has a public health system, providing free or low cost health care for those contributing to Spanish social security, plus their families and retirees (including those from other EU countries). However, although big improvements have been made in the last few decades the public health service is hugely over-burdened and there are long waiting lists to see specialists and have non-urgent operations in most areas. If you don't qualify for health care under the public health system, it's essential to have private health insurance (in fact, you won't usually get a residence card without it). This is often advisable in any case if you can afford it, in order to circumvent the shortage of public health services and waiting lists in some areas. Visitors to Spain should have holiday health insurance if they aren't covered by a reciprocal arrangement.

The Spanish are among the world's healthiest people and have an average life expectancy of 80 for women and 74 for men, the highest in the EU. The incidence of heart disease in Spain is among the lowest in the world, a fact partly contributed to their diet (which includes lots of garlic, olive oil and red wine). They do, however, have a high incidence of liver problems and other complaints associated with excess alcohol. The infant mortality rate of around nine deaths per 1,000 births is still relatively high (although improving) and smoking-related ailments and deaths are a serious problem. Smoking is the leading cause of death among adults in Spain, directly causing some 50,000 deaths a year (Spain rates second highest in the number of smokers per capita in western Europe after Greece).

Among expatriates, common health problems include sunburn and sunstroke, stomach and bowel problems (due to the change of diet and more often, water, but they can also be caused by poor hygiene), and various problems caused by excess alcohol (including a high incidence of alcoholism). Some health problems are exacerbated by the high level of airborne pollen in spring in many areas, which affects asthma and hay fever sufferers, and noise and traffic pollution (particularly in Spain's major cities). If you aren't used to Spain's fierce sun, you should limit your exposure and avoid it altogether during the hottest part of the day, wear protective clothing (including a hat) and use a sun block. Too much sun and too little protection will dry your skin and cause premature aging, to say nothing of the risks of skin cancer. Care should also be taken to replace the natural oils lost from too many hours in the sun and the elderly should take particular care not to exert themselves during very hot weather.

Spain's climate is therapeutic, particularly for sufferers of rheumatism and arthritis, and those who are prone to bronchitis, colds and pneumonia. Spain's slower pace of life (plus the *siesta*) is also beneficial for those who are prone to stress (it's difficult to remain up-tight while lying in the sun), although it takes most people some time to adjust. The climate and lifestyle in any country has a marked effect on mental health and people who live in hot climates are generally happier and more relaxed than those who live in cold, wet climates (such as northern Europe). When you've had a surfeit of Spain's good life a variety of health cures are available at spas and health 'farms'.

Health (and health insurance) is an important issue for anyone retiring to Spain (the Costa Blanca and Costa del Sol have the highest percentage of retired persons in the world, which puts a huge strain on local health services). Many people are ill-prepared for old age and the possibility of health problems. There's a dearth of welfare and home-nursing services for the elderly in Spain, either state or private, and many foreigners who are no longer able to care for themselves are forced to return to their home countries. There are few state residential nursing homes in Spain and hospices (usually funded by private donations) for the terminally ill, although there are an increasing number of private sheltered homes and developments. Spain's provision for handicapped travellers is also poor, and wheelchair access to buildings and public transport is well below the average for western Europe.

A useful phrase booklet (*Tell the Doctor*) for foreigners who don't speak Spanish is available from Jenny Bussey, C/El Moreral, 3, 03792 Parcent, Alicante (tel. (96) 558 1165). Another booklet entitled *Enjoying Good Health Care on the Costa del Sol* (by Ronald Elliott) is available free of charge from medical centres, doctors offices, expatriate clubs and many businesses on the Costa del Sol.

There are no special health risks in Spain (apart from over indulgence and falling sick in August when all the doctors are on holiday) and no immunisations are required. You can safely drink the water, although it sometimes tastes terrible and many people prefer bottled water — when not drinking red wine (which is not only tastier, but beneficial to your health **when consumed in moderation!**). *¡Salud!*

EMERGENCIES

The action to take in a medical 'emergency' depends on the degree of urgency. The emergency medical services in Spain are excellent. **Keep a record of the telephone numbers of your doctor, local hospitals and clinics, ambulance service, first aid, poison control, dentist and other emergency services (fire, police) next to your telephone.** In some cities (and provinces) you can dial a special number for the emergency services (*Servicios de Urgencias*), e.g. for most of the Costa del Sol it's 061 for an ambulance, 080 for the fire service and 091 for the police. If you're unsure who to call, ask operator information (003) or call your local police station, who will tell you who to contact or call the appropriate service for you. Whoever you call, always give the age of the patient and if possible specify the type of emergency so that the ambulance can bring a doctor if necessary. Some useful words are accident (*accidente*), serious illness (*enfermedad grave*), heart attack (*ataque cardiaco*), ambulance (*ambulancia*) and doctor (*médico*).

• In a life-threatening emergency such as a heart attack or a serious accident, you should call for an ambulance and mention the nature of the emergency. There may be a special three-digit number in a city, or you should call your local social security clinic (*ambulatorio, clínica de salud*) or the Red Cross (*Cruz Roja*). (You can become a member of your local Red Cross centre for around 3,000 ptas a year.) There are also 24-hour private medical centres (*centros médicos*) in resort areas with ambulance services. The numbers are listed at the front of your telephone book and should be kept next to your telephone.

Private ambulance services provide a 24-hour service in most towns and are listed by town under *Ambulancias* in Yellow Pages, and most clinics and private hospitals operate their own ambulance services. Ambulances are equipped with emergency equipment such as oxygen and life-support systems, and drivers and staff are trained to provide first-aid (but little else, as paramedics aren't recognised in Spain). Social security patients don't pay for ambulance services and private patients are usually reimbursed by a private health insurance policy. If you need to pay, the cost will depend on the type of ambulance required (intensive care ambulances are more expensive) and the distance travelled. Private ambulances cost from around 5,000 ptas for a short trip in a standard ambulance up to 25,000 or more for a journey of say 25 to 30km in a fully-equipped intensive care ambulance.

Taxis must, by law, transport medical emergencies to hospital when requested to do so. In an emergency an ambulance will take a patient to the nearest hospital equipped to deal with the particular emergency. A private car can claim priority when transporting a medical emergency by switching on its hazard warning lights and displaying a piece of white material from a window.

- In some areas there are emergency helicopter evacuation services such as *helicópteros sanitarios* on the Costa del Sol, who also provide a home doctor service and operate their own fleet of ambulances. Membership of *helicópteros sanitarios* (tel. (95) 281 6767) costs 15,000 ptas for a family (all unmarried members) or 33,000 ptas with the home doctor service and 6,500 ptas for an individual (14,500 with the home doctor service).

- If you're physically capable, you can go to a hospital emergency or casualty department (*urgencia*) or a 24-hour public health clinic (*ambulatorio* or *casa de socorro*). The telephone numbers of first aid stations are listed at the front of telephone directories and many are equipped with ambulances. Check in advance which local hospitals are equipped to deal with emergencies and the quickest route from your home. This information may be of vital importance in the event of an emergency, when a delay may mean the difference between life and death. In an emergency a hospital must treat you, regardless of your ability to pay. Most pharmacies post a list of local clinics and hospitals where emergency medical treatment is available. Note that if you're initially treated at a state medical centre (*centro de salud*) or out-patient clinic (*ambulatorio*) you will usually be referred to a public hospital for treatment (which you may not want if you have private health insurance).

- If you're ill and unable to visit your doctor's surgery, your doctor will visit you at home (in Spain, doctors make house calls at any time of day or night). If you need a doctor or medicine in a non-urgent situation and are unable to contact your doctor, ring the telephone information service (003) or your local police station, either of whom will give you the telephone number of a doctor on call or the address of a pharmacy that's open.

SOCIAL SECURITY HEALTH BENEFITS

If you pay Spanish social security (*Seguridad Social*) contributions, you and your family are entitled to free or subsidised medical and dental treatment on the same terms as Spaniards. Over 90 per cent of the population are covered by the *Instituto Nacional de la Salud (INSALUD)*, Spain's public health scheme, including retired EU residents (with a residence card) in receipt of a state pension. If you aren't entitled to public health benefits through payment of Spanish social security or being in receipt of a pension from another EU country, you must usually have private health insurance and must present proof of your insurance when applying for your residence card. If you're an EU national of retirement age, who *isn't* in receipt of a pension, you may be entitled to public health benefits if you can show that you cannot afford private health insurance.

Anyone who has paid regular social security contributions in another EU country for two full years prior to coming to Spain (e.g. to look for a job) is entitled to public health cover for a limited period from the date of their last social security contribution made in their home country. Social security form E-106 must be obtained from the social security authorities in your home country and be presented to the local provincial office of the *Instituto Nacional de la Seguridad Social (INSS)* in Spain. Similarly, pensioners and those in receipt of invalidity benefits must obtain form E-121 from their home country's social security administration. You will be registered as a member of INSALUD and will be given a social security card (*cartilla*), a book of vouchers, a list of local medical practitioners and hospitals, and general information about services and charges. If you're receiving an invalidity pension or other social security benefits on the grounds of ill-health, you should establish exactly how living in Spain will affect those benefits. In some countries there are reciprocal rights regarding invalidity rights, but you must confirm that they apply in your case.

Public health benefits include general and specialist medical care, hospitalisation, laboratory services, discounted drugs and medicines, basic dental care, maternity care, appliances and transportation. Note, however, that social security covers only around 75 per cent of the cost of treatment and the other 25 per cent must be paid by the patient or a supplementary insurance scheme (see page 260). Completely free treatment is available in certain hospitals only, where waiting lists can be very long. Members must also pay a percentage of the cost of certain treatment and items such as drugs and medicines (see page 239).

INSALUD places the emphasis on cure rather than prevention and treats sickness rather than promotes good health. There's little preventive medicine under INSALUD such as regular health checks and a comprehensive immunisation programme for children (preventable diseases such as TB, tetanus, diphtheria and typhoid haven't yet been totally eradicated in Spain). The public health service has limited resources for out-patient treatment, nursing and post-operative care, geriatric assistance, terminal illnesses and psychiatric treatment. Perfunctory treatment due to staff shortages, long waiting lists as a result of a shortage of hospital facilities and a general dehumanisation of patients are frequent complaints made against Spain's social security health system. Many problems are related to crippling bureaucracy, bad management and general disorganisation. Attempts at reform have had only limited success or have failed miserably.

When you receive your social security card, you will usually be assigned a general doctor (*médico de cabecera*) in the area where you live. You may be able to switch to another doctor in the same area, depending on availability and a doctor's number of patients. No payment is made when visiting a public health service doctor and members are simply required to produce their social security card.

DOCTORS

There are excellent doctors (*médicos*) throughout Spain, although finding a doctor who speaks good English can be a problem, particularly in rural areas. However, there's a number of English-speaking Spanish and foreign doctors (and other medical practitioners) practising in Spain, particularly in the major cities and most resort areas, including American, British, German and Scandinavian doctors. Many embassies and consulates in Spain maintain a list of English-speaking doctors and specialists in their area (or doctors speaking their national language) and your employer, colleagues, friends or neighbours may be able to recommend someone. **Note that if you wish to see a doctor who's contracted to Spain's public health service, you may have little or no choice of doctor.** Tourist offices may also keep a list of English-speaking doctors and the names and telephone numbers of English-speaking doctors and dentists are often listed in local English-language newspapers and magazines. Doctors are permitted to advertise their services in Spain and a number advertise in the expatriate press. General practitioners (GPs) or family doctors (*médicos de cabecera*) are listed in Yellow Pages under *Médicos* and specialists under their speciality such as obstetricians and gynecologists (*médicos obstetricia y ginecología*) and heart specialists (*médicos cardiología*).

The ratio of doctors to inhabitants in Spain is higher than many other western European countries, although it varies considerably from town to town and region to region. In most major cities and resort areas there are more than enough doctors, although in rural areas and some urbanisations (satellite towns) surrounding the major cities there's sometimes a shortage of doctors and those who practise there are often over-worked and can spare patients little time (some public health doctors see as many as 20 to 40 patients an hour!). This may also apply to some doctors working for Spanish insurance companies, although fees have increased in recent years and doctors are now able to spend more time with patients. Always try to choose a doctor who allocates you sufficient time and who will explain his diagnosis and recommended course of treatment. Note that if you don't speak Spanish, you may need a translator if you visit a Spanish doctor. If you take regular medication, are undergoing a course of treatment, or suffer from a long-term illness or disability, you should ask your present (i.e. overseas) doctor to provide a short statement about your case and have it translated into Spanish before arriving in Spain.

If you have private health insurance you can choose to see any doctor at any time and aren't required to register with a doctor or visit a doctor within a certain distance of your home. This also makes it easy to obtain a second opinion, should you wish to do so. If you need the services of a medical auxiliary such as a nurse, physiotherapist or chiropodist, you must usually obtain a referral or prescription from a doctor. Health insurance companies also usually insist on a referral from a family doctor (GP), but if you have a 'free choice' policy you can select your own specialist or other practitioner. In Spain, specialists don't require patients to have a doctor's referral, although a referral is necessary for public health patients and may also be required by a private health insurance company.

Note that if you attend a doctor at a health centre or clinic (public or private) certain tests including ECGs, scans, X-rays, and blood and urine analysis, may be conducted on the premises. Alternatively you may be given a form for X-rays, eye tests or special tests to be carried out at a local hospital or clinic (you may be given your X-ray plates to return to your doctor). Free flu (*gripe* vaccinations are given each autumn at clinics and medical centres.

Alternative medical practitioners aren't as common in Spain as they are in some other European countries or North America, although there are a number of expatriates practising in the major cities and resort areas (many advertise in Spain's English-language publications). Before choosing an alternative practitioner, you should check whether he's state registered. Note that it's normal practice to pay a doctor (preferably in cash) or other medical practitioner after each visit when you're a private patient, although some will bill you only after treatment is completed. A routine visit to a doctor's surgery usually costs between 4,000 and 8,000 ptas, a home day-time call 8,000 to 10,000 ptas and a home night-time call 10,000 to 15,000 ptas. A consultation with a specialist usually costs between 8,000 to 12,000 ptas.

If applicable, obtain a receipt for your insurance company. Surgery hours vary considerable between public health and private doctors and from day to day, e.g. private doctors' surgery hours may be from 0900 to 1200 and from 1700 until 1900 Monday to Friday, while public health doctors in health centres (*centro de salud* or *ambulatorio*) often work from 0800 until 1800 without a break. Some public health centres in resort areas provide a volunteer interpreter service for foreigners. It's usually necessary to make an appointment (*cita previa*), although many health centres operate a first-come, first served system, where patients are given a number and wait until it's called. Appointments with public health doctors can usually be made within 48 or 72 hours, although in some towns it can take a week or more. If your doctor is unavailable, his surgery will give you the name of a standby doctor. Most public health clinics operate a 24-hour service and there are also 24-hour private medical centres (*centros médicos*) in resort areas. If you're unable to attend surgery, doctors will make house calls, although if you live in a rural area you may have trouble getting a doctor to call on you unless you're an urgent case. If you rely on the public health service, try not to get ill in August when many doctors and specialists take a month's holiday. This is a serious point as a number of medical 'disasters' occur in August when doctors are away.

Note that although there are excellent antenatal facilities in Spain, there are no antenatal (or post-natal) organisations or clinics and you must make arrangements for regular check-ups through your family doctor. Children in Spain are issued with a green vaccination book (*carnet de vacunaciones*), which must be presented when starting school.

DRUGS & MEDICINES

Drugs and medicines (*medicinas/medicamentos*) prescribed by a doctor are obtained from a pharmacy (*farmacia*) denoted by the sign of a green cross. Most pharmacies are open from 0930 until 1330 and from 1630 until 2000 from Monday to Saturday. Outside normal opening hours, a notice is posted giving the address of the nearest duty pharmacy (*farmacia de guardia*) open after 2000 (a weekly roster may be displayed). There are 24-hour duty pharmacies in all towns (usually indicated by a red light), although there may also be duty day time (e.g. open from 0930 until 2200) and night-time pharmacies (e.g. open from 2200 until 0930 the following day).

When visiting a duty pharmacy outside normal hours, you must usually ring a bell, speak to the pharmacist behind a bullet-proof glass door and be served through a small hatch (this is particularly common in cities where crime is rife). In some areas you may even be required to take a policeman with you. Note that a duty pharmacy fills prescriptions (*recetas*) only and there may be a surcharge. In addition to being displayed in pharmacy windows, a list of duty pharmacies is published in local newspapers, and in some towns an annual schedule (and map) is published (available from tourist offices). A pharmacist in Spain must own and run his own pharmacy (chain pharmacies are illegal) and their numbers are strictly controlled.

If you have a prescription you must pay 40 per cent of the cost of medicines and drugs or nothing at all if you're a pensioner or handicapped. Many private health insurance schemes also reimburse members for drugs and medicines. Note that there's no refund for some prescribed medicines or for medicines purchased without a doctor's prescription. Prescription medicines in Spain are among the cheapest in the EU. However, pharmacies have a monopoly on non-prescription drugs in Spain, which are expensive compared with many other countries. General medication (such as aspirin, cough medicine and eye drops) which can be purchased in supermarkets in other EU countries can cost much more in Spain, e.g. 20 paracetamol tablets cost around 250 ptas in Spain or around five times the cost in Britain. It's advisable to buy non-prescription drugs abroad and stock up before arriving in Spain. In order to reduce the public health prescription bill of around 500 billion ptas a year, the public health service has removed almost 1,000 treatments previously available on social security prescriptions (it's estimated that some 30 per cent of medication on Spain is simply thrown away).

Pharmacists (*farmacéuticos*) in Spain are highly trained and provide free medical advice for minor ailments, although you will probably need to speak Spanish. They are often able to sell you the proper remedy without recourse to a doctor and will also recommend a local doctor, specialist, nurse or dentist when necessary. They can supply a wide range of medicines over the counter without a prescription, although some medicines sold freely in other countries require a doctor's prescription in Spain. Homeopathic and herbal medicines are stocked by most pharmacies, some of which specialise in homeopathy.

Note that brand names for the same drugs and medicines vary considerably from country to country, therefore if you regularly take medication you should ask your doctor for the generic name. If you wish to match medication prescribed abroad, you need a current prescription with the medication's trade name, the manufacturer's name, the chemical name and the dosage. Most foreign drugs have an equivalent in Spain, although particular brands may be difficult or impossible to obtain. It's possible to have medication sent from abroad and no import duty or value added tax (IVA) is payable. If you're visiting Spain for a limited period, you should take sufficient drugs to cover the length of your stay. In an emergency, a local doctor will write a prescription that can be filled at a local pharmacy or a hospital may fill a prescription from its own pharmacy.

Spanish pharmacies aren't cluttered with all the non-medical wares found in American and British pharmacies, although they also sell non-prescription medicines, cosmetics, diet foods and toiletries. Pharmacies are cheaper than a *perfumería* for cosmetics, but more expensive than a supermarket or hypermarket. A drugstore (*droguería*) sells non-medical items such as toiletries, cosmetics and household cleaning items, but not non-prescription medicines. A *droguería* shouldn't be confused with an American drugstore, which is a general store come fast food outlet (although there are also some of these in Spain). A health food shop (*herboristería*) sells health foods, diet foods and eternal-life-virility-youth pills and elixirs.

HOSPITALS & CLINICS

All Spanish cities and large towns have at least one hospital (*hospital*) or clinic (*clínica*), many of which are excellent modern establishments with highly trained staff and state of the art, high-tech equipment (most resort areas are particularly well endowed with good hospitals and clinics). However, in some areas (particularly poor rural areas) hospitals may be rundown, primitive and unhygienic, often with insufficient beds to cater for the local populace. There are long waiting lists for beds in some public hospitals (particularly the best ones) and patients occasionally die or are permanently disabled (e.g. cataract sufferers go blind) while waiting for a hospital bed or an operation. Generally large towns and resort areas have the best hospital facilities. Hospitals are listed in Yellow Pages under *hospitales* and indicated by the international hospital sign of a white 'H' on a blue background. A list of local hospitals and health centres treating social security patients is available from your local social security office.

There are many different categories of hospitals and clinics (often used to refer to all private hospitals) in Spain, including both public (*hospitales de la seguridad social*) and private hospitals (*hospitales privados*), plus day hospitals performing specialist tests and minor surgery. Spanish hospitals include general hospitals (*hospitales generales*), district hospitals (*hospitales distritos*), regional hospitals (*hospitales regionales*), provincial hospitals (*hospitales provinciales*), local hospitals (*hospitales comarcales/locales*), military hospitals (*hospitales militares*), nursing homes (*clínicas de reposo*), private clinics (*clínicas privadas*) and emergency clinics (*clínicas de urgencias*).

Many public hospitals are run by the Red Cross and are funded by private donations, although some towns contribute from public funds, and there are foreign-run private hospitals and clinics in major cities and resort areas. Major hospitals have an outpatients department (*consultas externas/departamento de enfermo externo del hospital*) and a *clínica de urgencia* provides a wide range of treatment including X-rays and electro-cardiograph (ECG) scans. Red Cross posts throughout the country (staffed by young men who have opted to do civil rather than military service) deal with minor accidents. Note that not all hospitals have an emergency department (*departamento de urgencias*) and public hospitals with emergency apartments are often swamped by patients faking emergencies in order to circumvent waiting lists.

Most private hospitals (*hospitales privados*) and clinics in Spain specialise in in-patient care in particular fields of medicine such as obstetrics and surgery, rather than being full-service hospitals. A number of private clinics advertise in the expatriate press in Spain. Many Spaniards and foreign residents have private health insurance (see page 260) and some 40 per cent of Spanish hospitals treat private patients only, including hospitals owned by Spanish health insurance companies which only treat patients covered by their policies.

In public hospitals in resort areas some 15 per cent of patients may be foreigners, many of whom are retired foreign residents who don't speak Spanish. Although the reception staff and telephonists at Spanish hospitals in resort areas and major cities often speak English (and other languages), medical staff may speak Spanish only. In hospitals with many foreign patients, local expatriates organise a team of volunteer interpreters (speaking a number of languages) for patients who are unable to speak Spanish. Note, however, that if you don't speak Spanish you may be given no information regarding the TV, phone, library, interpreting service, meal times and visiting hours, and will be very unlikely to receive any information in English or another foreign language. If your Spanish is poor, you may prefer to be treated at a private hospital or clinic with

English-speaking staff. The cost of a bed in a private hospital averages around 16,000 ptas a day in Spain, much less than in northern Europe, although specialists' fees may be higher (resulting in similar overall costs of around 30,000 ptas a day).

Except for emergency treatment, you're admitted or referred to a hospital or clinic for treatment only after a referral by a doctor or a specialist. If you're a social security patient, you're usually admitted to a hospital in your own province, unless specialist surgery or treatment is necessary which is unavailable there. If you wish to be treated in hospital by your personal doctor or specialist, you must check that he's able to treat you at your preferred hospital. You can usually leave hospital at any time without a doctor's consent by signing a release form.

Some public hospitals publish a guide (*guía del usario*) containing a hospital plan, public transport and road connections, department phone numbers, details of services such as cafeteria opening hours, cashpoint, visiting hours and other miscellaneous information. Public hospitals may have a library with books in a number of languages (including English) and may provide a mobile library for bed-ridden patients. The facilities provided in public hospitals are often limited compared with private hospitals and there may be no private rooms. If you wish to have a private room, you must pay a supplement, which may be paid by your private health insurance. You can usually rent a radio, television or telephone for a small daily fee (if not already included in the room fee) and must usually provide your own pyjamas, robes, towels and toiletries. Public hospitals often have a pay TV (shared with your fellow roommates, who if they are Spanish are likely to monopolise it) and a pay-phone operated by a special key.

Except in the case of emergencies, you must present your social security card or, if you aren't covered by social security, you must provide evidence of your health insurance or the ability to pay. If your private insurance company doesn't have an arrangement with a Spanish hospital to pay bills direct, you will have to pay the bill yourself (credit cards are usually accepted) or seek assurance from your insurance company that they will pay the bill. Note that if you have an appointment for treatment or surgery in a public hospital you may have to wait long past your appointment time before you eventually get a bed (beds in public hospitals are rarely left empty for long). Note also that in a hospital with an accident apartment, a non-urgent operation may be cancelled a number of times while priority is given to emergency cases.

Families were traditionally expected to look after their relatives, both while they were in hospital and after they had gone home. Although this is generally no longer the case, you may still be largely ignored by nursing staff (many of whom seem appear to have had a TLC bypass) and find your treatment is cold and impersonal, particularly compared with hospitals in northern Europe and North America. Hospital accommodation in public hospitals is usually basic (in rooms with two to four beds) and can be very noisy with visitors chattering and the TV blaring (it's quieter in a market place). Food is variable and at its worst is terrible (you will be spared if you're to have an operation, as you will immediately be put on a glucose drip and won't receive any meals). Note that pre-meds aren't usually given to patients before operations in Spain and you may even be required to walk to the operating theatre and climb on the table!

If you need crutches or other appliances you will need to obtain them yourself and a public hospital won't provide them even if you offer to pay (and you won't be discharged until you have them). In Spain patients are expected to convalesce at home, not in a hospital, and they are often discharged earlier than would be the case in many other countries. In many areas, back-up and nursing care is provided by the local community or expatriate groups. If you need to attend a public hospital out-patient department, bear in mind that it's likely to be totally chaotic (like a main railway station during rush hour). Take a thick book (and earplugs) and be prepared to wait a number of hours even if you have an appointment.

Footnote: Despite the criticisms included above, most foreigners are very satisfied with their treatment in Spanish hospitals and expatriate newspapers often carry letters from former patients praising their treatment. Many people also report that the difference between the standard of accommodation and treatment varies little between the best public and private hospitals and clinics.

DENTISTS

There are excellent dentists (*dentistas*) throughout Spain, although finding a dentist who speaks good English can be a problem, particularly in rural areas (although *Aaargh!* is the same in any language). However, there are many foreign and Spanish English-speaking dentists practicing in Spain (particularly in major cities and resort areas) including American, British, German and Scandinavian dentists (although their fees may be much higher than a Spanish dentist). Many embassies and consulates in Spain maintain a list of English-speaking dentists in their area (or dentists speaking their national language) and your employer, colleagues, friends or neighbours may be able to recommend someone.

Many tourist offices also maintain a list of English-speaking dentists and dentists may be listed in local English-language newspapers and magazines. Dentists are permitted to advertise their services in Spain and a number advertise in the expatriate press and are listed in Yellow Pages under *Dentistas Odontólogos*. Usually only names, addresses and telephone numbers are listed, and information such as specialities, surgery hours and whether they treat children (some don't) isn't provided. Many 'family' dentists in Spain are qualified to perform special treatment, e.g. endodontics (*endodoncia*) or periodontics (*periodoncia*), carried out by specialists in many countries.

Dentists' surgery hours vary considerably but are typically 0930 or 1000 to 1400 and 1700 to 2000. Some dentists have Saturday morning surgeries, e.g. 0900 to 1200. You must make an appointment. Many dentists provide an emergency service and there are special emergency dental services in major cities and resort areas. Note that only extractions and emergency treatment after an accident are available free of charge under the Spanish public health service (treatment may be performed in a public health clinic or a public hospital). If you need emergency treatment under INSALUD, first visit your doctor. Dentists expect to be paid in cash after treatment is completed, although if you're having expensive treatment such as a crown or a bridge made, your dentist may ask for a deposit in advance. Some dentists operate a time payment (instalment) scheme for expensive treatment. Always obtain an itemised bill if you intend to claim on insurance.

The cost of treatment varies wildly but as a rough guide you can reckon on around 5,000 ptas for an extraction and 5,000 to 10,000 for a filling. Before committing yourself to a large bill, it's advisable to obtain a written quotation for expensive treatment (if you don't receive a written quotation, the final bill is likely to be much higher than estimated). A verbal estimate will often be much lower than the final bill, even for a simple filling. If you or your family require expensive cosmetic dental treatment, e.g. crowns, bridges, braces or dentures, you may find it cheaper to have treatment abroad. Alternatively, you can ask your dentist if he can reduce the cost by reducing the work involved. As in most countries, dental treatment can be very expensive in Spain, so it will pay you to keep your mouth shut during dental visits. See also **Dental Insurance** on page 264.

OPTICIANS

As with other medical practitioners in Spain, it isn't necessary to register with an optician or optometrist (*óptico*); simply make an appointment with the optician of your choice. Ask your colleagues, friends or neighbours if they can recommend someone. Opticians are listed in the Yellow Pages under *óptica* and ophthalmologists under *médicos oftalmologías*. Eye tests and a prescription for spectacles are available free under the public health system, and low-income families and pensioners also receive free (basic) spectacles. Public health eye tests are generally performed at a public hospital and patients need a referral from their family doctor. Note that many opticians also carry out free eye tests.

The optical business is highly competitive in Spain. Prices for spectacles (*lentes*) and contact lenses (*lentillas de contacto*) aren't controlled, so it's wise to shop around and compare costs. Increased competition has reduced prices in recent years, although you may find that special spectacle lenses and contact lenses are more expensive in Spain than in some other European countries. Always obtain an estimate for lenses and ask about charges for such things as eye tests, fittings, adjustments, lens-care kit and follow-up visits. Note that the cost of tinted and special lenses (e.g. high index) increases the cost of spectacles considerably. Ask the cost of replacement lenses; if they're expensive, it may be worthwhile taking out insurance. Many opticians and retailers offer insurance against the accidental damage of spectacles for a nominal fee or even free for a limited period. Disposable and extended-wear soft contact lenses are also available in Spain, although medical experts believe they should be treated with extreme caution, as they greatly increase the risk of potentially blinding eye infections. **Obtain advice from an ophthalmologist before buying them.** (An ophthalmologist is a specialist medical doctor trained in diagnosing and treating disorders of the eye, performing sight tests, and prescribing spectacles and contact lenses.)

It's advisable to have your eyes tested before arriving in Spain and to bring a spare pair of spectacles and/or contact lenses with you. You should also bring a copy of your prescription in case you need to obtain replacement spectacles or contact lenses urgently. **Note that many people find it essential to wear sunglasses all year round in Spain.** Always buy a good pair that will protect your eyes from the sun's harmful ultra-violet rays.

COUNSELLING & SOCIAL SERVICES

Counselling and help for special health and social problems isn't as widely available in Spain as in many other European countries. However, there are a number of public and private organisations providing help for various health and health-related problems including drug rehabilitation; alcoholism and related problems; gambling; dieting; smoking; teenage pregnancy; attempted suicide and psychiatric problems; rehabilitation; homosexual related problems; youth problems; parent-child problems; child abuse; family violence (e.g. battered wives); runaways; marriage and relationship counselling; and rape.

In the first instance you should contact your family doctor, who can usually offer advice and put you in touch with an appropriate organisation or professional counsellor. In times of need there's usually someone to turn to and all services are strictly confidential. There are expatriate self-help groups in all areas, particularly for alcoholism (e.g. Alcoholics Anonymous), drug dependency and weight control (e.g. Weight Watchers). Voluntary groups are also common among expatriate communities, particularly organisations helping the elderly and infirm. There are English-language telephone help lines in some cities and resort areas manned by volunteers, e.g. Madrid has a help line operating from 1900 to 2300 (tel. (91) 559 1393).

One of Spain's major health problems is alcoholism, which is directly responsible for the loss of thousands of lives each year. The legal age for drinking alcohol in Spain is 18, although there's virtually no enforcement and children are readily served and sold alcohol everywhere (however, there has been a clamp down and high fines have been introduced for offenders). Alcoholism is a particular problem among expatriates in Spain, many of whom have little to do but lie in the sun and drink alcohol all day long. If you already drink more than is good for you, you should take care not to over-indulge in Spain. There are English-speaking Alcoholics Anonymous groups throughout Spain, many of which advertise in the expatriate press. Al-Anon is an organisation which originated in the USA and helps the families and friends of alcoholics to accept and deal with the condition. There are groups on both the Costa Blanca (tel. (96) 640 4184) and the Costa del Sol (tel. (95) 278 8903).

Spain has a relatively small number of social workers and there are few state-funded homes for the mentally and physically handicapped, or residential nursing homes for the elderly. In fact, services for the handicapped and elderly are generally poor. There are three kinds of social security homes (operated by INSERSO) for the elderly in Spain; homes for those able to look after themselves, residences for invalids or the chronically ill, and mixed residences. To qualify for entry you must be aged over 65 (or 60 if an invalid or widowed) *and* be in receipt of a Spanish state pension or be the spouse of a Spanish pensioner. Foreigners who aren't in receipt of a Spanish pension aren't admitted to INSERSO homes, but may be admitted to homes operated by provincial authorities.

SEXUALLY-TRANSMITTED DISEASES

As in many western countries, the spread of Aids (called *SIDA* in Spanish) is causing increasing anxiety in Spain. Spain has far more cases of Aids and HIV (human immunodeficiency virus), the virus that causes Aids, than any other EU country. The HIV virus is transmitted by sexual contact, needle sharing among drug addicts (injecting drug-users account for two-thirds of Spain's victims), and less commonly, through transfused blood or its components. The spread of Aids is accelerated by prostitutes, many of whom are also drug addicts. Since 1990, Aids has primarily been transmitted by drug users in Spain, where the number of intravenous drug-users with Aids is over 100 per million inhabitants and by far the highest in Europe (in Britain it's two per million, Germany three and France 22). Aids and HIV is rife in Spain's prisons, where drug use and the sharing of needles is widespread. There are also as many children infected with Aids in Spain as in all other EU countries combined.

Many heterosexuals don't take the threat of Aids seriously, particularly as most of its victims to date (in the western world) have been homosexuals and drug addicts. There's no cure for Aids, which is always fatal. The most common protection against Aids is for men to wear a condom, although they're not foolproof (against Aids or pregnancy) and the only real protection is celibacy. In an attempt to combat Aids, the use of condoms (*preservativos*) has been encouraged and they are widely available from pharmacies and vending machines in public toilets. Apparently only some 35 per cent of Spaniards use contraceptives in casual encounters (how do researchers know? — "er, excuse me for intruding, but are you wearing a condom?"). With the growing problem of Aids, opposition to contraception from the Catholic church has been muted. A lack of resources and political indifference are considered by medical experts to be the biggest hurdles to curbing the spread of Aids in Spain.

BIRTHS & DEATHS

Births and deaths in Spain must be registered at the Civil Registry (*registro civil*) at the town hall of the district where they take place. Registration applies to everyone irrespective of their nationality or whether they are residents of Spain or just visitors.

Births: Registration of a birth must be made within eight days at the local civil registry and may be done by the hospital or clinic where the child was born, or by the midwife when a birth takes place at home. Parents are, however, responsible for ensuring that this is done and may have to do it themselves. There are two forms of birth certificate in Spain; a short certificate (*extracto de inscripción de nacimiento* or *certificado simple*), showing only the date of birth, the names of the child and parents, and the inscription number; and a full certificate (*certificado literal de nacimiento*). Foreigners should always get the full one, which costs only a little more (both are inexpensive) and may be necessary to register your child at your home country's consulate or embassy in Spain (to obtain a birth certificate and passport for a child).

A birth certificate must state whether a child is legitimate or illegitimate (a *legitimate* child is one born at least 180 days after its parents' marriage or within 300 days of a divorce, annulment of a marriage or the death of the father). Note that the suspected father of a child can be compelled to undergo a biological test (at a cost of 150,000 to 200,000 ptas) to prove whether or not he's the father. Tests are supposedly almost foolproof (99.9 per cent accurate) and are accepted as such by a court of law. Spain has one of the lowest birth rates in the world at around 1.3 children per family.

Although legalised in 1986, abortion remains a contentious issue in Spain, and is fervently opposed by the Catholic church and right-wing circles. It's currently available during the first 12 weeks in certain circumstances, e.g. when a pregnancy threatens the mother's life, the foetus is severely deformed or the pregnancy was the result of rape. Previously Spanish women who wanted an abortion needed to go abroad or resort to 'illegal' abortionists (it's estimated that some 40,000 illegal abortions were performed annually in Spain) and a woman who had an illegal abortion could be jailed for up to a year.

Deaths: A death must be registered within 24 hours at the town hall of the district where it took place. If the deceased was a foreigner, the town hall will need his passport or residence card (*residencia*) and the death must also be registered at the deceased's local consulate or embassy in Spain. A death needn't be reported to the police unless it was as a result of an accident or crime (or the death occurred in suspicious circumstances). A death certificate must be prepared and signed by the doctor who attended the death (either in a hospital or elsewhere) and be legally certified by a judge. In the case of a foreigner, it must be presented to the deceased person's embassy or consulate in Spain to obtain a certificate valid in the deceased's home country. The certificates are required for insurance claims and to execute a will.

A body can be buried or cremated in Spain or flown to another country for burial. It's expensive (e.g. 250,000 to 500,000 within Europe) to fly a body to another country for burial, but the cost may be covered by an international insurance policy which includes repatriation. In Spain, a burial must take place through an undertaker (*funeraria*), who will arrange everything including death certificates. A full service funeral costs between 250,000 and 400,000 ptas, including five years rent on a cemetary niche (*nicho*). The cost of cremation is cheaper than a full-service funeral at 50,000 to 100,000 ptas, although there aren't many crematoria in Spain. Note that family members aren't permitted to attend the cremation itself but may attend a service (with the body present) before the actual cremation or after it with the urn containing the deceased's ashes (which may be scattered at sea or in the countryside in Spain). A body cannot be interred sooner than 24 hours after death. However, burial usually takes place within 48 hours of death and where there's no refrigeration a burial *must* take place within 72 hours. Refrigeration is, however, available in most areas and costs around 5,000 ptas a day.

Although cemeteries in Spain are mostly Catholic, a person of any creed can be buried there. There are also foreign cemeteries in some cities and towns, e.g. there's a British cemetery in Malaga and an international cemetery in Benalmádena (Costa del Sol). Burials and cremations can be made in official cemeteries only. In most Spanish cemeteries, internment is above ground and bodies are placed in niches set into walls, which are rented for a number of years, e.g. 5 to 50 (the rent is around 6,500 to 10,000 ptas a year). The cheapest 'graves' are in municipal cemeteries where typical rentals are around 25,000 ptas for five years, 100,000 ptas for 25 years and 200,000 ptas for 50 years. After the rental period has expired, bodies are interred in a common burial ground within the consecrated cemetery grounds. After a number of years (e.g. 25) all graves are exhumed in some areas and the remains buried in a large communal tomb, although this occurs mostly on the islands where land is at a premium. To avoid this you must buy a plot outright which can cost 500,000 ptas or more. Note that cemetaries in Spain often have limited opening hours and aren't open to the public at all hours as they are in most countries.

Dying is an expensive business in Spain and is best avoided if at all possible (undertakers only get one bite of the cherry and need to make the most of it). Always check the cost of a funeral in advance and make sure that you aren't paying for anything you don't want. The cost of a full service funeral is around 200,000 to 300,000 ptas, depending on the area and town, and there may also be extra costs for transportation and cemetery fees. Embalming isn't common in Spain and is expensive, e.g. 150,000 to 200,000 ptas. Note that it may be necessary to engage a local funeral company, so you may not be able to shop around for the lowest price (and anyway undertakers' fees are roughly the same in most areas). Most undertakers expect to be paid in cash. It's possible to take out an insurance policy (*seguro de decesos*) for funeral expenses with a Spanish or foreign insurance company, although it's very expensive.

When a resident of Spain dies, all interested parties must be notified (see **Chapter 19**). You will need several copies of the death certificate which are required by banks and other institutions.

MEDICAL TREATMENT ABROAD

If you're entitled to public health benefits in Spain or another European country, you can take advantage of reciprocal health care agreements in other European countries. Everyone insured under Spanish social security is covered for medical expenses while travelling abroad, providing certain steps are taken to ensure reimbursement. In some cases you must obtain a form from your local social security office before leaving Spain. **This also applies to foreign residents of Spain planning to visit their home EU country.**

Full payment (possibly in cash) must usually be made in advance for treatment received abroad, although you will be reimbursed on your return to Spain. This applies to all EU countries except Britain, where everyone receives free emergency health care. You're also reimbursed for essential treatment in countries not mentioned above, although you must obtain detailed receipts. Note that reimbursement is based on the cost of comparable treatment in Spain. In certain countries, e.g. Canada, Japan, Switzerland and the USA, medical treatment is very expensive and you're advised to take out travel or holiday insurance (see page 267) when visiting these countries. **This is advisable wherever you're travelling as it provides considerably wider medical cover than reciprocal health care agreements (and includes many other things such as repatriation).** If you do a lot of travelling abroad, it's worthwhile having an international health insurance policy (see page 262).

Visitors to Spain: If you're an EU resident visiting Spain, you can take advantage of reciprocal health care agreements. Nationals of non-EU countries are also entitled to free health care under the Spanish public health service, providing their home country has a reciprocal agreement with Spain. EU residents should apply for a certificate of entitlement to treatment (form E-111) from their local social security office at least three weeks before planning to travel to Spain. **The E-111 is valid for three months only and must be validated by being stamped prior to departure.** On arrival in Spain you must take your E-111 form to the provincial office of the Spanish social security (*Instituto Nacional de la Seguridad Social/INSS*) where you're issued with a Spanish medical card and a book of vouchers to use when claiming medical assistance. Note that these are valid for emergency or urgent medical treatment only and not, for example, for prescriptions or dental treatment.

If you use form E-111 in Spain, you present the form plus a photocopy to the medical practitioner who's providing treatment and pay for treatment in cash. The original is returned. You must apply for reimbursement to your home country's social security department (instructions are provided with the form), which can take a number of months. If you travel to Spain or to another EU country *specifically* for medical treatment or maternity care in a public hospital, you need form E-112, and prior authorisation from your country's social security department. Form E-112 authorises treatment in a Spanish or other EU public hospital without pre-payment (although it's difficult to obtain). Note that E-forms issued in other EU countries cover visitors to Spain only and *not* residents of Spain (although many foreign residents who aren't covered by Spanish social security use form E-111 illegally in Spain). However, Spanish residents covered by Spanish social security can use E forms in other EU countries.

British visitors or those planning to live in Spain can obtain information about reciprocal health treatment in Spain from the Department of Social Security, Overseas Branch, Newcastle-upon-Tyne, NE98 1YX, UK.

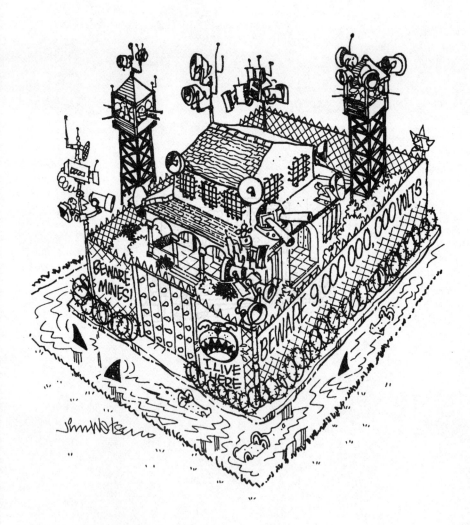

13.
INSURANCE

The Spanish government and Spanish law provide for various obligatory state and employer insurance schemes. These include health, sickness and maternity; work injuries; state pensions; disability; and unemployment insurance. However, the average Spaniard is more prone to taking risks than many other nationalities and carries less insurance than, for example, northern Europeans (although the market has grown tremendously in the last decade, particularly in private health and life insurance). Most Spanish and EU residents and their families receive health treatment under the Spanish social security system. If you don't qualify for health care under the Spanish national health system, it's essential to take out private health insurance (and is obligatory for many non-EU residents). Spanish employees have considerable protection under social security and are entitled to higher benefits than employees in many other EU countries (although in most cases you would be unwise to rely solely on social security to meet your needs).

Ensure that your family has full health insurance during the interval between leaving your last country of residence and obtaining health insurance in Spain. One way is to take out a travel insurance policy. However, if possible it's better to extend a private health insurance policy to cover you in Spain, rather than take out a new policy. This is particularly important if you have an existing health problem that won't be covered by a new policy. There are a few occasions in Spain where insurance for individuals is compulsory including third party car insurance, third-party property liability insurance for tenants and home owners, and mortgage life insurance for mortgage holders. If you lease a car or buy one on credit, a lender may insist that you have comprehensive car insurance. Voluntary insurance includes private pensions, disability, health, household, dental, travel, car breakdown and life insurance.

It's unnecessary to spend half your income insuring yourself against every eventuality from the common cold to being sued for your last peseta, but it's important to insure against any event that could precipitate a major financial disaster, such as a serious accident or your house falling down. As with anything connected with finance, it's important to shop around when buying insurance. Just collecting a few brochures from insurance agents and making a few telephone calls, **could save you a lot of money.** Regrettably you cannot insure yourself against being uninsured or sue your insurance broker for giving you bad advice.

In all matters regarding insurance, you're responsible for ensuring that you and your family are legally insured in Spain. Bear in mind that if you wish to make a claim on an insurance policy, you may be required to report an incident to the police within 24 hours (in some cases this may be a legal requirement). Obtain legal advice for anything other than a minor claim. Spanish law is likely to differ from that in your home country or your previous country of residence, so never *assume* that it's the same. See also **Car Insurance** on page 203 and **Motor Breakdown Insurance** on page 229.

INSURANCE COMPANIES & AGENTS

Until the 1980s, Spain had a relatively undeveloped insurance market, when many foreign companies stepped in to fill the vacuum and now control some 50 per cent of the market. There are numerous Spanish and foreign insurance companies to choose from, providing either a range of insurance services or specialising in certain fields only. Many of the British and other foreign insurance companies operating in Spain cater particularly for the needs of expatriates, with major insurance companies having offices or agents throughout Spain (many are also 'direct' telephone insurers). Insurance agents, brokers (*corredor de seguros*) and companies are listed in the Yellow Pages under *Seguros* and many advertise in the expatriate press in Spain. Most insurance companies or brokers will provide a free appraisal of your family's insurance needs.

There are many independent brokers in Spain, including many British and other foreign brokers in resort areas, who can offer you a choice of policies and save you money. However, as in many countries, it's often difficult to obtain completely independent unbiased insurance advice as brokers may be influenced by higher commission offered for selling a particular policy. As with all financial matters in Spain, be very careful who you choose as your broker and the company you insure with, as a number of companies have gone bust in recent years (particularly in the motor insurance sector) and insurance fraud isn't unknown. **When buying insurance, particularly car insurance (see page 203), shop until you drop!** Obtain recommendations from friends, colleagues and neighbours (but don't believe everything they tell you!). Compare the costs, terms and benefits provided by a number of companies before making a decision. Note that premiums (*premios*) are sometimes negotiable.

From 1st July 1994, Spanish residents have been free to insure their car, home or life with any insurance company registered in the European Union, *without* the need for the insurer to be registered in Spain. The company must be registered in its home country and insurance cover must correspond to the minimum legal requirements. Note, however, that should a dispute arise over a claim, it will usually be dealt with in the country where the insurance company is registered. Under EU law there should eventually be a Europe-wide insurance market, although at the moment relatively few companies operate internationally.

If you have a complaint regarding an insurance policy, you should complain in the first instance to the company; large companies usually have a complaints department (*defensores del asegurado*). If you don't receive satisfaction you can send a complaint to the *Servicio de Reclamaciones*, Dirección General de Seguros (DGS), Paseo de la Castellana, 44, 28046 Madrid (tel. (91) 575 4800). Note that the DGS concerns itself with Spanish insurance companies and foreign companies with a registered office in Spain.

INSURANCE CONTRACTS

Read all insurance contracts before signing them. If you don't understand Spanish, have your legal advisor check a policy and don't sign it until you clearly understand the terms and the cover provided. Many foreign insurance companies operating in Spain provide policies and information in English and other foreign languages. Note, however, that an insurance policy issued in Spain is usually written under Spanish law and that the Spanish document is always the legal one. Like insurance companies everywhere, some will use any available legal loophole to avoid paying out in the event of a claim and therefore it pays to deal with reputable companies only (not that this provides a foolproof guarantee). Policies often contain legal loopholes in the small print and if you don't understand them you should obtain independent professional legal advice before signing a contract.

If you believe that you have a valid claim you should always persevere, despite any obstacles placed in your path. The wheels of justice grind very (*very*) slowly in Spain and it may take you a number of years to gain satisfaction, but if you have a

legitimate claim you will usually eventually receive compensation (plus interest from the date of the claim).
Always check the notice period required to cancel (*cancelar/anular*) a policy. Note that in Spain, most insurance policies are automatically extended for a further period (usually a year) if they aren't cancelled in writing by registered letter two or three months before the expiry date. You may cancel an insurance policy before the term has expired if the premium has increased, the terms are altered, e.g. the risk is diminished, or an insured object is lost or stolen. This must, however, still be done in writing and by registered post. Cancellation is also permitted at short notice under certain circumstances including when changing jobs, redundancy, retirement, marriage and divorce (and death!). You're usually entitled to a refund of any unused premiums paid.

If you wish to make a claim, you must usually inform your insurance company in writing by registered letter within two to five days of the incident (e.g. for accidents) or 24 hours in the case of theft. Thefts should also be reported to the local police station within 24 hours as the police report (*denuncia*) constitutes evidence of your claim. Usually an insurance company will send an adjuster to evaluate the extent of damage, e.g. to your home or car.

One of the advantages of taking out a policy with a foreign insurance company is that you will have a policy you can understand (apart from all the legal jargon) and can make claims in your own language. This is usually a good option for the owner of a holiday home in Spain. However, bear in mind that insuring with a foreign insurance company may be more expensive than insuring with a Spanish company and in certain cases a policy may still need to be written under Spanish law.

SOCIAL SECURITY

Spain has a comprehensive social security (*seguridad social*) system covering over 90 per cent of the population. It includes health care (plus sickness and maternity); industrial injuries; unemployment insurance; old age (pensions), invalidity and death benefits. Social security benefits in Spain are among the highest in the EU, as are social security contributions. The total contributions per employee are an average of some 30 per cent of gross pay, some 25 per cent of which is paid by employers. With the exception of sickness benefits, social security benefits aren't taxed.

Two thirds of social security spending is on cash benefits such as pensions (old age, disabled, orphans and widows), sickness, housing and unemployment benefits, distributed through the *Instituto Nacional de Seguridad Social (INSS)*. Less than a third of revenue is spent on health services, administered through the *Instituto Nacional de Salud (INSALUD)*, and social services, which are the responsibility of the *Instituto de Servicios Sociales (INSERSO)*. Spain has a separate social security system for members of the civil service and the armed forces, and special schemes for farm workers, seamen, the self-employed, domestic servants and other groups.

As in many other European countries, the Spanish social security system is under severe financial strains (partly due to widespread fraud). An ageing population and increasing unemployment have contributed to a huge increase in spending on health care, pensions and unemployment benefits in recent years. Cutbacks in government spending have resulted in reduced unemployment benefits, pensions and other social security benefits in the last few years. Most analysts agree that present levels of social security benefits (particularly pensions) are unsustainable, and payments need to be slashed if the system isn't to be bankrupted.

For more information contact your local social security office or the *Instituto Nacional de la Seguridad Social*, Subdirección General de Relaciones Internacionales, Padre Damian, 4, Madrid 28036 (tel. (91) 564 7681). Free telephone information is available on 900-166565 (mainland and the Balearics), 900-103535 (Las Palmas) and 900-103838 (Tenerife).

Eligibility & Exemptions

All foreign employees working for Spanish companies and self-employed foreigners in Spain must usually contribute to Spanish social security. Generally if you're an employee in Spain, you will be insured under Spanish social security legislation and won't have any liability for social security contributions in your home country or country of domicile. However, social security agreements exist between Spain and over 40 countries, including all EU countries and the USA, whereby expatriates may remain members of their home country's social security scheme for a limited period. EU nationals transferred to Spain by an employer in their home country can continue to pay social security abroad for one year (form E-101 is required), which can be extended for another year in unforeseen circumstances (when form E-102 is needed). This also applies to the self-employed. However, after working in Spain for two years, EU nationals *must* contribute to the Spanish social security system.

To qualify for social security benefits, you must have been employed in Spain for a limited period and have made certain minimum contributions. If you're retired and living in Spain and receive a state pension from another EU country, or from a country with a social security agreement with Spain, you and your spouse are automatically entitled to health benefits under Spanish social security (if a wife aged 60 or over is entitled to public health treatment, then a husband aged under 65 may also be entitled to it). You must prove your entitlement to a pension by obtaining form E-121 from your home country's social security administration, which must be produced when registering with Spanish social security. Form E-121 has indefinite validity and doesn't require renewing. If, however, you retire to Spain before reaching the Spanish retirement age, you must have private health insurance.

If you qualify to pay social security contributions abroad, it may be worthwhile doing so, as contributions in some countries are lower than those in Spain. If you or your spouse work in Spain but remain insured under the social security legislation of another EU country, you can claim social security benefits from that country. If the spouse and children of an EU national employed in Spain remain in their home country, they will continue to be covered by the social security system of that country.

If you need to claim benefits in Spain and have paid contributions in another EU country, those contributions are usually taken into account when calculating your right to benefits. If you're receiving an invalidity pension or other social security benefits on the grounds of ill-health, you should establish exactly how living in Spain will affect those benefits, as they may cease when you take up residence in Spain. In some countries there are reciprocal rights regarding invalidity, but you must confirm that they apply in your case before going to live in Spain. Note that the payment and right to foreign (e.g. from other EU countries) social security benefits (apart from pensions) usually ends when you take up permanent residence in Spain. Citizens of an EU country who visit Spain as tourists can also use the Spanish public health system (see page 248).

In Britain, information regarding social security rights within the EU is provided in two booklets: *Social Security for Migrant Workers* and *Your social security, health care and pension rights in the European Community* (SA29), available from the Department of Social Security, Overseas Branch, Newcastle-upon-Tyne NE98 1YX, UK (tel. 0191-285 7111).

Registration

If you're working in Spain, your employer will usually complete the necessary formalities to ensure that you're covered by social security. If he doesn't do it, you must obtain an attestation that you're employed in Spain and register at the nearest social security office to your home. Your local town hall will give you the address of your local office or it will be listed under *Seguridad Social* in your local Yellow Pages. If you're in receipt of a state pension in another EU country and move to Spain, you must take both copies of your form E-121 (see above) to the pension department at your local social security office in Spain. One copy will be retained and the other stamped and returned to you. You will need to produce passports and (certified) birth certificates for all dependants and a marriage certificate (if applicable). You may also need to provide copies with official translations (but check first as translations may be unnecessary). You will also need proof of residence such as a property deed of sale (*escritura*) or a rental contract.

After you have registered you will receive a registration card (*cartilla de la seguridad social* or *tarjeta sanitaria*), usually by post around four to eight weeks later. A married couple with one partner working are covered by the same social security card and number, as are all dependants (e.g. children under 16) who are listed on your social security card. When applying for benefits or for social security reimbursements, you must always apply to the office listed on your social security card and quote your social security number or produce your card. Note that there's a compulsory waiting period before a new subscriber can claim certain social security benefits, which varies depending on the particular benefit.

If you contribute to social security, your dependants will receive the same benefits. Dependants include your spouse (if he isn't personally insured); your children supported by you under the age of 16 (or under the age of 20 if they are students or unable to work through illness or invalidity); and ascendents, descendants and relatives by marriage supported by you and living in the same household. Separated, divorced and widowed persons continue to receive benefits for at least one year after the 'event', or in the case of separated persons, for as long as their spouse is employed providing they aren't eligible for benefits from other sources.

Contributions

Social security contributions (*cuotas*) for employees are calculated as a percentage of their taxable income, although for certain contributions there's a maximum salary level. Contributions start as soon as you start work in Spain and not when you obtain your residence card (*residencia*). Social security contributions for both employees and employers are based on the official salary limit (*nómina*) for a specific occupation. The minimum annual salary on which you must usually pay social security contributions is around 70,000 ptas, of which 31.6 per cent is calculated as the monthly payment for social security. A small proportion, i.e. around 6 per cent of the 31.6 per cent, is deducted from the employee's salary and the remainder is paid by the employer. The minimum contributions are around 32,000 ptas a month for employees (*cuenta ajena*) and are higher than those for self-employed persons, as employees are entitled to unemployment benefits if they lose their jobs.

The self-employed (*cuenta propia*) pay a minimum of around 30,000 ptas a month (the maximum is around 110,000 ptas), which is subject to a 20 per cent surcharge if you don't pay it on time. Note that any self-employed person, even if he works only part time, must contribute to social security. If you don't work for a minimum of a calendar month you aren't required to pay social security during that period, e.g. if you operate a business in Spain and close for the month of January. Note that if you're self-employed and have a number of separate jobs, you require two sets of papers and must pay social security twice. Domestic workers (*empleados de hogar*) who are self-employed and work part-time for a number of employers pay reduced social security contributions of 17,384 ptas a month. However, if they're employed full-time by one employer, they must receive the minimum wage (see page 32) and pay normal employee contributions.

Benefits

Social security benefits are paid as a percentage of your salary, rather than as a flat rate, and are subject to minimum and maximum payments. You must earn a certain minimum salary to qualify for benefits. Spanish social security includes benefits for health, sickness, maternity, work injury, housing, unemployment, retirement, invalidity and death.

Health Benefits: Public health benefits include general and specialist care, hospitalisation, laboratory services, drugs and medicines, basic dental care, maternity care, appliances and emergency transportation. Note, however, that social security covers only around 75 per cent of the cost of treatment and the other 25 per cent must be paid by the patient or a supplementary insurance scheme. Completely free treatment is available only in certain hospitals, where waiting lists are very long. Members must also pay a percentage of the cost of certain treatment and items such as drugs and medicines (see page 239). See also **Social Security Health Benefits** on page 237.

Sickness Benefits: When an employee is ill, he continues to receive a percentage of his salary. A self-employed person can also receive 75 per cent of the *minimum* salary of 66,630 ptas a month, i.e. 49,972 ptas, providing he obtains a doctor's certificate stating that he's incapable of carrying out his usual occupation.

Unemployment Insurance Benefits: Unemployment in Spain is the highest in western Europe and although membership of the state social security system is mandatory, only some 50 per cent of the unemployed qualify for benefits (young people who have never been employed don't qualify for unemployment benefits). There's no such thing in Spain as supplementary benefit (e.g. as in Britain) or supplemental security income (e.g. as in the USA), although many regions pay a 'social wage' to the unemployed who don't qualify for unemployment benefits. There's a 'safety net' for agricultural workers who can claim the minimum unemployment benefit if they can prove that they have been employed for at least 35 days a year (most agricultural workers can find seasonal work for a maximum of just three months a year).

Until 1992, unemployed workers received 80 per cent of their previous salary in unemployment benefits, even when they had been employed only on a short-term contract for six months. However, huge deficits in public spending have forced the government to reduce benefits to 75 per cent of the *minimum* salary of 66,630 ptas a month, irrespective of former earnings. Unemployed persons who haven't been employed for at least one year receive only 75 per cent of this sum and don't receive any credit against their state pension. Under a new system, benefits have been cut and the period during which the newly unemployed are eligible for state assistance has been reduced to four months for every year worked. Entitlement to unemployment benefit ceases after one or two years, except in the case of families who receive a much reduced benefit for a further two years. An unemployed person intending to carry on a professional activity as a working member of a labour co-operative or an employee-owned company can collect the aggregate unemployment benefit as a one-time payment.

Note that social security payments made in another EU country are taken into account and credited to EU workers in Spain, so that they are eligible to full unemployment benefits during a period of unemployment. If you're entitled to unemployment benefits in another EU country and have been claiming unemployment for at least four weeks, you can continue to receive unemployment benefit (at your home country's rate) in Spain for up to three months while looking for work. You must inform the unemployment office in your home country that you intend to seek work in Spain well in advance of your departure. If you qualify for transfer of benefits to Spain, your home country's unemployment service will provide a certificate of authorisation, which is necessary to register in Spain.

You must register for work at the nearest office of the INEM (see page 23) in Spain within seven days of leaving your home country, so that your eligibility for benefits isn't interrupted. Note, however, that there may be a delay of up to three months before you actually start to receive benefits, so you must be able to finance yourself during your job search in Spain. During this period you're entitled to health care in Spain, for which you require a certificate of entitlement (form E-119). Note that Spanish bureaucrats aren't very co-operative with this scheme (i.e. even more obstructive than usual!) and you must persevere to obtain your rights. If after three months you don't have a job you must leave Spain, as you're permitted to remain for three months only without a residence card (and a residence card won't be issued if you don't have a job or an adequate income).

Old Age, Invalidity & Death Benefits: The Spanish state retirement (*jubilación*) pension is paid at 65 for men and 60 for women. Contributions are paid by both employers and employees and vary depending on your income. Spanish state pensions are the highest in Europe after Sweden and there was no restriction on the maximum pension until 1983, when it was set at 187,000 ptas a month. In 1997, the minimum pension (after 15 years' contributions) at age 65 was 64,505 ptas a month for a couple and 54,825 ptas a month for a single person. The maximum monthly pension was 284,198 ptas. Spanish pensions are indexed to take account of rises in the cost of living. Pensioners, like salaried employees, receive 14 payments a year instead of 12, with an extra payment in July and December (since 1992 this has also included retired self-employed persons).

A worker earning over 384,630 ptas a month can choose to pay the maximum contributions (around 110,000 ptas a month for a self-employed worker) in order to receive the maximum pension of over 250,000 ptas a month after 35 years' contributions. No extra contributions can be paid on income above 384,630 ptas a month. A worker's final pension is principally based on his payments during the eight years prior to his retirement, during which period only controlled increases in base payments are permitted.

The minimum number of years you must pay into the system to qualify for a pension was increased from 10 to 15 years in 1974. This means that foreigners who contribute for less than 15 years receive no Spanish state pension. Early or partial retirement is permitted under Spanish law and anyone with sufficient credits can choose to retire early. Since 1992, the widowed partner of a state pensioner has been entitled to the full pension payable to the deceased's spouse, while dependent children are entitled to an additional 20 per cent. When there's no surviving parent, dependent children are also entitled to the widow's pension.

If you move to Spain after working in another EU country (or move to another EU country after working in Spain), your state pension contributions can be exported to Spain (or from Spain to another country). Spanish state pensions are payable abroad and most countries pay state pensions directly to their nationals resident in Spain. Under EU regulations, the total contributions paid into different member states' insurance systems are taken into account when accessing an individual's rights to a state pension (also applies to invalidity pensions). The number of years' contributions paid in different countries are added together and each country pays the percentage for which it's liable, e.g. if you worked 20 years in Britain, 5 years in Germany and 15 years in Spain, Britain would pay 50 per cent, Germany 12.5 per cent and Spain 37.5 per cent of your state pension. Contributors can ask the authorities in the relevant countries to calculate their entitlements and opt to choose the highest amount. Contact your home country's social security administration for information.

If you retire to Spain before your home country's state retirement age, it's advisable to continue to contribute to the state pension scheme in order to qualify for a pension, otherwise your state pension could be reduced. In some countries (e.g. Britain) there are special contributions for those who aren't employed, who can pay contributions annually in one instalment. Most countries pay state pensioners living in Spain the same pension that they would receive in their home country, with annual increases indexed to the cost of living.

If you plan to retire to Spain, you should ensure that your income is (and will remain) sufficient to live on, bearing in mind devaluations if your pension or income isn't paid in pesetas, rises in the cost of living and unforeseen expenses such as medical bills or anything else that may reduce your income (e.g. stock market crashes). Anyone living in Spain who's in receipt of a state pension in any EU country is entitled to the benefits of Spanish social security. Various organisations, such as the *Fondo Nacional de Asistencia Social (FONAS)*, provides old age pensions for those who don't qualify under other schemes.

Future Prospects: As in all western European countries, state pensions are under pressure from governments that can no longer afford to pay them, due to the ever dwindling number of workers who are supporting a growing number of retirees. There were around 6m pensioners in Spain in 1997, which was expected to reach 6.5m by the year 2000 and 7.5m by 2015. For every 100 Spaniards over the age of 14, over 60 are inactive (the average for the EU as a whole is around 50). Spain has particular problems, as state pensions remain far too generous (for the government — pensions are *never* too high for pensioners), despite reductions in the last few years, and more people receive their income from the state than from the private sector. The state pension fund in Spain is almost bankrupt and it's possible that future contributor's won't receive the pension they have been promised at retirement age (the fund is expected to run into problems in around 15 years time). The Spanish government is trying to shift some of the burden onto private insurance companies, so far without much success. There are proposals to raise the pension age and the number of years required to qualify and drastically reduce benefits.

SUPPLEMENTARY PENSIONS

Until recent years, supplementary or private pensions (*planes de pensiones*) were unusual in Spain. However, with the long-term future of state pensions in doubt and attempts by the government to encourage company and private pensions, many people are taking out supplementary pensions. Many employees in Spain pay into private insurance schemes that top up their social security benefits, which may be combined with a private health insurance scheme. In many cases the combined state and supplementary pensions are equal to an employee's final salary.

It's important for anyone who doesn't qualify for a state pension or who will receive only the minimum state pension to consider contributing to a supplementary or private pension fund. Note that you must contribute to Spanish social security for 15 years before you're entitled to a state pension. There are a wide range of private pension funds in Spain (many provided by banks) and it's also possible to continue to contribute to a personal pension plan abroad or an offshore fund. Note, however, that contributions to foreign pension schemes aren't tax deductible in Spain. Many major European private pension companies have offices or agents in Spain.

Most experts advise that the best pension scheme for many people is one that doesn't require fixed monthly payments, but allows you to pay irregular lump sums. In Spain, there's usually a small minimum monthly payment, possibly as low as 5,000 ptas a month, and lump sum contributions are usually from 100,000 ptas. A pension should be index linked to insure that it keeps pace with inflation. With an index linked policy, capital is tax free after 15 years' contributions with a reducing scale for early surrender. If you have an offshore pension, there's no tax relief but all benefits are paid tax free. If you're a Spanish taxpayer, you can deduct pension contributions equal to 15 per cent of your income (up to a maximum annual limit of 750,000 ptas) from your net taxable income. Pensions paid to foreigners resident in Spain are taxed as regular salary income and a one-time payment is taxed as irregular income. The exception are civil service pensions, which are taxable in your home country and don't usually need to be declared to the Spanish authorities (this doesn't include United Nations pensions, as the UN cannot tax its former employees). Note, however, that civil service pensions are usually taken into account when calculating your Spanish tax rate if you have other income which is taxable in Spain.

HEALTH INSURANCE

The vast majority of people in Spain are covered for health treatment under social security (see page 237). However, most people who can afford it (some 6m people) take out private health insurance, which offers a wider choice of medical practitioners and hospitals, and more importantly, frees them from public health waiting lists. If you aren't covered by Spanish social security, it's **imperative** that you have private health insurance (unless you have a *very* large bank balance). The policies offered by Spanish and foreign companies generally differ considerably in the extent of cover, limitations and restrictions, premiums, and the choice of doctors, specialists and hospitals.

Note that the USA doesn't have a reciprocal health agreement with Spain and therefore American students and other Americans who aren't covered by social security *must* have private health insurance in Spain. Proof of insurance must usually be provided when applying for a visa or residence card (*residencia*). Note that some foreign insurance companies don't provide sufficient cover to satisfy Spanish regulations and therefore you should check the minimum cover necessary with a Spanish consulate in your country of residence.

Spanish Companies: There are a large number of Spanish health insurance companies, although their numbers have been considerably reduced in the last decade, during which literally hundreds of small companies went bankrupt (some as a result of fraud). Some companies such as Adeslas, Asisa, Previaso and Sanitas (owned by the British company BUPA) operate nationally, while others are restricted to certain cities or provinces only (although non-national policies have participating hospitals throughout Spain for emergency cases). Spanish insurance previously operated a coupon system, where policy holders were issued with coupons to give to their doctor or other medical practitioners, who then presented them to the insurance company for payment. However, this system has now been widely replaced by patient's membership cards. Insurance companies provide members with a list of contracted doctors, specialists and hospitals in their area that accept the company's cards. Some insurance companies also operate their own clinics. Usually it's impossible to freely choose your own doctor, clinic or hospital, although some companies offer a free choice of doctors and hospitals for a higher premium. The main disadvantage of the 'contract' system is that in some areas you may have to travel long distances to see a specialist or to be admitted to hospital. Note that if you're taken to a hospital in an emergency that isn't on your insurance company's list, you won't be covered by your policy.

Some companies offer a choice of plans which may include contracted doctors only; contracted doctors, specialists and other out-patient treatment; all out-patient consultations and treatment plus hospitalisation and surgery (with contracted practitioners and hospitals) for a limited period each year (say 50 days); and a free choice of practitioners and hospitals offering all services. An important consideration for many foreigners is being able to choose an English-speaking medical practitioner or a hospital with English-speaking staff (or staff that speak another language). This is impossible with Spanish insurance unless a policy allows a free choice of practitioners and hospitals.

Private health insurance used to be relatively inexpensive in Spain, although premiums have increased considerably in recent years and weren't not helped by a 4 per cent tax on private health insurance policies! Annual premiums for a family of four (two adults aged 40 years and two children aged under 16) range from around 175,000 to 300,000 ptas or from around 5,000 ptas a month for an individual. There may be an annual surcharge for those aged over a certain age, e.g. 60, which increases with age and supplements for certain services such as basic dental treatment or for a pregnant woman. Some Spanish insurance companies offer group policies to expatriate clubs and organisations at large savings over individual policies. Major Spanish insurance companies pay 90 per cent of medical expenses and policy holders pay the remaining 10 per cent. When a policy allows a free choice of practitioners and hospitals, clients may be expected to pay the first 20 per cent of bills.

When comparing the cost of Spanish health insurance with a foreign policy, always carefully compare the benefits and exactly what is included and excluded. All policies include limitations and restrictions, e.g. injuries as a result of participation in certain high risk sports aren't usually covered. Many Spanish companies limit costs for a particular specialist or treatment in a calendar year, in addition to having a total overall annual limit for all treatment. Some companies include very restrictive clauses, e.g. they may exclude dialysis treatment or may pay for a limited number of days a year in hospital only, e.g.

20 to 60. Steer well clear of policies with severe restrictions (such as a maximum 20-day hospitalisation period) and *always* have the small print checked.

Certain services aren't provided during the first six months cover, e.g. medical checkups and dental care, and some services may be included only for an extra premium and an excess payment. Most policies don't cover illnesses contracted within a certain period of taking out a policy or pre-existing illnesses for a period, e.g. one or two years (irrespective of whether you were aware of the illness or not). Many policies have clauses allowing annual increases bearing no relation to inflation or increases in the cost of living. **Spanish insurance companies can (and will) cancel a policy at the end of the insurance period if you have a serious illness with endless high expenses and some companies automatically cancel a policy when you reach the age of 65.** You should avoid such a company at all costs as to take out a new policy at the age of 65 at a reasonable premium is difficult or impossible. Some companies won't accept new clients aged over 60 while others accept new clients up to the age of 75.

It's important to note that Spanish health insurance policies are designed for those living permanently in Spain and most offer only emergency cover abroad. Emergency medical cover abroad is paid up to a limited amount only, e.g. 500,000 or 1,000,000 ptas, which is very little if you need to be hospitalised (international travel policies typically include medical expenses equal to 50m ptas or more). Spanish policies, not surprisingly, don't include repatriation to another country. The consensus among expatriates is that although Spanish health insurance may sometimes be cheaper, it doesn't offer wide cover and isn't good value for money compared with many foreign health insurance schemes.

Foreign Companies: There are a number of foreign health insurance companies with agents or offices in Spain including Baltica (Denmark), BUPA international, Exeter Friendly Society, PPP International, Columbus Healthcare and International Health Insurance (Denmark). These companies offer special policies for expatriates and usually include repatriation to your home country and international cover. If you aren't covered by Spanish social security and need private health insurance to obtain a resident permit, you must ensure that your health policy will be accepted by the Spanish authorities (those listed above are all accepted). The main advantages of a foreign health insurance policy is that treatment is unrestricted and you can choose any doctor, specialist, clinic or hospital in Spain and also usually abroad.

Most foreign policies includes repatriation (although it may be optional), which may be an important consideration as you may need treatment that's unavailable in Spain, but available in your home (or another) country. Repatriation may also pay for repatriation of your body for burial in your home country. Some companies offer policies for different areas, e.g. Europe, worldwide excluding North America, and worldwide including North America. A policy may offer full cover anywhere within Europe and limited cover in North America and certain other countries (e.g. Japan). Some policies offer the same cover worldwide for a fixed premium, which may be an important consideration for globetrotters. Note that an international policy allows you to choose to have non-urgent medical treatment in another country. Most companies offer different levels of cover, for example PPP International offer basic, standard, comprehensive and prestige levels of cover.

Usually there's an excess which may be per visit to a doctor or specialist, or per claim or illness. Obviously a per claim policy is better as the excess will include a visit to a family doctor, pharmacy medicines, a consultation with a specialist and hospitalisation, if they are all associated with the same illness. Cover for dental treatment, spectacles and contact lenses may be available as an option, although there may be a hefty excess, which usually means that you're better off paying bills yourself. A basic policy doesn't usually include maternity cover and may offer no benefits or restricted benefits for out-patient treatment (which means that you must pay for visits to a family doctor) and may also exclude out-patient drugs, medicines, dressings, surgical/dental appliances, spectacles, contact lenses or hearing aids. There may also be an annual limit on ambulance costs. Children (e.g. up to age 16) may be covered free on a parent's policy and children up to certain age (e.g. 26) may receive a 50 per cent premium reduction. Note that it's impossible to obtain insurance with some companies over a certain age, e.g. 75. Premiums are usually related to age, although some companies (such as the Exeter Hospital Aid Society) don't relate premiums to age providing you join before a certain age, e.g. 60 or 65.

There's always an annual limit on total annual medical costs (which should be at least around 60m ptas) and some companies also limit costs for specific treatment or costs such as specialist's fees, operations and hospital accommodation. Some policies also include permanent disability cover, e.g. 25m ptas, for those in full-time employment. A medical isn't usually required for most health policies, although pre-existing health problems are excluded for a period, e.g. one or two years. Claims are usually settled in all major currencies and large claims are usually settled directly by insurance companies (although your choice of hospitals may be limited). Always check whether a company will pay large medical bills directly. If you're required to pay bills and claim reimbursement from the insurance company, it may take you several months to receive your money (some companies are very slow to pay). It isn't usually necessary to translate bills into English or another language, although you should check a company's policy. Most companies provide 24-hour emergency telephone assistance.

The cost of international heath insurance varies considerably depending on your age and the extent of cover. Premiums can sometimes be paid monthly, quarterly or annually, although some companies insist on payment annually in advance. Annual premiums vary from around 150,000 ptas to as much as 500,000 ptas for the most comprehensive cover. Some companies have an excess of around 12,500 ptas per claim (or 20,000 ptas for dental treatment) and it may be possible to choose an increased voluntary excess of 40,000 to 125,000 ptas and receive a discount (e.g. 10 or 20 per cent). The maximum annual cover is usually up to 60m ptas per person, per year and may include permanent total disability cover up to 25m ptas. Payment may be accepted by Visa or Access. Policies usually include repatriation and limited worldwide cover, including North America.

When comparing policies, always carefully check the extent of cover and exactly what's included and excluded in a policy (often indicated only in the *very* small print), in addition to premiums and excess charges. In some countries, premium increases are limited by law, although this may apply only to residents in the country where the company is registered and not overseas policy holders. Although there may be significant differences in premiums, generally you get what you pay for and can tailor your premiums to your requirements. The most important questions to ask are does the policy provide the necessary cover and is it good value for money. If you're in good heath and able to pay for your own out-patient treatment, such as visits to your family doctor and prescriptions, then the best value for money policy may be one covering specialist and hospital treatment only.

If you have existing private health insurance in another country, you may be able to extend it to include Spain. If you already have a private health insurance policy, you may find you can save a substantial amount by switching to another company without losing any benefits (you may even gain some). To compare policies, it's best to visit an insurance broker offering policies from a number of companies. If your stay in Spain is limited, you may be covered by a reciprocal agreement between your home country and Spain (see **Medical Treatment Abroad** on page 248). Note that if you're a Spanish income tax payer, you can deduct 15 per cent of your total annual health care costs from your income tax bill.

Make sure you're fully covered in Spain before you receive a large bill. It's foolhardy for anyone living and working in Spain (or even visiting) not to have comprehensive health insurance. If you or members of your family aren't adequately insured, you could face some very high medical bills. When changing employers or leaving Spain, you should ensure that you have continuous health insurance. If you're planning to change your health insurance company, make sure that no important benefits are lost.

DENTAL INSURANCE

It's unusual to have full dental insurance (*seguro de dentista*) in Spain as the cost is prohibitive. Only extractions of bad teeth are possible under the Spanish public health service (see **Dentist** on page 243). Some Spanish insurance companies include coupons for basic dental care such as checkups, X-rays and cleaning in their standard premium, while others offer more comprehensive dental cover as an optional extra. Some foreign health policies include basic dental care and most offer optional (or additional) dental cover, although there are many restrictions and cosmetic treatment is excluded. Where applicable, the amount payable by a health insurance policy for a particular item of treatment is fixed and depends on your level of dental insurance. A detailed list of refunds is available from insurance companies.

Some dentists in Spain, including a number of foreign dentists, offer a dental insurance scheme. One such scheme costs around 10,000 ptas a year for one person, 15,000 ptas for a couple and 2,500 ptas for each child aged under 17. The fee includes two 6-monthly check-ups, a free scale and polish, and free consultations at any time. Insurance also entitles members to a discount of 50 per cent off the cost of fillings and 25 per cent off the cost of crowns, bridges and dentures, plus discounts on children's orthodontics. The cost of dental insurance may be dependent on the condition of your teeth.

HOUSEHOLD INSURANCE

Household insurance (*seguro de hogar*) in Spain generally includes the building, its contents and third-party liability, all of which are contained in a multi-risk household insurance policy. Policies are offered by both Spanish and foreign insurance companies and premiums are similar, although foreign companies may provide more comprehensive cover.

Building (*continente*): Although it isn't compulsory, it's advisable for home owners to take out property insurance that covers damage to a building due to fire, smoke, lightning, water, explosion, storm, freezing, snow, theft, vandalism, malicious damage, acts of terrorism, impact, broken windows and natural catastrophes (such as falling trees). Insurance should include glass, external buildings, aerials and satellite dishes, gardens and garden ornaments. Note that if a claim is the result of a defect in a building or its design, e.g. the roof is too heavy and collapses, the insurance company won't pay up (another reason why it's advisable to have a survey before buying a home). Property insurance is based on the cost of rebuilding your home and should be increased each year in line with inflation. **Make sure that you insure your property for the true cost of rebuilding.** It's particularly important to have insurance for storm damage in Spain, which can be severe in some areas. If floods are one of your concerns, make sure you're covered for water coming in from ground level, not just for water seeping in through the roof. Always read the small print of contracts. Note that if you own a home in an area that has been hit by a succession of natural disasters (such as floods), your household insurance may be cancelled.

Contents (*contenido*): Contents are usually insured for the same risks as a building (see above) and are insured for their replacement value (new for old), with a reduction for wear and tear for clothes and linen. Valuable objects are covered for their actual declared (and authenticated) value. Most policies include automatic indexation of the insured sum in line with inflation. Contents insurance may include accidental damage to sanitary installations, theft, money, replacement of locks following damage or loss of keys, frozen food, alternative accommodation cover, and property belonging to third parties stored in your home. Some items are usually optional, e.g. credit cards, frozen foods, emergency assistance (plumber, glazier, electrician, etc.), redecoration, garaged cars, replacement pipes, loss of rent, and the cost of travel to Spain for holiday home owners. Many policies include personal third-party liability, e.g. up to 50m ptas, although this may be an option.

Items of high value must usually be itemised and photographs and documentation (e.g. a valuation) provided. Some companies even recommend or insist on a video film of belongings. When claiming for contents, you should always produce the original bills if possible (always keep bills for expensive items) and bear in mind that replacing imported items in Spain may be more expensive than buying them abroad. Contents' policies always contain security clauses and if you don't adhere to them a claim won't be considered. If you're planning to let a property, you may be required to inform your insurer. Note that a building must be secure with iron bars (*rejas*) on ground-floor windows and patio doors, shutters and secure locks. Most companies give a discount if properties have steel reinforced doors, high security locks and alarms (particularly alarms connected to a monitoring station). An insurance company may send someone to inspect your property and advise on security measures. Policies pay out for theft only when there are signs of forcible entry and you aren't covered for thefts by a tenant (but may be covered for thefts by domestic personnel). All-risks policies offering a worldwide extension to a household policy covering jewellery, cameras and other items aren't usually available from Spanish insurance companies, but are available from foreign companies.

Community Properties: If you own a property that's part of a community development the building will be insured by the community (although you should always ensure that it's comprehensively insured). You must, however, be insured for third-party risks (*riesgo a terceros*) in the event that you cause damage to neighbouring properties, e.g. through flood or fire. Household insurance policies in Spain usually includes third-party liability up to a maximum amount, e.g. 50m ptas.

Holiday Homes: Premiums are generally higher for holiday homes, due to their high vulnerability, particularly to burglaries. Premiums are usually based on the number of days a year a property is inhabited and the interval between periods of occupancy. Cover for theft, storm, flood and malicious damage may be suspended when a property is left empty for an extended period. Note that you're required to turn off the water supply at the mains when vacating a building for more than 72 hours. It's possible to negotiate cover for periods of absence for a hefty surcharge, although valuable items are usually excluded (unless you have a safe). If you're absent from your property for long periods, e.g. longer than 30 days a year, you may be required to pay an excess on a claim arising from an occurrence that takes place during your absence (and theft may be excluded). **Note that (where applicable) it's important to ensure that a policy specifies a holiday home and not a principal home.** In areas with a high risk of theft (e.g. major cities and most resort areas), an insurance company may insist on extra security measures. It's unwise to leave valuable or irreplaceable items in a holiday home or a property that will be vacant for long periods. Note that some insurance companies will do their utmost to find a loophole which makes you negligent and relieves them of liability. You should ensure that the details listed on a policy are correct, otherwise your policy could be void.

Rented Property: Your landlord will usually insist that you have third-party liability insurance. A lease requires you to insure against 'tenant's risks', including damage you may make to the rental property and to other properties if you live in an apartment, e.g. due to floods, fire or explosion. You can choose your own insurance company and aren't required to use one recommended by your landlord.

Premiums: Premiums are usually calculated on the size (constructed area in square metres) of a property, its age, the value of the contents and the security protection, e.g. window protection at ground level, the number of entrance doors and their construction. As a rough guide, building insurance costs around 1,000 ptas a year per million pesetas of value insured, e.g. a property valued at 10m ptas will cost 10,000 ptas a year to insure. Contents insurance costs from around 2,500 ptas a year per million pesetas of value insured (e.g. a premium of 5,000 ptas for contents valued at 2m ptas) and may be higher for a detached villa than an apartment, e.g. up to 3,500 ptas per million pesetas insured. In general, detached, older and more remote properties cost more to insure than apartments and new properties (particularly when they are located in towns), due to the higher risk of theft. Premiums are also higher in certain high risk areas.

Claims: If you wish to make a claim, you must usually inform your insurance company in writing (by registered letter) within two to seven days of an incident or 24 hours in the case of theft. Thefts should also be reported to the local police within 24 hours, as the police report (*denuncia*), of which you receive a copy for your insurance company, constitutes irrefutable evidence of your claim. Check whether you're covered for damage or thefts that occur while you're away from your property and are therefore unable to inform the insurance company immediately. Take care that you don't under-insure your house contents and that you periodically reassess their value and adjust your insurance premium accordingly. You can arrange to have your insurance cover automatically increased annually, by a fixed percentage or amount, by your insurance company. If you make a claim and the assessor discovers that you're under-insured, the amount due will be reduced by the percentage by which you're under-insured. For example, if you're insured for 1m ptas and you're found to be under-insured by 50 per cent, your claim for 200,000 ptas will be reduced by 50 per cent to 100,000 ptas.

Insuring Abroad: It's possible and legal to take out building and contents insurance in another country for a property in Spain (some foreign insurance companies offer special policies for holiday home owners), although you must ensure that a policy is valid under Spanish law. The advantage is that you will have a policy you can understand and you will be able to handle claims in your own language. This may seem like a good option for a holiday home in Spain, although it can be more expensive than insuring with a Spanish company and can lead to conflicts if, for example, the building is insured with a Spanish registered company and the contents with a foreign based company. Most experts advise that you insure a Spanish home and its contents (*continente y contenido*) with a Spanish registered insurance company through a local agent.

THIRD-PARTY LIABILITY INSURANCE

It's common in Spain to have third-party liability insurance (*riesgo a terceros*). To take an everyday example, if your soap slips out of your hand while you're taking a shower, jumps out of the window and your neighbour slips on it and breaks his neck, he (or his widow) will sue you for around 50m ptas. With third-party liability insurance you can shower in blissful security (but watch that soap!).

Third-party liability insurance covers all members of a family and includes damage done or caused by your children and pets, for example, if your dog or child bites someone. Where damage is due to severe negligence, benefits may be reduced. Check whether insurance covers you against accidental damage to your home's fixtures and fittings (which may be covered by your household insurance). Third-party liability insurance is usually combined with household insurance (see above). If not included in household insurance, third-party liability insurance costs around 2,500 ptas for each 10m ptas of cover.

HOLIDAY & TRAVEL INSURANCE

Holiday and travel insurance (*seguro de viajes*) is recommended for all who don't wish to risk having their holiday or travel ruined by financial problems or to arrive home broke. As you probably know, anything can and often does go wrong with a holiday, sometimes before you even get started (particularly when you *don't* have insurance). The following information applies equally to both residents and non-residents, whether they are travelling to or from Spain or within Spain. **Nobody should visit Spain without travel (and health) insurance!**

Travel insurance is available from many sources including travel agents, insurance companies and agents, banks, automobile clubs and transport companies (airline, rail and bus). Package holiday companies and tour operators also offer insurance policies, some of which are compulsory, too expensive **and don't provide adequate cover.** You can also buy 24-hour accident and flight insurance at major airports, although it's expensive and doesn't offer the best cover. Before taking out travel insurance, carefully consider the range and level of cover you require and compare policies. Short term holiday and travel insurance policies should include cover for holiday cancellation or interruption; missed flights; departure delay at both the start *and* end of a holiday (a common occurrence); delayed, lost or damaged baggage; personal effects and money; medical expenses and accidents (including evacuation home); flight insurance; personal liability and legal expenses; and default or bankruptcy insurance, e.g. against a tour operator or airline going broke.

Health Cover: Medical expenses are an important aspect of travel insurance and you shouldn't rely on insurance provided by reciprocal health arrangements (see page 248), charge and credit card companies, household policies or private medical insurance (unless it's an international policy), none of which usually provide adequate cover (although you should take advantage of what they offer). The minimum medical insurance recommended by experts is around 50m ptas in Spain and the rest of Europe, and 250m ptas for the rest of the world (many policies have limits of between 300m to 500m ptas).

If applicable, check whether pregnancy related claims are covered and whether there are any restrictions for those over a certain age, e.g. 65 or 70 (travel insurance is becoming increasingly more expensive for those aged over 65, although they don't usually need to worry about pregnancy!).

Always check any exclusion clauses in contracts by obtaining a copy of the full policy document, as not all relevant information will be included in an insurance leaflet. High risk sports and pursuits should be specifically covered and *listed* in a policy (there's usually an additional premium). Special winter sports policies are available, which are more expensive than normal holiday insurance ('dangerous' sports are excluded from most standard policies). Third-party liability cover should be 500m ptas for North America and 250m ptas for the rest of the world. **Note that this doesn't cover you when you're using a car or other mechanically propelled vehicle.**

Cost: The cost of travel insurance varies considerably, depending on where you buy it, how long you intend to stay in Spain and your age. Generally the longer the period covered, the cheaper the daily cost, although the maximum period covered is usually limited, e.g. six months. With some policies an excess must be paid for each claim. As a rough guide, travel insurance for Spain (and most other European countries) costs from around 5,000 ptas for one week, 7,000 ptas for two weeks and 10,000 ptas for a month for a family of four (two adults and two children under 16). Premiums may be higher for those aged over 65 or 70.

Annual Policies: For people who travel abroad frequently, whether on business or pleasure, an annual travel policy usually provides the best value, but always carefully check exactly what it includes. Many insurance companies offer annual travel policies for a premium of around 20,000 ptas for an individual (the equivalent of around three months insurance with a standard travel insurance policy), which are excellent value for frequent travellers. Some insurance companies also offer an 'emergency travel policy' for holiday home owners who need to travel abroad at short notice to inspect a property, e.g. after a severe storm. The cost of an annual policy may depend on the area covered, e.g. Europe, worldwide (excluding North America) and worldwide (including North America), although it doesn't usually cover travel within your country of residence. There's also a limit on the number of trips a year and the duration of each trip, e.g. 90 or 120 days. An annual policy is usually a good choice for owners of a holiday home in Spain who travel there frequently for relatively short periods. **However, always check carefully exactly what is covered (or omitted) as an annual policy may not provide adequate cover.**

Claims: If you need to make a claim, you should provide as much documentary evidence as possible to support it. Travel insurance companies gladly take your money, but they aren't always so keen to pay claims and you may have to persevere before they pay up. Always be persistent and make a claim *irrespective* of any small print, as this may be unreasonable and therefore invalid in law. Insurance companies usually require you to obtain a written report and report a loss (or any incident for which you intend to make a claim) to the local police or carriers within 24 hours. Failure to do so may mean that a claim won't be considered.

LIFE INSURANCE

Although there are worse things in life than death (like spending a few hours with a life insurance salesman), your dependants may rate your death **without life insurance** (*seguro de vida*) high on their list. Some Spanish companies provide employees with free life insurance as an employment benefit, although it may be accident life insurance only. You can take out life insurance with numerous Spanish and foreign insurance companies. Note that Spanish policies are almost always for life *insurance* and not for *assurance*. An assurance policy covers an eventuality that's certain to occur, for example, like it or not, you must die one day! Thus a life assurance policy is valid until you die. An insurance policy covers a risk that *may* happen but isn't a certainty, e.g. accident insurance (unless you're *exceptionally* accident prone).

A large percentage of an annuity (life or fixed-period) is tax deductible (the actual amount depends on your age) and a life insurance policy can delay the payment of inheritance tax for unrelated beneficiaries. The beneficiaries of certain life insurance policies aren't liable to pay Spanish gift or inheritance tax. A policy intended to take advantage of Spanish law is best taken out in Spain to ensure that it complies with Spanish law. A life insurance policy can be useful as security for a loan and can be limited to cover the period of the loan. Non-smokers are usually offered a discount on life policies.

Finally, it's advisable to store a copy of all insurance policies with your will (see page 313) and with your lawyer. If you don't have a lawyer, keep a copy in a safe deposit box. A life insurance policy must usually be sent to the insurance company upon the death of the insured, with a copy of the death certificate.

14.

FINANCE

Spain is one of the poorest countries in the EU, with a per capita Gross Domestic Product (GDP) in 1996 of $15,522 per head compared with $20,900 in Britain, $27,600 in France, $29,600 in the USA and $30,300 in Germany. Although Spain's GDP has doubled since 1986, it's well below the EU average and likely to remain that way for some years. Spain was badly hit by the recession in the early 1990s and although the economy has recovered, unemployment remains very high, the cost of living has increased sharply and per capita personal debt has risen considerably. Like all western countries, Spain has extremes of wealth and poverty and there's a vast difference in prosperity between the rich north and the poor south and west of the country (an imbalance which regional policies and vast injections of EU aid have done little to alleviate. However, against most expectations Spain is on track to qualify for the single European currency (EMU) in 1999.

Although Spanish banks aren't renowned for their proficiency, they have improved hugely in the last two decades and are much more efficient and competitive than they were in the 1970s and early 1980s. Competition for your money (*dinero*) is considerable and financial services are offered by private and state clearing and commercial banks, savings banks, foreign banks, the post office, investment brokers and a range of other financial institutions. Compared to many other western countries, particularly Britain and the USA, Spain isn't a credit economy and the Spanish prefer to pay (and be paid) in cash rather than with a credit card or cheque. Never assume that a business accepts credit cards but check in advance.

If you're planning to invest in property or a business in Spain that's financed from abroad, it's important to consider both present and possible future exchange rates (don't be too optimistic!). If you wish to borrow money to buy property or for a business venture in Spain, you should carefully consider where and in what currency it should be raised. Note that it's difficult for foreigners to obtain business loans in Spain, particularly for new ventures, and you shouldn't rely on it. On the other hand, if you earn your income in pesetas, this may affect your financial commitments abroad, particularly if the peseta is devalued. List all your probable and possible expenses and do your homework thoroughly *before* moving to Spain — afterwards it may be too late!

When you arrive in Spain to take up residence or employment, ensure that you have sufficient cash, traveller's cheques, eurocheques, credit cards, luncheon vouchers, coffee machine tokens, gold coins, diamonds, etc., to last at least until your first pay day, which may be some time after your arrival. During this period you will find that an international credit card is useful (all major credit cards, e.g. American Express, Diners Club, Mastercard and Visa are widely accepted in Spain).

If you plan to live permanently in Spain you should ensure that your income is and will remain sufficient to live on, bearing in mind currency devaluations, rises in the cost of living, unforeseen expenses such as medical bills and anything else that may reduce your income (such as stock market crashes and recessions!). In the last two decades, Spain has become a member of the 'real' world and its cost of living and taxes have increased accordingly. It's no longer a low tax country as many people still believe — unless, of course, you come from Belgium, Holland or Scandinavia, when almost anywhere else is a low tax country. In the early 1990s many pensioners with a fixed income paid in a foreign currency saw it fall dramatically, as exchange rates worsened and the cost of living rose, although in the last few years some (such as the British) have made huge gains on the exchange rate. Despite the economic gloom of the last few years, the cost of living is still lower in Spain than in most other EU countries, inflation was just

3.6 per cent in 1996 (and is expected to be below 3 per cent in 1997) and for many the quality of life/cost of living ratio is unbeatable.

See also **Chapter 13** for information about social security, pensions and life insurance.

FISCAL IDENTIFICATION NUMBER

All residents and non-resident foreigners with financial affairs in Spain must have a foreigner's identification number called a *Número de Identificación de Extranjero (NIE)*. This is similar to the fiscal number (*Numero de Identificación Fiscal/NIF*) which all Spaniards have, that's the same as their identity card and passport numbers, and serves the same purpose. You can apply for an NIE at any national police station (*comisaría*) with a foreigner's department. Your NIE must be used in all dealings with the Spanish tax authorities, when paying property taxes and in various other transactions, e.g. without an NIE you cannot register the title deed of a property, open a bank account or take out an insurance policy in Spain. Anyone placing money or assets in deposits or other forms or receiving credits or loans in Spain must give their fiscal number to the bank within 30 days of the operation. A bank cannot issue a cheque against a deposit without reporting the fiscal number of the client and must report any activities where a fiscal number hasn't been provided. Banks and individuals can be heavily fined for non-compliance with the law regarding fiscal numbers.

SPANISH CURRENCY

As you're probably aware, the Spanish unit of currency is the peseta (colloquially called the *pela* or *cala*). Like many other European currencies, the value of the peseta has fluctuated wildly in the last 10 years. The government was forced to devalue three times in 1992/93 which was followed by a de facto devaluation when the European Exchange Rate Mechanism (ERM), which Spain joined in June 1989, widened the bands within which currencies are permitted to fluctuate on 2nd August 1993. In the last decade the peseta has lost considerable value against the US dollar and the strongest European currencies, although it has generally been stronger in recent years.

However, the peseta will eventually become obsolete if Spain qualifies for European Monetary Union (EMU), which looked a distinct possibility in late 1997, due to commence on 1st January 1999. In order to qualify for EMU, Spain must meet the following criteria: Inflation must be a maximum of 1.5 per cent above the average inflation rate of the three EU countries with the lowest inflation rates; the budget deficit must be a maximum of 3 per cent of GDP; general government gross debt must be a maximum of 60 per cent of GDP; and the government bond yield must be a maximum of 2 per cent above the average of the three EU countries with the lowest inflation rates. If Spain qualifies for EMU and introduces the Euro as legal tender on 1st January 1999, the peseta will circulate alongside the Euro for three years until 1st January 2002, when it will be withdrawn.

Spanish coins are minted in denominations of 1, 5, 10, 25, 50, 100, 200 and 500 ptas. The only valid coins are the small aluminium one peseta coin, the small bronze five (*duro*) peseta coin, the silver 10 peseta coin, the bronze 25 peseta coin (with a hole in the middle), the small silver 50 peseta coin ('dented edge'), the bronze 100 (*cien*) peseta coin (the only coin with no numbers on it), and the silver 200 and 500 peseta coins. Note that the 10, 50 and 200 peseta coins aren't in common use. Due to its low value, many people leave their one peseta coins behind if they're given them in change and many retailers (e.g. supermarkets) round the price up or down to the nearest five pesetas rather than give one peseta coins in change. Many old coins were taken out of circulation and ceased to be legal tender from 1st January 1997 (check that you don't receive old coins in your change).

Banknotes are printed in denominations of 1,000, 2,000, 5,000 and 10,000 ptas. **Beware of counterfeit notes, some of which are made with sophisticated colour laser copiers.** The peseta is usually written as pts or ptas (as used in this book). When writing figures (for example on cheques), a period (.) is used to separate units of millions, thousands and hundreds, and a comma to denote fractions.

It's advisable to obtain some Spanish coins and banknotes before arriving in Spain and to familiarise yourself and your family with them. You should have some pesetas in cash, e.g. 10,000 to 20,000 ptas in small bills, when you arrive, but you should avoid carrying a lot of cash. This will save you having to queue to change money on arrival at a Spanish airport (where exchange rates are usually poor and there are often long queues). It's best to avoid 10,000 peseta notes (unless you receive them as a gift!) which sometimes aren't accepted, particularly for small purchases or on public transport.

IMPORTING & EXPORTING MONEY

Exchange controls were abolished in Spain on 1st February 1992 (one year ahead of the EU deadline) and there are no restrictions on the import or export of funds. A Spanish resident is permitted to open a bank account in any country and to import (or export) unlimited funds in any currency. However, when a resident opens an overseas account his Spanish bank must routinely inform the Bank of Spain within 30 days of account movements over 500,000 ptas.

Declaration: Cash, notes and bearer-cheques in any currency, plus gold coins and bars up to the value of 1m ptas may be freely imported or exported from Spain by residents and non-residents without approval or declaration. However, if you intend to re-export funds you should declare them, as this will certify that the foreign currency was imported legally and will allow a non-EU foreigner to convert pesetas back into a foreign currency. Residents receiving funds from non-residents or making payments to them of over 1m ptas (or the equivalent in foreign currency) in cash or bearer cheques, must declare them within 30 days. A form must be completed (B-3) which includes the name, address and NIE of the resident, the name and address of the non-resident, and the reason for the payment.

Sums of 1m to 5m ptas (per person and journey) must be declared to the customs authorities (on form B-1) when entering or leaving Spain. For sums above 5m ptas, prior authorisation was previously required from the *Dirección General de Transacciones Exteriores (DGTE)* by completing form B-2 at your bank. However, although all sums above 1m ptas must be declared, the European Union ruled that the demand for prior authorisation was illegal under EU laws relating to the free transfer of capital between member states, and it now applies to non-EU nationals only. These regulations are designed to curb criminal activities, particularly drug-trafficking, and also apply to transit travellers stopping in Spain for less than 24 hours. **Note that if you don't declare funds, they are subject to confiscation.**

International Bank Transfers: When transferring or sending money to (or from) Spain you should be aware of the alternatives and shop around for the best deal. A bank-to-bank transfer can be made by a normal transfer or by a SWIFT electronic transfer.

A normal transfer is supposed to take three to seven days, but in reality it usually takes much longer (particularly when sent by mail), whereas a SWIFT telex transfer *should* be completed in as little as two hours (although SWIFT transfers aren't always reliable to and from Spain). One of the fastest and most economical methods of transferring cash between Britain and Spain is via the Royal Bank of Scotland's (RBOS) IBOS system and Banco Santander-Banesto. Note that it's usually quicker and cheaper to transfer funds between branches of the same bank or affiliated banks, than between non-affiliated banks.

If you intend sending a large amount of money to Spain or abroad for a business transaction such as buying a property, you should ensure you receive the commercial rate of exchange rather than the tourist rate (shop around for the best deal). Some banks levy high charges (as much as 4 per cent) on the transfer of funds to Spain to buy a home, which is the subject of numerous complaints, while others charge nothing if the transfer is made in pesetas. Always check charges and rates in advance and agree them with your bank (you may be able to negotiate a lower charge or a better exchange rate). If you have your pension paid into a bank in Spain from another EU country, you should have it transferred in pesetas, for which (under EU regulations) there should be no charge.

The cost of transfers vary considerably, not only the commission and exchange rates, but also the transfer charges (such as the telex charge for a SWIFT transfer). Shop around a number of banks. Many Spanish banks deduct commission, whether a transfer is made in pesetas or a foreign currency. However, some banks, including the Banco Popular, Banco de Andalucía and the Banco de Crédito Balear don't make any charges on transfers from certain countries including Belgium, Germany, Switzerland and the UK. An EU directive due to come into force in 1998 will limit banks in EU countries to being able to pass on to customers the costs incurred by sender banks only, and money will have to be deposited in customers' accounts within five working days.

Spanish banks (along with the Portuguese) are reportedly the slowest in Europe to process bank transfers. It isn't unusual for transfers to and from Spain to get stuck in the pipeline (usually somewhere in Madrid), which allows the Spanish bank to use your money for a period interest free. For example, transfers between British and Spanish banks sometimes take from three to six weeks and the money can 'disappear' for months or even completely! Except for the fastest (and most expensive) methods, cash transfers between international banks are a joke in the age of electronic banking when powerful financiers can switch funds almost instantaneously. If you routinely transfer large sums of money between currencies you should investigate Fidelity Money Funds, which operate free of conversion charges and at wholesale rates of exchange.

Bank Drafts & Personal Cheques: Another way to transfer money is via a bank draft (*giro bancario*), which should be sent by registered mail. Note, however, that in the event that it's lost or stolen, it's impossible to stop payment and you must wait six months before a new draft can be issued. Bank drafts aren't treated as cash in Spain and must be cleared like personal cheques. It's also possible to send a creditor a cheque (or a eurocheque) drawn on a personal account, although they can take a long time to clear (usually a matter of weeks) and fees are high. Some people prefer to receive a cheque direct (by mail) from their overseas banks, which they then pay into their Spanish bank (although you must usually wait for it to clear). **The main problem with sending anything by mail to or from Spain is that it leaves you at the mercy of the notoriously unreliable Spanish post office.** It's possible to pay cheques drawn on a foreign account into a Spanish bank account, however, they can take weeks to clear as they must be cleared with the paying bank (although some Spanish banks allow customers to make withdrawals against cheques drawn on foreign bank accounts from the day they are paid into an account).

Postcheques, Eurocheques & Eurogiro: Giro postcheques issued by European post offices can be cashed (with a guarantee card) for up to 25,000 ptas at main post offices and the *Caja Postal* in Spain. Holders of eurocheque cards can withdraw cash from cash dispensers in Spain and cash eurocheques (maximum 25,000 ptas) at most banks. You can also send money to Spain via the Girobank Eurogiro system from post offices in 15 European countries plus the USA to six Spanish banks (Banco de Andalucía, Banco de Castilla, Banco Crédito Balear, Banco de Galícia, Banco Popular and Banco de Vasconia).

Telegraphic Transfers: One of the quickest (it takes around 10 minutes) and safest methods of transferring cash is via a telegraphic transfer, e.g. Moneygram (tel. 901-201010) or Western Union (tel. freephone 900-633633), but it's also one of the most expensive, e.g. commission of 7 to 10 per cent of the amount sent. Money can be sent via overseas American Express offices by Amex card holders (using Amex's Moneygram service) to American Express offices in Spain in just 15 minutes.

Obtaining Cash: One of the quickest methods of obtaining (usually relatively small amounts) of cash in Spain is to draw cash on debit, credit or charge cards. Many foreigners living in Spain (particularly retirees) keep the bulk of their money in a foreign account (perhaps in an off-shore bank) and draw on it with a cash or credit card in Spain. This is an ideal solution for holiday-makers and holiday-home owners (although home owners will still need a Spanish bank account to pay their bills). Most banks in major cities have foreign exchange windows (and there are banks with extended opening hours at international airports and major railway stations in major cities) where you can buy and sell foreign currencies, buy and cash traveller's cheques, cash eurocheques, and obtain a cash advance on credit and charge cards.

Note that most banks charge around 1 per cent commission with a minimum charge of between 250 to 750 ptas, so it's expensive to change small amounts. However, some banks (such as the Caja Postal and Unicaja) charge a flat fee of 500 ptas and no commission, irrespective of the amount. There are numerous private *bureau de change* in Spain (including most travel agents), many of which are open long hours, and some stores (such as El Corte Inglés department stores) also provide a *bureau de change*. El Corte Inglés charge 1 per cent commission on cash (minimum 250 ptas) and 2 per cent commission on traveller's cheques (minimum 500 ptas). Note that banks at airports and railway stations often offer the worst exchange rates and charge the highest fees. There are automatic change machines at airports and in tourist areas in major cities that accept up to 15 currencies including US$, £Sterling, Deutschmarks, and French and Swiss francs.

Most *bureaux de change* offer competitive exchange rates and charge no commission (but always check) and are also usually easier to deal with than banks. If you're changing a lot of money you may be able to negotiate a better exchange rate. However, although commercial *bureaux de change* charge less commission than banks, they don't usually offer the best exchange rates and you're usually better off changing money at a bank. The posted exchange rates may apply only when changing high amounts (e.g. over 100,000 ptas), so ask before changing any money. **Note that no commission often equals a poor exchange rate.** The peseta exchange rate (*cambio*) for most European and major international currencies is listed in banks and daily newspapers, and announced on Spanish and expatriate radio and TV programmes. Always shop around for the best exchange rate and the lowest commission when changing a large amount, as they can vary considerably.

Traveller's Cheques: If you're visiting Spain, it's safer to carry traveller's cheques (*cheques de viaje*) than cash, although they aren't as easy to cash as in some other countries. They aren't usually accepted as cash by businesses, except perhaps in some major hotels, restaurants and shops, which usually offer a poor exchange rate. You may wish to buy traveller's cheques in pesetas in order to take advantage of a favourable exchange rate. Most banks charge a commission of 1 per cent when cashing foreign currency traveller's cheques with a minimum fee of between 500 and 750 ptas (so you should avoid changing small amounts). There's no commission when cashing peseta traveller's cheques. You must show your passport when changing traveller's cheques. Banks offer a better exchange rate for traveller's cheques than for banknotes.

Always keep a separate record of traveller's cheque numbers and note where and when they were cashed. Most cheque issuers offer a replacement service for lost or stolen cheques, although the time taken to replace them varies significantly. American Express claim a free, three-hour replacement service at any of their offices worldwide, providing you know the serial numbers of the lost cheques. Without the serial numbers, replacement can take three days or longer. Note that for Europeans travelling within Europe, eurocheques (or postcheques) are a useful alternative to traveller's cheques.

Footnote: There isn't a lot of difference in the cost between buying Spanish currency using cash, buying travellers' cheques or using a credit card to obtain cash in Spain. However, many people simply take cash when visiting Spain, which is asking for trouble, particularly if you have no way of obtaining more cash in Spain, e.g. with a credit card or eurocheques. **One thing to bear in mind when travelling anywhere is not to rely on one source of funds only!**

BANKS

Banking in Spain has changed out of all recognition in the last few decades, during which period the number of banks and branches has increased considerably (some have also gone bust). There are two main types of banks in Spain, clearing banks and savings banks (*cajas de ahorros*). The Spanish clearing banks with the largest branch networks are Banco Santander-Banesto, Banco Central Hispano, Banco Bilbao Vizcaya (BBV), Banco Popular and Argentaria. All banks in Spain are listed in the Yellow Pages under *Bancos*.

Many banks went broke in the 1970s and 1980s, since when Spain's banks have emerged from the dark ages and are now more efficient. Banking has become highly automated in recent years, although many Spanish banks remain frustratingly slow and inefficient compared with banks in many other EU countries. Where human involvement is concerned Spanish banks remain neanderthal, although with regard to electronic banking they compare favourably with other European countries and their ATMs (cash dispensers) are among the world's most advanced (how many other countries' ATMs 'talk' to you in a number of languages?). There are no drive-in banks in Spain. Many banks also offer home banking services via telephone. Confidence in Spain's banking system received a setback in 1994, when the country's fourth-largest private bank, Banco Español de Credito (Banesto) had to be rescued by the Bank of Spain (*Banco de España*) after it ran up a considerable capital shortfall. It has since been snapped up by Banco de Santander, creating Banco Santander-Banesto, Spain's largest bank.

In addition to clearing banks, Spain also has around 50 savings banks (*cajas de ahorros*), which were originally charitable organisations granting loans for public interest and agricultural policies. There are also some 100 co-operative savings banks (*cooperativas de crédito*), whose members are agricultural co-operatives, although they play only a small part in Spain's banking system and hold just a few per cent of total bank assets. Savings banks are similar to building societies in Britain and savings and loans in the USA, and hold around 45 per cent of all deposits and make some 25 per cent of personal loans. The three largest Spanish savings banks are La Caixa (some 3,700 branches), Caja de Madrid (almost 1,200 branches) and the Caja Postal (around 650 branches). In general, savings banks offer a more personal friendly service than clearing banks and are excellent for local business (many have limited regional branch networks). However, although they provide the same basic services as clearing banks, they aren't recommended for international business. A strange idiosyncrasy of some Spanish banks is that in addition to financial services they also sell goods (household appliances, bicycles, computers, etc.) and services (holidays, household insurance), which is rare in other countries.

There are also around 50 foreign banks operating in Spain, although there are fewer (with an overall smaller market share) than in most other European countries. However, competition from foreign banks is set to increase as EU regulations now allow any bank trading legitimately in one EU country to trade in any other EU country. Most major foreign banks are present in Madrid and Barcelona, but branches are rare in other cities. Among foreigners in Spain, the British are best served by their national banks, both in the major cities and resort areas. The most prominent British banks in Spain are, in order of the number of branches, Barclays (over 250 branches), Natwest (some 200) and Lloyds (around 50). These banks are full members of the Spanish clearing and payment system and can provide cheque accounts, cash and credit cards, and direct debit/standing order services. Note, however, that foreign banks in Spain operate in exactly the same way as Spanish banks, so you shouldn't expect, for example, a branch of Barclays in Spain to behave like a branch in Britain or any other country. Surprisingly, considering the size and spending power of foreign residents and tourists in Spain, most Spanish banks make few concessions to foreign clients, e.g. by providing general information and statements in foreign languages and having staff who speak foreign languages.

If you have a complaint regarding your bank, don't expect to receive a quick resolution or any resolution at all. A complaint should be addressed to the ombudsman (*defensor del cliente*, although the title may vary) of your bank. If a *defensor* doesn't exist or you don't receive a reply within two months, you should contact the Bank of Spain (Banco de España, Servicio de Reclamaciones, Alcalá, 50, 28014 Madrid, tel. (91) 338 5068).

Opening Hours

Normal bank opening hours in Spain are from between 0815 and 0900 until between 1330 and 1430, Monday to Friday, and from between 0830 and 0930 until 1200 or 1300 on Saturdays in winter (banks are closed on Saturdays from around 1st June to 30th September). Some branches in major cities remain open continually from the morning until 1600 or 1630 from autumn to spring, although they may close earlier on Fridays. Some banks are experimenting with longer hours at certain branches and opening from, for example, 0815 through to 2030 (or may open from around 0815 to 1400 and again from around 1630 until 1945). Banks in shopping centres may also open all day until late in the evening (some are open the same hours as hypermarkets, e.g. from 1000 until 2200). One of the drawbacks to longer opening hours is resistance from trade unions to their members working longer or irregular hours.

At major international airports and railway stations in major cities there are also banks with extended opening hours, although they often have long queues. Banks are closed on public holidays, including local holidays (when banks in neighbouring towns often close on different days), and may also close early during local *fiestas*. Note that many *bureaux de change* have long opening hours and some are even open 24 hours in summer in some resorts areas.

Opening an Account

You can open a bank account in Spain whether you're a resident or a non-resident. It's best to open a Spanish bank account in person, rather than by correspondence from abroad. Ask your friends, neighbours or colleagues for their recommendations and just go along to the bank of your choice and introduce yourself. You must be aged at least 18 and provide proof of identity (e.g. a passport), your address in Spain and your NIE (see page 273). If you wish to open an account with a Spanish bank while you're abroad, you must first obtain an application form, available from foreign branches of Spanish banks or direct from a Spanish bank in Spain. You need to select a branch from the list provided, which should preferably be near to where you will be living in Spain. If you open an account by correspondence, you need to provide a reference from your current bank.

Non-Residents: Since Spain became a full member of the EU on 1st January 1993, banking regulations for both resident and non-resident EU citizens have been identical. However, if you're a non-resident you're entitled to open a non-resident peseta account (*cuenta de pesetas de no residente*) or a foreign currency account only. An important point for non-resident, non-EU citizens to note is that when importing funds for the purchase of a property (or any other major transaction) in Spain, the transfer of funds must be verified by a certificate from your bank (*certificado de cambio de divisas*). This allows you to re-export the funds if (or when) you sell the property later. This is unnecessary for EU nationals. Although it's possible for non-resident home owners to do most of their banking via a foreign account using debit and credit cards and eurocheques, you will still need a Spanish bank account to pay your Spanish utility and tax bills (which are best paid by direct debit). If you own a holiday home in Spain, you can have all your correspondence (e.g. cheque books, statements, payment advices, etc.) sent to an address abroad.

Residents: You're considered to be a resident of Spain if you have your main centre of interest there, i.e. you live and work there more or less permanently. To open a resident's account you must usually have a residence card (*residencia*) or evidence that you have a job in Spain. Note that it isn't advisable to close your bank accounts abroad when you live in Spain, unless you're sure that you won't need them in the future. Even when you're resident in Spain, it's cheaper to keep money in local currency in an account in a country you visit regularly, rather than pay commission to convert pesetas. Many foreigners living in Spain maintain at least two cheque (current) accounts, a foreign account for international transactions, and a local account with a Spanish bank for day to day business.

Cheque Accounts

The most common account in Spain is a cheque or current account (*cuenta de ahorro con talonario/cuenta corriente*), which are provided by all Spanish banks, although paradoxically many Spaniards don't trust cheques and prefer to deal in cash. Personal cheques aren't usually accepted for payment by local retailers and cannot be guaranteed in Spain (although banks can issue a book of certified cheques). If you arrange to have your salary or pension paid into a Spanish bank account (called *domiciliación*) you may qualify for a choice of free gifts, entry in a grand draw to win a car or other prizes, and low or no-fee services such as a low-interest overdraft or free credit card.

Spanish banks levy some of the highest bank charges in Europe for normal day-to-day transactions such as writing cheques, standing orders, direct debits and credit card transactions. Always obtain a list of charges before opening an account and compare the charges levied by a number of banks. A number of entries (account transactions) a year are usually free (e.g. 30) after which there's a charge per entry (e.g. 30 ptas), although the manager can decide to waive certain charges. Cash dispenser cards (e.g. *Tarjeta 4B* or *Servired*) are routinely issued for cheque accounts (see page 282), although you usually need to ask for one. If you wish to change banks, don't abandon a bank account with a small amount of money in it as you will continue to be charged fees, but write a letter to your bank informing them that you're closing the account.

Spanish cheque accounts pay little interest on account balances, e.g. just 0.1 or 0.2 per cent interest on the average balance. Generally an interest paying cheque account (paying a 'normal' rate of interest) requires a minimum balance of around 250,000 ptas and even then it may pay interest only on the balance above this amount. So there's little point in keeping a lot of money in a cheque account when you can deposit your money in a deposit or savings account and earn interest on the whole balance. Spanish cheques (also *cheques* in Spanish but previously called *talones*) are probably different from those you're familiar with. Your account details (*Código cuenta cliente/CCC*) such as your bank, branch (*oficina*) and account number (*n. cuenta*) are printed at the top right of cheques and statements. This information is necessary when payments are to be made directly to or from your account, e.g. for direct debits.

When writing cheques, the payee's (*páguese a*) name is written in the top left-hand corner; it's usual to write *Sr. D.* in front of a man's name and *Sra. Da.* in front of a woman's name. The amount in figures is written in the top right hand corner. Many people put crosses like a hash (#) sign before and after the amount, e.g. #64.500#, so that it cannot be altered, although this isn't obligatory. The amount is also written in words (*Pesetas en letras*) on the line below the payee's name. The date must be written in words under the amount (in words) and after the town where the bank is located. Your signature is written at the bottom right hand side below the date. The amount and date in words must both be written in Spanish (although this may be waived in resort areas).

If a cheque is made out to the bearer, the words 'pay bearer for this cheque' (*Páguese al portador por este cheque*) must be added. When made out to a named person the word 'bearer' is replaced by his name, e.g. '*Páguese John Smith por este cheque*'. However, it isn't recommended to pay a cheque to the bearer, which is the same as writing a cheque for cash (although people will ask you to do this, so that the payment cannot be traced or so they can cash it immediately). It's usually better to pay someone in cash. A cheque made out to the bearer is regarded as currency and could change hands a number of times during its six-month validity period.

To ensure that a cheque can be paid into the account of the payee only, you must add '& Company' (*y Cia*) between diagonal lines on the front or add 'to be credited to the account of (*a abonar en cuenta*) before the name of the payee. Note that your bank isn't required to reimburse you for a falsified cheque if you have been negligent when writing it. If your cheque book is lost or stolen, you must notify your bank by telephone immediately and confirm the loss in writing. Once you have informed your bank of a loss, any cheques written after that time cease to be your responsibility.

In Spain, all cheques, including post-dated cheques, are payable on presentation (if the funds are available) and cheques are valid for six months from their date. If you write a cheque without sufficient funds in your account, your bank must pay out whatever is in your account as part payment, although this isn't always done. Your bank will also send you a 'notarial protest' (*declaración substitativo de impago/declaración equivalente*), which they must do within 15 days if the cheque is issued and payable in Spain (they have 20 days if it's issued in another European country and 60 days if it's issued outside Europe). You're obliged to pay a 10 per cent penalty of the unpaid amount of a cheque, e.g. if you write a cheque for 10,000 ptas and have only 8,000 ptas in your account, you must pay the 2,000 ptas shortfall plus a penalty of 10 per cent of this amount (200 ptas). Beware of accepting cheques from foreigners (even for small amounts) as they often bounce, resulting in a bank fee, e.g. 500 ptas, plus the loss of your money! **Note that it's illegal to overdraw a bank account in Spain without prior agreement and can lead to many problems.** You cannot stop payment of a cheque in Spain unless the cheque or cheque book has been lost or stolen, when a police report (*denuncia*) must be produced.

When buying something on credit in Spain, cheques aren't usually used to pay instalments. Instalments are made via bills of exchange (*letra de cambio*), one of which is issued for each payment due. You're required to sign one for each payment to be made, e.g. 24, if you're paying monthly for an item over two years, which are then presented to your bank for payment by your creditor each month. Make sure they are always made out in the name of the company that sold the goods and not an individual. If the funds aren't available to pay a *letra* you will receive a 'bill of exchange protest' (*letra protestada*) from your bank asking you to pay the amount due plus extra costs. You should never sign *letras* on behalf of a company or someone else as you will be personally held responsible for payment.

You can have your standing orders (*domiciliación de pagos*) and direct debits (*domiciliación bancaria*) paid by your Spanish bank by simply completing a form at your bank and giving them a copy of a bill. This is the best way to pay all regular bills such as electricity, gas, water, telephone, local taxes and community charges. You should check your statements to ensure that payments have been made, as banks cannot always be relied upon.

You can pay cheques drawn on a foreign bank into a Spanish account in all major currencies. Your bank may credit your account immediately, which means that you can draw on the money before the cheque has been cleared (which may take weeks). Many banks charge a flat fee per cheque (e.g. 1,000 ptas), so it pays to write cheques for large amounts, and you receive the exchange rate for cheques and traveller's cheques (which is higher than when changing cash).

All correspondence from Spanish banks is in Spanish and it's advisable to learn to interpret your statements and other correspondence you receive. Account statements (*estados* or *comunicaciones de movimentos*) are sent to customers monthly or quarterly, although you can request one at any time by asking for an *extracto* or an *avance*. The most common words used in statements are date (*fecha*), debit (*debe*), credit (*haber*), date of operation/transaction (*fecha operación/valor*), balance (*saldo*) and description (*concepto*).

Savings Accounts

It's possible to open a savings (*cuenta/libreta de ahorro*) or deposit account (*cuenta de imposición a plazo*) with all clearing and savings banks in Spain. Savings banks (*caja de ahorros*) are similar to British building societies and American savings and loan organisations, and offer savings schemes and loans for buying property and other purchases, although general banking services may be limited compared with clearing banks. The post office also offers a range of savings accounts (see page 119).

Most financial institutions offer a variety of savings and deposit accounts, with varying interest rates, minimum deposits, and withdrawal restrictions, depending on the type of account and the bank. For short-term savings and small amounts it's best to open a savings account where funds are on call and withdrawals can be made at any time. Interest is usually paid twice a year but is negligible unless the average balance is above a certain sum, e.g. 250,000 ptas. Funds in a term deposit account must be deposited for a minimum period or term (e.g. 7, 14, 30 or 90 days, 6 months or one year), which is the notice period you're required to give in order to withdraw funds without a penalty. The longer the period you're willing to have your money tied up, the higher the interest rate earned.

High interest accounts may require a minimum account balance of 250,000 or 500,000 ptas and can be as high as 1m ptas. These accounts can usually be in pesetas or a major foreign currency. Some accounts allow for the payment of standing orders and direct debits. There may be a maintenance charge, e.g. 500 to 1,000 ptas a year, for a savings account. Savings account holders usually receive a pass book in which all deposits and withdrawals are recorded. Savings and deposit account holders may also be issued with a cash card, a cheque book and a credit card, depending on the type of account.

For residents, the interest earned on bank accounts and deposits is subject to a 25 per cent withholding tax at source on account of personal income tax. The first 25,000 ptas of interest paid on bank deposits is tax-exempt and tax withheld at source can be deducted from tax payable when the next year's income tax return is filed. No tax is withheld from non-residents, who are paid interest gross.

Cash & Debit Cards

All Spanish banks offer customers combined cash and debit cards (*tarjeta de débito*), which are widely used and accepted throughout Spain. Purchases and cash withdrawals are automatically debited from your cheque or savings account. You don't receive a monthly statement and cannot run up bills with a cash or debit card. Cards allow holders to withdraw up to 100,000 ptas a day from automated teller machines or ATMs and obtain account balances and mini-statements (the amount you can withdraw from ATMs other than those located at branches of your own bank is restricted). There are three ATM networks in Spain, *Telebanco 4B* (indicated by a blue and yellow striped logo with the inscription 4B), *Red 6000* and *Servired*. Cash can also usually be obtained from the ATMs of other networks (other than the one your card belongs to), for which there's a fee. Most ATMs accept a bewildering number of Spanish and foreign cards, usually illustrated on machines, including credit (Eurocard, Mastercard, Visa), charge (Amex, Diners Club) and Eurocheque cards. Note that although foreign debit cards such as those belonging to the Visa network can be used to obtain cash in Spain, they are usually treated as credit cards and a charge made.

There are many thousands of automated teller machines (ATMs) in Spain, most of which are located outside rather than inside banks. In some cases they are located inside the bank or in a lobby, when you may need to run your card through a card reader to gain access. The procedure for withdrawing money from an ATM is usually as follows:

1. If the machine is in working order, a message such as *Introduzca su Tarjeta, por favor* will be displayed. If it's temporarily out of order, a message such as *Cajero Temporalmente Fuera de Servicio* will be displayed. Insert your card in the card slot face up with the black band to the right. Your card may be rejected by some machines for no apparent reason; try again and if it's still rejected try another machine.

2. Most machines permit you to choose the language in which instructions are displayed. If this is the case, the first screen will show a selection of languages, e.g. English, German, French, Portuguese and Spanish (may also include Catalan or another regional language). Press the button next to the language desired. Some machines are monolingual and display instructions in Spanish only.

3. Next you will be asked to enter your personal identification number (PIN) and press the green 'enter' (*anotación*) button. If you make a mistake, press the yellow 'erase' (*borrar*) button and re-enter your PIN. **As a security measure, if you enter the wrong PIN three times your card is retained by the machine and you must contact your bank for its return.**

4. Select the service required. e.g.:

   balance enquiry;
   statement enquiry;
   cash withdrawal.

5. If you have chosen to withdraw cash, the screen will display a choice of amounts, e.g. 5,000, 10,000, 15,000, 20,000 and 30,000 ptas. If the amount you wish to withdraw isn't displayed, you can press the 'other amounts' button and enter the amount required. If you make a mistake, press the yellow 'erase' (*borrar*) button and re-enter the correct amount. If you request more than your current credit limit (or account balance), you will be asked to request a smaller amount and the transaction will be terminated. A transaction will also be terminated and a message displayed if you select a service that's unavailable.

6. Remove your card, receipt (machines usually automatically issue a receipt) and cash when instructed.

The 'cancel' (*cancelar*) button can be used to terminate a transaction at any point. Your card will be returned and you can start again, if required.

Note that it's inadvisable to rely entirely on a cash or credit card to obtain cash in Spain, as your card may be 'swallowed' by an ATM and it may take a few weeks before it's returned via your bank. If you lose your cash card, you must report it to your bank as soon as possible.

Offshore Banking

If you have a sum of money to invest or wish to protect your inheritance from the tax man, it may be worthwhile looking into the accounts and services (such as pensions and trusts) provided by offshore banking centres in tax havens (*paraísos fiscales*) such as the Channel Islands (Guernsey and Jersey), Gibraltar and the Isle of Man (around 50 locations worldwide are officially classified as tax havens). The big attraction of offshore banking is that money can be deposited in a wide range of currencies, customers are usually guaranteed complete anonymity, there are no double-taxation agreements, no withholding tax is payable, and interest is paid tax-free. Many offshore banks also offer telephone banking (usually seven days a week).

A large number of American, British and other European banks and financial institutions provide offshore banking facilities in one or more locations. Most institutions offer high-interest deposit accounts for long-term savings and investment portfolios, in which funds can be deposited in any major currency. Many people living abroad keep a local account for everyday business and maintain an offshore account for international transactions and investment purposes. **However, most financial experts advise investors never to rush into the expatriate life and invest their life savings in an offshore tax haven until they know what their long-term plans are.**

Accounts have minimum deposits levels which usually range from the equivalent of around 125,000 to 2,500,000 ptas (e.g. £500 to £10,000), with some as high as 25m ptas (£100,000). In addition to large minimum balances, accounts may also have stringent terms and conditions, such as restrictions on withdrawals or high early withdrawal penalties. You can deposit funds on call (instant access) or for a fixed period, e.g. from 90 days to one year (usually for larger sums). Interest is usually paid monthly or annually; monthly interest payments are slightly lower than annual payments, although they have the advantage of providing a regular income. There are usually no charges providing a specified minimum balance is maintained. Many accounts offer a cash card or a credit card (e.g. Mastercard or Visa) which can be used to obtain cash from ATMs throughout the world.

When selecting a financial institution and offshore banking centre, your first priority should be for the safety of your money. In some offshore banking centres all bank deposits are guaranteed for a maximum amount under a deposit protection scheme, whereby a maximum sum is guaranteed should a financial institution go to the wall (the Isle of Man, Guernsey and Jersey all have such schemes). Unless you're planning to bank with a major international bank (which is only likely to fold the day after the end of the world!), you should always check the credit rating of a financial institution before depositing any money, particularly if it doesn't provide deposit insurance. All banks have a credit rating (the highest is 'AAA') and a bank with a high rating will be happy to tell you (but get it in writing). You can also check the rating of an international bank or financial organisation with Moody's Investor Service. You should be wary of institutions offering higher than average interest rates, as if it looks too good to be true it probably will be — like the Bank of International Commerce and Credit (BICC) which went bust in 1992.

CREDIT & CHARGE CARDS

Credit and charge cards are usually referred to collectively as credit cards (*tarjeta de crédito*) in Spain, although not all cards allow you to repay the balance over a period of time. Visa and Mastercard are the most widely acceptable credit cards in Spain and are issued by most Spanish banks. Other credit cards such as American Express and Diners Club aren't as widely accepted in Spain as they are in Britain and the USA (the Spanish wisely prefer cash, which cannot be traced by the tax authorities!).

The annual fee for a credit card varies depending on the issuing bank and is usually between 2,000 and 3,500 ptas a year for a standard Visa or Mastercard and between 7,500 and 10,000 ptas a year for a gold card. Always check annual fees and interest charges as they can vary greatly. Some credit cards provide free travel insurance (e.g. Europ Assistance) or accident life insurance when travel costs are paid for with the card, or operate a points system whereby you earn points every time you use a card. Before obtaining a credit or charge card, compare the costs *and* benefits. In some countries (e.g. Britain) credit card users are protected against a purchase going 'wrong', such as a company going bust or faulty goods (which may also apply to goods purchased overseas).

It's advisable to retain your foreign credit cards when you live in Spain, at least for a period. One of the advantages of using a credit card issued abroad is that your bill is usually rendered or your account debited around six weeks later, thus giving you a period of interest-free credit, except when cards are used to obtain cash, when interest starts immediately. You may, however, find it more convenient and cheaper to be billed in pesetas rather than a foreign currency, e.g. US$ or £Sterling, when you must wait for the bill from outside Spain and payments may vary due to exchange rate fluctuations.

All credit cards allow holders to obtain cash from ATMs (see above) in Spain and abroad (when you receive the wholesale rather than the tourist exchange rate). In order to withdraw cash from an ATM with a credit card, you need to obtain a PIN number from the issuing bank. Card holders can usually withdraw any amount up to their credit balance or personal limit. Note that using a foreign credit card to obtain cash in Spain is usually expensive as there's a standard charge (e.g. 1.5 per cent), plus a high interest rate is usually levied from the day of the withdrawal.

Major department and chain stores in Spain issue their own free account cards, e.g. Alcampo, Continente, El Corte Inglés, Cortefiel and Galerías Preciados. Some cards allow credit, where the account balance may be repaid over a period of time, although interest rates are usually high (however, the El Corte Inglés card allows three months free credit). Some supermarket chains issue their own 'credit' cards, which are in fact 'customer identity cards' allowing customers to pay with personal cheques. Never assume that a particular business (such as a restaurant) accepts credit cards or you may discover to your embarrassment that: 'that *won't* do nicely sir'! Note that in rural and resort areas, many small businesses don't accept credit cards.

If you lose a credit card or have it stolen, report it immediately by telephone to the issuing office or your bank (Spain is one of the riskiest EU countries for credit card thefts) and confirm the loss in writing by registered letter. Your liability is usually limited to around 25,000 ptas until you report a loss, after which you have no liability. Even if you don't like credit cards and shun any form of credit, they do have their uses, for example no-deposit car rentals, no prepaying hotel bills, safety and security, and above all, convenience (although you must always be wary of bogus charges and scrutinise statements). They are particularly useful when travelling abroad, when you should ensure you have your credit card issuer's emergency telephone number.

EUROCHEQUES

Very few Spanish banks issue eurocheques (EC) and eurocheque cards (*tarjeta Eurocheque*). However, many foreign banks operating in Spain issue them as do most banks in other EU countries. The eurocheque card has a variety of uses and can be used as a cash card and a cheque guarantee card in Spain. There's a fee of around 2,000 ptas for a eurocheque card, which is valid for up to two years. The main advantage of eurocheques is that they can be used as traveller's cheques to obtain cash at some 250,000 bank branches and post offices in Europe, and to pay bills in over five million outlets (such as shops, hotels, restaurants and garages) in some 40 European and Mediterranean countries.

Your bank guarantees to pay a eurocheque up to the value of 25,000 ptas (or the foreign currency equivalent) when supported by a eurocheque card, although you may write them for any amount. You may write eurocheques in most European currencies and send them abroad and also write them in English. You can even write them in US dollars but most US banks refuse them (no joke). If you don't have a $US account, it's better to buy a US$ cheque from a bank or make a direct transfer via your bank or the post office. When sending a eurocheque by mail, don't forget to put your card number on the back, as without it a eurocheque isn't guaranteed (some payees even send them back). When writing figures in Spain (or anywhere on the continent of Europe), the number seven should be crossed ($\neq$) to avoid confusion with the number one, which is written with a tail and looks like an uncrossed seven ($\mathcal{1}$) to many foreigners. The date is written in the standard European style, for example 10th March 1998 is written 10.3.98 and not as in the USA, 3.10.98.

When cashing a eurocheque in a Spanish bank, you must usually go to a special 'foreign' counter (staff may speak English), fill out and sign your cheque and show your passport (the number is noted on the form). You usually need to obtain your cash from a separate cash desk. Eurocheque cards can also be used to withdraw cash (in local currency) from ATMs (displaying the EC logo) in Spain and around 20 other European countries. The cash amount you can withdraw varies from country to country and is 25,000 ptas per day in Spain (or the equivalent in local currency abroad). Note that to withdraw cash from an ATM with a eurocheque card, you must obtain a PIN number from your bank.

The disadvantage of using the eurocheque card and eurocheques is the high fees and charges. There's a usage charge plus commission each time a eurocheque card is used to obtain cash from an ATM, a charge based on the face value of a cheque, plus commission and handling fees. When cashing a eurocheque in a bank abroad, there's a handling fee plus a fee of up to 1.6 per cent (the maximum permitted) of the cheque's value, depending on the country. Most banks charge a commission of 2.5 per cent with a minimum charge of around 400 ptas, so don't write eurocheques for small amounts. When sending money within Europe, it's often cheaper to make a post office giro transfer.

Although they are widely used and accepted in many European countries, eurocheques aren't popular in Spain. Some Spanish banks won't cash them (even when they display the EC logo!) and many small businesses (hotels, restaurants and shops) in Spain either refuse to accept eurocheques drawn on foreign banks or add five or 10 per cent because their banks levy a surcharge on them. Don't take it for granted that a business will accept a eurocheque and always ask if you don't see the blue and red EC sign.

Banks recommend that you don't keep your eurocheque card and cheques in the same place and that you never keep your card with a note of your PIN number. Don't leave them in your car and carry only as many cheques as necessary. If you lose both your card and cheques at the same time, or they are stolen and subsequently cashed, you may find that you're liable due to negligence. If you lose your EC card, notify the issuing bank as soon as possible.

LOANS & OVERDRAFTS

All Spanish banks provide loans (*préstamos*) and overdrafts (*giros en descubierto*), although they aren't as free with their money as banks in some other European countries, particularly regarding loans to foreigners. Most Spanish banks are happy to make loans to foreign residents in Spain, particularly if they are homeowners. However, some banks are reluctant to make loans to foreigners and may even refuse to lend you money, although if this is based purely on the fact that you're a foreigner, it's illegal. Note that overdrafts have no legal basis in Spain as all debts must be documented so that a bank can take legal action against a customer should he default on the repayments (a bank can place an embargo on your property or salary if a loan isn't repaid).

To calculate the cost of a loan you need to know the *tasa anual equivalente (TAE)*, which must be quoted by law. The TAE is the true rate of interest including all charges (e.g. documentation fees or maintenance charges) and varies depending on the frequency of payments. It pays to shop around for a loan as interest rates vary considerably depending on the bank, the amount and the period of the loan. Don't neglect smaller banks as it isn't always necessary to have an account with a bank to obtain a loan. Ask your friends and colleagues for their advice. If you have collateral, e.g. Spanish property or an insurance policy, or you can get someone to stand as a guarantor for a loan, you may be eligible for a secured loan at a lower interest rate than an unsecured loan. Some banks may require you to take out a life insurance policy to cover the term of a loan. The commission a bank can charge when a client pays off a loan before the due date is limited and interest on overdrafts is limited to 2.5 times the current interest rate.

Note that with the ending of exchange controls in Spain, both residents and non-residents can now obtain loans (and mortgages) in any EU country, in any currency (providing someone will lend to you).

MORTGAGES

Mortgages or home loans (*hipotecas*) are available from most Spanish banks (both for residents and non-residents), foreign banks in Spain, and overseas and offshore banks. In recent years, both Spanish and foreign lenders have tightened their lending criteria due to the repayment problems experienced by many recession-hit borrowers. Some foreign lenders apply stricter rules than Spanish lenders regarding income, employment and the type of property on which they will lend. Foreign lenders, e.g. offshore banks, may also have strict rules regarding the nationality and domicile of borrowers (some won't lend to Spanish residents) and the percentage they will lend (they may also levy astronomical charges if you get into arrears). If you raise a mortgage outside Spain for a Spanish property, you should be aware of any impact this may have on your foreign or Spanish tax liabilities or allowances.

Mortgage interest rates have traditionally been high in Spain, although they have fallen considerably in recent years and in 1997 were around 8 per cent (variable rate). Around 70 per cent of home loans in Spain have a variable (*interés variable*) rather than a fixed interest (*interés fijo*) rate and they have traditionally been set at 1 to 2 per cent above the base rate (Madrid inter-bank rate or MIBOR). Note that a low interest rate (which usually increases after one year) may be more than offset by increased commission charges. Always shop around for the best interest rate and ask the effective rate (*Tasa Anual Equivalente/TAE*) including all commissions and fees.

In Spain, it's customary for a property to be held as security for a home loan, i.e. the lender takes a charge on the property, which is recorded at the property registry. If a loan is obtained using a Spanish property as security, additional fees and registration costs are payable to the notary (*notario*) for registering the charge against the property. To obtain a mortgage from a Spanish bank, you must provide proof of your monthly income and all outgoings such as mortgage payments, rent and other loans or commitments. If a Spanish bank asks for security in the form of other property (e.g. located abroad), go to another bank. If you want a Spanish mortgage to buy a property for commercial purposes, you must provide a detailed business plan in Spanish. Note that a mortgage can be assumed by the new owner (called *subrogación*) when a property is sold, which is a common practice in Spain.

Mortgages are granted on a percentage of a valuation, which itself is usually below the market value. The maximum mortgage in Spain is usually 80 per cent of the purchase price for a principal home (*vivienda habitual*) and 60 or 70 per cent for a second home (*segunda residencía*). However, advertisements in Spanish real estate publications often offer mortgages with no down payment or as little as 500,000 to 1m ptas. The normal term is 10 to 15 years, although mortgages can be repaid over 5 to 25 years. The repayment period may be shorter for second homes. Repayment mortgages are the most common type in Spain, although endowment and pension-linked mortgages are also available. Payments can usually be made monthly or quarterly.

Note that you must add expenses and fees totalling around 10 per cent of the purchase price, to the cost of a property. For example, if you're buying a property for 10m ptas and obtain a 70 per cent mortgage, you must pay 30 per cent deposit (3m ptas) plus around 10 per cent fees (1m), making a total of 4m ptas. There are various fees associated with mortgages, e.g. most lenders levy an 'arrangement' fee (*comisión de apertura*) of 1 to 2 per cent which is usually a minimum of 50,000 to 75,000 ptas. Although it's unusual to have a survey in Spain, foreign (non-Spanish) lenders usually insist on a 'valuation survey' (usually costing between 30,000 and 50,000 ptas) for Spanish properties before they will grant a loan.

Buying Through an Offshore Company: This was popular among non-resident property buyers in Spain because they could previously avoid paying Spanish wealth tax, inheritance tax and capital gains tax. However, this is no longer possible and since 1st January 1992 the beneficial owners of such properties have been required to register their ownership with the Spanish authorities or pay an annual tax. Certain exemptions have been granted, but these expire in 1998.

Mortgages for Second Homes: If you have equity in an existing property, either in Spain or abroad, then it may be more cost effective to remortgage (or take out a second mortgage) on that property, rather than take out a new mortgage for a second home in Spain. It involves less paperwork and therefore lower legal fees, and a plan can be tailored to meet your individual requirements. Depending on your equity in your existing property and the cost of your Spanish property, this may enable you to pay cash for a second home. Note, however, that when a mortgage is taken out on a Spanish property, it's based on that property and not the individual, which could be important if you get into repayment difficulties.

Foreign Currency Loans: It's also possible to obtain a foreign currency mortgage, other than in pesetas (either in Spain or abroad), e.g. pounds sterling, Swiss francs, US dollars, Deutschmarks, Dutch guilders or even ECUs. In previous years, high Spanish interest rates meant that a foreign currency mortgage was a good bet for many foreigners. However, you should be extremely wary about taking out a foreign currency mortgage, as interest rate gains can be wiped out overnight by currency swings and devaluations. It's generally recognised that you should take out a mortgage in the currency in which you're paid or in the currency of the country where a property is situated.

In this case if the foreign currency in which you have your mortgage is heavily devalued, as happened with the £sterling in 1992, you will have the consolation of knowing that the value of your Spanish property will ('theoretically') have increased by the same percentage when converted back into pesetas. When choosing between a peseta loan and a foreign currency loan, make sure that you take into account all costs, fees, interest rates and possible currency fluctuations. Regardless of how you finance the purchase of a second home in Spain, you should always obtain professional advice. Note that if you have a foreign currency mortgage, you must usually pay commission charges each time you transfer foreign currency into pesetas or remit money to Spain. If you let a second home, you may be able to offset the interest (pro rate) on your mortgage against letting income. For example, if you let a Spanish property for three months of the year, you can offset a quarter of your annual mortgage interest against your letting income.

Payment Problems & Changing Lenders: If you're unable to meet your mortgage payments, lenders are usually willing to re-schedule your mortgage so that it extends over a longer period, thus allowing you to make lower payments. Note that if you stop paying your mortgage, your lender will embargo your property and could eventually repossess it and sell it at auction. Spanish banks have been extremely slow in reducing the interest rates charged to existing borrowers (after the dramatic drop in interest rates in recent years) and were obstructive in allowing existing lenders to transfer to another lender offering a lower rate.

This prompted the government to pass new legislation in 1994 which made it much easier for borrowers with fixed rate mortgages to change lenders or re-negotiate a mortgage with their existing lender. New regulations require all lenders to issue a list of conditions and interest rates (*hojas vinculantes*) which are binding on the lender for 10 days. This enables applicants to compare rates and allows existing mortgage holders to transfer their mortgage if their present lender cannot meet the terms offered by another lender. The new law established two ways of improving existing mortgage terms: by 'compulsory substitution' (*subrogación forzosa*), where the lender offering more favourable terms/interest rates takes over the existing mortgage, and by 'variation' (*novación modificativa*), where the existing lender offers a reduced interest rate or changes the repayment period. Some lenders offer to pay all the associated expenses if you switch your mortgage to them. In 1996 the government and the banks agreed that banks would charge a maximum of 2.5 per cent when a lender wishes to cancel a mortgage with fixed interest and make one with a variable interest (a common event when interest rates are falling). Note that if you're a Spanish tax payer you can claim a deduction for your Spanish mortgage against your tax liabilities.

INVESTMENTS

When looking for a profitable home for your cash, your decision will probably depend (among other things) on how much money you wish to invest (which may be a lump sum or a monthly amount), how quickly you need access to it in an emergency, whether you want income or capital growth, and whether you're a taxpayer. You also need to decide whether you're willing to speculate or want a guaranteed return on your money. Before you invest in anything remotely speculative, you should ask yourself: "Am I prepared to risk losing all or part of my investment?" If the answer is no, you should look for an investment offering a guaranteed return such as a time deposit. Lastly, you should consider the effect that inflation might have on your nest egg (inflation is the main enemy of anyone who relies on investment income, particularly if your income is fixed).

Financial advice is offered (often free) by numerous financial institutions and advisers (both in Spain and abroad), although the quality of advice is extremely variable and is highly unlikely to be independent. Any advice you receive should be tailored to your particular situation and requirements, and should not be the advisor's own standard packaged investment portfolio.

Be very, very careful where and with whom you invest your money. There have been many financial scandals in Spain in recent years and many investors have somehow managed to 'lose' ALL their clients' money - no mean feat, even in these turbulent times! Not for nothing is it said that the way to create a small portfolio is to come to Spain with a big one. Spain seems to have more than its fair share of 'crooks' and unscrupulous investment advisers, particularly on the Costa del Sol. Whoever you invest with, make sure that they have a good reputation (obtain references), extensive experience, a good track record (documented) and that you receive proper documentation. **Never invest in anything which sounds too good to be true, e.g. ostrich, emu or dodo farming, as it probably will be.** Bear in mind that many financial advisers in Spain are unregulated and anyone can set up business without any professional qualifications or experience. Also never be taken in by endorsements, as some people and businesses will endorse anything to make a buck.

When investing in anything you should always ask how much of your investment is gobbled up in fees (initial charges, annual fees, management fees, commission, administration fees, expenses, etc.). Don't allow yourself to be fobbed off with a lot of 'mumbo-jumbo' or talk about it being too complicated to calculate — insist on an answer in plain English. Whether you receive truly independent advice is usually impossible to determine. If you think that you aren't being told the truth, go elsewhere. There's no such thing as a guaranteed stock market investment; even a guaranteed return in a bank account won't necessarily protect you against inflation (in fact there's always a price to pay for a 'guarantee'). Most 'experts' agree that a balanced and well spread (internationally invested) portfolio is best, using as many financial instruments as possible. There's always a risk, although usually remote, that the company with which you invest will go broke. You should therefore choose a solid company and invest in a country where the bulk of your investment is covered by a deposit protection scheme.

Whatever advice you receive, you should do comprehensive personal homework, such as subscribing to specialist financial magazines and newsletters, some of which offer excellent advice. **The best thing to do in the first instance is nothing at all — until you know exactly what your long-term plans are and have investigated all the available investment options.**

VALUE ADDED TAX (IVA)

Value Added Tax (VAT or the 'Voracious Administration Tax'), called *Impuesto sobre el Valor Añadido (IVA)* in Spain, was introduced on 1st January 1986 when Spain joined the European Community. Most prices in stores are quoted inclusive of IVA, although sometimes prices are quoted exclusive of tax (e.g. office equipment). Bills usually show whether IVA is included (*IVA incluido*) or not (*más IVA*). Spain has the following rates of IVA:

Rate (%)	Applicability
4	**super reduced rate:** basic foodstuffs such as bread, flour, milk, cheese, eggs, fruit and vegetables; books, newspapers and magazines; pharmaceutical specialities; cars and prostheses for the handicapped; and subsidised housing;
7	**reduced rate:** food; drink (other than alcohol and soft drinks); fuel; water; communications; drugs and medicines; transportation; hotels; restaurants (excluding 5-fork rated restaurants); theatres and cinemas; certain sports services; and new dwellings;
16	**standard rate:** for goods and services which don't come under another rate including utility bills; rental cars; and 5-fork rated restaurants.

Certain goods and services are exempt from IVA including health care (e.g. doctors' and dentists' services); educational services; insurance, banking and certain financial services; social security services; sports and cultural activities; postal services; state lotteries; land and secondhand property; the letting of residential property; the transfer of a business (providing the buyer continues the existing business); and certain transactions that are subject to other taxes. Exports are also exempt from IVA.

In addition to IVA, special taxes are levied on automobiles, alcohol, petrol and tobacco products. VAT applies to the mainland and the Balearic Islands but isn't levied in the Canary Islands, Ceuta and Melilla, where the old sales tax remains. The Canary Islands has an indirect general tax (CIIGT) which is levied on goods and services at the rate of 4 per cent. (The Canary Islands, particularly Grand Canary and Tenerife, are something of a tax haven with 1 per cent company tax instead of the 35 per cent levied in the rest of Spain and no withholding tax on bank balances.)

All businesses in Spain must be registered for IVA. Businesses with a turnover of 1,000m ptas or more a year must file an IVA return monthly and pay the tax due within 20 days of the end of the month. Businesses with a turnover of less than 1,000m ptas a year must file a quarterly return and pay tax due within 20 days of the end of the quarter. IVA fraud is rife in Spain and payments are often made in cash to avoid IVA. **However, it's essential to have legitimate bills showing names and tax numbers (CIF, NIF, NIE) in order to reclaim VAT.**

IVA is payable on goods purchased outside the EU but not on goods purchased in an EU country where VAT has already been paid, although you may be asked to produce a VAT receipt. Persons resident outside the EU can obtain exemption from VAT on large individual purchases in Spain costing over US $500. Retailers can provide information and the necessary forms. You must show your passport and complete a form; the store will mail the refund to your home address, which must be outside the EU.

It's the declared aim of the European Union to eventually have just one universal rate of VAT for the whole community, although this will take some time to accomplish, particularly as only Denmark currently has one rate and Italy has seven! See also **Customs** on page 77 and **Shopping Abroad** on page 392.

TAXATION

Spain is no longer the tax haven it was in the 1960s and 1970s, when taxes were low and tax evasion was a way of life and almost encouraged! During the last decade Spain's taxes have increased dramatically, particularly income tax, although income tax and social security contributions remain among the lowest in the European Union. Before you decide to settle in Spain permanently, you should obtain expert advice regarding Spanish taxes. This will (hopefully) ensure that you take optimum advantage of your current tax status and that you don't make any mistakes that you will regret later.

Today it's much more difficult to avoid paying taxes in Spain and penalties are severe. However, despite the efforts of the authorities to curb tax dodgers, tax evasion is still widespread. Many non-resident home-owners and foreign residents think they should be exempt from Spanish taxes and are among the worst offenders. Many inhabit a twilight world as 'eternal tourists', not officially resident in any country, and some even have the effrontery to boast about not paying taxes. It has been estimated that around 20 per cent of foreign property owners in Spain live there permanently, which means there could be as many as 250,000 foreign residents not paying income tax in Spain. A common dodge for casual employees in Spain is to get paid 'cash in hand', thus avoiding paying value added tax (IVA) and income tax. Cash is preferred by many Spaniards in payment rather than by cheque or credit card, even when large sums are involved. Since 1986, when VAT was introduced, many Spaniards have been salting their money away from the prying eyes of the tax authorities.

As you would expect in a country with millions of bureaucrats, the Spanish tax system is inordinately complicated and most Spaniards don't understand it. In fact even the experts have difficulty agreeing with the tax authorities (*Agencia Estatal de Administración Tributaria*, previously known as *hacienda*) and tax advisers often give different advice. It's difficult to obtain accurate information from the tax authorities and just when you think you have it cracked (ho! ho!), the authorities change the rules or hit you with a new tax. Taxes are levied by three tiers of government in Spain: central government, autonomous regional governments and local municipalities. Government taxes are administered by the Ministry of Economy and Taxation (*Ministerio de Económica y Hacienda*), which has its headquarters in Madrid, and assessment and tax collection centres in provincial capital towns. There's a five-year statute of limitations (*prescripción*) on the collection of back taxes in Spain, i.e. if no action has been taken during this period to collect unpaid tax, it cannot be collected. Late payment of any tax bill usually incurs a surcharge of 20 per cent.

It isn't so much the level of taxes in Spain that's burdensome, but the number of different taxes for which individuals are liable. At the last count this was around 15, including those associated with buying and selling property and motoring. The most important taxes in Spain are listed below, where a reference is given to the page where they are discussed in detail.

Note that most taxes in Spain are based on self-assessment, meaning that individual taxpayers are liable to report and calculate any tax due within the time limits established by law. Tax forms must be purchased by taxpayers and are obtainable from a tobacconist's (*estanco*), although some are only available from tax offices (*agencia tributaria*). Penalties and interest are levied for late or non-compliance.

Residents:

*Income Tax (*impuesto sobre la renta de las personas físicas/IRPF*) is payable on world-wide income (see page 295).

Business Tax (*impuesto sobre actividades económicas/IAE*) is paid by all businesses including the self-employed once a year (formerly called *licencia fiscal*, see page 34).

Company or Corporation Tax (*impuesto sobre sociedades*) is paid at 35 per cent on profits by partnerships and registered companies such as a *Sociedad Anónima (SA)* or *Sociedad Limitada (SL)*.

*Property or Real Estate Tax (*impuesto sobre bienes inmuebles urbano*, formerly called *contribución urbana*) is paid by property owners (see page 304).

*Wealth Tax (*impuesto sobre el patrimonio*) is payable on capital assets, including property (see page 307).

*Capital Gains Tax (*impuesto sobre incremento de patrimonio de la venta de un bien inmueble*) is payable on the profits made on the sale of property and other assets located in Spain (see page 308).

*Inheritance and Gift Tax (*impuesto sobre sucesiones y donaciones*) is payable on worldwide assets (see page 310).

*Garbage Collection/Mains Drainage Tax (*basura y alcantarillado*) is an annual tax payable by property owners (see page 98).

Offshore Company Tax (*impuesto especial*) is an annual tax on offshore companies that don't declare the individual owner of property in Spain or the source of investment.

Social Security (*seguridad social*) isn't strictly a tax, but is payable by employees and the self-employed (see page 254).

Motor Vehicle Tax (*impuesto de circulación*) is paid annually by all vehicle owners on Spanish registration plates (see page 207).

Value Added Tax (*impuesto sobre el valor añadido*) is payable on a wide range of goods and services at varying rates (see page 290).

*   Also paid by non-resident property owners (see also below).

Non-Resident Property Owners:

Income Tax is payable on income arising in Spain and an imputed 'letting' or deemed property income tax based on property values is also payable (see page 295);

Capital Gains Tax is payable on the profits made on the sale of a property or other assets in Spain (see page 308);

Wealth Tax is payable on property and other assets in Spain (see page 307);

Inheritance and Gift Tax is payable on Spanish assets (see page 310);

There are other taxes concerned with building a property in Spain and property purchase, which include transfer tax (*derechos reales*) or value added tax (*impuesto sobre el valor añadido*) and 'land' tax (*plus valía*). Property buyers who purchase property in an urbanisation without the proper infrastructure may need to pay an exceptional municipal tax (*impuestos especiales municipales*) to bring the infrastructure up to the required standard.

Fiscal Representation

The term fiscal representation (as used here) refers to anyone who provides tax and other financial services including a fiscal representative (*representante fiscal*), accountant (*contable*) or tax adviser (*asesor fiscal*). Since 1994, it has no longer been necessary for non-resident owners of a *single* dwelling in Spain to have a fiscal representative, providing it's used as the address for communications from the tax authorities. If you have more than one asset in Spain, e.g. you have separate title deeds for a property and a garage or garden, or you own a commercial property, then you must still appoint a fiscal representative. A foreign company owning a property in Spain must also have a fiscal representative and a foreigner receiving income from a business in Spain may also need one. If you fail to appoint a fiscal representative you can be fined up to 1m ptas. All accountants and tax advisers in Spain act as fiscal representatives for their clients (see also **Appendix E**).

If you're a non-resident you should have someone in Spain to look after your financial affairs and declare and pay your taxes. This person would normally be your fiscal representative, to whom all communications will automatically be sent by the Spanish tax authorities. You can also have your fiscal representative receive your bank statements, ensure that your bank is paying your regular bills by standing order (such as electricity, water and telephone), and that you have sufficient funds in your account to pay them. Your fiscal representative can also apply for a fiscal number (*Número de Identificación de Entranjero/NIE*) on your behalf (see page 273).

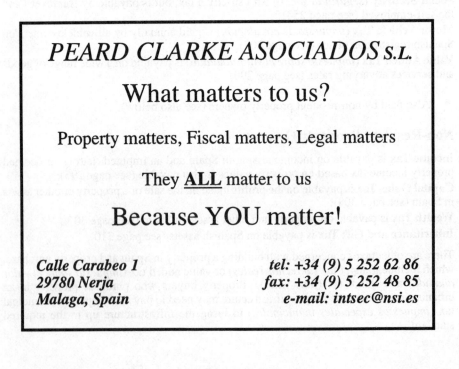

A fiscal representative can be a Spaniard or a foreign resident in Spain, an individual or a company (such as a bank). Your provincial office of the Ministry of Finance must be notified of the appointment of a fiscal representative within two months by letter and the representative must expressly communicate his acceptance of the appointment at the office where your taxes are to be paid. Before employing a fiscal representative obtain recommendations from friends, colleagues and acquaintances. However, bear in mind that if you consult a number of 'experts', you're liable to receive conflicting advice. **Note that some fiscal representatives fail to pay tax bills on time (or at all), thereby incurring their clients a fine equal to 20 per cent of the amount due.** You should always check with the town hall and tax authorities that your bills have actually been paid!

Fiscal representation usually costs from 20,000 ptas a year for a single person and up to double for a couple. Many representatives charge around 50 per cent more for a couple than they charge for a single person. A couple should pay around 30,000 ptas a year, depending on the services provided. There may be additional charges for tax administration and completing tax returns, with the cost depending on the complexity of your tax affairs. For the relatively small cost involved, most people (both residents and non-residents) are usually better off employing a fiscal representative to handle their Spanish tax and other financial affairs than doing it themselves, particularly as the regulations change frequently.

INCOME TAX

Income tax (*impuesto sobre la renta de las personas físicas/IRPF*) in Spain is below the EU average, although it has increased considerably the last few decades, particularly for high earners. However, it isn't supplemented by crippling social security rates as in some other EU countries (e.g. France). Belgians, Dutch and Scandinavians will find Spanish income tax low, while most other Europeans will pay around the same. Paying Spanish income tax can even be advantageous, as there are more allowances for some people than there are in other countries. If you're able to choose the country where you're taxed, you should obtain advice from an international tax expert. Employees' income tax (*retenciones*) is deducted at source by employers, i.e. pay-as-you-earn, and individuals aren't responsible for paying their own income tax. Self-employed people pay their income tax quarterly (*pago fraccionado*). Non-residents receiving an income from a Spanish source and non-resident property owners (see page 301) should instruct their fiscal representative to file an income tax declaration on their behalf (or do it themselves).

Moving to Spain (or another country) often provides opportunities for legal 'favourable tax planning'. To make the most of your situation, it's advisable to obtain income tax advice before moving to Spain, as there are usually a number of things you can do in advance to reduce your tax liability, both in Spain and abroad. Be sure to consult a tax adviser who's familiar with both the Spanish tax system and that of your present country of residence. For example, you may be able to avoid paying tax on a business abroad if you establish both residency and domicile in Spain before you sell. On the other hand, if you sell a foreign home after establishing your principal residence in Spain, it becomes a second home and you may then be liable to capital gains tax abroad (this is a complicated subject and you should obtain expert advice). You should inform the tax authorities in your former country of residence that you're going to live permanently in Spain.

Tax evasion is illegal and a criminal offence in Spain, for which offenders can be heavily fined or even imprisoned. On the other hand, tax avoidance, i.e. legally paying as little tax as possible (if necessary by finding and exploiting loopholes in the tax laws) is a different matter altogether. Although Spanish tax inspectors make a relatively small number of inspections, they target them at those among whom tax fraud is most prevalent, such as the self-employed. **Note that new legislation is being introduced to tackle fraud and it's expected that 'fiscal nomads' will find it more difficult to avoid Spanish taxation in future.** Note that residents have a number of opportunities to legally reduce their taxes, while non-residents have very few or none at all (at least legally).

You can obtain free tax advice from the information section (*servicio de información* or *oficina de información al contribuyente*) at your local provincial tax office in Spain, where staff will answer queries and assist you in completing your tax declaration (but won't complete it for you) via their PADRE computer system. Some offices, particularly those located in resort areas, have staff who speak English and other foreign languages. The tax office provides a central telephone information service from 0900 to 1900 (tel. freephone 900-333555). Tax clearance permits aren't required by those leaving Spain to live abroad.

Liability

You liability for income tax in Spain depends on whether you're officially resident there. Under Spanish law you become a **fiscal resident** in Spain if you spend 183 days there during a calendar year *or* your main centre of economic interest, e.g. investments or business, is in Spain. Temporary absences are included in the calculation of the period spent in Spain (or Spanish territories) unless residence is shown to have been in another country for 183 days in a calendar year. If your spouse and dependent minor children normally reside in Spain and have residence cards, and you aren't legally separated from him or her, you're also considered to be a tax resident in Spain (unless you can prove otherwise). Note that the 183-day rule also applies to other EU countries and many countries, e.g. Britain limit visits by non-residents to 182 days in any one year or an average of 91 days per tax year over a four year period.

If you're tax resident in two countries simultaneously, your 'tax home' may be resolved under the rules applied under international treaties. Under such treaties you're considered to be resident in the country where you have a permanent home; if you have a permanent home in both countries, you're deemed to be resident in the country where your personal and economic ties are closer. If your residence cannot be determined under this rule, you're deemed to be resident in the country where you have an habitual abode. If you have an habitual abode in both or in neither country, you're deemed to be resident in the country of which you're a citizen. Finally, if you're a citizen of both or neither country, the authorities of the countries concerned will decide your tax residence between them by mutual agreement.

If you intend to live permanently in Spain, you should notify the tax authorities in your previous country of residence. You may be entitled to a tax refund (*devolución*) if you depart during the tax year, which usually necessitates completing a tax return. The authorities may require evidence that you're leaving the country, e.g. evidence of a job in Spain or of having bought or rented a property there. If you move to Spain to take up a job or start a business, you must register with the local tax authorities soon after your arrival.

Double-Taxation: Spanish residents are taxed on their worldwide income, subject to certain treaty exceptions (non-residents are taxed only on income arising in Spain). Citizens of most countries are exempt from paying taxes in their home country when they spend a minimum period abroad, e.g. one year. Spain has double-taxation treaties with many countries, designed to ensure that income that has already been taxed in one treaty country isn't taxed again in another treaty country. The treaty establishes a tax credit or exemption on certain kinds of income, either in the country of residence or the country where the income is earned. Spain has double-taxation treaties with around 35 countries including Argentina, Australia, Austria, Belgium, Brazil, Bulgaria, Canada, China, the Czech Republic, Denmark, Ecuador, Finland, France, Germany, Hungary, India, Ireland, Italy, Japan, Korea, Luxembourg, Mexico, Morocco, the Netherlands, Norway, the Philippines, Poland, Portugal, Romania, Russia, Sweden, Switzerland, Tunisia, the United Kingdom and the USA. Where applicable, a double-taxation treaty prevails over domestic law.

However, even if there's no double-taxation agreement between Spain and another country, you can still obtain relief from double taxation. When there's no double-taxation agreement, tax relief is provided through direct deduction of any foreign tax paid or through a 'foreign compensation' (*compensación extranjera*) formula. Note that if your tax liability in another country is lower than that in Spain, you must pay the Spanish tax authorities the difference. If you're in doubt about your tax liability in your home country, contact your nearest embassy or consulate in Spain. The USA is the only country that taxes its non-resident citizens on income earned abroad (US citizens can obtain a copy of a brochure, *Tax Guide for Americans Abroad*, from American consulates).

Leaving Spain: Before leaving Spain, foreigners must pay any tax due for the previous year and the year of departure by applying for a tax clearance. A tax return must be filed prior to departure and includes your income and deductions from 1st January of the departure year up to the date of departure. Your local tax office will calculate the tax due and provide a written statement. When departure is made before 31st December, the previous year's taxes are applied. If this results in overpayment, a claim must be made for a refund.

Allowances & Deductions

Before you're liable for income tax, you can deduct social security payments and certain costs from your gross income and from the sum due after establishing your tax base. The resultant figure is your taxable income. If your earned, worldwide, annual income (i.e. income from work or pensions plus a maximum of 250,000 ptas from investments) is less than 1.1m ptas a year (1.2m ptas if you're a married couple declaring jointly or retired), you aren't required to make a tax declaration or pay Spanish income tax.

Income tax is payable on both earned and unearned income. Taxable income includes salaries, pensions, capital gains, property and investment income (dividends and interest), and income from professional, artistic, business or agricultural activities. It also includes employee benefits and perks such as overseas and cost of living allowances; contributions to profit sharing plans; bonuses (annual, performance, etc.); storage and relocation allowances; language lessons provided for a spouse; personal company car; payments in kind (such as free accommodation or meals); stock options; home leave or vacations (paid by your employer); and children's private education. If you own a property in Spain, your income also includes 2 per cent of its fiscal value (*valor catastral*). For example, if your Spanish property is officially valued at 10m ptas, then 200,000 ptas must be added to your income.

The following allowances and deductions apply to the fiscal year 1996, i.e. tax declarations made in 1997.

Deductions From Gross Income:

- any withholding tax paid during the previous year;
- all social security payments;
- 5 per cent of total income (maximum 250,000 ptas) is allowed as a general deduction for expenses that are difficult to itemise (this isn't applicable if your income is solely from investments);
- professional and trade union fees;
- property taxes (*impuesto sobre bienes inmuebles/IBI*);
- interest payments on loans or mortgages for buying or improving your principal residence (limited to 800,000 ptas for an individual and 1m ptas for a couple);
- Spanish company pension contributions up to a maximum of 15 per cent of earnings or a maximum of 750,000 ptas;
- a percentage of an annuity (life or fixed-period), which depends on your age;
- a divorced parent can deduct child-support payments made as a result of a court decision (alimony payments may be taxable subject to provisions made under court orders).

Deductions From Tax Due:

After making the deductions from your gross income (listed above) you apply the percentages shown in the tax tables on pages 300 and 301, which will give you the amount of tax due. For example, if a couple's income is 4m ptas and their deductions total 25 per cent, this leaves them with a taxable income of 3m ptas. For the 1996 tax year, the tax due on 3m ptas for a couple was 471,910 ptas. However, before arriving at your final tax bill you can make certain deductions from the tax due, including the following:

- 75 per cent of any *plus valía* tax paid as a result of a property sale;
- 40 per cent of the income from dividends on stocks and shares in Spanish companies;
- 15 per cent (maximum 100,000 ptas) of rental payments for your principal residence; to qualify your total income must be less than 3.5m ptas if you're single or 5m ptas for a married couple *and* your rent must exceed 10 per cent of your total income (this gives renters the same tax breaks as homebuyers);
- 15 per cent of medical or dental expenses incurred as a result of illness or accident including recovery after illness, orthopaedic apparatus, hospital costs for a person accompanying a sick person, travel associated with treatment, dental repairs, and spectacles or contact lenses (receipts must be provided);
- 15 per cent of expenses (maximum 25,000 ptas) for child care paid for all children aged under three of working parents; to qualify, a single parent's income must be under 2m ptas and a married couple's under 3m ptas;

- 15 per cent of the cost of the purchase or renovation of your principal residence (excluding additions such as a garage or swimming pool or normal maintenance and repairs);
- 15 per cent of the value of donations of cultural items to charities and public organisations and 10 per cent of cash donations (up to a maximum of 30 per cent of your taxable income);
- 15 per cent of the amount invested in a 'mortgage savings' account;
- 10 per cent of Spanish life premiums or premiums for an invalidity (critical illness) policy;
- 16,000 ptas if you're aged 65 or over;
- 16,000 ptas if you have a dependent parent or grandparent living with you (32,000 ptas if the parent or grandparent is over 75 years old);
- 21,500 ptas for the first two dependent children or grandchildren living with you (children must be under 30 years of age with an income below the Spanish minimum wage), 26,000 ptas for the third child, and 31,000 ptas for the fourth and subsequent children;
- 27,000 ptas for each salary-earner in the family if you work or receive a pension; 56,000 ptas if you (or any dependants) are an invalid with an income below the minimum wage; or 72,000 ptas if your income is less than 1,071,000 ptas (thus ensuring that a low-income person who's obliged to make a declaration doesn't actually pay any tax). If your income is between 1,071,001 and 1,971,000 ptas you must subtract 5 per cent of the difference between your income and 1,071,001 ptas from the 72,000 ptas allowance.

Any personal income taxes paid in another country will also be deducted from your tax base. Note, however, that if you pay higher tax abroad than would have been paid in Spain, you won't receive a rebate from the Spanish tax authorities!

Pensions

The taxation of pensioners changed in 1992, since when pensions have been taxed differently depending on the source:

Employment-based Pensions are taxed in the same way as salary income. You're entitled to the same deductions and personal allowances and the same tax rates apply. However, the situation isn't so straightforward if your pension is paid from a savings scheme, such as a pension fund established through an employment relationship with tax advantages in your home country.

Investment Capital Pensions, whereby you pay a sum of money or transfer assets such as property to another party in return for annuity payments (or a monthly income) for a fixed period or until death. This may give rise to capital gains and interest income, each of which are taxed differently in Spain.

Insurance Based Pensions are insurance schemes that permit you to choose between taking the whole amount accrued under the policy in one lump sum or to have it paid in the form of annuity payments. This income is taxed either as a capital gain or as ordinary income. The taxation of investment capital and insurance based pensions can be extremely complicated and you should obtain expert professional advice from an accountant or tax adviser *before* deciding where and how to receive your pension.

Civil Service Pensions are usually tax-free in Spain and don't need to be declared to the Spanish authorities if they are your only source of income, **although this depends on the country paying your pension and its double taxation treaty with Spain.** However, you may need to provide the tax office with proof that your pension is taxed at source. Civil service pensions don't include United Nations pensions, as the UN cannot tax its former employees (unlike individual countries). Note, however, that if you have other income which is taxable in Spain, your civil service pension is usually taken into account when calculating your Spanish tax rate and must usually be declared. If you pay tax in error on a pension that wasn't in fact taxable, you can claim a refund for the previous five years only, which is Spain's statute of limitations (if they aren't collected, taxes also usually lapse after five years).

Calculation

The tax year in Spain is the same as the calendar year (1st January to 31st December). Income tax rates for individuals (*persona física*) start at 20 per cent on income from 430,000 to 1,072,000 ptas and rises to 56 per cent on income above 10,222,000 ptas. For married couples, who can choose to be taxed individually or jointly (*conjunto de unidades familiares*), tax starts at 20 per cent on income from 857,000 to 2,142,000 ptas, rising to 56 per cent on income above 11,790,000 ptas. The tables below show the 1996 tax rates for individual and joint declarations (new rates are published annually in May):

Individual Declaration:

Taxable Income (Ptas '000)	Tax Rate (%)	Cumulative Tax* (Ptas)
0- 430	0	
430-1,072	20	128,400
1,072-1,682	22	262,600
1,682-2,292	24.5	412,050
2,292-2,902	27	576,750
2,902-3,512	30	759,750
3,512-4,122	32	954,950
4,122-4,732	34	1,162,350
4,732-5,342	36	1,381,950
5,342-5,952	38	1,613,750
5,952-6,562	40	1,857,750
6.562-7,172	42.5	2,117,000
7,172-7,782	45	2,391,500
7,782-8,392	47	2,678,200
8,392-9,002	49	2,977,100
9,002-9,612	51	3,288,200
9,612-10,222	53.5	3,614,550
over 10,222	56	

Joint Declaration:

Taxable Income (Ptas '000)	Tax Rate (%)	Cumulative Tax* (Ptas)
0- 857	0	
857- 2,142	20	257,000
2,142- 2,812	24.5	421,150
2,812- 3,482	27	602,050
3,482- 4,152	30	803,050
4,152- 4,822	32	1,017,450
4,822- 5,492	34	1,245,250
5,492- 6,162	36	1,486,450
6,162- 6,832	38	1,741,050
6,832- 7,502	40	2,009,050
7,502- 8,172	42.5	2,293,800
8,172- 8,842	45	2,595,300
8,842- 9,512	47	2,910,200
9,512-10,182	49	3,238,500
10,182-10,852	51	3,580,200
10,852-11,790	53.5	4,082,030
over 11,790	56	

*   In the above two tables the first column shows taxable income and the third column the cumulative tax payable on the maximum income in that band, e.g. 803,050 ptas is the tax payable on an income of 4,152,000 ptas. The second ('Tax Rate') column shows the tax rate payable on the band shown in the first column, e.g. if a couple's taxable income is 3,000,000 ptas, the tax payable on the first 2,812,000 ptas is 24.5 per cent (421,150 ptas) plus 27 per cent on the remaining 188,000 ptas (50,760 ptas), making a total of 471,910 ptas.

Income Tax for Property Owners

Residents: Property income earned by residents is included in their annual income tax declaration and tax is payable at their standard income tax rate. You're eligible for deductions such as repairs and maintenance; security; cleaning costs; mortgage interest (Spanish loans only); management and letting expenses (e.g. advertising); local taxes; insurance; plus an amortisation deduction of 1.5 per cent, per year of the value of the property. You should seek professional advice to ensure that you're claiming everything to which you're entitled.

Non-Residents: Non-resident property owners in Spain are liable for income tax at a flat rate of 25 per cent on any income arising in Spain, including income from letting a property. For short term letting, owners should obtain a form from the tourist authorities to apply for registration of their property (although few do so). Income must be declared on form 210 (*Impuestos Sobre la Renta de las Personas Físicas y Sobre Sociedades*) and paid quarterly to the tax authorities by your fiscal representative. There's a 10 per cent surcharge for late payment (reduced from 20 per cent in 1995). For the part of the year during which you don't rent, e.g. the winter, you must declare and pay tax using form 214 (see below).

From 1994, non-residents owning a single property in Spain have been able to be declare their income and wealth tax (see page 307) together on a single form at any time during the year, e.g. the declaration for 1996 could be made any time up until 31st December 1997. This is done on form 214 (*Impuesto sobre el Patrimonio y sobre la Renta de No Residente*), which is obtainable from a tax office (*agencia tributaria*) only and not from a tobacconist's (*estanco*). Note that if you own two or more properties in Spain, you cannot use form 214 and must make separate declarations for income and wealth tax between 1st May and 20th June (and you must appoint a fiscal representative in Spain).

Form 214 is a simple form and most homeowners should be able to complete it themselves (instructions are printed on the reverse). When a husband and wife own a property jointly they should both complete a separate form, although it's possible for a couple to make their declaration on one form (check with your fiscal representative). When a property is used partly for letting and partly for private use, an apportionment is made between the amount of time used for each purpose. You're supposed to be able to pay your tax at a bank, although most banks are unwilling to accept the tax forms and payment, in which case you must pay in cash or by a certified bank cheque at a tax office. This tax may be offset against taxes paid in other countries.

Income Tax on Deemed Letting Income: The tax that causes most confusion and resentment, particularly among non-resident property owners, is the income tax on deemed or notional 'letting income' (*rendimientos del capital inmobiliario*, usually referred to simply as *renta*). All property owners in Spain are deemed to receive an income of 2 per cent of the fiscal value (*valor catastral*) of their property (1.3 per cent if the fiscal value has been revised since 1st January 1994). Non-residents pay a flat rate tax of 25 per cent on this income. For example, if you own a property valued at 20m ptas, 2 per cent of that is 400,000 ptas, on which the 25 per cent 'income' tax is 100,000 ptas. There are no deductions. In the case of residents, the deemed letting income is added to other income for income tax purposes.

The *Agencia Tributaria* publish a booklet in English for non-residents entitled *Taxation of Non-Resident Individuals*, a copy of which can be obtained from local tax offices in Spain.

Declarations & Tax Bill

An annual income tax declaration (*declaración sobre la renta de personas físicas*) must be lodged between 1st May and 20th June by both residents and non-residents with income in Spain (other than income from property letting). If you're entitled to a refund (*devolución*) the deadline is extended until 30th June. Income tax is paid one year in arrears, e.g. the declaration filed in 1997 was for the 1996 tax year. The above deadlines also apply to declarations for property tax and wealth tax for residents.

If your earned personal income is below 1.1m ptas for an individual declaration or 1.2m ptas for couple making a joint declaration, then it isn't necessary to complete an income tax declaration. Note that if you're a Spanish resident, these limits apply to your worldwide family income wherever it arises, but don't include income taxed in another country. If you're resident in Spain, the authorities will ask to see your income tax declaration when you renew your residence card (*residencia*). Rather than try to explain that your income is below the tax threshold (and therefore possibly below the income necessary to obtain a *residencia*!), it's advisable to make a 'negative' tax declaration.

Tax returns aren't sent out by the tax office each year and must be purchased from a tobacconist's (*estanco*) for around 35 ptas each (they come with a set of instruction booklets). It you're unable to obtain a tax return from a tobacconist's, you can obtain one from a tax adviser or your local tax office (*agencia tributaria*). There are three kinds of tax declaration forms in Spain, an abbreviated declaration (*declaración abreviada*), a simple declaration (*declaración simplificada*) and an ordinary declaration (*declaración ordinaria*).

Abbreviated Declaration: The *declaración abreviada* (form 103) was introduced in 1996 and consists of just two pages. It can be used by an estimated 7m taxpayers whose income derives entirely from earnings or from pensions and investments which have already been subject to Spanish withholding tax. Note that if your income consists of a pension which has had some deductions made in another country and which you intend to subtract from your Spanish declaration, then you cannot use this form.

Simple Declaration: The *declaración simplificada* (form 101) consists of five pages and is for those with the same sources of income as for the abbreviated declaration, plus income from letting, certain business and agricultural income, or capital gains from the sale of a permanent home where the total gain will be invested in a new home in Spain. Form 101 is used for refunds and the declaration and payment of the first stage of income tax, while form 102 is used for the second payment.

Ordinary Declaration: The *declaración ordinaria* (form 100) consists of 13 pages and is for incomes from all other sources (other than those mentioned above), e.g. business or professional activities or if you have made a capital gain.

An instruction booklet is provided with returns and the tax office publishes a booklet, *Manual Práctico - Renta* (costing 125 ptas), containing practical examples of how to complete tax forms and an interpretation of the current finance act.

Married couples with separate incomes have the option of making separate tax returns. This is advisable if your joint income exceeds 4m ptas, when filing jointly would put you in a higher tax bracket than would be the case if you filed separately. Obtain advice from your accountant or tax adviser. Families with one income only must make a joint declaration, which includes the husband and wife and all children under 18.

If you can use the (*declaración abreviada*), you should be able to complete your own tax form, perhaps with a little help from the tax office. However, most people require professional help to complete the *simplificada* and *ordinaria* tax forms. Prior to the introduction of the *declaración abreviada*, only some 15 per cent of Spain's 14m taxpayers made their own tax declarations. If you need any assistance you can contact the information section (*servicio de información*) of your local tax office, which may have multi-lingual staff. Note, however, that tax offices won't help you complete an *ordinaria* tax form and you must make an appointment (tel. 901-223344). When you go to the tax office you should take along the following:

- your latest receipt for property tax (*impuesto sobre bienes inmuebles/IBI*), which you will need for your wealth tax (*patrimonio*) declaration;

- if you rent a property in Spain, you may qualify for a tax reduction, depending on your income; if this is the case, you need to produce your rental contract and rent receipts;

- your end of year bank statements (*estado de cuenta*) showing any interest received and your average balance (*saldo medio*);

- any papers relating to stocks, shares, bonds, deposit certificates or any other property owned, either in Spain or abroad;

- declarations and receipts for any taxes paid in another country (if you're seeking to offset payment against your Spanish taxes);

- your passport, residence card and NIE.

Income tax in Spain is self-assessed (*auto-liquidación*) and is paid at the same time as the tax declaration is made. You can pay either the whole amount when the form is filed or 60 per cent and the balance by the following 5th November. Tax returns should be submitted to the district tax office where you're resident for tax purposes or they can be filed (and payment made) at designated banks in the province. Note that payment must be made in cash and personal cheques aren't accepted, although if you're filing at a bank where you hold an account, they will make a transfer to the tax authorities. If no payment is due on a return, it must be filed at the tax office. If you delay filing your tax return by just one day, you must pay a surcharge on the tax due, although it's possible to request a payment deferral.

Large fines can be imposed for breaches of tax law and in certain cases forfeiture of the right to tax benefits or subsidies for a period of up to five years. The fraudulent evasion of 5m ptas in tax is punishable by fines of up to six times the amount defrauded and/or imprisonment (it is, however, rare for someone to be prosecuted for tax evasion in Spain). Fines have also been reduced in recent years, although they are usually higher when a taxpayer doesn't voluntarily pay his tax bill. You should retain copies of your tax returns for at least five years, which is the maximum period that returns are liable for audit by the Spanish tax authorities.

Unless your tax affairs are simple, it's prudent to employ an accountant or tax adviser (*asesor fiscal*) to complete your tax return and ensure that you're correctly assessed. There are 'foreign' tax assessors (*asesores de extranjero*) who specialise in filing returns for foreigners, particularly non-residents. The fees for filing tax returns vary and for residents are around 5,000 ptas for a simple return and 10,000 ptas for an ordinary return. The fee for filing a tax return for a non-resident is usually around 5,000 ptas. **However, always make sure that you obtain your tax return (stamped as proof of payment) from your advisor.**

PROPERTY TAX

Property tax or rates (*impuesto sobre bienes inmuebles urbana/rústica* or *IBI*, which replaced the *contribución urbana/rústica*), is payable by both resident and non-resident property owners in Spain. Property taxes go towards local council administration, education, sanitary services (e.g. street and beach cleaning), social assistance, community substructure, and cultural and sports amenities. Before buying a property, check with the local town hall that there aren't any outstanding local taxes for previous years (you should go back at least five years). As with all property related taxes and debts, if the previous years' taxes are unpaid the new owner becomes liable (you can, however, reclaim the tax from the previous owner — if you can find him!). A town hall has five years in which to either bill you or take legal action to recover unpaid taxes. Note, however, that it's now obligatory for the vendor to produce his last IBI receipt when completing a sale in front of a notary.

When you buy a property in Spain, you must register your ownership with the local town hall (take along your *escritura*). Registration must be done within two months of signing the deeds and there are fines ranging from 1,000 to 150,000 ptas for non-registration. At one time there were literally millions (three million were discovered in the last decade or so) of undeclared and untaxed properties in Spain, although most have now been registered as local authorities have clamped down. However, there remain tens of thousands of properties in Spain that simply aren't registered with the local council for local taxes.

Assessment: IBI is based on the fiscal or rateable value (*valor catastral*) of a property, which has traditionally been set at around 70 per cent of a property's actual market value. However, due to the sorry state of many municipalities' financial affairs (many are bankrupt), there have been huge increases in fiscal values in many areas in recent years (it may be worth checking the level of local government debt before buying a property). Due to the collapse of property values in recent years, this has resulted in the fiscal value being above the market value in some cases. Therefore it's advisable to check the *valor catastral* (see below) of a property before buying it, as if it has been over-valued it will result in increased taxes. A table of values (*ponencia de valores*) is used by local municipalities to assess the fiscal value of a property.

If the fiscal value of your property increases greatly, check that it has been correctly calculated. Property values are calculated according to a variety of measurements and evaluations including the area (in square metres) of the property (the built, terraces and land areas), building and zoning restrictions in the area, the quality of the building (whether it's classified as luxury, normal or simple), the date of construction, and the proximity to services and roads. To check that a property is correctly specified, go to the town hall or the *urbanismo* office and ask to see its dossier (*expediente*). This contains a number of official papers relating to a property and may also contain plans and photographs. Check that all the data recorded is correct as errors are fairly common.

If an error is made in your assessment it can take years to have it corrected, although it's important to persevere. You can appeal against the valuation of your property or an increase in valuation if you believe it's too high, particularly if it's higher than that of similar properties in the same area, although you have only 15 days in which to lodge an appeal (yet another reason for non-residents to have a local fiscal representative). **It's important that the fiscal value of your property is correct as a number of taxes are linked to this value (in addition to property tax) including deemed 'letting' income tax and wealth tax.**

Tax Rates: The IBI rate depends on both the population of the municipality and the level of public services provided, and can vary considerably for similar properties located in different areas. Rates tend to be higher in resort and coastal areas than in inland areas. Some municipalities have invested huge sums in recent years improving civic amenities, e.g. building indoor sports complexes (with swimming pools, gymnasiums, etc.) and cultural centres, and have increased property taxes to pay for them. General revisions are permitted once every eight years, but they can be adjusted annually in accordance with coefficients set annually by the state government in its budget. The basic IBI rate is 0.3 per cent for agricultural properties (*rústicas*) and 0.5 per cent for urban properties (*urbana*). However, provincial capitals, towns with over 5,000 inhabitants and towns providing 'special services' can increase the rate to 1.7 per cent. Rates are reduced if a property's *valor catastral* has been reviewed (*zona revisada*) recently. To calculate your property tax you simply multiply your fiscal value by the tax rate, e.g. if the fiscal value of your property is 10m ptas and the tax rate is 1 per cent, your IBI bill will be 100,000 ptas. IBI can be deducted from gross income by residents when calculating their income tax liability.

Payment: Payment of property taxes varies depending on the municipality, e.g. between 1st September and 31st October. **Town halls often don't send out bills and it's your responsibility to find out how much you have to pay and when.** Payment can usually be made in cash or by guaranteed bank cheque at the tax collection office, by postal giro at certain banks, and some municipalities accept payment by credit cards such as 4B, Mastercard and Visa. Non-resident property owners should pay their IBI (and other local taxes) by direct debit from a Spanish bank account. If the tax isn't paid on time, a surcharge (*recargo*) of 20 per cent is levied in addition to interest (plus possible collection costs). Note that some municipalities conveniently 'forget' to send non-residents' bills to their fiscal representatives so that they can levy surcharges for late payment. If you're unable to pay your property tax, you should talk to your local tax office. They will be pleased that you haven't absconded and will usually be willing to agree a payment schedule.

Some town halls have instituted a system of discounts to encourage residents to pay their bills early and thus spread the municipality's income throughout the year. For example, Mijas (Malaga) offers a discount of 9 percent for payments received in the first quarter, 6 per cent for payment in the second quarter and 3 per cent for payment in the third quarter. There's no discount for tax paid between October 1st and 20th November and a surcharge of 20 per cent for late payment after 20th November.

Non-Payment: In the past, many people have been able to avoid paying property taxes. Incredibly, many municipalities with a high proportion of foreign residents and non-resident property owners collect only 50 to 75 per cent of property and other local taxes (over 90 per cent of property tax debts in Spain are owed by foreigners). In the past some municipalities even considered they were doing well if around 65 per cent of taxes were collected! This *laissez-faire* attitude toward tax collection goes a long way towards explaining why most councils are so deeply in debt. Only some 70 per cent of taxes are paid voluntarily and authorities must take administrative steps to obtain payment for around a third of bills.

However, in recent years local municipal tax authorities have made strenuous efforts to collect unpaid property taxes. If you owe back taxes and refuse to pay them, your property can be seized and sold at auction, perhaps for as little as 10 per cent of its value. There have been many cases of foreigners arriving in Spain after a long absence to find that their homes had been sold to pay taxes. Using the threat of embargoes and the forced sale of properties, many town halls have collected hundreds of millions of pesetas in back taxes. Local authorities also have the power to seize vehicles and place garnishment orders on bank accounts. **There's little sympathy with those who blatantly avoid paying property taxes in Spain, which means that other owners must bear the burden (through increased taxes) or municipalities are forced to cut services.**

If you don't pay your local taxes, your name will be listed in your province's 'official bulletin' (*Boletín Oficial de la Provincia/BOP*), the official publication in which changes in provincial regulations are promulgated and where embargoes against properties are listed. If you're a non-resident owner it's essential that you know when an embargo has been placed on your property. The names of foreigners listed in the *boletines oficiales* in the 10 Spanish provinces with the most foreign property owners (Alicante, Almeria, Baleares, Gerona, Granada, Las Palmas, Malaga, Murcia, Tenerife and Valencia) are published by the *Institute of Foreign Property Owners* (see page 88) in their monthly newsletter.

Note that local authorities also levy fees (*tasas*) for services such as garbage collection (see page 98), street and beach cleaning, issuing documents, local parking restrictions and fire-fighting services (extinguishing fires).

WEALTH TAX

Spain levies a wealth tax (*impuesto extraordinario sobre el patrimonio*), commonly referred to simply as *patrimonio*, on both residents and non-resident property owners (unlike most other countries, which exempt non-residents). Your wealth is calculated by totalling your assets and deducting your liabilities. When calculating your wealth tax, you must include the value of all property including real estate, vehicles, boats, aircraft, business ownership, cash (e.g. in bank accounts), life insurance, gold bars, jewellery, stocks, shares and bonds. However, a percentage for the value of household goods and chattels (*ajuar doméstico*) is no longer added. If you fail to declare your total assets you can be fined. The value of real property is either the purchase price, its fiscal value (*valor catastral*) or a value assessed by the authorities, **whichever is the highest.**

Bank balances should be declared by producing your end-of-year bank statement (*estado de cuenta*) showing any interest you have received and your average balance (*saldo medio*). However, if you're a non-resident and your country of residence has a double-taxation treaty with Spain, then bank balances and interest are taxable only in your country of residence, not in Spain. Assets that are exempt from wealth tax include *objets d'art* and antiques (providing their value doesn't exceed certain limits); the vested rights of participants in pension plans and funds; copyrights (so long as they remain part of your net worth); and assets forming part of Spain's historical heritage. Deductions are made for mortgages (for both residents and non-residents), business and other debts, and any 'wealth' tax paid in another country.

Residents are exempt from paying tax on the first 17m ptas (20m ptas if their *valor catastral* has been revised since 1st January 1994) and if they make an income tax declaration and their worldwide assets total less than 17m ptas, they're exempt from making a wealth tax declaration. If a property is registered in the names of both spouses (or a number of unrelated people), they should make separate declarations and are each entitled to claim the 17m ptas exemption. Therefore if a resident couple's shared assets are valued at less than 34m ptas, they will be below the tax threshold after deducting the exemption. Assets are taxed on a sliding scale as follows:

Band Threshold (Millions Ptas)		Tax Rate (%)	Cumulative Tax* (Ptas)
up to	26.78	0.2	53,560
26.78 -	53.56	0.3	133,900
53.56 -	107.12	0.5	401,700
107.12 -	214.24	0.9	1,365,780
214.24 -	428.48	1.3	4,150,900
428.48 -	856.96	1.7	11,435,060
856.96 -	1,713.92	2.1	29,431,220
over	1,713.92	2.5	

* In the above table, the cumulative tax is the tax payable for each band threshold, e.g. 401,700 ptas is payable on assets of 107.12m ptas. If your assets are valued at 75m ptas, you pay 0.2 per cent on the first 26.78m ptas (53,560 ptas), 0.3 per cent on the next 26.78m ptas (80,340 ptas) and 0.5 per cent on the balance of 21.44m ptas (107,200 ptas), making a total wealth tax bill of 241,100 ptas.

Non-Resident Property Owners: Non-residents must pay wealth tax on their assets in Spain, which for most non-resident property owners consist only of their home. If a non-resident owns a home in Spain valued below 26.78m ptas, wealth tax is levied at one fifth of 1 per cent (0.2 per cent) of its value, e.g. for a property valued at 10m ptas wealth tax is 20,000 ptas. There's no exemption for non-residents. Non-resident property owners can have their fiscal representative in Spain make the declaration and arrange for payment on their behalf. When a husband and wife own a property jointly they should both complete a separate form, although it's possible for a couple to make their declaration on one form (check with your fiscal representative).

Declaration: Residents must make a declaration for wealth tax at the same time as they make their income tax declaration, i.e. between 1st May and 20th June. The declaration is made on form 714 (*Impuesto sobre el Patrimonio*), available from tobacconists and tax offices. The form must be presented with payment to your regional tax office or participating banks. Non-residents owning a single property in Spain can make their income tax (on deemed letting income, see page 302) and wealth tax declarations together on a single form at any time during the year, e.g. the declaration for 1996 could be made any time up until 31st December 1997. This is done on form 214 (*Impuesto sobre el Patrimonio y sobre la Renta de No Residente*). Note that it's no longer necessary for most people to declare their average balance (*saldo medio*) in Spain for wealth tax.

CAPITAL GAINS TAX

Capital gains tax (*impuesto sobre incremento de patrimonio de la venta de un bien inmueble*) is payable on the profit from the sale of certain assets in Spain including antiques, art and jewellery, stocks and shares, real estate and the sale of a business. Capital gains revealed as a result of the death of a taxpayer, gifts to government entities, donations of certain assets in lieu of tax payments, and the exchange of assets in return for a life annuity for someone aged over 65 aren't taxable. Spain's taxation system combines capital gains (*incremento de patrimonio*) and capital losses (*disminución de patrimonio*). Capital losses can be offset against capital gains, but not against ordinary income. Capital losses in excess of gains can be carried forward for offset against future gains for a five year period.

Property: A capital gain is based on the difference between the purchase price (as declared in the *escritura*) and the sale price of a property, less buying and selling costs (and the cost of improvements). In the past it has been common practice to under-declare the purchase price of a property, thus allowing the vendor to reduce his capital gains tax liability. However, if you agree to this, when you sell the property and the actual price is declared you will pay increased capital gains tax. A capital gain on property must be declared within three months. Note that the period of ownership (for capital gains tax purposes) starts from the day a property is registered or after a declaration of new work (*declaración de obra nueva*) if you make major improvements (perhaps to a ruin), so it's important to ensure that it's correctly registered. If you have a *declaración de obra nueva* in addition to your purchase *escritura*, you must make separate CGT calculations for the land and the house.

Deductions for assets purchased before 8th June 1996: A new capital gains tax law was introduced on 8th June 1996, which reduced the period over which capital gains are calculated from 20 to 10 years. As previously, all capital gains are taxed in full if assets have been owned for less than two years. However, after the first two years there's an annual deduction of 25 per cent for quoted shares, 14.28 per cent for 'general' assets (other than shares and real estate) and 11.11 per cent for real estate. This means that gains on these assets are free of tax after 5, 8 and 10 years respectively, as shown in the table below.

Years Held	Shares	General	Real Estate
1	100.00	100.00	100.00
2	100.00	100.00	100.00
3	75.00	85.72	88.89
4	50.00	71.44	77.78
5	55.00	57.16	66.67
6	00.00	42.88	55.56
7		28.60	44.45
8		14.32	33.34
9		00.00	22.23
10			11.12
11			00.00

Using the above table, it's easy to calculate your capital gains tax. For example, if you're a non-resident and sell a property after owning it for five years, the gain is reduced by one third (33.33 per cent) before tax is applied. Therefore if you made a profit of 2m ptas, your capital gains tax liability is 66.67 per cent of 2m ptas (1,333,400 ptas), which is taxed at 35 per cent if you're a non-resident, making a capital gains tax bill of 466,690 ptas.

Assets purchased after 8th June 1996: For gains arising from assets (including property) purchased after 8th June 1996, the above table *doesn't* apply. Instead a coefficient (inflation index) is applied when you sell, to allow for inflation and the loss of value of the amount originally invested. The difference between the purchase price (as declared in the *escritura*) and the sale price, after the application of the coefficient, is the capital gain. **The first 200,000 ptas of a capital gain is tax exempt.** For example, if you buy a property for 10m ptas after 8th June 1996 and sell it for 15m ptas after five years, the difference is 5m ptas. Assuming a coefficient of 25 per cent (5 per cent a year), this is then applied to the purchase price leaving 12.5m ptas, which is subtracted from the sale price of 15m ptas. The exemption of 200,000 ptas is deducted from the balance of 2.5m ptas, making a capital gain of 2.3m ptas, on which you're taxed.

Tax Rates: Non-residents are taxed at a flat rate of 35 per cent, as shown in the above example. Capital gains made by residents are treated as income and taxed in the year in which the gain was made. Prior to 8th June 1996, all capital gains were taxed at your maximum income tax rate; however, since 8th June 1996, CGT **for residents** has been limited to a maximum of 20 per cent (less if your maximum rate of income tax is below 20 per cent). If you're a resident and sell your principal home in Spain and plan to buy another there, you have three years after the sale (from the date on the *escritura*) to do so and are taxed only on the amount that isn't re-invested. **Note that it's important not to buy a new home until you have sold the old one, otherwise you may not be entitled to this concession.**

Buying From a Non-Resident: Anyone buying a property in Spain from a non-resident is required to subtract 5 per cent from the purchase price and pay it to the Spanish Ministry of Finance within 30 days of the transaction. A declaration must be made on form 211 (*impuestos sobre la renta de las personas físicas y sobre sociedades*). The payment is a 'guarantee' against a vendor trying to avoid paying capital gains and other taxes that are due (as thousands did before this system was introduced).

The 5 per cent deduction must be made by the buyer only when the vendor is a non-resident, irrespective of whether the buyer is a resident or not. Providing the buyer deducts 5 per cent from the purchase price and pays this to the tax authorities within 30 days, he cannot be pursued for additional capital gains tax if the seller's liability was greater than the 5 per cent deducted (and he fails to pay it). **However, if the buyer fails to subtract and pay the 5 per cent, he is liable to pay any capital gains tax due on the sale and could also be heavily fined.** After paying the 5 per cent to the tax office, the buyer must give the vendor a copy of form 211. The vendor must then apply (on form 210) for a return of the difference between his 5 per cent deposit and his CGT liability within three months of the payment. **If he doesn't, the tax office will keep the money (if the buyer is responsible for the delay, he will be responsible for the vendor's loss).** If a representative or agent obtains the refund for you, you should request copies of the above forms and a statement showing the tax paid and the agent's fees.

Where applicable, the 5 per cent deposit is supposed to be repaid within six months of the documentation being completed, although it often takes vendors up to a year to get their money back. Although a non-resident who has owned his Spanish home for over 10 years is exempt from CGT, he must still pay the 5 per cent deposit, which also covers his income and wealth tax. When a non-resident sells a property in Spain, he may be asked for proof that he has paid his wealth and income tax for the previous five years before the deposit is repaid.

INHERITANCE & GIFT TAX

As in most countries, dying doesn't free you (or more correctly your beneficiaries) entirely from the clutches of the tax man. Spain imposes an inheritance and gift tax (*impuesto sobre sucesiones y donaciones*), called estate tax or death duty in some countries, on assets or monies received as an inheritance or gift. The estates of both residents and non-residents are subject to Spanish inheritance tax if they own property or have other assets in Spain. In Spain, inheritance tax is paid by the beneficiaries, e.g. a surviving spouse, and not by the deceased's estate (as in some other countries). The country where beneficiaries pay inheritance tax is usually decided by their domicile (see **Liability** on page 296). If you're domiciled in Spain, then Spanish inheritance tax is payable on an inheritance whether the inheritance is located (or received) in Spain or abroad.

Tax is payable by beneficiaries within six months of death if the deceased died in Spain, although it's possible to obtain a six month extension, or within 30 days following the transfer of a lifetime gift. If the deceased died abroad, the inheritance tax declaration and the payment of inheritance tax duties must be made within 16 months. Tax is assessed on the net amount received and accrues from the date of death or the date of the transfer of a gift. However, some people have managed to avoid inheritance tax by failing to inform the Spanish authorities of a death, although this is illegal (after five years and six months the tax can no longer be collected). However, if this is done, all other taxes must still be paid during this five year period.

From 8th June 1996, residents have received an exemption of 95 per cent of inheritance tax when their principal residence or family business (in Spain) is bequeathed to a spouse, parent or child who have been living with the deceased for at least two years prior to his death. The principal residence must be valued at a maximum of 20m ptas (there's no limit for a business) or the inheritance must not exceed 20m ptas per heir, above which normal inheritance tax rates apply. The inheritor must retain ownership of the property for a minimum of 10 years, although if he dies within the 10-year period no further tax is payable. However, if the property or business is sold during this period tax may be levied at the discretion of the relevant authorities, e.g. the regional government.

The amount of inheritance tax payable depends upon the relationship between the donor and the recipient, the amount inherited and the current (pre-existing) wealth of the recipient, shown in the tables below. Direct descendants and close relatives of the deceased receive an allowance before they become liable for inheritance tax, as shown below:

Relationship:

Group	Includes	Allowances*
1	direct descendants under 21 years	2,556,000 ptas plus 639,000 ptas for each year under 21 up to a maximum allowance of 7,668,000 ptas.
2	direct descendants over 21 years, direct ascendants (parents and up), spouse	2,556,000 ptas
3	relatives to third degree (and ascendants by affinity) including brother, sister, uncle, aunt, niece, nephew, etc.	1,280,000 ptas
4	unrelated persons and more remote relatives (including common-law spouses)	NIL

*   A handicapped person is entitled to an additional deduction of 7,668,000 ptas.

Net Value of Transfer:

Tax Band (Ptas)	Tax Rate (%)	Accumulative Tax (Ptas)*
up to 1,280,000	7.65	97,920
2,560,000	8.50	206,720
3,840,000	9.35	326,400
5,120,000	10.20	456,960
6,400,000	11.05	598,400
7,680,000	11.90	750,720
8,960,000	12.75	913,920
10,240,000	13.60	1,088,000
11,520,000	14.45	1,272,960
12,800,000	15.30	1,468,800
19,190,000	16.15	2,500,785
25,580,000	18.70	3,695,715
38,360,000	21.25	6,411,465
63,900,000	25.50	12,924,165
127,800,000	29.75	31,934,415
excess	34.00	

*   In the above table the first column shows the taxable inheritance band, the second column the tax rate for that band, and the third column the cumulative tax payable (for the band threshold). For example, if your taxable inheritance is 10m ptas, you must pay 913,920 ptas tax on the first 8,960,000 ptas plus 13.60 per cent on the remaining 1,040,000 ptas (141,440 ptas) making a total tax bill of 1,055,360 ptas.

Current Wealth

The table below is used to calculate the inheritance tax payable based on current wealth. If your current wealth is less than 64m ptas and your relationship to the deceased comes under group 1 or 2 (see table on page 311), then it doesn't influence an inheritance. However, if your relationship to the deceased comes under group 3 or 4 or your current wealth is greater than 64m ptas, your inheritance tax liability (shown in the above table) is multiplied by the figure shown in the table below:

Current Wealth (Ptas Million)	Relationship Group 1/2	3	4
0-64m	1.00	1.5882	2.0
64-321m	1.05	1.6676	2.1
321-643m	1.10	1.7471	2.2
over 643m	1.20	1.9059	2.4

It's important for both residents and non-residents with property in Spain to decide in advance how they wish to dispose of their Spanish property. Ideally this should

be decided even before buying property in Spain. Property can be registered in a single name; both names of a couple or joint buyers' names; the names of children, giving the parents sole use during their lifetime; or in the name of a Spanish or foreign company or trust. You should obtain professional advice regarding the registration of a Spanish property. It's advisable for a couple not only to register joint ownership of a property, but to share their other assets and have separate bank accounts, which will help reduce their dependants' liability for inheritance tax. Spanish law doesn't recognise the rights to inheritance of a non-married partner, although there are a number of solutions to this problem, e.g. a life insurance policy.

One possible way of reducing your liability to inheritance tax is to transfer legal ownership of property to a relative as a gift during your lifetime. However, this is treated as a sale (at the current market price) and incurs fees of around 10 per cent plus capital gains tax, which need to be compared with your inheritance tax liability. Whether you should will or 'sell' a property to someone depends on the value of the property and the relationship, and it may be cheaper for a beneficiary to be taxed under the inheritance laws. Take, for example, a couple jointly owning a property in Spain who wish to leave it to a child. When one of the parents dies the child inherits half the property and pays inheritance tax on that amount. Inheritance tax on the other half of the property is paid when the other parent dies. In this way little tax is paid on a property with a low value. If you're elderly, it may pay you to make the title deed (*escritira*) directly in the names of your children.

Spanish inheritance law is a complicated subject and professional advice should be sought from an experienced lawyer who understands both Spanish inheritance law and the law of any other countries involved. Your will (see below) is also a vital component in reducing Spanish inheritance and gift tax to the minimum or deferring its payment.

An information file called *The Spanish Inheritance* is published by the *Institute of Foreign Property Owners* (see page 88) in various languages including Dutch, English, German, Norwegian and Swedish.

WILLS

It's an unfortunate fact of life (or death) that you're unable to take your hard-earned money with you when you make your final exit (even if you plan to return in a later life). All adults should make a will (*testamento*) regardless of how large or small their assets (each spouse should make a separate will). If a foreigner dies intestate in Spain, i.e. without a will, his estate may be automatically disposed of under Spanish law and the law regarding compulsory heirs (see below) applied.

A foreigner resident in Spain is usually permitted to dispose of his Spanish assets according to the law of his home country, providing his will is valid under the law of that country. If you have lived in Spain for a long time, it may be necessary for you to create a legal domicile in your home country for the purpose of making a will. Although it isn't *necessary* to have a Spanish will for Spanish property, it's advisable to have a separate will for *any* country where you own property. When a person dies, assets can be dealt with immediately under local law without having to wait for the granting of probate in another country (and the administration of the estate is also cheaper). Having a Spanish will for your Spanish assets speeds up the will's execution and saves the long and complicated process of having a foreign will executed in Spain. Note that if you have two or more wills, you *must* ensure that they don't contradict or invalidate one another. You should periodically review your will to ensure that it reflects your current financial and personal circumstances.

Under Spanish law, a surviving spouse retains all assets acquired before marriage, half the assets acquired during the marriage, and all personal gifts or inheritances which have come directly to the spouse. The remaining assets must be disposed of under the law of 'obligatory heirs' (*herederos forzosos*). When a person dies leaving children, the estate is divided into three equal parts. One third must be left to the surviving children in equal parts and another third must also be left to the children, but the testator may decide how it's to be divided. A surviving spouse has a life interest in this second third and the children who inherit it cannot dispose of it freely until the surviving parent dies. The final third can be freely disposed of. If a child has died leaving children, they automatically inherit his share. If you have no children, your surviving parents have a statutory right to one third of your estate if you have a surviving spouse and half of your estate if you don't have a surviving spouse.

However, a will made by a foreigner regarding Spanish assets isn't invalidated because it doesn't bequeath property in accordance with Spanish law. In practice, Spanish law isn't usually applied and the disposal of property (real estate or land) in Spain is governed by the national law of the deceased's home country unless there's a dispute among the beneficiaries, when Spanish law is applied. See also **Inheritance & Gift Tax** above regarding ways to delay or circumvent the law of obligatory heirs and reduce inheritance tax. There are three kinds of Spanish wills, each of which is described below:

An **open will** (*testamento abierto*) is the normal and most suitable kind of will for most people. Its contents must be known to the notary and to three witnesses, who can be of any nationality, each of whom must sign the will. It's unnecessary to employ a lawyer to prepare an open will, although it's usually advisable. It must, however, be prepared by a notary who's responsible for ensuring that it's legal and properly drawn up. He will give you a copy (*copia simple* or *copia autorizada*) and send a copy to the general registry of wills (*Registro General de Actos de Ultima Voluntad*) in Madrid. The original remains at the notary's office. If you don't understand Spanish, you will need an official translation into a language that you speak fluently.

A **closed will** (*testamento cerrado*), where the contents remain secret, must be drawn up by a Spanish lawyer to ensure that it complies with Spanish law. You then take the will to a notary, who seals the envelope and signs it along with the witnesses, and then files and records it as for an open will.

An **holographic will** (*testamento ológrafo*) is a will made in your own handwriting. It must be signed and dated and must be clearly drafted in order to ensure that your wishes are absolutely clear. No witnesses or other formalities are required. It can be voluntarily registered with the registry of wills. On the death of the testator it must be authenticated before a judge, which will delay the will's execution. A verbal will can also be made in the presence of five witnesses, who must then testify to a notary the wishes of the deceased. The notary then prepares a written will and certifies it.

For anyone with a modest Spanish estate, for example a small property in Spain, an holographic will is sufficient. The cost of preparing a simple open or closed will is around 15,000 ptas or 30,000 ptas for a couple (each of whom must have separate wills). Spanish wills can be drawn up by Spanish lawyers and notaries abroad, although it's cheaper to do it in Spain. Note that where applicable, the rules relating to witnesses are strict and if not followed precisely can render a will null and void. In Spain, marriage doesn't automatically revoke a will as in some other countries.

Executors aren't normal in Spain and if you appoint one it may increase the inheritance tax payable. However, if you appoint an executor you should inform your heirs so that they will know who to notify in the event of your death. It isn't advisable to name a Spanish bank or a lawyer who doesn't speak Spanish as the executor, because they must instruct a Spanish lawyer (*abogado*) whose fees will be impossible to control. If you personally appoint a lawyer as your executor, he's only permitted to charge a fee equal to 5 per cent of the estate's value.

Your beneficiaries in Spain must produce an original death certificate or an authorised copy. If you die abroad, a foreign death certificate must be legally translated and legalised for it to be valid in Spain. The inheritance tax declaration and the payment of inheritance tax duties must be made within six months of your death if you die in Spain and within 16 months if you die abroad (otherwise a surcharge may result). Inheritance tax must be paid in advance of the release of the assets to be inherited in Spain and beneficiaries may therefore need to borrow funds to pay the tax before they receive their inheritance. Note that the winding-up of an estate can take a long time in Spain.

Keep a copy of your will(s) in a safe place and another copy with your lawyer or the executor of your estate. Don't leave them in a bank safe deposit box, which in the event of your death is sealed for a period under Spanish law. You should keep information regarding bank accounts and insurance policies with your will(s), but don't forget to tell someone where they are!

Note that Spanish inheritance law is a complicated subject and it's important to obtain professional legal advice when writing or altering your will(s).

COST OF LIVING

No doubt you would like to try to estimate how far your pesetas will stretch and how much money (if any) you will have left after paying your bills. Spain is no longer the inexpensive Eldorado that it once was and the cost of living has risen considerably in recent years. Inflation in Spain is low at around 3 per cent, although unemployment is very high and most Spaniards have seen a drop in their standard of living in recent years. According to a survey conducted by the charity Caritas, some 20 per cent of Spain's population (eight million people) live in poverty, defined as less than half the average income (around 80,000 ptas a month). Around 5 per cent of the population live in extreme poverty with an income below 20,000 ptas a month. There's a huge variation between average incomes in different regions of the country, e.g. GDP is an average of just 1.1m ptas a year in Extremadura and 1.2m ptas in Andalusia, compared with over 2m ptas a year in Catalonia and greater Madrid.

In the last few decades, inflation has brought the price of many goods and services in Spain in line with most other European countries. The devaluations of the peseta in recent years have increased prices of imported goods and have also made it more expensive for Spaniards (and anyone with an income in pesetas) to travel abroad. On the other hand, foreigners whose income is paid in currencies such as Deutschmarks or US$ (and £sterling in the last year) have seen their incomes rise considerably. Among the more expensive items in Spain are quality clothes (although fewer are needed in resort areas), cars and many consumer goods. However, many things remain cheaper than in northern European countries including property, rents, fresh food, alcohol, dining out and general entertainment.

With the exception of the major cities, where the higher cost of living is generally offset by higher salaries, the cost of living in Spain is lower than in most other western European countries, particularly in rural and coastal areas. Overall, the cost of living is around 10 per cent lower than in Britain, France and Germany and around the same as North America. A couple owning their home can 'survive' on a net income of as little as 50,000 ptas a month (many pensioners actually live on less) and most can live quite comfortably on an income of 100,000 ptas a month (excluding rent or mortgage payments). In fact many northern Europeans (particularly Scandinavians) who live modestly in Spain without over-doing the luxuries find that their cost of living is up to 50 per cent less than in their home country.

It's difficult to calculate an average cost of living in Spain as it depends on each individual's particular circumstances and life-style. The actual difference in your food bill will depend on what you eat and where you lived before arriving in Spain. Food in Spain costs around the same as in the USA, but is cheaper than in most northern European countries. Around 30,000 ptas will feed two adults for a month, including (inexpensive) wine, but excluding fillet steak, caviar and expensive imported foods. Shopping for expensive consumer goods such as hi-fi equipment, electronic goods, computers and photographic equipment in other European countries or North America can yield savings (you can also shop on the Internet),

A list of the approximate **MINIMUM** monthly major expenses for an average single person, couple or family with two children are shown in the table below, although many live on less (most people will agree that the figures are either too HIGH or too LOW). When calculating your cost of living, deduct the appropriate percentage for social security contributions and income tax (see page 295) from your gross salary. The numbers (in brackets) refer to the notes following the table.

MONTHLY COSTS (Ptas)

ITEM	Single	Couple	Couple with 2 children
Housing (1)	30,000	45,000	60,000
Food (2)	20,000	30,000	40,000
Utilities (3)	10,000	10,000	15,000
Leisure (4)	10,000	10,000	20,000
Transport (5)	7,500	7,500	10,000
Insurance (6)	5,000	7,500	10,000
Clothing	5,000	7,500	10,000
TOTAL	87,500	117,500	165,000

(1) Rent or mortgage payments for a modern or modernised apartment or house in an average small town or suburb, excluding major cities and other high-cost areas. The properties envisaged are a studio or one bedroom apartment for a single person, a two bedroom property for a couple, and a three bedroom property for a couple with two children.

(2) Doesn't include luxuries or liquid food (alcohol).

(3) Includes electricity, gas, water, telephone, cable or satellite TV, and heating and air-conditioning costs.

(4) Includes all entertainment, dining out, sports and vacation expenses, plus newspapers and magazines.

(5) Includes running costs for an average family car, plus third-party insurance, annual taxes, petrol, servicing and repairs, but exclude depreciation or credit costs.

(6) Includes 'voluntary' insurance such as inexpensive supplementary health insurance, household (building and contents), third party liability, travel, automobile breakdown and life insurance. Expensive private health insurance isn't included.

15.

LEISURE

If you want guaranteed sunshine, miles of sandy beaches, good food and wine, an abundant choice of entertainment and a wide variety of accommodation — and you don't want to pay the earth, then Spain is the place for you. Not for nothing do the Spanish claim to have 'Everything Under The Sun'! Although the vast majority of holidaymakers (and residents) come to Spain to recline on a beach, there's much (much) more to the country than the *costas* and a few islands. Spain offers infinite variety with something for everyone including magnificent beaches for sun-worshippers; spectacular unspoilt countryside for greens; a wealth of mountains and waterways for sports fans; a vibrant night-life for the jet set; bustling sophisticated cities for 'townies'; superb wine and cuisine for gourmets; a surfeit of art, culture and serious music for art lovers; numerous festivals and fiestas for inveterate party-goers; and tranquility for the stressed. Spain is a nation of *bon viveurs* with a insatiable thirst for fun and pleasure — nobody can throw a better party than the Spanish.

Tourism took off in Spain in the early 1960s, when tourist visas (for many) were abolished and Spain offered unrivalled cheap holidays in the sun. The number of visitors grew steadily throughout the next few decades and currently stands at around 65m a year (some 70 per cent from Britain, France, Germany and Italy). In 1996, Spain was the third most popular tourist destination (the most popular regions are the Balearics and the Canaries) in the world after the USA and France, and tourism accounts for some 10 per cent of both GDP and employment. However, although mass tourism saved Spain from economic disaster in the 1960s, it has also been responsible for destroying much of value and has irrevocably changed the face of the country. Spain has traditionally catered to the package-holiday market, although it's now attempting to attract a more up-market clientele.

Outside its beach resorts, Spain's main attractions are its lively cities, particularly Madrid and Barcelona, between which there's intense rivalry. Barcelona is Spain's most international and European city, elegant and compact, while Madrid is a sprawling metropolis and one of the world's most friendly and free-wheeling cities. Madrid has a wealth of world-class museums and art galleries and is blessed with magnificent parks and gardens, whereas Barcelona is an architectural masterpiece and one of the world's most handsome cities. Both offer superb cuisine and a bustling, vibrant night-life, and are just warming up when most other European cities are going to bed. Naturally there's much more to Spain than Madrid and Barcelona and the country has a wealth of other beautiful historic cities including Avila, Burgos, Cáceres, Cadiz, Cordoba, Cuenca, Gerona, Granada, Mérida, Palma de Mallorca, Pamplona, San Sebastian, Salamanca, Santander, Santiago de Compostela, Segovia, Seville, Toledo and Valencia, to name just a handful.

Spain's diverse regions accentuate a land of great culture with a colourful history; over the centuries it has been home to Phoenicians, Iberians, Romans, Visigoths and Moors, all of whom have left their mark and added to the country's heritage and culture. It's a land steeped in tradition with a wealth of artistic, cultural and historical treasures scattered throughout the length and breadth of the country. There are a surfeit of excellent art galleries and museums throughout Spain, and traditional fiestas and music festivals are staged in all regions and major towns throughout the year. One of the foremost attractions of Spain is its outstanding countryside (sadly enjoyed by few visitors). Spain's rugged beauty is unparalleled in Europe and harbours a wealth of unique flora, fauna and wildlife, and contains more (and larger) unspoilt areas than any other European country, many preserved as national parks and nature reserves.

Information regarding local events and entertainment is available from tourist offices and is published in local English-language newspapers and magazines. In most cities there are magazines and newspapers dedicated to entertainment, and free weekly or monthly programmes (e.g. *Guía del Ocio*) are published by tourist organisations in major cities and tourist resorts. Many towns produce a monthly cultural programme and some foreigners' departments also produce newsletters listing local cultural events. Many newspapers publish weekly magazines or supplements containing a detailed programme of local events and entertainment. Among the many excellent guides to Spain are Baedeker's Spain, the Michelin *Green Guide*, the *Blue Guide* (A&C Black), *Fodor's Spain*, and for budget travellers *Let's GO Spain and Portugal* (Macmillan) and *The Rough Guide to Spain*.

TOURIST OFFICES

Tourism is promoted at four levels in Spain: by the national Ministry of Commerce and Tourism (*Ministerio de Comercio y Turismo*) through overseas Spanish National Tourist Offices/SNTO (*Oficinas Nacionales de España de Turismo*), by regional and provincial governments and by local municipalities. The SNTO maintains offices in Argentina, Austria, Australia, Belgium, Brazil, Britain, Canada, Denmark, Finland, France, Germany (4), Italy (2), Japan, Mexico, the Netherlands, Norway, Portugal, Sweden, Switzerland (2) and the USA (4). There are tourist offices (*oficinas de turismo* or simply *turismos*) in all major cities and resort towns in Spain, which are operated by the SNTO in major cities and by provincial governments and local municipalities in other cities and towns. In cities, there's usually a variety of tourist information outlets, including tourist offices at airports and railway stations, and even street tourist guides during the peak season in some cities.

The quality of information dispensed by local tourist offices varies enormously, as do office opening hours. Offices in resort towns are usually open from around 0900 to 1300 or 1330 and from 1600 to 1900 or 2000 from Monday to Friday, and 0900 to 1300 on Saturday. In major cities, offices are open continuously, e.g. from 0900 to 1900 or 2000, Monday to Friday. Offices are usually closed on Sundays. Business hours vary depending on the time of year and are reduced in winter (except in ski resorts).

National, regional and local authorities publish a wealth of free brochures, pamphlets and beautifully detailed maps in many languages, available from SNTO offices worldwide and local tourist offices in Spain. The SNTO publish a free map (*mapa de comunicaciones*) of Spain and regional tourist authorities produce a local calendar of events. It's often advisable to collect information before arriving in Spain as local tourist offices often run out, and local and regional tourist offices don't provide information about places outside their area. Staff at tourist offices in major towns and resorts speak English and can recommend qualified multi-lingual guides. Note that Spanish tourist offices don't usually make hotel bookings, although there are hotel reservation offices at international airports and the main railway stations in major cities.

Tourist information is also available by telephone (*teléfono de información turística*) from 1000 to 2000 seven days a week (tel. (901) 300 600), with information available in English, French, German and Spanish (calls are charged at the reduced rate). You can write to local tourist offices in Spain for information, a list of which is available from SNTO offices. When writing for information you should include an international reply coupon and shouldn't expect a personal reply in English, although most office staff will understand a letter written in English.

HOTELS

There are thousands of hotels and hostelries in Spain, catering to all tastes and pockets, from sumptuous, grand luxury (*gran lujo*) five-star hotels to humble *pensiones* and *fondas*. If you want to rub shoulders with the real Spanish, start at the bottom rather than the top of the accommodation chain. Note, however, that it can be difficult to find good (or any) hotels in small villages and towns or on main roads in many areas, and Spain doesn't have a tradition of charming country hotels such as are found throughout Britain and France. Hotels (and other accommodation in Spain) are regulated by the government and all legally registered establishments must display a blue plaque showing their category and class in white letters, as listed below:

Category	Description
*H (*hotel*)	standard hotels as described on the following pages;
*HR (*hotel residencia*)	residential hotels without a restaurant;
*HA (*hotel apartamento*)	self-contained apartments or chalets with kitchenettes; they offer reasonable weekly or monthly rates but little service;
*RA (*residencia apartamento*)	similar to ordinary apartments except that they are mainly let for short periods to tourists and may provide breakfast;
*M (*motel*)	roadside lodgings for short stays, located on or close to motorways and other main roads;
**Hs (*hostal*)	basic accommodation and usually family-run; no public rooms, although a TV may be provided in the dining room/lounge; may provide meals;
**HsR (*hostal-residencia*)	similar to a hostel but usually for long-stay guests and without a restaurant;
**P (*pensión*)	a guesthouse with basic accommodation, possibly offering full board only;
CH (*casa de huéspedes*)	a guesthouse which is usually a private home with rooms to let (no star rating) and similar to *hospedajes* (literally 'lodgings');
F (*fonda*)	a small inn offering basic accommodation (no star rating).

*   one to five stars

** one to three stars

Many of the above categories of accommodation including hostels, pensions, guesthouses and *fondas* are described under **Budget Accommodation** on page 325. Residential hotels are generally cheaper than standard hotels and offer fewer services and public lounges. Residential hotels and hostals don't provide a restaurant service, but may offer breakfast or a cafeteria service. Hostals often provide better accommodation than inexpensive hotels and better value for money (a three-star hostal is roughly equivalent to a one-star hotel).

Hotels are officially classified with one to five star (*estrellas*) by the Ministry of Tourism, depending on the facilities they offer, rather than their price (although they are priced accordingly). Note that hotels within the same category can vary considerably in quality and comfort, and that ratings depend on the area, as all regions administer star ratings in different ways. A *rough* guide to room rates is shown below:

Star Rating	Price Range ('000s ptas)	Class
*****GL	50+++	great luxury
*****	15-65++	luxury
****	8-30	top class
***	4-20	very comfortable
**	3-12	comfortable
*	2-6	basic

The prices quoted above are for a double room with bath for one night (prices in Spain are almost always quoted per room and *not* per person). Value added tax (IVA) at 7 per cent is added to all hotel bills. In the Canaries, Ceuta and Melilla, a local tax (IGIC or ITE) of 4 per cent is added to bills. Prices should be quoted inclusive of tax and service charges. Room rates don't usually include breakfast, which usually costs 800 to 900 ptas for continental breakfast, and it's illegal to be forced to pay for it (it's usually better value at a local bar or café). Hotels are closely regulated by the government (except for the half-built ones) and room prices must be posted in the lobby and in rooms, include seasonal rates, and state whether they include tax and service.

Rates vary according to location as well as category, with hotels located in large towns and cities, coastal resorts and spa towns being the most expensive. Hotels are expensive in major cities such as Madrid and Barcelona, where rates are similar to other European cities. However, inexpensive hotels abound in most towns, where a single room (*habitación individual*) can usually be found for 1,500 to 2,500 ptas and a double (*habitación doble*) for 2,000 to 3,000 ptas (usually without a private bath or shower). Inexpensive accommodation is mostly found in the old quarter of town centres, often close to the main square or cathedral. Hotel rates vary considerably depending on the region and season and it's often worthwhile haggling over rates, particularly if you're on your own or during the low season. As in most countries, single rooms are rare and only marginally cheaper than doubles (they usually cost around 20 per cent less).

A double room usually contains two single beds, rather than a double bed (*cama matrimonial*), which should be requested if required. Many hotels have 'family' rooms for three or four guests at greatly reduced rates, or provide extra beds for children in a double room free of charge. An extra bed for an adult normally costs around 35 per cent of the double room rate or 60 per cent of the cost of a single room. Half and full board is common at hotels with restaurants, although it's usually restricted to guests staying three or more days.

Minimum and maximum rates are fixed according to the facilities and the season, although there's no season in major cities. In the Canaries and winter resorts, low season may be in summer (there's usually not much difference in rates). Rates are considerably higher in tourist areas during the high season (*temporada alta*) of July and August (and Easter), when rooms at any price are hard to find. On the other hand, outside the main season, particularly in winter, many hotels offer low half or full board rates, when a double room with bath including dinner (buffet) and breakfast can be had for 5,000 ptas for two. Many hotels have lower rates at weekends and special rates for groups, and some chains provide discount cards for regular clients reducing rates by 15 to 25 per cent.

It's always advisable to make a reservation (*reserva*) during the high season months of July and August, on public holiday weekends, and during international trade fairs, conventions, festivals and fiestas. At most other times it's usually unnecessary to book, particularly in rural areas and small towns. It's advisable to book at least two to three months in advance for summer in major cities (such as Madrid and Barcelona), and around two weeks in advance at other times. An hotel is required to retain a booked room only until around 1800, after which it can be let to someone else (unless you have paid in advance). If you plan to arrive later than this, you should advise an hotel of your estimated arrival time. Children and animals are usually welcome, although you should check when booking. A guide to hotels (*Viajando con Perros*) accepting dogs and other animals is published by Seiquer SL, Paseo de la Castellana, 62, 28046 Madrid (tel. (91) 411 0862). Note that staff and owners of small rural hotels don't usually speak English or other foreign languages.

You're required by law to show your passport or identity card (it isn't retained) and complete a registration form when registering at an hotel. If you're staying in a small hotel and wish to leave early in the morning, it's best to pay your bill (*cuenta*) the evening before and tell the proprietor when you plan to leave. Otherwise you may find the hotel locked up like Fort Knox and no-one around to let you out. Check out time is usually 1200 at the latest and if you stay any later you may be charged for an extra day. If required, hotels will store your baggage free of charge until later in the day.

You should always be shown a room. No Spaniard would dream of accepting a room without inspecting it first, especially the beds, which are often hard or lumpy and too short for anyone above average height. Beds usually have long, hard, sausage-shaped bolsters (*cabezales*) serving as pillows and running across a double bed, with the bottom sheet running around them and substituting for pillow-cases. Many foreigners find bolsters uncomfortable, although they are quite happily used by most Spanish guests. There may be pillows (*almohadas*) in the wardrobe, which like bolsters usually have no slips and are placed under the bottom sheet. Duvets aren't common in Spain, even in winter, when sheets (*sábanas*) and blankets (*mantas*) are normally used.

Most hotels are centrally heated in winter, although cheaper hotels are often miserly with the heating and hostels often lack heating altogether. Air-conditioning is generally found in 3 to 5-star hotels only (and is a blessing in summer). If you're staying in a city, it's advisable to ask for a quiet room, i.e. nowhere near the discotheque, bar or restaurant. With the exception of modern and luxury hotels, hotels rooms in Spain aren't always equipped with a radio or TV, irrespective of the price. Satellite TV is provided in top class hotels. All top class hotels provide tea and coffee-making facilities; a radio and colour TV; bath (*baño*) and shower (*ducha*) with a bidet; telephone; room service; and a mini-bar or refrigerator. Drinks from an hotel mini-bar are expensive, but they are handy for storing your own food and drinks. Many top class hotels also provide sports facilities such as tennis, squash, swimming pools (mandatory in summer), gymnasium (there may be a fee), billiards/pool, sauna and solarium, plus bars, restaurants, discos, cabaret and a TV/video room with big-screen video. In many mid-range 'tourist' hotels, all meals are served buffet-style. Luxury hotels often have excellent convention facilities.

Paradors: One national chain of hotels rating a special mention are *Paradores Nacionales de Turismo* (usually referred to simply as *paradores*), a state-owned chain of hotels housed in historic buildings such as castles, palaces, convents and monasteries, plus a few modern buildings with swimming pools and sports facilities. There are some 85 *paradores*, most in the three or four star category, providing comfortable (even luxurious) rooms and excellent regional cuisine and wines. They are expensive by Spanish standards, with rates between 8,000 and 15,000 ptas, although prices are lower outside the high season when they also have special offers ('golden days') for those aged over 60 staying a minimum of two nights. Reservations can be made through agents in many countries. For a free catalogue contact *Paradores Nacionales de Turismo*, Central de Reservas, C/Velázquez, 18, Apartado de Correos 50043, 28001 Madrid (tel. (91) 435 9700). You can become a 'friend of paradores' (*amigo de paradores*) and receive a complimentary drink on arrival, free garaging for your car and one point for every 500 ptas you spend (which can be exchanged for free accommodation).

Most guide books contain a selection of hotels and there are numerous Spanish hotel guides. The most comprehensive hotel (and restaurant) guide is the *Michelin Red Guide España Portugal*, which includes both the humblest and poshest of establishments, and lists weekly closing days and seasonal opening. Lists of hotels and other accommodation are published by local municipalities, and provinces and regions also publish hotel guides. The SNTO publish the *Guía de Hoteles*, containing every classified hotel and hostal in Spain (available from local bookshops).

Note that all official establishments offering accommodation must maintain a complaints book (see page 394) and you can also make a complaint to the local tourist office, who may intercede on your behalf to resolve a dispute.

BUDGET ACCOMMODATION

There's a variety of budget accommodation in Spain including hostels, pensions, guesthouses, *fondas*, and rooms and lodgings (see list on page 322). *Fondas* are village inns with basic facilities and rooms, usually located over the bar. The distinction between *fondas*, *pensiones*, *casas de huéspedes* (guesthouses), and *hospedajes* (lodgings) is often blurred. *Pensiones*, *casas de huéspedes* and *hospedajes* are similar to guesthouses or lodgings and usually prefer long-stay guests (*estables*). *Fondas* and *pensiones* are slightly upmarket of *casas de huéspedes* and *hospedajes*, and supposedly serve food (some may not offer rooms without full board), although this isn't always the case. Hostals (*hostales*) offer similar accommodation to hotels and are the poshest of budget accommodation with wash basins in all rooms, but they don't usually offer full board.

Spain doesn't have bed and breakfast accommodation as such, although some private homes (*casas particulares*) offer bed and breakfast off the beaten tourist track, and there are 'bed and breakfast' organisations in cities and large towns. Beds (*camas*) and rooms (*habitaciones*) are advertised in the windows of private houses, and above bars and roadside restaurants such as *ventas*, perhaps with the phrase *camas y comidas* (beds and meals). They often provide the cheapest of all accommodation (except for youth hostels) and are usually spotlessly clean. In country areas there are rural cottages and farmhouses (*casas rurales*, *casas rústicas* and *casas de labranza*), officially referred to as *agroturismo*, providing the opportunity to experience the Spanish country way of life and make contact with Spanish families. A guide (*Vacaciones en Casas de Labranza*) is available from the SNTO.

Other budget accommodation includes rooms in university dormitories (*colegios mayores* and *residencias*) during the summer holidays and rooms in monasteries. Monasteries offer basic lodgings in real working monasteries where prayer, silence and seclusion are the order of the day (plus a large helping of beauty, serenity, superb architecture and perhaps even Gregorian chant). They accept guests of both sexes or men only and payment is often in the form of a donation (e.g. 2,000 ptas per night) rather than a fixed fee. There are set meal times and reservations must usually be made in advance. Many monasteries have hospices or guest quarters (*hospederías*). If you're a fan of Gregorian chant, you may wish to visit the monastery of Santo Domingo de Silos (Burgos), although you will need to book 'years' in advance since the astounding success of their recording of Gregorian chant.

The cost of budget accommodation varies considerably, although the cheapest is around 3,000 ptas per person, per day for full board (*pensión completa*) consisting of breakfast, lunch and dinner. Half board (*pensión media*) may also be offered at a slightly reduced rate. Rates at rural cottages and farmhouses usually range from 1,500 to 3,000 ptas for a single or double room. Hostels charge from 1,500 to 3,000 ptas for singles and 2,000 to 4,000 ptas for doubles, plus an extra 500 ptas or so for a room with a bath or shower. The cheapest accommodation is generally found at *casas de huéspedes* and *hospedajes*. If a room doesn't have a private bathroom, which usually contains a shower rather than a bath, you may be charged an additional fee to use a communal bathroom. As with most accommodation in Spain, large discounts are usually offered for long stays during winter.

When booking budget accommodation you should always enquire about the exact location and the facilities provided, as standards vary from clean and homely abodes to 'fleapits' unfit for human habitation. Note that budget accommodation is often basic, usually lacks heating and guests are often subject to curfews. There's usually a wide variation in the standard of accommodation of establishments within the same category. Note that budget establishments seldom accept credit cards and 7 per cent IVA is added to all bills. A list of budget accommodation can usually be obtained from local tourist offices and rooms to let can also be found by asking at local bars and restaurants. When staying in budget accommodation, it's advantageous if you speak some Spanish as your hosts may not speak any foreign languages.

YOUTH HOSTELS

There are around 165 youth hostels (*albergues juveniles*) in Spain (around 100 open all year round, 65 in summer only), operated by the Spanish youth hostel association, *Red Española de Albergues Juveniles (REAJ)*, and providing the cheapest accommodation in Spain. IYHF membership is usually necessary and costs around 2,000 ptas from REAJ offices, offices of Viajes TIVE and other travel agencies. Cards can also be issued at some hostels.

Most hostels are housed in old buildings without modern plumbing or air-conditioning, and possibly no heating in winter in the south of the country. They are usually situated out of town, packed with schoolchildren, and residents are subject to curfews which excludes guests from making the most of Spain's extensive night-life. If you don't have a booking, you should arrive early (e.g. between 0800 and 0900) at some hostels, particularly those in Madrid, and you should always book for the peak months of July and August. Most hostels allow a maximum stay of around three days. However, unless you're a dedicated youth hosteller you may find they aren't worth bothering with as there's a wealth of budget accommodation throughout Spain and hostels can be more expensive than a *fonda* or *casa de huéspedes* for couples and groups. Costs vary depending on the actual hostel, although typical costs per person are as follows:

Service	Typical Prices (Ptas)	
	Under 26	Over 26
full pension	2,500	3,000
half pension	2,000	2,250
bed & breakfast	1,250	1,700
dinner	900	900
bed	1,000	1,200
sheet rental	400	400

For further information contact *Red Española de Albergues Juveniles/REAJ*, C/José Ortega y Gasset, 71, Apartado 208, 28006 Madrid (tel. (91) 401 1300). In mountain areas the Spanish Mountaineering Federation (*Federación Española de Montañismo*, C/Alberto Aguilera, 3, 28015 Madrid (tel. (91) 445 1382) maintain over 200 alpine huts (*refugios*). They are simple, inexpensive, dormitory huts for climbers and hikers, and are usually equipped with bunks and a basic kitchen only.

SELF-CATERING

There's a wealth of self-catering accommodation in Spain which is extremely popular, particularly with Spanish families. It includes apartments, town houses, villas, farmhouses (*casas de labranza*) and *fincas* (country houses). Note that standards vary considerably, from dilapidated, ill-equipped apartments to luxury villas with every modern convenience. You don't always get what you pay for and some properties bear little resemblance to their descriptions. Unless a company or property has been highly recommended, it's best to book through a reputable organisation such as Interhome or a tourist agency. The SNTO publish a guide to self-catering accommodation entitled *apartamentos turísticos*. Tourist apartments (*apartamentos turísticos*) in Spain are graded by one to four keys as show below:

Luxury (four keys): a top-quality building in a good location with air-conditioning, heating, 24-hour hot water, parking, reception and information desk, private telephone, bar service, and a restaurant or cafeteria. Lifts are provided if the building is higher than two floors.

First-Class (three keys): a quality building with heating and hot water, reception and information desk, telephone to reception, and lifts if the building is higher than three floors.

Second-Class (two keys): well-built structure with heating, hot water, a telephone at the reception desk and on each floor, and lifts if the building is higher than three floors.

Third-Class (one key): Hot water, at least a shower in all apartments and a lift if the building is higher than three floors.

Most accommodation is let for a minimum of seven nights (except for public holiday weekends such as Easter). The cost per night usually ranges from 2,500 ptas for a studio (sleeping two to four persons) in low season, to 6,000 per night in high season

(July-August). A two bedroom apartment or town house (sleeping four to six) costs from around 6,000 ptas per night in low season to 12,000 ptas per night in high season, although rates depend on the location and the quality of the accommodation. Rates usually include linen, gas and electricity, although heating in winter, e.g. gas or electric heaters, is usually charged extra. Note that it's illegal to install electricity coin meters in rental accommodation in Spain. **Beware of gas heaters with faulty ventilation ducts as they are responsible for a number of deaths in self-catering accommodation due to gas poisoning.** Extra beds, cots and TVs (e.g. 500 ptas per night or 3,000 ptas per week) can usually be rented.

In Madrid and other cities there are luxury serviced apartments costing around 7,500 to 20,000 ptas a night (50,000 to 120,000 a week) for a studio or one bedroom apartment sleeping two and 20,000 to 25,000 ptas a night (125,000 to 150,000 ptas a week) for a two or three bedroom apartment sleeping four to six. IVA at 7 per cent is added to bills and may be included in quoted rates. Note that pets are usually prohibited. During the low season, which may extend from October to May, rates may drop to as low as 40,000 to 60,000 ptas a month for a two-bedroom apartment, although there's usually a minimum let of two months. Naturally you can rent a wide variety of villas and luxury properties throughout Spain, the cost of which can be astronomical.

Properties in resort areas always have a swimming pool (shared for apartments and town houses), in use from around May to October, and most are also located close to a beach. Some properties have an indoor heated swimming pool and other facilities such as tennis courts. Most holiday apartments are fairly basic, often with tiny kitchens and bathrooms (perhaps equipped with a shower only), and have a combined lounge/dining room, a patio or balcony and are fairly well equipped. If you need special items such as a cot or high chair, you should mention it when booking.

Properties are generally well-stocked with cooking utensils, crockery and cutlery, although you should check before shopping. Some things that may come in handy are a decent cook's knife, a teapot (if you make tea in a pot), egg cups, a pepper mill, a filter coffee machine and a few of your favourite foods such as tea, instant coffee, and relishes and condiments you cannot live without. Most people take a few essential foods and supplies with them and buy fresh food on arrival.

It's essential to book during the high season and over holiday weekends (e.g. at Easter). There's usually a 25 per cent deposit with the balance payable on arrival. Normally you must arrive by 1700 on your first day and vacate the property by noon on your day of departure. Outside the high season of July and August, self-catering accommodation can usually be found on the spot by asking around in bars and restaurants or by obtaining a list from the local tourist office.

CARAVANS & CAMPING

Spain has over 800 campsites (*campings, campamentos*), two thirds of which are located on the coast, with a total capacity of over 400,000 places. Campsites are inspected and approved by the Spanish tourist authority and classified under four categories L (luxury), 1st, 2nd and 3rd class (1^a, 2^a or 3^a), according to their amenities. Many camps have a small capacity of 300 to 400 people and some cater exclusively to naturists.

Even the most basic camp grounds must have 24-hour surveillance; a fenced area; unlimited drinking water; first aid and fire prevention; toilets and showers (there may be a fee for hot showers); washing and washing-up facilities; and garbage collection. Most camps also provide a range of other services and facilities that may include a post office, playground, currency exchange, cable TV, telephones, safes, laundries, bottled gas, electricity/water hookups for caravans and motor caravans, swimming pools, tennis courts and other sports facilities, shops, supermarket, hairdresser, disco, restaurants and bars.

All campgrounds post their daily fees (usually from noon until noon the following day) at the entrance, which are calculated per car or caravan, per person and per tent. Fees are around 350 to 700 ptas per person a day plus 300 to 600 ptas for a car and around the same for a caravan or camping space (although fees can be as high as 2,000 ptas a day at a de-luxe site). There are reductions of around 20 per cent a day for children, e.g. aged from three to 10 years. Motor caravans are charged between 700 and 1,300 ptas a day and electricity hook-ups cost an additional 350 to 400 ptas a day. VAT (IVA) at 7 per cent must be added to all fees. Some sites charge extra for hot showers, sports (such as tennis courts) and the use of ironing facilities or a freezer. Most campsites offer special rates outside the high season of June to August, although many are open only during the 'summer' season, e.g. April or June to September. It's advisable to book during the high season, particularly for campsites situated in coastal areas in July and August. Note that many campsites don't accept dogs.

An international camping carnet isn't necessary in Spain when camping at registered sites, although it's required when camping 'wild'. However, it's advisable to have one as it's accepted as proof of identification by campsites. Before camping in open country you should check that wild camping is permitted and obtain permission from the owner of private land. Wild camping is often prohibited during the dry season due to the danger of fires or because there's an official campsite in the immediate vicinity (you aren't permitted to camp within one kilometre of an official campsite). Camping is forbidden on beaches, river banks and mountains, and you can be fined for camping illegally.

The Spanish Federation of Camping Sites (*Federación Española de Empresarios de Camping y Centros de Vacaciones*, C/General Oraa, 52 - 2° D, 28006 Madrid, tel. (91) 564 2199) publishes an annual guide (*Guía de Campings*) listing sites (by region), with illustrations and plans. The *Real Automóvil Club de España (RACE)* publish the *Guía Ibérica de Campings* for Spain and Portugal. Reservations can be made directly with campsites and through the Spanish Federation of Camping Sites. The SNTO publish a free camping map (*Mapa de Campings*) showing all official campsites and free regional and provincial maps are available from local tourist offices. If you're a newcomer to camping and caravanning, it's advantageous to join a camping or caravan club which provide useful information (e.g. the best guides to campsites), approved sites, caravan and travel insurance, travel services, rallies, holidays, reservations and a range of other benefits.

FESTIVALS & FIESTAS

Festivals and fiestas are an important part of cultural and social life in Spain, where over 3,000 are celebrated each year. The Spanish are inveterate revellers and almost every village and town has its annual fair (*feria*), lasting from a few days to a few weeks. They are usually held on the local saint's day (*patrón* or *patrona*), appropriately marked in red on Spanish calendars, when an effigy of the saint is paraded around the town in a procession. Village festivals often include a pilgrimage (*romería*) to a local shrine on horseback and in horse-drawn wagons, where a grand celebration is held. Foreigners are usually welcome to join in, although you may need an invitation to take part in some religious festivals. The first national celebration of the year is *Martes de Carnaval* (Spain's *Mardi Gras*), held in February and best experienced in Cadiz or Tenerife. Holy Week (*Semana Santa*) is a major tourist attraction in many cities and towns, particularly in Seville and the rest of Andalusia. The main attractions are huge religious processions with ornate floats depicting scenes from the Passion and masked men decked out in ghostly masked costumes with pointed hats (imitated by the Ku Klux Klan in the USA). Other major festivals include Corpus Christi in May or June; the feast day of Spain's patron saint, Santiago, on 25th July; and the Assumption of the Virgin (*la Asunción*) on 15th August. There are also numerous local fiestas for harvests, deliverance from the Moors, safe return from the sea, plus a variety of other obscure occasions (the Spanish will use any excuse to have a party!).

Essential ingredients for a fiesta include costumes, processions, music, dancing and feasting. Processions often include huge papier mâché statues called giants or bigheads (*gigantones* or *cabezudos*), which takes many months to create and may be ritually burnt during the festival (the most famous is the *fallas* fiesta held in Valencia in March). The largest festivals include bullfights, flamenco, funfairs, circuses, fireworks, plays, concerts, music recitals and competitions. In Extremadura, the Basque lands and Navarre, summer fiestas often feature loose bulls stampeding through the streets (*el encierro*). The most famous is the running of the bulls in Pamplona during the *Fiesta de San Fermín* (although there are many others), when the slow of foot and foolhardy (usually foreigners) are often injured or even occasionally killed. A *vaquilla* is the running of bulls, cows or calves through the streets of a town and includes the opportunity to 'fight' the animals. Another tradition, called the *toro del aguardiente*, is to set a table with a bottle of brandy and glasses in the middle of a bullring; those wishing to enjoy a drink must risk being tossed by a small bull (some people will do anything for a free drink!).

There's rarely any violence or serious crime at Spanish festivals and fiestas, which are a great occasion for all the family (children often stay up all night), and any drunkenness or hooliganism is likely to be among foreigners. Pickpockets and bag snatchers are, however, fairly common at major festivals, which tend to attract thieves in droves. Dates for most festivals are fluid and when they fall on a Tuesday or Thursday the day is usually 'bridged' with the preceding or following weekend to create a four-day holiday. Check exact dates with the SNTO and local tourist offices in Spain. The SNTO publish a number of brochures about festivals and fiestas including *Celebrating in Spain* and *Festivals of Special Interest to Tourists*.

FLAMENCO

Flamenco consists of a flamboyant dance accompanied by guitar music and song (*cante*), the heart of the art of flamenco, which at its best is the true classical performance art of Spain. It has been referred to as the soul of Spain and like bullfighting is an essential part of the country's culture and traditions. The history of flamenco, in particular the origin of the name (literally 'Flemish'), is obscure, although it's believed to have originated in the 18th century with the gypsies of Andalusia. Its songs of oppression, lament and bitter romance were taken up by the peasants of Andalusia and spread throughout Spain in the 20th century as they migrated in search of jobs.

Flamenco consists of two main groups of songs, the *cante chico* (small song), which is lively and cheerful, and the *cante jondo* (big or deep song, the genesis of flamenco), lamenting love, sadness, death, hardship and the struggle for life. The classical flamenco repertoire consists of some 60 songs and dances. Castanets, although symbols of Spain to many foreigners, are rarely used by the best dancers. The best flamenco singers tend to live tormented lives and many die of alcohol and drug abuse, including the revered El Camarón de la Isla who died in 1992 (fans are still mourning his loss). Antonio Ruiz Soler, Spain's most famous flamenco dancer, died in 1996 aged 74. In the last few years flamenco has increasingly been blended with music from other cultures such as the salsa, rumba and blues, which is known as the 'new flamenco' (*nuevo flamenco*) or 'flamenco fusion' (one of the most famous and controversial 'fusion' dancers is Joaquín Cortes).

Flamenco has been shamelessly exploited by the Spanish tourist industry and it's commonly performed in commercial tourist shows advertised as 'genuine flamenco fiestas', which although enjoyable are a pale imitation of the real thing. Generally the more commercially orientated the performance, the less authentic it's likely to be. In fact the idea of a staged performance is alien to the whole concept of flamenco, which is traditionally informal and spontaneous. Real flamenco is said to evoke the indescribable quality of *duende* (spirit or demon) that possesses performers and contains a primitive, ecstatic allure that embraces listeners.

Real flamenco can be experienced in specialist bars and small members-only clubs (*peñas*) in Andalusia and other regions of Spain, where unappreciative foreigners are rarely welcome or invited (although it's possible to find authentic places where guests are admitted). The best chance most foreigners have of experiencing authentic flamenco is at one of the big summer festivals held in Cadiz, Jerez, Granada, Malaga and Seville or during festivals and fiestas in small villages off the tourist track. Many books have been written about flamenco including *The Art of Flamenco* by DE Pohren (Musical News Services Ltd.), *In Search of the Firedance* by James Woodall (Sinclair-Stevenson), *Flamenco* by Hoger Mende (Editorial Castillejo) and *Framenco Deep Song* by Timothy Mitchell (Yale University Press).

BULLFIGHTING

A book about Spain wouldn't be complete without a 'few' words about bullfighting (*la lidia*), commonly referred to as the *fiesta nacional* ('bullfighting' is actually a poor translation). Foreigners generally either love or loathe bullfights and it provokes controversy even among Spaniards. To many it's a barbaric and sadistic blood sport with no merit whatsoever and should be banned. An article about bullfighting in the expatriate press is guaranteed to raise the hackles of many readers and it receives a vitriolic press from most foreigners. However, there are a surprising number of foreign bullfight *aficionados* (fans), many of whom are every bit as enthusiastic as their Spanish counterparts. It's claimed by those opposed to bullfighting that over 80 per cent of Spaniards are against it, although it remains highly popular with over 40m paying spectators a year and top fights being shown live on television (plus endless repeats). It is, however, banned in the Canary Islands and in a few towns in mainland Spain.

Each individual must make a personal decision about the morality of bullfighting. If you're opposed to it on moral and ethical grounds, it's best not to go as you certainly won't enjoy it and may well be distressed. If you feel you ought to watch it at least once, it's advisable to watch a bullfight on TV before deciding whether to see one in the flesh.

If you decide to go to a fight, you should *never* cheer for the bull, particularly if it has gored the matador, otherwise you can expect to be the object of some hostility from the crowd.

Bullfighting isn't considered a sport in Spain, but an art (the art of tauromachy), and is reported in the arts and culture section of newspapers. It's certainly not a contest as there can be only one 'winner', although *toreros* can and do get killed every year (in addition to some 8,000 bulls) and even some spectators (*espontáneos*) who jump into the ring to try their hand. Aficionados hail it as a spectacle encompassing colour, tradition, excitement, pageantry, beauty, danger, bravery, skill, blood and high drama. It's an essential part of Spain's heritage and culture and has probably had more influence on Spanish consciousness than any other phenomenon in the last few centuries. It's considered an essential part of fiestas in any town, irrespective of size, where main squares are turned into temporary bullrings in towns without a permanent bullring.

History: Andalusia is the birthplace of bullfighting, where Ronda is regarded as the cradle of modern bullfighting, and many of Spain's top bullfighters come from this region (in addition to most bulls). Pedro Romero (immortalised by Goya in his painting *Tauromaquia*) who developed the classical style used today is considered the father of modern bullfighting and ended his career in the 1820s at the aged of 72, having killed over 5,500 bulls without once being gored. Throughout the last two centuries there have been many famous *toreros* including Rafael Gómez (*El Gallo*), Manolete (Manuel Rodríquez Sánchez), Joselito, Espartero and Juan Belmonte. Many bullfighters have been hailed by their supporters as the greatest who ever lived including Manolete, Joselito and Belmonte. Among modern bullfighters one of the most famous was Manuel Benítez (El Cordobés), who made his name in the 1960s and 1970s. Over the years there have even been a few American and English bullfighters and even women are beginning to make their mark in the ring (after being banned during Franco's dictatorship). However, women find it hard to gain acceptance in what is the world's most *machista* 'profession', and some of Spain's top male bullfighters have refused to share a bill with Cristina Sánchez, Spain's leading female *torero*.

Season: The official bullfighting season runs from 19th March until 12th October, although fights are held outside these dates. The most popular day is Sunday and in central and southern Spain and Barcelona, bullfights are held on almost every Sunday and public holiday from Easter to November and during festivals. The most famous bullfighting fiestas are staged in Seville during the April Fair; San Isidro in Madrid (May) with 23 consecutive days of *corridas*; San Fermín in Pamplona (July); Valencia's *fallas* (March) and *fiesta* (July); Granada's Corpus Christi celebrations (June); Bilbao's *Semana Grande* (August); and Zaragossa's *Feria de Pilar* (October).

Bullrings: There are some 500 permanent bullrings in Spain. The most famous bullrings, which are almost 'always' exactly circular (although a few are square), are Madrid's *Las Ventas* (the biggest in Spain seating 25,000), Seville's *La Maestranza* and Pamplona, followed by Barcelona, Bilbao and Valencia. There are also rings in many smaller towns including the resort towns of Benidorm, Marbella and Torremolinos. Apart from Madrid and Barcelona, other towns holding over 10 *corridas* a year include Malaga, Seville, Valencia and Zaragossa.

A bullfight is held between 1600 and 1800 or 1700 and 1900 depending on the heat and time of the year, and is one of the few things in Spain that starts on time. Sometimes two fights are held on the same day, one in the afternoon and another in the evening. Bullfights are announced by posters stating whether it's a full bullfight with senior *matadores* (*corrida de toros*) and mature bulls, or a novice bullfight with younger bulls and junior *toreros* (a *novillada, gran novillada* or *corrida de novillos*). Matadors are listed on posters in order of seniority. Note that the posters sold outside bullrings as souvenirs rarely advertise the current fight and most feature famous dead or retired bullfighters.

Tickets: Ticket (*billetes*) prices vary considerably depending on the bullring, the bullfighters and the occasion. Tickets for small *corridas* usually cost from 1,000 to 15,000 ptas, although tickets for the cheaper seats in a *novillada* are usually less than 1,000 ptas. Tickets for top fights may be sold by touts (scalpers) for up to 10 times their face value. Note that ticket prices are generally high in tourist areas (e.g. Mijas and Puerto Banus near Marbella), typically between 5,000 and 15,000 ptas, although locals usually pay nothing like the prices charged to tourists. Seats are usually designated as being in the shade (*sombra*) or the sun (*sol*), with shaded seats being more expensive. Sun and shade (*sol y sombra*) seats are those that become shaded as the fight progresses. The closer you are to the action, the more expensive the seat, with ringside barrier (*barrera*) seats in the shade being the most expensive. Some rings have seats designated as *contrabarrera* which are the next rows to the barrier seats. The seats behind the ringside seats are called *tendidos* and may be divided into high (*alto*) and low (*bajo*) areas. The cheapest seats in the highest rows at the back are *gradas* or simply *filas*, costing around 1,000 ptas in a large ring. Cushions (*almohadillas*) can be rented for around 40 ptas and are essential as the 'seats' are usually stone or concrete. Children aren't admitted to bullfights.

Tickets show the section name and number (e.g. *tendido* 10), the row (*fila*) and the seat (*asiento*) number. It's best to purchase tickets from the box office (*taquilla*) at the bullring or at an official ticket office. Tickets sold by agents have a surcharge, e.g. a 20 per cent commission in Madrid. You should avoid buying tickets from touts, who will often tell you that bullfights are sold out when they aren't.

Participants: The official title of the bullfighter who kills the bull is *matador de toros* (literally killer of bulls), although it isn't used to refer to a bullfighter, who's called a *torero*, which also refers to anyone who fights a bull including *picadores* and *banderilleros*. Bullfighters are never called *toreadores*. A matador's assistants are called *peones* (footmen) and his team a *cuadrilla*, consisting of three *banderilleros* and two horsemen (*picadores*). Other players in the cast include *monosabios* (wise monkeys) who guide the picador's horses, *mulilleros* who drag the dead bull out with a team of mules or a tractor, and *areneros* who tidy the sand.

Dress: A matador is usually distinguished from his assistants by his satin suit of lights (*traje de luces*), which is usually decorated in gold; assistants usually wear suits decorated in silver. A matador's suit is hand-made, taking six people a month to create and costing from 250,000 to 400,000 ptas (the whole outfit usually often costs over 500,000 ptas). The most popular colours are red, black, green, white and blue. Yellow is never worn (even by spectators) as it's considered to be bad luck (toreros are highly superstitious). The suit is worn with a white shirt; narrow black tie; a red, green or black sash knotted at the waist; pink, knee-high stockings; black ballet-style slippers; and a black astrakhan *montera* (a kind of two-cornered hat). One final adornment is the pig-tail (*coleta*) which denotes a matador and is clipped to the back of the head (it's symbolically cut in the ring when a matador retires). The matador's cape (*capote de paseo*) is worn only in the parade (*paseíllo*) before a fight commences and is then hung on the fence in front of a friend or a distinguished spectator.

Novices: A novice bullfighter is called a *novillero* and fights not in a *corrida*, but in a *novillada* with young bulls (*novillos*). There are also *novilladas sin picadores* (a novillada without picadores), which aren't necessary to weaken young bulls, when nine bulls may be killed by nine different novillos. Novices don't dress in a suit of lights but in Andalusian riding clothes (*traje corto*) consisting of a black outfit of short waistcoat, tight-fitting trousers, high-heeled boots and a broad black hat. Young bullfighters often take chances in their eagerness to please and be recognised, and are frequently tossed or even killed. Most novices learn their trade in bullfighting schools (*escuelas de tauromaquia*) such as the Royal School of Bullfighting in Seville. To join the senior ranks and become a fully-fledged matador de toros, a novice must take his *alternativa*, a bullfight where a matador symbolically cedes the tools of the trade (the cape and sword) to the novice, thus giving him the right to kill fully grown bulls.

Programme: Each bullfight (*corrida*) comprises six 'brave' bulls (*seis toros bravos*) and three matadors (hopefully also brave), each of whom fights two bulls. The bulls are specially bred 'fighting' bulls, usually from the same bloodline (*ganadería*), and are at least four years old (*cuatreños*) and weigh between 500 and 800kg. They must never have faced a man on foot before they enter the bullring, otherwise they may charge the man rather than the cape. The selection of bulls (*sorteo*) is determined by drawing lots on the morning of the corrida. Bullfighting is allegedly the subject of widespread corruption, including weak and under-size bulls, drugged bulls, manipulated drawing of bulls and trimmed or shaved horns. Shaving a bull's horns (which is actually done by cutting through the horn with a hacksaw) completely disorients a bull and has been compared to pulling out a boxer's fingernails before a fight. Some experts believe that 80 per cent of bulls have their horns shaved. An attempt by the authorities to stamp out this practice by checking the horns after fights rather than several hours before them (after which they are shaved?) led to a strike by toreros in 1997.

The toreros perform in order of seniority with the senior matador going first and fourth, the second-ranked matador second and fifth and the least experienced fighting third and sixth. If a matador is gored and unable to continue, the senior matador must take his place and finish the fight. Each bullfight (*lidia*) is divided into three distinctive stages (*suertes*) or thirds (*tercios*) and lasts for around 20 minutes. A corrida starts with a parade of all the contestants and bailiffs (*alguaciles*) dressed in 17th century costume, who salute the president (*presidente*) of the fight. The president is an important official who controls a fight and can award trophies to a matador who performs well. A trumpet is blown to announce the first fight, when the matador and his team enter the ring, and to signal the end of each stage. The bailiffs receive the key (thrown to them by the president of the bullfight) to the gate (*toril*) through which the bulls enter the ring. The president then waves a white handkerchief to signal the entrance of the first bull into the ring.

Preliminary Phase: During the preliminary phase the footmen, *peones* or *capeadores* (banderillos often accompanied by the matador) work the bull with large magenta and yellow capes (*capotes*), while carefully appraising its agility, intelligence, dangers, sight, strength and idiosyncracies. It's important for the matador to determine the animal's qualities such as whether it favours one horn or the other (e.g. hooks to the right or left) or swings its horns up at the end of each pass and how it charges (e.g. long smooth charges or swerves about rapidly). Sometimes a bull is reluctant to fight and if it cannot be enticed to charge or is judged 'unfit', it will be withdrawn on the sign of a red handkerchief from the president (a good sign is when the bull charges into the ring and attacks anything that moves). Toreros don't take any chances during the preliminary phase as this is when the bull is at its most dangerous, and at the merest hint of danger will retreat behind a barrier (*barrera* or *burladero*). If the matador (whose bull it is) gives his permission, you may see the other two matadors play the bull during the first or second stages, so don't be surprised if you see three matadors (wearing gold dress) in the ring at the same time.

First Stage: The first stage of a fight is called the *suerte/tercio de varas* or *suerte/tercio de picar* in which the picadores, mounted on padded and blindfolded horses (whose vocal cords are cut to stop them screaming) provoke the bull to attack them. The aim is to plunge their lance (*garrocha* or *pica*) into the bull's neck thus weakening its strong neck muscles. This causes it to lower its head, without which the matador couldn't perform the *coup de grâce* in the final part of the fight. Horse and rider are often lifted into the air and horses are occasionally injured or killed (always the case before they were padded). Usually three pics (*puyazos*) are given depending on the bull's strength (it may be more or less). A delicate balance is required as if a bull is 'over-picced' and loses too much blood, it may be too weak in the later stage of the fight. It's the most distasteful, misunderstood and thankless part of the proceedings and is even disliked by most aficionados.

Second Stage: When the bull has been sufficiently weakened by the picadores the *suerte/tercio de banderillas* stage commences, during which barbed darts (*banderillas*) 75cm (30 inches) long and decorated with coloured ribbons are placed in the bull's neck. The *banderillero*, carrying a *banderilla* in each hand, runs towards the charging bull at an angle and skillfully evading its horns, leans over the bull's head and places the banderillas in its neck. Some reckless banderilleros snap them in half and they are sometimes planted by the matador himself, although this is rare. Usually two banderilleros plant a total of two or three pairs of banderillas, one or two of which often fall out. They aren't designed to weaken the bull but to correct any tendency to hook, regulate the carriage of the head and slow it down.

Final Stage: the final stage of a bullfight is called the *suerte/tercio del muerte* and ends with the death of the bull. It begins with the matador removing his hat, saluting the president and asking for permission to perform with (and kill) the bull. He may dedicate (the *brindis*) the bull to somebody in the crowd (e.g. the president, a friend, pretty girl or even the whole crowd). Sometime the matador will toss his hat over his head; if it lands upside down it's supposed to be bad luck. The matador, armed with a sword and dark red cape (*muleta*), then begins to create a series of passes (of which there are over 40) using artistic and graceful movements, all the time bringing the bull closer and closer to his body (but hopefully not too close!). The two most basic passes include the right-handed pass (*derechazo*), in which the sword is used to expand the cloth, and the left-handed *natural*. Other common passes include the *verónica* when the cape is drawn over the bull's head, the *molinete* when the matador spins round making a colourful whirlpool, the *delantal* where the cape is spread out before the matador like an apron, the kneeling *farol* and the following *chicuelina* pass. A flamboyant matador who knows he's in control will turn his back on the bull and may even grasp the bull's horns as it rests between charges or kneel down in front of the bull. After each pass the crowd usually shouts *¡Olé!* (bravo!) in unison.

The Kill: When the matador realises the bull is weak and unable to charge much longer he will reach for his killing sword (*estoque*) and seek to manoeuvre it directly in front of him with its head down, so that he can administer the death stroke (*estocada*). The matador looks down the sword to sight the target, leans over the horns and attempts to insert it between the cervical vertebra (a three-inch wide opening between the shoulder blades) and into the bull's heart. It's extremely rare to see a clean, first-time kill and it often involves a number of failed attempts. If executed poorly it can become a wretched and ugly spectacle of attempted stabbing and gouging (after a few failed attempts, matadors often look at their swords as if they are blunt).

If the matador's death blow is deemed fatal, his seconds will play the bull until it drops to its knees, after which it may be despatched by a *punterillo* who thrusts a dagger (*puntilla*) into the back of its neck or brain. After repeated failures to despatch the bull with his estoque, a matador may be obliged to administer the *coup de grâce* with a shorter sword with a cross-bar close to the tip (called a *descabello*). In this case the death blow is directed between the base of the skull and the first vertebra, producing instant death by severing the animal's spinal cord. A messy and bloody kill instead of the desired swift death plunge with the sword will ruin an otherwise good performance and can even set back an aspiring matador's career.

Finale: If the matador has performed well and made a quick and clean kill he will be applauded, do a lap of honour, and be showered with flowers, wineskins (*odre/bota de vino*), hats, cushions and anything else to hand (some women throw their underwear). The crowd demonstrates its approval of a fight by waving white handkerchiefs, which are a signal to the president to award the matador a trophy. He can award the matador one or both of the bull's ears (*orejas*) and on extremely rare occasions its tail (*rabo*) also. A matador who performs well but had difficulty with the kill may be applauded and invited to make a lap of the ring. A matador awarded a trophy (ear or tail) will do a lap of honour holding his bloody prize up to the crowd, which he will milk for every drop of adulation (he may even be carried from the ring on the crowd's shoulders). However, if its a bad fight and end, the matador will receive a shower of cushions, whistles and abuse from the crowd (cowardly toreros have even on occasion been physically attacked). Note that barely one in 10 bullfights are good from the spectators' point of view.

If the bull has put up a good fight, its carcass too will receive a lap of honour (signalled by a blue handkerchief from the president) and a rousing posthumous cheer as it's dragged from the ring by a tractor (*arrastre*) or team of mules. If a bull is exceptionally brave or strong and the matador is unable to kill it, it may be spared and be allowed to return to its stud farm to live out its life in peace, although this is rare.

Live bullfights are shown on Spanish television almost daily throughout the season and recorded fights are screened twice weekly in the off-season. Top bullfighters are huge stars and feted like pop stars or star footballers and can command fees of anywhere between 3 and 30m ptas. Scores of books about bullfighting are published each year and magazines and newspapers devote many pages to it. Among the many books written about bullfighting are *Death in the Afternoon* by Ernest Hemingway (Grafton), *Or I'll Dress You in Mourning* by Larry Collins & Dominique Lapierre (Simon & Schuster) and *Blood Sport: A History of Spanish Bullfighting* by Timothy Mitchell.

MUSEUMS, ART GALLERIES, ETC.

Spain has over 800 museums (*museo*) and important collections, particularly in Madrid and Barcelona, and there has been an explosion in the number of art galleries (*galerías de arte*) in the last decade throughout the country, particularly contemporary art. Spain has a distinguished history in the field of art and has produced many of the world's greatest artists including Goya, El Greco, Ribera, Velázquez, Zurbarán, Cano, Murillo, Picasso, Dalí, Miró and Juan Gris, although it surprisingly had virtually no art market until the mid-1960s. Modern art is a passion with the Spanish and the annual Contemporary Art Fair (ARCO) in Madrid is a popular event.

Spain's premier art gallery is the Museo Nacional del Prado (called simply the Prado) in Madrid, housing one of the world's richest art collections. It contains over 5,000 paintings, each one a masterpiece, including an unrivalled collection of Spanish masters (but is able to display only a fraction of its total works). Complementing the Prado are many other celebrated art collections including the Museo Lazaro Galdiano, the Museo Thyssen-Bornemisza (which Baron Heinrich Thyssen moved from Switzerland to Spain in 1992 thanks to the influence of his wife, Carmen Cervera, a Spaniard) and the Museo Nacional Centro de Arte, Reina Sofía. Although housed in an ugly characterless building, whose only virtue is its monumental 12,500 square metres of exhibition space, the Reina Sofía is set to become Europe's top museum of contemporary art.

Although it isn't so richly endowed with museums as Madrid, Barcelona boasts a number of important collections including the Museu Picasso, the Museu d'Art de Catalunya, the Fundació Joan Miró, the Museu d'Art Modern and the Barcelona Museum of Contemporary Art (MACBA), which opened in 1995. Modernism is particularly strong in Barcelona which is the capital of modernist architecture. One of its major attractions is the Parc Güell designed by Spain's greatest architect Antoni Gaudí and housing the Casa-Museu Gaudí. Also not to be missed are Gaudí's masterpiece Casa Milà apartment building and his most famous work, the remarkable unfinished Temple Expiatori de la Sagrada Familia. The Museu Dalí (Dalí Theatre-Museum), itself a surrealist work of art, is located in Figueras (the birthplace of the artist) on the Costa Brava, and is the second most visited museum in Spain after the Prado. A new futuristic '21st-century' art gallery funded by the Guggenheim Foundation is under construction in Bilbao and will be one of Europe's top venues.

Most major museums (including the Prado) open from 0900 to 1900 from Tuesday to Saturday and from 0900 until 1400 on Sundays. Most are closed on Mondays. Smaller museums may open only from between 0900 and 1000 until 1400 or 1430, although some reopen after the siesta from 1600 to 1900. Some museums have extended opening hours in the summer. Opening times vary considerably and are subject to frequent change, so always check in advance (they are usually listed in guide books). Many smaller museums disregard 'official' opening hours and open erratically.

Entrance fees to Spain's museums, galleries and other sites are very reasonable and are usually between 200 and 400 ptas. The entrance fee of 400 ptas to the Prado is a bargain and entrance is free to students with an international student card and to all EU nationals under 21. Many museums provide free entrance to students, some have reduced fees for students and senior citizens, and a few provide free entry on one day a week (including the Prado), usually Sundays. A pensioner's card (*tarjeta de pensionista*) allows free entry to state museums and monuments (operated by the *Patrimonio Nacional*) and discounts elsewhere. In 1983, the Socialists made entry to Spain's national museums free for all Spaniards, foreign residents of Spain and those under 21. However the European Court of Justice ruled this discriminatory and now everyone must pay except students.

Note that most cathedrals, monasteries and famous churches, many of which house great works of art, charge admission fees to non-worshippers which go towards their upkeep. Student admission is usually half price or less and children under 14 may be admitted free. It's also possible in Spain to visit numerous businesses, particularly those connected with the food and drink industry such as vineyards, distilleries, breweries, mineral water springs, farms and dairies. Spain has some 27 zoos, the best of which are Barcelona, Jerez and Madrid (although many others keep animals in appalling conditions).

CINEMAS

Spain has over 2,000 cinemas (*cines*) nationwide and around 1,300 cinema clubs. Although it has lost a lot of its former popularity to television and many cinemas have closed in the last few decades, cinema remains popular in Spain where over 10 per cent of adults see a film each week. In major cities, most cinemas have three or four performances (*sesiones*) a day, at two or three hour intervals, e.g. 1630, 1830, 2030 and 2230 (some have an extra performance on Saturdays and holidays, shown in listings as S y F). Tickets prices are among the lowest in Europe and are generally around 500 to 700 ptas (or less in small towns). On certain days, e.g. Wednesdays in Madrid (designated the *día del espectador* or 'spectator's day'), tickets are reduced to 300 to 400 ptas for the first performance. Most cinemas are fairly small, although a number of multi-screen cinemas (e.g. with 15 screens) are planned. There are outdoor and drive-in cinemas in the summer in many areas and free films are also sponsored in some cities, e.g. in the Parque del Retiro in Madrid.

Most foreign films are dubbed into Spanish (including foreign names), usually indicated by the letters V.E. (*versión española*). Under Franco, the dubbing of foreign films was compulsory so that they could be censored more easily. However, a number of private theatres in the major cities and resort towns specialise in screening original soundtrack films, indicated by the letters V.O. (*versión original*), with Spanish subtitles (*subtitulada*). Restricted films that aren't recommended for children (minors) less than a certain age (e.g. 13 or 18) are listed as *no recomendada para menores de 13/18 años*, while a film with no age restrictions is classified as *todos los públicos*. Cinema programmes are published in daily newspapers and entertainment guides.

There has been a revival of Spanish film since censorship ended and some 30 per cent of films shown in Spain are now Spanish-made, with the rest being imports dubbed into Spanish. Spain stages some 40 film festivals each year, notably in Barcelona, Gijón, Madrid, San Sebastian and Vallodolid. However, Spanish film makers (like the French) are under serious threat from US-made films. In order to protect its indigenous film industry the Spanish government introduced a highly unpopular quota system in 1994, forcing cinemas to screen one day of European films for every two or three of US-made pictures.

THEATRE, OPERA & BALLET

The vast majority of theatres in Spain are in Madrid and Barcelona, although there has been a huge theatre building programme throughout the country in the last decade and many smaller towns now have municipal-sponsored theatres (*teatros municipales*) housed in cultural centres. The main theatres in Madrid include the Teatro de Zarzuela, Teatro Español, Teatro de la Comedia, Centro Dramático Nacional, Teatro María Guerrero, Centro de Nueva Tendencias Escénicas, and the Compañía Nacional de Teatro Clásico, a number of which are sponsored by the state or city. Spain has a long tradition of drama and a number of prolific playwrights such as Lope de Vega (who wrote or co-wrote almost 2,000 plays) and Tirso de Molina (who created Don Juan). Classical and contemporary Spanish and foreign plays are performed throughout Spain and experimental theatre is particularly popular in Catalonia.

Theatre tickets are inexpensive, usually costing between 500 and 2,000 ptas, with reduced prices on certain days, e.g. Wednesdays or Thursdays. Some offer student discounts. There are often two performances in the same evening at 1900 or 1930 and 2200 or 2230 and 'matinee' (afternoon) performances on Saturdays, Sundays and public holidays, starting around 1630. In summer, outdoor plays are performed in many cities, including free sponsored plays, e.g. in Madrid in July and August. There are also a number of English-language amateur dramatics' groups in the major cities and resort towns, performing in local theatres and 'supper theatre' in restaurants.

Opera is popular in Spain which has produced some of the world's leading performers including Victoria de los Angeles, Teresa Berganza, Montserrat Caballé, José Carreras, Plácido Domingo and Alfredo Kraus. Regular performances are held in Madrid, Barcelona, Oviedo, Bilbao and other cities, although only Barcelona has a 'proper' opera house, the Gran Teatro del Liceu (1847), considered second worldwide only to La Scala in Milan. The season in Barcelona lasts from September to July. Madrid's Teatro Real was reopened as the *Teatro de la Opera* in 1992 and stages opera, symphony, ballet and zarzuela. The National Ballet of Spain performs in the Teatro de la Zarzuela or the Teatro Monumental in Madrid, and the Teatro de la Zarzuela in Madrid stages opera from January to July and ballet from December to January. A new opera and symphony theatre (*Teatro de la Maestranza*) with 1,800 seats was opened in Seville in 1992.

MUSIC

Music of all kinds, from flamenco to rock, jazz to classical, is extremely popular in Spain and an essential ingredient of any festival or fiesta. Spain has a wealth of traditional folk music and dance, particularly flamenco (see page 330) and classical guitar, which are popular throughout the country. It's renowned worldwide for its classical guitar made famous by (among others) Andrés Segovia, Carlos Montoyo, Manuel de Falla, Joaquín Rodrigo and Narciso Yepes. An international festival of the guitar is held in Córdoba in July.

Rock and pop music is popular with young Spaniards and there are many excellent home-grown bands, although the most popular music is American and British. Among the most popular forms of Spanish pop music are root-rock (*rock-con-raíces*), a sort of rock version of flamenco singing, and rave music (*bacalao/baKalao*). Madrid has the most lively and varied music scene, although the Catalans are recognised as Spain's most serious music lovers, particularly with regard to opera, jazz and Catalan song, which was revived after Franco's death. Jazz has a large following in Spain and jazz festivals are staged in many cities in summer including Barcelona, San Sebastian, Santander and Sitges.

Spain's most popular crooner is Julio Iglesias, who has sold more records in more languages than any other musical artist in history (over 160m albums) and has earned some 200 gold and platinum records. However, one of Spain's biggest national and international hits in recent years was surprisingly the Benedictine monks of Santo Domingo de Silos (Burgos), whose album of Gregorian chant (*Las Mejores Obras del Canto Gregoriano*) has topped music charts around the world selling some 5m copies.

Madrid, Barcelona and Valencia all stage classical music seasons in winter. Major classical concerts in Madrid are held at the magnificent Auditorio Nacional de Música, home of the Spanish national orchestra (*Orquesta Nacional de España/ONE*), where tickets for most concerts cost between 500 and 2,500 ptas. Annual concert cycles are also performed by the National Orchestra and Choir of Spain, and Spanish Radio and Television at the Teatro Real in Madrid. Free open air concerts are held in summer by the city band in the Templete del Retiro in Retiro Park. One of the most popular forms of music in Madrid is *Zarzuela*, a form of light opera or comic operetta in the style of Gilbert & Sullivan, performed in the Teatro de Zarzuela. In Barcelona major concerts are held at the eccentric art nouveau Palau de la Música.

Spain also stages a wealth of excellent music festivals including a festival of religious music (*Semanas de Música Religiosa*) in Cuenca at the end of March; the international festival of music and dance (*Festival Internacional de Música y Danza*) in Granada in June/July (Spain's most important musical event including concerts, operas, operettas, and classical and modern ballet); the Santander international festival (*Festival Internacional de Santander*) of music, dance and drama in July/August; the international music festival (*Festival Internacional de Música*) in Barcelona in September/October; and the Autumn festival in Madrid from mid September until the beginning of October (includes concerts, opera, drama and ballet). Top international soloists, bands and orchestras give concerts in Spain throughout the year.

SOCIAL CLUBS

There's a wealth of expatriate clubs and organisations in major cities and resort areas in Spain catering for all nationalities. In addition to a multitude of social, sports and special interest clubs, there are also branches of international clubs in most major towns including Ambassador Clubs, American Women's and Men's Clubs, Anglo-Spanish Clubs, Business Clubs, International Men's and Women's Clubs, Kiwani Clubs, Lion and Lioness Clubs, and Rotary Clubs. Club listings and announcements are made in English-language and other expatriate publications in resort areas, and many embassies and consulates in Spain maintain lists.

Most clubs organise a variety of activities and pastimes such as chess, bridge and whist evenings; sports activities and outings; art, music, theatre, cinema and local history outings; informal dances; and various other social events. Some clubs have their own facilities such as a clubhouse, library, bar and restaurant. Annual membership fees vary considerably, e.g. from 1,500 to 10,000 ptas, and some offer daily, weekly and monthly membership for visitors. Many clubs provide important information for new arrivals, organise free or inexpensive Spanish language lessons, and provide foreign newspapers to keep members in touch with home.

Joining a local club is one of the best ways for newcomers to meet people and make friends in Spain. If you want to integrate into your local community or Spanish society in general, one of the best ways is to join a local Spanish club. Most towns also have social centres for retired people (*jubilados*) and pensioners' clubs (*club de pensionistas*) open to residents with a pensioner's card (*tarjeta de pensionista*), available from your local town hall.

NIGHT-LIFE

Spain is famous for its vibrant night-life, which extends until dawn and beyond in major cities such as Madrid and Barcelona (not for nothing are nocturnal *Madrileños* known as 'the cats' or *los gatos*). In major cities and resort areas there's a wide choice of night-life for all ages including jazz clubs, cabarets, discos, sex shows, flamenco clubs, music clubs and bars, nightclubs, music halls, and restaurants with floor shows (*tablaos*). Karaoke is popular in many pubs and clubs in resort areas (particularly with drunken Brits). For many Spaniards the day doesn't begin until nightfall and most clubs and discotheques don't start to warm up until after midnight (raving is ironically referred to as 'the bad life' — *la mala vida*).

Many young Spaniards literally rock around the clock and in the major cities and resorts some discotheques *open* at daybreak, while others are in business non-stop from Friday night until Monday afternoon (when do people sleep?). Not surprisingly, Spaniards (especially *Madrileños*) reportedly sleep less than other Europeans. Ibiza is the spiritual home of the Euroraver and is *the* place to be in summer, when it boasts Europe's most vibrant nightlife and biggest and boldest dance clubs. The authorities in Madrid and Barcelona have been forced to restrict Spain's incessant day and night life in some cities, in an attempt to reduce drug use (particularly amphetamines and ecstasy) and the resulting high number of fatal car accidents. Bars in these cities must now close at 0230 and discos at 0430 (relatively early by Spanish standards), although most owners ignore the new regulations unless forced to close by the police. Some towns are also cracking down on discos making excessive noise.

Discos are found in the smallest of towns, although they may be no more than a bar with music and a dance floor. The entrance fee is usually around 1,000 ptas but can be as high as 3,000 ptas for the most exclusive places (women often obtain free entry or are charged less than men). Some discos have early evening sessions for teenagers with an entrance fee of 250 to 1,000 ptas. Live music is common in music bars which have a small dance floor and offer free entrance or charge a small fee, e.g. 200 to 300 ptas. The disco cover charge often includes a drink, although some have no cover charge but *very* expensive drinks, which usually cost between 500 and 1,000 ptas. It's important to be fashionably dressed to gain access to the most exclusive discos, although usually any casual dress is acceptable including jeans and T-shirts. There's usually a 'bouncer' on the door checking that guests are suitably attired and haven't had too much to drink.

Discos, night-clubs, music bars and clubs, dinner/dancing venues and cabarets are listed in English-language publications and in Spanish newspapers under *salas de fiestas* and *espectáculos*.

GAMBLING

The Spanish are a nation of gamblers and bet a higher proportion of their income than almost any other nation (over a million are addicted). It's estimated that the Spanish gamble well over 3 trillion pesetas a year equal to around 80,000 ptas per head each year or some 15 per cent of the average net household income. They will bet on almost anything including lotteries, football and racing pools, horse racing (Illegal betting shops, where punters bet on foreign horse and greyhound racing, are common in resort areas), bingo, slot machines (in bars and cafés), casinos, and the big jai-alai games in the Basque lands and Madrid. Prizes can be huge running into hundreds of millions of pesetas. In today's frenetic get-rich atmosphere in Spain it's hard to believe that gambling was actually banned under Franco!

The most popular form of gambling in Spain is the state national lottery (*Lotería Nacional*) run in aid of charities (such as the blind and the Red Cross) and the Catholic church. Lottery tickets are sold at lottery offices at face value or can be purchased for a 10 per cent commission from street vendors throughout Spain and through ONCE (the society for the blind) kiosks manned by blind people. ONCE takes some 10,000 ptas a year from every Spaniard (39m) and has a massive turnover many companies would be proud of.

Spain's and the world's biggest lottery, 'the fat one' (*El Gordo*), is held at Christmas and consists of 108 series of 66,000 tickets, each costing 30,000 ptas. Not surprisingly, 30,000 ptas is too much for most people and tickets are divided into 10 shares (*décimos*) costing 3,000 ptas each. Many clubs and charities buy a *décimo* and offer shares (called *partcipaciones*) for a few hundred pesetas, usually adding a small surcharge. The total amount wagered on *El Gordo* is over 200,000,000,000 ptas (over $1.5 billion), some 70 per cent of which is paid in prizes, with the rest going in expenses and profits. The top prize is around 300m ptas, the second 150m ptas and the third 75m ptas, each of which is multiplied by the number of series' of tickets (there are usually over 100).

Tickets are usually sold out long before the draw on the 22nd December, which is televised live (it takes three hours) and traditionally made by the children of the San Ildefonso school in Madrid. Winning numbers are published in newspapers on 23rd December and the list is posted in lottery offices for three months following the draw. Note that winners must claim their winnings and aren't sent them automatically (unclaimed winnings revert to the state). If you win a big prize you can take your ticket to a Spanish bank, who will give you a receipt and collect your winnings on your behalf. Lottery prizes are free of all taxes. Spain's second largest lottery is called the kid (*El Niño*) after the baby Jesus and takes place on 5th January.

Note that winning the lottery isn't a guarantee of a happy life and it can cause huge upheavals in small towns, particularly when disputes arise over the ownership of tickets. For example the town of Campello (Alicante) was torn apart when 5,000 of its 11,400 inhabitants shared 21 billion pesetas in 1993, setting neighbour against neighbour, friend against friend, and even splitting families. When it comes to easy money the Spanish are as avaricious as anyone else and it may be advisable to buy your own ticket, as sharing can have unfortunate consequence (one man who won 49m ptas stabbed his sister to death after an argument about how to share the winnings among the family). The good news is that you have a better chance of being struck by lightning than winning the lottery.

Spain has some 20 casinos located in Torrelodones (Madrid), Sant Pere de Ribes (Barcelona), Villajoyosa (Alicante), Puzol (Valencia), El Puerto de Santa María (Cadiz), Lloret de Mar (Gerona), Benalmádena Costa (Malaga), Marbella (Malaga), Calviá (Majorca), Alfajarin (Zaragossa), Isla de Toja (Pontevedra), Corunna Santander (Cantabria), Playa de San Augustín (south Gran Canaria), Santa Catalina (Gran Canaria), Puerto de la Cruz (Tenerife), Adeje (Tenerife), Ibiza, San Sebastian (Guispúzcoa), Peralada (Gerona), La Manga (Murcia) and Boecillo (Valladolid). There's also a casino in Gibraltar. The most common casino games are American and French roulette, black jack, *punto y banca* and *chemin-de-fer*, plus the ubiquitous slot machines and private gaming rooms. There's usually an entry fee, e.g. 600 ptas, and visitors must show their passports (to identify professional gamblers). Most casinos are open from late afternoon until the early hours of the morning, e.g. 1700 until 0400 or 0500. Dress code is smart casual (no jeans, sandals or t-shirts).

BARS & CAFES

One of the delights of living in Spain is the many excellent pavement cafés and bars, and in particular, their delicious coffee and inexpensive prices. Few countries (if any) can match Spain for the variety, quality, economy and number (it's said that Spain has more bars than the rest of Europe put together) of its watering holes. Drinking habits vary considerably from region to region, although it isn't uncommon to see Spaniards drinking wine or beer at breakfast time or taking a brandy with their morning coffee (a common continental habit).

Bars: Spain's cities and resort areas contain a wealth of bars and pubs including over 8,000 in Madrid alone (one for every 600 residents) and reportedly more than the whole of Norway (which you will hardly find surprising if you've ever tried to get a drink there!). They include cocktail bars, piano bars, disco bars, live-music bars (e.g. jazz, rock or flamenco), bar-cafeterias, bar-restaurants, cabaret bars, casino bars, beach bars, bodegas, taverns (*tabernas*), *mesónes* (a bar specialising in serving wine and *tapas*), *tascas*, *cervecerías* (a bar specialising in beer, usually with a wide selection of imported beers on tap), gay bars, roof-top bars, pool-side bars, youth bars, topless bars (*not* roofless bars, although there are some of those also) and a huge variety of foreign bars and pubs. *Pubs* in Spain tend to be flashy bars often with live music, satellite television, expensive drinks and often no food.

For homesick Britons there are numerous pseudo British bars in resort areas, almost always equipped with huge satellite television systems showing English football, cricket and other sports events (ladies be warned!). Television can be even more obtrusive in Spanish bars, where customers are fed a constant diet of soccer, bullfights, game-shows and dubbed foreign films. Don't expect to have a quiet conversation in a bar with a TV. Note that it's cheaper to drink while standing at the bar; sitting at a table may be 50 per cent more expensive and a table on a pavement terrace (*terraza*) can double the bar price. You may not be permitted to buy a drink at the bar and take it to a seat outside. Eating at a bar is also cheaper than at a table. Bars are usually open from 1200 to 1600 and from 2000 until 2400 or later, although some are open all day while others open in the evenings only. In resort areas, many bars (and restaurants) are closed outside the high season. There are no official licensing laws in Spain and closing time is usually when the owner decides to shut up shop or when the last customer goes home (or falls off his bar stool), which is usually in the early hours of the morning (although some town halls fix bar closing times, e.g. 2am).

Cafés: Traditional café life can still be found in Spain, where a café is rarely simply somewhere to grab a cup of coffee and a pastry. Its myriad roles include a locale in which to read the newspaper (without buying one); a convenient place to make a telephone call or go to the toilet (due to the dearth of public toilets in Spain); somewhere to pass the time; a business or social meeting place; a place to write or study; an academic or debating arena; a refuge from the sun or rain; or simply somewhere to watch the world go by. Around 1700 is the hour of *tertulia*, the café get-together that's a national institution. Note that it's customary to buy a drink when you use the toilet in a bar or café, although owners don't usually mind non-customers using their facilities. Cafés often have a billiard room and some even entertain customers with a live orchestra or chamber music.

To attract the attention of a waiter (*camarero*) or waitress (*camarera*) in a busy bar or café, it's customary to call out 'attention, please' (*¡oiga, por favor!*) or simply to shout your order at the waiter. In small family bars and cafés you will usually be served by the landlord or landlady (*dueño/dueña*), who won't usually accept tips. Tipping is, however, common in bars, although tips (*propinas*) are usually small and often consist of the small change left in saucers. Tips are often kept in a communal tin or box (*bote*) and shared among the staff, although this practice isn't common in restaurants, where waiters prefer to keep their own tips.

Coffee: Spain is a mecca for coffee lovers and Spanish coffee is invariably superb and the best value in Europe. It's served in cafés, ice-cream parlours (*heladerías*), bars and restaurants and is freshly made, piping hot and actually tastes of coffee beans (unlike American and British dishwater often served in British bars). A 'normal' coffee in Spain is an expresso which is served black (*café solo*), while a coffee made with all milk is a *café con leche*, usually drunk by Spaniards for breakfast. Coffee with a dash of milk is a *café cortado*. If you want a large black coffee ask for a *doble* or a *grande*. Should you wish to drink weak milky coffee ask for a *manchada*, which is literally 'stained milk', i.e. milk with a small amount of coffee added. Decaffeinated coffee (*descafeinado*) is widely available, although it's likely to consist of a sachet of instant coffee poured into a cup of hot milk. Iced coffee (*café con hielo*) is also available and is usually served black. In some areas a coffee is routinely accompanied by a glass of cold water. A coffee usually costs between 125 and 175 ptas and even in tourist haunts and fashionable *terrazas* rarely goes above 175 ptas. It's often served spiked with brandy, whisky or anisette, when it's called a *carajillo*, and may be served with a small slice of lemon and a coffee bean floating on top.

Tea: Tea (*té*) is available in most bars and cafés and is usually drunk black or served with a slice of lemon (*té con limón*). If you want tea with milk it's best to ask for tea with a little cold milk (*té con un poquito de leche fría*), as if you ask for tea with milk you're likely to get tea made with half water and half hot milk. However, it's best not to drink tea in bars and cafés at all as it's invariably awful. Herbal teas such as camomile (*manzanilla*) and mint (*menta*) are also widely available. There are tea salons (*salones de té*) in the major cities and afternoon tea is often served in luxury hotels, perhaps to a background of live classical music.

Soft Drinks: A wide variety of non-alcoholic 'soft' drinks (*refrescos*) are available in Spain including ubiquitous international brands such as pepsi, coca cola and seven-up. Other common drinks include sweetened fruit juice (*zumo* or *jugo*), fresh juice (*zumo natural*), iced fruit juices made from fruit syrups or coffee (*granizados*), orange (*naranja*), lemon (*limón*), tonic (*tónica*) and bitter (*kas*). Mineral water is sold in sparkling (*con gas*) and still (*sin gas*) versions. A popular thirst-quenching drink is a *horchata de chufa*, an orgeat made from the tuberous root of the *chufa* (known in English as 'earth almond') and served with crushed-ice (often served in special cafés called *horchaterías*). Others include a black and white (*negro y blanco*), a combination of ice cream (*helado*) and coffee, and creamy milk shakes (*batidos*).

Beer: Beer is extremely popular in Spain and somewhat surprisingly most Spaniards prefer it to wine. In general a bar serves one brand of local draught beer and possibly a few different bottled beers. A *cervecería* is a bar that specialises in beer and usually has several brands on tap and a wide range of bottled beers, including imported brands. Spanish beers come in light (*dorada*) and dark (*negra*) varieties, the most famous brands including *San Miguel, Cruzcampo, Dorada, Aguila, Estrella* and *Mahou Five Star*. Bars also serve non-alcoholic beer, inappropriately called *sin* (literally 'without'). A small bottle of beer (300ml) is a *botellín*, while a small glass of draught beer is called a *caña*. A *caña doble* is twice as large as a *caña* (and is often served when you don't ask for a *caña*) and a large beer is a *tubo* (tube) or *jarra* (mug or jar), although this can also mean a large jug or pitcher. In tourist resorts customers who ask for a beer are often served a *tubo*. Draught beer is generally cheaper than bottled beer and costs around 125 to 150 ptas for a small glass (*caña*). Note that Spanish beer is quite strong and is usually around 5 per cent alcohol by volume. For something lighter try *clara*, a refreshing shandy made with beer and sweetened seltzer (*gaseosa*).

Cocktails & Spirits: Cocktails and spirits are much cheaper in Spain than in most other countries and are served in larger measures (the Spanish don't use official measures when pouring drinks, although EU regulations are supposed to end this practice). An aperitif at midday or in the evening is a ritual in Spain and many people have a brandy (*brandy* or *coñac*) as an accompaniment to a mid-morning coffee (or at any time). Most spirits are ordered by brand name as there are generally cheaper Spanish (*nacional*) equivalents for most international brands. When drinking cocktails, most people notice little difference between Spanish gin, vodka and rum, and more expensive imports. However, Spanish whisky is terrible and to be avoided. Some bars and discotheques reportedly buy inexpensive spirits in bulk to refill well-known brand bottles and charge higher prices. Whisky (scotch, bourbon or rye) is less likely to be substituted as it's difficult to reproduce the flavour of a particular whisky and it's less likely to be drunk in a cocktail. Drinks are usually served with lots of ice (*hielo*), which those with sensitive stomachs may wish to avoid (depending on the water source).

Other Drinks: Wine (*vino*) is sold by the glass (*copa*) in bars and cafés and is ordered by simply asking for a glass of red, white or rosé (*una copa de tinto/blanco/rosado*). If you don't specify the colour, you will usually be served red wine. It's inexpensive by northern European standards, costing as little as 100 ptas for a glass of house wine (*vino de la casa* or *vino del lugar*) often served from a barrel or a glass jug. If you fancy trying your hand at drinking from a wineskin (*odre/bota de vino*) or *porrón* (a glass carafe with a pouring funnel) don't wear your best clothes. Note that red wine is sometimes served chilled in bars; if you want it at room temperature ask for *no frío* or *normal*.

Table wine (*vino corriente* or *vino de mesa*) is often drunk mixed with sparkling mineral water, soda or lemonade, called *tinto de verano* (literally 'summer red') when made with red wine. *Sangría* is a delicious red-wine punch made with peaches, oranges, seltzer, sugar, red wine and a dash of brandy. It's available everywhere and can be surprisingly strong, although it isn't usually well made in bars. A similar drink is *zurra* made with white wine, brandy, vermouth and sugar, garnished with orange and lemon segments and diluted with water and ice. Sherry (*jerez*) is popular, particularly in the south, and cider (*sidra*) is a common drink in the north of Spain. Pacharán, made from sloes, is an increasingly popular after-dinner drink.

Food: Bars and cafés in Spain aren't just somewhere to get a drink, and many serve snacks and complete meals from morning until late at night. In addition to *tapas* (see below), bars (and cafés) serve a variety of snacks including sandwiches and rolls (*bocadillos*), toasted sandwiches (*tostadas*) and various egg dishes including fried eggs (*huevos fritos*) and cold omelette (*tortilla*). In local bars there's often no menu and you just ask the patron what he has to eat. There will invariably be something, usually what the family is eating such as a homemade stew, grilled seafood or fresh salad. You can also find a wide selection of appetising snacks in food shops such as *panaderías* and *croissanterías*.

Tapas: *Tapas* (meaning 'lids', as they were originally little saucers of snacks served on top of a drink) are a way of life in Spain and the world's greatest snack food. They are a way of life throughout Spain, although more common in the south and the major cities, where it's customary to drop into a bar after work to have a drink accompanied by tapas. Tapas consist of small dishes usually eaten at the counter in a bar with a glass of draught beer or wine, although they may also be eaten as an *entrée* before a meal.

Among the best places to eat tapas is a traditional *mesón* or *tasca*, many of which are also restaurants, with a whole counter full of hot and cold appetisers. If you don't speak Spanish, it's best to choose a bar where the dishes are displayed along the bar, rather than one where they're simply listed on a blackboard. A dirty floor is the sign of a good tapas bar, as everything that's left is simply dropped on the floor including leftovers, seafood shells, olive stones, nutshells, cigarette ends and serviettes.

Tapas are served in various sizes: a standard tapa is an appetiser-like serving, a *pincho* or a *porción* a slightly larger serving, and a *ración* is the same size as an entree (it's also possible to order half a ración (a *media ración*). Always remember to state the size of serving you want. Tapas *variadas* is a selection of tapas and an excellent introduction for the uninitiated. Most tapas can also be ordered as sandwiches (*bocadillos*) in French bread. There are many varieties of tapas including olives, mushrooms, pickled vegetables, kebabs (*pinchos morunos*), ham, seafood (baby eels, tuna, squid, octopus, clams, mussels, lobster, prawns, anchovies), garlic potatoes, pieces of *tortilla* (omelette), meatballs, tripe, huge potato crisps, peanuts, Russian salad, cheese, salami, nuts, pickled carrots, sausage, snails, stewed pimento, cubes of pork in sauce, pig's ear and pickled artichoke hearts (to name but a few). In southern Andalusia a favourite tapa is *huevos revueltos*, softly scrambled eggs made with a variety of flavourings including wild asparagus, shrimps, ham, beans and mushrooms. Tapas are usually accompanied by draft beer, wine or sherry.

Some bars automatically serve free tapas with every drink (although they may not offer them to tourists), midday and evening, although this custom is not so widespread nowadays. However, it's still possible to find places where you can get a small glass of wine (*chato*) and a tapa for 100 to 150 ptas. Tapa etiquette dictates that you don't usually choose free tapas. When not served free, tapas cost around 100 to 200 ptas for a serving (you may be billed by the toothpick count).

Paying: In a bar or café it's usual to 'run a tab' and pay for your drinks when you leave, although you may be asked to pay when you're served in a busy establishment or a tourist spot such as a beach bar. Your account may be chalked on the counter itself or written on a pad kept behind the bar. If your waiter is going off duty, he'll also ask you to pay. Service and tax is included in the price and it's unnecessary to tip, although most people leave their small change (e.g. 25 ptas) and a party may leave 100 ptas after an evening's drinking. When Spaniards have a drink together, usually the one who made the invitation or suggestion will pay (although they may argue about it). The foreign habit of trying to work out who has drunk what and splitting the bill is alien to the Spanish and they don't run a mental bill and make sure that everyone pays in turn, although that's often the case in practice. If you're invited for a drink by a Spaniard, he will invariably insist on paying, even when he's of modest means.

The legal age for drinking in Spain is 18, although it isn't always enforced (children under 18 are permitted on licensed premises with an adult, but cannot consume alcohol). Although Spaniards are comparatively heavy drinkers by most standards, you will rarely see them intoxicated. Drunkenness is associated with a loss of dignity and anyone who cannot hold his drink is scorned. Alcoholism is a serious problem in Spain, particularly among expatriates, many of whom are unable to control their drinking. Newcomers should be particularly wary of drinking too much, which is all to easy with Spain's low prices and generous measures. A surfeit of sun and alcohol can be deadly. See also **Alcohol** on page 382 and **Restaurants** below.

RESTAURANTS

Like most latins, Spaniards live to eat (and drink) and one of the greatest pleasures of living in Spain is its abundant variety of inexpensive eating places. In fact, anyone who loves good food and wine is guaranteed a happy life in Spain, which boasts one of the healthiest diets in Europe. Dining out is a popular social occasion and a source of great pleasure and it's common for Spaniards to entertain their friends at a restaurant rather than at home. You will often see whole families dining together, perhaps represented by three or four generations, and including children of all ages (children are welcome in all but the most exclusive restaurants in Spain). However, the restaurant trade has been hard hit by live TV football matches, which are now screened six nights a week in Spain (the most extensive coverage in Europe).

Spain offers a huge variety of restaurants to suit all tastes and pockets. Spanish cities and towns offer a wealth of eating places from luxury international restaurants (with matching prices) to humble *bodegas* and *cantinas* serving homely fare at bargain prices. Traditional eating and drinking places include *mesónes* in urban areas, *ventas* in the countryside, and *merenderos*, *chiringuitos* and *chamboas* (specialising in sea-food) at the beach. *Paradores* (see page 325) and *refugios* specialise in regional cooking. A *marisquería* is a an up-market fish restaurant, *cocederos* and *freidurías de pescado* are basic places to enjoy fresh fried fish, while an *asador* specialises in roast meat, poultry or fish. It's also possible to 'dine out at home' in many towns, where restaurants and caterers provide gourmet take-away meals complete with simple cooking instructions, or a chef and waitress will cook and serve dinner in your home for a moderate charge.

Anyone who says Spanish food is boring or always swimming in garlic and olive oil hasn't ventured far off the tourist trail. Spanish cuisine is among the most varied and sophisticated in Europe and is greatly influenced by other Mediterranean countries and Arab cooking. Each region serves its own specialities (*platos típicos*) based on local produce, meats and fish, and every province and most large towns boast their own culinary delights, even if it's just a local sausage or cheese. Spanish cooking largely consists of simple, wholesome fare and is noted for its high-quality fresh ingredients. Spices, particularly hot spices, are used sparingly and the best Spanish cooking is a subtle combination of ingredients and sauces intended to enhance (rather than smother) the flavour.

Generally, the further north you go in Spain, the better the food, with the majority of *haute cuisine* restaurants being situated in the Basque lands, Madrid and Barcelona. Basque cuisine is the finest in Spain, where San Sebastian (heavily influenced by France and vice versa) is the gastronomic capital, with around six Michelin-rated restaurants. San Sebastian is also famous for its all-male gastronomic societies (*sociedades populares/cofradías*), where members do the cooking in turn. In addition to the Basque lands, Asturias, Catalonia and Galicia are also noted for the excellence of their cuisine.

Spain isn't noted for its international cuisine, although there's an abundance of good foreign restaurants in Spanish cities and resort areas, including a plethora of fast food outlets such as hamburger joints (*hamburgueserías*) and British 'restaurants' that for some strange reason serve 'full English breakfast all day' (perhaps Brits are inclined to sleep all day and breakfast in the evening), although you're unlikely to find any in rural areas. Foreign restaurants cater mostly to foreigners (with menus in English or German, although it's illegal not to also have a menu in Spanish) as the Spanish generally prefer to stick to Spanish cuisine. Although Spanish food can sometimes be terrible, particularly in some tourist establishments on the *costas*, it usually offers better value-for-money (and often better quality) than foreign cuisine. In general, it's best to follow the locals' example. In resorts, restaurants that open year round may offer better service and value for money than seasonal and beachside restaurants catering primarily to tourists.

Spain's most famous dishes include *gazpacho* (cold tomato, cucumber and onion soup from Andalusia, although the recipe varies depending on the region), *paella* (a seafood saffron rice dish originally from Valencia), and *tortilla española* (Spanish omelette from Castile), found on tourist menus throughout Spain. However, there's much more to Spanish cooking than a few stereotypes and the country boasts many other delicacies including roast suckling pig (*cochinillo asado*) and lamb (*cordero asado*); superb casseroles and stews such as *cocido madrileño* made from salt pork, beef and stewing hen; 'exotic' dishes like bull's tail (*rabo de toro estofado*) cooked in a sauce of onions and tomatoes; and mouth-watering game such as partridge braised with ham, tomatoes, wine and anchovies (*perdices al torero*). Spain also has a wide variety of desserts (*postres*), although in budget establishments dessert may consist of fresh fruit or the Spanish 'flan' (*créme caramel* or *crema catalana*) only.

The Arab habit of adding fruit and nuts to meat and fish dishes is common in Spain, as are unusual combinations of meat, fish and fowl. Meat is usually excellent throughout Spain particularly the pork (Spanish cured ham is rated by many as the best in the world) and chicken (often free-range). When ordering steak you should specify how you want it cooked, i.e. *very* rare (*vuelta y vuelta*, literally 'turned'), rare (*poco hecho*), medium (*hecho*) or well done (*muy hecho*). Vegetarians are an endangered species in Spain, where there are few vegetarian restaurants (usually run by foreigners) outside the major cities. However there's something vegetarian on most menus and many foreign restaurants serve vegetarian dishes. Note that many soups and vegetable dishes in Spain contain bacon, ham or sausage and food is often cooked in pork fat. Your safest bet is salad and eggs, although if you eat fish you will have an abundance of dishes to choose from.

Spain is noted for the quality and variety of its fish (*pescados*) and shellfish (*mariscos*), and fish lovers will think they have died and gone to heaven. The average Spaniard eats over 20kg of fish each year and the average Basque over 40kg (compared, for example, with an average off around 10kg per head in France). Seafood is excellent throughout Spain, even in Madrid and other inland cities, although its best in the north (particularly Galicia) and the southwest region of Andalusia. However, fish and seafood is rarely cheap and in up-market restaurants can be expensive (fish is usually priced per 100g). In coastal areas there are numerous seafood restaurants (*marisquerías*) exclusively serving fish and other seafood, and unpretentious open-air, beach restaurants such as *merenderos* or *chiringuitos* serving inexpensive fried fish and chips (although some are sophisticated and expensive). Good fish restaurants often keep a variety of live fish and shellfish in tanks from which you can choose your meal.

The most common seafood dish in Spain is *paella*, usually eaten by Spaniards at lunchtime only, and best (and most authentic) in Valencia where it originated. The quality and variety of seafood in Spain is unrivalled and includes sea bream, grouper, trout, tuna, salmon, swordfish, turbot, angler fish, sea bass, hake, eels, cod, squid, king crabs, spider crabs, jumbo shrimp, scallops, mussels, lobster, cockles, oysters, prawns, crayfish, octopus, cuttlefish, clams and the most prized of all shellfish, *percebes* (goose barnacles), costing up to 10,000 ptas a kilo.

Menus: Menus (*el menú* or *la carta*) are usually written in two or three languages in resorts and some cities, e.g. Spanish plus English and/or German, although in Barcelona they may be written in Catalan only, particularly in high-class establishments. All restaurants must offer a menu of the day or house menu (*menú del día, cubierto* or *menú* *de la casa*) at lunch time at 80 per cent of the price each course would cost separately. The house menu is usually written on a blackboard outside restaurants and may not be listed on the menu inside. It usually consists of three courses (e.g. starter, main course with vegetables and a sweet) and may include a glass or small carafe of house wine and bread, although these are usually an extra. Many restaurants serve a selection of *tapas* before the first course as part of a set menu. Menus usually cost from 600 ptas in small restaurants, bodegas and bars, up to 2,500 ptas or more in high class restaurants. Many restaurants have a 1,000 ptas set menu and some also have a 2,500 ptas set menu. Note that prices, quality and the choice of dishes on a set menu vary enormously. In resort areas and major cities, many establishments offer tourist menus (*menú turístico*), with a choice of set meals including a quarter to half a litre of wine or a beer, service and other charges. Many restaurants, particularly those catering to foreign residents and tourists in resort areas, provide special menus at Christmas and New Year.

Wine: Wine (*vino*) is inexpensive in Spanish restaurants by northern European standards and costs just 200 to 500 ptas for a bottle (*botella*) or carafe (*garafa*) of house wine (*vino de la casa*) in a modest establishment. However, the price increases rapidly as you go up market, although a good bottle can be purchased in most quality restaurants for 1,000 to 2,000 ptas (the markup on wines in Spain is usually around 100 per cent of the supermarket price and can be as low as 50 per cent). Wine is sometimes included in set menus, when two people may receive a bottle between them and one person a half bottle (*media botella*) or a quarter to half a litre. Most house whites and rosés are drinkable and may be produced locally. However, the quality of house red wine varies considerably from reasonable to terrible.

Buying wine by the glass is quite expensive at between 150 and 250 ptas a glass, especially considering it's usually cheap 'plonk' which costs 200 to 300 ptas a bottle in a supermarket. If you drink more than a few glasses you're better of ordering a bottle (or half bottle, although these are rare in Spain) from the wine list. In an inexpensive rural establishment there may be no choice of wine and you'll be served whatever comes out of the barrel. If you just order *vino* it's understood to mean red wine, which is often served chilled and drunk with everything from red meat to fish. Spaniards don't drink a lot of alcohol with their meals and many prefer mineral water (*agua mineral*) or lemonade. If you want tap water ask for *agua del grifo* or *agua corriente*.

Meal Times: The Spanish eat much later than other Europeans, with lunch (*comida* or *almuerzo*) usually being taken between 1400 and 1600 and dinner (*cena*) between 2100 and 2300 (or as late as midnight at weekends!). People in Barcelona tend to eat dinner around an hour earlier than those in Madrid (which has the latest eating hours in Europe), while in tourist resorts dinner is usually served from 1900 or 2000. Most establishments serve meals from 1300 until 1600 and from 2000 until midnight, and outside these hours the only restaurants that may be open are those catering to foreigners (or those serving 'snacks' rather than full meals). Most restaurants close on one day or evening a week, usually Sunday evening and possibly also the whole of Monday or Tuesday. Many restaurants close for holidays in January or August for at least two weeks and some also close for a few days at Easter and over Christmas. In resort areas, many restaurants and bars close for the whole of the winter.

Ratings/Prices: Spanish restaurants are officially rated by their number of forks, from one to five, with five denoting the top grade, although they aren't necessarily a sign of quality cooking, but facilities, décor, length of menu and price. Prices per head range from 800 ptas in the cheapest bar-restaurants to around 2,000 ptas in a two or three-fork restaurant, where two people can dine well for around 3,000 to 5,000 ptas including a bottle of good wine. You don't always receive value for money in Spain, where the best value is often found in inexpensive, unpretentious restaurants, particularly the *comedores* (dining rooms) of bars, *pensiones* and *fondas*, many of which may serve food at lunchtimes only.

There are also budget *cafeterías* (often self-service) in major cities and resort areas graded with one to three cups depending on their facilities. The emphasis is usually on bland 'international' fare, although many serve traditional Spanish dishes and they provide unbeatable value for money, e.g. 700 to 800 ptas for all you can eat. *Cafeterías* also offer set meals called *platos combinados* (literally 'combination plates'), which are also available in many bars and inexpensive restaurants, consisting of one-course meals such as egg and chips, steak and/or fish with chips, and calamares (squid) and salad. *Platos combinados* usually include bread and possibly a drink and cost from 500 to 1,000 ptas. There are many excellent pizza places in resort areas (e.g. Telepizza), where scrumptious 'real' pizzas are made in proper wood-burning ovens and usually cost around 500 to 800 ptas (some claim that pizzas were invented in Catalonia).

Breakfast: Breakfast (*desayuno*) isn't usually an important meal in Spain and is often skipped altogether. When eaten it's generally of the continental variety consisting of coffee or hot chocolate and rolls (*bollos*), toast, croissants (*croisantes*), fried fritters (*churros*) or small sponge cakes (*magdalenas*). However, most hotels and many cafés and bars serve a cooked breakfast (*desayuno completo*), particularly in resort areas.

Lunch: Lunch is the most important meal of the day in Spain and is usually eaten between 1400 and 1600. It consists of an appetiser or starter (*entrada*) of soup or salad, a first course (*primer plato*), possibly followed by an *entrée* or second course (*segundo plato*), often consisting of egg dishes (e.g. omelettes) or vegetables, a main course (*plato fuerte*) of fish or meat with vegetables or salad, followed by fruit or cheese and occasionally a dessert (*postre*). Often you will need to order vegetables separately and in small family restaurants a salad may be routinely served. Note that modest establishments expect customers to use the same knife and fork for all courses.

Dinner: Dinner is usually served from 2100 until 2400, although it's served earlier in resort towns, e.g. from between 1900 and 2000, and in Spanish cities many restaurants remain open until well after midnight. Usually dinner is a lighter meal than lunch, although judged by international standards it's certainly no snack. There's often little difference between lunch and dinner menus, except that there isn't always a set menu in the evening and rural establishments may serve dinner only by prior arrangement. A meal eaten late in the evening, perhaps after visiting the cinema or theatre, is called supper (*cena*) and is often eaten in the early hours of the morning in major cities.

It's always advisable to book for high class restaurants or any restaurant in a popular resort during the high season. Note, however, that many budget restaurants don't accept reservations and may not even have a telephone. If you're allergic to smokers, bear in mind that it's unusual to find a non-smoking section in a Spanish restaurant (and many Spaniards smoke throughout a meal). Restaurant bills usually include a 15 per cent service charge (plus 7 per cent value added tax or 16 per cent in 5-fork restaurants), usually shown on the bill as *servicio incluido*. Even when service isn't included the Spanish rarely tip (*propina*) much and may leave a few small coins only. However, many foreigners follow international practice and tip as they would in other countries. Note that not all restaurants accept credit cards, particularly budget restaurants, so it's prudent to check in advance.

There are many excellent guides to Spanish cuisine and restaurants including a number published (in Spanish) by the Spanish *Club de Vinos Gourmets* who also publish an annual guide to Spanish wines (*Guía Práctica de los vinos de España*) and a monthly magazine entitled *Gourmentour*. *Vinoselección* (Conde de la Cimera, 4, 28050 Madrid, tel. (91) 535 2267) is Spain's largest wine club (30,000 members) and publishes the gourmet food and wine magazine *Sobremesa*. Others guides include *The Wine and Food of Spain* by Jan Read with Maite Manjón and Hugh Johnson (Weidenfeld & Nicolson), *The Spanish Table* by Marimar Torres (Ebury Press), *Cooking in Spain* by Janet Mendel (Mirador), the *BMW Gastronomic and Tourist Guide to Spain*, the pocket *Essential Food & Drink Spain* (Automobile Association), *Floyd on Spain* by Keith Floyd (Penguin) and the Michelin *Red Guide España and Portugal*. See also **Alcohol** on page 382 and **Bars & Cafés** on page 342.

¡Que aproveche! (enjoy your meal/*bon appétit*)

LIBRARIES

Spain has poor public libraries, which bear no comparison to the excellent library systems in, for example, Britain and the USA. Most Spaniards don't do a lot of reading and most homes possess few books, which is reflected in the poor public library system. However, Spanish public libraries often have an international section mostly containing English-language books, but also with books in Danish, Dutch, French and German (the selection may depend on the predominant resident expatriate community). There's usually a small annual membership fee, e.g. 500 ptas, but you may not be able to loan books or browse among the bookshelves. Usually you must know in advance what you want and ask for it at a counter. Opening times are usually severely restricted and libraries may open only for a few hours a day, usually in the morning, on just two or three days a week. The largest library in Spain is the National Library in Madrid containing over 2m volumes. The Instituto Cervantes and the Hispanic and Luso Brazilian Council have offices in many countries with extensive Spanish reference (open to non-members) and lending libraries.

Foreign residents will be pleased to know that there are private libraries in many towns run by expatriate organisations and social clubs. There are also secondhand bookshops in resort areas, where you can swap books. Like public libraries, private libraries open for a few hours only on two or three days a week, usually including Saturdays. Annual membership normally costs 500 to 1,500 ptas a year or perhaps a few hundred pesetas more for non-residents (short-term membership is usually available). There may also be a small fee (e.g. 25 ptas) for each book borrowed. Private libraries welcome new members of all nationalities, both residents and non-residents, and are grateful for donations of unwanted books.

16.

SPORTS

Sports facilities in Spain vary considerably depending on the town or area and are usually excellent in major cities and resort areas, although sparse in rural areas. Many towns have municipal all-weather sports complexes (*polideportivos*) and there's a wealth of private country clubs, sports centres and gymnasiums in cities and resort areas, most of which allow guests to use their facilities. All community developments in resort areas have swimming pools and many also have communal tennis courts and other sports facilities. The cost of participation in most sports in Spain is reasonable and less than in most other EU countries, with annual membership of a sports or country club usually between 50,000 and 100,000 ptas a year. Most towns have sports centres and organise a wealth of sports activities and courses at all levels during the summer and other school holidays. Fees are low and are usually between 200 and 500 ptas a session or a few thousand pesetas a month (annual season tickets are also available).

Sports facilities in Spain have been greatly improved in the last decade and now rival most other European countries. Many improvements have been tourist-driven, particularly regarding golf, skiing and water sports. Most Spaniards aren't great sports participants and are more at home watching a soccer or basketball match on TV in a bar than working up a sweat. In general Spaniards are more relaxed in their attitude towards sports and pastimes and they don't work so fervently as northern Europeans and North Americans to enjoy themselves.

Sport in Spain received a huge boost from the 1992 Barcelona Olympic Games, where Spain's athletes won more medals than the total accumulated in all previous games. Spain's athletes are prominent in many world sports including soccer, basketball, tennis, golf and cycling. Other popular sports include swimming, handball, fishing, hiking, horse riding, jai-alai, boules, hunting, motor sports, volleyball and squash. Spain is a mecca for water sports enthusiasts and sailing, waterskiing and wind-surfing have a large following, as do aerial sports such as hang-gliding and paragliding. However, football is Spain's national sport and top teams such as Real Madrid and Barcelona have a vast following throughout the world.

General information about sports facilities and events can be obtained from the SNTO (see page 321), while local information is available from regional, provincial and local tourist offices, all of which publish information regarding special sports events and local sports venues. Many towns also publish an annual sports' programme (*programa de actividades deportivas*). Numerous newspapers and magazines devoted to sport are published in Spain, including three daily sports newspapers in Barcelona alone, although they tend to concentrate mostly on football. Note that a player's licence (which covers all sporting accidents) is necessary to participate in competitive sports in Spain. Information about particular sports can be obtained from the Spanish Sports Council (*Consejo Superior de Deportes*), Avda Martín Fierro s/n, 28003 Madrid (tel. (91) 449 7300).

FOOTBALL

Football (*fútbol*) or soccer is Spain's national sport and easily the country's most important participant and spectator sport. Spanish soccer fans are among the most dedicated and fervent in Europe and are matched in their fanaticism only by the Italians (football isn't just a matter of life and death in Spain — it's far more important!). Every town in Spain has a football pitch and team, and indoor football (*fútbol de sala*) is also played in sports centres throughout the country. Spanish children learn to play football almost as soon as they can walk, with the most promising players being snapped up by the major clubs and coached from an early age in special football schools. Not surprisingly, Spain has many sports newspapers devoted almost exclusively to football, where every aspect of the players' public and private lives are analysed and debated.

The Spanish league is one of the most competitive in Europe and Spanish teams have enjoyed considerable success in European competitions, although the glory days of Real Madrid and Barcelona in the '50s and '60s are long gone and the successes of Spanish clubs have been overshadowed in recent years by the Italians. Spain has never been able to repeat its clubs' successes at international level and the Spanish national team is a constant source of disappointment. The progress of the national team hasn't been helped by the influx of foreign stars in recent years (some 150 play in the first division alone) which makes it difficult for promising young Spanish players to get a game.

The Spanish league is divided into three main divisions, two of which are sub-divided into regional competitions. Division 1 (with 22 teams) and division 2a are national leagues. Division 2b is divided into four regional leagues (I central, II north, III east and IV south) and division 3 consists of local groups regionalised for financial reasons. Spanish clubs also compete in the Spanish Cup (*Copa del Rey*). The Spanish football season runs from September to June, with a break from Christmas eve until the end of January (in common with many other European countries). Matches are usually played on Sundays (occasionally Saturdays), starting at 1700, and evening matches (many televised) are also held most weeks starting as late as 2130. Generally you must queue to buy tickets on match days, although tickets for major games are sold in advance at ticket agencies in department stores such as El Corte Inglés and Galerías Preciados in Madrid. Tickets for the top matches start at around 1,000 ptas (standing) and go up to 10,000 ptas or more for seats. Hooliganism and violence is rare at Spanish football grounds and families can safely take their children to matches.

There's a huge gulf between the top Spanish clubs and the rest regarding every aspect of the game, not least their stadiums. Real Madrid and Barcelona (Barça) in particular stand head and shoulders above the rest. Real Madrid play at the imposing 130,000-seat Santiago Bernabeu stadium, while Barcelona's home is the equally impressive 120,000-seat Nou Camp stadium. Outside the top handful of clubs, attendances at most first division matches are low. A number of division one matches are shown live on TV each week, invariably involving either (or both) Real Madrid or Barcelona, and are screened in bars throughout Spain. Gambling on football is also popular and is organised through a tote system called the *Quiniela*. Spanish football is dominated by arch rivals Real Madrid and Barcelona, with few other teams getting a look in. The current top dog is Real Madrid, who won the first division championship in 1995 and 1997, following four consecutive titles for Barcelona (1991-94). Other top teams include Deportivo La Coruña, Atlético Madrid (who won the first division championship in 1996), RCD Español, Valencia and Atlético Bilbao.

In the early 1990s, Spanish football went through one of the worst periods in its history, during which bad management, lack of European success, excessive spending on expensive foreign players and their salaries, and massive spending on stadiums all took their toll. However, like British premiership clubs, the finances of Spanish clubs have been rescued by the vast revenue from televised football matches in the last few years. Spanish clubs have been awash with money in recent years spending over US$300m in 1997, when unfashionable Real Betis (Seville) paid US$35m for Brazilian international Denilson with an annual salary of US$3.3m and a contract buy-out clause of US$425m! Top clubs demand instant success and tend to swap their coaches almost as often as their players change their shirts. Real Madrid has had eight coaches in the last 10 years, which looks like secure employment when compared with Atlético Madrid's 28 coaches in seven and a half years! Barcelona has also had its fair share of managers in the last few decades (Johan Cruyff lasted longer than most).

Spanish football is renowned for its gifted players and fluent attacking style, although there are a surprising number of sterile one-sided games, lacking in excitement and passion, when teams appear paralysed by the fear of losing. Spanish football is equally noted for its cynical 'gamesmanship' (i.e. cheating) which includes every underhand trick in the book, e.g. obstruction, body-checking, shirt-pulling, elbowing, diving, 'accidental' tripping and collisions, and faked injuries, all of which Spanish players have perfected. Players often do their utmost to get opposing players booked or sent off.

The cheats are aided and abetted by Spanish referees who are often terrible and wildly inconsistent, wither handing out red and yellow cards with abandon or losing control of matches and allowing players to get away with anything short of murder. However, their job isn't helped by players diving to the ground whenever an opposing player comes within tackling distance, although referees are guilty of falling for the most outrageous play-acting which often leads to penalties and players being sent off. The hapless referees are crucified by TV replays, which gleefully highlight their every mistake.

SKIING

Skiing (*esquí*) is a popular sport in Spain, where it's growing faster than in any other European country. Spain is the second most mountainous country in Europe after Switzerland and has over 30 ski resorts in 14 provinces, where the season extends from December to April or May. The most popular form of skiing is naturally downhill (*esquí de descenso*), although cross-country (*esquí nórdico*) skiers are also catered for in many resorts. With Andorra, Spain offers the cheapest skiing holidays in western Europe and is becoming increasingly popular with beginners and intermediate skiers wishing to avoid the high cost of skiing in the Alps. However, most of Spain's resorts aren't sophisticated or developed and most don't offer sufficient challenges to satisfy the demands of advanced skiers, particularly regarding off-piste skiing.

The majority of Spain's resorts are located in the Pyrenees in the provinces of Gerona (Nuria and La Molina), Huesca (Astún, El Cadanchú, Cerler, Formigal and Panticosa), and Lérida with Baqueira-Beret (Spain's most fashionable resort, popular with the Spanish royal family, and Europe's most extensive ski resort outside the Alps), and Boí-Taüll, Masella, La Molina and Supert-Espot. Other skiing regions include the Cordillera Cantábrica region (with the resorts of Alto Campoo, San Isidro, Valdezcaray and Valgrande Pajares), the Guadarrama and Gredos mountains north of Madrid (includes La Pinilla, Navacerrada, Puerto de Navacerrada, Valcotos and Valdesquí), Galicia (Cabeza de la Manzaneda), the Sierra de Gúdar (Turuel) and the Sierra Nevada (Granada).

Although encompassing a relatively small area, the Sierra Nevada (also called 'Sol y Nieve') near Granada is Spain's most famous resort and was the venue for the 1996 World Cup Skiing championships (they were scheduled for 1995, but were cancelled due to lack of snow). The Sierra Nevada is Europe's most southerly winter sports resort and a common boast is that you can ski there in the morning and swim in the Mediterranean in the afternoon (although you would need to be a masochist to swim in the cold waters of the Mediterranean during the skiing season). The resort is centered around the village of Paradollano at 2,100m, with undercover parking for 2,800 vehicles. It has 20 lifts with a capacity of over 30,000 passengers an hour, around 60km of pistes and 30 runs, and skiing up to a height of 3,400m (11,155ft). A ski-lift pass (*forfait*) costs around 3,500 ptas per day (17,500 ptas for six days) in high season, with discounts on certain days, special mid-season rates, package deals and a 50 per cent discount for the over 65s. Snow is generally guaranteed as the resort has an extensive network (over 100) of snow-making machines covering some 20km of pistes (tel. (958) 249119 for snow and weather conditions, given in English and Spanish).

Although cheaper in Spain than many other countries, downhill skiing is an expensive sport, particularly for families. The cost of equipping a family of four is around 160,000 ptas for equipment and clothing, or around 40,000 ptas a person. If you're a beginner it's better to rent ski equipment (skis, poles, boots) or buy secondhand equipment until you're addicted, which, if it doesn't frighten you to death, can happen on your first day on the pistes. Most sports shops in Spain have pre-season and end of season sales of ski equipment.

Most resorts have a range of ski lifts including cable cars, gondolas, chairlifts and draglifts. Pistes in Spain are rated as green (very easy, *muy fácil*), blue (easy, *fácil*), red (difficult, *difícil*) or black (very difficult, *muy difícil*). Adult ski passes cost between 2,000 and 4,000 ptas a day or 10,000 to 20,000 ptas for six days, depending on the number of lifts provided, with passes for children costing around one third less. Ski rental costs around 1,500 ptas a day or 6,000 ptas for six days and boots around half this (the smaller the resort, generally the lower the cost of ski and boot rental). Most resorts have ski schools and the larger resorts such as Sierra Nevada have both Spanish and international ski schools.

Most resorts offer a variety of accommodation including hotels, self-catering apartments and chalets. Accommodation is more expensive during holiday periods (Christmas, New Year and Easter), when ski-lift queues are interminable and pistes are often overcrowded. These periods (and school holidays in February) are best avoided, particularly as the chance of collisions are greatly enhanced when pistes are overcrowded. Outside these periods and particularly on weekdays, resorts are generally free of crowds and queues (not that the Spanish believe in queuing).

Mono-skiing and surfing are particularly popular in Spain and are taught in most resorts, where there are generally few restrictions on where you can practice them. Other activities may include paragliding, parasailing, hang-gliding, ice-skating, snow-shoe walking, sleigh rides, climbing, snow scooters and snowmobiles. Heli-skiing, where helicopters drop skiers off at the top of inaccessible mountains, is possible in Spain. Many winter resorts also provide a variety of mostly indoor activities including tennis, squash, curling, heated indoor swimming pools, gymnasiums, saunas and solariums. The Pyrenees have excellent food influenced by both Basque and French cuisine, and skiers are amply provided with mountain restaurants in most resorts. There's also an excellent choice of restaurants and bars in Spanish resorts which have the most lively and cheapest (with Andorra) night-life of any country in Europe. Spaniards aren't such fanatical skiers as other Europeans and many tend to rave all night and ski in the afternoons only (when their hangovers have cleared), rather than ski from dawn to dusk. There's also night skiing on floodlit runs in some resorts.

For further information about skiing and other winter sports in Spain contact the *Asociación Turística de Estaciones de Esquí y Montaña*, C/Juan Ramón Jiménez, 8, Edificio Eurobuilding, 28035 Madrid (tel. (91) 458 1557) or the *Federación Española de Deportes de Invierno*, C/de Claudio Coello, 32, 28001 Madrid (tel. (91) 575 8943). The latest weather and snow conditions are broadcast on Spanish television and radio, published in daily newspapers, and are available direct from resorts (which provide recorded telephone information). The SNTO publish a number of brochures for winter sports fans including *Winter Sports in Spain, El Turismo de Nieve en España* (in Spanish) and a skiing map (*Mapa de Estaciones de Esquí*).

CYCLING

Spain is one of the foremost cycling countries in Europe, where cycling is both a serious sport and a relaxing pastime. Bicycles (*bicicletas*) are inexpensive in Spain, where you can buy a men's 21-speed mountain bicycle (*bicicleta de montaña*) for as little as 40,000 ptas from a supermarket. Bicycles should be fitted with an anti-theft device such as a steel cable or chain with a lock. If your bicycle is stolen, report it to the local police but don't expect them to find it. Bicycles can be rented in major cities and most resorts by the hour or day (e.g. 1,000 to 1,500 ptas). Not surprisingly in a country with so many hills, mountain biking is a popular sport and bikes can be rented in many mountain resorts and can even be taken on specially-adapted chair lifts to the tops of mountains.

Cycling in Madrid and other cities can be dangerous and isn't recommended (if you cycle in cities, you should wear a smog mask and a crucifix). In addition to the hazards of traffic and pollution in towns and cities, cyclists must contend with the often debilitating heat, interminable hills and poor roads in many areas. However, cycling is usually pleasant in coastal areas and the flatlands outside high summer. Cyclists must use cycle lanes where provided (although there are few in Spain) and mustn't cycle in bus lanes or on footpaths (although people do). Spanish motorists usually give cyclists a wide berth when overtaking, although tourists aren't always so generous, particularly those towing caravans.

It isn't necessary to wear expensive sports clothing when cycling, although a light crash helmet is advisable, particularly for children, and much cheaper than brain surgery. Head injuries are the main cause of death in bicycle accidents, most of which don't involve accidents with automobiles, but are a result of colliding with fixed objects or falls. Always buy a quality helmet that has been approved and subjected to rigorous testing. Reflective clothing is also advisable when riding at night. Take *particular* care on busy roads and don't allow your children onto public roads until they are competent riders.

Cycling is a popular competitive sport in Spain where over 5,000 annual cycling races and events are staged at all levels throughout the country. These include many professional races such as the tour of Spain (*Vuelta de España*) — held over three weeks in April-May and the third most important world cycle race after the tours of France and Italy — and the tour of Andalusia. Spain has a number of top cycling teams including ONCE and Banesto, whose leading rider Miguel Induraín (from Villaba near Pamplona) retired in 1996 after winning the Tour de France for a record five years in succession (1991-95).

Madrid has an annual bicycle fiesta in May when the roads are closed to vehicles and taken over by some 300 to 400,000 cyclists of all ages. There are road and track cycling clubs throughout Spain, although aspiring champions should bear in mind that they need to be extremely fit to join organized trips over mountain routes. For information about clubs and competitions contact the Spanish Cycling Federation (*Federación Española de Ciclismo*), C/de Ferraz, 16-5°, 28008 Madrid (tel. (91) 242 0434). Many companies organise cycling holidays in Spain, including Turespaña, Spain's national tourism board.

HIKING

Spain has some of the finest hiking (*excursiones*) areas in Europe and few countries can offer its combination of good weather and spectacular, unspoilt countryside. Spain is unrivalled in Europe for its diversity of landscape, profusion of flora and fauna, and its variety of native animals and birds, many unique. Serious hikers can enjoy mountain walking in some of the most spectacular scenery in Europe. Spring and autumn are the best seasons for hiking in most of Spain, when the weather generally isn't too hot or too cold, although winter is the best time in the south of Spain. Note, however, that some paths can be extremely dangerous in winter and are only safe in summer.

Hiking isn't a popular sport among the Spanish, although Spain is a favourite destination for foreign hikers. It has a wealth of hiking areas including the Basque country, Cantabria and Asturias in the north (an area often described as 'Switzerland by the sea', containing the Picos de Europa), the Basque mountains and the Cantabrian Cordillera — all areas of outstanding beauty. The Pyrenees and the Ebro region are Spain's most popular and accessible hiking regions, assisted by the abundance of winter sports resorts and skilifts that whisk you to the mountain tops. The north of Spain has many outstanding hiking routes, the most famous of which is the old 'pilgrim's way' from Le Puy in France to Santiago de Compostela in Galicia, designated a *Grande Randonnée* (GR65) by the French. It offers some of the most beautiful scenery in Spain and takes two or more months to complete the whole route, although most hikers complete just a small section at a time.

In central Spain, outstanding hiking areas include the Gredos and Guadarrama Sierras, the Alcarria region, the Sierra of southern Salamanca, the Las Hurdes of northern Extremadura, El Bierzo of western León and the Sierra Morena in the south. Andalusia also has an abundance of spectacular hiking areas including the Alpujarras and the Sierra Nevada in Granada, the Sierra de Grazalema running from Cadiz to Malaga, and the Serranía de Ronda. Spain has nine national parks (four in the Canary Islands), including the Coto de Doñana near Cadiz, Europe's largest nature reserve, and numerous other areas designated as natural parks. For information contact the National Institute for the Conservation of Nature (*Instituto Nacional para la Conservación de la Naturaleza/ICONA*), Gran Vía de San Francisco, 35, 28071 Madrid (tel. (91) 347 6000).

There are tens of thousands of kilometres of official footpaths throughout Spain, most of which are marked with parallel red and white stripes painted on rocks and trees, and accompanied by arrows when the direction changes. The sign of two crossed lines indicates that you should *not* go in that direction. Where paths cross they are shown by different colours, e.g. green and yellow instead of red and white. The best hiking maps are published by the *Instituto Geográfico Nacional (IGN)* and the *Servicio Geográfico del Ejército (SGE)* in scales of 1:200,000, 1:100,000, 1:50,000 and occasionally 1:25,000. The SGE series are generally considered to be more accurate and up to date than those published by the IGN, although neither are up to the standards of the best American and British maps. *Editorial Alpina* produces 1:40,000 and 1:25,000 map booklets for the most popular mountain and foothill areas of Spain and the *Mapa Topográfico Nacional de España* produce a series of 1:50,000 scale maps covering the whole of Spain and showing most footpaths and tracks. Hiking booklets containing suggested walks are published by some regional tourist organisations and maps showing city walks are available in many cities.

In mountain areas, there are over 200 refuge huts (*refugios*) for climbers and hikers, equipped with bunks and a basic kitchen, where overnight accommodation costs as little as 200 ptas. Some are staffed in spring and summer and provide food, although most are unstaffed and you must therefore carry your own food, sleeping bags, cooking utensils and other essentials. Note that many huts are kept locked and enquiries should be made in advance about where to obtain the key. For information contact the Spanish Mountaineering Federation (*Federación Española de Montañismo*), C/Alberto Aguilera, 3° iz, 28015 Madrid, tel. (91) 445 1382).

Dangers: Hiking in Spain is no more hazardous than in other countries, although you should be aware of the dangers. Wherever you walk in Spain, you need to be on the alert for savage dogs. Carry a stick or walking cane to defend yourself (pointing it at a dog is usually enough to prevent it attacking you). Don't venture too far off official paths during the hunting season, when you risk being shot by a trigger-happy hunter. Other 'natural' hazards include encounters with wild animals such as bulls, bears, wild horses, wolves, wildcats, snakes, scorpions, tarantulas and a variety of insects, e.g. mosquitoes, horseflies, ants, wasps and fleas. Your chances of meeting a wild animal or being attacked or bitten are remote, although you should take standard precautions such as checking your clothing and shoes before dressing when camping, wearing protective clothing and using insect repellent. You should also take precautions against the heat and sunstroke and be careful not to start fires, the lighting of which is strictly forbidden in most areas of Spain. If you don't speak Spanish, you should carry a phrase book when hiking in remote areas as few people speak English (or other foreign languages).

Take care when walking on roads in country areas as many have loose gravel and stones, on which it's easy to lose your footing. On narrow, winding country roads you should walk on the side of the road which affords the best view of the road ahead, as many roads have blind corners and some drivers keep close to the edge. This is the one exception when it pays to ignore the 'walk facing the traffic rule', but take care to listen for traffic approaching from behind.

A number of books about hiking in Spain are published in English including *Trekking in Spain* by Marc Dubin (Lonely Planet), *Walking Through Spain* by Robin Nellands and *On Foot Through Europe: A Trail Guide to Spain and Portugal* by Craig Evans (Quill). There are also many books dedicated to walking in particular regions. The SNTO publish a booklet, *Rutas de Montaña y Senderismo* (500 ptas), featuring around 50 mountain walks throughout Spain. Hiking tours and holidays are organised for hikers of all ages and fitness levels throughout Spain, and there are expatriate groups of ramblers in resort areas throughout the country. See also **Camping** on page 328.

MOUNTAINEERING, ROCK-CLIMBING & CAVING

Those who find hiking a bit tame might like to try mountaineering (*alpinismo*), rock-climbing or caving (subterranean mountaineering), all of which are popular in Spain. Sport climbing, where climbs are previously 'equipped' with bolts, is predominant in Spain and is the safest form. Spain is a great country for amateur rock-climbers and mountaineers, and provides a wealth of challenges and some of the best areas in Europe outside the Alps. Around 10,000 caves have been discovered in Spain, many with prehistoric rock paintings and stalactites. Note, however, that some caves are long and dangerous and should be explored only with an experienced guide.

If you're an inexperienced climber, it's advisable to join a club and 'learn the ropes' before heading for the mountains. There are over 750 climbing clubs in Spain, many maintaining their own mountain huts and refuges. Information can be obtained from the

Spanish Mountaineering Federation (*Federación Española de Montañismo/FEM*), C/Alberto Aguilar, 3-4° iz, 28015 Madrid, tel. (91) 445 1382). The FEM also produce 1:50,000 scale maps for mountain areas (see also **Hiking** on page 359 for information regarding maps and refuges). A number of climbing books are published for the most popular regions of Spain.

It's important to hire a qualified and experienced guide when climbing in an unfamiliar area, which are available through climbing clubs and schools throughout Spain (if you find a guide other than through a recognised club or school, ensure that he's qualified). It's important to note that Spain *doesn't* have the sophisticated mountain rescue services provided in Alpine countries and if you get into trouble you will need to rely on your own resources and those of your companions. Many climbers lose their lives each year, often through their inexperience and recklessness. **Needless to say, it's extremely foolish, not to mention highly dangerous, to venture into the mountains without proper preparation, excellent physical condition, adequate training, the appropriate equipment and an experienced guide.**

RACQUET SPORTS

Racquet sports are popular in Spain, particularly tennis. Tennis' popularity has grown tremendously in the last few decades and there are now thousands of courts at tennis and country clubs, hotels, urbanisations, and municipal and private sports centres. Courts have a variety of surfaces including tennis-quick (fast cement court), clay (*arcilla*), cement (*hormigón*), artificial grass and plexipave, many of which are floodlit. There are also indoor courts in the north of Spain, although these are rare in the south and the islands, where the weather permits outdoor tennis to be played all year round. Many tennis clubs offer a variety of other sports facilities including swimming pools and a gymnasium or fitness centre.

Most private clubs and hotels allow guests to use their courts, with fees ranging from a few hundred pesetas an hour at an hotel to 5,000 ptas for daily use of tennis courts and other facilities at a private tennis club, perhaps with a lesson and a 'free' meal included. Courts at private clubs cost from around 500 ptas an hour during the day (750 ptas floodlit) to around 1,500 ptas an hour (2,000 ptas floodlit) for members and up to double for non-members. Most clubs open from early morning until as late as 2300 or 2400. Many urbanisations have private tennis courts which can be used free of charge by residents (they are maintained through community fees), although floodlit lighting must usually be paid for via a coin meter. Courts are usually available on a first come, first served basis, although there may be a booking system in the peak summer season when demand is high.

Annual membership of a private club usually costs from 50,000 to 100,000 ptas a year in a resort area, although fees can be astronomical at exclusive clubs in major cities. Weekly, monthly and six-monthly membership may also be available. Most clubs have special rates for families, children (e.g. under 18) and possibly senior citizens. Many clubs provide saunas, whirl-pools, solariums and swimming pools, and most have a bar and restaurant. All clubs organise regular tournaments and provide professional coaching (individual and group lessons), and many clubs and hotels offer resident tennis schools throughout the year. Individual lessons costs from around 2,500 ptas an hour. Information regarding competitions and tennis clubs can be obtained from the Royal

Spanish Tennis Federation (*Real Federación Española de Tenis*), Avda Diagonal, 618, 08028 Barcelona (tel. (93) 201 0844).

Tennis was long regarded as an elite sport in Spain and although it remains so in some private clubs, it's now a sport of the people and Spain's most popular participant sport after soccer. In the last few years Spain has become one of the world's strongest tennis countries with top male tennis players including Sergei Bruguera, Carlos Costa, Alberto Berasategui, Carlos Moya, Alex Corretja and Jordi Arrese, supported by top 10 female players Arantxa Sánchez Vicario and Conchita Martínez. The majority of top players come from Catalonia, the powerhouse of Spanish tennis.

Squash is gaining popularity in Spain with the increasing number of courts in many areas. There are now squash clubs in most large towns in Spain and many tennis clubs and sports centres have a number of squash courts. However, the standard is low due to the lack of experienced coaches and top class competition, although it's continually improving. Racquets and balls can be rented from most squash clubs for the American version of squash, called racquet ball, which is played in Spain on a squash court. Badminton isn't widely played in Spain and facilities are rare, although some sports centres have badminton courts and there are badminton clubs in some areas.

SWIMMING

Not surprisingly, swimming (*natación*) is a favourite sport and pastime in Spain, with its glorious weather, 2,000km (1,240miles) of beaches (*playas*), and a profusion of swimming pools (*piscinas*). The beach season in Spain lasts from around Easter to October, although many people sunbathe on beaches all year round in the south of Spain, and the Canaries offer year round beach weather. Most people find the Mediterranean too cold for swimming outside June to September and the Atlantic is generally warm enough only in July and August (in northern and southern Spain). Spanish beaches, almost all of which are public, vary considerably in size, surface and amenities. Surfaces include white, grey and even red (fine and coarse) sand, shingles, pebbles and stones. Beaches are generally kept clean and well-groomed all year round, particularly in popular resorts, although in some areas they are covered in garbage and large stones and look more like waste areas than public beaches.

Nevertheless, it's difficult to find a totally unspoilt beach in Spain as pollution and high-rise buildings blight most Spanish beaches, although there are a few in remote areas of the mainland and the islands. The best beaches are to be found on the smaller islands in the Balearics (e.g. Formentera and Menorca) and in the Canaries (e.g. Fuerteventura), where it's even possible to find a deserted beach outside the main tourist season. Beaches are extremely crowded in summer and during school holidays, when bodies are packed in like sardines (or there's standing room only). Beaches away from the main resorts are less crowded and if you have a boat you can visit small coves that are inaccessible from the land. Most beaches have municipal guards, first-aid stations, toilets, showers, bars and restaurants, and some have special paths for those in wheelchairs. Deck chairs, beach-beds and umbrellas can be rented on most beaches, and a wide range of facilities are usually available in summer including volleyball, pedallos and boats for rent, and facilities for most water sports. Note that dogs and camping are forbidden on most beaches in Spain.

Many resorts have made a huge effort to clean up their beaches in recent years and the number of resorts awarded the coveted EU 'blue flag' (*bandera azul*) has risen in all areas.

A total of 329 blue flags were awarded in 1996 which was a quarter of the total for Europe. The SNTO publish an annual list of blue flag beaches and marinas in Spain (tel. (901) 300600 for information). Note, however, that many beaches are still dangerously polluted by untreated sewage and industrial waste, and bathing in some areas (particularly close to industrial towns and cities) isn't advisable. The pollution count (which cannot always be believed) must be displayed at the local town hall: blue = good quality water, green = average, yellow = likely to be temporarily polluted, and red = badly polluted.

Topless and nude bathing is widespread and there are a number of official nudist beaches (*playas naturale/playas de nudistas*) in Spain such as the Costa Natura village situated near Estepona (Malaga) on the Costa del Sol and Almanat near Almayate (Vélez-Málaga), while on the Balearic island of Formentera it's almost standard practice. Topless bathing is permitted on all Spanish beaches, many of which have a section for nude sunbathing. Note, however, that it's possible to get arrested for nude sunbathing on some beaches. Topless bathing is less acceptable at swimming pools, although there are naturist pools in some cities and resorts.

Swimming can be dangerous at times, particularly on the Atlantic coast where some beaches have lethal currents. Swimmers should observe all beach warning signs and flags. Most beaches are supervised by lifeguards who operate a flag system to indicate when swimming is safe; a green flag means that it's safe (calm sea), yellow indicates possible hazardous conditions (take care) and red (danger) means bathing is prohibited. The Red Cross (*Cruz Roja/Puesto de Socorro*) operate first-aid posts on most Spanish beaches during the summer season. There are stinging jellyfish in parts of the Mediterranean. A description of all Spanish mainland and island beaches is provided in *Baedeker's Spain*.

Most Spanish towns have a municipal swimming pool (*piscina municipal*), including heated indoor pools (*piscina acalorado cubierta*) and outdoor pools (*piscinas al aire libre*). The entrance fee to a pool varies considerably (e.g. 250 to 1,000 ptas for adults) depending on whether it's an outdoor or indoor pool and its facilities and location. Many pools offer reduced-price, multiple-ticket options. Opening hours may vary from day to day and most municipal pools don't open during the evenings. Heated indoor pools are open all year round and most outdoor pools are open during the summer only, e.g. from June to September. Public pools in cities are usually overcrowded, particularly at weekends and during school holidays, while pools in hotels and private clubs are less crowded, although more expensive.

There are strict safety regulations at all public and community swimming pools. Regulations usually depend on the depth of a pool, its size (surface area in square metres) and the number of properties it serves, and are established and enforced by local municipalities. They usually include such matters as water quality and treatment, and the provision of showers, non-slip pathways, life belts, first-aid kits and lifeguards. It's usually compulsory to wear a cap in a public or community pool. Usually a lifeguard must be on duty whenever a public or community pool is open (very large pools may require two lifeguards). Note, however, that many hotels and communities have dangerous pools without lifeguards. **It's important to ensure that young children don't have access to swimming pools and private pools should be fenced to prevent accidents (also take extra care around rivers and lakes).**

Most swimming pools and clubs provide swimming lessons (all levels from beginner to fish) and run life saving courses. Spain also has many water parks (*parque acuático*) and water sports centres where facilities include indoor and outdoor pools, water slides, flumes, wave machines, river rapids, whirlpools and waterfalls, sun-beds, saunas, solariums, jacuzzis, hot baths and a children's area. Most water parks are open during the summer season only, e.g. from June to September.

It's important to protect yourself against the sun in Spain to prevent sunburn and heatstroke, which includes using a high protection sun cream, a sun block on lips and nipples, and drinking plenty of water. On some beaches a body spray service is provided where you can be sprayed head to toe with sun tan lotion. If you aren't used to Spain's fierce sun, you should limit your exposure and avoid it altogether during the hottest part of the day in summer, wear protective clothing (including a hat) and use a sun block.

WATER SPORTS

Spain is a mecca for water sports enthusiasts, which is hardly surprising considering its immense coastline (7,880km/4,896miles), many islands, numerous lakes and reservoirs, and thousands of kilometres of rivers and canals. Popular water sports include sailing, windsurfing, waterskiing, jet-skiing, rowing, canoeing, kayaking, surfing, rafting and subaquatic sports. In addition to the Atlantic and Mediterranean, many reservoirs and lakes are also popular venues for sailing, water-skiing and wind-surfing. Note that coastal resorts often have designated areas for wind-surfing, waterskiing and jet-skiing, and it's forbidden to operate outside these areas. Wet suits are recommended for wind surfing, waterskiing and subaquatic sports, even during the summer. Rowing and canoeing is possible on many lakes and rivers, where canoes and kayaks can usually be rented. Spain's premier canoeing event is the 22km Descenso del Sella down the Sella river in Asturias (from Arriondas to Ribadasella), which takes place on the first Saturday in August. Surfing is popular along the Atlantic coast of the Basque Lands and Cantabria: however, Lanzarote in the Canaries is the Hawaii of the Atlantic to surfers and Fuerteventura is also good. Spain also has Europe's foremost windsurfing area at Tarifa. There are clubs for most water sports in all major resorts and towns throughout Spain and instruction is usually available.

Scuba-diving is a popular sport in Spain, where there are many diving clubs offering instruction and equipment and boat rental. **Note, however, that scuba-diving can be dangerous and safety is of paramount importance. For this reason, many experts don't recommend learning to dive while on holiday. Holiday divers should in any case dive only with a reputable club, and, due to the dangers of decompression, stop diving 24 hours before taking the flight home.** A diving permit (costing around 1,000 ptas) is required to dive in Spanish waters and is obtainable from clubs and schools. Among the best areas for scuba divers are the seas around the Balearic and Canary islands. For information contact the Spanish Subaquatic Federation (*Federación Española de Actividades Subacuáticas*), C/Santaló, 15, Barcelona (tel. (93) 228 8796).

Spain has some of the world's best windsurfing areas including Fuerteventura in the Canaries (claimed by many to offer the best windsurfing in the world), El Mádano in south Tenerife, and Tarifa at the southernmost tip of Spain on the Strait of Gibraltar. Tarifa is a windsurfers' paradise and Europe's windiest place, where winter winds from the southwest or northeast can reach up to 120 kph (75 mph) and the average wind speed is 34 kph (21 mph). A new sport to hit Spain in recent years is canyoning, a combination of abseiling and white-water rafting consisting of descending gushing rivers, waterfalls and canyons with the aid of ropes. It can be dangerous and only 'lunatics' need apply. The best white-water area in Spain is Ribadesella in Asturias.

Be sure to observe all warning signs on lakes and rivers. Take particular care when canoeing as some rivers have 'white water' patches that can be dangerous for the inexperienced. It's always wise to wear a life-jacket when canoeing, irrespective of whether you're a strong swimmer or not. All water sports equipment can be rented, although you're usually required to leave a large deposit and should take out insurance against damage or loss. Unless you're an experienced rider, it's advisable to steer well clear of jet-skis, which are deadly in the wrong hands.

Spain has a wealth of yacht marinas and harbours, many with over 1,000 berths (including Benalmádena and Puerto Banús on the Costa del Sol), which are scattered liberally along Spain's coasts. Puerto Banús near Marbella is Spain's answer to St. Tropez where the rich go to sea and be seen, full of vast ostentatious yachts, flash cars and beautiful people. There are also numerous sailing clubs (*club náutico*) based at marinas and sports harbours, all of which offer tuition and courses. Both crewed and uncrewed yachts can be rented in resorts, although you need a skipper's certificate or a helmsman's overseas certificate to rent an uncrewed yacht. If you have a few million pesetas to spare and wish to impress your friends, you can even rent a luxury yacht with crew.

Despite the large number of marinas, berths can be difficult to find in summer in some areas, although temporary berths can usually be found on public jetties and harbours. Moorings can be expensive, particularly in the most fashionable resorts such as Marbella. The cost of keeping a yacht on the Atlantic coast is cheaper than on the Mediterranean or in the islands, although even here it needn't be too expensive providing you steer clear of the most fashionable berths (e.g. from as little as 1,000 ptas a day for an 8 x 3 metre berth in low season to 4,000 ptas a day for a 20 x 5 metre berth in high season). Races take place in many classes (such as dinghies) all year round, while yacht racing is generally restricted to between April and October, during which period there are big regattas in the Balearics (where the most prestigious event is the Copa del Rey which takes place off Palma de Mallorca in August) and the Bay of Cadiz. Boating holidays are popular in Spain, where boats of all shapes and sizes can be rented in harbours and coastal resorts. For information about marinas and competitions contact the Spanish Sailing Federation (*Federación Española de Vela*), C/Juan Vigón, 23, 28003 Madrid (tel. (91) 533 5305).

Spain is a good place to buy a yacht as prices are very competitive. However, since 1993, the 'wandering yacht' hasn't been able to escape VAT as it must be levied on all yachts purchased in EU countries by EU citizens at the time of sale. Note that VAT is paid in the country of registration or destination and therefore you should compare Spain's 16 per cent VAT (IVA) with the country of purchase. EU residents aren't permitted to register their vessels abroad simply to avoid paying VAT, and any vessel registered outside the EU must be located there and is liable for import duties if berthed in an EU port. Previously owners could escape paying VAT by keeping their yachts harboured for less than six months a year in a particular EU country. Note than all vessels kept permanently in Spain must be registered. Buyers from non-EU countries remain exempt from VAT, providing they export their yachts to non-EU waters. However, a foreign-registered boat can be kept in Spain and used there for six months a year, but must be sealed (*precintar*) when it isn't being used. Boats can also be operated on Spanish tourist flag registration to avoid paying Spanish taxes.

AERIAL SPORTS

Spain is an outstanding country for all aerial sports including light-aircraft flying, gliding, hang-gliding, paragliding, parachuting, sky-diving, ballooning and microlighting. Spain's many mountain ranges, particularly the Pyrenees, are excellent venues for aerial sports such as hang-gliding and paragliding, due to the strong air currents that allow pilots to stay aloft for hours. Paragliding, which entails jumping off a steep mountain slope with a parachute, is technically easier than hang-gliding. The Pyrenees are reckoned to be the best mountains in Europe for hang-gliding and paragliding, with their warm summers and wide valleys. Participants must complete an approved course of instruction, after which they receive a proficiency certificate and are permitted to go solo. Competitions are held throughout the country, often with cash prizes. If you employ an instructor for any aerial sport, always ensure that he's qualified.

A flight in a balloon is a marvelous experience, although there's no guarantee of distance or duration and trips are dependent on wind conditions and the skill of your pilot. A flight usually costs around 20,000 ptas (often including a champagne breakfast) and is made either at dawn or in the evening when the air is more stable. There are balloon meetings and competitions throughout Spain, particularly in summer. It is, however, an expensive sport and participation is generally limited to the wealthy (lawyers and politicians get a reduction for supplying their own hot air). A list of ballooning clubs is available from the SNTO and local tourist offices in Spain.

There are flying clubs at most airfields in Spain, where light aircraft and gliders can be rented. Parachuting and freefall parachuting (sky-diving) flights can also be made from many private airfields in Spain. The south of Spain is an excellent place to learn to fly as it's rarely interrupted by bad weather. The latest craze to have taken off in Spain is microlight (or ultralight) flying, which is a low-flying go-cart with a hang glider on top and a motorised tricycle below, and one of the cheapest and most enjoyable ways to experience real flying. For information about aerial sports in Spain contact the *Real Aero Club de España*, Carretera San Jerónimo, 15, 28014 Madrid (tel. (091) 429 8534) or the *Asociación Española de Pilotos*, C/ Alfredo Truan, 11, 9A, 33205 Gijón (Asturias).

Before taking up aerial sports, you're advised to make sure that you have adequate health, accident and life insurance and that your affairs are in order. Why not try fishing instead? A nice, sensible, <u>SAFE</u> sport (unless, of course, you're a fish).

FISHING

Spain is a paradise for fishermen and with 2,119km (1,317miles) of mainland coastline, over 75,000km of rivers (46,000miles) and thousands of lakes and reservoirs, it can keep even the keenest of anglers busy for a few weeks. There's excellent fishing (*pesca*) in inland waterways including rivers, lakes and reservoirs, where a permit (*permiso de pesca*) is required. Permits are issued by the local provincial office of the National Institute for the Conservation of Nature (*Instituto Nacional para la Conservación de la Naturaleza/ICONA*), Avda Gran Vía de San Francisco, 35-41, 28071 Madrid (tel. (91) 347 6000).

The fishing season varies depending on the particular species of fish, e.g. the trout season starts in March and the salmon season commences on the first Sunday in March. The salmon season closes on the second Sunday in July and the trout season at the end of August or September. On most rivers there are restrictions on the number of licences issued each day and on the size of fish (and often the number) that may be caught, and the bait and technique that can be employed. The most common freshwater fish include various species of trout, barbel, pike, carp, bogue, black bass, mullet, sturgeon, bream, tench and perch. Salmon are found in streams and rivers in the Cantabrian range and in Galicia, and trout are common in the upper reaches of rivers throughout Spain. Information about local fishing areas and fishing permits is available from local town halls and tourist offices. Tourist offices may also provide a fishing map (*Mapa de Pesca Fluvial*) showing where to fish and what you may catch, plus details of seasons and licences.

Sea fishing is also popular in Spain and you can fish without a licence from anywhere along Spain's coastline or rent a boat and go out to sea. Many Spaniards fish from beaches in winter (but don't seem to catch much). Common saltwater fish include grouper, sea-bream, mackerel, cod, tuna, mullet, bonito, swordfish and various species of shark, although sea fishing is declining in popularity as Spanish waters are largely fished out (particularly the Mediterranean). Boat rental, perhaps with a local fisherman as a guide, and deep-sea fishing trips can be arranged throughout Spain. Sea fishing is prohibited from one hour after sunset until one hour before dawn and deep-sea fishermen need a licence from the provincial *Comandancias de Marina*. For more information about fishing in Spain contact the National Fishing Federation (*Federación Nacional de Pesca*), C/Navas de Tolosa, 3, 28013 Madrid (tel. (91) 532 8353).

HUNTING

Hunting (*caza*) is extremely popular in Spain, which has some 35m hectares of hunting land including national parks, national hunting reserves, national preserves, and numerous private big and small game reserves. The best hunting areas are the Atlantic coast, the Pyrenees and parts of Andalusia, where big game includes mountain goat (*cabra hispánica*), various species of deer, ibex, roebuck, chamois, stag, wild boar, wolf and big-horned mountain sheep. Certain animals such as bears and lynx are in danger of extinction and are completely protected (although it doesn't stop people shooting them).

The hunting season for all game is strictly defined and there are large fines for anyone caught hunting out of season. The hunting season for small game runs from mid-October to early February (although some game can be hunted all year round) and includes grouse, quail, ring dove, turtle dove, red-legged partridge (the most common prey), pheasant, duck, geese, bustard, water fowl, pigeon, hare and rabbit. Like the French and Italians, the Spanish kill thousands of songbirds each year, which are considered a delicacy by many people and are unprotected. There's no tradition of conservation in Spain and most hunters are inclined to shoot anything that moves. Although they won't deliberately shoot you (unless you're a conservationist), it's advisable to steer clear of the countryside during the hunting season.

There are several kinds of hunting land, ranging from free zones where only a general licence (*permiso de caza*) is necessary, to municipal-owned local reserves, private reserves and national reserves, where a special licence is required. To hunt in a national reserve you need a hunting permit issued by the provincial office of the National Institute for the Conservation of Nature (*Instituto Nacional para la Conservación de la Naturaleza/ICONA*), Avda Gran Vía de San Francisco, 35-41, 28071 Madrid (tel. (91) 347 6000). Special permission is also required to hunt in a private reserve (*coto privado de caza/coto vedado de caza*). The best way to hunt in Spain is to join a local club. When hunting is prohibited, it's usually denoted by a square sign divided diagonally into black and white halves.

Hunters need a medical certificate obtainable from special clinics (*Centros de Reconocimento Médico para Conductores y Armas todas las Categorías*), a firearms permit (*permiso de armas*) and third party insurance. Guns must be broken and bagged when transported on public land and they may not be used within 500 metres of a house or in any urban zone (often ignored). Non-resident hunters may import their own firearms, although they need to obtain an import certificate from their local Spanish consulate abroad (take your current firearms certificate to the consulate with a photocopy and your passport). On arrival in Spain the import certificate and gun must be taken to the local police station, who will issue a Spanish gun permit.

There are a number of magazines devoted to hunting in Spain and regional tourist offices publish hunting leaflets and maps. Hunting trips and holidays for hunters are organised on private estates throughout Spain (the most popular regions are Castille-La Mancha, Andalusia, Extremadura and Castille & Leon). For further information about hunting contact the Spanish Hunting Federation (*Federación Española de Caza*), Avda Reina Victoria, 53, 28006 Madrid (tel. (91) 553 3495).

GOLF

Golf is one of the fastest growing sports in Spain and is becoming increasingly popular with the Spanish, although it's still regarded by many as an elite game for rich businessmen, tourists and the elderly. Spain has around 150 courses with many more planned, but still trails well behind other 'new' golfing nations such as France, Germany and Sweden, and ranks around 12th in the world in the number of courses. Most courses are concentrated in the main tourist areas and islands and include Europe's biggest concentration of golf courses along the western Costa del Sol from Malaga to Cadiz, dubbed the 'Costa del Golf'. With the exception of a few months in the summer when it's too hot, southern Spain has the perfect climate for golf, particularly during the winter. There's even a floodlit golf course for insomniacs on the Costa del Sol (the *Dama de Noche*) open 24-hours a day (a minimum of 10 golfers are needed to book the course at night).

Spanish golf courses are invariably excellent and beautifully maintained. Most courses are located in beautiful settings (sea, mountain and forest), many designed by famous designers such as Robert Trent Jones, Jack Nicolas and Severiano Ballesteros and linked with real estate development. Properties on or near golf clubs (often including 'free' life membership) are popular with foreigners seeking a permanent or second home in Spain and are among the cheapest golf properties in Europe. Some golf clubs offer golf shares for around 1 or 2m ptas, usually providing members with a number of free rounds or even free golf for life. Many golf clubs are combined with country or sports clubs and offer a wide range of sports and social facilities including swimming pools, tennis, squash, gymnasium, snooker/pool, and a bar and restaurant.

Spain has courses to suit all standards, although there are few inexpensive public courses and it's an expensive sport. Golf used to be relatively inexpensive in Spain but has become much dearer in recent years, although fees remain lower than in many other European countries. Most courses are owned by syndicates and have annual membership fees of from around 200,000 ptas for a single person (couples 350,000 to 400,000 ptas) and seasonal and daily fees for non-members. Most clubs don't have a waiting list for new members or strict handicap requirements for non-members, although they usually insist on golfers wearing suitable attire.

Green fees vary depending on the club and the season, and on the Costa del Sol are usually from around 5,000 ptas in winter and from 4,000 in summer (not as popular due to the extreme heat) for 18 holes. In the north of Spain, fees may be cheaper in winter than in the summer or remain the same all year round. Fees at an exclusive club such as Valderrama (Cadiz) can be as high as 20,000 ptas a round and you may be restricted to teeing off at certain times only, e.g. between 1200 and 1400. Green fees are often reduced early in the morning, e.g. for rounds starting within one hour of opening or anytime before noon, and late in the afternoon, e.g. between 1500 or 1700. Many clubs offer reductions to couples, senior citizens and groups and have weekly rates. Note, however, that many clubs restrict non-members to off-peak times and it's often difficult for non-members to get a game at weekends and during school holidays. Playing with a member usually entitles guests to a reduction on green fees. Third party accident insurance is obligatory and costs around 200 ptas a day.

You can rent golf clubs (e.g. 2,000 ptas), golf trolleys/carts (around 300 ptas a round or 1,200 ptas for an electric trolley) and electric golf buggies (3,000 to 4,000 ptas a round) at all clubs. The golf cart has virtually made the caddie extinct in Spain and some courses are built in difficult terrain where it's almost mandatory to use a buggy. Most clubs have a pro shop with a club professional, driving ranges, practice putting and pitching greens, and offer individual and group instruction and a full programme of competitions. Clubs and a growing number of golf schools hold regular clinics for all standards from beginner to expert. Clubs are usually members of the Royal Spanish Golf Federation (*Real Federación Española de Golf*), C/Capitán Haya, 9-5°, 28020 Madrid (tel. (91) 555 2682), who produce a detailed map of Spanish golf courses showing their vital statistics and an annual competition calendar (*Calendario Oficial de Competiciones*).

Spain hosts more regular PGA European Tour events than any other country, mostly during the beginning and end of the season when the weather in northern Europe is unreliable. Valderrama hosts the Volvo Masters Tournament in autumn, the last and richest event in Europe, and was the venue for the 1997 Ryder Cup (between teams from Europe and the USA), the first time it has been held outside the USA and Britain. Spain is the second strongest European golfing country after Britain, although it's now having to beat off a strong challenge from Sweden. In the last few decades it has produced many top male professional golfers including Severiano Ballesteros, José María Olazábel, Miguel Angel Jiménez, Manuel Piñero, José María Cañizares, Miguel Angel Martín, Ignacio Garrido, Diego Borrego and José Rivero, to name but a few, plus a number of top women golfers.

Golf holidays are popular in Spain and a major source of revenue for clubs, most of which welcome visitors and often offer special rates. Some hotels cater almost exclusively for golfers and offer golf holiday packages inclusive of green fees (or reduced green fees). A guide to Spanish golf courses (*Guía de Golf—España*) is available from SNTO offices or the Secretaria General de Turismo, C/de María de Molina, 50, 28006 Madrid (tel. (91) 411 4014) and many regions and provinces publish golf guides (*Golf Guía Práctica*) with maps. A number of free and subscription golf magazines are published in Spain, most with articles printed in both Spanish and English, including *Andalucía Golf* and *Costagolf*.

OTHER SPORTS

The following are a selection of other popular sports in Spain:

Athletics: Most Spanish towns have local athletics (*atlético*) clubs which organise local competitions and sports days, including fun runs, half-marathons and marathons. Jogging is (surprisingly) more popular in Spain than in many other countries and there are reportedly twice as many joggers in Spain as in Britain. In recent years (since the Barcelona Olympics in 1992) Spain has become a force in middle and long-distance running.

Basketball: Basketball (*baloncesto*) is extremely popular in Spain (second only to football in Barcelona) and there are amateur clubs in all large towns and cities. Barcelona and Real Madrid are among Europe's top professional clubs and play in the European Clubs Championship group A, with matches being regularly televised.

Billiards and Snooker: Many hotels, bars and sports clubs have billiard or snooker tables and there are billiard and snooker clubs in the larger towns where billiards, snooker and American pool can be played. Many pubs and snooker clubs in resort areas organise leagues and competitions with cash prizes for both men and ladies.

Bungee Jumping: If your idea of fun is jumping off a high bridge or platform with an elastic rope attached to your body to prevent you merging with the landscape, then bungee jumping may be just what you're looking for. Although late starters, the Spanish have taken to bungee jumping with a vengeance. Most venues employ purpose-built platforms and cranes (rather than natural locations) which are sometimes erected on beaches in summer.

Gymnasiums & Health Clubs: Spain has a wealth of gymnasiums (*gimnasios*) and health clubs in cities and resort areas where dedicated masochists go to torture themselves. Most clubs have tonnes of expensive bone-jarring, muscle-wrenching apparatus, plus saunas, jacuzzis, steam baths and beauty treatments. Many gyms are part of a larger sports complex where facilities may include a swimming pool, tennis, paddle tennis, martial arts and squash, plus a bar, restaurant and children's playground or crèche. Dance, training and exercise classes are also offered by many sports centres and clubs.

Most clubs offer weekly, monthly or annual membership or you can just pay for individual classes on a pay-as-you-go basis. Fees vary considerably and start at around 5,000 ptas a month for a single person in a resort area. There are usually reduced fees for couples, and children (e.g. under 16) accompanied by a parent may be admitted free. Individual classes are usually around 1,000 ptas a session. Most clubs permit visitors, who usually pay a daily membership fee of between 500 and 1,000 ptas (although it can be as high as 3,000 ptas at exclusive clubs). Many clubs offer a one-day free trial or a free introductory class. Clubs are usually open from around 0800 to between 2200 and 2400, seven days a week, although some close on Sundays. Note that some clubs are small and extremely crowded, particularly during lunch hours and early evening, and it's advisable to check the numbers at the times you wish to attend before becoming a member.

Handball: Handball is a popular sport in Spain, as it is throughout continental Europe, and it has some of the top teams in Europe. It's played indoors on a pitch similar to a five-a-side soccer pitch, where players pass the ball around by hand and attempt to throw it into a small goal. It's particularly popular among footballers with two left feet.

Horse Riding: Horse riding is widespread in Spain, which has a long history of horse breeding and horsemanship. The Spanish or Andalusian thoroughbred is among the most famous breeds in the world and the art of horsemanship is demonstrated in many equestrian schools (such as the *Real Escuela Andaluza del Arte Ecuestre* in Jerez). Spain has numerous ranches, riding centres and schools (*picaderos*) where you can hire a horse by the hour or day. Instruction is provided and cross country and mountain treks on ancient shepherd's paths are organised, including day trips and tours lasting a number of weeks. The SNTO provide information about riding holidays in Spain, and regional and municipal tourist offices provide details of local schools and riding centres. For more information contact the Spanish Riding Federation (*Federación Hípica Española*), C/Monte Esquinza, 8, 28010 Madrid (tel. (91) 419 0233).

Lawn Bowls: Lawn green bowls was introduced to Spain in 1976 and there are now clubs (around 20) in all popular resort areas where winter and summer championships are held, including both league and cup knockout competitions. Clubs offer short-term membership to non-residents. Indoor bowls isn't played in Spain as lawn bowls can be played throughout the year in most areas. The Spanish play their own version of bowls (*bolas*) which bears little resemblance to *boules* or *pétanque* played in France (and none at all to lawn bowls).

Motor-Racing & Motor-Cycling: The Spanish are great motor racing fans and Spain stages many international races including the Spanish formula one grand prix held at various circuits including the Circuito de Jarama race track north of Madrid, the Montmeló Circuit de Catalunya in Barcelona or Jerez de la Frontera. Spain has no top formula one drivers but has produced some leading rally drivers including two-time world rally champion Carlos Sainz. Four-wheel driving is a popular sport in the mountains of southern Spain. Motor-cycling also has a large following in Spain, which has a long tradition of producing world motor-cycling champions and is one of Europe's top motor-cycling nations.

Pelota (or Jai Alai): Pelota was invented by the Basques, who comprise many of the best players in north America, and it's their national sport. Every town of any size in the Basque lands (on both sides of the border) has a *frontón*, the three-sided court on which pelota is played, and it's also played in other parts of Spain. It's played by two or five players who throw a ball against the end wall usually with a woven basket (*chistera*) strapped to an arm, although a leather glove or even bare hands are also used (there are over 20 versions played in some 25 countries). The *chistera* combines the functions of glove and catapult, in which the ball is caught and hurled back against the wall at speeds of up to 200kmh (124mph). Pelota is the fastest ball game in the world and players sometimes wear crash helmets to protect themselves if they're hit on the head by the ball. However, the real purpose of pelota is a vehicle for gambling and huge sums are wagered on top games. For information contact the *Federación Española de Pelota*, C/Lo Madrazo, 11-5°, 28014 Madrid (tel. (91) 521 4299).

Miscellaneous: Many foreign sports and pastimes have a group of expatriate (and also Spanish) fans in Spain including American football, baseball, boccia, boules, ten-pin bowling, cricket, croquet, polo (which has a long history in Spain) and rugby. Cricket is popular in many parts of Spain, where it's mainly played by zealous expatriate Brits with a few eccentric Spaniards to make up the numbers. There are a number of cricket clubs in Spain competing in leagues and knock-out competitions between March and November. Polo is also a popular sport in Spain and is played throughout the year at a number of clubs. For information about local sports facilities and clubs, enquire at tourist offices, town halls, and embassies and consulates (see **Appendix A**).

17.

SHOPPING

Spain isn't renowned as one of Europe's great shopping countries, either for quality or bargains, although the choice and quality of goods on offer has improved considerably since Spain joined the European Union. Prices of many consumer goods such as TV and stereo systems, computers, cameras, electrical apparatus and household appliances have fallen dramatically in recent years and are now similar to most other EU countries. Furthermore, if you're fortunate enough to get paid in a currency that has increased in value against the peseta in recent years, you will be pleasantly surprised how far your money will stretch.

Small family-run stores (*tiendas*) still constitute the bulk of Spanish retailers, although the shopping scene has been transformed in the last decade with the opening of numerous shopping centres (many beautifully designed) and hypermarkets, and the effects of the recession in the early 1990s. Following the trend in most European countries there has been a drift away from town centres by retailers to out-of-town shopping centres (malls) and hypermarket complexes, which has left some 'high streets' run down and abandoned. The biggest drawback to shopping in cities and towns is parking, which can be a nightmare. Note that some British 'catalogue' stores also operate in Spain such as British Mail Order Services (includes Argos and Kays) which has four stores on the Costa Blanca and two on the Costa del Sol. Customers can order from catalogues and pay in pesetas or £sterling, although there's a surcharge of 15 per cent.

With the exception of markets, where haggling over the price is part of the enjoyment (except when buying food), retail prices are fixed in Spain and shown as PVP (*precio de venta al público*). It's important to shop around and compare prices in Spain as they can vary considerably, not only between small shops and hypermarkets, but also among supermarkets and hypermarkets in the same town. Note, however, that price differences often reflect different quality, so make sure you're comparing similar products. The best time to have a shopping spree is during the winter and summer sales (*rebajas*) in January-February and July-August respectively, when bargains (*gangas*) abound and prices are often slashed by 50 per cent or more (the best bargains are usually clothes). If you're looking for bargains, you may also wish to try the cut-price shops which sell everything at 100 (or 200/300) pesetas (*todo a 100/200/300 pesetas*); most items couldn't even have been manufactured for this price (much of it's bankrupt stock).

Among the best buys in Spain are the diverse handicrafts which include antiques, cultured pearls, shawls, pottery, ceramics, damascene, embroidery, fans, glassware, hats, ironwork, jewellery, knives, lace, suede and leather, paintings, porcelain (e.g. Lladró from Valencia), rugs, trinkets and carved woodwork. Although the number of artisans has fallen dramatically in the last few decades, arts and crafts have survived the 20th century better in Spain than in most other western European countries.

Shopping 'etiquette' in Spain may differ considerably from what you're used to, particularly in market places and small stores. The Spanish (and many tourists) don't believe in queuing and people often push and shove their way to the front. Don't expect shop assistants to serve customers in order; you must usually speak up when it's your turn to be served. You also shouldn't expect service with a smile, except perhaps when you're being served by the owner. Shop assistants in supermarkets and hypermarkets can be surly and unhelpful, and some staff give the impression they couldn't care less about your custom. On the other hand, in small shops where you're a regular customer, you will be warmly received and many shopkeepers will even allow you to pay another day if you don't have enough money with you.

In major cities and tourist areas you *must* be wary of pickpockets and bag-snatchers, particularly in markets and other crowded places. *Never* tempt fate with an exposed wallet or purse or by flashing your money around. The Spanish generally pay cash when shopping, although credit and debit cards are widely accepted. However, personal cheques (even local ones) aren't usually accepted. Don't be surprised if you don't receive any one peseta coins in your change as prices are usually rounded up or down to the nearest five pesetas.

For those who aren't used to buying articles with metric measures and continental sizes, a list of comparative weights and measures are included in **Appendix C**. For information about pharmacies (chemists) see **Drugs & Medicines** on page 239.

SHOPPING HOURS

Shopping hours in Spain vary considerably depending on the region, city or town and the type of shop. There are no statutory closing days or hours for retail outlets, except in Catalonia where shops must close by 2100. However, Spain's hitherto unrestricted opening hours were curtailed in 1994 by a new law restricting opening on Sundays and public holidays, designed to protect small retailers. Large stores may open on a maximum of 12 Sundays and public holidays (*festivos*) a year (fines start at 2m ptas for those who break the law!), although a new national law of free commercial hours is due to come into effect in the year 2001.

However, the law can be relaxed by regional governments in designated 'tourist' zones (which may permit Sunday opening in July and August) and hypermarkets can open on certain public holidays and Sundays, e.g. in December. Stores located in zones of 'great tourist influence' (beach resorts and historic towns) can apply to open their shops all year round, not just during the summer months (some food stores even remain open 24 hours a day). As in other European countries, small shopkeepers (who close for siestas and at weekends) are having increasing difficulty competing with hypermarkets and department stores, which previously opened seven days a week.

A big surprise for many foreigners is the long afternoon *siesta*, when most small shops close from 1330 or 1400 until around 1700. Apart from department stores and many large supermarkets, there's no such thing as afternoon shopping in Spain. The *siesta* makes good sense in the summer when it's often too hot to do anything in the afternoon, but it isn't so practical in winter when evening shopping must be done in the dark. However, foreigners are often divided over Spain's shopping hours, some seeing them as a inconvenience, others a bonus. Many people actually find they prefer to shop in the evening when they get used to it.

Most small shops open from between 0830 and 0930 (or earlier for food shops) until between 1300 and 1400 and from around 1700 until between 1930 and 2100, Monday to Friday, and from 0930 until 1400 on Saturdays. Note, however, that in some areas most shops are closed on Monday mornings. In the south of Spain, the *siesta* generally lasts from 1330 or 1400 until 1700. Department stores, hypermarkets and many supermarkets are open continually (without a break for a *siesta*) from around 0930 or 1000, until between 2000 and 2200 from Monday to Saturday. Department stores and hypermarkets may also open on Sundays (e.g. 1000 to 1500 or 1200 to 2000) and public holidays (e.g. 1000 to 2000). During the summer, shops in resort areas (particularly food shops and tobacconist's) often remain open until 2200 or 2300 (except in Catalonia). Shops in resort areas may also remain open longer on Saturdays and open on Sunday mornings in the summer. In major cities such as Madrid and Barcelona and some resort towns there are

24-hour, American-style, drugstores comprising a supermarket, cafeteria, tobacconist's and restaurant.

In general, shops close for one whole day and one half day each week, usually on Saturday afternoon and Sunday (some shops also close on Mondays or Monday mornings). In Madrid and other cities some shops close for the whole of August, when everyone is on holiday.

SHOPPING FOR FOOD

The hallmark of Spanish cooking is the use of fresh local produce and not surprisingly, shopping for food (and eating) is a labour of love in Spain, where the range and quality of fresh food is unsurpassed. Many Spanish housewives shop daily, not because it's necessary but out of enjoyment and the opportunity to socialise. The Spanish housewife has traditionally preferred to shop in small specialist food shops and markets, rather than in large soulless supermarkets and hypermarkets, although this is changing. Some 70 per cent of food in Spain is now purchased in self-serve supermarkets and hypermarkets and the days of the family-run shop are numbered. Those that remain survive by offering a friendly and personal service (advice, tastings, etc.), stocking local fare and providing better quality than supermarkets.

If you wish to save money on your weekly food bill, it isn't only what you buy, but where you shop that's important. In general it's best to shop at markets and small stores where the Spanish shop. It takes more time but is better value than shopping at supermarkets and the quality is also usually better. It helps if you speak some Spanish, although it's easy to point and say *un kilo* or *medio kilo* (half a kilo). A freezer is useful and allows you to buy in bulk, although you also shouldn't be concerned about buying small amounts as the Spanish often buy in small quantities, e.g. multiples of 100 grammes. In some areas foreign food shops operate clubs allowing members to buy food at wholesale prices.

The Spanish haven't developed a taste for foreign foods and are parochial in their food tastes. Consequently Spain doesn't import a lot of foreign foods, although there are specialist imported food shops in major cities and resorts with many foreign residents, and most supermarkets offer a selection of foreign foods (but don't expect to find shelves full of imported meat, cheese or wine). **Note that if you insist on buying expensive imported foods, your food bill will skyrocket.**

Meat: Many villages and all towns have a butcher's shop (*carnicería*) selling all kinds of meat, although generally speaking pork is the preserve of the *charcutería* (see below). Pork (*carne de cerdo*) is the most widely consumed meat in Spain and with chicken provides the best value for money. Veal (*carne de ternera*) is also fairly common, although expensive. Beef (*carne de vaca*) and lamb (*carne de cordero*) are expensive and not particularly good. Chicken (*pollo*) and eggs (*huevos*) are also sold in special shops called *pollerías* and eggs may be sold in a *huevería* (egg shop). Baby suckling pig (*cochinillo*) and baby lamb (*cordero*) are favourite dishes in central Spain, where they are roasted in a wood or clay oven. Game is plentiful outside summer and fresh rabbit is available throughout the year. Kebab meat for barbecues is sold cubed and marinated.

Meat is cut differently in Spain than in many other countries and is seldom pre-cut and packaged in a butcher's shop (as it is in supermarkets). Meat is usually purchased 'on the bone' and minced on the spot if you wish. Cold cuts of meat are sold by weight (kg) or by the slice (*rodaja*). Like most foods in Spain, the range of meat on sale depends on the region and butchers are happy to give advice on its preparation and cooking. A *casquería* sells offal such as a bull's testicles (considered a delicacy in Spain) and also the meat of bulls (*toro/carne de lidia*) killed during bullfights, which isn't sold in an ordinary butcher's shop (but is available in some supermarkets). There are horse meat butchers (*carnicerías de equino*) in some towns.

Pork: Pork can also be purchased from a special pork butcher (*charcutería*), who also sells cold meats (*fiambres*) and cheese (*queso*). Spanish raw ham is renowned and among the best in the world, although the best types are expensive. The finest Spanish ham is named after the town where it's produced, e.g. *jamón de Serrano* and *jamón de Jabugo*. It's similar to Parma ham and is widely used in Spanish recipes. Cured processed ham (*jamón de York*) is also good and much cheaper than raw ham. You can buy smoked bacon (*beicon*) in Spain, although its usually of the streaky variety. Spain is also famous for its sausages such as *chorizo* (spicy paprika) and *morcilla* (blood, perhaps with nuts). The large *chorizo* sausage is similar to salami and is intended for slicing and eating raw; a red string indicates hot and a white string mild.

Fish: The Spanish are great fish eaters and generally eat fish around three times a week, which is usually bought from a fishmonger (*pescadería*). Shellfish may be sold in a special seafood restaurant (*marisquería*) selling both cooked and uncooked seafood plus *tapas* (see page 345). Fish is surprisingly expensive in Spain due to poor local catches and restrictive EU quotas and consequently must be caught in remote fishing grounds. Shellfish is reasonably priced. Fish is invariably excellent throughout Spain, even in Madrid, where fresh fish is delivered daily from the coasts.

The most common fish include bass, dorado, hake, grouper, monkfish, mullet, sea bream, salmon, sardines and trout, although they vary depending on the region. Note that the same fish may have different names in different parts of Spain or the same name may be used for several different kinds of fish. The best areas for price and variety are Galicia and the Basque Lands, where most of Spain's fish is landed. Fish is cut (*cortado*), cleaned (*limpiado*), gutted (*destripado*) and scaled (*descamado*) on request. Fish are usually sorted by size and sold in fillets (*filetes*) or slices (*rodajas*) for larger fish such as swordfish and tuna. In inland towns and villages, fish is commonly sold frozen. Canned fish is also popular, particularly tuna of which there are numerous varieties.

Bread and Cakes: Bread (*pan*) is sold in a *panadería* in Spain and is usually baked on the premises, even by supermarkets. A wide variety is available, although there are two main types; country bread (*pan chapata*), which is heavy and round and lasts several days, and *pan de barra*, which is a long, thin, crusty loaf similar to a French *baguette* that will stay fresh for a few hours only. Among the many other types of bread available are *pan cateto*, *integral* (wholemeal), *hogaza* (round peasant bread), *gallegos* (round bread) and *pan alemán* (German bread), which is an extremely tasty dark wholegrain bread often sold in supermarkets. There are also many regional styles of loaves, usually referred to simply as *pan*.

Sliced bread (*pan de molde*) isn't sold in a bakers, although most will slice bread free on request. Bread is sold by weight and prices are similar throughout Spain. Many supermarkets have a bread counter where bread is often baked on the premises. Bakers also sell French-style *croissants*, cakes and tarts. A *bollería* sells bread and rolls (*bollos*). Traditionally, bread and pastries weren't sold in the same store in Spain, although bakers nowadays sell a wide range of cakes and biscuits. If you want pastries you must usually go to a pastry or cake shop (*pastelería* or *confitería*) which sells sweet breakfast rolls, cakes, gateaux, fruit tarts, pastries, biscuits and sweets, but usually not bread. The best Spanish cakes and pastries are found in Catalonia and Majorca, although in general

Spanish cakes aren't up to the standards of northern European countries. The larger pastry shops often incorporate a bar or tea room (*salón de té*).

A unique Spanish treat is fried doughnuts or long fluted shapes of lightly fried dough or fritters called *churros*, usually sold at a *churrería* and costing around 60 ptas a serving. They are traditionally eaten with a cup of thick, sweet, hot chocolate in which it's 'obligatory' to dip your *churros*. They are an essential part of Spanish life, particularly on winter Sunday mornings.

Fruit & Vegetables: Fruit and vegetables are best purchased from a market or a fruit and vegetable shop (*frutería*), rather than from supermarkets, where produce is often past its best. The variety and value (they practically give them away) of locally-grown fruit and vegetables in Spain is second to none, and most are available throughout the year (vegetarians can live cheaply in Spain). However, don't be influenced by the low prices and buy more than you can eat within a few days, as fruit and vegetables go off quickly in hot weather (unless stored in a refrigerator). It's easy to buy too much, particularly when prices are low, e.g. oranges at 100 ptas a kilo, strawberries 200 ptas a kilo, apples 150 ptas a kilo, tomatoes 150 ptas a kilo and iceberg lettuces for 100 ptas each. Note that in small shops, you shouldn't handle the produce unless invited to do so, although you can usually serve yourself.

Olive Oil: Olive oil (*aceite de oliva*) is part of the staple diet of Spaniards and merits a special mention. Spaniards consume around 10 kilos of olive oil per head each year (compared with around a third of a litre in many northern European countries) and have one of Europe's lowest number of deaths from heart disease (along with France, Italy and Portugal — all large consumers of olive oil). The finest quality is classified as *virgen* and is made by a single cold pressing. There are two grades of *virgen* oil, *extra* and *fino*, both green in colour. *Extra* has the least acidity and is the most expensive. Among the best olive oils are *Sierra de Segura* from Jaén and *Borjas Blancas* from Lérida, although most people have their own particular favourites. The finest oil is always classified as pure olive oil (*aceite puro de oliva*). Refined (*refinado*) oil is blended with *virgen* oil and is light yellow in colour. *Puro* is a mixture of *virgen* and refined oil.

There are four controlled areas of production (*denominación de origen*) in Spain (although fine olive oil is also produced in other areas) and some 60 varieties. Olive oil can be purchased direct from producers, when you will usually be treated to a tasting as if you were buying wine. Olive oil has varying acidity (*acidez*), e.g. 0.4 or 0.5 degrees, which are tasteless in salads and odourless in cooking. If you want more flavour choose an acidity of 1.0 degrees. Apart from its use in cooking and as a salad dressing, olive oil is also used in rolls instead of butter, which goes off quickly in hot weather, and eaten on bread sprinkled with salt.

Cheese: There are some 300 varieties of cheese (*queso*) in Spain, although most are produced in tiny quantities and many are unknown outside Spain or the area of production. Despite the fact that cheese has been produced in Spain for over 3,500 years, the Spanish have the lowest consumption of cheese in Europe and over the years many varieties have simply vanished. Spanish cheese is mainly hard and cheddar-like and most are an acquired taste. The hard salty *manchego* and similar cheeses are the most common (often served as a *tapa*) and can be old and ripened (*añejo*) or young (*tierno*). Other common cheeses are *el cigarral*, similar to a mild English cheddar, *cabrales*, a delicious blue sheep's cheese from Asturias, and *idiazabel* from Navarra. Although cow's cheese (*queso de vaca*) is the most common, Spain is renowned for its sheep (*queso de oveja*) and goats' (*queso de cabra*) cheeses, which are widely available. Soft fresh cheeses are also made in many areas, although they aren't often seen in shops. A range of foreign cheeses are widely available in supermarkets including Brie, Camembert, Cheddar, Danish Blue and Edam, plus numerous processed cheeses. Note that dairy products are generally more expensive in Spain than in other European countries.

Miscellaneous Food Shops: A general store (*alimentación* or *ultramarino*) sells dairy foods, hams and other cured meats, wine, canned and packaged goods, and sometimes fresh produce and meat. In towns, many general stores have become small self-service supermarkets. A *bombonería* is a sweet shop or candy store selling a delicious assortment of hand-made chocolates, truffles and candies, all guaranteed to wreck your diet and your teeth. A *heladería* is an ice cream parlour, often combined with a café or bar. They are popular and ubiquitous in resort areas. A *herbario* is a herb and spice shop, a *lechería* a dairy shop and a *mantequería* a delicatessen selling dairy foods, wines and liqueurs (often combined with a bar). Remote areas are served by mobile shops (*ventas ambulantes*), which travel around the countryside selling fresh bread, meat, fish, fruit and vegetables in addition to preserved foods.

MARKETS

Markets (*mercados*) are a common sight in towns and villages throughout Spain, and are an essential part of Spanish life, largely unaffected by competition from supermarkets and hypermarkets. They are colourful, entertaining and fun, and an experience not to be missed, even if you don't plan to buy anything. Markets thrive throughout Spain and are the centre of life in towns and villages. Some towns have markets on one or two days a week only (always the same days), while others have daily fruit and vegetable markets from Monday to Saturday. In rural and coastal areas, market days are varied in local towns so that they don't clash (a list of local markets may be available from the local tourist office). There are also Sunday markets in some towns.

There are generally three kinds of markets in Spain: indoor markets, permanent street markets and travelling open-air street markets (*venta ambulante*) that move from neighbourhood to neighbourhood on different days of the week or month. There are some 8,000 travelling markets in Spain (most are in Andalusia and Extremadura), each with from 50 to 200 stands. The most popular wares are textiles and fruit and vegetables, plus shoes, perfume and toilet articles, and general household goods. Prices are generally around 20 per cent lower than in shops, although much depends on your bargaining skills. There's often a large central market (*mercado central*) in cities, and many towns and neighbourhoods of large cities have indoor or covered markets. Municipal markets (*mercados municipales*) controlled by the local council are found in most towns and many large villages. Markets usually operate from 0900 until 1400, although in cities and some towns they occasionally re-open on Fridays after the *siesta*, e.g. from 1700 or 1730 until 1930 or 2000.

A variety of goods are commonly sold in markets including food, flowers, plants, clothes (markets are best for inexpensive clothes), shoes, ironmongery, crockery, hardware, cookware, linen, ceramics, cassettes/CDs, arts and crafts, household wares, carpets, jewellery, watches and leather goods. Specialist markets in Madrid and other cities sell antiques, books, clothes, stamps, postcards, medals, coins, flowers, birds and pets. **You should beware of bargain-priced branded goods in markets such as watches, perfume and clothes, as they are usually fakes.**

Food markets remain highly popular, despite the proliferation of supermarkets and hypermarkets in recent years. They are generally divided into sections for fresh meat, fish and shellfish, cheese and cooked meats, fruit and vegetable, and general groceries. Food is invariably beautifully presented and encompasses fruit and vegetables (including many exotic varieties), fish, meat, dairy products, bread and cakes, and pickled vegetables, herbs and olives, usually sold in different sections. Food is always cheaper and fresher in markets than in supermarkets, particularly if you buy what's in season and grown locally. You should arrive early in the morning for the best choice, although bargains can often be found late in the day when stallholders are packing up.

All produce is clearly marked with its price per piece or per kilogramme. There's no haggling over food prices, although at the end of the day an offer may be accepted. When shopping for food in markets, vendors may object to customers handling the fruit and vegetables, although you needn't be shy about asking to taste a piece of cheese or fruit. It's advisable to take a bag when buying fruit and vegetables as carrier bags aren't usually provided. When buying fruit and vegetables in markets check that the quality of produce you're given is the same as that displayed, which isn't always the case. Queues are a good sign. Note that local people also sell home-grown produce on the fringes of markets.

Antique and flea markets (*rastros*) are common throughout Spain, although you shouldn't expect to find many (or any) bargains in the major cities, where anything worth buying is snapped up by dealers. However, in small towns you can turn up some real bargains. Note that you should never assume that because something is sold in a market it will be a bargain, particularly when buying antiques (*antigüedades*), which aren't always authentic. In many cases local shops are cheaper, particularly those selling to local residents rather than tourists. Always haggle over the price of expensive items. To find out when local markets are held, enquire at your local tourist office or town hall.

SUPERMARKETS & HYPERMARKETS

There are supermarkets (*supermercados*) and hypermarkets (*hipermercados*) in or just outside most towns in Spain. The big advantage of supermarkets is the convenience of doing all your shopping in one place, free parking, all day opening, and you don't need to speak a word of Spanish — a big advantage for many foreigners. Hypermarkets and large supermarkets are generally open all day from 0930 or 1000 until between 2100 and 2200 from Monday to Saturday and don't close for lunch or a *siesta*. Some also open on Sundays, although this may only be in the summer months in resorts and before Christmas. Smaller supermarkets generally open at around 0900 and close earlier than hypermarkets, e.g. 1900 or 2000, or perhaps later on Fridays. Some supermarkets close for lunch, e.g. 1330 or 1400 until 1600 or 1700, although not usually on Saturdays. Supermarkets and hypermarkets are often located in shopping centres with a variety of small shops, key cutting, shoe repair, newsagents, banks or ATMs, cafés and restaurants (often including a self-serve restaurant), toilets, public telephones, a huge free car park, and possibly a petrol station and car wash.

Supermarkets and hypermarkets have transformed the way the Spanish shop in the last few decades and now account for over a third of Spain's retail business and some 70 per cent of food sales. In addition to food and drink, most supermarkets sell household products, tableware, clothes, toiletries and hardware. The name *hipermercado* is used fairly loosely in Spain and many *hipers* are in fact small supermarkets selling a few non-food items and nothing like, for example, the vast French hypermarkets.

A 'real' hypermarket is similar to a department store (although usually on one floor) and sells everything you would expect to find in a supermarket plus books, CDs, cassettes,

TVs, music systems, computers, cameras, furniture, textiles, household goods, gardening equipment and furniture, domestic electrical apparatus, do-it-yourself, motoring accessories, white goods (e.g. refrigerators, freezers, washing machines), sports equipment, jewellery, bicycles, tools, kitchenware, clothes and shoes, toys, magazines and newspapers. French-owned hypermarkets such as Alcampo, Continente and Pryca dominate the Spanish market, the main competition coming from Hipercor owned by El Corte Inglés. National supermarket chains include Más y Más, Dia, Dunnes Stores, Lidl and Spar, plus many smaller regional chains (e,g, Aldi, Cayetano and Euromarket on the Costa del Sol). There are also wholesale or cash and carry outlets in Spain such as Makro, where you need a membership card (note that some wholesale outlets don't accept credit cards).

The cost of food in Spain is slightly less than the average for western Europe. A couple with two children can expect to spend around 10,000 ptas a week on food. Note that prices often vary (even in different branches of the same supermarket) depending on the level of local competition. All supermarkets and hypermarkets have food counters for meat, fish, bread (often located outside the main hall) and cheese. The Spanish generally don't like to buy pre-packaged meat, fish, cheese, fruit or vegetables, but prefer to buy them to order. Some supermarkets use a number system (whereby you take a number from a roll) at certain counters (e.g. meat and cheese) to ensure customers are served in the correct order (make sure you know what it is in Spanish or alternatively just hold it up).

Fruit and vegetables in supermarkets are often a disappointment, with poor quality second class produce well past its best. It's often said that the Spanish export all their best produce, which isn't difficult to believe judging by the quality in some supermarkets. Fruit and vegetables are usually weighed by an assistant and *aren't* weighed at checkouts. It's best to avoid packaged fruit and vegetables, which often contain bad produce. Note that produce in supermarkets is often well past its sell-by date, particularly during very hot weather when it's difficult to keep food fresh. Always check the 'sell-by' date (*fecha de caducidad*) or date of minimum duration (*fecha de duración mínima*), particularly when buying slow-selling foods such as pre-packaged foreign cheeses and meats, as it's common to find food is out of date (and mouldy). Sometimes a 'preferably consume before date' (*consumir preferentemente antes de 'date'*), production date (*fecha de fabricación*) or packaged date (*fecha de envasado*) is shown, which mean little without a shelf-life date.

There's a huge choice of tinned vegetables and meats in Spanish supermarkets, but few frozen vegetables. While there's generally an excellent selection of fresh foods, there's a poor choice of frozen and convenience (fast) foods, and microwave meals are rare. Although the production of frozen foods has increased in the last decade, there's still a poor choice compared with American and British supermarkets (which to the Spanish simply confirms their poor taste). Frozen and convenience foods are also expensive and the quality leaves much to be desired. Many supermarkets cater for the tastes of foreigners, particularly in resort areas where there are many foreign residents. Note, however, that imported foods are generally expensive. If you live on the Costa del Sol you can visit Gibraltar and stock up on British foods from stores such as Marks and Spencer and Safeway.

Fresh milk is available in most supermarkets, although it may be close to or past its sell-by date (a sure sign is a bulging carton) and goes off quickly in summer. Most Spaniards and the majority of foreigners buy UHT long-life milk, which initially usually tastes awful (particularly in tea), but most people get used to it. It usually comes in skimmed (*desnatada*) and semi-skimmed (*semi-desnatada*) versions and is sold in one litre and half-litre cartons.

Although some smaller supermarkets still price items individually, most use barcode scanning. Barcodes make it difficult to check your bill (unless you have an exceptional memory), although most till receipts list all items with their name and price. Mistakes are common (usually in the retailer's favour) and you should at least verify the price of special offers. You can pay with a debit card (issued by all Spanish banks) or credit card in most supermarkets and hypermarkets. Some supermarkets have their own purchase cards (*tarjetas de compra*) offering customer discounts and supermarkets may also offer free scratch cards (and other gimmicks) where you can win small prizes.

In some supermarkets you're required to leave your shopping bags at a special counter (*consigna*) before entering, in return for which you're given a numbered disc. Most Spanish supermarkets provide free plastic bags (*bolsas*), although they shouldn't be filled with too many heavy items such as bottles of wine. Checkout staff don't bag your purchases and take them out to your car for you, although some supermarkets have a home delivery service (sometimes you can also order by phone), which may be free when your purchases exceed a certain sum, e.g. 5,000 ptas. Note that it's essential to have a 100 peseta coin to obtain a trolley. You insert the coin in a slot to release the chain connecting it to the next trolley. When you've finished with it, return it to the trolley park, lock it into another trolley and remove your coin.

All supermarket and hypermarket chains publish regular brochures and leaflets (which may be distributed to local mailboxes) featuring special offers. See also **Shopping for Food** on page 376.

ALCOHOL

Drinking is an integral part of everyday life in Spain, where most people have a daily tipple. Low taxes mean that Spain has the cheapest alcohol in the EU — even cheaper than buying it duty-free. Whatever your poison, you'll find something to suit your taste among the many excellent wines, beers, spirits and liqueurs produced in Spain or the numerous imported beverages. Spain is, however, most famous for its wine, particularly its sherry.

Sherry: Sherry (*jerez*) is world famous and Spain's most celebrated export and has been produced for hundreds of years (dominated by the English since the 16th century). Sherry takes its name from Jerez de la Frontera in Andalusia where it's produced and where three-quarters of the population is employed in its production in some way or another. It's produced from the Palomino grape (although other grapes are used for colouring and sweetening), which is also the only vine that the chalky soil in the southwest region of Spain will support. Sherry is matured in oak barrels and produced from a variety of vintages, using the unique *solera* method of production of progressively blending young and old wines.

There are various types of sherry to suit most tastes and occasions (it can apparently be drunk with almost any dish). Dry (*fino* or *seco*) and the medium dry *amontillado* are usually drunk chilled as an aperitif, while the sweet *oloroso* and *dulce* (brown, cream or amoroso) are drunk at room temperature as after dinner drinks. There's also a dry (*seco*) variety of *oloroso*. The very dry *manzanilla* has a slightly salty after taste, attributed to the salty soil of the coastal area in Sanlúcar de Barrameda where it's produced. Sherry lovers can tour the wineries (*bodegas*) in Jerez for a few hundred pesetas and enjoy tastings.

Wine: Spain has a 2,000 year history of wine production and has more acres (around 20m) of vineyards than any country in the world (although it rates third after France and Italy in wine production). An extraordinary diversity of wines are produced in Spain, due to the country's different climatic and soil conditions, matched by few other nations. While most aren't as famous as the wines of France and some other countries, the best Spanish wines compare favourably with many classic foreign wines. Although Spain still produces oceans of mediocre 'plonk' and Spanish wine has a generally poor international reputation, it also makes some of the best value-for-money wines in Europe, including many great wines. The quality of Spanish wine has improved enormously in the last few decades, during which modern methods of production and the introduction of new grape varieties (such as chardonnay and cabernet sauvignon) have transformed wine production. Note, however, that some cheaper red wines (including some Riojas) are unreliable and it isn't unusual to find bad (e.g. corked) bottles.

Classification: Spain has some 60 wine-producing regions, 40 of which are officially designated areas with a *Denominación de Origen (DO)* classification, indicated by a small map on the back label (labels also contain official seals, such as Rioja's 'stamp'). Regulations relating to DO regions include the type of grape that can be used, yield per hectare, minimum alcohol strength, permissible amount of natural sugar, maturity process and period, bottling and labelling. Wine from another region cannot be mixed with a DO wine. There's also a further quality classification, *Denominación de Origen Calificada (DOC)*, which has so far been awarded only to Rioja. The designation *vino de mesa* applies to blended wine or wine made from grapes grown in unclassified vineyards, while *vino de la tierra* is local wine from a defined area that doesn't qualify for a DO. Note, however, that there are many excellent Spanish wine producers who choose not to belong to a *Denominación de Origen* or who produce wines that contain grape varieties which aren't permitted under DO regulations.

Production Areas: Nearly every region of Spain produces wine, from sweet dessert whites to dry reds, modest table wines to fine vintages. Spanish wine regions fall into three main areas; the north, where the best Spanish wines are produced, containing the regions of Rioja, Penedés, Tarragona, Ribera del Duero and Galicia; the central zone including La Mancha, Valdepeñas and the coastal region of the Levante, containing half of Spain's total vineyards and producing some 35 per cent of its wine (mostly table wines); and the dry southern zone which produces (almost exclusively) apéritif and dessert wines, including sherry.

Rioja: The most famous Spanish red (*tinto*) wine is Rioja, a strong wine high in tannin, often with a distinctive oaky flavour (from the oak barrels). Some 40 per cent of Rioja is aged in barrels (age is usually more important in a Rioja wine than its vintage or *cosecha*), the rest being drunk within one or two years of bottling. Few Spanish wines can match Rioja for price and quality and many connoisseurs believe that vintage Riojan wines can hold their own with the best France (or anywhere else) has to offer. You usually cannot go wrong with Rioja and even the cheapest young wines are usually highly palatable. Excellent white (*blanco*) wines are also produced in Rioja, which is subdivided into three geographical areas of production: Alavesa, Alta and Baja.

Like the best French wine-producing regions, Rioja declares an annual vintage, classified as follows: poor (*mediana*), normal, good (*buena*), very good (*muy buena*) and excellent (*excelente*). Rioja declared excellent vintages in both 1994 (heralded as the wine of the century) and 1995 (the largest harvest of all time), an unprecedented event as two excellent years have never before been declared in succession. Prior to 1994 there had been only eight excellent vintages in the previous 70 years, the last being in 1982. 1996 was also a very good year.

Riojas are generally released at their optimum drinking date and some may begin to deteriorate within a few years (the longer a wine has been aged, the longer it will keep). Riojan red wines are divided into four categories depending on the amount of aging they have undergone. The best Riojan wines are labelled *reservas* or *gran reservas* and they can reach high prices for exceptional years (i.e. those rated very good or excellent). *Gran reservas* (which account for just 3 per cent of total production) spend a minimum of two years maturing in oak barrels and four more in the *bodega* before being sold. A *reserva* spends at least a year in the barrel and three in the *bodega* and a *crianza* at least a year in the barrel and another in the bottle. A *sin crianza* or *conjunto de varias cosechas (CVC)* wine isn't aged (it spends no time in oak and is fermented in stainless steel vats) and is made from a combination of vintages.

There's a huge number and variety of Riojan red (and white) wines and many of excellent quality and value for money. Some good value and quality wines that you should be able to find throughout Spain include Campo Viejo (CVC, crianza and reserva), Carta de Plata (CVC), Faustino VII, V and I (CVC, reserva and gran reserva), Cune (crianza and reserva), Glorioso (crianza and reserva), Puerta Vieja (crianza), Marqués de Murrieta (reserva and gran reserva), Marqués de Riscal (reserva and gran reserva), Monte Real (reserva and gran reserva) and Viña Tondonia (gran reserva). Note, however, that like all wines, not all Riojas are of top quality — part of the enjoyment is experimenting and finding those that best suit your palate and pocket!

Other Wines: Other regions worthy of special mention include Penedés, where two-thirds of Catalonia's wine is produced. Penedés is renowned for its white wines, although it also produces fine reds and much of Spain's premier sparkling wine (*cava*). The most famous producer in Penedés is Torres, who produce celebrated red (including Sangre de Torre and Gran Coronas) and white wines (e.g. Gran Viña Sol). The main difference between the wine produced in Rioja and Penedés is that vintage Riojan wines are aged in oak and Penedés wines in the bottle. However, Spain's most exclusive and expensive wines are produced by Vega Sicilia in the Ribera del Duero wine district. They cannot be purchased in shops and are allocated by the producer (there's a waiting list). Navarra is noted for producing the best rosé wines in Spain (and is also becoming known for its reds), while Albariños of the Rías Baixas district in Galicia produces what many consider to be the best white wines in Spain. Tarragona makes excellent dessert wines (*vinos generosos*) and the world's strongest red wine (up to 18 per cent proof), *Priorato*.

Sparkling Wines: Spanish sparkling wine made by the *méthode champenoise* or *método tradicional* is called *cava* and is often as good as French champagne (some are even judged superior) and at around 1,000 ptas a bottle it's much cheaper. *Cava* was actually marketed as champagne (*champán* or *méthode champenoise*) for many years, although this was prohibited after complaints from the French. It isn't, however, an inferior Spanish 'champagne' but a quality sparkling wine in its own right (it's also made with different grapes to champagne). It's usually less than a few years old and vintage *cava* is rare. Among the best known producers are Castellblanch, Codorníu and Freixenet (Carta Nevada and Cordón Negro are top brands). *Cava* is classified by its sweetness which includes very dry (*brut de brut*, *brut nature*, *brut reserva*, *vintage*), dry (*brut*), fairly dry (*seco*), semi-dry (*semiseco*), semi-sweet (*semidulce*) and sweet (*dulce*). *Rosado* or *Rose* denotes a pink wine. All *cava* wines come under the same DO, irrespective of where they are produced. Spain also produces lesser sparkling wines (*vinos gasificados*), which are carbonated white and rosé wines, and aren't highly rated.

Buying Wine: Most people buy their wine from supermarkets and hypermarkets, although the quality and range of wines on offer isn't usually outstanding. A liquor store (*bodega*) usually has a larger selection of wines and other drinks than a supermarket, and the prices are usually comparable. Supermarkets (and department stores) often have special offers, particularly around Christmas and New Year, when prices are reduced across the board from table wine to the best gran reservas (a good time to stock up your cellar). However, you should avoid buying expensive vintage wines from a supermarket as they are often badly stored (upright and too warm). Nowhere are the Spanish more parochial and nationalistic than when it comes to wine, and supermarkets stock few imported wines.

The Spanish are unpretentious when it come to wine and don't generally take it seriously. They drink mostly young table wines (*vino corriente*) at home, which are free of tannin. At the lower end of the quality range, wine is cheaper in Spain than in many other countries, although quality wines can be as expensive as in France. At the bottom end of the market wine is sold in cartons (*briks*) at around 100 ptas a litre (cheaper than milk), some of which tastes worse than vinegar. Inexpensive red (*tinto*), white (*blanco*) and rosé (*rosado*) wines costing around 200 ptas a litre are better and include names such as *Don Simón* and *Elegido*. Slightly up market table wines (*vinos de mesa*) from Soldepeñas, Valdepeñas and Valencia (e.g. Castillo de Liria) cost around 250 to 350 ptas a bottle. The cheapest Riojan red wines start at around 350 ptas, while a reasonable bottle costs 400 to 500 ptas. If you like dry white wine, you cannot go wrong with Rioja from around 350 ptas a bottle.

Not so many years ago Spaniards would take an empty jug or bottle to the wine merchant for a refill of *vino corriente* from a cask inscribed with the colour and the alcohol content; *tinto* (full-bodied), *clarete* (light red) and *blanco* (white), although this practice isn't common nowadays. Buying wine in bulk direct from producers is possible in Spain, although it isn't common. If you live near a winery you can buy wine in bulk in small glass carboys. You pay an initial deposit for the carboy and thereafter you exchange your empties for full ones (or you can bring your own container and have it filled). In many wine-producing regions villages have a *bodega* producing strong, inexpensive wine for local consumption. It's possible to visit most Spanish bodegas (usually by appointment) and wine festivals are held throughout the year, particularly at harvest time. **Note that you shouldn't leave wine in a car for long periods during hot weather, which will ruin it.**

Education: There are numerous books about wine, a few of which are dedicated to Spanish wine, such as *Spanish Wines* by Jan Read (Mitchell Beazley). There are also many Spanish guide books such as *Guía de Vinos Gourmets* and *Guía Peñin de los Vinos de España*. For those who don't know when they've had enough, there's *Floyd on Hangovers* (Michael Joseph) and if you feel guilty about drinking too much wine, *Your Good Health: The Medicinal Benefits of Wine Drinking* by Dr. E. Maury (Souvenir Press) may make you feel better. Note, however, that while it's true that drinking red wine reduces heart disease and the risk of certain cancers (and may also delay the onset of Alzheimer disease), drinking excessive amounts of alcohol destroys your brain and causes cirrhosis of the liver!

Spirits & Liquors: Spirits and liquors are extremely cheap in Spain and the cheapest in western Europe. There are generally cheaper Spanish equivalents (*nacional*) for most imported spirits and liquors, some of which are excellent. If you want the 'real thing', don't be fooled by Spanish brands in look-alike bottles with similar brand names. Spain even produces its own gin and whisky. Spanish gin, particularly Larios (around 1,000 ptas a litre), is usually excellent, although it's only a few hundred pesetas cheaper than Gordons, the international market leader (which has been reduced considerably in price in recent years). Spanish whisky is terrible and to be avoided. Imported gin and scotch whisky (unknown blended brands) are available in supermarkets from around 700 ptas for a 70cl bottle. Johnny Walker scotch costs around 1,400 ptas a bottle, Smirnoff vodka around 1,000 ptas and Bacardi rum around 1,200 ptas.

If you're making cocktails you may as well buy Spanish gin, vodka and white rum as most people cannot tell the difference between them and more expensive imports. Many famous French liquors are made in Spain under licence including Benedictine, Cointreau, Marie Brizard and Pernod. They are made exactly as in France but from Spanish wine (Chartreuse was made exclusively in Spain for over 35 years and is as much a Spanish liquor as French). Spanish liquors include Cuaranta y Tres (similar to Southern Comfort), Ponche (made of brandy and herbs) and Pacharan, which is made from bilberries. There's even a liquor made from artichokes called *Cynar* (it tastes dreadful, although some people obviously like it).

Spanish brandy (labelled *brandy* for legal reasons but often referred to as *coñac*), has a vanilla flavour and is very good. Popular brands include *Magno, Torres Solera Selecta*, *Soberano* and *Bobadillo 103*. It's often drunk in coffee (for breakfast!) and in cocktails. A litre bottle of Spanish brandy costs around 1,000 ptas. Aguardiente (aquavits) is a strong spirit distilled from grape leftovers, skins and pips, and is one of the strongest drinks in the world (80 per cent proof). It may puts hairs on your chest but will removes your skin if you spill it and should always be drunk sitting down. *Anís*, an aniseed-flavoured drink, is also popular in Spain.

Beer & Cider: Spanish beer is brewed in light (*dorada*), similar to the ubiquitous export lager, and dark (*negra*) varieties and is usually good. It may come as a surprise to many foreigners to find that most Spaniards prefer beer to wine. Beer is usually sold in 300ml bottles (*botellines*) but also comes in large one litre bottles. It's strong stuff and usually contains between 4.5 and 5.5 per cent alcohol by volume. Many imported beers are available in supermarkets, although is isn't usually worth paying the extra. Among the best known Spanish beers are *San Miguel, Dorada, Aguila, Estrella* and *Mahou Five Star*. Local regional beers are often even better than the national ones. The finest Spanish cider (*sidra*) is made in Asturias (it's also made in Galicia and León) and is best drunk served from a barrel, although it's also bottled and sold throughout Spain. It's dry (not sweet) and a little cloudy and is stronger than beer. Supermarkets frequently have special offers on beer and some brands can be bought in returnable one litre bottles, which is cheaper than buying small bottles. Some supermarkets have a special store (*consigna*) where you return your empties. However, most bottles are now non-returnable and are taken to bottle banks or simply thrown away.

Health: Considering the low cost of alcohol in Spain, it may come as a surprise to find that the Spanish don't have a huge problem with alcoholism or drunkenness, which is more than can be said for many tourists and foreign residents. Expatriates who like the odd drink (or two) should carefully monitor their alcohol intake, as alcoholism is a big problem among foreign residents (there are numerous expatriate Alcoholics Anonymous groups in Spain).

DEPARTMENT & CHAIN STORES

There are few department stores (*grandes almacenes*) in Spain and only two national chains, El Corte Inglés with around 35 stores and Galerías Preciados with 30 (which are now both owned by El Corte Inglés). El Corte Inglés is a Spanish institution and operates Spain's largest and best department stores with branches including Alicante, Barcelona (two stores), Bilbao, La Coruña, Las Palmas de Gran Canaria, Madrid (four stores), Malaga, Murcia, Seville, Valencia, Vallodolid, Vigo and Zaragossa. It's one of Spain's most successful companies and is Europe's second-largest department store chain in terms of gross sales, despite the fact that it has far fewer stores than its rivals. However, what it lacks in numbers it makes up for in size and operates huge stores with thousands of square metres of floor space.

El Corte Inglés is more upmarket than Galerías Preciados and stocks the best and most famous Spanish and international products. Stores pander to the needs of free-spending foreign shoppers and provides multi-lingual information desks, interpreters, international mailing, tax-refunds, travel services and money changing (outside banking hours). Stores are open throughout the day from 1000 until 2000 or 2100 and some are also open on Sundays and public holidays (e.g. from 1200 to 2000). In addition to the usual departments found in department stores, El Corte Inglés stores also have excellent (but expensive) food markets.

Galerías Preciados has more outlets than El Corte Inglés, although its stores are much smaller. Branches include Alicante, Barcelona, Bilbao, Granada, Palma de Majorca, Madrid (3 stores), Murcia, Oviedo, Santa Cruz de Tenerife, Seville, Valencia, Vitoria and Zaragossa. Galerías Preciados is cheaper than El Corte Inglés and provides a 10 per cent discount card for foreign shoppers. Both stores accept telephone orders and provide free delivery for orders above a certain value, e.g. 15,000 ptas, or for a fee (e.g. 1,000 ptas) below this amount. All major credit cards are accepted and both El Corte Inglés and Galerías Preciados issue their own credit cards, although interest rates are high.

A number of foreign chain stores have outlets in Spain including Adam's (children's clothes), Benetton, Body Shop, C & A, Dorothy Perkins, Marks & Spencer (six stores), Mothercare and Presto. Britons living on the Costa del Sol can satisfy their yearning for their home high street by taking a day trip to Gibraltar, where there are branches of many British chain stores including the Body Shop, British Home Stores, Marks and Spencer, Mothercare, Olympus Sports and Safeway.

TOBACCONISTS'

Tobacconists' (*estancos*) are conspicuous by their yellow and dark red paintwork, and a sign depicting the letter 'T' (for Tabacalera, the state-owned tobacco company) on a stylised tobacco leaf. Tabacalera SA is the state-owned tobacco monopoly which supplies and owns the official tobacconists' (established in 1637) who in turn supply everyone else (also a plan to introduce some competition is in the offing). Cigarettes can also be purchased from machines in bars and cafés and from street kiosks (*quioscos*), although these are a little more expensive than a tobacconist's.

Spanish cigarettes are usually made of strong black tobacco (*tabaco negro*) with a high nicotine content, although cigarettes made with 'blond' or Virginia tobacco (*tabaco rubio*) are also available. Note that imported brands are up to three times the price of local brands, which is why there's a lively smuggling trade (most of it through Gibraltar) costing Spain billion of pesetas in lost duty annually. A few foreign brands are produced in Spain under licence and are cheaper than imports. The best-selling Spanish brands are Ducados and Fortuna. Good inexpensive Spanish cigars are made in the Canary islands and imported Cuban cigars are also excellent value for money.

Tobacconist's are a unique institution in Spain. Not only are they the sole authorised vendors of cigarettes and other tobacco products, but they are also mini-stationers and the source of official government forms (e.g. for tax, contracts and official medical certificates) and 'state paper' (*papel del estado*), used to pay official fees for permits and licences. Note, however, that few if any tobacconist's stock the whole range of forms or *papel del estado* and you may have to obtain them from an official government office. A tobacconist's also sells postage stamps at face value, postcards, single envelopes and writing paper, gifts and souvenirs, cigarette lighters, photographic film, and other odds and ends.

FASHION

Spanish fashion has made huge strides in the last few decades and has a growing reputation on the international scene, particularly cities such as Madrid and Barcelona (which naturally hold rival fashion weeks). Spanish fashion reflects the Spanish character and is audacious, colourful and stylish, with vibrant colours and styles influenced by the 'gypsy' folklore of the south and the sober elegance of the north. The 1980s spawned a whole generation of exciting, talented, young fashion designers in Madrid, Barcelona, Galicia and Seville.

There's a relaxed dress code in Spain, although the Spanish are invariably well-dressed and scornful of slovenly foreigners (particularly those who dress scantily in public places away from the beaches). Spanish fashion caters mostly for the expensive and cheap ends of the market, with little in between. If you want moderately-priced durable fashion wear, you're usually better off shopping abroad. If you live on the Costa del Sol, you can visit Gibraltar and stock up on British clothes at stores such as Dorothy Perkins, Evans, Marks and Spencer, Topman and Topshop. Spain isn't generally a good place to buy quality clothes at reasonable prices, although the annual sales in January and July throw up some bargains. Ready-made children's clothes are excellent but are also expensive. Spain lacks the bargain-basement clothes shops common in the USA, Britain and France, where you can buy last season's fashions at knock-down prices and there are also few 'vintage' (secondhand) or charity clothes shops. Markets are the best place for inexpensive clothes, but you must watch out for counterfeit brands.

Spanish leather goods are excellent quality (but are no longer cheap) and include leather and suede coats, jackets, handbags, belts, boots and shoes (a shoe shop is a *zapatería*). Loewe are one of the best-known and most expensive brand names. Spanish shoes (usually produced in Alicante and the Balearic islands) are good value, although they are generally made in one width (medium) only. Spanish clothing and shoe manufacturers don't cater for the large sizes and fittings widely available in other European countries and North America.

El Corte Inglés department stores sell most internationally famous fashion and design labels and international fashion stores such as Bally, Benetton and Charles Jourdan have outlets throughout Spain. Other shops of note are Cortefiel (branches in some 25 cities) selling middle of the road fashion at reasonable prices; Don Algodón for fun fashion clothes for children and teenagers; Zara for inexpensive fashion clothes for men, women and children; and Tokio which has a good selection of assessories such as hats, gloves, socks and swimwear. The celebrated British chain store Marks and Spencer have six stores in Spain (two in Madrid and Barcelona, and stores in Seville and Valencia).

NEWSPAPERS, MAGAZINES & BOOKS

Newspapers and magazines are sold at a tobacconist's (*estanco*), newsagents, street newsstands, railway station kiosks, and in supermarkets and hypermarkets. Spain has had a free press only since 1978 after over 30 years of censorship under Franco's dictatorship, which along with Spain's relatively high illiteracy rate and lack of development is responsible for the low circulation figures. The Spanish aren't great newspaper readers and circulation is much lower than in most other European countries (only the Greeks, Portuguese and Albanians read fewer newspapers). Reading a newspaper in Spain is largely a middle-class habit and there's no popular tabloid or gutter press (*prensa amarilla*), as is common in many other European countries. Only eight newspapers nationwide sell over 100,000 copies daily and only one in each 10 Spaniards buys a newspaper. However, each copy tends to be read by more people than in other countries, so the sales figures don't accurately reflect the total readership.

Franco's death in 1975 heralded the re-birth of a free popular daily press, since when there has been an explosion of new newspapers and magazines (if not readers). Spain's most popular daily newspaper is *El País* (the country), founded in 1976 and published in Madrid. It's the only serious Spanish newspaper for political analysis and the best for international news. It's a liberal newspaper (although aligned with the socialist party) with a national circulation of around 400,000 from Monday to Saturday and 200,000 on Sundays, including various regional editions. *ABC*, which also publishes some regional editions (e.g. Andalusia), is also published in Madrid and is Spain's second-largest selling newspaper. It's conservative, traditional and right wing.

Leading newspapers in Barcelona include *La Vanguardia*, *El Periódico*, *Avui* (the largest selling) and *Diari de Barcelona*, the last two written in Catalan. In the Basque lands there are the Basque newspapers of *Deia*, *Eja* and *Egin* (supporters of ETA), which are mostly written in Basque (Euskera). Other major newspapers include *Diario 16* (centrist), the Catholic *Ya* (right) and *El Alcázar* (extreme right-wing). The regional press is often right-wing and supportive of regional autonomy. Most weekly newspapers in Spain are also published on Sundays with a colour supplement. In addition to general daily newspapers, a number of popular sports newspapers are published such as *AS* and *Marca*, dedicated entirely to sports coverage (mostly soccer). Some newspapers publish free entertainment supplements with their Thursday or Friday editions listing art shows, exhibitions, theatre, cinema, concerts and other leisure activities.

Numerous magazines (*revistas*) are also published in Spain and are generally more popular than newspapers. Spain publishes countless glossy women's magazines, referred to as the 'press of the heart' (*prensa de corazón*). Magazines such as ¡*Holá*!, *Diez Minutos*, *Semana*, *Pronto*, *Lecturas* and *Garbo* are among the 10 most popular magazines in Spain, selling over 2.5m copies a week. Although they cover the private lives of the rich and famous and often epitomise bad taste, they are rarely controversial or scurrilous. Other popular magazines include *Cambio 16* (weekly news magazine) and *Blanco y Negro* (current affairs).

Many foreign newspapers are available in the main cities and resorts by the afternoon or the following morning. A number of British newspapers including the *Daily Express*,

Daily Mail, Daily Mirror, Star and *Sun* are printed in Spain and available on the morning of publication. Many other English-language daily newspapers are widely available on the day of publication including *USA Today, International Herald Tribune* (edited in Paris), *Wall Street Journal Europe* and the *European Financial Times*. The *European* weekly newspaper is also sold throughout Spain from Fridays. Many English and foreign newspapers produce weekly editions including the British *International Express, Guardian Weekly* and *Weekly Telegraph*, all of which are available on Spanish newsstands. Note that foreign newspapers cost around three times the price in their country of origin.

Many English-language newspapers are published in Spain including the *Costa Blanca News, Costa del Sol News, Iberian Daily Bulletin, Iberian Daily Sun* and the *Majorcan Daily Bulletin*. Spain also has a number of English-language monthly magazines including *Lookout* magazine, available from newsagents throughout Spain (see **Appendix A** for addresses). Note that many Spanish and foreign newspapers and magazines can be purchased on subscription from the publishers, often at large savings over local retail prices.

Free local English-language newspapers and magazines are published in most areas and contain a wealth of information about local events, restaurants, bars, entertainment, services and shops. These include *The Reporter* (monthly), *The Entertainer* (regional versions, weekly), *Sur in English* (Costa del Sol weekly) and the *Marbella Times* (monthly). Other free newspapers and magazines are published in Dutch, Finnish, French, German and Swedish.

There are English-language bookshops (*librerías*) in Spain's major cities and resort towns. Some (like Bookworld España, Las Palmeras, 25, 29670 San Pedro de Alcántara, Malaga, tel. (95) 278 6366) publish a seasonal catalogue and provide a mail order service (post-free on orders over 10,000 ptas) for English-language books. There are also many secondhand bookshops in resort towns that buy, sell and exchange secondhand books. Most have books in various languages including English, Danish, Dutch, French, German and Swedish. In small towns there are usually a few small shops selling a limited selection of books, rather than one well-stocked large bookshop. Most Spanish bookshops have a poor selection and don't stock many English-language books.

In major cities there are bi-annual book fairs and regular secondhand book markets for collectors. Generally, the price of imported books is lower in Spain than in many other European countries, although Americans will be shocked at the prices. Many expatriate organisations and clubs run their own libraries or book exchanges and some Spanish public libraries keep a small selection of English-language books.

FURNITURE & FURNISHINGS

Many foreigners who decide to live permanently in Spain find that it's better to sell their furniture (*muebles*) abroad, rather than bring it to Spain. In any case, foreign furniture often isn't suitable for Spain's climate and house styles (antique furniture in particular often doesn't stand the heat well). Many holiday homes sold by foreigners are sold furnished, particularly apartments, although furniture may be of poor quality and not to your taste. However, buying a furnished property can represent a real bargain. If you're buying a property as an investment for letting, most developers or agents will arrange to furnish it for you.

The kind of furniture you buy will depend on a number of factors including the style and size of your home, whether it's a permanent or holiday home, your budget, the local climate, and not least, your personal taste. If you intend to furnish a holiday home with antiques or expensive modern furniture, bear in mind that you will need adequate security and insurance. If you intend to live permanently in Spain in a few years time and already have a house full of good furniture abroad, there's little point in buying expensive furniture in Spain. It may pay you to compare the cost of buying furniture abroad with the cost in Spain. If you're buying a large quantity of furniture, don't be reluctant to ask for a reduction, as many stores will give you a discount. The best time to buy furniture and furnishings is during the sales (particularly in winter), when prices of many items are slashed (some stores have half price sales in winter). Many stores offer furniture packages costing from around 600,000 ptas for a two-bedroom apartment and it's possible for residents to pay for furniture (and large household appliances) over 12 months interest-free or over five years (with interest).

A wide range of modern and traditional furniture is available in Spain at reasonable prices. Modern furniture is popular and is often sold in huge stores in commercial centres. Reasonably priced furniture can also be purchased from large hypermarkets and more exclusive furniture from department stores such as El Corte Inglés. Pine and cane furniture is inexpensive and widely available. If you're looking for classic modern furniture, you may wish to try Roche Bobois, which has 150 showrooms in 15 countries, or Universo de la Piel (80 stores in seven countries) for quality leather suites. If you're looking for antique furniture at affordable prices, you may find a few bargains at antique and flea markets in rural areas. However, you must drive a hard bargain as the asking prices are often ridiculous. There's a large market for secondhand furniture in Spain and many sellers and dealers advertise in the expatriate press (there are also specialist newspapers for secondhand goods). There are do-it-yourself hypermarkets such as Texas Hiperhogar in most areas, selling everything for the home including DIY, furniture, bathrooms, kitchens, decorating and lighting, in addition to tool rental and wood cutting.

HOUSEHOLD GOODS

Household goods in Spain are generally of high quality and although the choice isn't as wide as in some other European countries, it has improved considerably in recent years. Electrical items have traditionally been more expensive in Spain than in many other European countries, although the gap has narrowed and prices are now comparable (particularly in hypermarkets and supermarkets). Spanish-made appliances, electrical apparatus and consumer goods are usually of good quality, although they are sometimes of eccentric design and not always as reliable as imported brands, which are widely available.

Bear in mind when importing household goods that aren't sold in Spain, that it will be difficult or impossible to get them repaired or serviced (however, should you need to get something repaired, there are strict rules to protect consumers). If you bring appliances with you, don't forget to include a supply of spares and consumables such as bulbs for a refrigerator or sewing machine, and spare bags for a vacuum cleaner. Note that the standard size of kitchen appliances and cupboard units in Spain *isn't* the same as in other countries and it may be difficult to fit an imported dishwasher or washing machine into a Spanish kitchen. Check the size *and* the latest Spanish safety regulations before shipping these items to Spain or buying them abroad, as they may need expensive modifications. Spanish washing machines take in cold water only and heat it in the machine, which makes machines that take in hot water (such as those sold in the USA) obsolete.

If you already own small household appliances it's worthwhile bringing them to Spain, as usually all that's required is a change of plug. However, if you're coming from a country with a 110/115V electricity supply such as the USA, you'll need a lot of expensive transformers (see page 101) and it's usually better to buy new appliances in Spain. Small appliances such as vacuum cleaners, grills, toasters and irons aren't expensive in Spain and are of good quality. Don't bring a television or video recorder without checking its compatibility first, as televisions made for other countries often don't work in Spain without modification (see page 142). If your need is only temporary, many electrical and other household items (such as TVs, beds, cots/highchairs, electric fans, refrigerators, heaters and air conditioners) can be rented by the day, week or month. Tools and do-it-yourself equipment can also be rented in most towns. There are DIY hypermarkets such as Texas Hiperhogar in most areas, although DIY equipment and supplies are generally more expensive than in other EU countries (most items are imported).

If you need kitchen measuring equipment and cannot cope with decimal measures, you will need to bring your own measuring scales, jugs, cups and thermometers. Foreign pillow sizes (e.g. American and British) aren't the same as in Spain, although various sizes can be purchased in stores such as El Corte Inglés. Spanish textiles are often of inferior quality or more expensive than in other European countries.

SHOPPING ABROAD

Shopping abroad includes day trips to Andorra, France, Gibraltar, Portugal and Morocco, as well as shopping excursions further afield. A day trip abroad makes an interesting day out for the family and can save you money, depending on what and where you buy. Don't forget your passports or identity cards, car papers, children, dog's vaccination papers and foreign currency. Most shops in border towns gladly accept pesetas, but usually give you a lower exchange rate than a bank. Whatever you're looking for, always compare prices and quality before buying. Bear in mind that if you buy goods that are faulty or need repair, you may need to return them to the place of purchase. From 1993 there have been no cross-border shopping restrictions within the European Union for goods purchased duty and tax paid, providing all goods are for personal consumption or use and not for resale. Although there are no restrictions, there are 'indicative levels' for items such as spirits, wine, beer and tobacco products, above which goods may be classified as commercial quantities.

Gibraltar: Considerable savings can be made on cigarettes, petrol, foodstuffs, luxury goods (e.g. perfumes) and various consumer goods in Gibraltar. Spanish residents and visitors are permitted to import goods up to the value of 28,500 ptas (14,900 ptas for under 14s), exclusive of duty-free items (see below). Note that there are often long delays for vehicles at the border crossing into Spain as Spanish customs officers allegedly check them for drugs and tobacco (it's mostly just obstruction due to Spain's long-running dispute with Britain over Gibraltar's ownership). It's often advisable to park on the Spanish side of the border and get a bus or taxi (or walk) into Gibraltar town. **However, make sure that you lock and secure your car against theft, as cars are often stolen while their owners are shopping in Gibraltar!** Shopping hours are usually from 0900 until 1900 Monday to Friday and 0900 to 1300 on Saturdays (most shops are closed on Sundays).

Andorra: Andorra is Europe's biggest duty-free shop and considerable savings can be made on almost everything including alcohol, tobacco products, cheese and other foodstuffs, clocks and watches, cameras, film, electrical goods, perfume, luxury goods and petrol.

Never attempt to import illegal goods into Spain and don't agree to bring a parcel into Spain or deliver a parcel to another country without knowing exactly what it contains. A popular confidence trick is to ask someone to post a parcel abroad (usually to a post restante address) or to leave a parcel at a railway station or restaurant abroad. **THE PARCEL USUALLY CONTAINS DRUGS!** Many foreign truck drivers are languishing in Spanish jails having been the unwitting victims of drug traffickers (who conceal drugs in shipments of goods).

DUTY-FREE ALLOWANCES

Under European Union (EU) rules, duty-free (*libre de impuestos*) shopping within the EU is to remain until 1st January 1999. Duty-free allowances are the same whether or not passengers are travelling within the EU or from a country outside the Union. From 1993, for each journey to another EU member state, travellers aged 17 or over (unless otherwise stated below) are entitled to import the following duty-free goods:

- one litre of spirits (over 22 degrees proof) *or* two litres of fortified wine, sparkling wine or other liqueurs (under 22 degrees proof);
- two litres of still table wine;
- 200 cigarettes *or* 100 cigarillos *or* 50 cigars *or* 250g of tobacco;
- 60cc/ml of perfume;
- 250cc/ml of toilet water;
- other goods including gifts and souvenirs to the value of 28,500 ptas (14,900 ptas for under 14s).

Duty-free allowances apply on both outward and return journeys, even if both are made on the same day, and the combined total (i.e. double the above limits) can be imported into your 'home' country. **Note, however, that it's rarely worthwhile buying duty-free alcohol when travelling to Spain, as it's much cheaper in Spanish supermarkets and liquor stores.**

Special rules apply when shopping in duty-free areas such as Andorra and Gibraltar. In Andorra the duty-free limits for those aged over 17 are:

- 1.5 litres of alcohol over 22 degrees proof or 3 litres of alcohol under 22 degrees proof;
- 5 litres of still table wine;
- 300 cigarettes *or* 150 cigarillos *or* 75 cigars *or* 400g of pipe tobacco;
- 75g of perfume and 375ml of toilet water;
- up to 175 ECUs (around 30,000 ptas) worth of other 'agricultural' goods, although there are limits for some products such as milk (6 litres), butter (1kg), cheese (4kg), sugar (5kg), coffee (1kg) and tea (200g);

- up to 525 ECUs (around 85,000 ptas) worth of manufactured goods.

Duty-free allowances for Gibraltar include 200 cigarettes, 1 bottle of spirits and 200 litres of petrol, plus other purchases to the value of 28,500 ptas (14,900 ptas for under 14s).

If you're resident outside the EU, you can reclaim value added tax (IVA) on single purchases over 15,000 ptas. An export sales invoice is provided by retailers listing all purchases, which must be confirmed by a customs officer when leaving Spain (so don't pack purchases in your checked baggage). Your refund will be posted to you later or paid to a credit card account (at major airports it can also be reclaimed at a special Europe Tax-Free Shopping refund window). With certain purchases, particularly large items, it's better to have them sent directly abroad, when IVA won't be added. Large department stores such as El Corte Inglés have a special counter where non-EU shoppers can arrange for the shipment of goods.

RECEIPTS

When shopping in Spain, always insist on a receipt (*recibo* or *factura*) and keep it until you have left the shop or have reached home. This isn't just in case you need to return or exchange goods, which may be impossible without the receipt, but also to verify that you've paid if an automatic alarm sounds as you're leaving a shop or any other questions arise. Generally speaking, a complaint won't be entertained without a receipt (so make sure that you receive one). Under Spanish law, all products sold must be suitable for the use for which they are intended. If they aren't, you're entitled to exchange them or obtain a refund. It's illegal for traders to use 'small print' to try to avoid liability. You have the same legal rights whether goods are purchased at the recommended retail price or at a discount during a sale. It's advisable to keep the receipts and records of all major purchases made while you're resident in Spain, particularly if your stay is for a limited period only. This may save you both time and money when you finally leave Spain and are required to declare your belongings in your new country of residence.

CONSUMER PROTECTION

Spain has become more aware of consumer rights in recent years and there are strict consumer protection laws (particularly concerning the vital tourist industry). If you have a complaint (*reclamación*) about a product or service you should always make it in the first instance to the supplier or manufacturer, if possible in person. Failing that make a complaint in writing and keep a copy of all correspondence. Note that there are special procedures for complaints against many companies including utility companies, the post office, Telefónica, public transport companies, banks, insurance companies, hotels, restaurants, bars and the public health service. Your local town hall can advise you how to make a complaint.

All businesses are required by law to keep a complaints book or complaints forms (*libros/hojas de reclamaciones*), which must be produced on demand. These vary depending on the region and may be printed in both Spanish and English. The form has three pages, one or two of which you receive. A request for a complaints form (or book) often results in a speedy and satisfactory outcome to a dispute, as all complaints must be forwarded to the authorities within 48 hours and businesses can be penalised if they are in the wrong.

If you fail to obtain satisfaction regarding a complaint against a local business you should contact the Ministry of Health and Consumer Affairs (*Ministerio de Sanidad y Consumo*) through their local office (*Oficina Municipal de Información al Consumidor (OMIC)*). OMIC offices are established in liaison with town halls in most towns; if there isn't a local OMIC office contact your town hall. A serious complaint may be referred to the OMIC regional office (*Oficina Regional del Información al Consumidor*) in the regional capital town and a business can be fined up to 2.5m ptas if a complaint is upheld.

OMICS are supported in many areas by local housewives associations (*Asociaciones de Amas de Casa*), which have both watchdog and educational roles. The main consumer organisation in Spain is the *Unión de Consumidores de España (UCE)*, Aptdo de Correos 53238, 28080 Madrid (tel. (91) 435 4252), which has provincial offices. The UCE also runs a programme to inform tourists of their rights and help them deal with problems.

18.

ODDS & ENDS

This chapter contains miscellaneous information. Most of the topics covered are of general interest to anyone living or working in Spain, although admittedly not all are of vital importance. However, buried among the trivia are some fascinating snippets of information.

BUSINESS HOURS

Business hours for offices in Spain are generally from 0900 or 0930 until 1330 and from 1630 or 1700 until 2000. In summer, many businesses work from 0800 through to 1500 (the end of the working day) without a break. However, in recent years many companies, particularly those operating globally have switched to 'international' working hours, e.g. from 0900 until 1700, with a break for lunch from 1300 to 1400. It's often difficult to determine business hours in Spain and most people therefore try to do business involving telephone calls or visits in the mornings (which is why the telephones are always engaged), rather than the afternoons. Note that government establishments are meticulous in keeping to their official working hours. When dealing with small businesses or the self-employed, making telephone or personal calls during *siesta* hours should be avoided.

CITIZENSHIP

Your eligibility for Spanish citizenship depends upon your parentage, your current nationality and how long you have lived in Spain. You automatically acquire Spanish nationality if one of your parents is Spanish; you were born in Spain and one of your parents was also born there (parents don't need to be Spanish); or you were born in Spain of foreign parents who have no nationality (or you aren't entitled to claim their nationality).

Most foreigners must have held a residence card (*residencia*) for 10 years before they can apply for Spanish nationality. The main exceptions are those who have been granted political refuge or asylum, who can apply after five years, and nationals of Latin American countries, Andorra, the Philippines, Equatorial Guinea, Portugal and Jews of Spanish origin, all of whom qualify after just two years. A one-year residence period is sufficient for someone born in Spain or born outside Spain with a Spanish mother or father, or anyone married to a Spanish citizen (even if the marriage has been dissolved). In all cases the period of residence in Spain must have been immediately prior to the application. Marriage to a Spanish citizen doesn't entitle you to a work permit, although an application for one will usually be granted and expedited. Foreign children aged under 18 who are adopted by Spanish parents automatically become Spanish citizens, although an adopted child aged 18 or older at the time of adoption must decide whether to choose Spanish nationality in the two years following adoption.

An application for Spanish citizenship must be made to the Minister of Justice, who can refuse it on grounds of public order or national interest. In order to apply for Spanish nationality you require your birth certificate, marriage certificate (if applicable), and your parents' birth and marriage certificates, all of which must be officially translated into Spanish. You also require a certificate of good conduct from the police, a statement from two Spanish citizens supporting your application, and must show that you're a good citizen and integrated into Spanish society. Most people find it necessary to employ a lawyer to handle the paperwork involved.

Spanish law doesn't recognise dual nationality for adults and therefore a child who's entitled to choose between Spanish and another nationality must make a choice at the age of 18. A foreigner must usually renounce his former nationality (exceptions include Portuguese and Latin Americans), swear allegiance to the King of Spain, and swear to abide by the Spanish constitution and laws. Some countries (e.g. Britain) don't recognise a renunciation of nationality, irrespective of whether its citizens have taken another nationality. It's always advisable to take legal advice before renouncing your nationality and becoming a Spanish citizen.

CLIMATE

Hardly surprisingly, the overwhelming attraction of Spain for most foreigners is its excellent climate. Spain is the sunniest country in Europe and the climate (on the Costa Blanca) has been described by the World Health Organisation as among the healthiest in the world. Spain's Mediterranean coast, from the Costa Blanca to the Costa del Sol, enjoys an average of 320 days sunshine each year. When northern Europe is being deluged or frozen you can almost guarantee that the south of Spain will be bathed in sunshine (except in winter in recent years — see below). In general May and October are considered the best months for touring as they are generally dry and not too hot in most regions.

The price to pay for all those hot, dry days is a shortage of rainfall in many areas. In summer 1995 the reservoirs in central, southern and eastern Spain were almost empty after four years of severe drought, during which water was rationed for millions of people. However, the drought was broken in dramatic fashion in the winter of 1995/96, when torrential rain caused widespread flooding throughout Spain, which was repeated again in 1996/97. The winter of 1996/97 was the wettest on record and many areas in the south of the country experienced two months of almost constant torrential rainfall. Storm damage topped 15,000m ptas in the province of Malaga alone and many roads were closed by subsidence, rockfalls, landslides and collapsed bridges.

Continental Spain experiences three climatic zones: Atlantic, Continental and Mediterranean, in addition to which some areas, particularly the Balearic and Canary Islands, also have their own distinct micro-climates. In coastal areas there can be huge variations in the weather simply by travelling a few kilometres inland and up into the mountains. On some islands such as Majorca, rainfall varies from 300 to 400mm in the South to over 1,200mm in the north and some areas experience strong winds in winter, while others are sheltered.

The **Atlantic** or green coast (*costa verde*) embraces the northwest region of the country including Galicia (which has a mild and humid climate), the Cantabrian coast of Asturias, Cantabria and the Basque Country, and the Pyrenees separating Spain and France. The region from Galicia's border with Asturias along the coast to the Pyrenees is the wettest region of Spain, although even here there are some 1,800 hours of sunshine a year (much more than in northern Europe). Summer coastal temperatures average around 25°C (77°F) and spring and autumn are mild. However, the region experiences high rainfall (from 900 to 2,000mm a year), particularly in winter on the coast, and inland it's cold with frequent snowfalls (Teruel and Soria provinces generally have the worst winter climate). Contrary to the popular saying, the rain in Spain certainly doesn't fall mainly on the plain — the plains are very dry and most rain falls along the northern and western coasts. Heavy snowfalls are common above 1,200m in winter and although snow is rare outside the mountainous areas, the north of Spain and the Balearics occasionally experience snowfalls.

The **Continental** zone encompasses the central part of Spain, called the meseta (tableland), and the Ebro river valley. It embraces the provinces of Castile/La Mancha, Castile/Leon and Extremadura, plus part of Aragon and Navarre, and is baking hot in summer and freezing cold in winter. Madrid is in the centre of the meseta and has the lowest winter temperatures in Spain ranging from an average low of -20°C (-4°F) to an average high of 11°C (52°F). Annual rainfall in Madrid is 300 to 600mm. The further you travel away from Madrid in winter the warmer it becomes (except in mountainous regions), with, for example, Seville experiencing temperate winters. Seville also experiences the hottest summers in Spain, where the temperature averages around 34°C (93°F) in July and August, and often exceeds 40°C (104°F). The temperature in Ecija, between Cordoba and Seville, has exceeded 47°C (117°F) and is known as the frying pan of Andalusia (*el sartén de Andalucía*).

The **Mediterranean** zone embraces the coastal regions of Spain from the French to the Portuguese borders and is usually split into three regions. Catalonia (including the Costa Brava) has relatively mild winters but is also quite humid, with 500 to 800mm of rain and between 2,450 and 2,650 hours of sunshine a year. Summers are pleasant without very high temperatures. The central eastern part of the Mediterranean coast, from around Alicante to Tarragona (known as the Levante) and including the Costa Blanca (plus Valencia and Murcia), is warmer in winter than Catalonia and has lower rainfall (300 to 425mm). The annual hours of sunshine are between 2,700 to 3,000 and temperatures in summer can be extremely high at over 30°C (86°F). The southern coast of Andalusia (including the Costa del Sol) has slightly higher temperatures than the eastern coast (in both winter and summer) and between 2,900 and 3,000 annual hours of sunshine. Annual rainfall is just 230 to 470mm. In winter the daytime temperature on the Costa Blanca and Costa del Sol often reaches a pleasant 15 to 20°C (59 to 68°F), when the Spanish habitually dress in overcoats and the foreigners in shorts or bathing costumes.

Andalusia includes the most arid part of Spain in the province of Almeria and also the area with the highest rainfall in the whole of Spain (Spain is a country of oases and deserts). Most rain in Andalusia falls in the winter months, with some areas having as little as 200mm (8 inches) a year, which may all fall in one or two days causing flash floods. The Mediterranean coast is also subject to cold winds from the north and northeast which bring snow to the Pyrenees and the meseta in winter. The Costa del Sol can be extremely windy in winter (it was originally called the 'windy coast' or *Costa de Viento*) and parts of the Atlantic coast of Cadiz experience a strong wind called the *levante*, which can blow for days at a time (great for windsurfers). The mountain ranges of the hinterland help to protect the coastal regions from climatic extremes and funnel warm air from the meseta to the coast in summer.

The **Balearic Islands** have a Mediterranean climate with mild winters and hot summers, tempered by cool sea breezes. Annual sunshine is similar to the Levante, while annual rainfall is higher at between 450 and 650mm. The **Canary Islands** boast the best year-round climate with warm winters and temperate summers, and temperatures of between 20 to 27°C (68 to 81°F) throughout the year. Rainfall is low and varies from less than 100mm a year on Fuerteventura and Lanzarote to 750mm in the inland areas of Gran Canaria and Tenerife. The inland region of Tenerife experiences around 3,400 annual hours of sunshine a year, the highest in Spain (most areas have over 3,000 hours a year).

Winds, Earthquakes, Fires, Floods, Etc. Spain experiences many violent, cold, dry winds, including the *sirocco* in southern Spain, the *tramontana* in the Pyrenees and

Catalonia, the *solano* in Cadiz, and the *tramontana* in Menorca (Balearics). Although they are rare, southern Spain is prone to earthquakes; however, the strongest usually measure a maximum of around 5.0 on the Richter scale and they usually cause no (or very little) damage. In summer, forest fires are a danger throughout the country and along with droughts, pose a serious long-term threat to the landscape, which resembles a desert in many areas (some 15 per cent of the country's surface has a serious erosion problem). Flash floods can be very dangerous, particularly in mountainous areas, e.g. over 80 people died in August 1996 when a flash flood struck a campsite in Biescas (Huesca) in northern Spain.

Approximate average daily maximum/minimum temperatures for some major cities are shown below in Centigrade and Fahrenheit (in brackets):

Location	Spring	Summer	Autumn	Winter
Barcelona	18/11 (64/52)	28/21 (82/70)	21/15 (70/59)	13/6 (55/43)
Cadiz	20/13 (68/55)	27/20 (81/68)	23/17 (73/63)	15/9 (59/48)
Granada	20/7 (68/45)	34/17 (93/63)	23/10 (73/50)	12/2 (54/36)
Madrid	18/7 (64/45)	31/17 (88/63)	19/10 (66/50)	9/2 (48/36)
Malaga	21/13 (70/55)	29/21 (84/70)	23/16 (73/61)	17/8 (63/46)
Palma	19/10 (66/50)	29/20 (84/68)	18/10 (64/50)	14/6 (57/43)
Santander	15/10 (59/50)	22/16 (72/61)	18/12 (64/54)	12/7 (53/45)
Seville	24/11 (75/52)	36/20 (97/68)	26/14 (79/57)	15/6 (59/43)
Tenerife	24/17 (75/62)	28/20 (83/68)	28/21 (82/69)	20/14 (68/58)
Valencia	20/10 (68/50)	29/20 (84/68)	23/13 (73/55)	15/6 (59/43)

Frequent weather forecasts (*pronósticos* or *el tiempo*) are given on television, radio and in daily newspapers. A quick way to make a *rough* conversion from Centigrade to Fahrenheit is to multiply by two and add 30 (see also **Appendix C**).

CRIME

Spain's crime rate is among the lowest in Europe, although in common with most other European countries it has increased dramatically in the last decade. The Spanish generally have a lot of respect for law and order, although 'petty' laws (such as illegal parking and making too much noise) are usually ignored. In villages away from the tourist areas crime is almost unknown and windows and doors are usually left unlocked. As in other countries, major cities have the highest crime rates and Barcelona, Madrid and Seville are among the worst. Seville is notorious for 'petty' crime such as handbag snatching, pickpockets and thefts of and from vehicles. Stealing from cars, particularly those with foreign registrations, is endemic throughout Spain. You should *never* leave anything on display in your car, including your stereo system, which should be removed when parking in cities and towns (in some areas it will be gone within 15 minutes). Even storing valuables in your boot (trunk) isn't advisable as thieves may force them open and steal the contents (better to leave them unlocked and empty). In cities it's advisable to park in 'guarded' car parks, although they take no responsibility for a car's contents.

The most common crime in Spain is theft, which embraces a multitude of forms. One of the most common is the ride-by bag snatcher on a motorbike or moped. Known as the 'pull' (*tirón*), it involves grabbing a hand or shoulder bag (or a camera) and riding off with it, sometimes with the owner still attached (occasionally causing serious injuries). It's always advisable to carry bags on the inside of the pavement and to wear shoulder bags diagonally across your chest, although it's better not to carry a bag at all (the strap can be cut) and wear a wrist pouch or money belt. You should also be wary of bag-snatchers in airport and other car parks, and never wear valuable jewellery and watches in high-risk areas. Motorcycle thieves also smash car windows at traffic lights to steal articles left on seats, so always stow bags on the floor or behind seats.

Tourists and travellers are the targets of some of Spain's most enterprising criminals, including highwaymen, who pose as accident or breakdown victims and rob motorists who stop to help them. Don't leave cash or valuables unattended when swimming or leave your bags, cameras or jackets lying around on chairs in cafés or bars (*always* keep an eye on your belongings in public places). Beware of gangs of child thieves in cities such as Madrid and Barcelona, pickpockets and over-friendly strangers. Always remain vigilant in tourist haunts, queues and anywhere there are large crowds, and *never* tempt fate with an exposed wallet or purse or by flashing your money around. One of the most effective methods of protecting your passport, money, travellers cheques and credit cards is with an old-fashioned money belt.

Foreigners are often victims of housebreaking and burglary, particularly holiday home owners, which is rife in resort areas. Always ensure that your home is secure (see page 94) and that your belongings are well insured, and never leave valuables lying around. It's advisable to install a safe if you store valuables or cash in your property. Even having a guard dog may not help as professional thieves may cut its throat to keep it quiet and cut telephone lines to prevent owners from calling the police. In some areas it isn't unusual for owners to return from abroad to find their homes ransacked. Many developments and urbanisations are patrolled by security guards, although they usually have little influence on crime rates and may instill a false sense of security. It's advisable to arrange for someone to frequently check you property when it's left unoccupied. Petty theft by gypsies, who wander into homes when the doors are left open, is common in some parts of Spain.

Violent crime is still relatively rare in Spain, although armed robbery has increased considerably in the last decade or so. However, despite the fact that there's an estimated 3m guns in Spain, they are rarely used by crooks. Muggings at gun or knife-point are also rare in most towns, although they are becoming increasingly common in some areas. There are no particular dangers for women travelling alone in Spain, although hitch-hiking isn't recommended. Sexual harassment is no longer a big problem, although women (particularly blondes) may be the subject of unwanted attention in some areas. It's advisable for lone women to use taxis rather than public transport late at night.

The most common source of violent crime in Spain comes from ETA (*Euskadi ta Azkatasuna*, meaning 'Basque homeland and liberty'), the Basque terrorist organisation, which has been waging a struggle for independence since 1959. ETA has lost much of its support in recent years due to indiscriminate bombings, kidnappings and murder, and isn't supported by the vast majority of Basques (the ETA political party, Herri Batasuna, receives around 15 per cent of the vote). ETA's campaign of violence has claimed over 800 lives in the last 25 years and it continues to murder members of the police and security forces (and random other victims). It isn't, however, a threat to most foreigners in Spain and its activities are largely confined to Madrid and the north of Spain.

Drug dependency is the motivation for most crime in Spain's major cities, where as much as 80 per cent of crime is drug related. Drug addiction is a huge and growing problem throughout Spain, and drug addicts (and prostitutes) are a common sight in many towns and cities. Spain is the major gateway for cocaine and hashish into Europe and drugs are easy to obtain, particularly in the cities (sometimes with the collusion of the local police). It's an offence to possess soft drugs such as hashish (which was legalised for a period in the 1980s), although the law tends to turn a blind eye to its use and it's openly smoked in many bars and clubs. However, the possession and use of hard drugs such as heroin and cocaine is strictly prohibited. Spain is particularly harsh in its treatment of foreign drug dealers (of whom there are many), who can be held on remand for years without trial (much of the organised crime in Spain such as drugs and prostitution is run by foreigners). **Foreigners travelling to and from Spain in private or commercial vehicles must take particular care when exporting goods or freight from Spain, as cargoes are frequently found to contain hidden drugs.**

Spain rates third in the number of prisoners per 100,000 inhabitants in Europe after Hungary and Britain, and the prison population has almost doubled in the last decade or so (Spanish prisons house some 30 per cent more prisoners than they were designed for). There are conflicting reports about the treatment of prisoners, with some claiming it to be inhumane and others exemplary. While conditions in Spanish prisons vary considerably, most are no worse than those in other European countries and many foreigners actually prefer to do their time in Spain. Spain houses over 6,000 foreigners in its jails (one in six prisoners), a large percentage of whom are serving sentences for drug offences.

The Costa del Sol has earned an unsavoury reputation as a refuge for criminals and fugitives from justice, hence its nickname the 'Costa del Crime'. Spain previously had no extradition treaty with most other European countries, although this has changed with Spain's entry into the EU. A new threat in recent years has come from foreign organised crime syndicates, who take advantage of open frontiers and use Spain as a safe haven from the law in their home countries. Much organised crime (particularly money laundering and drug trafficking) on the Costa del Sol is centred on Marbella and mostly involves foreigners, including the Russian mafia (the police have identified around 20 different criminal organisations or 'gangs' on the Costa del Sol in recent years). There has recently been a an increasing number of murders connected with organised crime.

One of the biggest dangers to most foreigners in Spain isn't from the Spanish, but from their own countrymen and other foreigners. It's common for expatriate 'businessmen' to run up huge debts, either through dishonesty or incompetence, and cut and run owing their clients and suppliers millions of pesetas. In resort areas, confidence tricksters, swindlers, cheats and fraudsters lie in wait around every corner and newcomers must constantly be on their guard (particularly when buying a business). Fraud of every conceivable kind is a fine art in Spain and is commonly perpetrated by foreigners on their fellow countrymen. Always be wary of someone who offers to do you a favour or show you the ropes or anyone claiming to know how to 'beat the system'. **If anything sounds too good to be true, you can bet it almost certainly is.** It's a sad fact of life but you should generally be *more* wary of doing business with your fellow countrymen in Spain than with the Spanish.

Although the increase in crime in Spain isn't encouraging, the crime rate remains relatively low, particularly violent crime. **This means that you can usually safely walk almost anywhere at any time of day or night, and there's absolutely no need for anxiety or paranoia about crime.** However, you should be 'street-wise' and take certain elementary precautions. These include avoiding high-risk areas, particularly those frequented by drug addicts, prostitutes and pickpockets. When you're in an unfamiliar city ask a tourist office, policeman, taxi driver or local person whether there are any unsafe neighbourhoods — and avoid them! You can safely travel on public transport in Spanish cities at night. As with most things in life, prevention is better than cure. This is particularly true when it comes to crime prevention in Spain, where only a small percentage of crimes are solved and the legal process is agonizingly slow. It's also important to have adequate insurance for your possessions. Report all crimes to the police but don't expect them to take any interest in your case.

See also **Car Theft** on page 220, **Household Insurance** on page 264, **Home Security** on page 94, **Legal System** on page 410 and **Police** on page 417.

ECONOMY & TRADE

Spain has been transformed in the last three decades from a rural, backward agricultural country into a nation with a diversified economy and strong manufacturing and service sectors (although the country's bureaucracy remains firmly rooted in the 19th century). Between 1961 and 1973 (the so called years of development or *años de desarrollo*) the Spanish economy grew at 7 per cent a year (second only to Japan) and in 1963 the per capita income reached $500 a year, thus elevating Spain from the ranks of the developing nations (as defined by the United Nations). After joining the European Union (EU) in 1986 Spain again had one of the world's fastest-growing economies with annual growth averaging over 4 per cent until being hard hit by the recession in the early 1990s. However, three depreciations of the peseta helped contribute to a vastly improved balance of payments and economic reforms introduced by a new Conservative government in 1996 initiated a strong recovery. In 1997, growth was running at over 3 per cent, inflation was under 2 per cent, the budget deficit had fallen to below 3 per cent of GDP (down from 7.5 per cent in 1993.) and the Bank of Spain's bench mark interest rate had fallen to just 5.5 per cent. Nevertheless (although falling) unemployment remains a huge concern and is the highest in the EU (over 20 per cent and double the EU average), and the country has an accumulated national debt of 60 per cent of GDP.

Spain has the fifth-largest economy in Europe and accounts for around 10 per cent of EU output. However, GDP per head remains one of the lowest in the EU at $14,268 in 1996, only exceeding that of Portugal and Greece. Spain's main trading partners are France, Germany and Italy for exports, and Germany, France and Italy for imports. Some 70 per cent of exports are to EU countries, who also provide around 65 per cent of imports. Spain also has close economic ties with South America, its natural trading partner where language is concerned. The Basque country and Catalonia are Spain's main industrial regions and just five of Spain's provinces (Barcelona, Madrid, Navarre, Oviedo and Vizcaya, all situated in the north and east) produce over half the country's industrial output. Catalonia, where some 85 per cent of companies are located in Barcelona, is Spain's economic powerhouse and one of Europe's most important industrial regions.

Spanish industry has lost competitiveness in the last decade or so and productivity is well below the European average (it rates around 30th in the world). Adding to Spain's problems in recent years was the ending of its seven-year, European Union, 'honeymoon' transition period in 1993, during which its tariffs and quotas on EU imports were phased out, thus exposing the economy to the full force of EU competition. However, huge investment has been made in Spain's infrastructure in the last decade (assisted by $billions in EU subsidies) including its roads, railways, airports, water supply and communications, while at the same time the country has tightened its economic belt.

Spanish industry is firmly rooted in small and medium-sized family concerns and has only a few companies in Europe's top 100. It's significant that Spain hasn't got one manufacturer among Europe's largest companies and most manufacturers are too small to compete globally. Spain has relied heavily on foreign investment (three-quarters of it in Barcelona and Madrid) for much of its recent growth, although many investors turned their backs on Spain during the recession. Over 30 per cent of Spanish industry is foreign-owned, including some 50 per cent of its food production (mostly French owned). Spanish industry is handicapped by its lack of modern machinery and technology (much of Spain's industrial plant is antiquated and needs replacing), particularly computer technology, coupled with poor efficiency and organisation. It has yet to create a silicon (computer) economy that's the engine of so much growth elsewhere. Most of Spain's largest companies remain state-owned (by the *Instituto Nacional de Industria/INI*) and loss-making (some 500 billion ptas a year!), and include banking, duty-free shops, construction, coal mines, shipyards, airlines, capital goods, aerospace, railways, TV and radio, munitions, paper pulp, electricity, gas, electronics, aluminium, insurance, tobacco and ferry services. However, the privatisation of state industries begun in the late 1980s is continuing apace under the conservative government and many more are expected to be sold off in the next few years.

Spain's dependence on agriculture has diminished in the last few decades, while tourism and other service industries have grown considerably in importance. In 1995 agriculture accounted for around 3.5 per cent of GDP and employed some 10 per cent of the workforce, almost half of the figure for 1985 (and down from over 25 per cent of GDP in 1960, when around 40 per cent of the population was employed in agriculture). In 1997, one third of the workforce was employed in industry, while services accounted for around 60 per cent of jobs. Spain's most important industries include tourism; chemicals and petro-chemicals; heavy industry such as iron and steel castings; food and beverages; and electrical and automobile manufacturing (Spain is Europe's fifth-largest car manufacturing country after Germany, France, Italy and Britain). The principal growth areas include tourism, insurance, property development, electronics and financial services. Tourism is one of Spain's most important industries, earning around 10 per cent of GDP and employing over 10 per cent of the workforce (directly and indirectly). In 1996, Spain welcomed some 42m visitors and in terms of tourist revenue was second only to the USA.

Despite its often antiquated farming methods Spain is the world's largest producer of olive oil, fourth-largest of dried fruit and the sixth largest of citrus fruits. Spain's vineyards are the largest in the world and some 60 per cent larger than France's, although it's only the fourth largest producer of wine-grapes and ranks third in wine production. Other important crops include barley, wheat, maze, rice, potatoes, sugar-beet, peppers, avocados, tomatoes, tobacco, hops, oil-bearing fruits, cork, esparto-grass and raw materials for textiles (cotton, flax and hemp). The most valuable produce is fruit and vegetables. Spain has over three million hectares of land under irrigation and employs widespread 'artificial' watering, which often isn't cost-effective. Spanish farmers have been badly hit by falling prices, drought, frost and hailstorms in recent years.

The farmers' plight has been exacerbated in recent years by French anarchists destroying Spanish trucks and produce (such as strawberries) on its way to French markets. Spanish fishermen have also had violent clashes with British and French fishermen over fishing quotas and the alleged use of illegal drift nets. Spain is Europe's largest producer of shellfish and has the second largest fishing fleet in the world after Japan (60 per cent of which is based in Galicia on the Atlantic coast), although it's being reduced as part of an EU agreement to conserve fish stocks. Spanish fishing grounds are, like most European waters, largely exhausted and Spanish deep-sea boats comb the seas to fill their holds. Fishing and agriculture (one of the main beneficiaries of EU funds) account for around 8 per cent of GDP and employ some 10 per cent of the workforce.

In the last few years Spain has been forced to live within its means and state spending has been slashed to control the soaring budget deficit. Like many European countries, Spain has found that it can no longer afford to pay the high social security benefits that its citizens have become accustomed to in the last few decades. Fiscal policy was tightened by the new (conservative) government in 1996, which has made qualification for EMU one of its main priorities. Against all the odds and to the dismay of many, Spain is expected to qualify for the European single currency in 1999. The down side of Spain's strong economic recovery in recent years is that it could become a victim of its own economic success and lose valuable EU cohesion and structural funds.

GEOGRAPHY

Spain or the Kingdom of Spain (*reino de España* or *Estado Español*) is the second largest country in western Europe after France, and is often referred to as 'the old bullhide' (*la piel de toro*), because a map of the country resembles a stretched out bullhide. It covers an area of 492,463km2 (190,154sq miles) of the Iberian Peninsula or 504,749km2 (194.898sq miles) including the Balearics and the Canary Islands. The mainland is 805km (500miles) from north to south and 885km (550miles) from east to west. Spain's mainland coastline totals 2,119km (1,317miles).

The Balearic Islands off the eastern coast comprise the islands of Majorca, Ibiza, Menorca and Formentera and cover an area of 5,014km2 (1,936sq miles), while the Canary Islands, situated 97km (60miles) off the west coast of Africa, cover an area of 7,272km2 (2,808sq miles). Spain also has two North African enclaves, Ceuta and Melilla, administered by the provinces of Cadiz and Malaga respectively. They have been held by Spain since the 15th century and are, not surprisingly, claimed by Morocco. The small islands of Peñón de Vélez, Alhicemas and Xhafarinas off the Moroccan coast also 'belong' to Spain.

The Pyrenees in the north form a natural barrier between Spain and France and Andorra, while to the west is Portugal. To the northwest is the Bay of Biscay and the province of Galicia, with an Atlantic coast. In the east and south is the Mediterranean. The southern tip of Spain is just 16km (10miles) from Africa across the Straight of Gibraltar. The ownership of Gibraltar (a British colony) has long been a thorn in the side of Spain's rulers and on occasion it flares up, notably during the France era when the border was closed from 1969 until 1985. Although relations have improved since then, they remain strained and in recent years Spain has increased its diplomatic efforts (and obstruction) in its efforts to regain sovereignity over Gibraltar. Spain also has concerns over the high level of crime associated with Gibraltar including tobacco smuggling, drug-running and money-laundering. The smuggling of cigarettes and hashish is carried out openly in Gibraltar under the eyes of the local police, although there have been crackdowns in recent years.

Spain consists of a vast plain (the meseta) surrounded by mountains and is the highest country in Europe after Switzerland, with an average altitude of 650m (2,132ft) above sea level. The vast plateau of the meseta extends over an area of over 200,000km2 (77,000sq miles) at altitudes of between 600 and 1,000m (2,000 and 3,300ft). Mountains hug the coast on three sides with the Cantabrian chain in the north (including the Picos de Europa), the Penibetic chain in the south (including the Sierra Nevada with the highest peaks in Spain) and a string of lower mountains throughout the regions of Catalonia and Valencia in the east. The highest peak on the peninsula is the *Pico de Mulhacén* in the Sierra Nevada range (3,482m/11,423ft), which is topped by Mount Teide (3,718m/12,198ft) on the Canary island of Tenerife.

Spain's main river is the Ebro, from which the Iberian peninsula gets its name, and the only Spanish river flowing into the Mediterranean. Others include the Douro, Guadalquivir, Guadiana, Tagus and Tajo, all of which flow into the Atlantic. Half of Spain's soil is unproductive or barren and some parts of the southeast are almost desert (inland from Almeria is where many Spaghetti westerns were made). At the other extreme the *huerta* of Valencia and the Guadalquivir valley are extremely fertile and the northern coast of Cantabria, Asturias and Galicia are green and lush with forests and pasturelands.

GOVERNMENT

Following the death of General Franco on November 20th 1975, which heralded the end of 36 years of crippling dictatorship, Spain has become a parliamentary democracy. A year after Franco's death political parties were legalised, the Socialists in February 1977 and the Communists in April. The first general elections was held in 1979 and won by the *Unión de Centro Democrátia (UCD)* led by Adolfo Suárez, who was largely credited with transforming Spain from a dictatorship into a democracy. The new Spanish constitution of 31st October 1978, arguably the most liberal in western Europe, heralded a radical transformation from a dictatorship to a democratic government. The most important task of the constitution was to devolve power to the regions which were given their own governments, regional assemblies and supreme legal authorities. The central government retains exclusive responsibility for foreign affairs, external trade, defence, justice, law (criminal, commercial and labour), merchant shipping and civil aviation. Spain has been a member of the United Nations (UN) since 1955, the North Atlantic Treaty Organisation (NATO) since 1982 and the European Union (EU) since 1986, and is also a permanent observer member of the Organisation of American States (OAS).

Parliament: The national parliament (*las Cortes Generales*) has two chambers, the lower of which is the **Congress of Deputies** (*Congreso de los Diputados*) and the upper the **Senate** (*senado*). The Congress consists of 350 members representing Spain's 50 provinces and the North African enclaves of Ceuta and Melilla. Each province is an electoral constituency, with the number of deputies depending on its population. Members of Congress are elected by a system of proportional representation for four years. The Senate has 254 members, directly elected by a first-past-the-post system. Each province provides four members plus additional members in the Balearic and Canary islands, where extra members represent the various islands, making a total of 208 members. The 17 autonomous regions also elect one senator each and an additional member for each one million inhabitants, totalling a further 46 members. The Senate has the power to amend or veto legislation initiated by Congress.

Under Spanish law, the official result of a general election is made public five days after the vote, in order to allow sufficient time for recounts and disputed results. After the members have been sworn in, the King of Spain meets with the party leaders and asks one of them (usually the leader of the largest party) to form a government, which must then be ratified by parliament. The leader of the party of government becomes the president (*presidente*) of Spain and has his official residence in the Moncloa Palace in Madrid.

The **Constitutional Court** (*el tribunal constitucional*) is responsible for ensuring that laws passed by parliament comply with the constitution and international agreements to which Spain is party. The **Judiciary** is independent of the government, with the highest legal body being the 'General Council of Judicial Power' (*Consejo general del Poder Judicial*), which has 20 independent members and is headed by the president of the supreme court (*tribunal supremo*).

Present Government: Following a general election in March 1996, the conservative (right-wing) *Partido Popular (PP)* led by José Maria Aznar won a narrow victory over the Socialists (*Partido Socialista Obrero Español/PSOE*) who had governed Spain since 1982. However, the PP were 20 seats short of an overall majority, and like the Socialists before them, were forced to enter into a coalition with regional parties. The United Left (*Izquierda Unida*) is the third largest national party and there are also important regional parties in Catalonia (*Covergencia i Unio/CiU*) and the Basque lands (*Partido Nacionalista Vasco/PNV*). The PP rely on the support of the CiU (led by Jordi Pujol, dubbed the 'King of Catalonia') and PNV to retain power, in return for which they received even greater autonomy (they had already squeezed concessions from the Socialists for their support in previous coalitions) over fiscal matters at the expense of poorer regions.

Autonomous Regions: Spain has 17 autonomous regions (*comunidades autónomas*), shown on the map in **Appendix D**, each with its own president, government (*gobierno* or *junta*), administration and supreme court (plus its own flag and capital city). The regions are funded by the central government and the regions of the Basque Lands, Catalonia, Galicia and Andalusia are responsible for matters such as economic development, education, health, environment, police, public works, tourism, culture, local language and social security. The other regions have less autonomy and fewer responsibilities. The people of the Basque Lands, Catalonia and Galicia have also been recognised as separate ethnic groups and have the right to use their own languages in education and administration, as declared in the Statute of Autonomy of 1983 accepted throughout Spain in a referendum. With the increasing influence of the Basque and Catalan regional parties in national politics after the general election of 1996, the whole question of regional power and autonomy has taken on a new significance. Catalonia and other regions have obtained the right to retain a greater share of their taxes, which means less money for Spain's poorer regions and will exacerbate their already dire economic situation.

Provinces: Each province has its own administration (*diputación*) which is responsible for a range of services including health (hospitals, nursing homes), public works (including roads), sports facilities (such as public swimming pools) and social clubs (e.g. for youths and the elderly). The civil governors (*gobernadores civiles*), who were head of the provincial governments, have been replaced by sub-delegates (*Subdelegados del Gobierno*) who coordinate the work of the different government offices in the provinces.

Municipalities: A municipality is run by a council consisting of a number of councillors (*concejales*), each of whom is responsible for a different area of local services. The council is headed by the mayor (*alcalde*), some of whom are autocratic and run their towns like feudal fiefdoms, and has its offices in the local town hall (*ayuntamiento*). The official population of a municipality includes everyone who's registered in the list of inhabitants (*padrón municipal*). Entry in the *padrón municipal* is a prerequisite for inclusion on the electoral roll (*censo electoral*) and the right to vote in local elections every four years. Although it isn't mandatory for foreigners to register in their community, it's important to register as the funds that municipalities receive from central and regional governments is based on the official number of inhabitants. Theoretically the more government funds a municipality receives, the lower the local taxes.

The responsibilities of municipalities include garbage collection, street cleaning, street lighting, drinking water, sewage disposal/treatment, road access and maintenance, public health controls, cemeteries, schools, urban planning, traffic control, consumer protection and policing. Municipalities with over 5,000 inhabitants must also provide public parks, a public library and markets, and those with over 20,000 also need to provide civil protection, social services, fire prevention, public sports facilities and a municipal slaughterhouse.

Many town halls have a chronic liquidity problem, due to a combination of inefficiency (many Spanish communities are among the worst run in the EU), over-manning and a failure to collect taxes. It's ironic that while municipalities are quick to fine residents for late payments, they are themselves the worst payers of bills in Spain and have run up debts of many billions of pesetas. Some are so bad at paying their bills that they have great difficulty in finding companies willing to supply or work for them, and municipal workers often have to strike to get paid (some towns cannot even afford to insure their police cars). The financial situation of many councils is critical, many of whom are paying millions of pesetas a day in interest charges on their debts, and has been described as a financial time-bomb. As a result of the town halls' debts, property taxes have risen sharply in recent years and are expected to go even higher.

Corruption: One of the most topical issues in Spain during the last few years has been corruption among public officials including illegal financing of political parties, tax avoidance, fraud, bribery, institutionalised sleeze, nepotism, misappropriation of public funds, illegal patronage, influence-peddling and kickbacks. Spain has been described (in the Spanish press) as the most corrupt society in the EU and corruption permeates political and public life at every level (many Spaniards lack a sense of ethics when it comes to bribery, which is often accepted as a perk of the job). In 1994 the Socialist government was rocked by a number of corruption scandals (which did much to lose them the 1996 election), when every day seemed to bring to light new cases involving national, regional or local officials.

Foreign Voting Rights: The voting rights of non-EU residents depend on whether a bilateral agreement exists between Spain and their home countries. Foreigners must be registered on the electoral roll to vote in local elections. Foreign nationals of EU countries resident in Spain will be able to vote and stand as councillors in local elections from 1999. Candidates must be able to express themselves in a dignified manner in Spanish and have a good knowledge of their municipality and the local government laws in Spain. The non-political organisation *Ciudadanos Europeos* has long promoted voting rights for European Union citizens resident in Spain and in other European countries, and plans to field candidates in local elections in 1999.

With the new voting rights for foreigners, it's expected that they will be taken more seriously by their town halls in future (at least in municipalities where there's a sizeable resident foreign population). Many town halls already have employees who speak English and other foreign languages, and in municipalities where there are a large number of foreign residents there are often special foreigners' departments (*departamentos de extranjeros*). However, foreigners usually pay a disproportionate amount of taxes for what they receive in return, particularly non-resident home owners, and their investment in Spain has been out of all proportion to the number of votes they receive. Local councils in resort areas often ignore the needs of certain communities and urbanisations, particularly those mainly populated by non-resident foreigners, and spend (waste) the vast bulk of their revenue beautifying their main town centre.

European Parliament: EU Residents of Spain are allowed to vote in European elections for Members of the European Parliament (MEPs), but cannot vote in Spanish general elections.

LEGAL SYSTEM

If you're seeking legal advice, always ask around among local residents and obtain recommendations. This way you will usually find out not only who to employ, but more importantly who to avoid (wrong legal advice is often more expensive in the long term than having none at all). Always obtain an estimate (*presupuesto*) of costs in advance, if possible in writing, and shop around and compare fees from a number of lawyers, as they can vary considerably. The estimate should detail exactly what the lawyer will do for his fees. Note, however, that if you consult a number of legal 'experts' about the same matter, you're highly unlikely to receive exactly the same advice.

The Spanish legal system is excruciatingly slow (i.e. largely at a standstill) and there's a backlog of hundreds of thousands of cases throughout Spain, which means that it takes years for many case to come to court. Even local courts can take five years to hear a case, although delays are usually up to two years for minor offences and up to four years for serious offences. **This means that you should do everything possible to avoid going to court by taking every conceivable precaution when doing business in Spain, i.e. obtaining expert legal advice in advance.** If things do go wrong it will almost certainly take years to achieve satisfaction and in the case of fraud the chances are that those responsible will have either gone broke or disappeared (or even died!). Note that even when you have a foolproof case there's no guarantee of winning and it may be better to write off a loss as experience. Local courts, judges and lawyers frequently abuse the system to their own ends and almost anyone with enough money or expertise can use the law to their own advantage. In recent years public confidence in Spain's legal system has been rocked by a succession of scandals.

Lawyers: If you're buying property in Spain, investing in or starting a business, applying for a work permit or making a will, you should employ the services of an experienced Spanish lawyer (*abogado*). You may be able to obtain a list of lawyers from your local embassy or consulate (see **Appendix A**). Suggested lawyer's fees are set by provincial professional bodies (*Ilustre Colegio de Abogados*), although individual lawyers often set much higher fees. However, fees are usually lower than those charged by lawyers in northern European countries, with a simple consultation of less than half an hour costing around 5,000 ptas. When preparing contracts involving a sum of money, e.g. property or land purchase, fees are calculated as a percentage of the sum involved. 'No win, no fee' lawsuits are illegal in Spain.

Always try to engage a lawyer who speaks your mother tongue. In some areas English-speaking lawyers (and lawyers speaking other foreign languages) are common and lawyers are used to dealing with foreigners and their particular problems. In cases where a lawyer is obligatory (which depends on the sum involved in a civil case) and your income is below double the Spanish minimum wage (see page 32), you can apply for free legal assistance (*abogado de oficio*). The college of lawyers will appoint a lawyer to assist you, although he won't take as much interest in your case as a private lawyer would. In cases involving large sums (e.g. over 800,000 ptas) the services of a barrister (*procurador*) is required. If you don't receive satisfactory service you can complain to the local professional college. Common complaints include long delays, poor communication, high fees and overcharging (particularly with regard to property transactions involving foreigners). **Bear in mind that in Spain, lawyers are often part of the problem rather than the solution (aren't they always?)!**

Gestor: A *gestor* is an official agent licensed by the Spanish government as a middleman between you and the bureaucracy. This speaks volumes for the stifling and tortuous Spanish bureaucracy, which is so complicated and cumbersome that it's necessary for citizens to employ a special official simply to do business with the government! It's a profession found only in Iberia and Latin America (enough said) and is a throwback to the days when most people were illiterate and needed professional help with official paperwork. It isn't *compulsory* to employ a *gestor*, but without one you will usually need to speak fluent Spanish (or have an interpreter), possess boundless patience and stamina, and have unlimited time to deal with the mountains of red tape and obstacles that will confront you. However, if you have the time and can speak reasonable Spanish, you will find it extremely educational to do your own paperwork.

A *gestor's* services aren't generally expensive and most people find it worthwhile employing one. He usually works in a *gestoría* (*gestor's* office), where a number of experts may be employed dealing with different matters including employment and residence permits; establishing and registering a business; obtaining a driving licence, tourist plates or registering a car; social security; and property contracts. A *gestor* can help you in your dealings with any government body or state-owned company such as an electricity company. Note that the quality of service provided by *gestores* can vary considerably and that they cannot always be relied upon to do a professional job (some have been known to take their clients' money and do absolutely nothing).

Notario: A *notario* (notary) is a public official authorised by the government, who's most commonly engaged in property transactions. He doesn't deal with criminal cases or offer advice concerning criminal law. *Notarios* have a monopoly in the areas of transferring real property, testamentary (e.g. of wills) and matrimonial acts, which by law must be in the form of an authentic document, verified and stamped by a *notario*. In Spain, property conveyancing is strictly governed by Spanish law and can be performed only by a *notario*. In respect to private law, a *notario* is responsible for administering and preparing documents relating to property sales and purchases, inheritance, wills, establishing limited companies, and buying and selling businesses. He also certifies the validity and safety of contracts and deeds. If you need irrefutable proof of delivery of a letter or other documents, they should be sent via a *notario*, as nobody can deny receiving a document delivered through his offices.

Property Administrator: A property administrator (*administrador de fincas*) is a licensed professional who's qualified to handle all matters connected with owning and managing property in Spain, particularly property in an urbanisation where there's a community of owners. His duties include calling meetings, taking minutes, advising residents, collecting fees, paying taxes and paying bills.

Courts: Like French law, Spanish law derives from the *Code Napoléon*. The lowest court is the justice of the peace (*juez de la paz*), dealing with simple matters such as property complaints between neighbours. Neither party need have legal counsel and simple cases are usually resolved at this level. Civil cases are decided by a *juzgado/tribunal de primera instancia*, where most cases start. The next highest court is a district court presided over by a district judge (*juez de distrito*), where you will need a lawyer. It handles more serious matters, e.g. unpaid debts for goods and services or failure to meet the conditions of a contract. Criminal cases are held before a local *tribunal de primera instancia e instrucción*, followed in order of importance by an *audiencia provincial*, *audiencia territorial*, *audiencia nacional*, *tribunal superior de justicia* and the Supreme Court (*tribunal supremo*) in Madrid. Trial by jury for criminal trials was reintroduced in 1996 after 57 years absence. A jury consists of nine people, seven of whom must agree to establish a guilty verdict. You have the right of appeal in all cases.

Arrest: If you're arrested you have the right to make a statement in the presence of your lawyer, or one nominated by the police if you don't have one, and the right to an interpreter. You also have the right to advise a member of your family or another person of your arrest or in the case of a foreigner to contact your consul. You can be held for up to 72 hours without charge after which you must be charged and brought before a court or freed. You cannot be held longer without a judicial order. Note, however, that if you're remanded in custody, you can be held for years while a case is being 'investigated'. Wrongful imprisonment isn't uncommon and any innocent person unlucky enough to be caught up in the drug trade can look forward to a long stay in prison.

Complaints: If you have a complaint against someone, for example your neighbour for making too much noise or your local authority for not collecting your garbage, and your appeals fall on deaf ears, you can make an official complaint (*denuncia*) to the police. There are ombudsmen in most regions who handle certain complaints and queries, many with staff who speak English and other foreign languages. If you have a complaint concerning the way EU laws are interpreted or are being broken in Spain, you should complain to your European member of parliament. You can also bring a lawsuit against the Spanish state. However, you should expect to wait a long (long) time for your case to be heard.

Never assume that the law in Spain is the same as in any other country as this often *isn't* the case and some Spanish laws are bizarre. Note that it's illegal for anyone to be without some form of personal identification in Spain and you should carry your residence card (if applicable) or passport at all times (you can be asked to produce it by a policeman). Certain legal advice and services may also be provided by your embassy or consulate in Spain, including for example, an official witness of signatures (Commissioner for Oaths). A useful book for Spanish residents and property owners is *You and the Law in Spain* by David Searl (Santana). See also **Consumer Protection** on page 394, **Crime** on page 401 and **Police** on page 417.

MARRIAGE & DIVORCE

Despite the falling number of marriages and church attendances in Spain, a church wedding with all the trimmings remains the dream of most Spanish girls. Marriage bureaux are common in cities, with applicants (of all ages) paying a fee of from 25,000 to 40,000 ptas to meet an unlimited number of prospective partners with no time limit. Surprisingly, 70 per cent of Spaniards below the age of 30, both married and single, live with their parents.

To be married in a Roman Catholic church in Spain at least one partner must be a Roman Catholic; a divorcee isn't permitted to marry in a Spanish church if the previous marriage was solemnised in church. A certificate of baptism is required plus a declaration from your former parish priest that you're a Roman Catholic and are free to marry. You receive a certificate from the priest which must be presented within one week to the local civil registry in order to obtain an official marriage certificate. Couples also receive a 'family book' (*libro de familia*) when they marry in Spain, which is the official registration of a couple and their children. It's necessary for children to present this when they apply for their own identity card, social security card and when they marry or divorce (or when someone dies).

In order for two non-Catholic foreigners to marry in Spain, one must have lived (and have been domiciled) in Spain for at least two years. Marriages are held at Spanish civil registry offices and are presided over by a judge (church weddings for non-Catholics in Spain aren't legally recognised). If you're divorced or widowed, you must produce an official divorce or death certificate. A divorced person requires a legal declaration (*certificado de ley*) drawn up by a lawyer and legalised by a Spanish consul in the country of origin. Some foreigners will find it easier to get married abroad, e.g. Britons and Americans can get married in Gibraltar, where couples are married in a registry office in front of two witnesses. Many foreigners can also be married at their country's embassy in Spain.

Unmarried couples (including homosexuals) can register their union (without getting married) at a special registry in some towns and receive a formal certificate allowing them to claim social security and benefit from life insurance policies. Note, however, that common-law partners have no property rights in Spain and are treated as unrelated individuals if they don't have official documentation. A new bill which was intended to give equal rights to unmarried couples, both heterosexual and homosexual, was blocked by parliament after the vote was deadlocked. A parliamentary commission will now consider the rights of some 400,000 Spaniards in 'de facto' marriages

Divorce: Under Franco divorce was impossible in Spain, but was eventually legalised in 1981. Foreigners who were married abroad can also be divorced in Spain and only one of the partners need be a resident. A couple must have been married for one year before they can file for divorce, the simplest form of which is when a couple wish to divorce or separate by mutual consent. The separation must be legalised before a Spanish notary (*notario*) and you usually need to employ a lawyer. After two years of legal separation, a divorce is automatically granted, providing the situation remains the same. Apart from mutual consent, the usual grounds for divorce are adultery, cruelty, desertion, mental disorders, and alcohol or drug addition. In cases where the separation wasn't by mutual consent, the period of legal separation before a divorce is granted is five years.

MILITARY SERVICE

Since the end of the civil war until well into the 1970s, the Spanish army was a sinecure for officer civil war veterans and consequently was grossly top heavy with around one officer to every 10 soldiers. However, since Franco's death in 1975 the status and influence of the military has been considerably reduced. The vast majority of Spain's soldiers are male conscripts (paid around 1,500 ptas a month) for whom service starts at the age of 18 and continues for nine months (women can volunteer to serve in the military). Spain's conscripts work the longest hours for the lowest pay of any in the 15 EU member states. Those selected to do military service are chosen at random by a nationally televised lottery, when balls inscribed with the day and month of the year are drawn (the Spanish love lotteries, although this one isn't popular with the winners!)

Conscription is a big issue among the young and some two-thirds of Spaniards are opposed to it (there's a vigorous *Mili No* campaign to end it) and there has traditionally been a higher than average death rate due to accidents and suicides among Spanish conscripts. The government maintains that compulsory military service is necessary as there isn't the mentality for a professional army and there wouldn't be enough volunteers (it would also be very expensive). The biggest threat to conscription is from the number of people refusing military service on the grounds of conscientious objection, which was finally recognised in 1985 (prior to which objectors were jailed). In the Basque country and Navarra there's an objection rate of some 70 per cent. Conscientious objectors (*objetores*) do 13 months social service such as driving ambulances and working as paramedics on beaches. Since 1985 the number of objectors has soared and is growing six times as fast as the available social services' places. In fact over half of all objectors avoid service of any kind as there isn't enough social work to go round. Those who refuse to do any kind of national service, termed 'unsubmissives' (*insumisos*), can be jailed for two years, four months and one day.

Spain is a signatory to the treaty banning nuclear weapons and has been a member of NATO (*OTAN* in Spanish) since 1982, although there has been widespread opposition, particularly to American bases in Spain. A referendum on whether to remain in NATO was held in 1986 and received a small majority in favour of membership. In the 1980s, US forces in Spain were cut, culminating in the closure of the huge Torrejón airbase near Madrid (more for strategic reasons than pressure from Spain). In 1996, a Spaniard, Javier Solana, became NATO's Secretary-General. Defence spending in Spain is around 2 per cent of GDP and less than 20 per cent of what Britain, France or Germany spend.

PETS

If you plan to take a pet (*animal de compañía* or *mascota*) to Spain, it's important to check the latest regulations. Make sure that you have the correct papers, not only for Spain but for all the countries you will pass through to reach Spain. Particular consideration must be given before exporting a pet from a country with strict quarantine regulations, such as Britain. If you need to return prematurely, even after a few hours or days in Spain, your pet must go into quarantine, e.g. for six months in Britain. Apart from the expense this is distressing for both pets and owners. Norway and Sweden abolished quarantine on 1st May 1994 (but have strict vaccination regulations) and it's possible that Britain will follow suit (animals imported into Britain by professional breeders and other approved establishments were exempted in 1994).

A maximum of two pets may accompany travellers to Spain. A rabies vaccination is usually compulsory, although this *doesn't* apply to accompanied pets (including dogs and cats) entering Spain directly from Britain or for animals under three months old. However, if a rabies vaccination is given, it must be administered not less than one month or more than 12 months prior to export. A rabies vaccination is necessary if pets are transported by road from Britain to Spain via France. Pets over three months old from countries other than Britain must have been vaccinated against rabies not less than one month and not more than one year before being imported. If a pet has no rabies certificate it can be quarantined for 20 days. An official certificate is also required declaring that the area where the animal is normally kept is free from animal diseases and rabies. All certificates must be legalised and stamped by a Spanish consulate (there's a small fee). Some animals require a special import permit from the Spanish Ministry of Agriculture and pets from some countries are subject to customs duty.

British pet owners must complete an *Application for a Ministry Export Certificate for dogs, cats and rabies susceptible animals* (form EXA1), available from the Ministry of Agriculture, Fisheries & Food (MAFF), Animal Health (International Trade) Division B, Hook Rise South, Tolworth, Surbiton, Surrey KT6 7NF, UK (tel. 0181-330 4411). A health inspection must be performed by a licensed veterinary officer, after which you receive an export health certificate, which must be issued no more than 15 days before your entry into Spain with your pet. If you're transporting a pet to Spain by ship or ferry, you should notify the ferry company. Some companies insist that pets are left in vehicles (if applicable), while others allow pets to be kept in cabins. If your pet is of nervous disposition or unused to travelling, it's best to tranquilise it on a long sea crossing. A pet can also be shipped to Spain by air.

If you intend to live permanently in Spain, most vets recommend that you have a dog vaccinated against rabies before arrival, which saves you having to get your dog vaccinated on arrival in Spain. Dogs should also be vaccinated against leptospirosis, parvovirus, hepatitis, distemper and kennel cough, and cats immunised against feline gastro-enteritis and typhus. Note that there are a number of diseases and dangers for pets in Spain that aren't found in most other European countries. These include the fatal leishmaniasis (also called Mediterranean or sandfly disease), processionary caterpillars, leeches, heartworm, ticks (a tick collar can prevent these), feline leukemia virus and feline enteritis. Obtain advice about these from a veterinary surgeon (*veterinario*) on arrival in Spain. Take extra care when walking your dog, as some have died after eating poisoned food in rural areas. Poisoned bait (e.g. meat laced with strychnine) is laid in some areas by hunters and poachers to control natural predators such as foxes, wolves and lynx (poisons are also laid in some urbanisations to keep down the feral cat population).

Veterinary surgeons are well trained in Spain, where it's a popular profession, and emergency veterinary care is also available in animal clinics (*clínica veterinaria*), many of which provide a 24-hour emergency service. Veterinary surgeons and animal clinics advertise in English-language publications in Spain. Health insurance for pets is available from a number of insurance companies. The premium is around 10,000 ptas a year for a dog and 7,500 ptas for a cat, which covers owners against veterinary fees (e.g. up to 250,000 ptas a year), travel abroad, complementary medicine, third party liability (e.g. 10m ptas), accidental death and theft.

There are kennels and catteries (*residencias para animales de compañía*) throughout Spain, many of which advertise in Spanish English-language publications in resort areas (make sure they are registered and bona fide establishments). Book well in advance if you plan to leave your pet at a kennel or cattery, particularly for school holiday periods. Fees are around 500 ptas a day for a cat and from 600 to 1,000 ptas a day for a dog, depending on its size (there may be a small discount for more than one pet). Pets must be vaccinated.

There may be discrimination against pets when renting accommodation, particularly when it's furnished, and the statutes of community properties can legally prohibit pets. Many hotels accept pets such as cats and dogs, although they aren't usually permitted in restaurants, cafés or food shops (except for guide dogs). A guide to hotels (*Viajando con Perros*) accepting dogs and other animals is published by Seiquer SL, Paseo de la Castellana, 62, 28046 Madrid (tel. (91) 411 0862).

A dog registration scheme operates in Barcelona and Madrid and is being introduced in municipalities throughout Spain. Owners are required to register their dogs and have them either tattooed with their registration number in an ear or have a microchip inserted in their neck (it's a painless process, apart from the bill). Registration costs around 3,000 to 5,000 ptas and there are fines for owners who don't have their dogs registered. Regardless of whether your dog is microchipped, it's advisable to have it fitted with a collar and tag with your name and telephone number on it and the magic word 'reward' (*recompensa*). All municipalities have rules (*ordenanzas*) regarding the keeping of dogs, which require a health card if they are older than three months. In public areas, a dog must be kept on a lead (and muzzled if its dangerous) and wear a health disc on its collar. Dogs are prohibited from entering places where food is manufactured, stored or sold; from sports and cultural events; and are banned from beaches.

It's common in Spain for owners to let their dogs roam free (in Spain dogs go for a walk on their own), although owners of unsupervised dogs are held responsible for any damage they cause. Dogs that chase cyclists and mopeds are a nuisance in some towns and Spain has a growing problem with bands of wild dogs attacking sheep and other domestic animals (stray cats are also a problem in many areas). One of the most unpleasant consequences of dog ownership in Spain is the vast amount of excrement deposited on Spanish streets, which is an increasing health hazard, particularly for young children. You must *always* watch where you walk in Spain and keep an eye on young children. It's illegal not to clean up after your dog in a public area, although few people do so. Note that the chemicals used in swimming pools are a health hazard for dogs and if you allow your dog to swim in your pool, you should hose it down afterwards.

Much has been written about the Spaniard's attitude towards animals, particularly his (seemingly) heartless attitude towards animal suffering (Spain is the only EU country where there's no specific legislation against cruelty to animals). The Spanish aren't sentimental about animals and aren't a nation of animal lovers, which is confirmed by the many owners who simply abandon their pets when they go on holiday. Many Spaniards (and foreigners) own dogs simply to guard their homes and many bark continually, particularly at night. They are often tied up for 24 hours a day, although fed and watered regularly, and may be left on their own for days or weeks at a time (apart from when being fed). Note that keeping a large dog isn't a guarantee against burglary and it isn't uncommon for thieves to poison dogs to gain access to homes (it's best to keep a dog inside the house where thieves cannot get at it). However, the Spanish aren't a nation of animal abusers and most Spaniards love and care for their pets as much as owners in any other western European country. There are animal protection organisations and animal shelters run by foreigners in many resort areas.

Most criticism is reserved for Spain's treatment of its working animals (among the worst in the EU) and the ritual abuse of animals in what have been described as 'barbaric medieval practices'. Among the targets of animal rights' campaigners are bullfighting, where horses are often killed in addition to the bulls; the use of live ponies on roundabouts (the 'living carousel'), who are often forced to work for hours on end without a rest or food or water; and stone-pulling competitions by horses and donkeys in the Basque lands, where many die in the attempt to haul huge stones weighing hundreds of kilogrammes. The World Wildlife Fund for Nature has stated that most Spanish zoos should be closed down or radically overhauled because animals are kept in appalling conditions.

POLICE

Spain has a high ratio of police officers to inhabitants and three police forces, often with confusing and overlapping roles. The main forces are the local municipal police (*policía municipal/local* or *guardia urbana*), the national police (*policía nacional*) and the civil guard (*guardia civil*), all of whom are armed (although they rarely use their guns to shoot foreigners). Some autonomous regions have their own police forces, including the Basque Lands (where they wear red *boinas* or berets), Catalonia (the *Mosses d'Esquadra*) and Andalusia, where regional police protect government buildings, politicians and functionaries. Spain also has an elite special operations group (*Grupo Especial de Operaciones*) responsible for combating terrorism and dealing with other extreme situations, in addition to guarding Spanish ambassadors and embassies abroad. Other 'police' forces include the port police (*policía de puerto*) in sea ports, whose jurisdiction is limited to the property of the local *junta del puerto*, and armed guards (*vigilantes jurados*) employed by banks and security companies.

Municipal Police: The municipal police (*policía municipal/local* or *guardia urbana*) are attached to local town halls in towns with a population of over 5,000. They wear blue uniforms with white-chequered bands on their hats and sleeves, and usually patrol in white or blue cars. *Municipales* deal with minor crime such as traffic control, protection of property, civil disturbances and the enforcement of municipal laws. In large cities, municipal police often have multi-lingual offices and some towns have mounted police.

They are the most sympathetic Spanish police force and even under Franco were never regarded as a repressive force. In resort areas the local police often speak English and during the summer spend most of their time dealing with drunken (mostly British) tourists. On the spot fines are imposed for a range of offences. Note that in some towns local police are heavy-handed and can be a law unto themselves and aren't adverse to using illegal methods.

National Police: The national police (*policía nacional* or *cuerpo nacional de policía*) 'replaced' the despised *policía armada* (literally 'armed police'), who were reorganised and renamed in 1978 and given new brown uniforms in an effort to rehabilitate them. The *policía armada* were much hated and feared for their repression and violence under Franco, but the (*policía nacional* are now 'quite popular' (if that could ever be said of policemen in Spain). They are stationed in towns with a population of over 20,000 and deal with serious crime such as theft, rape and muggings, and are also used to control demonstrations and crowds. Other duties include guarding embassies, railway stations, post offices and army barracks in most towns and cities, when they are armed with submachine guns. The *policía nacional* are housed in a police station (*comisaría de policía*), many of which have a 'foreigners' (*extranjeros*) department dealing with matters such as residence cards. There are also plain clothes policeman (*cuerpo superior de policía*) in urban areas.

Civil Guard: The civil guard (*guardia civil*) patrol Spain's highways and rural areas, often on motorcycles (which always operate in pairs), and deal with road accidents. They also act as immigration officers and frontier guards and use helicopters to combat crime. In villages there isn't usually a national police station (*comisaría*) but a *guardia civil* barracks (*cuartel*). The *guardia civil* is a military force and was traditionally headed by a general, although this is no longer the case. Under Franco they were a reactionary force and very unpopular, with a fearsome reputation for aggression. They wear avocado green uniforms and olive-green caps, which have replaced the black, patent-leather, tricorn hats now worn on ceremonial occasions only. They are one of the world's most efficient police forces and have a reputation for honesty and courtesy.

Despite their fearsome (and nowadays undeserved) reputation, Spanish police are generally extremely helpful and will go out of their way to be of assistance. However, corrupt policemen dealing in drugs, prostitution and other organised crime are not uncommon, and a disturbing number of policemen have run amok with their guns. There have been reports of stolen goods disappearing into thin air after having been 'recovered' by the police (they are supposed to be displayed at police departments, e.g. for 18 months, after which they are sold at auction if not claimed). Note that Spanish police are sometimes colour prejudiced, particularly in regard to Africans.

If you need to contact the police in a emergency, you can dial 091 for the *policía nacional* or, in some towns, 062 for the *guardia civil*. You must usually dial a local number for the *policía municipal*, although dialling 092 may get you connected to the local police station or will get your message relayed. The telephone numbers of local police stations are listed at the front of telephone directories. If you lose anything or are the victim of a theft, you must report it in person to the local police and make a complaint (*denuncia*). This must usually be done within 24 hours if you intend to make a claim on an insurance policy. The report form, of which you receive a copy with an official stamp for your insurance company, may be printed in both English and Spanish. Note that if you don't speak Spanish you should have a fluent Spanish speaker with you, although in some tourist areas you can make a *denuncia* in a number of foreign languages.

See also **Car Theft** on page 220, **Crime** on page 401, **Legal System** on page 410 and **Traffic Police** on page 211.

POPULATION

The population of Spain is around 40m and has steadily increased over the last 20 years, unlike some other European countries, notably France and Germany, where it has fallen. Part of the increase is due to the influx of foreign residents from Africa and retirees (from Britain, Germany, Belgium, the Netherlands and Scandinavia). However, during the last three decades the population of half of Spain's provinces has decreased as people have abandoned the countryside for the cities, particularly during the 1960s and 1970s. Now just nine provinces are home to half the population, and Madrid and Barcelona alone account for over 25 per cent of Spain's population. Some 75 per cent of the population is concentrated on the perimeters of Spain (including the Balearic and Canary Islands) and Madrid.

Spain has an average population density of around 80 inhabitants per km2 (200 per square mile), one of the lowest in Europe and just one sixth of the Netherlands' and one third of Britain's. However, it varies enormously from region to region. For example the regions of the Basque Lands and Madrid comprise just over 3 per cent of the land area and are home to some 16 per cent of the population, while the regions of Extremadura, Castile/La Mancha, Castile/Leon, Aragon and Navarre make up half of Spain's land area and have a smaller population than the Basque Lands and Madrid. Some 75 per cent of Spaniards live in towns of over 10,000 inhabitants. In resort areas the population figures don't include the often large number of foreigners who live in Spain all year round, but don't register as residents.

The largest conurbations are Madrid, Barcelona, Bilbao and Valencia and the largest cities Madrid (3.2m), Barcelona (1.75m), Valencia (765,000), Seville (674,000) and Zaragossa (593,000). The most densely populated areas are the provinces of Madrid and Barcelona, both of which have around 600 inhabitants to the km2 (some 1,600 per sq mile). Barcelona is the fourth most densely populated city in the world. The most sparsely populated areas are the provinces of Soria, Teruel and Guadalajara with 10 to 12 inh. per km2 (26 to 31 per sq mile).

RELIGION

Spain is a Christian country with some 96 per cent of the population belonging to the Catholic church and less than 1 per cent Protestant. The majority of the world's religious and philosophical movements have religious centres or meeting places in the major cities and resort areas, including English (e.g. Anglican) and American churches. The right to freedom of religion is guaranteed under the Spanish constitution, although some extreme sects are prohibited.

There have traditionally been close relations between the state and the church, although Catholicism is no longer the state religion and the Catholic church has lost much of its previous influence under Franco. In fact Spain is fast turning its back on its Catholic past and increasingly passing laws contrary to the church's teaching (such as divorce and abortion). Like a number of other countries, Spain is finding it difficult to attract new recruits to the priesthood and has had to resort to importing priests from Latin America (while convents have imported teenage nuns from India). The shortage is reaching crisis proportions, with some 3,000 priests retiring each year and just 250 new ordinations. However, although many Spaniards are ambivalent about religion and church attendances are falling, around 20 per cent of the population attends mass regularly and many Spanish families still spend some 300,000 ptas on a child's first Holy Communion.

Spain has a wealth of historic churches and cathedrals, many in desperate need of restoration including the cathedral of Santiago de Compostela, one of the most important holy places in Christendom (it once rivalled Rome) and a place of pilgrimage since the ninth century. It's necessary to dress appropriately to enter places of worship and if you're wearing shorts (short trousers to Americans, not underwear!), a vest or have bare feet, you won't be admitted. Women may also be refused entry if they're wearing short skirts or 'scanty' tops. Like churches, shrines and sanctuaries are holy places and should be treated with respect.

Foreign church services are listed in English-language publications such as *SUR in English* on the Costa del Sol, and include all major and many minor religions. Notices of Catholic services are posted outside churches and at strategic points in towns (mass is held in foreign languages in some churches).

SOCIAL CUSTOMS

All countries have their own particular social customs and Spain is no exception. As a foreigner you will probably be excused if you accidentally insult your host, but you may not be invited again.

- When you're formally introduced to a Spaniard you should say good day (*buenos días señor/señora/señorita*) or good evening (*buenas tardes*) and shake hands (a single pump is enough). Spanish men shake hands on meeting and again on departing, whether it's a casual meeting in the street or a formal occasion. If you're in doubt as to whether a woman is married or single, wedding rings are worn on the fourth finger of the right hand (not the left), although mature women should always be addressed as *señora*. *Buenas tardes* is used instead of *buenos días* after lunch (which can *start* as late as 1500) until 2100 or 2200. *Buenas noches* (good night) is usually used when going to bed or leaving a house late at night. Goodbye is *adiós* or less formally *hasta luego* (see you later).

  ¡Hola! (hi or hello) is used among close friends and young people, often accompanied by *¿qué tal?* (how are you?) or *¿qué hay?* (what's new?). In more formal language 'how are you?' is *¿cómo está usted?*, to which the reply is usually *muy bien, gracias, ¿y usted?* (fine, thank you, and you?). A common reply when being formally introduced is *encantado* (delighted). Elderly friends are often addressed as *don* (male) and *doña* (female), followed by their Christian name (considerable courtesy and respect are shown to women and the elderly in Spain). When someone thanks you (*gracias*), it's polite to reply *de nada* (literally 'it was nothing' and the equivalent of the American 'you're welcome'). Note that when talking to a stranger it's polite to use the formal form of address (*usted*) and not the familiar form (*tú*) or someone's Christian name until you're invited to do so. However, nowadays the *tú* form is much more widely used and *usted* is reserved mainly for business and when addressing older people.

- Male and female acquaintances kiss each other, usually on both cheeks. If a lady expects you to kiss her she will offer her cheek. The 'kiss' is deposited high up on the cheek, never on the mouth (except between lovers), and isn't usually really a kiss but a delicate brushing of the cheeks. Close family and male friends embrace.

- You should always introduce yourself before asking to speak to someone on the telephone. Although the traditional siesta is facing a battle for survival, it isn't advisable to telephone between the siesta hours (e.g. 1400 to 1700) when many people have a nap. If you call between these times, it's polite to apologise for disturbing the household.

- Family surnames are often confusing to foreigners as the Spanish often have two surnames (possibly linked by 'and', e.g. y or i in Catalan), the first being their father's and the second their mother's. When a women marries she may drop her mother's name and add her husband's, although this isn't usual. Spanish children are usually named after a saint and a person's saint's day (*santo*) is as important a celebration as their birthday (*cumpleaños*), both of which are occasions on which it's traditional to entertain your family and friends.

- If you have an appointment with a Spaniard don't expect him to arrive on time, although being later than 15 minutes is considered bad manners. If you're going to be more than 15 minutes late for an appointment you should telephone and apologise.

- The Spanish always say good appetite (*que aproveche*) before starting a meal. If you're offered a glass of wine, wait until your host has made a toast (*¡salud!*) before taking a drink. If you aren't offered a (another) drink it's time to go home.

- Spanish men and women are almost invariably well groomed and style and fashion are important, although they often dress casually. It's advisable to dress conservatively when doing business or visiting government offices on official business. There are few occasions when formal clothes are necessary and there are very few dress rules in Spain (except in respect to places of worship). Spaniards consider that bathing costumes, skimpy tops and flip-flops or sandals with no socks are strictly for the beach or swimming pool, and not for example, the streets, restaurants or shops (although foreigners and their 'eccentric' behaviour are tolerated).

THE SPANISH ROYAL FAMILY

The King (*el Rey*) of Spain is Juan Carlos I, who's married to Queen (*la Reina*) Sofía of the Greek royal family. They have one son, Prince Felipe, Prince of Asturias and heir to the throne, and two daughters, the Princesses Elena and Cristina. Princess Elena, the Infanta, was married to Jaime de Marichalar amid much pomp and ceremony in Seville cathedral in March 1995, Spain's first royal wedding for 89 years (King Juan Carlos and Queen Sofía were married in Athens in 1962). Princess Cristina was engaged in 1997. However, Prince Felipe's failure to find a suitable mate is causing concern among the Spanish royal family (part of the problem is that he's supposed to marry a princess rather than a commoner, although most Spaniards believe that he should marry whoever he wishes).

The royal family live in the Palacio de la Zarzuela, a few miles to the northwest of Madrid and also have use of the Palacio de Marivent in Palma de Mallorca. The King pays taxes and the Spanish royal family is one of the least expensive to maintain in Europe. The King is the supreme commander of the armed forces and has a considerable personal influence on politics, although his powers are strictly limited by the constitution. His duties include the promulgation of laws and decrees, the calling of elections and referendums, and the appointment of ministers.

In addition to the royal family, the Spanish aristocracy comprises numerous hereditary and non-hereditary title holders, many of whom received their titles from the King. The leading nobility in Spain number some 400 and have the title of *grandee* (*los grandes de España*) in addition to their other titles. There are also some 2,500 nobles (including marquises, counts, viscounts, barons and lords) who don't merit the title of *grandee*, and a large number of 'knights' (*hidalgos*), although the title is no longer used. A title confers no economic or legal privileges on the holder, although they have considerable social cachet in the right circles.

The Spanish monarchy was restored to the throne in 1975 after 44 years, following the deposition of King Alfonso XIII in 1931 and 39 years of dictatorship under General Franco, who named King Juan Carlos I as his 'heir' (in preference to his father and heir to the Spanish throne, Don Juan de Borbón, the Count of Barcelona). On his assumption of the throne, King Juan Carlos was loathed by the left as Franco's puppet and despised by the extreme right due to his father's liberal credentials and Anglophilia. However, the King energetically supported the transition to democracy and his courageous opposition to the attempted army coup in 1981 provoked a wave of popular support for the monarchy that remains largely intact to this day (he's apparently more popular in Spain than the Pope).

TIME DIFFERENCE

Like most of the continent of Europe, most of Spain is on Central European Time (CET), which is Greenwich Mean Time (GMT) plus one hour. The exception is the Canaries, which from October to March are on Western European Time or GMT and from April to September on CET. The Spanish mainland changes to summer time in spring (the end of March) when they put their clocks forward one hour. In autumn (at the end of September) clocks are put back one hour for winter time (i.e. spring forward, fall back). Time changes are announced in local newspapers and on radio and television.

Times in Spain, for example in timetables, are almost always written using the 24-hour clock, when 10am is written as 10h and 10pm as 22h. Midday (*mediodía*) is 1200 and midnight (*medianoche*) is 2400; 7.30am is written as 07.30. Note, however, that *medio día* can also refer to lunchtime, which can be anytime between 1400 and 1600. The 24-hour clock is never referred to in speech, when 7am is *las siete de la mañana* and 7pm is *siete de la tarde*. The international time difference in winter (October to March) between Madrid at noon (1200) and some major international cities is shown below:

MADRID	LONDON	JO'BURG	SYDNEY	AUCKLAND	NEW YORK
1200	1100	1300	2200	2400	0600

TIPPING

Tipping isn't a common practice among the Spanish. Hotel, restaurant and café bills usually include a 15 per cent service charge (plus 7 per cent value added tax/IVA or 16 per cent for 5-fork restaurants), usually shown on the bill as *servicio incluido*. When it isn't indicated most people assume that service is included. However, even when service isn't included the Spanish rarely tip, although they may leave a few small coins. The only exception to this rule is in expensive or fashionable establishments where 'tips' (*propinas*) may be given to secure a table (or guarantee a table in future). Many foreigners follow international practice and tip as they would in other countries.

The 'no tipping' practice usually extends to other businesses and services including taxi drivers, porters, hotel staff, car park attendants, cloakroom staff, shoeshine boys, ushers (cinema, theatre, bullring) and toilet attendants, although you can give a small tip if you wish. Even at Christmas the Spanish rarely give tips, although Spanish employers usually give their employees a hamper or a few bottles of wine. If you're unsure whether you should tip someone ask your Spanish neighbours, friends or colleagues for advice (who will probably all tell you something different!). Large tips are considered ostentatious and in bad taste in Spain (except by the recipient, who will be your friend for life).

TOILETS

Although it has had a poor reputation in the past for its public toilets (*aseos públicos*), Spanish toilets are now among the cleanest in Europe and most are spotlessly clean (although toilet paper is sometimes a luxury). However, you will still find the occasional dirty toilet, possibly without a seat, and there are some Turkish-style squat toilets in use in rural areas. The Spanish have a number of words for the toilet including *servicios* (the most commonly used), *baño* (literally bathroom), *aseos*, *W.C.*, *retretes* and *sanitarios*. To ask where the toilet is you say *¿Dónde están los servicios por favor?* or simply *¿Hay servicios por favor?*. The usual signs are *damas* (ladies) and *caballeros* (gentlemen), although you may also see *señoras* (women) and *señores* (men). Doors may also be marked simply with a 'C' (*caballeros*) and 'S' (*señoras*) or with signs depicting the silhouette of a man or woman.

Public toilets are few and far between in Spain, although there are toilets in bars, cafés, restaurants, hotels, department stores, supermarkets, shopping centres, railway stations, museums and places of interest, on beaches and near markets. Note that bars, hotels, cinemas and department stores must, by law, offer their facilities free of charge to anyone (although it's customary to buy a drink when using the toilet in a bar or café). There are modern coin-operated public toilets with soap, hot water, towels and air-conditioning in some cities and resort areas.

Note that many cafés and restaurants have their toilets located at the rear of the building with access from outside (not from the restaurant) and some public toilets have an automatic, timed light switch, where you're plunged into darkness after around one minute. Toilets at petrol stations are usually locked and you need to ask the attendant for the key. The latest craze in night clubs in Barcelona are designer communal toilets for men and women, which may even have see-through glass doors on the cubicles! Note that toilet paper (*papel higiénico*), which is usually very thin in Spain, isn't provided in many toilets and it's advisable to carry some with you when travelling. One of the reasons is that many Spanish toilets are unable to handle paper, which should be deposited in the basket provided.

19.

THE SPANISH

Who are the Spanish? What are they like? Let's take a candid and totally prejudiced look at the Spanish people, tongue firmly in cheek, and hope they forgive my flippancy or that they don't read this bit (which is why it's hidden away at the back of the book).

The typical Spaniard is courteous, proud, enthusiastic, undisciplined, tardy, temperamental, independent, gregarious, NOISY!, honest, noble, individualistic, boisterous, jealous, possessive, colourful, passionate, spontaneous, sympathetic, fun-loving, creative, sociable, demonstrative, disrespectful, irritating, generous, cheerful, polite, unreliable, honourable, optimistic, impetuous, flamboyant, idiosyncratic, quick-tempered, arrogant, elegant, irresponsible, an *aficionado*, hedonistic, contradictory, an anarchist, informal, self-opinionated, corrupt, indolent, frustrating, vulgar, voluble, helpful, friendly, sensitive, a traditionalist, insolent, humourous, fiery, warm-hearted, chauvinistic, bureaucratic, dignified, kind, loyal, extroverted, tolerant, macho, frugal, self-possessed, unabashed, quarrelsome, partisan, a procrastinator, scandal-loving, articulate, a *bon viveur*, inefficient, conservative, nocturnal, hospitable, spirited, urbanised, lazy, confident, sophisticated, political, handsome, chaotic and a football fanatic.

You may have noticed that the above list contains 'a few' contradictions (as does life in Spain), which is hardly surprising as there's no such thing as a typical Spaniard. Apart from the differences in character between the inhabitants of different regions such as (for example) Andalusia, the Basque Lands, Catalonia, Galicia and Madrid, the population also includes a potpourri of foreigners from all corners of the globe. Even in appearance, fewer and fewer Spaniards match the popular image of short, swarthy and moustached (particularly the women!), and the indigenous population includes blondes, brunettes and redheads. However, while it's true that not *all* Spaniards are stereotypes, I refuse to allow a few eccentrics to spoil my arguments . . . .

Although not nearly as marked or rigidly defined as the British or French class systems, Spain has a complex class structure. The top drawer of Spain's aristocrats are the 400 or so *grandees*, who are followed at a respectable distance by myriad minor nobles, all of whom tend to keep to themselves and remain aloof from the *hoi polloi*. Next in pecking order are the middle class professionals, the lower middle class white-collar workers, the blue-collar working class and the peasant underclass. These are followed by assorted foreigners, a few of whom have been elevated to the status of 'honorary' Spaniards (usually after around 100 years' residence). At the bottom of the heap, below even the despised drunken tourists, are the gypsies (*gitanos*), Spain's true aristocrats. Gypsies are treated as lepers by many Spaniards (except when they are celebrated flamenco artists or bullfighters) and are even less desirable as neighbours than the 'Moros' (Moroccans).

Spaniards are often disparaging about their compatriots from other regions. Nobody understands the Basques and their tongue-twister of a language, the Galicians are derided as being more Portuguese than Spanish, and the Andalusians are scorned as backward peasants by other Spaniards. However, the most marked antagonism is between Madrid and Barcelona, whose inhabitants argue about everything from the economy to sport, history to politics, culture to language. Catalans claim that Madrileños are half African, to which they reply that it's better than being half French. However, although they are proud of their regional identity, the Spanish aren't nationalists or patriotic and have little loyalty to Spain as a whole.

Most Spaniards live in harmony with the foreign population, although many foreigners (colloquially dubbed *guiris*, from the word *ghirigay* meaning gibberish) live separate lives in tourist 'ghettos', a million miles away from the 'real' Spain. The Spanish don't consider the concrete jungles of the Costa del Sol, Costa Blanca, Majorca and the Canaries to be part of Spain, but a plastic paradise created for and by foreigners so that pasty-faced tourists can lie in the sun and drink cheap booze. However, although the Spanish aren't generally xenophobic they are becoming more racist and many would happily eject the gypsies, Arabs and North Africans from their country. They also don't care much for the Portuguese either, who are the butt of their jokes (when not making jokes about the Andalusians). It's an honour for a foreigner to be invited to a Spaniard's home, although it's one rarely granted. Nevertheless, Spaniards do occasionally marry foreigners, much to the distress of their parents.

Usually when Spaniards and foreigners come into contact (conflict) it concerns official business and results in a profusion of confrontations and misunderstandings (few foreigners can fathom the Spanish psyche) and does little to cement relations. Spain has the most stifling (and over-staffed) bureaucracy in western Europe (worse than the French!) and any encounter with officialdom is a test of endurance and patience. Official offices (if you can find the right one) often open for only a few hours on certain days of the week; the person dealing with your case is always absent; you never have the right papers (or your papers and files have disappeared altogether); the rules and regulations have changed (again); and queues are interminable (take along a copy of *War and Peace* to help pass the time). It's all part of a conspiracy to ensure that foreigners cannot find out what's going on (and will hopefully therefore pay more taxes, fines, fees, etc.).

Official inefficiency has been developed to a fine art in Spain, where even paying a bill or using the postal service (a truly world-class example of ineptitude) is an ordeal. The Spanish are generally totally disorganised and the only predictable thing about them is their unpredictability. They seldom plan anything (if they do the plans will be changed or abandoned at the last moment), as one of the unwritten 'rules' of Spanish life is its spontaneity. Spain has been described as part advanced high-tech nation and part banana republic, where nothing and nobody works (ouch!).

Almost as infuriating as the bumbling bureaucracy is the infamous *mañana* syndrome, where everything is possible (*no problema*) tomorrow — which can mean later, much later, sometime, the day after tomorrow, next week, maybe next week, perchance next month, possibly next year or never — but **never, ever** tomorrow (the Spaniards' motto is 'never do today what you can put off until *mañana*'). When a workman says he will come at 11 o'clock, don't forget to ask which day, month and year he has in mind. Workmen don't usually keep appointments and if they do deem to make an appearance they're invariably late (and won't have the right tools or spares anyway). The Spanish are good at starting things but not so good at finishing them (hence the numerous abandoned building sites in Spain).

The Spanish are dismissive of time constraints and have no sense of urgency, treating appointments, dates, opening hours, timetables and deadlines with disdain (it's said that the only thing that begins on time in Spain is a bullfight). If you really need something done by a certain date, *never* tell a Spaniard your real deadline. It's significant, however, that the Spanish have a much lower incidence of stress-related disease than north Europeans, which is somewhat surprising in the noisiest country in Europe and the second loudest in the world (after Japan) — maybe creating a din is the Spanish way of releasing tension?

Over half the inhabitants of Spanish cities endure noise levels well in excess of the World Health Organisation's 'healthy' limit of 65 decibels. Most noise is caused by traffic, lustily supported by pneumatic drills, jack hammers, chain-saws, mopeds, (usually without silencers), car horns, alarms, sirens, radios, televisions, *fiestas*, fireworks, car and home music systems, discos, bars, restaurants, incessantly barking dogs, loud neighbours, screaming children and people singing in the streets. In Spain, a normal conversation is two people shouting at each other from a few feet apart (not surprisingly Spaniards are terrible listeners). Spanish cities are the earthly equivalent of Dante's hell, where inhabitants are subjected to endless noise (surely even Spaniards *must* sometimes yearn for the sound of silence?). Spaniards don't care to waste time sleeping (except in the afternoons) when they can party and cannot see why anyone else should want to.

Spanish men are world champion hedonists and are mainly interested in five things: sex, football, food, alcohol and gambling (not necessarily in that order). The main preoccupation of the Spanish is having a good time and they have a zest for life seldom matched in other countries. They take childish pleasure in making the most of everything and are energetic about having a good time and grasp every opportunity to make merry. The Spanish are inveterate celebrators and when not attending a *fiesta*, family celebration or impromptu party, are to be found in bars and restaurants indulging in another of their favourite pastimes (eating and drinking).

Spaniards have a passion for food, which consists largely of *paella* and *tapas* and is always swimming in garlic and olive oil. Like the French, they eat all the disgusting objectionable bits of animals that civilised people throw away (e.g. pigs' ears and bulls' testicles) and will eat any creatures of the deep, the more exotic and revolting looking the better (e.g. octopus and squid). They are particularly fond of baby food (baby suckling pig, baby lamb, baby octopus), which is preferable to 'grown-up' food as it's easier to fit into the ubiquitous frying pan (when not eaten raw like their ham, all food is fried in Spain). Contrary to popular opinion, the Spanish are a nation of animal lovers and will eat anything that moves. They do, however, have an unsavoury habit (at least most foreigners think so) of 'playing' with their food and can often be seen chasing their steak around a ring before dinner (*¡Olé!*).

When not eating (or playing guitars or flamenco dancing) the Spanish are allegedly having sex — Spanish men have a reputation as great lovers (or have a good publicist), although their virility isn't confirmed by the birth rate which is one of the lowest in the world. In any case most of their conquests are drunken tourists (only too keen to jump into the sack with anything in trousers), so their reputation doesn't bear close scrutiny. However, the carefully nurtured *Don Juan* image was shattered by a recent survey which found that the average Spaniard makes love badly and infrequently (just 71 times a year or 1.4 times a week) compared with the world average of 109 (how do they know these things?). Nevertheless, contraceptives are carried in wallets just in case (when you only 'score' 1.4 times a week, you've got to grab your chances when you can!). Even their macho image has taken a pounding in recent years as women have stormed most male bastions and today are as likely to be found in the university, office, factory, professions or the government, as in the home or the church.

Most Spaniards are anarchists and care little for rules and regulations, and generally do what they want when they want, particularly regarding motoring (especially parking), smoking in public places, the dumping of rubbish and paying taxes. Paradoxically they have taken to democracy like ducks to water and are passionate Europeans, firmly believing in a united Europe and a single currency (so would you if you had the peseta!). However, like most sensible people they care little for their politicians, whose standing has plummeted to new lows in recent years following a succession of corruption scandals.

The Spanish are sensitive to criticism, particularly regarding their history and traditions. Whatever you do, don't ask an old man 'what he did in the civil war' or take sides — you never know which side he fought on (while we're on the subject, don't mention Franco, the Falklands or Gibraltar either). Spaniards are intolerant of other people's views and criticism of Spain is reserved for the Spanish (who do it constantly) and isn't something to be indulged in by ignorant foreigners.

Since throwing off the shackles of dictatorship in 1975, Spain has resolutely turned its back on the past and embraced the future with gusto. Since those heady days it has undergone a transformation influencing every facet of Spanish life. However, although most changes have been for the better, many people believe that the soul of traditional Spain has been lost in the headlong rush towards economic development. The modern Spaniard is more materialistic than his forebears and has taken to the art of making a fast buck as quick as any North American immigrant ever did. Progress has, however, been purchased at a high cost and has led to a sharp increase in crime, drug addiction, alcoholism, poverty, begging, and the devastation of unspoilt areas by developers hell-bent on smothering the country in concrete and golf courses.

How Spain transformed itself in a flood of hedonism and liberalism was the European success story of the 1980s. However, just when the Spanish had 'joined' Europe and thought that the future looked rosy, it was hit by the recession, which shook the country to its core and left many fearful of the future. It precipitated an explosion in unemployment, already the highest in western Europe, and the most serious problem facing Spain as it approaches the new millennium (along with modernising the bloated civil service, slashing the bankrupt welfare system and disposing of the terminally inefficient state-owned businesses that undermine the whole economy). However, a booming economy has lifted the gloom in the last few years and in 1997 Spain had one of the most encouraging outlooks of any EU country.

Despite its manifest problems, the Spanish enjoy one of the best lifestyles (and quality of life) of any European country, or indeed, any country in the world; in Spain work fits around social and family life, not vice versa. The foundation of Spanish society is the family and community, and the Spanish are noted for their close family ties, their love of children and care for the elderly (who are rarely dumped in nursing homes). Spain has infinitely more to offer than its wonderful climate and rugged beauty, and is celebrated for its arts and crafts, architecture, fashion, night-life, music, dance, gastronomy, design, sports facilities, culture, education, health care and technical excellence in many fields.

For sheer vitality and passion for life the Spanish have few equals and whatever Spain can be accused of, it's *never* plain or boring. Few other countries offer such a wealth of intoxicating experiences for the mind, body and spirit (and not all out of a bottle!). Spain is highly addictive and while foreigners may occasionally complain, the vast majority wouldn't dream of leaving and infinitely prefer life in Spain to their home countries. **Put simply, Spain is a great place to live (providing you don't have to do business).**

However, the real glory of Spain lies in the outsize heart and soul of its people, who are among the most convivial, generous and hospitable in the world. If you're willing to learn Spanish (or at least make an effort) and embrace Spain's traditions and way of life, you'll invariably be warmly received by the natives, most of whom will go out of their way to welcome and help you.

¡Vivan los españoles! ¡Viva España!

20.

MOVING HOUSE OR LEAVING SPAIN

W hen moving house or leaving Spain, there are numerous things to be considered and a 'million' people to be informed. The check lists contained in this chapter will make the task easier and may even help prevent an ulcer or nervous breakdown — providing of course you don't leave everything to the last minute.

MOVING HOUSE

When moving house *within* Spain the following items should be considered:

- If you're renting accommodation, you must usually give your landlord one or two months notice (refer to your contract) and have your deposit refunded. Your notice letter should be sent by registered mail (*certificado*).
- Inform the following, as applicable:
  - Your employer.
  - Your present town hall and the town hall in your new municipality.
  - Your local social security and income tax offices.
  - If you have a Spanish driving licence or a Spanish registered car and are remaining in the same province, you should return your licence and car registration document (*permiso de circulación*) and have the address changed (see page 195). If you're moving to a new province you should inform both your current and new provinces.
  - Your electricity, gas, telephone and water companies.
  - Your insurance companies (for example health, car, house contents, private liability, etc.); hire purchase companies; lawyer; accountant; and local businesses where you have accounts. Take out new insurance, if applicable.
  - Your banks and other financial institutions such as stockbrokers and credit card companies. Make arrangements for the transfer of funds and the cancellation or alteration of standing orders (regular payments).
  - Your family doctor, dentist and other health practitioners. Health records should be transferred to your new practitioners.
  - Your children's and your schools. If applicable, arrange for schooling in your new community (see **Chapter 9**). Try to give a term's notice and obtain copies of any relevant school reports and records from current schools.
  - All regular correspondents, subscriptions, social and sports clubs, professional and trade journals, and friends and relatives. Arrange to have your mail redirected.
  - Your local consulate or embassy if you're registered with them (see page 79).
- Return any library books or anything borrowed.
- Arrange removal of your furniture and belongings, or rent transportation if you're doing your own removal.
- **Ask yourself (again): 'Is it really worth all this trouble?'.**

LEAVING SPAIN

Before leaving Spain for an indefinite period the following items should be considered *in addition* to those listed above under **Moving House:**

- **Check that your own and your family's passports are valid!**
- Give notice to your employer, if applicable.
- Check whether any special entry requirements are necessary for your country of destination by contacting the local embassy or consulate in Spain, e.g. visas, permits or inoculations. An exit permit or visa isn't required to leave Spain.
- You may qualify for a rebate on your income tax (see page 295) and social security payments (see page 254).
- If you have contributed to a supplementary pension scheme, a percentage of your contributions may be repaid (see page 260), although the pension company will require proof that you're leaving Spain permanently.
- Arrange to sell anything you aren't taking with you (house, car, furniture, etc.) and to ship your belongings. Find out the procedure for shipping your belongings to your country of destination (see page 96). Check with the local embassy or consulate in Spain of the country to which you're moving. Special forms may need to be completed before arrival. If you've been living in Spain for less than two years, you're required to re-export all personal effects imported duty-free from outside the EU, including furniture and vehicles (if you sell them you may be required to pay duty).
- If you have a Spanish registered car which you intend to take with you, you can drive on your Spanish registration plates for a maximum of three months.
- Pets may require special inoculations or may have to go into quarantine for a period (see page 415), depending on your destination.
- Arrange health, travel and other insurance (see **Chapter 12**).
- Depending on your destination, you may wish to arrange health and dental checkups before leaving Spain. Obtain a copy of your health and dental records.
- Terminate any Spanish loan, lease or hire purchase contracts, and pay all outstanding bills (allow plenty of time as some companies are slow to respond).
- Check whether you're entitled to a rebate on your road tax, car and other insurance. Obtain a letter from your Spanish motor insurance company stating your no-claims bonus.
- Make arrangements to sell or let your house or apartment and other property in Spain.
- Check whether you need an international driving licence or a translation of your Spanish or foreign driving licence for your country of destination.
- Give friends and business associates in Spain an address and telephone number where you can be contacted abroad.
- Buy a copy of *Living and Working in ********* by David Hampshire before leaving Spain. If I haven't written it yet, drop me a line and I'll get started right away!

¡Buen Viaje!

APPENDICES

APPENDIX A: USEFUL ADDRESSES

Embassies

Embassies are located in the capital Madrid and many countries also have consulates in other cities (British provincial consulates are listed on page 438). Embassies and consulates are listed in the Yellow Pages under *Embajadas*. Note that some countries have more than one office in Madrid and before writing or calling in person you should telephone to confirm that you have the correct office.

Algeria: C/General Oráa, 12, 28006 Madrid (tel. (91) 562 9705).

Angola: C/Serrano, 64, 28001 Madrid (tel. (91) 435 6166).

Argentina: Paseo de la Castellana, 53, 28046 Madrid (tel. (91) 442 4500/442 4732).

Australia: Paseo de la Castellana, 143, 28046 Madrid (tel. (91) 579 0428).

Austria: Paseo de la Castellana, 91, 28046 Madrid (tel. (91) 556 5315).

Belgium: Paseo de la Castellana, 18, 28046 Madrid (tel. (91) 577 6300).

Bolivia: C/Valázquez, 20, 28001 Madrid (tel. (91) 578 0835).

Brazil: C/de Fernando el Santo, 6, 28010 Madrid (tel. (91) 308 0459).

Bulgaria: C/Travesia de Santa Maria Magdalena, 15, 28016 Madrid (tel. (91) 345 5761).

Cameroon: C/Rosario Pino, 3, 28020 Madrid (tel. (91) 571 1160).

Canada: C/Núñez de Balboa, 35, 28001 Madrid (tel. (91) 431 4300).

Chile: C/Lagasca, 88, 28001 Madrid (tel. (91) 431 9160).

China: C/Arturo Soria, 113, 28043 Madrid (tel. (91) 519 3680).

Colombia: C/General Martinez Campos, 48, 28010 Madrid (tel. (91) 310 3800/310 3804).

Costa Rica: Paseo de la Castellana, 164, 28046 Madrid (tel. (91) 345 9521/345 9622).

Croatia: C/Velázquez, 44, 28001 Madrid (tel. (91) 577 6881).

Cyprus: C/Serrano, 43-45, 28006 Madrid (tel. (91) 435 9630).

Czech Republic: C/Caidos de la División Azul, 22-A, 28016 Madrid (tel. (91) 350 3604).

Cuba: Paseo de la Habana, 194, 28036 Madrid (tel. (91) 359 2500).

Denmark: C/Claudio Coello, 91, 28006 Madrid (tel. (91) 431 8445).

Dominica: Paseo de la Castellana, 30, 28046 Madrid (tel. (91) 431 5395).

Ecuador: C/Príncipe de Vergara, 73, 28001 Madrid (tel. (91) 562 7215/562 7216).

Egypt: C/Velázquez, 69, 28006 Madrid (tel. (91) 575 8764).

El Salvador: C/Serrano, 114, 28006 Madrid (tel. (91) 562 8002).

Equatorial Guinea: C/Claudio Coello, 91, 28006 Madrid.

Finland: Paseo de la Castellana, 15, 28046 Madrid (tel. (91) 319 6172).

France: C/Salustiano Olózaga, 9, 28001 Madrid (tel. (91) 435 5560).

Gabon: C/Angel Diego Roldán, 14-16, 28016 Madrid (tel. (91) 413 8211).

Germany: C/Fortuny, 8, 28010 Madrid (tel. (91) 319 6310/318 5866).

Greece: Avda. Doctor Arce, 24, 28002 Madrid (tel. (91) 564 5819).

Guatemala: C/Rafael Salgado, 3, 28036 Madrid (tel. (91) 344 0347).

Haiti: C/Marqués del Duero, 3, 28001 Madrid (tel. (91) 575 2624).

Honduras: C/Rosario Pino, 6, 28020 Madrid (tel. (91) 579 3149/579 0251).

Hungary: C/Angel de Diego Roldán, 21, 28016 Madrid (tel. (91) 413 7011).

India: Avda. Pío XII, 30-32, 28016 Madrid (tel. (91) 345 0265).
Indonesia: C/Agastia, 65, 28043 Madrid (tel. (91) 413 0294/413 0394).
Iran: C/Jerez, 5, 28016 Madrid (tel. (91) 345 0112).
Iraq: C/Ronda de Sobradiel, 67, 28043 Madrid (tel. (91) 759 1282).
Ireland: C/Claudio Coello, 73, 28001 Madrid (tel. (91) 576 3509).
Israel: C/Velázquez, 150, 28002 Madrid (tel. (91) 411 1357).
Italy: C/Lagasca, 98, 28006 Madrid (tel. (91) 577 6529).
Ivory Coast: C/Serrano, 154, 28006 Madrid (tel. (91) 562 6916).
Japan: C/Joaquin Costa, 29, 28002 Madrid (tel. (91) 562 5546).
Jordan: C/General Martinez Campos, 41, 28010 Madrid (tel. (91) 319 1100).
Korea: C/Miguel Angel, 23, 28010 Madrid (tel. (91) 310 0053).
Kuwait: Paseo de la Castellana, 141, 28046 Madrid (tel. (91) 572 0162).
Latvia: C/Pedro de Valdivia, 9, 28006 Madrid (tel. (91) 563 1745).
Lebanon: Paseo de la Castellana, 178, 28046 Madrid (tel. (91) 345 1368).
Libya: C/Pisuerga, 12, 28002 Madrid (tel. (91) 563 5753).
Luxembourg: C/Claudio Coello, 78, 28001 Madrid (tel. (91) 435 9164).
Malaysia: Paseo de la Castellana, 91, 28046 Madrid (tel. (91) 555 0684).
Malta: C/Maria de Molina, 39, 28006 Madrid (tel. (91) 411 2006).
Mauritania: C/Velázquez, 90, 28006 Madrid (tel. (91) 575 7007).
Mexico: Carrera de San Jerónimo, 46, 28014 Madrid (tel. (91) 369 2814).
Monaco: C/Villanueva, 12, 28001 Madrid (tel. (91) 578 2048).
Morocco: C/Serrano, 179, 28002 Madrid (tel. (91) 563 1090).
The Netherlands: Avda. del Comandante Franco, 32, 28016 Madrid (tel. (91) 359 0914).
New Zealand: Plza. de la Lealtad, 2, 28014 Madrid (tel. (91) 523 0226).
Nicaragua: Paseo de la Castellana, 127, 28046 Madrid (tel. (91) 555 5510).
Nigeria: C/Segre, 23, 28002 Madrid (tel. (91) 563 0911).
Norway: Paseo de la Castellana, 31, 28046 Madrid (tel. (91) 310 3116).
Pakistan: Avda. Pío XII, 11, 28016 Madrid (tel. (91) 345 8986).
Panama: C/Claudio Coello, 86, 28006 Madrid (tel. (91) 576 5001).
Paraguay: C/Eduardo Dato, 21, 28010 Madrid (tel. (91) 308 2746).
Peru: C/Príncipe de Vergara, 36, 28001 Madrid (tel. (91) 431 4242).
Philippines: C/Claudio Coello, 92, 28006 Madrid (tel. (91) 576 5403).
Poland: C/Guisando, 23 bis, 28035 Madrid (tel. (91) 373 6605).
Portugal: C/Pinar, 1, 28006 Madrid (tel. (91) 561 7800).
Qatar: Paseo de la Castellana, 15, 28046 Madrid (tel. (91) 319 8400).
Romania: Avda. Alfonso XIII, 157, 28016 Madrid (tel. (91) 350 4436).
Russia: C/Velázquez, 155, 28002 Madrid (tel. (91) 411 0807).
Saudi Arabia: Paseo de la Habana, 163, 28036 Madrid (tel. (91) 345 1250).
Slovenia: C/Salustiano Olózaga, 5, 28001 Madrid (tel. (91) 575 6556).
South Africa: C/Claudio Coello, 91, 28006 Madrid (tel. (91) 435 6688).
Sweden: C/Caracas, 25, 28010 Madrid (tel. (91) 308 1535).
Switzerland: C/Núñez de Balboa, 35, 28001 Madrid (tel. (91) 431 3400).
Syria: Pza. Platerías Martinez, 1, 28014 Madrid (tel. (91) 420 1602).

Thailand: C/Segre, 29, 28002 Madrid (tel. (91) 563 2903).

Tunisia: Pza. de Alonso Martinez, 3, 28004 Madrid (tel. (91) 447 3508).

Turkey: C/Rafael Calvo, 18, 28010 Madrid (tel. (91) 319 8064).

United Arab Emirates: C/Capitán Haya, 40, 28020 Madrid (tel. (91) 570 1001).

United Kingdom: C/de Fernando el Santo, 16, 28010 Madrid (tel. (91) 319 0208/319 0200).

United States of America: C/Serrano, 75, 28006 Madrid (tel. (91) 577 4000).

Uruguay: Paseo Pintor Rosales, 32, 28008 Madrid (tel. (91) 542 8038).

Venezuela: C/Capitán Haya, 1, 28020 Madrid (tel. (91) 555 8452).

Yugoslavia: C/Velázquez, 162, 28002 Madrid (tel. (91) 563 5045).

Zaire: C/Doctor Arca, 7, 28002 Madrid.

British Provincial Consulates in Spain

Alicante: British Consulate, Plaza Calvo Sotelo, 1/2, 03001 Alicante (tel. (96) 521 6022/521 6190).

Barcelona: British Consulate-General, Edificio Torre de Barcelona, Avda. Diagonal, 477-13, 08036 Barcelona (tel. (93) 419 9044).

Benidorm: Honorary British Vice-Consulate, Edificio Paris, 1E, C/Ruzafa, 03500 Benidorm (tel. (96) 585 0123).

Bilbao: British Consulate-General, Alamada de Urquijo, 2-8, 48008 Bilbao (tel. (94) 415 7600).

Ibiza: British Vice-Consulate, Avenida de Isidoro Macabich, 45, 07800 Ibiza (tel. (971) 301 818/303 816).

Madrid: British Consulate-General, Centro Colón, Marqués de la Ensenada, 16, 28004 Madrid (tel. (91) 308 5201).

Malaga: British Consulate, Edificio Duquesa, C/Duquesa de Parcent, 8-1, 29001 Malaga (tel. (95) 221 7571).

Palma de Mallorca: British Consulate, Plaza Mayor, 3D, 07002 Palma de Mallorca (tel. (971) 712445).

Menorca: Honorary British Vice-Consulate, Sa Casa Nova, Cami de Biniatap, 30, Es Castell, 07720 Menorca (tel. (971) 363373).

Las Palmas: British Consulate, Edificio Cataluña, Luis Morote, 6-3, 35007 Las Palmas (tel. (928) 262 5080).

Santa Cruz de Tenerife: British Consulate, Plaza Weyler, 8-1, 38003 Santa Cruz de Tenerife (tel. (922) 286863).

Santander: Honorary British Consulate, Paseo de Pereda, 27, 39004 Santander (tel. (942) 220000).

Seville: British Consulate, Plaza Nueva, 8B, 41001 Seville (tel. (95) 422 8875).

Tarragona: Honorary British Consulate, C/Real, 33, 1-1, 43004 Tarragona (tel. (977) 220812).

Vigo: British Consulate, Plaza Compostela, 23-6, 36201 Vigo (tel. (986) 437133).

English-Language Newspapers & Magazines

Costa Blanca News, Apartado, 95, 03500 Benidorm (Alicante), Spain.

Costa del Sol News, Apartado, 95, 03500 Benidorm (Alicante), Spain. Fortnightly newspaper.

Costa Española International, ATCF Publicaciones SL, C/Ronda Sur, 6 bis, 03730 Jávea (Alicante), Spain.

The Entertainer, The Entertainer, Plaza de la Constitucion, 15, Atico, 29640 Fuengirola (Malaga), Spain. Free weekly newspaper.

For Sale/Se Vende, Avda. Miguel Cano, 10, 29600 Marbella, Spain. Property magazine.

Iberian Daily Sun, San Felia, 25, Palma, Majorca, Spain.

In Spain Magazine, Doctor Esquerdo, 35, 1F, 28028 Madrid, Spain. Monthly lifestyle magazine.

The Island Gazette, C/Iriarte, 43, 2°, Puerto de la Santa Cruz, Tenerife, Canary Islands, Spain.

Lookout, Lookout Publications SA, Urb. Molino de Viento, C/Rio Darro, Portal 1, 29650 Mijas Costa (Malaga), Spain. Monthly lifestyle magazine.

The Mallorca Daily Bulletin, San Feliu, 25, Palma de Mallorca, Mallorca, Balearics, Spain.

The Marbella Times, Alonso de Ojeda, 2, 1°, Km 188 Crta de Cadiz, 29660 Marbella (Malaga), Spain.

Private Villas, 52 High Street, Henley-in-Arden, Solihull, West Midlands B95 5BR, UK. Monthly magazine advertising properties to let in Spain and other countries.

The Reporter, C/Los Naranjos, 5, Pueblo Lopez, 29640 Fuengirola (Malaga), Spain. Free monthly news magazine.

Spanish Property News, 2 Paragon Place, Blackheath, London SE3 0SP, UK. Monthly property magazine.

Sur in English, Diario Sur, Avda. Doctor Marañón, 48, 29009 Malaga, Spain. Weekly free newspaper.

Villas & . . . España, SKR Española SL, Apartado 453, 29670 San Pedro Alcántara (Malaga), Spain. Monthly property magazine.

World of Property, Overseas Property Match, 532 Kingston Road, Raynes Park, London SW20 8DT, UK. Quarterly property magazine.

APPENDIX B: FURTHER READING

The publications listed in this appendix are only a selection of the hundreds of books written about Spain. For example, in addition to the general tourist guides listed below, there are also numerous guides covering individual cities and regions of Spain. The publication title is followed by the author's name and the publisher's name (in brackets). Note that some titles may be out of print but may still be obtainable from bookshops, libraries or secondhand bookshops. Books prefixed with an asterisk (*) are recommended by the author.

General Tourist Guides

AA Essential Explorer Spain (AA)
Andalucía Handbook, Rowland Mead (Footprint)
Andalusia, Michael Jacobs (Viking)
*Baedeker's Spain (Baedeker)
Berlitz Blueprint: Spain (Berlitz)
Berlitz Discover Spain, Ken Bernstein & Paul Murphy (Berlitz)
*Blue Guide to Spain: The Mainland, Ian Robertson (Ernest Benn)
Cadogan Guides: Spain, Dana Facaros & Michael Pauls (Cadogan)
Collins Independent Travellers Guide Spain, Harry Debelius (Collins)
Excursions in Eastern Spain, Nick Inman & Clara Villanueva (Santana)
Excursions in Southern Spain, David Baird (Santana)
*Fodor's Spain (Fodor's)
*Frommer's Spain and Morocco on $40 a Day (Simon & Schuster)
Guide to the Best of Spain (Turespaña)
*Inside Andalusia, David Baird (Santana)
The Insider's Guide to Spain, John de St. Jorre (Moorland)
*Insight Guides: Spain (APA Publications)
Lazy Days Out in Andalucía, Jeremy Wayne (Cadogan)
*Let's Go Spain & Portugal (Macmillan)
*Madrid, Michael Jacobs (George Philip)
Madrid: A Traveller's Companion, Hugh Thomas (Constable)
*Michelin Green Guide Spain (Michelin)
*Michelin Red Guide to Spain and Portugal (Michelin)
Off the Beaten Track: Spain, Barbara Mandell & Roger Penn (Moorland)
*Paupers' Barcelona, Miles Turner (Pan)
*Rough Guide to Andalucía, Mark Ellingham & John Fisher (Rough Guides)
The Shell Guide to Spain, David Mitchell (Simon & Schuster)
Spain: A Phaidon Cultural Guide (Phaidon)
Spain at its Best, Robert Kane (Passport)
Spain: Everything Under the Sun, Tom Burns (Harrap Columbus)
Spain on Backroads (Duncan Petersen)
*Spain: The Rough Guide, Mark Ellingham & John Fisher (Rough Guides)

Special Places to Stay in Spain, Alistair Sawday (ASP)
Time Off in Spain and Portugal, Teresa Tinsley (Horizon)
Time Out Madrid Guide (Penguin)
Travellers in Spain: An Illustrated Anthology, David Mitchell (Cassell)
Welcome to Spain, RAN Dixon (Collins)
*Which? Guide to Spain (Consumers' Association and Hodder & Stoughton)

Travel Literature

*As I Walked Out One Midsummer Morning, Laurie Lee (Penguin)
*Between Hopes and Memories: A Spanish Journey, Michael Jacobs (Picador)
*The Bible in Spain, George Borrow (Century Travellers Series)
*Cider With Rosie, Laurie Lee (Penguin)
Gatherings in Spain, Richard Ford (Dent Everyman)
*Handbook for Travellers in Spain, Richard Ford (Centaur Press)
Iberia, James A. Michener (Fawcett)
*Jogging Round Majorca, Gordon West (Black Swan)
*In Spain, Ted Walker (Corgi)
*A Rose for Winter, Laurie Lee (Penguin)
*Spanish Journeys: A Portrait of Spain, Adam Hopkins (Penguin)
*South from Granada, Gerald Brenan (Penguin)
*A Stranger in Spain, H.V. Morton (Methuen)
Two Middle-Aged Ladies in Adalusia, Penelope Chetwode (Murray)
*A Winter in Majorca, George Sands

Living & Working in Spain

*The Bottlebrush Tree, Hugh Seymour-Davies (Black Swan)
**Buying a Home in Spain, David Hampshire (Survival Books)
Choose Spain, John Howells & Bettie Magee (Gateway)
Introducing Spain, B.A. McCullagh & S. Wood (Harrap)
Life in a Spanish Town, M. Newton (Harrap)
*Madrid Inside Out, Artur Howard & Victoria Montero (Frank)
Simple Etiquette in Spain, Victoria Miranda McGuiness (Simple Books)
Spain: Business & Finance (Euromoney Books)
Spanish Property Owners Community Handbook, David Searle (Lookout)
*You and the Law in Spain, David Searle (Santana)

Food & Wine

*AA Essential Food and Drink Spain (AA)
*The Best of Spanish Cooking, Janet Mendel (Santana)
The Complete Spanish Cookbook, Jacki Passmore (Little Brown)
*Cooking in Spain, Janet Mendel (Santana)
Delicioso: The Regional Cooking of Spain, Penelope Casas (Knoff)

*Floyd on Spain, Keith Floyd (Penguin)
The Food and Wine of Spain, Penelope Casas
404 Spanish Wines, Frank Snell (Lookout)
*The 'La Ina' Book of Tapas, Elisabeth Luard (Schuster)
*Spanish Cooking, Pepita Aris (Apple Press)
*The Spanish Kitchen, Nicholas Butcher (Macmillan)
The Spanish Table, Marimar Torres (Ebury Press)
*Spanish Wines, Jan Read (Mitchell Beazley)
The Spanishwoman's Kitchen, Pepita Aris (Cassell)
Tapas, Silvano Franco (Lorenz)
*The Wine and Food of Spain, Jan Read & Maite Manjón (Wedenfeld & Nicolson)
The Wine Roads of Spain, M&K Millon (Santana)

History

The Assassination of Federico García Lorca, Ian Gibson (Penguin)
*Blood of Spain, Ronald Fraser (Pimlico)
Casa, Elizabeth Hilliard (Pavillion)
Concise History of Spain, Melveena McKendrick (Cassell, 1972)
*The Face of Spain, Gerald Brenan (Penguin)
*Federico García Lorca: A Life, Ian Gibson (Faber & Faber)
*Franco: A Biography, Paul Preston (Harper-Collins)
A History of Spain & Portugal, William Atkinson (Penguin)
*Homage to Catalonia, George Orwell (Penguin)
Memories of the Spanish Civil War, Colin Williams (Alan Sutton)
*Moorish Spain, Richard Fletcher (Phoenix)
*A Moment of War, Laurie Lee (Viking)
*Red Sky at Sunrise, Laurie Lee (Penguin)
Spain: A Brief History, Pierre Vilar
*Spain, 1808-1975, Raymond Carr (OUP)
*The Spanish Civil War, Hugh Thomas (Penguin)
*The Spanish Labyrinth, Gerald Brenan (CUP)
*The Spanish Tragedy, Raymond Carr (Weidenfeld)
The Story of Spain, Mark Williams (Lookout)
*Tales of the Alhambra, Washington Irving (Sanchez)
Travellers in Spain, David Mitchell (Lookout)
A Traveller's History of Spain, Juan Lalaguna (Windrush)

Modern Spain

*Barcelona, Robert Hughes (Harvill)
*Fire in the Blood, Ian Gibson (Faber)
The Making of Spanish Democracy, Donald Share (Prueger)
*Modern Spain, Raymond Carr (Opus)

The Modern Spanish Economy, Keith Salmon (Pinter)
*The New Spaniards, John Hooper (Penguin)
*Spain, Jan Morris (Faber & Faber)
*Spain: A Portrait After the General, Robert Elms (Mandarin)
Spain Beyond Myths, Carlos Alonso Zaldívar and Manual Castells
Spain: The Change of a Nation, Robert Graham (Michael Joseph)
Spain: Dictatorship to Democracy, Raymond Carr & Juan Pablo Fusi (Allen)
*The Spanish Temper, VS Pritchett (Hogarth)
The Transformation of Spain: From Franco to the Constitutional Monarchy, David Gilmour (Quartet)
*The Triumph of Democracy in Spain, Paul Preston (Routledge)

Miscellaneous

The Art of Flamenco, DE Pohren (Musical News Services Ltd.)
*Blood Sport: A History of Spanish Bullfighting, Timothy Mitchell
Cities of Spain, David Gilmour (Pimlico)
Dali: A Biography, Meredith Etheringon-Smith (Sinclair-Stevenson)
*A Day in the Life of Spain (Collins)
*Death in the Afternoon, Ernest Hemingway (Grafton)
Gardening in Spain, Marcelle Pitt (Santanar)
The Gardens of Spain, Consuela M Correcher (Abrams)
*In Search of the Firedance, James Woodall (Sinclair-Stevenson)
The King, Jose Luis de Vilallonga (Weidenfeld)
*Nord Riley's Spain, Nord Riley (Lookout)
*On Foot Through Europe: A Trail Guide to Spain and Portugal, Craig Evans (Quill)
*Or I'll Dress You in Mourning, Larry Collins & Dominique Lapierre (Simon & Schuster)
La Pasionaria, Robert Low (Hutchinson)
Spain: A Literary Companion, Jimmy Burns (John Murray)
Spain's Wildlife, Eric Robins (Santana)
Trekking in Spain, Marc S. Dubin (Lonely Planet)
*Walking Through Spain, Robin Nellands
*Wild Spain, Frederic Grunfeld & Teresa Farino (Ebury)
*Xenophobe's Guide to the Spanish (Ravette)

APPENDIX C: WEIGHTS & MEASURES

Although most countries officially use the metric system of weights and measures, if you're from Britain or the USA (and a few other places) you may be more familiar with the imperial system, in which case the tables on the following pages will be of help. Comparisons shown aren't exact but are close enough for most everyday calculations.

Clothes sizes, apart from the different measurement systems used, can vary wildly depending on the manufacturer (as we all know only too well!). Try all clothes on before buying. Don't be afraid to return something if, when you try it on at home, you decide it doesn't fit or it's a different colour to what you imagined. Spanish shops will exchange most goods or give a refund, unless they were purchased at a reduction during a sale.

Women's clothes:

Continental	34	36	38	40	42	44	46	48	50	52
GB	8	10	12	14	16	18	20	22	24	26
USA	6	8	10	12	14	16	18	20	22	24

Pullovers: | **Women's** | | | | | | **Mens** | | | | | |

Continental	40	42	44	46	48	50	44	46	48	50	52	54
GB	34	36	38	40	42	44	34	36	38	40	42	44
USA	34	36	38	40	42	44	sm	medium	large	exl		

Note: sm = small, exl = extra large

Men's Shirts

Continental	36	37	38	39	40	41	42	43	44	46
GB/USA	14	14	15	15	16	16	17	17	18	

Men's Underwear

Continental	5	6	7	8	9	10
GB	34	36	38	40	42	44
USA	small	medium	large	extra large		

Children's Clothes

Continental	92	104	116	128	140	152
GB	16/18	20/22	24/26	28/30	32/34	36/38
USA	2	4	6	8	10	12

Children's Shoes

Continental	18	19	20	21	22	23	24	25	26	27	28
GB/USA	2	3	4	4	5	6	7	7	8	9	10

Continental	29	30	31	32	33	34	35	36	37	38
GB/USA	11	11	12	13	1	2	2	3	4	5

Shoes (Women's and Men's)

Continental	35	35	36	37	37	38	39	39	40	40
GB	2	3	3	4	4	5	5	6	6	7
USA	4	4	5	5	6	6	7	7	8	8

Continental	41	42	42	43	44	44
GB	7	8	8	9	9	10
USA	9	9	10	10	11	11

Weights:

Avoirdupois	Metric	Metric	Avoirdupois
1 oz	28.35g	1g	0.035oz
1 pound*	454g	100g	3.5oz
1 cwt	50.8kg	250g	9oz
1 ton	1,016kg	1kg	2.2 pounds
1 tonne	2,205 pounds		

* A metric 'pound' is 500g.
Note: g = gramme, kg = kilogramme

Length:

British/US	Metric	Metric	British/US
1 inch =	2.54 cm	1 cm =	0.39 inch
1 foot =	30.48 cm	1 m =	3.28 feet
1 yard =	91.44 cm	1 km =	0.62 mile
1 mile =	1.6 km	8 km =	5 miles

Note: cm = centimetre, m = metre, km = kilometre

Capacity:

Imperial	Metric	Metric	Imperial
1 pint (USA)	0.47l	1l	1.76 GB pints
1 pint (GB)	0.568l	1l	0.265 US gallons
1 gallon (USA)	3.78l	1l	0.22 GB gallons
1 gallon (GB)	4.54l	1l	35.21l fluid oz

Note: l = litre

Square Measure:

British/US	Metric	Metric	British/US
1 square inch .	6.45 sq. cm	1 sq. cm	0.155 sq. inches
1 square foot	0.092 sq. m.	1 sq. m.	10.764 sq. feet
1 square yard	0.836 sq. m.	1 sq. m.	1.196 sq. yards
1 acre	0.405 hect.	1 hectare	2.471 acres
1 square mile	259 hect.	1 sq. km.	0.386 sq. mile

Temperature:

Celsius	Fahrenheit	
0	32	freezing point of water
5	41	
10	50	
15	59	
20	68	
25	77	
30	86	
35	95	
40	104	

The Boiling point of water is 100 degrees Celsius, 212 degrees Fahrenheit.

Oven temperature:

Gas	Electric	
	F	**C**
-	225-250	110-120
1	275	140
2	300	150
3	325	160
4	350	180
5	375	190
6	400	200
7	425	220
8	450	230
9	475	240

For a quick conversion, the Celsius temperature is approximately half the Fahrenheit temperature (in the range shown above).

Temperature Conversion:

Celsius to Fahrenheit: multiply by 9, divide by 5 and add 32.
Fahrenheit to Celsius: subtract 32, multiply by 5 and divide by 9.

Body Temperature:

Normal body temperature (if you're alive and well) is 98.4 degrees Fahrenheit, which equals 37 degrees Celsius.

APPENDIX D: REGIONS & PROVINCES

The map opposite shows the 17 autonomous regions and 49 provinces of Spain (listed below).

1.	La Coruña	26.	Barcelona
2.	Lugo	27.	Tarragona
3.	Pontevedra	28.	Cáceres
4.	Orense	29.	Badajoz
5.	Asturias	30.	Guadalajara
6.	León	31.	Toledo
7.	Palencia	32.	Cuenca
8.	Burgos	33.	Ciudad Real
9.	Zamora	34.	Albacete
10.	Valladolid	35.	Madrid
11.	Soria	36.	Castellón
12.	Salamanca	37.	Valencia
13.	Avila	38.	Alicante
14.	Segovia	39.	Huelva
15.	Cantabria	40.	Seville
16.	La Rioja	41.	Córdoba
17.	Vizcaya	42.	Jaén
18.	Guipúzcoa	43.	Cadiz
19.	Alava	44.	Malaga
20.	Navarra	45.	Granada
21.	Huesca	46.	Almeria
22.	Zaragossa	47.	Murcia
23.	Teruel	48.	Baleares
24.	Lérida (Lleida)	49.	Canarias
25.	Gerona (Girona)		

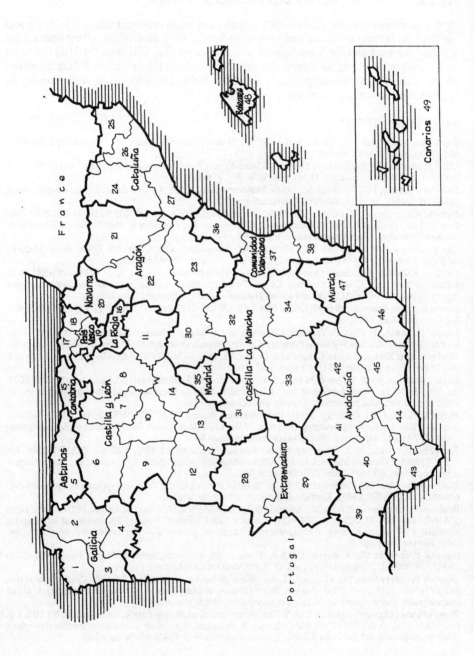

APPENDIX E: SERVICE DIRECTORY

This **Service Directory** is to help you find local businesses and services in Spain and the UK, serving residents and visitors to Spain. Note that when calling Spain from abroad, you must dial the international access number (e.g. 010 from the UK) followed by 34 (the country code for Spain), the area code without the preceding 9 (e.g. 5 and *not* 95 for Malaga), and the subscriber's number. Please mention *Living and Working in Spain* when contacting companies.

AGENTS (PROPERTY)

Bonin Sanso (Mahón) S.L., Carren Nou 14, 07701 Mahón (Menorca), Spain (tel. (971) 363462, fax (971) 363458). Contact: Colin Guanaria.

D.S.I. Properties (Nerja) Limited, Deerhurst House, Epping Road, Roydon, Harlow, Essex CM19 5DA, UK (tel/fax 01279-792162). Contact: David Scott B.Sc. FFOPDAC.

European Estates, Edificio Barambio, Avda. Mancomunidad, 35500 Arrecife de Lanzarote, Canary Islands (tel. (928) 804342, fax (928) 804341). Contact: Norma Lindes.

Eurosur, C/Los Hertos, 78, PO Box 164, 29780 Nerja (Málaga), Spain (tel. (95) 252-5051, fax (95) 252-1244). Contact: Ivan Jullit Navas. Nerja's estate agents. The best service, professional, multilingual staff and a wide variety of properties. **See advertisement on page 88.**

The Fielding Partnership, Urb. La Carolina, Edif. Commercial, Ctra Cádiz, km 178.5, 29600 Marbella (Málaga), Spain (tel. (95) 282 7754, fax (95) 282 9754). Contact: Cheryl Fielding.

Geoffrey Knight & Associates, Centro El Capricho, 29600 Marbella (Málaga), Spain (tel/fax (95) 283 2822, e-mail: rjjg@vnet.es). Contact: Geoffrey Knight (Director). Member of the National Association of Estate Agents (Overseas), FOPDAC, RIM and Abbey National (mortgage approved introducer).

Homes in Spain, Freepost BS 6095, Bristol BS8 3YY, UK (tel. 0117-955 3351, fax 0117-955 3595). Contact: Bill Cleaver or John Reynolds.

Images of Andalucía (Spain), Tara, Ctr. Colmenar, 29170 Solano (Málaga), Spain (tel/fax (95) 211 1178). Contact: Diana or Malcolm Williams (Partners). Country property estate agents. Member of ANAEA Overseas.

Marbella Real Estates, Centro Commercial Tembo, A3, Ctra. N-340, 29600 Marbella (Málaga), Spain (tel. (95) 286 6355, fax (95) 286 6651). Contact: Paul Goodman.

Mijas Properties, Avda. Virgen de la Peña, 8, Mijas Pueblo, 29650 Mijas (Málaga), Spain (tel. (95) 248-5025, fax (95) 259-0413). Contact: Susanne Terés (Co-Owner). Sales and Rentals. Established in Mijas 14 years - villas, apartments, land, businesses. Friendly professional service.

Philip Lockwood, 71 Coventry Street, Kidderminster, Worcs. DY10 2BS, UK (tel/fax 01562-745082). Contact: Philip Lockwood (Managing Director). Villas and village houses from the heart of England agents with over 20 years' experience. **See advertisement on page 86.**

Propertunities Ltd., 13-17 Newbury Street, Wantage, Oxon OX12 8BU, UK (tel. 01235-772345, fax 01235-770018). Contact: Maureen Knight (Office Manager). Main agents for Grupo Masa, Spain's largest developer. Costa Blanca/Calida. £20,000 to £65,000.

The Property Mart SL, Commercial II, Local III, Urb. La Siesta, 03180 Torrevieja (Alicante), Spain (tel. (96) 670 8983, fax (96) 670 8343). Contact: Reg Austin or Janiccée Wretman.

Realtors Sevicios Inmobiliarios SL, Apartado 508, 04638 Mojacar (Almeria), Spain (tel. (95) 047 8763/ (96) 574 8695, fax (95) 047 8529/ (96) 574 8695). Contact: Luis Gonzalez. Property developers and estate agents established 17 years offering a comprehensive range of commercial and residential property. **See advertisement on page 87.**

Sunway Properties SL, 1, Parque Cattleya, Playa de las Americas, Tenerife, Canary Islands (tel. (922) 790021/791900, (922) fax 795172). Contact: Barry MacDonald (Director).

Tenerife Property Shop SL, 117 Puerto Colon, Playa de las Americas, Adeje, Tenerife, Canary Islands (tel. (922) 794700, fax (922) 794720). Contact: Bruce Grindley or Mary Spencer. Specialists in property, land and business sales. Largest portfolio. Clear and unencumbered title is guaranteed.

Wessex Homes (Europe) Limited, Unit Y, The Enterprise Centre, Station Parade, Eastbourne BN21 1BE, UK (tel. 01323-733320, fax 01323-733390). Contact: R. Saunders. Specialists in country properties throughout Almeria, Andalucía and the Costa Blanca. Coastal properties from £19,500 fully furnished.

BUILDING SERVICES

Hartig SL, The Air Conditioning Centre, Ctra. Cádiz, km 178.2, 29600 Marbella (Málaga), Spain (tel. (95) 282 9900, fax (95) 286 2462). Contact: Helga Hartig (Manager). Cooling, heating and ventilation experts.

BUSINESS SERVICES

Sunway Properties SL, 1, Parque Cattleya, Playa de las Americas, Tenerife, Canary Islands (tel. (922) 790021/791900, (922) fax 795172). Contact: Barry MacDonald (Director).

FINANCIAL SERVICES

Blackstone Franks International Ltd., Barbican House, 26-34 Old Street, London EC1V 9HL, UK (tel. 0171-250 3300, fax. 0171-250 1793). Contact: Bill Blevins (Managing Director). Independent financial advisors who specialise in advising retired expatriates living in France, Spain and Portugal.

FISCAL REPRESENTATION

The Property Mart SL, Commercial II, Local III, Urb. La Siesta, 03180 Torrevieja (Alicante), Spain (tel. (96) 670 8983, fax (96) 670 8343). Contact: Reg Austin or Janiccée Wretman.

INVESTMENTS

Allied International, C/C El Capanario, 11, Sitio de Calahonda, 29647 Mijas Costa (Málaga), Spain (tel. (95) 283 3070, fax (95) 283 2736). Contact: Kevin White (Director). Independent offshore investment advisors. Specialist advice for the working and retired expatriate.

Blackstone Franks International Ltd., Barbican House, 26-34 Old Street, London EC1V 9HL, UK (tel. 0171-250 3300, fax. 0171-250 1793). Contact: Bill Blevins (Managing Director). Independent financial advisors who specialise in advising retired expatriates living in France, Spain and Portugal.

LANGUAGE SCHOOLS

El Centro Inglés, Apdo. de Correos, 85, 11500 El Puerto de Santa Maria (Cádiz), Spain (tel. (956) 850560, fax (956) 873804). Contact: Linda M. Randall (Principal/Owner). Bilingual preschool, primary, secondary, further education, Spanish in Spain for foreigners, summer school/camp/courses.

LEGAL SERVICES

Bennett & Co., Solicitors, 39 London Road, Alderley Edge, Cheshire SK9 7JT, UK (tel. 01625-586937, fax 01625-585362) and 19/20 Grosvenor Street, London W1X 9FD, UK (tel. 0171-493 3175, fax 0171-493 3384). Contact: Trevor T. Bennett. Specialising in Spanish legal matters, e.g. property transfers, inheritance, litigation for 15 years.

Cornish & Co, Urb. La Carolina, Edif. Comercial, Ctra. Cádiz, km 178.5, 29600 Marbella (Málaga), Spain (tel. (95) 286 6830, fax (95) 286 5320) and Lex House, 1-7 Hainault Street, Ilford, Essex IG1 4EL, UK (tel. 0181-478 3300, fax 0181-553 3418). Also an office in Gibraltar.

Fernando Scornik Gerstein, 32 St. James's Street, London SW1A 1HD, UK (tel. 0171-839 1581, fax 0171-930 3385). Contact: Alberto Perez Cedillo (Director of Office). Spanish law firm with offices in Madrid, the Canary Islands and 19 other cities. Practice includes real estate, conveyancing, probate, family law and litigation.

Gestoría Bocanegra, Avda Ricardo Soriano, 65, 2nd Floor, 29600 Marbella (Malaga), Spain (tel. (95) 277 0706, fax (95) 282 9932). Contact: Ricardo Bocanegra (Titular). Taxes, residence permits, business licences, social security, cars, and legal advice in general.

García Garrido & Dowen, Avda. Lepanto, 7, 03730 Javea (Alicante), Spain (tel. (96) 646 0859, fax (96) 646 0857). Contact: Susan Dowen (English Solicitor).

John Howell & Co., 17 Maiden Lane, Covent Garden, London WC2E 7NA, UK (tel. 0171-420 0400, fax 0171-836 3626, e-mail: info@lawspain.com). Contact: John Howell. Fully insured, specialist English solicitors with 12 years experience and 19 associate offices in Spain. **See advertisement on page 411.**

MOBILE HOMES

Meadowhead Parks, Meadowhead Ltd., Charterhall, Duns, Berwickshire TD11 3RE, UK (tel. 01890-840301, fax 01890-840651, e-mail: meadowhed@aol.com). Contact: Betty Gray (Marketing Director). Let your Spanish property and spend summer in a beautiful home in Scotland/Northumberland.

MORTGAGES

Conti Financial Services, 204 Church Road, Hove, Sussex BN3 2DJ, UK (tel. 01273-772811, fax 01273-321269, e-mail: 106033.3156@compuserve.com). Contact: Simon Conn (proprietor). Simon has specialised in arranging finance overseas for over 17 year in many countries.

PROFESSIONAL SERVICES

Blackstone Franks International Ltd., Barbican House, 26-34 Old Street, London EC1V 9HL, UK (tel. 0171-250 3300, fax. 0171-250 1793). Contact: Bill Blevins (Managing Director). Independent financial advisors who specialise in advising retired expatriates living in France, Spain and Portugal.

The Property Mart SL, Commercial II, Local III, Urb. La Siesta, 03180 Torrevieja (Alicante), Spain (tel. (96) 670 8983, fax (96) 670 8343). Contact: Reg Austin or Janiccée Wretman.

PROPERTY SERVICES

Barwell Leisure, Barwell Leisure Group, The Coach House, Elm Road, Chessington, Surrey KT9 1AW, UK (tel. 0181-397 4411, fax 0181-974 1442). La Manga Club Resort: Outstanding sporting facilities, P&O's prestigious Peninsular Club, average annual temperature of 67°F. **See advertisement on page 86.**

Key Property Services SL, Property Consultants, Local 7, Zona 4, Urb, San Luis, 03180 Torrevieja (Alicante), Spain (tel/fax (96) 571 3403). Contact: Marion Atkins NAEA (Director). Specialists in new and resale homes, plus fincas in Almeria. Assistance with purchase, bank accounts, wills and residencias.

Sunway Properties SL, 1, Parque Cattleya, Playa de las Americas, Tenerife, Canary Islands (tel. (922) 790021/791900, (922) fax 795172). Contact: Barry MacDonald (Director).

SCHOOLS/EDUCATION

American International School, C/Oratorio, 4, 07015 Portals Nous (Mallorca), Spain (tel. (971) 675850/675851, fax (971) 676820). Contact: James Berry (Director).

El Centro Inglés, Apdo. de Correos, 85, 11500 El Puerto de Santa Maria (Cádiz), Spain (tel. (956) 850560, fax (956) 873804). Contact: Linda M. Randall (Principal/Owner). Bilingual preschool, primary, secondary, further education, Spanish in Spain for foreigners, summer school/camp/courses.

Xabia International College, Ctra. Cabo la Nao, 21, Apartado de Correos 311, 03730 Jávea (Alicante), Spain (tel/fax (96) 647 1785). Contact: John Porteous. Accepts pupils aged from 3 to 18+ years.

SURVEYORS

The Fielding Partnership, Urb. La Carolina, Edif. Commercial, Ctra Cádiz, km 178.5, 29600 Marbella (Málaga), Spain (tel. (95) 282 7754, fax (95) 282 9754). Contact: Geoffrey Fielding (Director). Chartered Surveyors and estate agents. Offices: Marbella, Mijas Costa, Nerja, Ibiza and Majorca.

TRAVEL

Flightclub, Guildbourne Centre, Chapel Road, Worthing, West Sussex BN11 1LZ, UK (tel. 01903-231857, fax 01903-201225, e-mail: flightclub@clubs.itsnet.co.uk). Offers low cost flights worldwide from all UK airports. Incentives for overseas property owners/managers.

INDEX

D

E

T

SUGGESTIONS

Please write to us with any comments or suggestions you have regarding the contents of this book (preferably complimentary!). We are particularly interested in proposals for improvements that can be included in future editions. For example did you find any important subjects were omitted or weren't covered in sufficient detail? What difficulties or obstacles have you encountered which aren't covered here? What other subjects would you like to see included?

If your suggestions are used in the next edition of *Living and Working in Spain*, you'll receive a small gift as a token of our appreciation.

NAME: _____

ADDRESS: _____

_____

Send to: Survival Books, PO Box 146, Wetherby, West Yorks. LS23 6XZ, United Kingdom.

My suggestions are as follows (please use additional pages if necessary):

OTHER SURVIVAL BOOKS

There are other *Living and Working* books in this series including America, Australia, Britain, France, New Zealand and Switzerland, all of which represent the most comprehensive and up-to-date source of practical information available about everyday life in these countries. We also publish a best-selling series of 'Buying a Home' books including *Buying a Home Abroad* plus buying a home in Florida, France, Ireland (autumm 1998), Italy (autumn 1998), Portugal and Spain.

Survival Books are available from good bookshops throughout the world or direct from Survival Books. **Order your copies today by phone, fax, mail or e-mail from:** Survival Books, PO Box 146, Wetherby, West Yorks. LS23 6XZ, United Kingdom (tel/fax:44-1937-843523). E-mail: survivalbooks@computronx .com, Internet: computronx.com/survivalbooks. If you aren't entirely satisfied simply return them within 14 days for a full and unconditional refund.

BUYING A HOME IN SPAIN

Buying a Home in Spain is essential reading for anyone planning to buy a home there and is designed to guide you through the jungle and make it a pleasant and enjoyable experience. Most importantly, it is packed with over 200 pages of vital information to help you avoid the sort of disasters that can turn your dream home into a nightmare! Topics covered include:

- Doing Your Homework & Avoiding Problems
- Retirement, Working & Starting a Business
- Finding the Right Home & Location
- Choosing the Region
- Real Estate Agents
- Finance, Mortgages & Taxes
- Home Security
- Utilities, Heating & Air-Conditioning
- Moving House & Settling In
- Permits & Visas
- Renting & Letting
- Traveling & Communications
- Health & Insurance
- Renting a Car & Driving
- And Much, Much More!

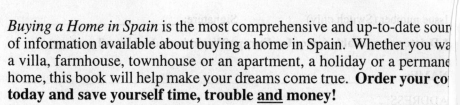

Buying a Home in Spain is the most comprehensive and up-to-date sour of information available about buying a home in Spain. Whether you wa a villa, farmhouse, townhouse or an apartment, a holiday or a permane home, this book will help make your dreams come true. **Order your co today and save yourself time, trouble <u>and</u> money!**

Order your copy today by phone, fax, mail (order form overleaf) or e-mail from: Survival Books, PO Box 146, Wetherby, West Yorks. LS23 6XZ, United Kingdom (tel/fax: 44-1937-843523, e-mail: survivalbooks@computronx.com, internet: computronx.com/survivalbooks).

ORDER FORM

Please rush me the following Survival Books:

Qty	Title	Price*			Total
		UK	Europe	World	
	Buying a Home Abroad	£11.45	£12.95	£14.95	
	Buying a Home in Florida	£11.45	£12.95	£14.95	
	Buying a Home in France	£11.45	£12.95	£14.95	
	Buying a Home in Ireland (autumn 1998)	£11.45	£12.95	£14.95	
	Buying a Home in Italy (autumn 1998)	£11.45	£12.95	£14.95	
	Buying a Home in Portugal	£11.45	£12.95	£14.95	
	Buying a Home in Spain	£11.45	£12.95	£14.95	
	Living and Working in America	£14.95	£16.95	£20.45	
	Living and Working in Australia	£14.95	£16.95	£20.45	
	Living and Working in Britain	£14.95	£16.95	£20.45	
	Living and Working in France	£14.95	£16.95	£20.45	
	Living and Working in NZ	£14.95	£16.95	£20.45	
	Living and Working in Spain	£14.95	£16.95	£20.45	
	Living and Working in Switzerland	£14.95	£16.95	£20.45	
	The Alien's Guide to France (winter 1999)	£5.95	£6.95	£8.45	
				TOTAL	

Cheque enclosed/Please charge my Access/Delta/Mastercard/Switch/Visa* card,

Expiry date _____ No. __ __ __ __   __ __ __ __   __ __ __ __   __ __ __ __

Issue number (Switch only) _____ Signature: _____

* Delete as applicable (price for Europe/World includes airmail postage)

NAME: _____

ADDRESS: _____

_____

_____

Send to: Survival Books, PO Box 146, Wetherby, West Yorks. LS23 6XZ, United **Kingdom or tel/fax/e-mail credit card orders to 44-1937-843523.**